W9-ATF-984

Revolutionary Mexico

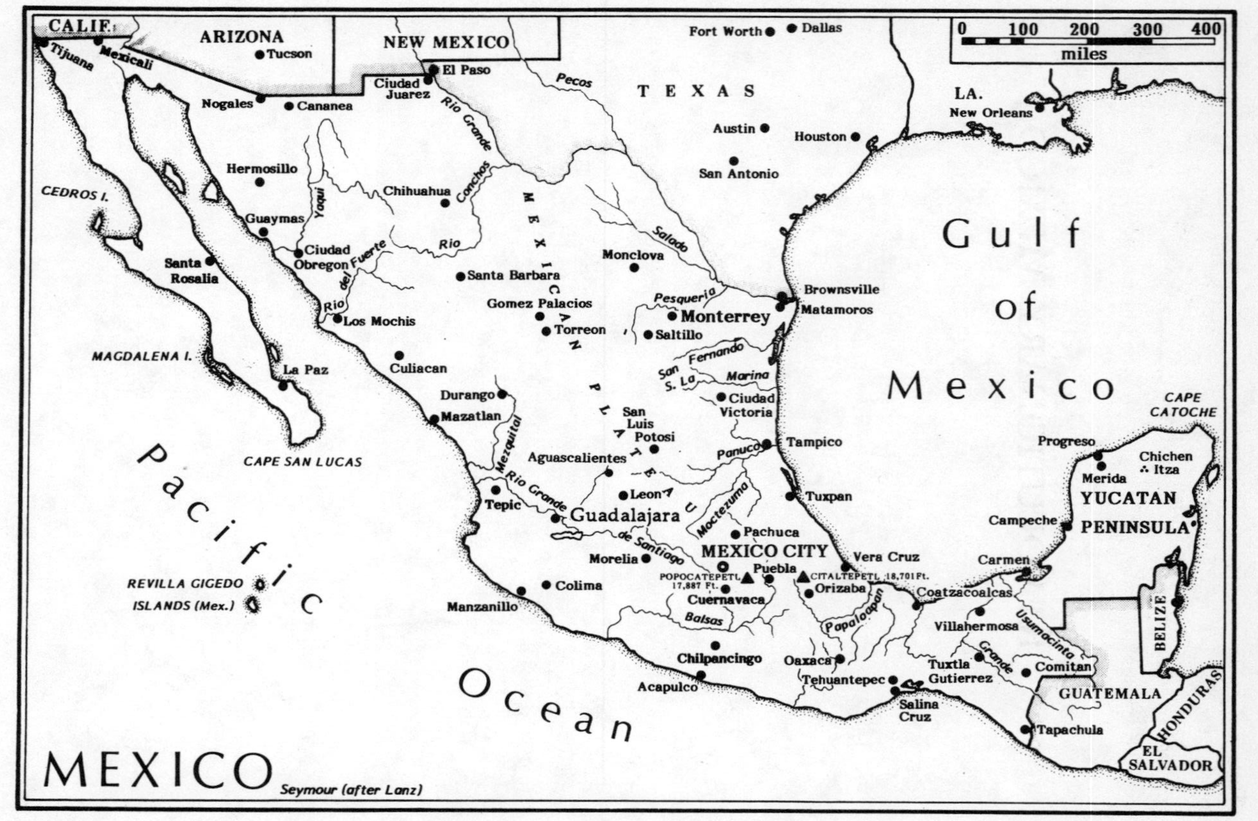
MEXICO
Seymour (after Lanz)
0 100 200 300 400
miles
CALIF.
ARIZONA
NEW MEXICO
TEXAS
LA.
Tijuana
Mexicali
Tucson
Nogales
Cananea
El Paso
Ciudad Juarez
Pecos
Fort Worth
Dallas
Austin
Houston
San Antonio
New Orleans
Rio Grande
Conchos
Chihuahua
Hermosillo
Guaymas
Yaqui
Ciudad Obregon
Rio del Fuerte
Rio
Los Mochis
CEDROS I.
Santa Rosalia
MAGDALENA I.
La Paz
CAPE SAN LUCAS
Culiacan
Santa Barbara
Gomez Palacios
Torreon
Monclova
Salado
Pesqueria
Monterrey
Saltillo
Brownsville
Matamoros
MEXICAN PLATEAU
San Fernando
S. La Marina
Ciudad Victoria
Durango
Mazatlan
Mezquital
San Luis Potosi
Aguascalientes
Panuco
Tampico
Rio Grande
Tepic
Guadalajara
Leon
Moctezuma
Tuxpan
Pachuca
de Santiago
MEXICO CITY
Morelia
Puebla
POPOCATEPETL 17,887 Ft.
CITALTEPETL 18,701 Ft.
Vera Cruz
Orizaba
Cuernavaca
Colima
Manzanillo
Balsas
Papaloapan
Coatzacoalcas
Chilpancingo
Oaxaca
Tehuantepec
Acapulco
Salina Cruz
Villahermosa
Usumacinta
Grande
Tuxtla Gutierrez
Comitan
Tapachula
GUATEMALA
HONDURAS
EL SALVADOR
BELIZE
Carmen
Campeche
Progreso
Merida
Chichen Itza
YUCATAN PENINSULA
CAPE CATOCHE
Gulf of Mexico
Pacific Ocean
REVILLA GIGEDO ISLANDS (Mex.)

Revolutionary Mexico

The Coming and Process of the Mexican Revolution

John Mason Hart

University of California Press
Berkeley • Los Angeles • London

University of California Press
Berkeley and Los Angeles, California

University of California Press, Ltd.
London, England

First Paperback Printing 1989

Tenth Anniversary Edition 1997

Library of Congress Cataloging in Publication Data

Hart, John M. (John Mason), 1935–
Revolutionary Mexico.

Bibliography: p.
1. Mexico—History—Revolution 1910–1920—Social aspects. 2. Mexico—History—1867–1910. 3. Social conflict—Mexico—History—20th century. 4. Argentina—Economic conditions. 5. Mexico—Foreign relations—United States. 6. United States Foreign relations—Mexico. 7. Title.
F1234.H3 1988 972.08 87-5399
ISBN 0-520-21531-1

Printed in the United States of America

1 2 3 4 5 6 7 8 9

The paper used in this publication meets the minimum requirements of American National Standard for Information Sciences—Permanence of Paper for Printed Library Materials, ANSI Z39.48-1984. ♾

To the martyrs of Veracruz who gave their lives
in the defense of national integrity.

Contents

Preface to the Tenth Anniversary Edition

During the first years of the twentieth century, before the Russian Revolution and the emergence of the Soviet Union, a wave of political upheavals swept across important areas of the Third World. In Russia and Iran in 1905, China in 1898 and 1911, and Mexico in 1910—all sites of ancient civilizations—revolutionaries tempered modernization with the desire to retain traditional practices that served their interests.

Modernization created highly divisive forces in those societies. The growth of the commercial economy created larger and articulate pequeña burguesías while propaganda increased public expectations for greater well-being and political democracy. At the same time, however, new communications and transportation facilities greatly increased the power of dictatorial central governments against state and local entities. Obtaining concessions from the national governments, foreigners established and controlled railroad, shipping, telegraph, and telephone services, leaving the peripheral undertakings to local capitalists. Meanwhile, the privatization of land in order to promote commercialized agriculture altered ages-old land tenure systems that previously granted resident laborers considerable control over governance and farming output. In all four countries, foreigners led the way in developing modernized ranching and agricultural enterprises. In Mexico they became the owners of most of the land used for the production of cattle, cotton, sugar, and timber for export, and they controlled the marketing of henequen.

The new investors also reorganized industrial production. Artisans and less skilled workers moved from small self-managed patios into factories often administered by foreign supervisors who enjoyed wage differentials as great as 20 to 1. After 1900, wage increases ended while foreign workers with comparable skills enjoyed preferential treatment through segregated housing, higher salaries, and more prestigious work assignments in the oil fields and mines. Mexican miners resisted, but by 1910 all but a few had been forced to give up piece work and accept hourly wages.

The uprisings stemmed from three fundamental causes. First, economic setbacks and even famines dashed the hopes of people who had been led to expect greater well-being by the the promises of their governments and western business leaders. Second, the national governments extended dictatorial controls rather than leading the way toward expected democracies. And third, the growth of foreign economic power, political influence, and cultures instead of the development of autonomous national strength gave rise to nationalism.

In all of these insurgencies, as well as in the Balkans, Cuba, the Philippines, and South Africa, the western powers intervened and either crushed the insurrections or prevented the revolutionaries from resolving the conflicts on their own terms. The forces for democracy, nationalist control of their economies, social justice for industrial and urban workers, and village-based agrarian and rural political reform in China, Russia, and Iran failed in their efforts to overthrow the dictatorships. It was only in Mexico that they achieved their goal and established a stable government. Having ended the regime of General Porfirio Díaz, who had taken power in 1876, the Mexican revolutionaries could not reconcile their differing aspirations for the future and waged a civil war that endured for nine years.

THE REVOLUTIONARIES

The divisive nature of the alliance that toppled General Díaz followed classic revolutionary lines. Its roots are found in the contradictory class and cultural backgrounds of the leaders. Three interest groups emerged in the revolutionary struggle against Díaz: the provincial elites and pequeña burguesía, the rural working classes, and the urban and industrial workers.

The first group was reflected by Francisco Madero, a scion of the richest family in the state of Coahuila, and later by Coahuila Governor Venustiano Carranza; they and their supporters comprised the provincial elites and pequeña burguesía. Madero envisioned a government based on local constituencies under the tutelage of provincial elites and pequeña burguesía, responsive to the needs of Mexicans rather than to the demands of foreign interests. He also wanted to modify social relations by creating a government influenced rather than controlled by unions, and a system of agrarian resettlements in which the rural population that insisted on community landholding would be given vacant properties largely in undesirable areas far removed from the lands of their ancestors.

The provincial elite and most pequeña burguesa revolutionaries banded together in support of a democratic republic with the rights of states and regions to be administered by local leadership, and a nationalism that sought cooperation with, rather than subordination to, their hegemonic American neighbors. At that point, out of the nation's 485-million-acre surface, U.S. investors owned 130 million acres, concentrated on the coasts and frontiers. Some 154 U.S. individuals and companies held almost 100 million of those acres.

In commerce, industry, and banking the provincial elites and pequeña burguesa revolutionaries also sought parity with the Americans and Europeans, who held some 90 percent of the incorporated capital in the Mexican economy. In sum, this interest group sought a more balanced distribution of power between themselves, the national government, and the foreigners. The provincial elites and their pequeña burguesa supporters were diverse and would carry out personalist and ideologically based struggles among themselves once the major fights against the metropolitan regime and the rural, urban, and industrial workers had been successfully terminated.

The second leadership group derived from the rural working classes, the sugar plantation laborers, mechanics, and village leaders of the Zapatistas, and the cowboys, miners, dirt farmers, lumberjacks, and pueblo leaders of the Villistas. Their share of land ownership nationwide had fallen from 25 percent to 2 percent during the Díaz privatization program. They sought the return of privatized lands to the rural working class on the basis of the communities they lived in, with local political control to be in their hands through the creation of "municipios libres." They also sought parity in wages and opportunities for workers.

The third leadership group comprised the independent union chiefs and militants of the industrial and urban working class who formed the 150,000-member Casa del Obrero Mundial and contributed 5,000 men as soldiers and hundreds of women as field nurses to the revolutionary cause. They wanted workers' self-management in the factories, land for the peasants, and a greatly reduced role for the government and foreign capitalists. The divergent interests and consciousness of these leaderships and their supporters led to the civil war.

THE RIVALRIES

Madero quickly alienated his agrarian and leftist followers. The Zapatistas, centered in the sugar plantations south of Mexico City, declared war and demanded the restoration of local political rights and most of the land taken from them during the Díaz era. Ultimately, the army eliminated Madero, whose assassination led to civil war. The rebel leaders rallied a cross-section of the Mexican public against military dictatorship.

In Chihuahua the leadership fell to Francisco Villa, the most effective military chief, because the army had assassinated Governor Abraham González, and the Chihuahua oligarchy supported the military dictatorship, leaving a vacuum at the top. Villa, who ran a provisioning company for the mines in the Sierra, secured quick victories in Chihuahua and confiscated cattle in order to buy arms in El Paso. He tried to maintain good relations with the Americans, but his men drove several thousand of them out of the state and seized their properties. His forces marched southward, sweeping the enemy before them. They soon became known as the División del Norte, counting some 60,000 members. The Zapatista leaders liked their Villista counterparts and formed an alliance. The allies however, had enemies among the other revolutionary leaders.

The rebels in Coahuila and Sonora, led by Venustiano Carranza, claimed the title of "First Chief" of the Revolution. Carranza's recognition by the United States as a belligerent enabled Villa, as his subordinate, to obtain arms legally from American dealers. Using the safer locale of Sonora, Carranza escaped Villa's growing military power on the central plateau, including Coahuila. He combined forces with the Sonoran mining and ranching oligarchy, which had organized to fight for power against the army and to protect themselves from the ill-armed, pro-Villista Yaqui Indians and mine workers. The Sonorans put together a powerful army, while on the Gulf Coast another force, led by Carranza's son-in-law, Cándido Aguilar, gained control of a large area around the oil fields being worked by American petroleum companies.

By the summer of 1914, the stage was set for the war against the army to change into a fight between the revolutionaries. First the military surrendered and turned over Mexico City to forces loyal to Carranza that were able to enter central Mexico, passing south of Villa's forces because the American authorities at El Paso and Eagle Pass refused to allow the coal used to fuel the División del Norte's trains to cross the border. The Villistas watched in frustration as the Carrancistas occupied Mexico City.

Carranza and his principal supporter, Alvaro Obregón Salido, a marginal but dynamic member of the Sonoran oligarchy, decided to fight rather than to accept dictates from the stronger Villistas and Zapatistas. In a monumental step, Obregón Salido, who conveniently dropped the oligarchical Salido from his name, recruited the Casa del Obrero Mundial. He stressed the cultural backwardness of the peasantry and promised the Casa leaders that they could organize the working class wherever the army went as the "first step toward the world-wide proletarian revolution." Carranza, Obregón Salido, and their supporters then fled to Veracruz, where an American invasion force held the port.

General Frederick Funston, acting on virtually the same orders given by President Woodrow Wilson to General William Graves at Vladivostok during the Russian Civil War, resupplied the Carrancista forces. The importance of the American supplies and the soldiers provided by the Casa came into evidence at the El Ebano, where the Villistas and Carrancistas fought for control of the oil fields. A force of some 8,000 ragged Villistas marched into battle with mismatched guns and ammunition and obsolete brass field guns. Their opposition, including several thousand "Red Battalion" troopers from the Casa, met them with high impact artillery, machine guns, and field radios. After their defeat the Villistas dragged themselves away on foot with mules, and the forces under Obregon Salido entered El Ebano with new trucks hauling their artillery.

Unfortunately for the Villistas, the Zapatistas were militarily weak and lacked equipment, training, and the desire to leave their homeland. The Villistas fought without their allies. At Celaya and León, indirect artillery and machine gun fire inflicted a decisive defeat on them. During the retreat the División del Norte dissolved. Soldiers became cowboys, miners, farmers, and lumberjacks again. Reduced to guerrilla warfare, Villa passed agrarian reform and labor laws regulating social relations in the mining and timber industries.

In 1916, with the Villistas and Zapatistas incapable of strategic military actions, Carranza demobilized the Red Battalions and after a series of general strikes and disturbances he dissolved the organization. Obregón Salido rejected the Casa leaders when they appealed to him for aid and told them to disband. Shortly thereafter, the government chose a union to represent the workers.

The second American intervention came in the wake of the Villista attack on Columbus, New Mexico. On that occasion the U.S. officers carried maps indicating a zone of military occupation, or protectorate, extending from the border to a line running from the oil fields around Tampico west to Mazatlán on the Pacific Coast. The same maps indicated Parral in southern Chihuahua would be the headquarters for the American occupation forces. The Villistas, who were never caught; the Carrancistas, who defeated an American unit at the Carrizal; the citizenry of Parral, who rioted when some American troopers entered the city; even Carranza, who threatened war if the American forces advanced further; and the deepening crisis with Germany—all combined to inflict a public relations defeat on the "Punitive Expedition."

The Constitution of 1917 symbolizes revolutionary goals, successes, and failures. It promised land reform and municipal autonomy for the rural population, nondiscrimination and full freedoms for the industrial workers, federalism, full voting rights for adult males, and national ownership of sub-soil resources, coasts, and frontiers. By 1962 the land reform program had returned almost 30 percent of the nation's surface to the peasantry, but local autonomy had become a hollow pledge. Official unions organized millions of workers but reduced them to virtual dependency on the state. Civilianized generals headed a vast "revolutionary" party and bureaucracy numbering in the hundreds of thousands until 1946, when the first civilian became president. Political participation was available between the 1920s and the 1980s through membership in the party, a union, an agrarian junta, or business organization. In 1953 women gained the right to vote in national elections. Federalism finally emerged with the rise of opposition parties in the 1980s. In the 1990s the nation is moving toward multiparty democracy.

From the 1920s to the early 1980s the government spent 20 percent of its annual outlays on public education. In the 1930s segregated housing and discriminatory salaries and work assignments ended while the government seized most of the lands along the coasts and borders, nationalized the oil, transportation, and communications infrastructure, and created 50–50 partnerships in high-tech businesses. In the 1990s Mexico restored foreign participation and even dominance over high-tech communications, transportation, and oil production.

In sum, the Revolution temporarily accomplished the goal of Mexico for the Mexicans. The failures of the revolutionaries, however, constitute a tragedy. Enormous income and wealth disparities place Mexico among the most inequitable societies in the world, where a few enjoy unimaginable wealth in the midst of squalor and misery.

What can we learn from the Mexican Revolution? That modernization provokes nationalism if the public experiences economic and political losses in powerful cultures such as Mexico, Iran, China, and Russia. That significant foreign control of real property at the expense of provincial elites such as the Maderos or mullahs will result in denunciations of the government and demands for national sovereignty. That sacred lands associated with ancestral village leaders can be privatized only at the cost of rural working class unrest. That industrial workers with small shop experience and cultural pride will resist ethnic inequality and the extremes of the factory regimen. And, that foreign interests commonly favor security through dictatorship when confronted with revolutionary nationalism.

John Mason Hart
October, 1997

Preface

The ideas for this book had their beginnings during the mid-1960s in the free and stimulating debates that took place in Robert N. Burr's Latin American History seminar and in the study of the Spanish Civil War with Stanley G. Payne at the University of California, Los Angeles. It was apparent early that the historiography of the Mexican Revolution suffered from an overdose of impressionistic narrative and lack of theory. The revolution, it seemed, had happened because of a presidential interview, a candidate's book, because people were poor, because some were "left out," or because President Díaz had grown old and suffered from a toothache. The prevailing explanations of the revolution clearly lacked causative analysis.

I began this work with a study of Mexican labor and then researched agrarian history, an approach through which I hoped to explode the myth of working-class irrelevance by demonstrating the underlying nature and long history of Mexican social conflicts. That investigation led to the discovery of a large and radical nineteenth-century industrial labor movement and vast wave of agrarian unrest that intensified and spread across the nation for one hundred years before becoming revolutionary. I then studied the historical development of elite alienation and the crisis of the Porfirian political economy that brought about the seemingly controlled mobilization of the lower classes by elements of the elites. At that point, in 1980, I anticipated that my research work was done; the revolution was "territorio ya explorado," already examined in thousands of books.

However, some of the standard explanations of the revolution itself did not stand up to critical questioning. To my surprise, I found unexamined archival resources as vast as those previously ignored collections that I had studied to understand the origins of labor, agrarian, and provincial elite unrest. A new reality emerged: American investors and "pioneers" owned more than 22 percent of Mexico's surface in 1910. Hundreds of Mexican campesino groups, many of them based on communities with long histories of unrest, independent of direct Zapatista or Villista influence, assaulted the American-owned properties and those of other foreigners and Mexicans on a nationwide scale between 1910 and 1916. The alarmed American government decisively affected the outcome of the revolution through a secret and massive infusion of arms during its 1914 intervention at Veracruz.

Mexican events took on greater significance as part of a larger picture; causative factors leading to political economic destabilization, foreign intervention, and class alignments paralleled the other great revolutions at the turn of the century. All this forced me to reinterpret the events of the revolution, giving it a new framework.

In recent years two important books on the Mexican Revolution have appeared. *The Great Rebellion* by Ramón Eduardo Ruiz is based on the author's impressive command of Mexican historical writing and literature from the Porfiriato to the present and upon a lifetime of research. Ruiz and I agree in many areas of interpretation and fact regarding the 1910 upheaval. The many achievements of the revolution, however, preclude deeming it only a rebellion. During and after the violence the Mexican public rejected the strong caste bias that prevailed before the revolution and still characterizes those parts of Latin America with large Native American populations. In addition, the land redistribution program that shifted property ownership from latifundistas to agrarians, the forcible expulsion of massive American interests including the companies that controlled the nation's communications and transportation infrastructure, and the seizure of the assets of U.S. landowners and oil companies, all give evidence to the transformation of property ownership that justifies Mexico's claim to revolution.

The Mexican Revolution by Alan Knight is a synthesis of the massive body of historical monographs produced over the last fifteen years and offers many interpretive insights. Knight's work was not available to me when this book was written. It is a thoughtful analysis which should be considered by any student of the revolution. I disagree, however, with Knight's contention that American interests in Mexico were marginal and that Mexican nationalism was an afterthought.

I am indebted to many people, scholars, and friends for their assistance in the completion of the work. Among them, Thomas O'Brien, Paul Hart, Friedrich Katz, Sue Kellogg, and Steven Mintz read and critiqued the manuscript. William Beezley, Charles Harris III, David La France, Dirk Raat, Ray Sadler, Paul Vanderwood, James Wilkie, David Walker, and Mary Wolf spared me from making many errors by sharing their knowledge or making editorial suggestions. David Pfeiffer and Fred Pernell of the Washington National Records Center; Nettie Lee Benson, Carmen Cobas, Laura Guttierrez de Witt, Jane Garner, and Lisa J. Hart of the Benson Latin American Collection; and dozens of archivists in the United States and Mexico provided research leads and made materials available to me.

The University of Houston, the American Philosophical Society, the University of Texas at Austin Latin American Center, and the Social Science Research Council contributed important research support without which this study could not have been completed. Mary Hart offered special encouragement and Colin MacLachlan rendered advice and counsel throughout.

THE PORFIRIATO

Ah, distinctly I remember it was in the bleak December,
And each separate dying ember wrought its ghost upon the floor.
Eagerly I wished the morrow;—vainly I tried to borrow
From my books surcease of sorrow—sorrow for the lost Lenore—

For the rare and radiant maiden whom the angels name Lenore—

Nameless here for evermore.

—Edgar Allan Poe, *The Raven and other Poems*

Introduction

The ancient *velador* paces the streets between eleven at night and four in the morning in one of Uruapan's oldest and most dangerous quarters. It is an area stalked by gangs of *porros,* antisocial youths who prey upon their helpless victims in the darkness. Yet in all the years of the velador's lonely rounds, the gangs have never molested him. He is a living representation of Uruapan's enduring cultural heritage. The Mexican people, even the porros in their way, have an abiding respect for their pre-Columbian and Spanish cultural traditions. The defense of the sovereignty and economy of Mexico's national, state, and local regimes was the essence of the social revolution of 1910 and the nineteenth-century provincial uprisings that preceded it.

This study is an analysis of both the development of those forces whose interaction brought about the Mexican Revolution and the pursuit by the revolutionaries of their respective interests during that conflict. It examines each major social group—industrial and urban workers, peasants and *campesinos, pequeña burguesía* and provincial elites—in the context of its prerevolutionary development and its role in the unfolding revolutionary process until the basic social resolution achieved by 1924.

Understanding the Mexican Revolution requires analysis of why both socially conservative elites and restless lower-class groups chose to overthrow their government. By this analysis Mexico's social conflicts and the national economy will be placed in long-term, short-term, and global contexts. Those dimensions necessarily measure the sociopolitical effects of foreign-engendered domestic economic growth between 1867 and 1910 and assess the importance of increased foreign indebtedness and dependence on foreign investment during the economic crisis between 1900 and 1910.

The revolution itself will be examined in the context of the contending forces vying for control of Mexican society between 1910 and 1917. Four major social groups inside Mexico—the peasantry, industrial and urban workers, pequeña burguesía, and provincial elites—manifested distinct revolutionary objectives during the struggle. Their visions included violently contradictory goals as well as reconcilable ones. In this way the interactions of the revolutionaries with elements of the ancien régime and foreign interests and governments provide an essential dimension for understanding the ultimate outcome of the revolutionary process.

THE BACKGROUND

During the last decade of the ancien régime long-standing social, economic, political, and cultural conflicts exacerbated by an international economic crisis intensified to a point of national upheaval. In the long term Mexico's revolutionary unrest derived from internal stresses rooted in the castelike inequalities established by the Spanish conquest of the sixteenth century. The basis for those conflicts, however, deepened during the last hundred years of the Spanish colony and the first half-century after political independence. Then, between 1876 and 1910, the impact of the global economy upon the national social fabric dramatically increased. During the last ten years of the Porfirian regime the society entered deep crisis. Recurring foreign economic and financial contractions between 1899 and 1910 seriously undermined Mexico's well-being, especially after 1907. Displaced peasants and unemployed workers faced deprivation while the nationalistic pequeña burguesía and regional elites saw their economic opportunities increasingly limited and their federalist-democratic principles trampled upon by a government unable or unwilling to stem foreign competition.

The long-term development of Mexican social conflict began in the late seventeenth century when metropolitan and outside-controlled commercial estate agriculture and industry progressively encroached upon quasi-independent pueblos and local societies, destabilizing them. The resulting competition for land and water rights led to peasant revolts. In many cases the rural indigenous people had experienced prolonged periods of relatively autonomous isolation and social stability prior to the disruption of their economic, political, and cultural lives by the outsiders.

For most of the colonial era a sharing of benefits engendered common interests among provincial and metropolitan elites vis-à-vis the indigenous and *mestizo* working classes. As a result, the leadership of the regional uprisings derived from elements of the residual indigenous village and local elites, not from the relatively high-status provincial landowners and political power brokers. In the late eighteenth century, however, the growth of metropolitan-controlled commercial agriculture and mining and the extension of state power provoked unrest among provincial and local political elites. This potent group demonstrated its political capacity by rallying the displaced classes and castes—the village peasant and artisan producers, Indians, blacks, and mestizos—to its side.[1]

Between 1810 and 1876 regional and local elites frequently used the militias of their respective territories to guard their economic and political privileges against outsiders. Absentee estate owners in Mexico City and provincial capitals sought profit through export agriculture in the center, south, and far north. The expansion of their enterprises and the intrusion of their supervisors was accompanied by the growth of small-scale businesses in the *pueblos*. The changing economic and cultural milieu often challenged the prerogatives of village communal holders and the traditional authorities of local regimes.

Meanwhile, Mexico's growing global economic involvement meant more outside competition for domestic industry. The gradual opening up of trade and the influx of high-technology goods eroded local artisanry. Agricultural and industrial dislocation created widespread public unrest, giving regional elites and local citizenries the popular base they needed for countless insurrections and successful political revolutions in 1853–1854 and 1876.

The process of economic intrusion and resulting regional multiclass and caste rebellions that characterized the revolution of 1910 first surfaced when commercial estate agriculture made rapid gains in the Chiapas-Isthmus of Tehuantepec region during the late seventeenth century. Absentee landlords in Mexico City created and controlled a new complex of industrial export agriculture, producing tobacco, cotton, sugar, hemp, and cacao. The principal estate involved, the enormous and expanding Marquesana hacienda, was once part of the Cortes heirs' Marquesado *latifundia*. The trouble began when hacienda owners seized lands claimed by the Isthmian Zapotec pueblos. Some local elites, suppliers, buyers, administrative personnel, and officials including *caciques* benefited from the development of the large-scale commercial and export-oriented great estates, but some did not. The result was a change in the balance of power in local political and economic hierarchies.

Conflict arose between those most closely associated with the still intact

Zapotec peasant-indigenous society and the beneficiaries and participants in the new order. Starting in 1707, ten years of violence rooted in deepening political, economic, and cultural conflict swept the Chiapas-Tehuantepec region in the form of village risings. Displaced and threatened local elites, mestizo townsmen, village peasants, and rural estate workers formed the core of the unrest.

In 1780 new violence erupted near the town of Izúcar in present-day southwestern Puebla. The recent introduction of large-scale commercial sugar production had transformed land tenure in the area. Although the estate owners made their homes in Mexico City, their local representatives undermined the traditional political hierarchy, indigenous cultural traditions, and peasant economy of their respective areas. The clash between the commercial landowners and formerly communal peasants reflected an early, isolated, but important emergence of capitalism when the latter complained of *"raquiticos salarios"* (feeble salaries). The Izúcar rebellion comprised a multiclass and caste alliance of rebels who fought to restore village autonomies, regional political authority, and usurped pueblo landholdings and to gain better wages for their part- and full-time labor on the estates.

In a similar manner the 1810 Independence Revolution in the Bajío resulted from regional social destabilization brought about by massive increases followed by erratic contractions in mining and commercial agriculture during the eighteenth century. The mining boom encouraged the development of estate agriculture in the region. A century of mining prosperity ended, however, with a severe contraction between 1800 and 1810. That crisis, characterized by industrial layoffs and falling silver production, compounded the region's prolonged problems of peasant displacement and endemic famine. The revolutionary alliance included political officials, factory owners, shopkeepers, village curates, displaced peasants, unemployed mine workers, and "villagers" from estate rancherías who claimed land usurpation at the hands of the growing estates.[2]

The local Creole elite led the principal revolutionary forces; smaller groups displayed mulatto, mestizo, and Indian village and tenant farmer leadership. As the revolution spread southward through the present-day states of Michoacán, Guerrero, and Morelos, it took on contrasting aspects. In the following years a professional class—pequeña burguesía—and ranchero (commercial middle holder) leadership characterized the main forces. However in the countryside, the village and rural farm worker population carried out a generalized attack against outside-controlled commercial agriculture and political interference.

Between 1832 and 1854 rural unrest continued with three major regional uprisings that swept the 60,000-square-mile area between the highly commercialized Tehuantepec region in the south and the new citrus-producing zones of the Balsas River basin in Michoacán and the sugar centers of Morelos and Izúcar, Puebla, to the north. The third revolt, that of 1853–1854, became national in scope and led to the overthrow of President Antonio López de Santa Anna and his replacement with southwestern provincial strongman Juan Alvarez.

Commercial agriculture grew rapidly during the eighteenth century, and the southwest was one of its focal points. Peasant displacement associated with the growth of the great estates advanced rapidly in the most commercially developed areas. The Marquesana hacienda in the Isthmus of Tehuantepec and the hacienda San Marcos located between Acapulco and Oaxaca were the region's largest. The latter reached 500,000 acres in size.

During the peasant offensives of the independence struggle between 1810 and 1821 the great estates in the southwest suffered heavy losses, but after the war with Spain they began to reconsolidate. The absentee estate owners residing in faraway Mexico City continued to exercise considerable power, and their efforts constituted a threat to the increased leadership role desired by provincial Creole elites as well as to the landholdings claimed by the village peasantry. The ongoing lower-class unrest was finally harnessed by the regional *caudillo* Juan Alvarez and his southwestern provincial elite allies, who used it during their seizure of national political power in 1854.

Many of Alvarez's Liberal party supporters shared a desire to emulate the political and economic success of the United States. They longed for the capital and technology of the North Atlantic power to undo a sense of defeat engendered by over forty years of chaos since 1810. Some carried their vision to the extreme of membership in the growing republic to the north. Most sought economic cooperation between the two nations. The close and unequal economic relationship formed between American investors and Mexicans became a critical element in the coming of revolution in 1910.

During the second half of the nineteenth century peasant and provincial rebellions shifted northward in association with railroad, commercial agriculture, timber, and mining investments. Major peasant and regional uprisings in the affected areas took place between 1868 and 1883. By the 1890s the pattern of intrusion and revolt had reached previously remote Chihuahua and Coahuila. The self-governing semiautonomous mestizo towns established in earlier times as frontier buffer colonies against marauding Indians were transformed from quasi-independence toward tenant farmers and laborers. During the economic prosperity that prevailed until 1899 the regional elites took part in only a few of the struggles.

In 1876, Porfirio Díaz, long a rebellious provincial caudillo from the southwestern state of Oaxaca, had rallied the provincial elites with the Revolution of Tuxtepec. Named after a small town in Puebla, the uprising began in earnest in January 1876 from Díaz's headquarters in Brownsville, Texas. Openly supported with cash and arms by important American capitalists, military commanders, and large-scale Texas landowners, Díaz was able to sustain his revolution for six months along the Río Bravo between Laredo-Nuevo Laredo and Brownsville-Matamoros. By June state governors and provincial garrison commanders had joined the movement to topple the destabilized and "anti-American" government of President Sebastian Lerdo de Tejada.

In the early years of its tenure the Díaz regime created a broad base of elite support. Its partisans included representatives of the state oligarchies including Evaristo Madero of Coahuila. They participated in an economic expansion dominated by North American and European capitalists. Now in direct contact with outside markets via the growth of the railroads and extractive industries, the northern oligarchs lost their political autonomy, but new wealth showered upon them. For the most part the fighting that took place during the Porfiriato involved the army and peasant villages suffering from land enclosure in isolation from the upper strata of provincial society.

By 1900 the situation was changing. The national government had centralized political authority to an unprecedented extreme, while increasing ties between the regime and foreign capital led to an influx of American colonists claiming title to Mexican land and resources. That situation was frightening to the northern provincial elites, who had witnessed the earlier loss of Texas to American colonists and the ensuing economic takeover of the territories that later became the southwestern United States. Those concerns, combined with a fiscal crisis that reduced the government's ability to provide sinecures through public works contracts, led provincial elites to feel they were being denied the opportunity to participate in the country's economic growth. After 1900, government-sponsored foreign commercial intrusion into provincial society reached an unprecedented magnitude, especially in the far north, often in competition with local landowners, businessmen, and artisans. By 1910, American real estate holdings totaled 130 million acres and encompassed much of the nation's most valuable mining, agricultural, and timber properties.

Because the financing of Porfirian capitalist growth was foreign and not produced by dynamic internal processes, the increasing number of centers of commercial agriculture and industrial activity were superimposed on an otherwise peasant population in the countryside. The result was a crazy quilt of contrasting societies in rural Mexico. In five areas the conflicting forces of economic intrusion and traditional society were especially strong: Morelos and parts of Guerrero and Puebla in the center-south of the country; the Pacific coast from Sonora to Chiapas; Tamaulipas, Veracruz, Tabasco, and Campeche on the Gulf coast; the Isthmus of Tehuantepec; and the northern border states of Coahuila, Chihuahua, and Sonora. These became the starting points of the Mexican Revolution. Two of them—the center-south and the far north—became the focal points of sustained lower-class-led revolutionary activity.

An indigenous cohesion existed in Morelos, unlike much of the north, Gulf coast, and in the more developed areas. Over 20 percent of the rural population in 1910 still spoke only Nahuatl and even more were bilingual. In contrast to the nation's generally thinly distributed countryside population, Morelos was the most densely populated rural place in Mexico, and its strong Indian-mestizo village society was concentrated within one of the most intensely commercial agricultural zones. A legendary thirty-eight families controlled the state's sugar mills and plantation fields. Many of the absentee owners, some of them foreigners, resided in Mexico City. Competition between the estates and villages for acreage during the 1880s and 1890s resulted in victories for the great estate owners. By 1910 they claimed almost 98 percent of the arable land. Many of the pueblos faced the prospect of extinction. To increase sugar profitability and production, two railroad lines were constructed connecting the state to the Mexico City metropolis and the export centers of Veracruz and Acapulco. The furtherance of commercial ends also resulted in the nation's finest rural road system. The byways crisscrossed the state, bringing the ordinarily remote and disparate peasant villages into ready contact. News traveled fast in Morelos, and so did peasant guerrilla armies.

Located a mere 50 miles from Mexico City, the Morelos peasantry were affected not only by the efforts of metropolitan and foreign capitalists but also by the diffusion of European radical ideas. Nationalism, anarchism, and liberalism found a receptive audience there. Zapata acknowledged his debt to them in his myriad proclamations, "al pueblo Mexicano," while incorporating anarchist advisors from the revolutionary workers' organization, the Casa del Obrero Mundial. Ringed by rugged, inpenetrable mountains narrowly embracing fertile lowland fields, Morelos became the ideal location for a sustained peasants' war. Its rugged topography contrasted sharply with the easily accessible Gulf coast-Isthmus of Tehuantepec zone of rebellion in Tamaulipas, Veracruz, Tabasco, southern Oaxaca, and Campeche.

Along the Gulf and Pacific coasts and in the Isthmus of Tehuantepec, an equally large revolution among fieldworkers on the great estates began in 1910–1911 and raged out of control in late 1912 through 1916. A high degree of commercialization had occurred centuries earlier, however, and the residual village communal regimes were weak. Only a remnant of small-scale landowning Mexican local elites remained to offer the insurrection cohesive leadership. On the coasts thin population dispersal and lack of intact traditional village hierarchies denied the unrest a sustaining basis. The flat, easily traversed coastal areas offered maximum opportunities to the conventional army and made guerilla actions more difficult, if not impossible. The repeated rebellions in the Gulf and Pacific coast zones were quelled by government forces in 1913, in late 1914–1915, and again in 1919–1920. In the Isthmus of Tehuantepec the fragmented rebels, remote from the nation's metropolitan center, achieved their ends by expelling hundreds of American landholders and companies. Uncontested, they satisfied their countryside revolutionary aims by reestablishing much of their pre-Porfirian land tenure system.

In Morelos the dense infrastructure of peasant villages, with their partially intact pre-Columbian cultural heritage and social and authority structures, came into conflict with an insistent, heavy-handed economic intrusion of outsiders, many of whom were concentrated in nearby Mexico City, to create a volatile situation. The state's rugged terrain and unique transport and communications systems combined with its wide exposure to outside revolutionary ideas dedicated to the liberation of oppressed peoples to make it a center of uncontrollable peasant-based guerrilla unrest.

In the north commercially oriented provincial elites became active in the political opposition because of the economic and political threat posed by growing national government and American domination. By 1902 more than 23 percent of all U.S. investments in Mexico were concentrated in those three rural states (Coahuila, Chihuahua, and Sonora) whose total population constituted only 1.5 percent of the nation's citizenry. Nationwide, Americans and other foreigners dominated industry, transportation, mining, and timber production and, holding more than 120 million highly capitalized acres, challenged the Mexicans in landownership. Americans were an important bloc among the cattle raisers and the new commercial farming elite. Despite their close trade ties to American entrepreneurs across the border, the nationalistic northern elites were well aware that U.S. commercial and landowning hegemony in the affected regions had preceded the loss of Texas and, in 1848, of the massive territory that became the southwestern United States.

The politically sophisticated northern elites had exercised semiautonomous control of their provinces since colonial times and enjoyed geographical remoteness from the national government until the railroad and telegraph of the Porfiriato placed them under the thumb of the ruling operatives in Mexico City. In the meantime, an avalanche of new American capital seized control of most northern economic resources, orienting production toward foreign export. This occurred at the expense of local competitors while creating Mexican-owned support industries. Regional elite protest arose in the face of increasing American landholdings across the nation and exploded in revolution when financial contractions in the United States provoked a deep depression in the Mexican north after 1907.

During the second half of the nineteenth century the Industrial Revolution produced a potentially powerful industrial working class. Worker unrest rooted in colonial-era immiseration and artisan leadership found anarcosyndicalism a solution. Nationalistic industrial labor strikes and uprisings plagued Mexico after 1900. Directed against French, American, and Mexican owners, the workers' violence helped to undercut the regime's political legitimacy.

The factors that brought about the revolution of 1910 were active during most of the nineteenth century in diminished scale or on a regional level and included the following:

—the national government's failure to satisfy the nationalistic public demand to meet the overwhelming political, cultural, and economic challenges of foreign intruders;
—regional elite competition with an expansive central government and metropolitan ruling class for control of local resources;
—increasingly restricted access to public works contracts and polity;
—resentment of the government's overwhelmingly powerful foreign entrepreneurial allies;
—national government fiscal crises brought about by increasing interest burdens on debts and the need for infrastructure development;
—pequeña burguesa disillusionment with dictatorship and boss rule;
—imported revolutionary working-class ideologies;
—peasant displacement through the expansion of export agriculture far

out of proportion to the ability of new technology and industrial growth to absorb them through new employment; and
—peasant and industrial working-class repression and deprivation.

Between 1707 and 1910 the focus of political, economic, and cultural conflict—with the exception of Sonora and Yucatán, where almost continuous struggle took place—assumed a general pattern of movement from south to north. It did so in response to the rate of change and social dislocation in the countryside that began with metropolitan investments in tropical export agriculture and ended with an overwhelming takeover by the Americans. Throughout the process the loci of unrest paralleled the growth of commercial export croplands, mining, railroads, and timber until the onset of the revolution. The ever growing regional uprisings of the eighteenth and nineteenth centuries anticipated the essence of the much larger conflagration of 1910.

In the short term, those critical ten years after 1900, the historically resistant agrarian and industrial working classes confronted food shortages, rising prices, and growing unemployment, which contributed to worsening living conditions. The peasants experienced new levels of displacement as 15,000 American colonists armed with property titles and rifles occupied large areas of Chiapas, Chihuahua, Coahuila, Puebla, Sonora, Sinaloa, San Luis Potosí, Tamaulipas, Veracruz, and the Isthmus of Tehuantepec. Apart from the colonists, American corporations bought massive land tracts in the north, Campeche, Chiapas, Colima, Durango, Tabasco, Veracruz, and Zacatecas.

Simultaneously, the frustrated Mexican pequeña burguesía and local and provincial elites saw their own social position eroded and the national government politically overwhelmed by foreign economic invasion, their federalist-democratic principles abused by the resulting dictatorship and boss rule, and opportunities for social and economic success increasingly limited by erratic downturns endemic to the economy with new foreign competitors often working in cooperation with the national government. Mexico's vulnerable and dependent position in the world economy caused a foreign-controlled, excessively narrow, unbalanced pattern of economic growth, with centers of American, British, Belgian, French, and German prosperity protected by armed *rurales* juxtaposed to and often combined with increasing native deprivation.

The Porfirian commercial and industrial revolution transformed traditional peasants and artisans, creating agrarian and industrial workers. It forged an army of technocrats and administrators, while small businessmen proliferated. Regional elites acquired unprecedented riches from commercial agriculture and mining. Yet as time went on, foreign investment and the ever-stronger national government foreclosed on provincial elite autonomy and competed with it for local opportunities. In the first ten years of the twentieth century elements of all four classes—peasant, industrial worker, pequeña burguesía, and provincial elites—separately espoused the revolutionary doctrines of anarchism, liberalism, or democracy. In the context of growing foreign economic, political, and cultural domination and deepening economic crisis, however, all four could and did rally to nationalism.

In the long and short term, the causes of the Mexican Revolution of 1910 were comparable to those that engendered contemporary multiclass upheavals in the transitional societies of China, Iran, and Russia. The nationalistic autonomy-minded Mexican provincial elites and their pequeña burguesa allies, like their counterparts in China, Iran, and Russia, led workers and peasants in the demand for increasingly effective representation of their interests by the national government in its dealings with foreigners. With their expectations crushed by an overwhelming foreign economic and political presence meshing with the policies of their national governments, the excluded provincial elites and pequeña burgesía found no peaceful means to enter the national political arena.

In all four countries the restricted political base of the national governments became obsolete as economic growth created new economically and technologically important, yet politically excluded, social groups. As transitional societies China, Iran, Russia, and Mexico shared a common dependence upon foreign financial support for their industrialization. Immediately prior to their early twentieth-century upheavals these nations experienced deep socioeconomic and political trauma when their sources of financial support in Western Europe and the United States were cut off by banking crises between 1899–1904 and 1907–1908.

In the midst of general socioeconomic instability, rising foreign influence, political dissent, and fiscal crisis, the Porfirian government gradually lost its ability to rule. Foreign companies' increasing power coupled with the cost of public indebtedness dictated the regime's inability to respond to the complex economic and political problems that arose in the first ten years of the twentieth century. The regime's subordinate-dependent relationship to foreign capital precipitated a confrontation between the metropolitan elites and the provincial elites led by Francisco I. Madero over the issues of home rule, a more open political system, and the disbursement of local economic opportunities. In order to gain lower-class support for his insurrectionary cause, Madero offered industrial workers the right to organize freely and peasants the opportunity to reclaim usurped lands.

As a consequence of elite crisis a partially paralyzed state could not activate the traditional mechanisms of social control with full efficiency, and a nationwide conflagration broke out. Foreign revolutionary ideologies—nationalism, liberalism, anarchism, and socialism—offered the alienated groups both explanations of and solutions to their dilemmas. Between 1910 and 1920 the rival classes clashed in a series of struggles that shook the nation, threatened the interests of foreign companies and governments, provoked foreign intervention, and reshaped the society and state.

This study is an analysis of both the development of those forces whose interactions brought about the Mexican Revolution and the revolutionaries' pursuit of their respective interests during that conflict. It examines each major social group—industrial worker, peasant-campesino, pequeña burguesía, and provincial elite—in the context of its prerevolutionary development and its role in the unfolding revolutionary process until the basic social resolution achieved between 1916 and 1924.

THE STRUGGLE

The Mexican Revolution comprised the same social forces and groups that carried forward the first massive popular uprisings of the twentieth century (between 1905 and 1911) in Iran, Russia, and China. Peasants, industrial workers, pequeña burguesía, and provincial elites mobilized, challenging the government while meeting the threats presented by foreign intruders and one another. In all four of these early twentieth-century national revolutions, formally constituted political parties possessed little of the organizational strength and unity between peasants and industrial workers that characterized later struggles in Russia and China. In Mexico, although anarchosyndicalism was strong among the revolutionary industrial workers and influenced the Zapatistas and Villistas, there were no Marxist-Leninist cadres. As a result, the organizational strength and resources of the pequeña burguesía, provincial elites, and their foreign supporters, reinforced by the latter's geographical proximity, proved decisive.

In the course of the revolution an olio of contending forces arose, each setting forth demands and perceptions rooted in its historical development. The peasants, industrial workers, pequeña burguesía, regional elites, foreign capitalists, and metropolitan Porfirian oligarchy all behaved in accordance with patterns and interests established earlier. Their experience and behavior prior to the onset of national crisis is a major dimension of this study and essential to understanding the revolution.

The roles and importance of the various interest groups that brought about the Mexican Revolution can be discerned during the course of the struggle itself in the context of three phases. The first phase, that of *elite crisis and mass mobilization,* began with the emergence of the Mexican Liberal party and heightened with the revolt of landowner-businessman Francisco Madero in 1910 and endured until 1914. It involved a mutually destructive rivalry between provincial and national ruling elites for control of the government in Mexico City. In the vacuum created by that strife the long repressed and rebellious peasants of the center-south were able to organize a formidable armed force, the Zapatistas, which also challenged the government. In 1911 the fall of the far-removed border town of Ciudad Juárez triggered riots in Mexico City. Meanwhile, countless rural insurrections against commercial and foreign property owners were carried out by local peasants, agricultural workers, and miners across the country; and the mobilization of American troops along the border hurried the shaken president into exile without a real fight.

Unable to control the demands and actions of revolutionary peasants and workers, Madero failed to reconcile the resentful oligarchy and foreigners to his upstart rule. For about fifteen months Madero attempted to govern while confronted by a rising tide of revolt in the countryside and violent labor-organizing efforts in the urban areas. The fall of 1912 brought a nationwide wave of campesino assaults against foreign-owned properties that reached a peak in 1914. The attacks were frequently led by local small landowners and other men of note, who usually called themselves Villistas and Zapatistas but who were in fact outside any organized authority. In the face of rising unrest, army commander General Victoriano Huerta overthrew Madero in February 1913. The new regime, backed by the oligarchy and foreigners—including the Americans, who provided Huerta with large-scale arms aid—faced a new insurrection led by the northern elites in Sonora and Coahuila and lower-class leaders in Chihuahua.

Eventually victorious, the Constitutionalist faction, led by the great estate owner and governor of Coahuila, Venustiano Carranza, and backed by part of the Sonoran state oligarchy, waged a civil war against Huerta. As a result of the northern oligarchy's incomplete control, tens of thousands of townspeople, peasants, and agrarian workers mobilized in Chihuahua in 1913 and 1914 under the lower-class leadership of Francisco

Villa. Dozens of groups calling themselves Zapatistas and Villistas carried out raids in the countryside. Zapatista raiders appeared in Tamaulipas, Sinaloa, and Sonora. Groups self-identified as Villista operated as far south as Chiapas, Oaxaca, and Campeche. Invariably they were made up of local campesinos, miners, artisans, and rancheros. Some operated in the manner of bandits; others seized claimed lands and occupied them or destroyed foreign (especially American) mining, ranching, and farming properties.

Temporarily allied under Carranza's titular leadership, the larger but disparate northern revolutionary groups gained crucial American neutrality in the summer of 1913 and open support in the winter of 1914. The initial elite crisis-mass mobilization phase of the revolution ended early in the summer of 1914 with the defeat of Huerta. At that point tens of thousands of fighters were arrayed in two coalescing and hostile groups while independent groups still stalked the countryside.

The critical second phase of the revolution, that of *class confrontation, American intervention, and workers' defeat,* began with a struggle that surfaced in mid-1914 between the victorious provincial elite- and pequeña burguesa-led forces arrayed with Carranza and the populist northern rural cohorts of Villa with their initially ranchero, artisan, and rural lower-class leaders. The basically peasant followers of Zapata and the most extreme of the radical agrarian reform leaders such as Eulalio Gutierrez of San Luis Potosí quickly rallied to Villa. During the ensuing civil war the organized urban workers, pequeña burguesía, the bulk of the intelligentsia, and, subtlely, the American companies and government supported the broad-based reformist appeal of Alvaro Obregon Salido, the military commander of the Constitutionalist forces, and Venustiano Carranza.

The American intervention at Veracruz in April 1914 constituted the focal point of the U.S. government's effort to control events in Mexico. It began with an attempt to oust Huerta but quickly became a means to gain concessions from Carranza. The Americans controlled an immense strategic stockpile of arms there. The military equipage included over 4,500 crates of armaments and filled three warehouses to overflowing, each of which measured 57.5 yards in width and length and over 21 feet in height. More arms including machine guns and artillery were placed in reinforced depositories, among them the Baluarte of Veracruz, the Benito Juárez lighthouse, and the San Juan de Ulloa fortress. In the meantime American ships quietly supported the beleaguered Constitutionalist forces by entering the ports of Mazatlán, Manzanillo, Acapulco, Salina Cruz, and Guaymas, maintaining the flow of supplies without entering into hostilities.

The American authorities at Veracruz, led by presidential envoy John

Lind and U.S. Army General Frederick Funston, also contributed to the maintenance of "law and order" in Campeche and Tabasco by shipping weapons to "police and planters" there. Four American companies owned over 3 million acres of hardwood forest and henequen and rubber plantations in Campeche alone. Another company held a 3.5 million-acre timber concession in Quintana Roo and Yucatán. The American properties extended in a solid body north from the Guatemalan border to the Gulf of Mexico at Carmen and on to the capital of the state. After August 1914, the onset of World War I made Campeche's supply of rubber, already a strategic material, even more central to U.S. government concerns. The United States was the world's largest consumer of raw rubber, and Mexico was an important producer.

The provincial elite- and pequeña burguesa-led Constitutionalist and industrial worker alliance was crucially aided by freely imported American munitions and the massive quantities of arms stockpiled at Veracruz. Equipped with modern artillery, machine guns, barbed wire, trucks, radio transmitters, and rifles, they quickly succeeded in defeating the much larger but less well-equipped Villista and Zapatista main forces directed by mostly rural working-class leaders. They achieved strategic domination of the Villistas and Zapatistas by mid-1915, although the fighting continued for another five years.

The second stage of the revolution continued when the urban working class and the bourgeoisie turned on each other in mid-1915 after the military collapse of the Villistas in the Bajío and north-central Mexico. The Constitutionalist government, supported by foreign companies and the most important industrialists of Mexico City, violently opposed the plans of the principal industrial labor organization, the Casa del Obrero Mundial.

The Casa planned eventually to seize control of Mexico's private enterprises and to reorganize them on an anarchosyndicalist basis. The government refused urban labor demands for relief from inadequate salaries, the elimination of script currencies by private enterprises, price controls to stop inflation, and the resolution of widespread unemployment. Increasingly militant and large-scale strikes, mass demonstrations and street violence continued for fifteen months. Factories closed while armed workers maintained barricades and angry crowds surged through the streets. The unrest finally ended in August 1916 when troops broke the second general strike of that year, smashed the various Casa centers located in the nation's cities, and with them the power of the revolutionary urban labor movement.

During the final phase of the revolution, that of *elite synthesis and sociopolitical reorganization* between 1916 and 1924, diminished bloodshed characterized the struggle for power. The basically pequeña burguesa-led army and the Sonoran oligarchy supported Alvaro Obregon Salido and Plutarcho Elías Calles against Carranza's narrowing alliance of Coahuila and northeastern elite, governmental bureaucratic, and industrialist backers. The resulting synthesis in government forestalled violent changes of power. The process began with the workers' defeat in August 1916, featured the promulgation of a corporatist and nationalistic constitution in 1917, the pacification of most of the myriad countryside insurgencies, and ended with a successful Bonapartist coup d'état carried out by Obregon Salido in 1920. Soldiers killed President Carranza when he fled the capital for Veracruz.

During the period 1916–1924 violence abated as the society underwent political restructuring and the elite was being reorganized. Demoralized elements of the defeated Villista, Zapatista, and industrial/urban labor movements joined pacified groups from the Porfirian regime in a new order dominated by the victorious military leadership. The leaders began to translate their military power into civil and economic dominance. While the ambivalent American businessmen and government looked on and prepared to negotiate, the pequeña burguesa winners elaborated a new and sophisticated basis for social control in their liberal, nationalistic, and unifying Constitution of 1917. Through that instrument and the will of the winners the masses made striking gains, eliminating most of the vestiges of caste and archaic social relations that still plague much of Latin America, and opening society for public education and individual mobility. The organizational structure and methods of operation that emerged between 1916 and 1924 established a working order that became the basis of rule in the sixty years that followed.

In the 1920s and 1930s the government isolated and coopted violently dissident agrarian, labor, military, business, and Church groups. Their revolutionary or dissenting tendencies removed, the defeated groups joined the new hierarchy as subordinate parts. In the meantime the state reached a series of accommodations with the American companies and government. The result of this mode of operation during the last forty years has been a widely based, solidly entrenched sociopolitical order. The new regime, in conjunction with the rapid growth of the capitalist economy, has given power to a resurgent bourgeoisie and left the Mexican working classes in deplorably poor economic conditions.

STASIS

The deep conflicts between the United States and Mexico and between the rival social groups prior to and during the Mexican Revolution have long suffered from misunderstanding. Traditional elite attitudes on the part of the Mexican intelligentsia have too often portrayed the working classes in novels and historical essays as passive, fatalistic, and "*inconsiente.*" An ahistorical approach neglected and even denied the long revolutionary experience of the Mexican peasantry and industrial working classes and the chaos resulting from the countless attacks on rural commercial properties by small groups of workers and peasants in the countryside between 1911 and 1920. The magnitude of American-owned properties and the nationwide assault against them has been totally overlooked.

There has been a tendency to emphasize widespread passivity among the majority of the population during the revolution. Examination of the revolutionary actions of thousands of peasants and rural workers operating outside the authority of the constituted Villista, Zapatista, and Constitutionalist leaderships, however, reveals that countryside masses were actively involved in the revolution. Another misguided theme is the emphasis placed on the cross-class support enjoyed by the Constitutionalists to explain their eventual success. This approach obscures the divergent interests manifested by the revolutionary participants during the course of the struggle. Multiclass allegiances to elite-led factions have taken place in all revolutions. That common phenomenon does not point to victory any more than it mutes evident class dichotomies. Merely stressing cross-class involvement lends no insight regarding the processes of the Mexican Revolution. Analysis of the wider rivalries based upon the social status and vested interests of the factional and local leaderships and their differing designs yields striking results.

Understanding of the Mexican Revolution has been confounded in the past by successful Constitutionalist and postrevolutionary government efforts to legitimize their rule. The search for legitimacy led to the formulation of a unifying "revolutionary" ideology that explains events and allegiance to the regime of formerly antagonistic groups defeated during the struggle. In the quest for postrevolutionary stability the new government celebrated the defeats of the agrarian working-class Zapatistas, provincial lower-class Villistas, and industrial and urban workers of the Casa del Obrero Mundial, with the formation of the progovernment Partido Agrarista for the campesinos and the equally loyal Confederación Regional del Obrero Mexicano (CROM) and its political corollary, the Partido Laborista for the industrial working class. These first-generation semigovernmental organizations and those that followed have claimed legitimacy through their links to the regime as "revolutionary" participants and as representatives of the masses. They are portrayed by the regime and often by scholars as "revolutionary institutions." In fact, they serve as ideological tools that have been used with great success since 1920 as a facade by an elite stratum.

The agrarian reforms and strengthening of government structures during the era of President Lazaro Cárdenas (1934–1940) have been portrayed similarly as revolutionary. In addition to sowing confusion among scholars who talk of "continuing revolution," "peaceful revolution," and "institutionalized revolution," their most significant role in the development of postrevolutionary Mexico has been as successful mechanisms of elite social control over historically restless and revolutionary segments of society.

The Mexican Revolution was no anomaly. The causes of unrest and its course of development were on a grander scale but still rooted in the colonial-era and nineteenth-century patterns of economic intrusion and social displacement that engendered earlier upheavals. In part it represented the first Third World uprising against American economic penetration and control. It is hoped that this study will demonstrate the unique as well as the classic and universal patterns of dissent and struggle that took place in the coming and process of the Mexican Revolution.

Part I

The Ancien Régime

ONE

The Peasantry

Peasant resistance to outside intrusions into local economies, culture, and policy was a major aspect of Mexican experience from pre-Columbian times until the outbreak of the revolution. Village and regional revolts against the Maya, Zapotec, Mixtec, Teotihuacani, Toltec, and Aztec empires were frequent and sometimes helped bring down the state. Early in the Spanish colonial epoch the *campesinaje* again demonstrated its will to resist.

Soon after the collapse of Aztec and Tarascan power, the Yopes located inland from Costa Chica south of Acapulco rebelled in a sporadic but major uprising against the Spaniards that endured twenty years. Then the indigenous population of the near northwest revolted during 1540–1541 in the Mixton War, a serious uprising that required the commitment of Spanish armed forces from as far away as Guatemala to quell. Contemporary Maya resistance, based upon the rural village infrastructure of Maya society, against the Spanish intrusion into Yucatán was intense for more than thirty years and continued in periodic flare-ups during the remainder of the colonial era. Maya resistance, however, was that of an intact Indian society.

THE COLONIAL ERA

For most of the Mexican rural populace the time between 1519 and 1630 was a postconquest debacle. The people underwent a demographic catastrophe caused by disease, famine, forced labor, and war in which the total population dropped an estimated 95 percent from 25 to 1.3 million. Disease and famine were by far the most serious problems, the former brought on by the Indians' lack of immunities and the latter by food shortages engendered by the imposition of Spanish pastoralism on the ecosystem of the densely concentrated hydraulic populations of Mesoamerica. After the 1630s the rural Indian population stabilized and began a gradual but steady recovery. Between 1640 and 1810 the rural populace increased to over 5 million, of which 2.5 million were classified as Indians. The once recessive village societies throughout most of Mexico regained lost strength. Between the 1550s and early eighteenth century, indigenous countryside revolts outside of Yucatán were quite small.[1]

Then, two hundred years before the revolution, Mexico began to experience increasingly frequent and growing village-based regional peasant uprisings. These political, economic, and cultural conflicts took place in an evolving countryside characterized by the penetration and disruption of local regimes by alien commercial agriculturalists, which transformed quasi-independent peasants into tenant farmers and laborers. Rapidly growing landed estates producing for consumption outside their immediate environs competed with the villages for land. They did so in response to the burgeoning demands of a prospering European economy for silver, gold, cacao, coffee, sugar, hemp, and other exportable raw materials. The Spanish Empire and the Mexican colony were closely tied to the European market, and the increased profitability of those products began the transformation of Mexican land tenure. In the eighteenth century absentee owners developed their commercial estates most rapidly in the old but again booming zones of support for the mines of the Bajío and Sultepec-Taxco, in the export crop areas around the port cities of Veracruz and Acapulco, and in the south, where large-scale export agriculture quickly destabilized the smaller and relatively less commercialized holdings of local elites and the Indian village land tenure regimes in general.[2]

A salient and illustrative episode within the pattern of regional uprisings resulting from rural commercialization that reached its apogee in the conflagration of 1910 began with the 1707 revolt of largely Zapotec peasants around Ixtepec in the Isthmus of Tehuantepec. Although the fighting centered on the *municipio* of Ixtepec, violent encounters took place as far away as Suchilapan some seventy-five kilometers to the north alongside the transisthmian road that runs north to south from the Gulf of Mexico to the Pacific Ocean. Other incidents occurred in the municipio of Tehuantepec thirty kilometers to the west of Ixtepec and some fifty kilometers to the east of the center of the rising near the present border dividing the states of Oaxaca and Chiapas.[3]

The absentee owner of the hacienda La Marquesana, originally part of the Marquesado del Valle estate holdings of Hernán Cortés, had successfully moved against pueblo communal lands in Ixtepec's district, including those of Ixtepec itself. Offers of purchase had been made in the late seventeenth century, followed by the denunciation and occupation of the properties in the 1690s. By 1707 the estate's administrators controlled a number of plots giving them frontage on and direct access to the transisthmian road between Juchitán on the Pacific coast and Suchilapan in the interior. Given the increased traffic on the road and marketability of goods including coffee, cacao, sugar, cotton, hemp, and timber, the properties meant an agricultural and speculative bonanza for the estate owners. Some of the isthmus village hierarchies, including the prosperous merchants of Juchitán, in contrast to Ixtepec and its allies, compromised with the estate owner, accepting cash and tenant farming arrangements. Other less commercially oriented pueblos such as Ixtaltepec that chose litigation rather than violence remained in limbo for decades while the Spanish courts adjudicated the ensuing disputes. Some of those properties were occupied de facto by estate operatives.[4]

By 1707 the handling of the land dispute between the pueblos around Ixtepec and the commercial export-oriented estates resulted in a compromise settlement that caused the peasants of the Ixtepec communes to resort to armed resistance that swept the southern half of the isthmus. Local officials, the courts, and finally the Audiencia in Mexico City had bowed to the Marquesaña estate owner's power and the need to generate export earnings. Unrest continued in the isthmus with periodic violations of the peace for the rest of the century. The ameliorating effect of the Crown's "Indian Courts" and its system of protective laws undoubtedly eased the blow and reduced the violence of the response, but even the Spanish court system could not prevent land redistribution in one of Mexico's most capitalistically advanced commercial and agricultural zones.[5]

During the next sixty-five years wars were fought by the Yaqui Indians of the northwest and by the Maya in Yucatán and Chiapas. Those struggles involved resistance by Indian regimes to outside economic, political, and cultural intervention and presaged their violent resistance to outside intruders in the mid- and late nineteenth century. In the case of the Sonoran Yaqui, the Spanish Crown exacerbated the unrest by expelling the Jesuits from its American empire. That action upset the balance between the Yaqui and their secular Spanish and Mexican neighbors, removing an element of political, economic, and religious leadership. The Jesuit missions, established in the seventeenth century, were centers of syncretic religion blending Yaqui mysticism and Catholicism. The missionaries and Indian wisemen, though frequently in conflict, had worked out a functioning relationship. The missionaries' role was rooted in the insular economic and political function of the missions as centers of self-sustaining indigenous agriculture and diplomatic contact with the world.[6]

The Yaqui leadership understood that removal of the Jesuits eliminated important allies in the struggle to protect their Yaqui River bottomlands and extensive territories from interlopers. Between 1767 and 1770 the Yaqui fought to defend their domain and special relationship with the Jesuits. Between the 1767 uprising and the revolution of 1910 frequent hostilities broke out between the Yaqui and an expansive secular society, economy, and government.[7]

On the southern periphery the Maya, like the Yaqui, enjoyed geographic and topographic remoteness from the global economy and the authority of Mexico City. In the eighteenth century they continued a self-sufficient rural forest-peasant economy and culture rooted in the millennia of a highly integrated civilized past. The Crown sent the missionaries to "Hispanize" the Indians who lived in the nearly inaccessible interior. They helped create a syncretic amalgam of native and European religious beliefs under the aegis of the Catholic Church.[8]

The Maya slash-and-burn peasant agricultural economy and village infrastructure remained intact. The violence that began in the northern and coastal zones during the 1520s continued into the interior over a period of centuries. At first it was aimed at establishing Spanish authority over centralized regimes, such as the one at Petén Itzá, which finally fell in 1657. Then the nature of outside intrusion became more social and economic. Spanish settlements and agriculture gradually spread. The peasantry resisted, amalgamated with the newcomers, or retreated deeper into the interior. During the eighteenth century violence in the south took on new meaning as it shifted from a frontier war into periodic peasant risings. Sporadic Mayan peasant rebellions swept southern Mexico as expanding commercial estate agriculture displaced native villagers from Chiapas to the Caribbean during the century.

While periodic warfare raged on the southern and northern peripheries, new forms of social unrest appeared in central Mexico between the 1770s and 1810. There was a geometric increase in rural crime. Most startling was the growing number of robberies and assaults carried out by groups of lower-caste individuals against men of property. The authorities reported more murders in 1809 than in any previous decade. In 1810 there were more reported homicides in the first nine months than for all of 1809. As the incidence of economic crime increased, so did law enforcement efforts.

The Acordada, the imperial constabulary, gained note for dispensing summary justice to robbers along the rural byways.[9]

A multiclass and multicaste rebellion broke out in the Izúcar area in 1780–1781. Its leaders—Creoles, mestizos, mulattos, and members of the Indian village hierarchies—cited the contemporaneous Tupac Amaru rebellion in Peru, vowing to overthrow Spanish authority and create an "Indian" nation. The triggering incident was all too common throughout Spanish America: a Crown official's abuse of an Indian village authority. That incident occurred because of the diminished role of the village hierarchy in an economy that had moved from peasant tenure to a system of large export-oriented commercial agricultural estates in the possession of absentee owners in Mexico City who used large numbers of day laborers. Given the new mode of production, the radius of village authority was correspondingly reduced from the surrounding countryside to the immediate living zone of the pueblo.

Many of the Indian towns were now integrated societies with a cross-section of castes, workers, artisans, state employees, and merchants all living among the indigenous population. In many towns the *"commune de Indios"* was a recessive minority in the midst of the growing number of newcomers. Conflicts were inevitable, and the Indian caciques were consistent losers, although in some cases they translated their old power over communal holdings into private properties in the new regime.

By 1780 the process of commercialization had advanced in the area of Izúcar for more than three-quarters of a century. The resident Indian peasant tenure was all but eliminated in the face of expanding sugar production. The majority of Indian workers, still remembering their communal rights, had joined the other castes as cane cutters and field hands on the great estates' lands that they still regarded as pueblo property. The workers' common identity as villagers and their collective grievances against the estate administrators transcended caste differences and their differing aspirations to live as communal pueblo landholders and private farmers.

The long-range intent of the rebellion was not well planned. During their interrogation after the fighting was over the captured leaders reduced it to a mere case of outrage at the excesses of a local official. The citing of the Tupac Amaru independence rebellion in Peru by the revolutionaries during the rising, however, indicated to the Spanish authorities that this was no minor incident. The averred intention of creating an Indian nation in Mexico and destroying the white caste demonstrated that the peasant-Indian majority in the countryside could be harnessed as a revolutionary force. The realization of what the events at Izúcar might mean sent a tremor of concern through Spanish authorities in New Spain.[10]

Despite the rising levels of violence in central Mexico before 1810, peasant unrest was minuscule in proportion to that which ensued during the century that followed. The peasant wars of the nineteenth century and 1910 resulted from the same formula for the overturning of social peace that had occurred at Ixtepec and Izúcar: the displacement of local elites and peasant regimes by the development of absentee-owned commercial economies. The social peace that had prevailed for over two centuries rested on a continued balance between peasant and capitalist production in the countryside.

The social peace of the mature colonial era after 1570 resulted from three basic Crown programs that were eventually undermined by the commercialization of the economy that overtook the empire in the eighteenth century. First, the Spanish Crown allocated and then protected Mercedes land grants to the villages. These donations greatly ameliorated the conflict between the peasantry and the great estate owners. The landholdings that were formed were generally quite large relative to the population involved. Technically the land grants were given to the village religious brotherhoods, the *cofradías,* which were associated with the parish church. In practice, with the passage of time the holdings came to be regarded by the villagers as common or corporate property.

Second, the Crown's court system contributed to countryside tranquility by frequently deciding land disputes between pueblos and estates in favor of the communes, especially in those cases of blatant commercial estate land invasions. The courts were flawed with indecision and excessive bureaucracy, however, and local jurisdictions were often corrupt. The inevitable appeals process was slow and sometimes took generations, only to fail in resolution of the dispute. Local police enforcement of court decisions favoring the villages or harmful to *hacendado* interests was unreliable.[11]

Indigenous revolts in central Mexico during the colonial era were small and peasant village based, the result of new global economic forces, changing ownership of the mines and landed estates, and delays and imperfections in the judicial process. Some revolts were triggered by unfavorable court rulings. The rural population of New Spain gave at least limited recognition to the legitimacy of Spanish authority through taking its first recourse in the redress of grievances to the judiciary.

Third, the Church in its Hispanizing function played an insular role, protecting the Indians from secular opportunity seekers and reducing the degree of friction between the two groups. Unlike local Crown officials whose positions could be compromised, the religious orders were relatively invulnerable to domination by the local landed elites. Churchmen introduced utensils, language, and beliefs to the Indian villages, helping to create a Hispanic peasantry. The priests represented the villages in litigation. In most places they became an integral part of village life.[12]

During the three centuries of Spanish rule countryside villages were usually satisfied with pacific attempts to solve their problems. During the course of the eighteenth century, however, serious uprisings in what later became focal points of unrest provide ample evidence that the agrarian population was despairing of its confidence in the Spanish authorities. The general reliance upon and belief in the overburdened and inefficient Spanish court system that seemed to prevail for so long deteriorated during the late seventeenth- and eighteenth-century boom in mining and commercial agriculture. The abandonment of long-standing rural authority figures such as the cacique, the elders, the clergy, and especially the Jesuits and their replacement by frequently insensitive and corrupt outsiders created new tensions. The general feeling of distrust soon turned into hatred of Spanish authority and unrest. The situation was exacerbated by the continued growth of the indigenous population, which began a comeback in the middle of the seventeenth century from its earlier greatly reduced numbers. The result was a population-land crisis that presaged the tumult of the nineteenth and early twentieth centuries.

Social banditry and Catholic millenarianism were important manifestations of conflict between the urban and rural sectors of society and of a separate, distinctive, and economically exploited society in the hinterlands of New Spain. Social banditry, religious millenarianism, and the revolts were inarticulate forms of peasant opposition to the ever increasing metropolitan control of the agricultural economy, culture, and society via the growth of the great estate.[13]

Mexican social banditry as a preideological form of agrarian protest did not consciously threaten the political, social, or economic system; rather, with its dramatic raids upon haciendas and the local headquarters of various Crown officials, it constituted a coherent manifestation of hostility toward an unsatisfactory local condition or administration. Little is known of Mexico's colonial period banditry other than its rural population base, increasing prevalence during the late eighteenth century and especially between 1800 and 1810, and involvement in traditional crimes such as highway robbery. Despite the fact that bandit activities in Río Frío, Morelos, Izúcar, Durango, and Chihuahua accounted for the only counterflow in the otherwise continuous drainage of wealth from the countryside to the city, thus far it has been examined only as a police problem. The attacks upon local representatives of outside authority increased in the latter part of the eighteenth and peaked in the early nineteenth century. The areas of most intense bandit activity geographically coincided with those regions that later supported the agrarian uprisings of the late nineteenth and early twentieth centuries.

Catholic millenarianism among Mexico's campesinos was another important symptom of the differences between the agricultural population and the European-oriented culture and economy of urban society. The millenarian idea was originally brought to Mexico by the early contingents of Catholic missionary priests. The most famous millenarian agricultural commune was attempted with Indians at Santa Fe just west of Mexico City in the 1530s by Vasco de Quiroga. Contemporary sixteenth-century Catholic millenarianism stressed the virtue of communal property, condemned private property as a sin, and rejected human authority. Men were to live as equalitarian brothers in a classless society under the rule of God after a successful class war that would defeat the rich and powerful.

Millenarianism gave the campesinaje the expectation that some day everything would be changed for the better and the long sought ideal of social justice would prevail. In the midst of growing rural desperation the image included a return of the Aztec ruling family, the restoration of village lands, and the expulsion of aliens. Nineteenth-century religious-campesino uprisings in central Mexico, led by priests, actually sought these goals in the states of Morelos, Hidalgo, and Chihuahua. Millenarian belief was expressed as well in the land-reforming religiosity of some contingents in the independence revolutionary armies of Miguel Hidalgo, José María Morelos, and Ignacio Rayón. It was repeated by the Zapatista forces, who, like their independence revolutionary predecessors, invoked the Virgin of Guadalupe while carrying out widespread pueblo-initiated land reform without the authorization of the leadership.

The basis for large-scale conflict in the countryside was the free village versus the great estate, although other tensions resulted. Local village and pueblo elites comprising rancheros (the owners of middle-sized landholdings) and *arrendatarios* (tenant farmers) on the great estates often led revolts when changes of ownership of the haciendas led to cancellation of land rentals, increases in rents, or boundary disputes. The new owners were generally more financially solvent than their predecessors. They frequently sought to consolidate estates that had been sold piecemeal by their former owners. Frequently they sought to streamline production and to reduce costs. In pursuit of those objectives they introduced new crops and canceled land rent and labor contracts.

The tenant laborers who lived in the rancherías (the worker settlements on the haciendas) protested the land shortages that resulted from commercialization. With their own leaders, agrarian workers fought against forced transfers brought about by hacendado attempts to resolve "overpopulation" through relocation of labor resources to other parts of the estate or outright expulsion. While the haciendas grew, reduced wages and land availability for tenant farming provoked the hacienda agrarian working class.[14]

The free villages only rarely transcended their natural rivalries over land, water rights, and areas of political jurisdiction to achieve unity among themselves. They were divorced from the tenants and workers on the great estates because of the latter group's basic dependence on the great landowners. Municipio leadership was usually divided in times of confrontation because the caciques often owed their status to the local representatives of the Spanish Empire and accordingly opposed rebellious elements from rival local elites and from the lower social strata of indigenous society. Ethnic and racial antagonisms compounded these differences. Indian and mestizo villages were often in competition, and the uneven effects of European acculturation separated them further. These phenomena frequently divided the smaller settlements or *poblados* from the larger and usually more European-oriented towns or villas. Villages fought one another over land, water rights, and political jurisdictions.

Ranchería residents on the haciendas and their free village neighbors living in traditional locales on the peripheries of the great estates frequently resented one another. Sometimes the hacendado employers paid resident employees more than they did the part-time free village workers for identical tasks; other times the balance was reversed. In addition, the patron often assumed the hacienda resident workers' tax burden. When this was not done, the "unfree" hacienda residents paid the same rate of taxes or even higher levies than their free neighbors. Because of the close supervision imposed on them, it was more difficult for them to escape the levies than the more mobile "free" villagers. Some hacienda workers were sharecroppers. Others were tenant farmers. Their incomes and status varied widely. Debt peons resented the ability of their free neighbors to come and go as they chose. The result of this system in central Mexico and other intensive commercial farming areas was a divided, multitiered rural working class in a state of perpetual self-defeating rivalry.

Despite the peasantry's growing alienation, it was unable to assert itself with notable force until the Independence Revolution. Its limited access to weapons, lack of adequate military and political leadership, and the notoriously poor communications of the countryside left most incidents of unrest isolated. Then, beginning in 1810, the rural populace of the Bajío and the villages of the west and southwest rallied to the provincial elite and pequeña burguesa revolutionary leadership of Hidalgo, Allende, Aldama, Morelos, and Rayón.

In 1810 a state of deep social crisis existed in the greater Bajío region, an area that extended three hundred miles from Querétaro in the east to the border of Jalisco in the west. Between 1700 and 1800 the area had been the center of a mining and manufacturing boom. The key to prosperity was the success of the silver mines. During those hundred years silver coinage increased from 1.5 million pesos per year at the Mexico City mint to almost 24 million pesos per year. The greater part of the increase came from the mines of the Bajío, although the Sultepec-Taxco and Real del Monte complexes were also enjoying a renaissance. The Mexico City mercantile elite, encouraged by incentives offered by the Spanish government, provided the new capital and purchased the technology that renovated old mines long moribund in the seventeenth century and stimulated the digging of new ones. Agricultural production had also leaped ahead in the Bajío, as it did in other mining support zones, for more than a half-century. In the thirty-five years before 1810, however, the region experienced periodic crop failures and even famine as the population outgrew local production.

The industrial success of the area attracted an enormous influx of workers seeking employment in the mines, with the support industries in towns such as Dolores and San Miguel and on the great estates providing foodstuffs for both the towns and mines. Almost all newcomers went through a transitional state upon arrival, resulting in a large homeless population on the fringes of the towns and easily exhausting support services. During mining layoffs engendered by flooding, breakdowns, and the exhaustion of veins, the transient population in the towns swelled with laid-off workers. The manufacturing sector of the economy was similarly unstable. Mining slowdowns meant reduced or canceled orders for supplies and inevitable layoffs. Industrial labor unrest was endemic. Given the economic instability of the region, relations between absentee mine owners and locally based manufacturers and suppliers were also strained.

From 1800 to 1810 mining shutdowns became even more frequent and prolonged as a result of overexpansion. The decade was a time of instability and a 7 percent decline in output. The vulnerable provincial manufacturing elites, always distrustful and resentful of Mexico City and its use of autocratic power to favor Spanish mercantile importers while inhibiting the production of manufacturers in the colony, became openly hostile. The Aldama and Allende family-owned factories first reduced output and then, faced with canceled orders, shut down. The underlying factor for massive peasant and lower-class revolution in the Bajío was in agriculture.

During the eighteenth century the fallow farmlands of the once underpopulated Bajío filled with tenant farmers. Then increasing profitability caused the land to be reorganized for commercial production under direct control of the owners. Tenant farmers who wanted to remain on the land and not lose their higher social status and ancestral homesites moved to the hillsides, away from the irrigated fields. In years of adequate rainfall they scraped out a bare existence, but in times of drought they had no base of sustenance. Lower-paid newcomers brought in as day laborers replaced them. Before the boom the tenant farmers had lived on estate rancherías—at least that is how legal documents described the settlements. They were largely a people of mixed blood, descended from sixteenth-century workers brought by the Spaniards to work in and support the silver mines, because the area's underpopulation during the late pre-Columbian era left no resident Indian basis for labor.

During the ensuing generations tenant farmers adopted a way of life and value systems consistent with those of the Crown's legally recognized autonomous villages of central Mexico. Lacking a legal foundation, they built homes and churches and farmed the lands of the estate owners on a renewable contract basis. The plots of land they farmed were recognized by custom to pertain to a particular settlement, to the heirs of a particular family. They paid for livestock grazing and water rights at long-established rates. They aspired to be an autonomous peasantry. They believed themselves to be a peasantry. Their displacement during the economic bonanza of the eighteenth century was within Spanish law. Fortunately, expanding mine and industrial employment softened the blow. Then economic breakdown came to mining and manufacturing; desperation and anger replaced hope. The displaced peasantry were among the most alienated and ready to rebel.[15]

The first signs of social crisis appeared with drought and crop failure in the mid-1770s and famine in 1777–1779. The problem reappeared in 1792–1793 and 1799. It threatened ominously in 1806 and again in 1810. Many of the tenant farmers were forced to give up their lands and settlements and migrate to the already overpopulated towns. Beggars were omnipresent. Then industrial decline set in with layoffs, shutdowns, and reduced hours and wages. Industrial workers joined displaced peasants in the streets. The scions of local industrialist families, the Allende and Aldama, and the leading intellectual of the province, Padre Miguel Hidalgo de Costilla of Dolores, when faced with impending arrest for their insurrectionary conspiracies with the provincial elite at Querétaro, rallied the displaced peasants and workers to revolution.

The revolt swept across the Bajío. Spaniards, state authorities, and great estates were the targets of attacks. Displaced tenant farmers joined by unemployed miners and industrial workers and disgruntled great estate agricultural workers from the rancherías rose up and seized the properties. By the time the revolution reached Jalisco and Michoacán, on the western and southern peripheries of the Bajío, it had become much more than an independence movement under a unified command. It was a decentralized peasant counterattack against the expansive great estates, involving countless village-based mini-insurrections. In Jalisco and Michoacán villages peasants participating in the revolution sought redress of earlier unsatisfactorily resolved land disputes with the private great estate owners. Local middle- and smallholders went largely untouched. In Michoacán, where the Tarascan ethnicity of a great part of the peasantry compounded economic differences, the fighting was particularly acute. In both Michoacán and the Altos of Jalisco geographic remoteness and the topographic difficulty of the terrain abetted prolonged resistance to government troops even after Hidalgo's main forces had been defeated.[16]

The peasant war underpinning of the independence insurrection cost the rebellious Bajío regional elites any hope of metropolitan Creole backing against the Spanish government. The Creole elite was concentrated in Mexico City and environs. Its economic strength lay in absentee large-scale commercial landholding, which was the principal contradiction between the peasantry and the regime. José María Morelos recognized this contradiction during his tenure as the principal insurrectionary leader between 1812 and 1815 and disciplined the villages under his control in Michoacán, Guerrero, and Morelos for agrarian excesses. The metropolitan elites, however, correctly viewed the revolution on the periphery as hostile to their interests. They opted to support the monarchist Creole militia commander Agustin de Iturbide's military coup d'état and his rapprochement with the insurgent leaders, hacendados Vicente Guerrero and Guadalupe Victoria. Independence found the country economically depleted. Its revenue-generating industries were largely shut down, communications and commerce severely impaired by guerrillas and bandits, and the ravaged great estates lying fallow or partially in the hands of the subsistence-oriented peasantry.[17]

THE HACENDADO COUNTERATTACK: 1821–1910

Despite widespread restoration of the fields to peasant control during the independence struggles, the campesinos failed to influence the national government. At first the new regime came under the control of the more "conservative" Creoles of Mexico City. The Conservatives' principal rivals for power were the Liberals. Both groups included important hacendado contingents no longer constrained by protective Crown land, Indian, and Church laws dating from the sixteenth century. The Conservatives, in their defense of colonial-era privileges, used the support of pueblo rights as a means to build a national alliance between the autocratic right wing of the metropolis and the mass of lower communal village peasantry. Yet during the era of their rule local and state ordinances were enacted enabling hacendado seizures of pueblo lands.

The Liberals, led by provincial elites including hacendados, businessmen, and professionals, were frequently hostile to the pueblo communes. The Liberal emphasis on individual ownership challenged the interests of the lower peasantry. Their national program, which called for a more open society, posited the need for public schools, and higher levels of agricultural production through private ownership. It offered middle peasant mestizo and Indian property holders greater individual political and social participation including the hope for public education and lower prices through free trade. The Liberal push to abolish head taxes engendered support from all levels of peasant society.[18]

After independence the hacendados, now in political power and stimulated by the ever-present profitability of agricultural exports, attempted to restore their estates. That effort brought about nearly a century of intermittent campesino revolutions. The restoration of hacienda and plantation agriculture meant an increased flow of rural productivity and wealth away from the hinterlands to the cities. Peasant landholdings, political independence, and cultural values once again came under attack.

That change especially disturbed the Indo-peasantry, which, until the uninvited intrusion, had an almost insular experience and satisfaction with the products of the land. The preference for their own way of life mitigated the Indo-peasantry's need for the outside world and the goods available in its cash economy. The Mexican campesino had to be acculturated and recruited before new needs could be felt. With the passage of time some peasant villages accommodated the new ways, but in many places they demonstrated unrest for more than two centuries extending from 1707 to the 1930s. In 1910 the precapitalist structure was still capable of violently resisting the alien intrusion.[19]

In 1832–1834 the first major peasant uprising since the Independence Revolution spread from Nochistlán, Oaxaca, where village-private estate land disputes were under way, across southwestern Mexico into the Balsas River basin areas of southern Michoacán. It involved dozens of villages and countless pueblos that complained of land seizures by outside and local private estate owners, court decisions, and the various "anti-clerical" laws passed in 1828 and 1829. That legislation, they complained, enabled the denunciation of fallow lands and the properties of those pueblos with unclear or undocumented titles. Many of the lands that were legally Church property were in fact used by the pueblos.

By the time troops reached the remote sites of the initial rebellion, unrest had grown out of hand. It spread northeasterly through the rural expanses of southeastern and southern Guerrero, where estate agriculture was regaining its former hold through the production of sugar, cotton, livestock, and timber, into the new citrus zones of the Balsas River basin on the border between Guerrero and Michoacán. A related but isolated rising led by the village priest at Yautepec in Morelos also broke out at this time. Millenarian in character, the rebellion sought to reestablish the Aztec empire in a glorious new order under the aegis of an Indian prince with seven wives. Many of these villages had supported the insurgency during the independence wars between 1811 and 1821. The lack of a centralized leadership and the poor coordination of efforts between village-based rebellious zones exhibited in the 1832–1834 fighting established a pattern that continued into the 1910 Revolution.[20]

In 1842–1845 the same area of southwestern Mexico served as the center of an even larger peasants' war with all the characteristics of the 1910 revolution. It was an agrarian war characterized by provincial elite, local elite, and peasant-led formations which encompassed 60,000 square miles, involved hundreds of pueblos between Ixtepec in the Isthmus of Tehuantepec and the Balsas River basin of southern Michoacán, and bordered by the Pacific Ocean and Sultepec-Taxco, Cuernavaca, and Izúcar regions in the nation's center. It began at Tecoanapa in the Costa Chica south of Acapulco. Tecoanapa was a minor crossroads town on the route between Oaxaca and Acapulco comprising the mixed-blood descendants of black slaves, mestizos, and village Indians who worked full- or part-time on the vast San Marcos hacienda during the colonial era. Its claim to pueblo status, like those of other settlements in the region, was not supported by documents.

Between the 1740s and 1770s the entrepreneurial José Gallo controlled the San Marcos hacienda, the largest commercial estate in central and southwestern Mexico. Gallo, who commanded the Acapulco garrison, owned truck and large commercial farms on the peripheries of Guadalajara and Matamoros. His brother operated a complex of commercial estates around Mexico City. Utilizing his control over the Aduana of Acapulco, Gallo made the San Marcos hacienda the principal source of provisions for the Philippine-Asian fleets. He supplied timber, beef, salt, twine, and other needed products to the silver mines of Sultepec and Taxco and even conducted cattle drives to the much larger market of Mexico City.

The San Marcos estate, reduced by peasant land occupations during the independence wars, was regenerating under the ownership of a Spanish merchant of Mexico City. He had already subjugated the other populated sites nearer its center after rejecting their claims to sharecropping rights and outright ownership. No longer enjoying the fruits of the Philippine-Asian trade and having lost its fruit orchards along the Oaxacan border, the estate administration moved to create a more specialized production system. Specifically, the owner was intolerant of *acasillado* demands for land set aside for corn and bean production. In addition local administrators, known if not trusted by the indigenous populace, had been replaced by outside professionals from Mexico City. Salaries were replacing sharecropping arrangements while water, salt, and land rights were intensely disputed. Tecoanapa was descended in part from black slaves, many of whom had fought in the independence wars. The town, located some thirty kilometers from the estate *casco,* and other nearby villages and pueblos sensed a serious threat.[21]

Elite crisis between the provincial Liberal general Juan Alvarez and the national administration helped trigger the peasants' war and increased its magnitude. With the peasants already apprehensive about the expansionist program of the San Marcos hacendado, the Santa Anna government in Mexico City promulgated a political redistricting plan that created new states and changed local jurisdictions. The territory involved coincided to a considerable extent with the zone of peasant uprising, a large segment of Guerrero extending from Tlapa to Chilapa southward to the Pacific. The political reorganization was designed to replace the influence of Alvarez with the Conservative cacique and hacendado of Chilpancingo, Nicolas Bravo. Alvarez and his elite allies in the states of Mexico and Puebla stood to lose heavily and worked actively to prevent the redistricting. Part of Alvarez's effort included a tour of the Costa Chica, warning the peasants of a threat to their interests. Whether or not he expected a rebellion is unclear; however, the extent of peasant violence forced him to move against them.[22] (For map of 1840s Southwestern peasant war, see p. 79.)

The citizenry of Tecoanapa was thrown into panic by the possibility of its delivery into the arms of Bravo and the San Marcos estate owner. Rioting broke out after a town meeting. Then, joined by peasants from nearby communities, they attacked the great estate, burned the big house, and killed the administrator. When the rebellion was a few weeks old Alvarez finally sent his dragoons to quell the rising. They razed Tecoanapa and dispersed the rebels, but by then the contagion had spread.

The principal area of warfare was in the southern half of the Chilapa district encompassing several municipio jurisdictions and between thirty and forty insurgent pueblos. The social divisions in the conflict anticipated the revolution of 1910. The center of the fighting was Ayahualulco, the mostly Nahuatl former district capital during Aztec and colonial times which Bravo had replaced with Chilapa, a commercial crossroads and mestizo town where a number of hacendados resided. Landowners in the area, depending on their affluence, lived in Chilapa, Chilpancingo, or Mexico City. They were largely political supporters of Bravo, although the ranchero José de Abarca, a leader of Ayahualulco and one of the insurrectionary chiefs, later became an officer in Alvarez's Liberal army that ousted Santa Anna in 1854. In the years following independence, Ayahualulco lost its bottom lands to the caciques of Chilapa, the Moctezuma heirs. That land dispute, followed by the loss of timberlands and hilltop properties, caused Ayahualulco to participate in the 1832–1833 uprising. The town was defeated, however, and faced economic disaster.

In 1842, Ayahualulco fought again, exercising its traditional leadership over the pueblos of a county-sized area of two dozen settlements. The rebellion continued for two years before a compromise was negotiated by Alvarez, ending the fighting. The pueblos were left in dire straits. Ayahualulco was sacked and burned at least twice during the war. The town remained the *"mata de la indígena"* of Nahuatl central Guerrero, but all hope of containing the hacendados and the growing commercial-political power of Chilapa ended.[23]

Within weeks of the outbreak around Ayahualulco the Yope and Tlapaneca peasantry to the east in the neighboring districts of Atlixtac and Tlapa revolted with their own leadership. The basis of conflict was the same except that Alvarez was one of the commercial landowners in the Tlapa area. Three thousand peasants laid siege to Tlapa for six weeks. Unable to take the city, they annihilated a relief column of mixed cavalry and infantry sent from Puebla. While intermittent fighting continued throughout Guerrero, the uprising spread into new areas. Revolts broke out at the mining center of Sultepec-Taxco, the sugar-producing regions to the southeast of Cuernavaca and between Tlaxiaco in Oaxaca and Izúcar in Puebla, in the citrus zones of Michoacán, and along the Oaxacan Pacific coast to the Isthmus of Tehuantepec, where coffee and tropical export industries were displacing the resisting village populace. At the end of 1844 most of the fighting lapsed. In 1845 new flare-ups occurred near Zirandero on the Michoacán-Guerrero border because of new head taxes and in the Isthmus of Tehuantepec between 1847 and 1849 because of continued Marquesana estate incursions against Zapotec peasantry land tenure.[24]

Throughout the uprisings Alvarez offered sympathy to peasant claims of land despoilation. He fought their rebelliousness at Tecoanapa but offered his services at the negotiating table while the government forces served his interests at Tlapa. Meanwhile he recruited a massive local elite and peasant following over a wide area between Chilapa, Acapulco, and Oaxaca. In 1853 he used the goodwill generated by his maneuvering in the 1840s to obtain support for his Guerrero-Oaxaca regional elite-led revolution of Ayutla, which began in the heart of the peasant rebellious zone near Tecoanapa, and overthrew Santa Anna in 1854. The basis of popular support for the 1854 revolution was remarkably similar to the larger regional elite-led uprising of 1910 and the social revolution that followed.

In 1849 and again in 1856–1857 extensive peasant uprisings swept across the center and south of the nation. The 1849 revolts started at Acambay in the state of Mexico and spread into neighboring states as peasants resisted land seizures by the hacendados who promptly settled their *asalariados* (employees) on the pueblo lands. The later rebellions opposed the Liberal government's Ley Lerdo, which outlawed communal properties in 1856, and its constitutionalization in 1857. Village peasants and agrarian workers in states extending from San Luis Potosí and Sinaloa in the north to the Isthmus of Tehuantepec in the south were involved. In 1858–1860 they supported the Conservative counterrevolution that succeeded in driving the Liberals temporarily from power.

The Ley Lerdo not only outlawed corporate landholdings but established procedures for their partition among private landholders. While it enhanced opportunities for local elites, rancheros, and hacendados, it diminished the condition of lower peasants and agrarian laborers by reducing their lands. It vastly increased the number of competitors for tenant farming contracts among the rural population. The Mexican government, in its physiocratic search for national prosperity through the promotion of commercial agriculture, came into open conflict with most of the communal pueblo peasantry.

During the French intervention between 1862 and 1867 the Mexican agrarian population was beset by ambivalence. Disdain and hatred for the Liberals on the part of the communal, Catholic, most intensely traditional and lower peasants was balanced by resentment of the French on the part of villages in areas such as the north, where Mexican nationalism and middle-sized commercial land tenure had already taken hold. In some parts of central Mexico, especially Suchilapan and the Gulf coast of the Isthmus of Tehuantepec, campesinos welcomed the French-imposed Emperor Maximilian as liberator. Maximilian attempted to solidify his regime with village support. He created the Junta Protectora de las Clases Menesterosas in order to relieve peasant misery engendered by the massive land seizures that accompanied the Ley Lerdo in 1856–1857. Although his maneuver succeeded in capturing village backing, it proved politically and militarily disadvantageous because it drove the overwhelming majority of regional elites, basically hacendados, with their state militias and irregular forces into the opposing Juárez-led liberal camp.

During the years 1868–1870, shortly following the French departure and the Liberal reconquest of Mexico, a wave of peasant unrest swept central Mexico and included pueblos in the states of Chiapas, Morelos, Mexico, Oaxaca, Puebla, Tabasco, Tlaxcala, Veracruz, Hidalgo, San Luis Potosí, Querétaro, Guanajuato, Michoacán, and Jalisco. There were at least five distinct movements and geographical divisions in the unrest. The largest and most important uprising was led by revolutionary anarchist Julio Chávez López whose main force numbered fifteen hundred men. Its sphere of activity centered along the eastern edge of the Valley of Mexico and ranged south into Morelos, east into Puebla, Tlaxcala, and Veracruz, and north to Actopan in Hidalgo.

The pueblos of this region had reaped great benefits from Maximilian. On 19 June 1866 the emperor issued a land grant to Xico, which became a hotbed of violence between 1868 and 1872, returning land that the pueblo claimed had been usurped by a hacienda. Another center of the uprising, Coatepec, near Chalco, also received a grant restoring its lost commons. The Juárez government immediately restored the lands to the liberal politicians of the area including Mariano Riva Palacio and General Rafael Cuellar. The towns of Xico, Tlalmanalco, Coatepec, Hueypostla, Tianguistengo, and Amecameca in the state of Mexico, San Lucas Nextitelco near Cholula in Puebla, and San Agustín Tetlama, which lost properties to the hacienda of Temisco, supported the rebellion with men, horses, and supplies.[25]

Chávez López was a "hacienda worker," probably a worker and tenant farmer in one of the many olive orchards in the area, from near Texcoco. Anarchist organizers from Mexico City proselytized him at a campesino political action center in the important municipio of Chalco, long a center of social bandit activity. Anarchist graduates of the Colegio de San Ildefonso, the best school in Mexico City at the time, wrote the agrarian manifesto issued in his name. It was the first of a series of published revolutionary agrarian programs. Rising against an intensive land enclosure movement, the 1868–1870 Chávez López uprising initiated the beginning of ideological agrarian revolution. Its consistent proagrarian worker and independent village and anticentral government and landed estate ideology established the fundamental demands for peasant insurrection that held through the Zapatista revolution in 1910. It blamed government, Church, Spaniards, and expansionist landowners for the hardships of the campesinos and called for the overthrow of the government, locally controlled land redistribution, and the establishment of village autonomy, the *"municipio libre."*

A three-century-long modus vivendi had been upset in Chalco, the fishing pueblo of Xico, and the eastern valley during the late 1860s by the construction of the Mexico City-Veracruz railroad in the northern portion of the area which caused an inflation of land values. The drainage of Lake Chalco in the south and the general commercialization of landholdings ranging from wheat and grapes to olive cultivation by entrepreneurial farmers compounded the problem. Liberal politicians, land developers, and contractors competed for tracts of land leased by estate owners from Mexico's ruling political and economic elite, while tenant farmers and communal villagers were driven off their land, presented with higher taxes, and forced to join a surplus labor force desperately seeking ever dearer tenant farming contracts.[26]

Chávez López's main force, recruited from small-scale commercial olive orchard and vineyard operations and free villages and hacienda rancherías, defended its water rights and land while resisting new taxes and displacement. It still aspired to maintain autonomous status for its pueblos. Chávez López's forces were smashed in battle by the Federal Army at Actopan,

Hidalgo in 1869, but his movement had already introduced an articulate revolutionary agrarianism into Mexico's campesino unrest. The revolutionary Chávez López was executed, but the region of his operations continued to experience widespread disorders, and smaller military engagements went on for more than a year.[27]

Another serious agrarian revolt in 1868–1869 centered in San Luis Potosí, Querétaro, Hidalgo, and the northern part of the state of Mexico. These forces, like those to the south, had a mix of local elite-ranchero leadership and Indian and mestizo, free village, and ranchería-resident hacienda worker support. Alienated local elites displaced by new economic forces and unrepresented in Mexico City led the movement and attempted to maneuver as a conventional army. They mobilized local support by demanding the return of lost communal landholdings and recognition of various ranchería claims to autonomous rights against the haciendas. They carried out a number of land occupations. They, too, were defeated by the Federal Army.

A third region of campesino unrest in 1868–1869 developed in the western half of the state of Mexico, the Sierra Gordo highlands of southern Querétaro, and in parts of the states of Guanajuato and Michoacán. In this case clusters of villages complained of land "despoilation" and attacked "Spanish" towns and the Augustinian monastery at Dehedó. They did not constitute a strategic military threat, but at one stage the capital of the state of Mexico, Toluca, was surrounded by an angry horde of campesinos who closed the roads and began a seige. The army sent relief columns to provide the state capital with foodstuffs and water.

The Sierra Gordo of Querétaro was the site of many violent clashes over land from the 1840s through the 1880s. When Otomí Indian peasants and estate workers attacked the Augustinian monastery near Dehedó, they claimed its lands. On several occasions troops were sent from Mexico City to disperse the rebels. In Jalisco the rebellious peasants complained of land "alienations by outsiders" and resorted to violent resistance after petitions failed. In the Bajío, Guanajuato peasants formed an agrarian league and vowed to fight for the restoration of their lands, which they complained had been despoiled. Expansive commercial estates increasingly dominated agriculture there.

A fourth region of peasant unrest centered on the long-resistant indigenous stronghold of Juchitán in the Isthmus of Tehuantepec. Finally, a far-south zone of indigenous-peasant resistance to land enclosures extended from Chiapas across Campeche and part of Tabasco.[28]

During the 1870s radical *agraristas* in the Mexican urban labor movement, recognizing the need to link the resistance of the rural working classes with that of the industrial workers, became increasingly assertive. Using their press, they attacked the government's policies of support for the hacendados and advanced the idea of agrarian as well as industrial cooperatives as counterforces. They hoped that the cooperative movement would better organize the peasants against capitalism.

Late in the decade Mexico City anarchist and agrarian revolutionaries formed organizing committees that attempted to assist campesino leaders through emissaries and legal representation going as far as the Supreme Court. In one Supreme Court case government lawyers accused the radical attorney representing a confederation of litigious villages of being one of the "communists" who had agitated them to revolution and urged his arrest for sedition.

The most important group of urban agraristas, the Gran Comité Conmunero, included radical Mexico City lawyers and teachers. Led by anarchist Francisco Zalacosta, it affiliated with a group of attorneys led by Tiburcio Montiel and a few radical army officers. Montiel had helped organize and represented litigious villages in the Chalco area against neighboring haciendas. The Gran Comité played a coordinating role in the agrarian uprisings of 1878–1883.[29]

Between 1878 and 1883 a wave of peasant unrest swept across north and central Mexico. The Mexico City revolutionaries actively provoked peasant uprisings in the eastern part of the Valley of Mexico and parts of Hidalgo and Querétaro. In 1880 the army executed Zalacosta in Querétaro. In the meantime, the Gran Comité organized regional village conventions in the states of Mexico, Hidalgo, and Guanajuato. The Gran Comité Conmunero continued court litigations on behalf of the expelled tenant farmers and the multiplying villages losing their commons to private denunciation. In the midst of land seizures associated with the planning of the new railroad system, peasant uprisings ranged from Chihuahua in the north to Oaxaca in the south. A peasant league emerged from regional conventions held in Mexico, Hidalgo, and Guanajuato. Finally, a gathering attended by representatives of forty villages and pueblos from the states of Guanajuato, Michoacán, Querétaro, Hidalgo, and Mexico met at La Barranca in Guanajuato. La Barranca was a ranchería lacking de jure pueblo status, but its citizens believed theirs was a legal pueblo. Whatever their legal status, they were losing tenant farming and water use rights to new, more commercially oriented landowners. The campesino delegates called upon the government to carry out agrarian reforms in order to avert a revolution. The army restored discipline. During the ensuing five years of fighting the Mexico City Gran Comité Conmunero encouraged agrarian rebels from Hidalgo to southern Chihuahua to western Michoacán.[30]

The initial land seizures preliminary to railroad construction were the reverse of what the peasants had expected from the young Díaz regime. The mobilized peasantry commonly believed that the new government was violating promises of agrarian reform made on their behalf in Porfirio Díaz's Plan of Tuxtepec, issued during his struggle to overthrow the government in 1876. Actually the plan did not spell out an agrarian reform program at all, but Díaz, in leading a broad-based political movement, convinced mutually antagonistic social groups, ranging from Rio Grande Valley ranchmen in Texas and northern Mexican elites to industrialists and workers and landowners and campesinos, to support him by posing as a representative for each of their interests. Indeed, the Plan of Tuxtepec, with its vague idealism, its promise to end political corruption, and the promise of its presidential candidate Porfirio Díaz to serve only one term, seemed to offer all things to all people. The result was a violent confrontation of the government with the unhappy campesinos and the radical urban labor movement.

The 1878–1883 revolts enjoyed some initial success because during the 1876 Revolution of Tuxtepec the rural constabulary, the rurales, who were vital to maintaining tranquillity in the countryside, supported President Sebastian Lerdo de Tejada and were destroyed as an effective force. In 1878 the new government had not yet restored the rurales' previous level of vigor or efficiency.[31]

Despite the land seizures, overwhelming defeats, and demoralization suffered by the peasants, the 1878 unrest produced significant advances for Mexican agrarianism. A higher degree of unity had been achieved than ever before. That consciousness produced the Ley del Pueblo in Puebla, a state whose land tenure regime and traditional balance of social relations had been completely upset by the growth of absentee-owned depersonalized great estate export agriculture.

The Ley del Pueblo was written by members of the local elite and pequeña burguesía, the agrarista radicals Alberto Santa Fe, Manuel Serdán, and Jesus Laguna of Puebla. It was the most complete agrarian program that Mexico had yet seen. Porfirio Díaz called Santa Fe a communist. The *ley* proclaimed all of humankind spiritually equal and entitled to equal rights. All male heads of campesino families with less than three thousand pesos in total wealth were to receive parcels of land 276 × 184 rods in size. The ley provided for the municipios to take charge of hacienda properties and administer the land allocations to their member citizenry. The hacendados were to receive compensation through the presentation of receipts to an Agricultural and Industrial Bank (Banco Agrícola y Industrial), which was to be entrusted with the duties of financing the resurrection of Mexican agriculture besides handling the details of the agrarian reform process. Those details included low-interest 6 percent loans to the campesinos to make possible initial land purchases and to provide a material basis for increased peasant agricultural production.[32]

In the northern zone of revolt unrest focused on the state of San Luis Potosí and the Huastecan areas of the Sierra Madre Oriental. Its causation and indigenous composition was comparable to the 1840s peasants' war of the southwest. Unrest in the north was linked to the intrusion by railroads, the accompanying inflation of land values, and the commercialization of agriculture in the mountain valleys. New *jefes políticos* displaced local elites in power while large investors in the United States, Mexico City, and the state capitals seized lands adjoining or within reach of the rail system beginning construction.[33]

The San Luis Potosí revolt, however, contrasted with the others. Rather than exploding outward against metropolitan Mexico and its provincial capitals, it turned away from the center and metropolitan Mexico. The rebels moved from the Río Verde Valley deep into the mountainous Huasteca Indian zones, across the Sierra Madre Oriental to Ciudad del Maíz. Importantly, the exclusiveness of Huastecan nationalism caused the revolution to implode rather than to expand into other, alien areas. Later, despite the massive Zapatista uprisings that occurred there, that desire for apartness would isolate the Huasteca from the greater arena of conflict during the 1910 revolution.

In 1886 scattered agrarian uprisings triggered by land disputes swept the states of Hidalgo, San Luis Potosí, and Veracruz. Isolated incidents of campesino unrest took place in the west. They had no connection with the radical and liberal agraristas of Mexico City. The government suppressed these disorders with little difficulty. For the Mexican campesinaje the 1880s were a dark period of land seizures, loss of tenancy and water rights, more formalized alienating latifundia labor, migration, rurales, and armed discipline.

In 1888 the aggressive sugar hacendados of eastern Morelos greatly increased their holdings. In that year the owner of the El Hospital hacienda seized properties to the east and north of its principal acreage, lands that were regarded by the fairly large town of Yautepec, the villa of Ayala, and the pueblo of Anenecuilco as their own. The result was a series of petitions by the municipalities to the local, state, and national governments protesting the intrusions by the "Spaniards." Armed men from the hacienda prevented the villagers from reentering the disputed land.[34]

In 1892 the villages sent a committee that included Emiliano Zapata to Mexico City for an audience with President Díaz. Such a hearing would normally have been impossible, but a prominent Mexico City lawyer supported the villages and arranged for the delegates to meet with the president. Díaz heard their complaints and promised to take action. When Díaz did act, however, he deported the delegation leader to serve a penal term at forced labor in Yucatán, and Zapata was forcibly conscripted into the army. The 1888 hacienda occupation became the justification for the Anenecuilco defense committee's 1910 insurrection under the command of Zapata. Years later Zapata's friend and fellow villager Francisco Franco wrote President Lázaro Cárdenas and the Mexican Agrarian Commission to tell them that it was the 1888 El Hospital land seizures that made Anenecuilco and Zapata revolt.[35]

Between 1888 and 1892 peasant unrest seethed in the greater Tomochic area of southwestern Chihuahua, providing an added dimension to the ongoing warfare in the nation's northwest between the Mexican government and the countrypeople in the Sierra Madre Occidental, the Yaqui in Sonora, and the Mayo in Sinaloa. The Tomochic rebellion of 1892 was economically and culturally linked to the other conflicts in the region. Railroad, mining, ranching, and timber interests from the United States had established hegemony over the economy of the northwest, with some British and Canadian participation.

The uprising resulted mainly from the intrusion of lumbermen and the Northwestern Railroad into the once remote setting. Foreign lumbermen gained access to Tomochic's land in 1889 and 1890 via leases from Secretary of the Treasury Limantour, who had just acquired it from the government through a trade of land he had obtained illegally in Baja California. The railroad management became interested in the Tomochic region because of its timber, mineral, and mining resources. Two of the principal concerns in the area were the British Pinos Altos and Palmarejo Mining Companies. The Northwestern Railroad, a U.S.-chartered concern, controlled by Canadian electrical power magnate Fred Stark Pearson, gained a right-of-way across Tomochic's lands in the late 1880s.

A statewide revolution in real estate values was under way in which elements of the state elite shared in the bonanza with Pearson and American investors including the Cargill Lumber Company, the Thomas Wentworth Peirce estate, Edwin Morgan, heir to the Morgan steamship line, and a complex of Louisiana and east Texas railroads, the Denver and Rio Grande

Railroad interests, Phoebe and William Randolph Hearst, Edwin J. Marshall (founding treasurer of the Texas Company), and ex-governor A. C. Shepherd of Washington, D.C. Other American investors rushed to join in the land speculations in the years that followed. The Tomochic spur to the Northwestern's main line was never built, but the effect of the 1889 timber leases by foreigners of the Limantour tract that dominated Tomochic destabilized the region. The first peasant rising in southwestern Chihuahua, in what became the Porfirian government's most embarrassing confrontation, broke out at nearby Cusihuiriachic.[36]

Like the 1910 revolution, the growing unrest in western Chihuahua had a cultural and millenarian dimension in addition to the economic one. Desperation engendered an indigenous religious movement featuring trances and visions. The inspiration for the new religiosity was Teresa Urrea de Cabora of Sonora, known as Santa Teresa or Teresita by her adherents. Her visions, like the contemporary escapist Ghost Dance of the American Plains Indians, could be shared through trances. While in that detached state her beleaguered peasant followers of northwestern Mexico could see utopia—the intruders would go away. It was not going to be that easy.[37]

The Tomochic rebellion began with outright rejection of the state's authority and religion by the townfolk. It was followed by the defeat of a small contingent of troops and a large-scale invasion that overwhelmed the town, killing its three hundred adult males and a good portion of the women, children, and elderly. For the next eighteen years the press, famed novelist Heriberto Frías, and the political opposition combined to make Tomochic one of the most embarrassing imbroglios of the Díaz administration.

In 1909 campesinos from Janos and Casas Grandes invaded and occupied the disputed river bottom lands of the 979,000-acre Corralitos hacienda in Chihuahua. The Corralitos was owned by an American company headed by Edwin Morgan, Thomas Wentworth Peirce II, and stockholders of the Denver and Rio Grande Railroad. The peasants took action because of a land dispute that developed after land surveyor Henrique Muller, an American citizen working for St. Louis bankers, first seized 133,000 acres of Janos's lands in the 1880s and then sold them to the powerful Corralitos operators. In 1760, Janos and Casas Grandes had each received viceregal grants of four leagues of land in each direction from the church *capilla*.

Meanwhile, during the 1880s the Terrazas family, the dominant element of the Chihuahuan oligarchy, had seized half the territory claimed by the ranchers of Casas Grandes located to the pueblo's southwest. The citizens of Casas Grandes and Janos appealed in the courts and eventually took their complaints to President Díaz. All of their efforts failed. Praxedis Guerrero of the Partido Liberal Mexicano (PLM) and ensuing revolutionaries found a ready revolutionary spirit among the angry people of the two towns.

By 1909 the two pueblos had been reduced to the "urban zones" of streets and houses in their localities. The Corralitos hacienda had gained three-fourths of its land through private purchases and denunciations of communal properties. In 1909 the Corralitos's boundaries extended from ten miles south of Casas Grandes northward past the town to the edge of neighboring Janos, west ten miles beyond both Janos and Casas Grandes, and east to the range of mountains that embraced the valley.[38]

Led by anarchist Guerrero of the PLM, campesinos of the two pueblos began raiding the Corralitos hacienda in 1907. Following their 1909 river bottom land occupations they fought government efforts to oust them, initiating an era of violence that continued there for over ten years. Following the attack on the American hacienda, a cross-section of the rural populace of western and southern Chihuahua lent heavy support to efforts to oust American landholders and overthrow the governments of Díaz and Huerta. They successively supported the lower-class and local elite revolutionary leadership of the PLM, then Pascual Orozco, and finally Francisco Villa and his allies in the state in their struggle with rival upper-class-led revolutionary factions after the fall of the ancien régime.

The fighting in Chihuahua complemented a large uprising in 1891 and again in 1896 at Papantla, Veracruz. In the bloody 1896 rising, campesinos outraged by land despoilation for the purpose of developing vanilla, cacao, sugar, coffee, and rice production burned the town. The intruders were foreign and Mexico City investors whose "surveying" companies carried contractual rights to claim about one-third of the land delineated and purchase the remainder at auction prices. About a thousand men participated in the revolt, which was complicated by the racial antagonisms between peasant Huastecan Indians and the mestizo-Caucasian commercial farmers and local elites. The mestizo and Caucasian private property holders of the Papantla region lived in the town and controlled the municipal government. Yet some of the local elite supported the rebellion. They were being displaced as well. Casualties were heavy; hundreds were lost.[39]

The Papantla conflict was a microcosm of the developing agrarian conflict in Mexico. It was a struggle for political and economic power that involved the land and racial and cultural friction. It was complicated by political rivalries between pueblo and town and alliances of local elites with lower and middle peasants versus outside intruders. The late timing of unrest in Papantla was consistent with its Gulf coast remoteness from the capital and strong residual ethnic culture. The arrival of foreign investors, large-scale commercial agriculture, and political intrusion was finally getting under way, and the population of the Papantla region reacted just as the well-entrenched peasant societies in other areas of Mexico had reacted earlier. The army quickly dispersed the campesino main forces, but the rebels in Veracruz continued to fight as guerrillas with radical pequeña burguesa leadership and local elite support throughout the remainder of the Porfiriato until 1910, when they joined in the revolution.[40]

The struggle around Papantla paralleled the intense land, cultural, and political conflicts of the countrypeople in southwestern Chihuahua, the Yaqui in Sonora, the Mayo in Sinaloa, and the Maya in Yucatán. These were ongoing confrontations that in the long-range view began with the sixteenth-century Spanish intrusion but which were rekindled in the 1880s by the ancien régime's land denunciation policies. Those land policies opened up vast tracts of communal and "vacant" or "public" properties for colonization by American settlers.

Over seven thousand American settlers poured into the northern tier of states, putting up fences on what they regarded as inexpensive private property. Those properties were considered by the indigenous campesino population to be their own. The most publicized land transfer and colonization case was the acquisition by the Richardson Construction Company of Los Angeles, California, of 993,650 acres of Yaqui River Valley property long regarded by the Yaqui Indians as their national homeland. A Mexican short-term private holder sold it after acquiring it by denunciation procedures from the government. A tract totaling 1,450,000 acres on the headwaters of the Yaqui River lay adjacent to the Richardson holdings and extended to the Chihuahua border. It was owned by the Phoenix-based Wheeler Land Company controlled by Stanton Hyer of Rockport, Illinois, and a consortium of Chicago capitalists.[41]

The American Smelting and Refining Company, Phelps Dodge, William Greene, Edwin Marshall, American railroads, the Los Angeles Times Company, The Corralitos Company, William R. Hearst, Cargill, Edward Doheny, and the Texas Oil Company joined other prominent U.S. interests and benefited in the acquisition of cheap lands totaling 130 million acres. More important, the sale of these lands by ensuing American development companies to fifteen thousand settlers beginning on a large scale in 1903 displaced Mexican tenants and informal farm occupants extending from Chiapas to Chihuahua. One American described the situation:

> Yes sir. There was sometimes a little difficulty. You know, the natives down there are in the habit of planting, or putting up a house, or starting up a little farm of their own just wherever they want to, and of course, an American goes down there and buys his property and pays his taxes and lives according to the law. He wants his property, and he will have a little difficulty in getting these people off, keeping them off.[42]

The Díaz regime's land policies brought it under attack during the first decade of the twentieth century from radical liberals and the agraristas in Mexico City. The newspaper *El Hijo del Ahuizote* became the capital city's principal literary vehicle for the protest against alleged transgressions committed against the peasantry and foreign ownership of the nation's resources. The newspaper's banner declared "Mexico for the Mexicans," a slogan adopted during the revolution by the Mexican Gran Liga of Railroad Conductors shortly before it ordered the American railroad conductors to leave the country.

In 1906 indigenous resistance intensified through uprisings at Chinameca, Minatitlan, and Ixhuatlán in Veracruz, all zones undergoing commercialization of agriculture toward the production of rubber and ixtle. Members of the Partido Liberal Mexicano of Ricardo Flores Magón participated in organizing and leading the unrest. In September 1906, three hundred men, most of them campesinos led by Donato Padua, attacked Acayucan, Veracruz, a center of American agricultural investment and colonists. Repulsed by the defenders, they retreated into the countryside and continued to fight until the revolution of 1910, when they merged with larger forces. During the period 1906–1910 their range of operations included the area of textile labor strife at Rió Blanco-Nogales and later spread southward into the state of Tabasco. In October 1910, in alliance with the campesino insurgents commanded by Santana Rodríguez ("Santanon"), they conducted a series of attacks on large towns in Veracruz. Some survivors of the Papantla, Chinameca, Minatitlan, and Ixhuatlán struggles eventually joined the combined Padua-Santanon PLM forces. The pequeña burguesía demonstrated increasing revolutionism, taking the lead of peasant forces, for several years before the revolution.[43]

By 1910 the most advanced forms of capitalism, technically sophisticated mining, and large-scale timbering, ranching, and rubber processing had emerged in conjunction with the railroads. The trains brought in manufactured products from the United States. The result was the transformation of the quasi-independent peasants and artisans of Mexico into tenant farmers and laborers. Agrarian unrest against the encroachment and the alienation of labor was manifest in the northern states of Sonora and Chihuahua, the Gulf coast from Yucatán to Tamaulipas, Veracruz, Puebla, Hidalgo, San Luis Potosí, Tlaxcala, the eastern side of the Valley of Mexico, and Morelos. In the Cuautla region of eastern Morelos, dominated by "Spanish"-owned sugar haciendas (in the minds of the campesinos), the peasant villages, including Yautepec, Anenecuilco, and Ayala, had already organized defense committees. The Anenecuilco defense committee numbered about forty men armed with machetes, pistols, and a few primitive rifles. Emiliano Zapata led them.

When the starving peasants occupied the bottomlands of the Corralitos in 1909, they repulsed the unenthusiastic attempts by the local authorities to dislodge them and planted beans, corn, and chile. As the revolt in the north grew it involved peasants, farmers, miners, cowboys, rancheros, and artisans who had been displaced by political centralization, socioeconomic transformation, and ensuing depression. Pequeña burguesa PLM leader Guerrero led the unrest at Corralitos until he died during an armed engagement with government forces at Janos on 30 December 1910.[44]

By the end of the Porfiriato growing endemic unrest characterized the far north, where American holdings were the strongest. In the Yaqui Valley of Sonora and the interior of the state, Yaqui Indians resisted the intrusions of the Richardson and Wheeler Companies, whose combined holdings totaled 2,443,000 acres. The Anaconda Company also held large properties in the state, including 350,000 acres directly north of the Richardson and Wheeler terrain and east of the 1.5 million acres owned by Robert Vick of San Antonio, Texas. The Anaconda properties consisted of the Greene Cananea Copper complex, of which company president John D. Ryan had gained full ownership well before the outbreak of the revolution. Adjacent to and to the east of the Anaconda holdings, Louis Booker held another 360,000 acres that bordered on the 2.5 million-acre Las Palomas Ranch of Edwin Marshall. The Las Palomas property extended to a point near Ciudad Juárez immediately south of El Paso. The Corralitos hacienda and other American holdings including several Mormon properties that together totaled over 1.5 million acres coincided with the Las Palomas tract to the south. In all, American holdings in Chihuahua exceeded 15 million acres, comprising part of a vast expanse of American-owned properties extending almost unbroken from the Yaqui Valley and the Sea of Cortez eastward across the Sierra Madre Occidental of Chihuahua and southward along the mountains from the U.S. border at El Paso to the state of Durango. In Durango, American landownership was omnipresent, including a hacienda of 427,000 acres. Immediately west of Durango and south of the Yaqui Valley, Edwin Marshall, William Lemke, and the other American landowners in Sinaloa owned more than 5 million additional acres, including all of the fertile Rió Fuerte Valley. Further east of Ciudad Juárez in Chihuahua the Riverside Ranch comprised another 1,237,000 acres extending to Ojinaja. In Yucatán the Mengel Company held a ten-year lease on 3.5 million acres of hardwood timberland. In the Isthmus of Tehuantepec, American companies owned 1.5 million acres, and most of both northern and coastal Chiapas were in American hands.

In Baja California the Colorado River Land Company and other American interests held well over 1.5 million acres extending from Tijuana to Sonora and along both sides of the Colorado River from Yuma to the Sea of Cortez. Near Ensenada the Circle Bar Ranch of San Diego held renewable twenty-year leases on over one million acres of the holdings of the Baja California Colonization and Development Company. Several American colonies of property owners sprang up between Mexicali, Tijuana, and Ensenada, as did the much larger American colonies in Sonora, Chihuahua, Coahuila, Tamaulipas, Veracruz, Oaxaca, and Chiapas. The usual displacement of poor local Mexican farmers and small ranchers lacking documents ensued.[45]

Francisco Villa, the PLM, and other revolutionaries capitalized on the widespread, almost universal lower-class and ranchero dissent that resulted from the American takeovers and colonization process. A dozen or more American communities sprang up in Chihuahua and Sonora claiming hundreds of thousands of acres and evicting Mexican "squatters" who lacked papers granting legal entitlement to the land. The Mexican peasantry soon attributed to Villa the Robin Hood label of robber of the oppressive rich and giver to the poor. Independent bands of rural attackers from Chiapas to the U.S. border invoked his name during thousands of acts of violence. They especially sought out and devastated the properties of the rich Americans. Anti-Americanism highlighted a general resentment toward the intrusive outsiders of all nations who dominated industry and the land and who created more commercial farming. Villa and the other revolutionaries enjoyed refuge from the authorities in the mountains and small villages of southern and western Chihuahua while his proximity to the United States enabled him to purchase arms.

Despite the growing magnitude and frequency of peasant revolts resulting from agricultural commercialization and political centralization between 1707 and 1910, none had the programmatic capability to overthrow and replace the Mexican government. The desire on the part of the southern and central village peasantry and the Indians and ranchers of the north for political decentralization and municipal economic autonomy had divorced them from other sectors of society. The socioeconomic dislocations of 1876–1910, however, were on a national rather than a regional scale. The development of national and cross-class alliances would have a telling effect on the coming of the Mexican Revolution.

TWO

The Industrial and Urban Workers

Based upon a heritage of immiserated living and harsh working conditions, deep castelike class divisions, labor militancy, and the inculcation of foreign revolutionary ideologies, the emergent industrial working-class movement developed strong revolutionary propensities during the late nineteenth- and early twentieth-century rise of Mexican industrial capitalism. Industrial and urban working-class unrest, rooted in the labor struggles of colonial and postindependence Mexican society, played a major role in the coming and process of the Mexican Revolution.

During the Spanish colonial era working-class riots or *tumultos* directed against the state executive, the viceroy, swept the downtown sector of Mexico City in 1624 and 1692 while mine worker unrest flared periodically on the peripheries of central Mexico. The leaders of the industrial urban working-class crowds of Mexico City in the seventeenth century were Creole and mestizo artisans and politically involved priests who provided the working class with strong direction and a severely limited focus on issues. The crowds were particularly hostile toward the Spanish merchants. They comprised skilled and unskilled workers who suffered chronic unemployment, low wages, and crowded inadequate housing, and the *leperos* who literally had nothing to lose, being the propertyless bottom 16 percent of the population. The latter lived in clapboard shacks and, without a regular income, often lacked the resources to survive.

In the colonial era the working classes could unite over specific complaints: rising food prices, food shortages, and control of available food supplies by a small ethnically and economically identifiable group of "Spanish" middlemen. Charges of government corruption in the distribution of food during famines and shortages provoked working-class violence comparable to the pattern of so-called preideological working-class unrest in Europe.

Artisan leadership played a central role in the nature of working-class mobilization from colonial times through the revolution of 1910. Artisan discontent was fed by colonial control of wholesale and industrial goods distribution. Artisan conflict with Spanish merchants and manufacturers deepened the antagonism between imperial and colonial producers. The artisans, however, were severely limited in their capacity to lead lower industrial workers in confronting capital on a class basis because improved wages and working conditions for factory, large shop, transportation, and raw materials-producing industrial workers meant higher basic materials and production costs for them. The public assertion of urban working-class unrest thus was made possible only by food crises and breakdowns in the jointly administered clerical and secular Mexico City authority structure.[1]

In 1624 the secular authority represented by the viceroy as the king's agent was in conflict with the Church, led by the archbishop and the Franciscan order. Following his excommunication the vulnerable viceroy was attacked in his palace, which was burned down by a crowd composed of a social, cultural, and occupational cross-section of Mexico City's working class: among them artisans, skilled and unskilled laborers, and unemployed leperos. Friars were among the crowd's leaders. They shouted support for and loyalty to the king while demanding an end to the bad government of the viceroy and his administration.

The tumulto of 1692, caused by food shortages and rising staple prices, was triggered by the same elite crisis between the Church and secular authorities. Once again the clergy participated as leader of the crowds, but this time the rioters went further than merely attacking the Viceregal Palace. The crowd shouted denunciations of the Spanish nobility and mercantile economic elite. Animosity ran deep between the artisan industrial working-class producers of the city and the Spanish merchants who controlled the supply of raw materials and even the tools used in artisanry. In the artisans' view the merchants were foreign gougers and opportunists. In times of famine they were even seen as oppressors. Among the structures selected for destruction were the Cortés family mansion, Spanish business establishments, shops in the marketplace, government buildings, and the Viceregal Palace. One indication of emergent Mexican nationalism was the anticolonial shout, "Death to the Gachupines who eat all of our maize!"[2]

There is no evidence, however, that the industrial and urban working class of Mexico City actively supported the independence revolution during the eleven years of civil war. When Hidalgo's forces marched to the gates of the city, the urban lower classes were silent. It is likely that some artisans were even prepared to take up arms in defense of the city, or at least of their homes. The sacking of Dolores and Guanajuato by the revolutionaries had been highly publicized by both Church and state. The fact that some working-class citizenry in Valladolid had been recruited to the rebel forces during Hidalgo's stay there indicates the rebels' attractability. Some provincial elites also joined the revolutionary fold, but the antimetropolitan bias and provincial base of the revolutionaries alienated all but a very few in Mexico City.[3]

The Bajío rebels were not attuned to or a part of metropolitan life. As citizens of the capital the artisan working class participated in a collective urban experience that included amenities such as Sunday promenades, parks, outdoor music, fountains, and paved streets and lighting. Despite the differences between rich and poor the city's public life had a unifying effect vis-à-vis provincial elites, rural miners, and campesinos. Hidalgo's attack on the Spanish mine-owning elite of the Bajío, the abolition of slavery, and his proclamation for the return of farmlands from the commercial estates to the villages pleased unemployed mine workers, a few Creole nationalists, blacks, and peasants, but he alienated slave owners, many of whom were artisans, and the metropolitan Creole hacendados. Once again, because of their position in the economy between the lower workers and the Spanish mercantile elite, the artisans did not support revolutionary change that might grant greater power and wages to laborers producing basic materials.[4]

Without the support of the Mexico City artisans, Hidalgo's revolution had no hope of recruiting other urban workers. The failure of the less affluent workers to demonstrate revolutionary zeal reflected the lack of artisan interest. The artisan-led urban working class exhibited no affinity with the propeasant, clearly antimetropolitan bias of the Bajío revolutionaries. They also failed to support actively the rural proindependence forces that persisted on the periphery after the demise of Hidalgo. The urban working classes' refusal to support the Hidalgo revolution critically undercut the radical impulse in the independence movement. The defeat of the strong peasant-based revolts delivered the new nation to the Creole landholding and mercantile elite while the master and journeymen artisans maintained their status and well-being. Independence ended de jure caste limitations on social mobility but brought few other changes to the urban economic and social order.

During the second quarter of the nineteenth century the working-class tumulto became an even more important aspect of Mexico City labor unrest. By the 1830s the crowds, stimulated by social inequality and economic hardship, adopted a more political orientation. They were mobilized by leaders ranging from Conservative President Anastacio Bustamante to Jacobin Liberals such as Valentin Gómez Farías. They helped topple the Gómez Farías government and other regimes in support of revolutionary political plans.

Rival sectors of the elite still instigated the crowds, but now, as parts of movements seeking to control an independent government, their rallying points included far-reaching programs and theories that promised to cure the ills of society. Elite Conservative and Liberal politicians alike were involving the Mexican urban working class, albeit through manipulation, in the selection of national leadership. To the Conservatives' chagrin the Mexico City crowds became increasingly pro-Liberal in their political orientation as the century progressed. By the mid-1850s the Liberals could count on popular support in Mexico City. The growth of factory-based industry and of a proletariat was responsible for the leftward trend in Mexico City working-class unrest. It stimulated new modes of organization that rendered the tumulto obsolescent.[5]

in the 1860s and 1870s the emergent urban labor movement adopted new tactics and forms of worker organization that reflected an emerging new mode of production. The artisans with their guild tradition were vulnerable to the growth of factory production and were at the forefront in the creation of modern Mexican urban labor groups. The politically experienced artisans were severely damaged by the introduction of mass production and by the lowering of internal provincial and town tariff barriers that encouraged the consumption of cheaper goods.

In the mid-1850s the artisans began to lose their secure position in social, economic, and political life. They faced proletarianization. Foreign financiers and industrialists introduced capital-intensive textile factory production, which reduced the number of producers. Between 1876 and 1910 the number of *sastres,* artisans of the textile industry, decreased from 42,000 to 8,000. During the same period the number of textile workers increased from 8,000 to 32,000. The number of textile producers decreased by 10,000 despite a 67 percent increase in the population. Instead of controlling his own workplace or working among an intimate group of ten or fewer producers, the former artisan now found himself part of an impersonal mode of production.

Many of the new factory workers lived in barracks or company compounds. They answered bells and whistles that told them when to work, rest, eat, or return home. Administrative supervision replaced personal direction. The artisans were losing their individual identity in a new mode of production and joining displaced campesinos in a workplace most of them despised. As a result, the threatened artisans provided the industrial and urban working-class movement with most of its domestic radical leaders between the 1860s and 1920. Technological transformation helped create radicalism among the tailors, typesetters, stonemasons, stonecutters, and hat makers.[6]

The combination of social inequality, economic hardship, and the presence of foreign anarchists, most of them from Spain, contributed a strong revolutionary tendency to the Mexican industrial labor movement that developed during times of governmental instability from the 1860s through the revolution of 1910. Labor radicalism in Mexico has never been able to withstand concerted opposition from a strong government, but in the 1860s Mexico suffered foreign invasion and civil war. The resultant political vacuum made revolutionary industrial labor organizing feasible.

In 1867, when the Liberals reoccupied Mexico City, they found the principal urban labor group, La Sociedad Artística Industrial, in the hands of an amalgam of foreign-born and domestic anarchists and radicals. The radicals were already organizing workers' "resistance societies" among the artisan trades and in the textile factories. The imperial government of Maximilian had allowed this condition to develop because of its preoccupation with the civil war. The only decisive action it took was to create the Gendarmería Imperial, which was used to break strikes.[7]

By 1868 La Sociedad succeeded in organizing some of the largest textile factories in the Mexico City region, and in July the first successful factory labor strike took place. That success caused groups of factory workers to approach La Sociedad for help; several new workers' "resistance societies" resulted, including some in the artisan trades. The next step for the radicals was to form a workers' council, the Círculo Proletario, the objective of which was to further working-class organizing. In 1869 Círculo leaders contacted the Geneva Congress of the European First International Workingmens Association. In September 1870 the radicals brought the important workers' groups of central Mexico together in one organization, the first central workers' council of Mexico City, the Gran Círculo de

Obreros de Mexico. In 1871 branch círculos were created by the industrial workers in San Luis Potosí and Toluca.[8]

The Liberal government did not stand by passively and allow the development of a revolutionary urban and industrial labor movement. A group of conservative artisan trade union advocates, some of them personal friends of President Benito Juárez, joined La Sociedad and the Círculo, both of which had open memberships. With government financial support these pro-Liberals vied with the radicals for control of the workers' councils and slowly gained ground in the Círculo's elections. In 1872 the radical leader of the Círculo, anarchist Santiago Villanueva, died and shortly afterward the pro-Liberals gained a majority of the officerships in the organization. Immediately after their electoral victory they suspended official Círculo organizing efforts among the factory workers.[9]

The radicals remained in the group and occasionally won elections, but they continued to organize factory workers. They anticipated later Mexican anarchist labor-organizing tactics by continuing to form workers' resistance societies through the activities of La Social, a secret Bakuninist group. By "Bakuninist" they referred to the Russian anarchist leader Mikhail Bakunin, whose revolutionary theory called for the creation of underground workers' societies led by deeply committed revolutionaries to undertake the education and organizing of the masses. During the early 1870s a number of communist-led strikes took place at the Real del Monte mine near Pachuca, Hidalgo, and at the Miraflores textile factory in the small town of Tlalmanalco near Chalco in the southeastern corner of the Valley of Mexico.[10]

These rural industrial strikes by workers in open contact with radicals from the Círculo and La Social occurred simultaneously and in immediate proximity with agrarian uprisings aided by La Social and the Gran Comité Conmunero. The contemporaneous strikes and peasant uprisings in the Valley of Mexico during the late 1860s and 1870s with their mutual links to the Gran Comité Conmunero and La Social parallel the presence of PLM peasant guerrillas in the Río Blanco area at the moment of the 1906 industrial worker uprising. These violent risings demonstrate the presence of organizationally linked industrial and agrarian labor unrest long before the 1910 revolution.

During the early and middle 1870s radical working-class ideas circulated in the relatively open political climate of Mexico City. Labor spokesmen published newspapers and called for the reorganization of society around self-managed workers' control of production—libertarian socialism. They attacked the Liberals, guilds and trade unions, and mutualist societies as inadequate and demanded the organization of factory workers. They labeled the capitalists "blood suckers," "vampires of gold," and "enemies of the working class." They chided capitalists for asking workers "to live on their knees." Despite the wishes of the Liberals in the Círculo, the radicals continued to fill its ranks with factory laborers. By 1876 it had about 10,000 members.[11]

The labor spokesmen's goal of a workers' revolution required the creation of a national labor federation. The growth of the urban working-class movement in Mexico City and in other developing Mexican industrial centers such as San Luis Potosí, Querétaro, Puebla, Veracruz, and Monterrey made that step feasible. On 5 March 1876 the first meeting of the Mexican Labor Congress, the Congreso General Obrero de la República Mexicana, convened in Mexico City with thirty-five of seventy-nine authorized delegates present. In its opening manifesto the labor congress declared the need for workers to reorganize into cooperatives in order to escape the "capitalist yoke."[12]

Five delegates represented anarchist La Social, including Soledad Sosa, the first woman to take part in the industrial and urban labor movement's leadership. Sosa's admission to the Congreso came after heated debate. A small but vocal minority among the less radical delegates objected to the seating of a woman because it "violated precedent." Between 1876 and 1882 the anarchists provided a strong radical impetus to the national labor organization.

The 1876 tripartite political civil war between the armies of President Lerdo de Tejada and the rival insurgents José María Iglesias, Chief Justice of the Supreme Court, and General Porfirio Díaz, inevitably involved the industrial working-class movement. Both rebel leaders leveled charges against the Lerdo government based upon the already well-established *puro*-Liberal critique of the less programmatic and what they regarded as misguided nationalism of the Lerdo Liberals. They wanted to reduce tariffs, abolish local tariffs and taxes, attract foreign investment capital, and develop a transportation and communications network. They opposed the reelection of the president as unconstitutional and appealed for action on behalf of the industrial and agrarian working classes.

Díaz was especially assertive in his radical critique and attracted the support of Liberal politicians and moderates in the industrial workers' movement. The provincial elites gave him wide support across the nation. They included radical-Liberal General Manuel González of Tamaulipas; Trinidad García de la Cadena, caudillo of Zacatecas; and Miguel Negrete of Puebla. García and Negrete were both active in support of the labor movement, and Negrete had even supported the agrarian insurrection of Julio Chávez López at Chalco and the Ley del Pueblo in Puebla.[13]

The ensuing strife divided the industrial working-class movement into three factions: supporters of Díaz; those who backed Lerdo; and the most radical, who argued that none of the rival factions actually supported the working class and were merely taking advantage of it. In October criticism of Lerdo published in the working-class press resulted in the forced closing of *El Hijo del Trabajo,* the most radical labor newspaper. Following Díaz's victory the labor movement remained divided, but the trade unionist pro-mutualist moderates lost much support because of their identification with the new government's policies, which quickly came into conflict with organized workers.

In 1877 and 1878 the radical labor leaders challenged the procapital, antistrike policies of the Díaz government. Police actions on behalf of property and business during the growing labor unrest of the late 1870s brought a barrage of criticism. With the overthrow of Lerdo some members of the working-class organizations incorrectly anticipated a freer political atmosphere and acted on it. By 1880 the National Labor Congress had 50,000 members.

The radicals of Mexico's industrial working-class movement, however, did not restrict themselves to the confrontation between the state and labor. They assailed the government's new agrarian land policies, which they felt favored the hacendados and violated Díaz's preincumbency promises to the village peasantry. The most controversial case involved the violently resisted expulsion of ranchería sharecroppers and estate workers from the Hacienda de Bocas in San Luis Potosí.[14]

The Díaz regime began a program of active repression, attempting to deunionize and discipline Mexican labor as part of its effort to attract foreign investment. Mexican industrial working-class belligerency contrasted sharply with the *empresario* contracts being offered multinational industrial concerns in Western Europe's African and Asian colonies and the spheres of influence available in China. At the same time, most of Mexico's sister Latin American republics featured the low costs of their own coercive labor systems in their competitive search for outside capital.

Radical labor leaders insisted upon the independence of working-class organizations from government and sensed impending repression. In 1878 the Díaz government became increasingly hostile toward working-class organizing; some of the radicals retreated to Zacatecas, where they obtained the protection of the puro-Liberal, General García de la Cadena. The Zacatecas exiles set up a new workers' council and a subsidiary organizing group in Mexico City known as the Primer Sucursal (First Branch). The most radical Mexico City textile unions, including workers' associations in Tlalpan, San Ildefonso, Contreras, Río Hondo, and La Colmena, joined the Zacatecas workers' central.[15]

The 1878 alliance of anti-Díaz forces in the Primer Sucursal, however, was short lived. It broke up in 1879 after the discovery that García de la Cadena was using it to launch a presidential campaign against Díaz's selection, General Manuel González. The urban labor anarchists and radicals felt betrayed. They could not accept involvement in the political process they considered detrimental to working-class interests and in the service of provincial sectors within the Mexican elite. The National Labor Congress refused to endorse García de la Cadena. A series of meetings and large street demonstrations in Mexico City were held in December 1879 in order to convince the National Labor Congress to stay out of politics. The radical faction of the industrial working-class movement regarded both the broad-based elite support for the Díaz administration and the northern provincial elite-backed García de la Cadena movement as inimical to the workers' interests.

The anarchists regained dominance in the Mexican labor movement in the late 1870s because of their uncompromised demands for working-class political autonomy, labor participation in management decisions, and grass-roots factory worker organizing which coincided with the emergent mode of production. They had built up a wide base of support. La Social counted sixty-two regional units organizing workers throughout most of the nation. The anarchist newspaper *La Internacionalista* publicized their program, which included autonomous municipal governments, workers' *falanges,* abolition of the wage system, equality of property possession, and the abolition of national boundaries through the creation of a "universal social republic." By 1878–1879 the anarchists were in complete control of the Labor Congress. In 1881 the Mexican Labor Congress, with its 100 affiliated societies and 50,236 registered members, officially joined the anarchist International Workingmens Association headquartered in Amsterdam.[16]

Anarchist domination of both the National Labor Congress and the reorganized Mexico City Gran Círculo and the desire to please foreign investors brought government repression in 1881. Díaz surrendered his presidential power to protégé Manuel González from 1880 to 1884. One of González's charges was to suppress worker and peasant unrest without tainting Díaz while the latter promoted U.S. investment in the Mexican economy. Díaz's effort included a capital recruitment tour of the United

States in 1881 with meetings with Colis P. Huntington, former president U. S. Grant, Jay Gould, Thomas Wentworth Peirce, and others. Suppressed by the government, the Círculo disbanded that year. Confronted by increasing pressure, the Labor Congress attempted to survive by publicly promising to obey "the laws of the land," but its pledge to revolt only when "the rights of man were taken from him" did little to blunt the government's drive for deunionization. Following an all-time high in the number of enrolled members in 1882, the Labor Congress disappeared in 1883. Increased control of the press prevented public accounts of the event.

The government exercised more than force in its drive to deunionize the working class, however. It practiced the most effective forms of cooptation. In 1883 the only labor organization that claimed national stature was the newly created TRUE Labor Congress (TRUE Círculo y Congreso de Obreros), which endorsed the government and welcomed foreign investment. In 1884 the TRUE Congress endorsed Díaz for reelection and supported a number of government-endorsed candidates in the various states. Use of the English "true" coincided with its willingness to cooperate with the Americans. Many former radicals and anarchist leaders became prominent TRUE Congress directors. Some later achieved appointive and elective government offices.[17]

The TRUE Congress worked closely with the Díaz regime in the creation of several rural cooperatives colonized by European immigrants. Elite Mexican thinkers believed that European farmers were racially superior and more productive than Mexican peasants and laborers. Intellectuals offered dietetic and educational reasons for the seeming discrepancy in abilities between Mexicans and Americans. These ideas followed the thinking of an active body of scholars in the United States. Meanwhile the TRUE Congress ceased organizing factory and mine workers, advocating cooperatives for the artisans instead.

In 1885 strikers at the Tlalpán, Tizapan, and La Magdalena textile factories were dismissed from their jobs; strike leaders at Tlalpán and Tizapan disappeared amid charges that they had been encarcerated at the fortress of San Juan de Ulloa in Veracruz and at the Belém penitentiary. Defeated, the leading radicals and labor revolutionaries fell silent. Plotino Rhodakanaty, the demoralized Greek mentor of both Villanueva and Zalacosta and founder of La Social, returned to Europe in 1886. By the mid-1880s an employer-government offensive had dissolved the large radical working-class organizations in central Mexico.[18]

During the 1880s and 1890s radical labor activists formed numerous secret but small workers' councils and factory unions and even staged some wildcat strikes. In 1883 workers struck at the Cerritos factory in Orizaba. Between 1885 and 1895 La Magdalena in Contreras, La Victoria, La Colmena in Tlalnepantla, and the large Hercules textile mill at Querétaro underwent paralytic strikes. The rurales intervened on these occasions. The underground "sociedad de resistencia" formed by the textile workers at Río Blanco in 1892 carried on self-help activities during the 1890s and survived until the rebellion there in 1906. No independent workers' central could function for long, however. The foreign-dominated growth of the national economy provided stability to the government and temporarily put the working-class movement on the defensive.

Strikes were rare and usually desperate defensive reactions by workers to arbitrary dismissals, reduced pay rates, or suddenly extended working hours resulting from short-run downturns in the economy. Some of the most violent instances of worker belligerency took place in the Mexico City industrial suburbs of Tlalnepantla and Tlalpán and among textile workers at the San Antonio de Abad plant near downtown. Throughout the nation the strikes were uncoordinated and the great majority, unmitigated failures.

In one case, in 1892 Pedro Ordoñez, once a young anarchist and former independent labor leader who had joined the TRUE Congress and became a Mexico City councilman, helped to gain relief from a fine levied against the striking workers at the San Antonio de Abad factory by the owners. He arranged an agreement under which the workers' fine went to the Casa del Obrera, a charity run for the benefit of working-class women bereft of the means of sustenance. Police intervention and the use of strikebreakers from Puebla had ruined the strike. Sixteen strikers were incarcerated. Violent strikes were in the minority and usually handled by police forces at the disposal of the local jefes políticos or the rurales who were often stationed at or near the larger factories. Only a small number of strikes required the intervention of the army. "Industrial peace" through a mix of cooptation of leaders and strong labor discipline by the government prevailed for fifteen years.[19]

In 1900 the era of Porfirian "industrial peace" began to crumble when a strike that began at the El Mayorazgo textile factory in Puebla spread across the state, which was a national center of textile production. At its peak the strike involved three thousand workers. Rapid economic growth in Western Europe and the resulting world market financial contraction of 1899–1904 reduced available funding for the French-owned Mexican mills. Although unplanned, the shutdown had the effect of a general strike.

It turned nineteenth-century radical theories about the general strike into a twentieth-century reality. It was the turning point in the ancien régime's economic expansion and successful dealing with the industrial working class. The shutdown heralded the onset of economic destabilization and revealed Mexico's extreme vulnerability to foreign economic crises.

The economic inequality of native workers vis-à-vis their American counterparts and sudden hardship combined to produce the 1 June 1906 miners' strike and rebellion at Cananea in the northwestern state of Sonora. That episode had a major impact on the development of Mexican industrial working-class revolutionism. The miners were part of an enclave economy, a highly capitalized enterprise devoted to the extraction of raw materials, controlled by foreigners. Its only impact on Mexican society other than the workers' salaries was a wealth of tax revenues. The miners' strike, the two-day gun battle and confrontation with the authorities and American vigilantes that ensued caused a nationwide sensation. The nationalistic public saw the Cananea uprising and American intervention as a Mexican challenge to the omnipotent foreigners in which the government sided with the aliens against its own people.

Like the labor unrest in central Mexico, economic contraction formed the material basis of the Cananea workers' alienation. Lying 62 kilometers south of the border and surrounded by mountains and desert, Cananea was supplied by the Southern Pacific Railway of Mexico and the old wagon road, both running to Naco, Arizona. In addition to all machinery and industrial products, a wide variety of consumer goods were imported in their entirety from the United States. These products included roofing, paper, fuel oil, rice, eggs, apples, canned milk, prepared cereals, and canned vegetables. Imports of American hay, barley, flour, beans, salt, and sugar dominated local sales as well. Because of a basic undersupply to the north, corn and chile, among other staples, came from domestic sources. Chinese merchants handled most of the retail sales at Cananea in league with their ethnic counterparts who dominated the southward export trade from southern Arizona.

In 1905 Mexican devaluation of the peso by 50 percent, which resulted from the slowdown of American and European investments during the U.S. banking panic of 1902–1903 and the Western European financial crisis of 1899–1904, devastated the real wages of the miners at Cananea. They faced the immediate loss of half of their buying power because their American employer insisted upon paying them in Mexican and non-gold-based script monies instead of gold or U.S. dollars. They depended heavily on U.S. imports for their staples, the cost of which suddenly doubled in

Mexican prices. Besides blaming the Chinese merchants for the inflated peso prices of essential consumer goods, the Cananea work force demanded higher wages as compensation for their lost real earnings. The Greene Cananea Copper Company, however, had also suffered badly during the 1902–1903 U.S. banking crisis. By 1906, unable to find passive financial backing, the company was deeply in debt to the Anaconda Corporation.

Greene's arrogance toward Mexican workers and his inability to act freely because of Anaconda managerial strategies combined to exacerbate the miners' grievances. Workers protested the discriminatory wages paid in devaluing Mexican scripts and currency, inequitable work assignments, and inferior living accommodations relative to the American personnel. The Americans received their pay inside Mexico in stable, ever more powerful U.S. currency and enjoyed higher wages to begin with, better employment status, and superior housing in their segregated quarters.

The workers' actions at Cananea carry special importance for the revolution of 1910 because they challenged a combination of powerful foreign interests aligned with the Mexican government. It was the first major case of industrial working-class unrest since the unplanned statewide textile strike in Puebla in 1900. It stirred widespread nationalist outrage because of foreign intervention and government repression. It took place six months before the next workers' rebellion, at Río Blanco.

Among the significant contending forces at the Cananea strike were some of the highest-ranking officers in the national government, including Vice-President Ramón Corral, whose political ally Governor Rafael Izábal was in charge of restoring order at the mines. The governor's notorious reputation preceded the occupation of his haciendas during the revolution and the discovery of torture chambers on the premises used for Yaqui Indians whom he kept there to perform forced labor. He did not suffer working-class rebellion at Cananea gladly.

An impressive foreign element also favored law and order at Cananea. At the time of the strike, William D. Greene, the financially distressed promoter of the mine, was only a joint owner of the company; it was actually controlled by John D. Rockefeller's Anaconda Copper Company. Anaconda became a minority owner of the mine in 1904–1906 when it purchased the shares of the John "Bet a Million" Gates, Edwin Hawley, H. F. Huntington, and E. H. Harriman group that had been acquired before and during 1903.

In addition to various public stock issues, Gates and Hawley bought 80,000 shares from George Mitchell and two other men who had been associated with Greene earlier in time. Then they purchased 100,000 shares of unissued Cananea Copper treasury stock from the nearly bankrupt Greene. By 1903 the Gates-Hawley group held at least seven of the Cananea Copper Company's directorships. They also occupied three seats on the board of directors executive committee. "Greene retained his company for the time being and acquired a great source of capital, but the Gates-Hawley group began quietly replacing members of the board of directors with their own representatives."

Harriman and the Rockefellers were closely associated through their directorships in the National City Bank held by William Rockefeller and Harriman, and through City Bank chairman of the board James Stillman's and Gates's earlier association in the financing and management of Arthur Stilwell's Kansas City, Pittsburg and Gulf Railroad. When Rockefeller's Anaconda bought out the Cananea shares of Gates, Hawley, Huntington, and Harriman, it was a transaction between longtime business associates. The overmatched Greene was forced constantly to seek new financing because of overexpansion. His flamboyant reputation caused Anaconda's management to exercise caution in the handling of cash.

By 1906 Anaconda president John D. Ryan of Duluth, Minnesota, was handling important monetary decisions and loans for the financially beleaguered Greene by telegraph. Ryan served as one of Rockefeller's most trusted aides and strategists. Ryan also carried heavy influence with the territorial governor of Arizona, Joseph H. Kibby. Ryan's company, Anaconda, was the largest business concern in the Arizona Territory, and Ryan had supported Governor Kibby's appointment. The governor commanded the Arizona Rangers.[20]

Those who challenged the forces of foreign property and state authority in Cananea made up three separate elements. The Partido Liberal Mexicano had chosen Cananea as an organizing point months before the outbreak. During the spring of 1906 Lázaro Gutiérrez de Lara of the PLM organized an underground group, the Club Liberal de Cananea. Another secret group formed the Unión Liberal Humanidad shortly afterward. The Unión Liberal planned to create a local unit of a new nationwide miners' union that would give the PLM a significant working-class base of support. The PLM planned to make the fledgling union, the Liga Minera de los Estados Unidos Mexicanos, an official branch of the party. The Unión Liberal provided much of the negotiating leadership after the strike and revolt were already under way. Another important group were the dozen or more working-class revolutionaries from the Industrial Workers of the World and other radical workers from the mine fields of the American southwest. They came to Cananea, obtained jobs, agitated for Mexican workers' rights, and then led assaults on mines and property in the area after the outbreak began.

The events at Cananea took place only after the largest and most important group, the Mexican mine workers themselves, seized the initiative. On 1 June suddenly and without prior warning to employers, authorities, or union organizers, they went on strike and precipitated an armed conflict that continued for two days and a stalemated confrontation that was not settled until 6 June.

Cananea mine workers demanded an eight-hour workday, higher wages, and an end to racial discrimination in housing, job promotions, and rates of pay. In the first hours of the strike the aggressive manager of the company store fired into a crowd that had gathered in front of the premises to protest his alleged earlier abuse of a woman customer. The crowd exploded with rage. Workers killed the manager and an employee and then burned the hated company store. The crowd then attacked other buildings. The initial outbreak of violence was interrupted by negotiations, which broke down when Greene was unable to make any of the needed concessions.

For two days the main force of workers attacked buildings and exchanged scattered gunfire with company guards and local police. Then the main group of workers retired to the residential area, set up barricades, and exchanged random shots with their enemy while members of the Unión Liberal Humanidad negotiated a ceasefire. Uninvolved in the initiation of the uprising, the Unión Liberal sought a peaceful compromise. Meanwhile small bands composed of radical Mexican and American workers raided and sabotaged outlying mine shafts and equipment belonging to the company. They also approached workers in other mines in the area, attempting to recruit more support.

The suddenness of events surprised leaders from the Unión Liberal, but soon they took over and opened negotiations with the authorities. Their settling effect on the workers helped stop the spread of the revolt. They probably also spared many of the workers from execution by the government after order was restored, but they were hardly the militant revolutionary heroes they later claimed to be. The American mine management and local Sonoran state officials at first underestimated the workers' unrest. Their violent and contemptuous reaction to the strike and initial attempt to break it precipitated much of the fighting.

Within two days the state government perceived the Cananea events as a serious political confrontation with potential nationwide impact. The armed forces were largely committed far away in southern Sonora to the war with the Yaqui Indians, however, and troop transport to Cananea was indirect and not immediately available. A period of several days was required in order to place troops on the scene. In the meantime Greene sent a telegraph message to Arizona with the exaggerated claim that Americans were being killed. In fact no Americans had been killed since the outbreak at the company store. Approximately seventy men armed with rifles and commanded by Captain Thomas Rynning and five other Arizona Rangers boarded a train, crossed the border at Naco, and went to Cananea to protect American lives and property. Despite appeals to prevent escalation of the fighting and the possible massacre of the largely unarmed Mexican mine workers, the territorial governor did nothing to stop the border violation until the Rangers were already en route. His effort at that point was merely a disclaimer that the men were "on their own."

Border crossings had ample precedent. An agreement between the nations had allowed U.S. cavalry to pursue Apache Indian bands into Mexico for more than a decade. This time, however, the Ranger crossing constituted intervention by American vigilantes against Mexican citizens on their own soil. Mexican nationalists viewed the Americans' action as an arrogant, racially biased lynch mob acting in the service of its capitalist leaders against the just demands of the workers. The Cananea management, panicking over delays in the arrival of Mexican troops, desired American intervention. Local Sonoran officials went along with the arrangement.

Workers and local authorities agreed upon a truce before the Americans arrived at Cananea. During negotiations the Americans stood guard over company property and were placed between a crowd of Mexican workers and the general offices of the Cananea Company. Only hours after arriving, the Americans departed when invited to leave by alarmed and embarrassed higher state officials, but the political damage had already been done. Cooperation between the American entrepreneurs and the Mexican state for the issuance of building permits, development contracts on the site, operating licenses, and the treatment of Mexican workers was well established. For those who objected, the coordinated use of force between the Mexican and American authorities and American owners was indisputable.

On 6 June Governor Izábal, backed by two thousand troops, ordered the workers to end their belligerency or face conscription into the war against the tenacious Yaqui in the Sonoran highlands. The strike-rebellion came to an end. Estimates vary, but between thirty and one hundred Mexican workers and four Americans were killed in the fighting. The number of wounded is unknown. Seven American workers and nine Mexicans were identified as agitators and saboteurs. The government apprehended the Unión Liberal leaders and incarcerated them in the dungeons of San Juan de Ulloa in Veracruz.[21]

Cananea was the first wave in a growing tide of working-class combativeness. Despite its isolation some fifteen hundred miles from Mexico City, Cananea had a traumatic effect on public opinion in central Mexico. Pequeña burguesa and intellectual criticism of the government for allowing foreign intervention against Mexican workers led to charges of treason on the part of the more outraged. The PLM benefited from its images as the representative of the workers in the incident. The party's prestige grew rapidly among the nation's industrial workers. The events that ensued at Río Blanco were a natural extension of Cananea en route to revolutionary worker participation in the revolution.

In 1901 the militant workers at the Río Blanco textile factory in the Orizaba region of Veracruz reactivated their almost moribund secret "resistance society" from its earlier function as a self-help group to one intended to regain workers' "lost rights." Río Blanco, like Cananea, was one of the largest production complexes of its kind in Mexico. The conditions of labor created a maximum sense of workers' alienation. Relative to the older and smaller mills and artisan shops, jobs were more formalized, with a structured administration and totally remote foreign ownership.

The workers felt a deep sense of hostility toward the French owners, the Spaniard who leased and operated the company store, and the administration staff. In 1903 the Río Blanco workers went on strike over the abuse of a shop supervisor. In 1904 they organized a Gran Círculo. Then, in the winter of 1906, José Rumbia, a radical anti-Catholic and antigovernment Protestant preacher opened a tabernacle near the factory. He recruited a sizable following of workers with his fiery sermons, which were a mix of fundamentalist Christianity and a radical critique of foreign exploiters, the Roman Catholic Church, and the bourgeoisie.

In the spring of 1906 José Neira, a workers' organizer, "Luchador Obrero," from the PLM, arrived in Río Blanco. He obtained a job in the factory, joined the Círculo, and attended tabernacle meetings. Soon Neira and Rumbia were working together. Rumbia delivered the sermons and Neira gave political lectures. On 2 April a group of twenty-seven Río Blanco workers secretly met with Rumbia and Neira at a private residence and formed the Gran Círculo de Obreros Libres (GCOL). They affiliated with the PLM and elected Neira GCOL president. Then they began publication of an underground newspaper, *La Revolución Social,* which denounced Church and government as corrupt and called for revolution.

They promised to "tumble that arrogant Frenchman [the owner] out of the clouds." The GCOL appeal worked, and the nearby Santa Rosa and Nogales factories were organized.

When the government discovered the existence of the GCOL, it declared the group subversive and ordered the apprehension of its leaders. On Jueves de Corpus (June or July) 1906 the rurales duly raided the Círculo meeting place. The government disbanded the GCOL, but many workers were already politicized. Rumbia and Neira eluded capture.

A few months later the government approved a new GCOL in order better to control the workers, employing a proven tactic of the Díaz regime. José Morales, a timekeeper in the Río Blanco plant, became its first president. Pledges of mutual support were exchanged by Morales, the local jefe político, the state governor, and President Díaz. The new union chief vowed that he would "support the governor." The Morales-led GCOL quickly organized many of the textile factories in Puebla, Orizaba, and Tlaxcala. While excluding radicals from union membership, Morales successfully recruited membership because the workers adopted a "something is better than nothing" attitude, and he promised to address "bread and butter" issues. Labor historian Luis Araiza has noted that Morales was "more concerned with the interests of the industrialists than those of the workers."

Meanwhile the predominantly French owners of ninety-three factories throughout central Mexico, in cooperation with the first-generation French-descended Minister of the Treasury José Ives Limantour, formed the Centro Industrial Mexicano. The Centro Industrial was an industrialists' group designed to standardize prices, set production quotas, lobby the government, and develop a common front in labor negotiations. Late in November the Centro Industrial prohibited uncensored reading materials in company towns and required identification passbooks, which were to include the discipline histories of each worker.

The GCOL and Centro Industrial negotiated between November and December 1906. Morales and the GCOL leadership were caught between the workers' indignation and the employers' power and intransigence. Morales could not yield to the Centro Industrial without losing prestige with the workers. For weeks the Díaz government refused GCOL requests for arbitration. On 22 December the Centro Industrial declared a lockout affecting 22,000 textile and related workers in Puebla, 10,000 in Orizaba, and 25,000 more in the rest of central Mexico. The Puebla-Orizaba workers suffered greatly, and over 2,000 of them migrated in the nine days that the lockout endured.

On 31 December the government finally agreed to arbitration, but the workers were already beaten. On 4 January 1907 the government promulgated its settlement, signaling defeat for the workers on all major issues. In the following two days workers in Puebla and elsewhere accepted the verdict with resignation. At the Puebla meeting the bishop blessed the document as "God's work," but in Orizaba a large minority at the union meeting shouted Morales down despite a narrowly won vote of approval for the contract. The meeting hall denunciations of Morales intermingled with the shouts "Death to Porfirio Díaz!" and "Down with the dictatorship!"

On 7 January textile workers in central Mexico returned to their jobs, but at 5:30 A.M. a stone-throwing crowd of men, women, and children diverted the first shift of the workers at Río Blanco from the front gate. Led by a woman worker, Margarita Martínez, the assembled workers marched to a company store and burned it down. When the jefe político arrived with a contingent of rurales, the crowd pelted him. The rurales, caught up in the workers' fervor, refused to act. The jefe político discreetly withdrew, an action which the governor's investigation concluded allowed the unrest to develop further. Soldiers arrived later, arrested the rurales, and opened fire on the crowd, killing seventeen and wounding eighty.

The crowd then divided into two factions. One group marched into the town of Río Blanco shouting "Death to Porfirio Díaz!" seized the jail, and released the prisoners. The other segment headed for the Nogales and Santa Rosa factories shouting "Long live liberty!" "Death to the dictator Porfirio Díaz!" and "Down with oppressors and company stores!" The Santa Rosa and Nogales workers joined them, and together the groups set fire to the company stores.

The workers that had gone to Nogales and Santa Rosa were intercepted by troops on the road back to Río Blanco. The troops opened fire, and although estimates vary widely, scores of workers were killed and even more wounded. Only scattered remnants of the Santa Rosa-Nogales workers' contingent were able to get back to Río Blanco, where the main fighting was under way.

In Río Blanco armed workers seized the railway station and telegraph office, tore up railway tracks outside of town, and cut down the telegraph lines. An angry crowd attacked and burned the houses within the compound where GCOL president Morales resided. Morales and the other GCOL leaders recognized the serious nature of the outbreak and had fled the area. Armed bands of workers engaged in uneven street battles with the army. The one-sided fighting continued all night before the workers retired.

On the morning of 8 January the army fired upon a crowd of workers in front of the Santa Rosa factory, killing five. Two militant Santa Rosa workers' leaders were also killed that morning. One account claims that the Santa Rosa leaders "fell in action." Another version asserts that troops took them prisoner and killed them inside or behind the burned-out Santa Rosa company store.

In total, the army killed almost two hundred workers, and the number of wounded defies estimate. Four hundred workers were taken prisoner. Armed workers killed approximately twenty-five soldiers in just over twenty-four hours of fighting. They wounded between thirty and forty soldiers. Eleven of the rurales arrested at the outset were later reported executed, although their fate is uncertain. The employers then removed over fifteen hundred workers in five factories from their jobs. The rebellious workers littered the countryside with smashed goods from the company stores. Government officials and the American consul from Veracruz noted that there was no stealing, just destruction. The Río Blanco affair began as a lockout; it turned into a workers' rebellion.

Despite the praise received from the American consul for "decisive action," the Mexican state was badly shaken by the events at Río Blanco. Its spokesmen at various times declared the Río Blanco episode "communist," the product of "anarchist propaganda," and a "rebellion." The "anarchist" PLM and "outside agitators" were accused of instigating the entire affair.[22]

The Río Blanco area experienced continued worker discontent. In April 1907 another strike closed the Nogales and Santa Rosa plants. In 1909, despite the insuperable odds created by the presence of troops and the use of imported peasant strikebreakers from poverty-ridden Oaxaca, the Río Blanco workers struck and closed the plant again. In July 1909 the Santa Rosa workers followed suit. With the agrarian revolutionary forces of Padua and Santanon operating in the area and continued industrial worker unrest, heavy troop concentrations were necessary in the Orizaba-Río Blanco region until the revolution began in 1910.

Between 1907 and 1910 worker unrest continued to simmer in central Mexico in the wake of Río Blanco and Cananea. In January 1907, simultaneous with events in Río Blanco, the workers in the La Magdalena textile factory in San Angel near Mexico City went on strike. The nearby La Hormiga plant followed suit. The San Angel strike was broken by the arrest of its leaders and occupation of the factories by rurales. In 1908 another strike that required army intervention took place in the San Angel factories. The workers in these plants first organized in 1876–1882 and carried out wildcat strikes during the 1880s and 1890s. In 1909 two strikes staged in defiance against reduced wages and dismissals closed the large San Antonio de Abad textile factory. Factory owners blamed "anarchist and communist agitators" from Río Blanco for the disturbances. Strikers complained of unfair treatment, wage and hour reductions, and foreign ownership.

From 1907 to 1910 the factory owners, government, and Church carried out a series of workers' control programs designed to quell the rising unrest. Security perimeters were established around the workers' living areas adjacent to factories. Guards were placed at entry points to record individual arrivals and departures. The despised black identification books and employment and disciplinary records were required of all employees. Special searches of company-owned workers' living quarters removed subversive reading materials and possible weapons. The Church sponsored labor conventions in attempts to ensure peace and, with the government's blessing, set out to form a Christian labor movement. Church officials deplored worker violence and sought to form "white" unions in order to achieve cooperation between capital and labor.[23]

Between 1900 and 1910 the Mexican industrial working class regained the organizational impetus of the 1860s, 1870s, and early 1880s. Encouraged by the radical-liberal pequeña burguesa organizers of the PLM and the propaganda of the PLM newspaper *Regeneración,* the workers at Río Blanco and Cananea became revolutionary when faced with increasingly difficult living and working conditions and the intransigence of the foreign owners and state. The caste divisions of Mexican society that had so long kept workers and the literate and professional classes apart were being removed by the growth of nationalism to counter the overbearing strength of foreigners in Mexico. Industrialization had created a larger working class with which the nationalistic pequeña burguesa could communicate. Modern communications, horizontal and vertical mobility, and growing nationalism combined to create a worker-pequeña burguesa alliance in a struggle with the state and foreign capital.

Despite an energetic repression, a rising tide of working-class militancy embraced greater Mexico City. The factory, construction, and artisan workers in central Mexico reorganized. A crisis-ridden national government revealed its weakness and allowed revolutionary workers' organizing groups to function that ten years earlier could operate only underground.

The organizing intensified when Francisco Madero called for a national revolution to oust Díaz. On that day in 1911 when the aged president left the capital, working-class crowds were rioting in wide areas of the city.[24]

At Cananea and Río Blanco class-based revolts from below struck out at foreign proprietary privileges and contributed directly to the growth of revolutionary nationalism. The clearest ideological expression of their class consciousness was anarchism. The workers' nationalism fused with other social groups, aggravated by the Mexican state's failure to protect them from foreign capitalist domination. In the international arena of competing states the most successful competitor for control of natural resources and labor power in the Mexican north was the United States. French capitalists, who dominated the textile industry, employed the largest single group of workers in the nation's urban areas. The enclave economy and discriminatory practices of the foreign owners at Cananea and Río Blanco, and the demands of the French-controlled Centro Industrial Mexicano, created the conditions that led to the workers' revolts.

The government's use of force at Cananea and Río Blanco and the factories of central Mexico to restore order against workers protesting discrimination in wages and employment conditions made the state appear as a mere pawn in the hands of foreign capitalists. The government's seeming subordination to foreign interests rallied the newly important and nationalistic pequeña burguesía and regional elites, who chafed under its heavy-handed economic and exclusionary political policies. The state lost its legitimacy among industrial workers, the general public, and its own cadres and therefore the ability to rule.

Between 1911 and 1920 nationalistic Mexican miners, resentful of American wealth and power, would assault, dynamite, and sack mines throughout the north. During the same period Mexican factory workers mobilized on a massive scale and staged the most violent and paralyzing strikes in the nation's history. Their Red Battalions were important to the Constitutionalist victory during the revolution. Their form of organizing and their leadership, anarchosyndicalist and artisan, were consistent with their history and carried forward the weaknesses of the past.

THREE

The Pequeña Burguesía and Provincial Elites

The alienation of and revolutionary participation by significant elements of the pequeña burguesía and regional elites played a crucial role in the coming and process of the 1910 revolution. Between 1821 and 1910 politically revolutionary segments of the Mexican local and provincial elites frequently challenged the metropolitan ruling class of Mexico City. Rivalries between segments of the provincial and local elites were rooted in Mexico's vast geographic, economic, cultural, and political diversity. During the last century of the colonial era the rise of metropolitan industrial, commercial, and political intervention disrupted local societies and promoted their defense by the affected local and regional elites. Between 1821 and 1910 elite competition intensified between the semiautonomous structures of the periphery and the metropolis with its direct ties to the global economy.

Elite participation in the eighteenth-century rebellions in the Isthmus of Tehuantepec and southwestern Puebla regions came about through reaction of intact village hierarchies to the intrusion of commercial estate managers, state officials, and transient agrarian workers, who eroded local authority and tax revenues while introducing a more monetized economy. The change represented more than the mere diminution of local elites; it entailed cultural homogenization. In the zones of economic transition it meant the end of an entire way of life affecting the ecosystem, diet, work regimen, economy, religion, language, politics, and lines of authority. The rebellions were restricted in size because in the early stages of intrusive commercial agriculture the areas of social disruption were localized. That factor combined with the Crown's desire to satisfy the demands of local hierarchies because of its own competition with the increasingly powerful Mexico City landholding elite. The Crown shared the provincials' desire to hold the capitaline aristocracy in check.[1]

The Independence Revolution of 1810 resulted from disruption of the delicate balance that had maintained stability during most of the colonial era. The causes and interplay of forces during the more limited and regionally based Independence Revolution of 1810 were a microcosm of the nationwide upheaval of the revolution of 1910. It resulted from the development in the Bajío of an intensely commercialized agricultural system, overconcentration of population that outstripped local food production, domination by outside investors, and external political control that overwhelmed provincial and local elites. Those problems became acute when they were exacerbated by a mining depression between 1800 and 1810. That depression was triggered by forces in the world marketplace beyond the Mexicans' control—the trade disruptions caused by the Napoleonic Wars.

In 1810 the Bajío was mired in a social crisis rooted in the changes of the past one hundred years. After 1700 the area experienced a mining and manufacturing bonanza that attracted a mass of hopeful immigrants. In the later part of the eighteenth century periodic crop failures brought famine. Then, between 1800 and 1810, mine closures, unemployment, bankruptcy, and endemic hunger brought the populace to an explosive state.[2]

Spanish merchants and the wealthy among the capital's Creole elite, inspired by burgeoning European trade and demand and the special privileges and tax exemptions offered by the Spanish government, sowed their metropolitan trading and absentee agricultural profits into the silver mining industry during a century of commercial and industrial growth. New capital replaced broken-down and obsolete machinery with improved technology. The miners drained and restored inoperative mines and developed new ones. Meanwhile agriculture and industry expanded as the support needs of the mines increased. The costs of rural agricultural properties increased, bringing about a revolution in ownership. Commercial crop production expanded, to the detriment of tenant farmers and sharecroppers who were displaced. Industrial growth turned the small towns of Dolores and San Miguel into employment centers, and increased output and trade gave the provincial cities Querétaro and Guanajuato added importance. Celaya, situated in the middle of the plains, became a produce center.

The expanding economy offered displaced peasants a chance to earn higher wages in mining and manufacturing. Wages created increasing demand for domestic and local production. Local shopkeepers, suppliers, and artisans lost political power and social status to the representatives of wealthy outsiders and omnipresent state and treasury officials, but they expanded their businesses and gained unprecedented profits. Local townspeople, increasingly crowded and ill-housed, were placated by prospects of employment as silver production doubled every twenty years for a century. The Bajío's regional elite experienced trepidation while their world changed and outside forces subordinated them, but industrial and commercial success softened the cultural and political insults.

The first signs of trouble came with crop failures in the 1770s that left the region chronically undersupplied. Then, near the end of the century, war in Europe dampened silver exports, and reduced yields because of deposit exhaustion brought on mine closings. Uncertainty in Europe brought lower profits, higher risks, and a slowed rate of outside investment. Lower production levels caused layoffs and cancellation of orders for provisions and machinery. The mining crisis hit hard at local manufacturers, artisans, shopkeepers, and commercial farmers. The latter laid off agricultural workers who still believed the lands concerned rightfully belonged to them.

When the source of investment and buying slowed, the momentum of the economy died. In the socially volatile and economically imbalanced Bajío the effects were widespread misery, a spectacular rise in the crime rate, and alienation among the region's elite. The wild economic fluctuations of the decade 1800–1810 mobilized the already hostile regional elites and pequeña burguesía.

In the case of Padre Hidalgo of Dolores and his aides, Ignacio Allende and Juan Aldama, the Bajío elites' conflicts with the Spanish empire and metropolitan ruling class forged a revolutionary leadership. It was imbued with the example of colonial independence set by the American Revolution. Hidalgo, the intellectual, viewed the social program of the French Revolution and the Enlightenment idea of a social contract between government and governed as models. To him they meant the abrogation of slavery, the caste system, and the great estates and the dismantling of the colonial economic system, which denied villages the right to free manufacturing and agricultural marketing.

Scions of the provincial elite, Allende and Aldama came from families that lost heavily in the difficult years after 1800. The Allende industrial plant at San Miguel closed. Some of their properties had been foreclosed by creditors. For Allende and Aldama the American Revolution, which won independence from England while resisting social change, held more interest than the social excesses of the French Revolution. Their provincial elite anger blamed the intrusive Spanish metropolitan elite for general economic failure, the financial demise of their families, and political exclusion.[3]

When the revolution reached Michoacán, Jalisco, and the present-day states of Guerrero and Morelos, it gained support from the owners of middle-sized ranches and professionals, men of Creole and mestizo background who felt excluded from power and success by the Spanish regime, to sustain a guerrilla-type war for ten years. The revolution enrolled village leaders and landowners in the west and southwest, where the inroads of commercial agriculture had already provoked pueblo-scale unrest in the eighteenth century.[4] It also attracted a sizable group of literati. These men, largely provincial lawyers, represented the growing nationalist sentiment of the Mexican professional classes and intelligentsia. In 1814 they promulgated Mexico's first constitution at Chilpancingo. The basic causative force behind provincial elite, pequeña burguesa, and village hierarchy participation in the protracted civil war carried out from 1810 to 1821 was their economically engendered disenchantment with the metropolitan-controlled Spanish regime.

In the era immediately following independence (1821–1854) conservatism and liberalism, the political expressions of the Mexican elites, vied for control of the government and adopted political positions that would prevail until the revolution of 1910. They reflected competing ideologies and regional and economic interests. The leadership of the Conservatives was a diverse but principally metropolitan group that included large merchants, absentee commercial landowners, army officers, and high clergy. From the Conservative ranks two political factions favoring political centrism emerged. One was an alliance of military officers and leading intellectuals, including Lucas Alaman and José María Tornel, that supported General Antonio López de Santa Anna. While defending colonial caste distinctions and aristocratic privilege, they favored programs designed to develop infrastructure and the economy. The other principal Conservative faction was less flexible. Led by the high clergy and promonarchist, foreign-oriented large mercantile capitalists, they despised Santa Anna and fought the Liberals.

The Liberals were also diverse in their composition but were composed of two important factions. One was led by progressive elements of the metropolitan Creole elite, including the Fagoáda family, and the urban intelligentsia. The other group comprised radical provincial lawyers, landowners, professionals, and army officers, many of whom had supported the insurgency. They stressed provincial and municipal semiautonomy through federalism.[5]

For thirty years the contending groups fought. Liberal president, former insurgent leader, and wealthy hacendado Vicente Guerrero was assassinated by Conservative generals in 1829. The Church press celebrated the departure of deposed Liberal president General Valentín Gómez Farías from Veracruz in 1835 by lamenting that he was not washed overboard during a Gulf tempest. In the minds of the more extreme antagonists, their adversaries held totally different and evil worldviews and aspirations. Among their many points of disagreement were answers to the following questions:

—Should the government be decentralized with "autonomous" states or centralized in Mexico City with presidentially appointed heads of departments?
—What degree of mass participation in polity and how much vertical economic mobility should be allowed?
—What and how much in the area of social services should the government provide?
—What should be the disposition of Church political power and properties, which the Liberals claimed constituted 48 percent of the nation's arable land?
—Should colonial era privileges be continued for the aristocracy, army officer corps, and Church officials?

Conservatives saw the old order as sacred and viewed liberalism with alarm: "The great capitalists give impulse to and rationalize labor, without them the poor would have nothing. You want to divide property by throwing the poor against us, undoing in a day what has taken centuries to bear fruit."[6] The Liberals left no doubt, however, of their own elite status: "You smear us by claiming we want equality of wealth. All we desire is the free flow of wealth. We seek its accumulation, but as a result of work and industry. On the contrary you want it to remain in a few hands, making it inaccessible due to inequality of class and inequitable conditions."[7]

In 1910 these issues remained only partly resolved. In practice most of the privileges of the Church, army officer corps, and upper classes remained. Vertical mobility was far too restrictive for a society undergoing industrial transformation. The Church still possessed vast wealth and political power. The dictatorship imposed rule on the states from Mexico

Limits and focal points of unrest during the 1840s uprisings

City and offered virtually nothing to the lower classes in the realm of social services. The issues posed in the elite disputes of the 1820s and 1830s and the violence they triggered haunted the nation until the revolution of 1910.

Two major elite confrontations illustrate the depth of their rivalry in the first half of the nineteenth century. The first took place when the Liberal Gómez Farías government seized the Church Indian mission properties in California and sold the lands to local elites while conducting an anticlerical, antiaristocratic political offensive in Central Mexico. In response the Conservatives rallied to Santa Anna's Plan de Cuernavaca. Gómez Farías was ousted and the centrist Santanista program constitutionalized in 1836. From the Liberal-regional elite and pequeña burguesa perspective, the most offensive aspect of Santa Anna's program was to abolish the states and to replace them with departments headed by presidential appointees. Many of the new department directors were Santanista aristocrats from the militias. The provincial elites and their pequeña burguesa allies rebelled but were quickly quelled, with the exception of Anglo-American Texas, which took the opportunity to seize independence. The fundamental elite crisis rested in the issue of local and provincial political-economic control. The regional elites would not tolerate powerlessness.[8]

The second illustrative elite conflict in the postindependence epoch took place in the state of Mexico (now Guerrero) during the 1840s southwestern peasants' war. In 1842 the eastern half of Guerrero, especially the Costa Chica zone, was a focal point of regional and local elite crisis. The rivalry between Acapulco caudillo Juan Alvarez and Santa Anna's government came to a head when the national administration attempted to reorganize the region politically under the aegis of the Conservative aristocrat Nicólas Bravo in Chilpancingo. Alvarez, as the local militia commander and a major landowner, held power over the Acapulco-Costa Chica area in virtual perpetuity. His real estate holdings and political influence, however, extended far beyond his immediate domain. He owned private estates as far away as two hundred miles in the Tlapa area, and his allies—landowners, village leaders, and militia chiefs—extended from Guadalajara to the Isthmus of Tehuantepec.[9]

Santa Anna's reorganization plan jeopardized Alvarez and provincial elites in the states of Mexico and Puebla. Alvarez attempted to rally village elites to his side in the Costa Chica, helping to spark the peasants' war, which broke out shortly thereafter at Tecoanapa. He maneuvered brilliantly as the conflict exploded across southwestern Mexico. He mediated between the village hierarchies and rural pequeña burguesía on the one side and the Conservative government on the other. He maintained a low profile when peasants attacked his own estates near Tlapa. During the course of the fighting, which continued on a broad scale for three years, Alvarez successfully acted as a popular tribune, an intermediary who observed legality but treated the insurgent peasantry with an evenhandedness to which they were unaccustomed. He emerged as a voice of reason trying to resolve local grievances against new national taxes and land seizures by the Mexico City elite and Conservative aristocrats.[10]

After the war Alvarez enjoyed a popular image in the southwest as "a friend of the people." His centrist rivals Santa Anna and Bravo, the absentee Spanish merchant San Marcos estate owner, and the Conservative party were linked in the minds of the country folk to foreign and metropolitan interests.[11] In 1853 Alvarez used his good standing in the region to pronounce against Santa Anna in the wake of national protest over the latter's sale of the Mesilla Valley to the United States. The Plan of Ayutla, named after a town located in the heart of the area of peasant rebellion, explained his purposes. An alliance of southwestern Liberal elites including the governor of Oaxaca, Benito Juárez, used their popular base of support to sweep Alvarez into the presidency in 1854.

The Revolution of Ayutla was the turning point that eventually brought about Liberal ascendancy over conservatism. The Liberals laid out their program in the Constitution of 1857. The document established states' rights, prohibited the reelection of the president, forced the sale of Church property, placed education and social services under the aegis of the government, abolished village collectives, and posited equal rights before the law.[12]

The experiences of the French Intervention (1862–1867) transformed Mexican politics and liberalism. Not only were the conservatives rejected by outraged nationalists after they collaborated with the French but the victorious Liberals perceived a new chance for Mexican social and economic development through government sponsorship of public education, communications and transportation infrastructure, and the application of advanced European technology and business practices. The empire established the practicality of national government services in the reorganization of the Mexican economy. With developmentalism as a prime motivating factor, special commissions had completed hacienda inventories at Maximilian's request in order to determine production levels and potential capacity, the impact of road construction, and the future placement of railroads. Despite the empire's bankrupt state and the ongoing frontier and guerrilla war with the Liberals, relatively large foreign investments were attracted by the opportunity to exploit Mexico's raw material resources. The modernization of Mexico City, the reconstruction of the Paseo de la Reforma, and the rapid extension of the Veracruz-Mexico railroad inland to the foothills gave Mexicans a new appreciation of what government could do. The Europeans' entrepreneurialism and their applied interaction of the national government with the economy impressed most Mexican elite observers.[13]

During the Restored Republic (1867–1876) presidents Juárez and Sebastían Lerdo de Tejada, while espousing faith in the doctrine of federalism, had come to believe in the necessity of centralized political and military power. Destructive provincial elite revolts in the late 1860s and early 1870s plagued the government. They were the result of long-standing rivalries in the Liberal hierarchy, an intense dispute over the interpretation and practical application of Liberal ideology, and the conflict between regional and national economic and political interests. A provincial elite leader in alliance with local hierarchies in opposition to the national government headed each of the revolts.

The serious San Luis Potosí, Zacatecas, and Puebla uprising of 1869 is the prime example of provincial elite rebellion. The revolt was led by Liberals Trinidad García de la Cadena of Zacatecas, Pedro Martínez and Francisco Antonio Aguirre of San Luis Potosí, and Miguel Negrete in Puebla. They had supported the presidential bid of Jesus González Ortega of Zacatecas in the mid-1860s and opposed the strong centralization of power under President Juárez. They espoused radical critiques of the Mexico City-based national government, charging it with dictatorial methods and electoral fraud. They supported more power for the states and the constitutional provision prohibiting reelection of the president.

All three states involved in the insurrection, especially once-rich Zacatecas, were suffering a severe economic decline at a time when the government favored abolition of internal tariffs (*alcabalas*) to open up trade. In crisis-ridden Zacatecas the alcabalas represented 43 percent of state income. In neighboring Durango the figure reached 68 percent; in San Luis Potosí and Puebla the figures were 36 percent and 68 percent, respectively. At the same time, investors in Mexico City were attempting to increase their control of transportation and communications, industry, and public services. Provincial and local elite protests went unheeded. In at least one case, the Negrete-led Puebla revolt, rebel leaders sought agrarian working-class support giving the campesino revolutionaries under Julio Chávez López at Chalco logistical aid in their struggle with the Federal Army.[14]

Suppression of the revolt demonstrated the ever greater concentration of power in Mexico City. As technological advances gave the national government more power, the idea grew in Mexico City that centralization was necessary in order to govern effectively, that political practicality required the abandonment of federalist theory.

Liberal political rivalries provoked by the increasing disparity between Mexico City and the hinterlands produced the 1872–1873 La Noria Revolution. Porfirio Díaz, a provincial elite leader in Oaxaca, headed the revolt. Manuel González (Tamaulipas), Pedro Martínez (San Luis Potosí), Miguel Negrete (Puebla), García de la Cadena (Zacatecas), Geronimo Treviño (Nuevo León), Luis Mier y Teran (Veracruz), and other provincial elites supported Díaz.

The rebels called for no reelection of the president coupled with an appeal for "less government and more liberties." They opposed the growth of central government, demanded the return of political and administrative authority to the states and municipalities, opposed excise taxes in order to stimulate trade and commerce, and advocated jury trials. After intense fighting the national government emerged victorious. Relative stability reigned for the next four years despite radical-Liberal protests by intellectuals such as Ignacio Ramírez against violations of a free press and the democratic process, and the use of force against dissenters. In 1876 President Sebastian Lerdo de Tejada, who succeeded to office when Juárez died in 1872, decided to run for another term.

An even larger array of radical-Liberal forces supported Porfirio Díaz's 1876 Revolution of Tuxtepec than had been the case for the La Noria rebellion but still based upon the ideas and interests of the group that had revolted in 1872. The main sources of military strength for the Tuxtepec alliance again came from Díaz, González, Treviño, and Negrete, with an important new source of support—the Americans. An alliance of provincial elites supported the insurgency, but their militias were quickly defeated everywhere except in Puebla and in the northeast, where they received sanctuary and aid in Texas.

The Plan of Tuxtepec, endorsed by a plethora of provincial elite Liberals including Evaristo Madero, was a major statement of late nineteenth-century puro-liberalism. It objected to the power of a national government dominated by metropolitan elites; called for a division of political responsibilities, a system of political checks and balances, states' rights, greater responsibilities and authority for municipal governments; and claimed that democracy had been crushed by a presidential dictatorship. After securing private American aid and conducting almost six months of successful guerrilla warfare in the northeast, Díaz traveled incognito through much of the nation in search of support. He made a sophisticated cross-class political appeal. Later, elements of the organized agrarian leagues and urban workers claimed that Díaz had promised them his support in their struggle against excesses committed by landowners and industrialists working in league with the government.[15]

Once in office, however, Díaz quickly recognized a unique opportunity. He used the amassed power of his allies who had overwhelmed President Lerdo and rival claimant to the presidency Supreme Court Chief Justice José María Iglesias in order to consolidate a new regime. During the next four years he established alliances in the provinces and abroad. Federal armies entered state conflicts and overwhelmed dissenting groups in every part of the nation. Cooperative elements among the provincial elites were given political power and new business opportunities in industry, trade, and real estate, associated with foreign-controlled railroad construction, mining, and commercial agriculture, as Díaz's political economy of national elite-foreign investor hegemony in transportation, trade industry, and banking took shape and began to prosper.

Between 1880 and 1900 the regime added a temporarily satisfied provincial elite to a docile working class to create a reputation for stability among foreign investors. The same tactics employed against challenges from the industrial and agrarian working classes defeated dissenting radical elements among the provincial elites. Using force only when necessary against the background of an expanding economy, the regime sponsored loyal appointees in the states and municipios, working-class leaders in the unions, and local jefes in the villages. The government used the rurales or the military in those cases in which authority broke down. The regime formed a stable and enduring base. The durability of the Díaz system of political alliances with subordinate provincial elites and the moderate elements of the working-class movement paralleled the vigor of the profitable, largely foreign-financed era of economic growth. The regime's survival rested upon the continued allegiance of the provincial elites, but that depended upon continued national economic success.

The Díaz regime encountered radical-Liberal opposition as soon as the new president announced his appointments and programs. Generals Miguel Negrete and Trinidad García de la Cadena formed an early and dangerous alliance of Liberal dissenters among the provincial elites in the military. Both men, in rebellious, economically declining provinces, had hopes of attaining the presidency. Both federalists, their ideological convictions and constituencies eventually overshadowed selfish interests. As governor of Zacatecas during the Restored Republic, García de la Cadena abolished debt peonage liberating 50,000 families "from conditions of slavery under the inhuman dominion of the hacendado." Even in old age García de la Cadena and Negrete still revolted. Radical-Liberal idealists, they opposed metropolitan-controlled latifundia in the provinces and presidential reelection while supporting state autonomy, free municipal government, agrarianism, and a strong industrial labor movement. In their dedication to liberalism they accepted capitalism as progress, desired the development of a national economic infrastructure, favored increased foreign and free trade and industrialization; yet they favored pluralistic decentralized government, the protection of artisan industry, and the preservation of peasant village agriculture as the basis of campesino dignity. Conversant with French physiocratic economic theory, they saw no contradiction between an agricultural system based on village collectives and smallholdings and capitalism. They did not seem to anticipate the demise of local economies or polity with the advent of foreign investment.[16]

Negrete first rebelled against Díaz in 1877 after resigning his position as military commander of the Federal District. His Plan of Buena Vista repeated provincial elite-federalist and radical-Liberal complaints. He singled out the tax act of 1877 for attack and declared the revolt because of "*miseria política*" and the "betrayal of the Plan of Tuxtepec." Included in the "betrayal" were the dictatorial methods of the president and Díaz's failure to honor promises made to the states to restore their powers and to the village governments to return their lands. After several military defeats he agreed to a truce.

In 1879 Negrete revolted again when Díaz announced the selection of confidant Manuel González as his choice to succeed to the presidency. In his *pronunciamiento* Negrete called for agrarian reform to be carried out by autonomous village governments (*municipios libres*). This proposal anticipated the Liberal complaints that resurfaced with the coming of the 1910 revolution and resembled the far-reaching agrarian reform program, the Ley del Pueblo, proposed by Negrete's political allies Colonel Alberto Santa Fe and Manuel Serdán in Puebla. For the urban workers he advocated government aid to the anarchist-dominated nationally organized Labor Congress for creation of a nationwide system of worker-controlled cooperatives. He violently denounced Mexico's subordination to foreign interests. He promised the restoration of democratic liberties and a free press.[17]

García de la Cadena opposed González in the 1880 presidential election and campaigned on the issue that, through the government, landowners and industrialists had mounted a concerted attack upon the agrarian and urban working classes. He openly supported labor against the Díaz regime and allowed the formation of the Zacatecas workers' círculo, led by union leaders from Mexico City who had fled government repression. Supported by Negrete, he demanded states' rights and village autonomy, declared that the principle of no reelection must mean a clean break with the previous administration, and called for the restoration of a free press.[18]

González swept into power via the 1880 election. When Negrete charged the regime with fraud and rebelled again, government troops crushed his forces. During the next four years foreign-controlled construction of the railroads began in earnest. Economic activity increased. The government effectively organized and radical-Liberal dissent was dispersed. In 1884, despite a fiscal crisis and financial scandal, Porfirio Díaz returned as president with barely a whisper of protest.[19] His new tenure in office continued until 1911.

In 1886 Negrete and García de la Cadena, the last important military figures to espouse nineteenth-century puro-liberalism, made yet another effort to overturn Díaz. On 26 June an aged Negrete promulgated his Plan of Loma Alta in Puebla. It promised cooperatives to the urban workers, municipios libres to the agrarians, and federalist autonomy for the states. García de la Cadena attempted to help Negrete, but the army captured and executed him in the field on the orders of Secretary of War Hinojosa. Negrete surrendered and was imprisoned. In 1892 he tried again, but his forces were defeated. After incarceration Díaz released his old and enfeebled comrade in arms of 5 May, 1862 to retirement in Puebla.[20]

During the economically successful late 1880s and 1890s the principal sources of pequeña burguesa and provincial elite criticism linked to later revolutionary aspirations came from the Liberal press, some reformers within the regime itself, the restless temporarily déclassé, democratically oriented university students, and the literary community. During the 1890s a renewed nationalistic economic, political, and moral critique of the government developed that sharpened in the first decade of the twentieth century and endured until the onset of revolution in 1910.

Nationalism grew among the pequeña burguesa intelligentsia between the 1880s and 1910. Literary expression during the Porfiriato mirrored the deepening alienation between the public and the regime. During the 1880s novelists expressed concern for a national reform, which they termed "regeneration." Realism surfaced as a literature of social criticism alongside positivism and escapist modernism, tendencies that apologized for the regime. During the 1880s and 1890s the otherwise supportive works of

Emilio Rabasa reflected the reformism of a still vital regime. The ensuing years of economic instability and social unrest witnessed growing literary criticism of political and social decadence. By 1908–1910 several important authors demanded extreme, even revolutionary, solutions for the resolution of the nation's ills.[21]

Two novels that introduced social analysis appeared simultaneous with the 1891 Liberal opposition Grupo Liberal Reformista of Mexico City, the 1892 reformist but progovernment Convención Nacional Liberal, and the student unrest and wild street demonstrations of the early 1890s. *La calandria* (1890) and *Angelina* (1892), by Rafael Delgado, reflected concern with the burgeoning social problems of a racially "unjust" industrializing society. Another novel, *Angel del campo,* described the hardships of a transitional society through the desperate life of displaced peasants and artisans in the swollen cities. In 1893 Heriberto Frías captured the plight of the campesinaje in his *Tomochic*. The title was taken from the town in the Chihuahua *sierra* that rebelled against increased state authority and the reallocation of lands to the Limantour family. In retaliation the army devastated Tomochic. Frías concluded that Mexico needed "regenerative" reforms, echoing the demands of the commentaries on the cities.[22]

During the late 1880s and 1890s the Liberal press opposition in Mexico City deeply concerned the government. In 1891 the Grupo Liberal Reformista, which included capitaline newspaper men, demanded government respect for a free press and enforcement of the inoperative anticlerical laws. During the late 1880s and continuing until 1893 two Mexico City newspapers, *El Demócrata* and *La República,* attacked the government as a heavy-handed tyranny that needed reform. In March 1893 *El Demócrata,* edited by Mexico City's dissident students, announced a plan to expose fully the government's brutal suppression of the agrarian rebels around Tomochic by publishing Frías's essay in serial form. Both newspapers tried to arouse public opinion, and later that year the government closed them. The government imprisoned the editors of the puro *El Hijo del Ahuizote*. On 13 August 1893 over fifty newspaper editors and writers were in Mexico City's Belem prison. The infusion of industry and infrastructure development from abroad, and the reinforcement of labor-coercive industrial export agriculture by foreign capital in a still basically agrarian society with a strong landowning class, ensured a weak bourgeoisie and defeated the peasantry and labor movement. The result was economic and political plutocracy, conditions described by Barrington Moore, Jr., in his analysis of emergent authoritarian regimes.[23]

Mexico's democratic forces showed strength, however. Student unrest in the early 1890s led to violent antigovernment demonstrations by the university students of Mexico City in the spring of 1892 and 1893. The demonstrations, which included mutualist societies and unions, were at first staged against presidential reelection and political tyranny. As the demonstrators encountered police and military suppression, however, they grew increasingly radical and broadened the scope of their attack to include foreign businessmen in Mexico, capitalism in general, the Church, and the progovernment press. In 1892 the leaders of the protest movements were arrested. The government detained, among others, Ricardo Flores Magón, the future leader of the Partido Liberal Mexicano. He served one month in jail. The following year he and his fellow student dissidents founded the short-lived *El Demócrata*. The newspaper's suppression focused even greater attention on the dissidents.[24]

In 1892 some of the best minds of the Díaz regime, including the celebrated Científicos (middle-level government and nongovernment experts, specialized functionaries, and intelligentsia), met in the Convención Nacional Liberal in Mexico City. Their purpose was to formulate a political platform in support of the president's reelection. Consistent with the regime's growing inability to accommodate upwardly mobile social groups or provincial elites, the Científicos rarely reached the higher councils of government. Their manifesto, however, revealed interest in high-level policy-making, much of the regime's thinking, and the directions its energy would take in the future. They noted the need for a more efficiently enforced tax collection system. They favored the total and final abolition of the alcabalas, which were the principal sources of local and state revenues, regarded by the government as "tax barriers," in order to "facilitate national trade and industry." The large-scale foreign industrialists and big merchants supported the latter measure, which was a disaster for local artisan and small factory production. It became law on 1 July 1896.[25]

The convention recommended the institution of a vice-presidency in order to provide an orderly succession for the presidency. It advocated the eventual establishment of political democracy after a prelude of law and order had achieved sufficient material and social progress. It urged an active public education program commensurate with Mexico's needs as an emerging industrialized nation. It favored jury rather than judge-decided verdicts for newspapers accused of violating constitutional restrictions on the press. Finally, it recommended smaller financial outlays for the military in favor of more rapid industrial development.[26]

Overall, the convention tried to bring forth a ringing endorsement of the president's reelection bid, but it implied reservations about a number of policy questions, including the level of support for the military, the education program, and freedom of the press. Just as important, had its writers been rewarded politically, it would have established a precedent for convention endorsements prior to elections. Díaz perceived the Científicos as a threat, and consequently few ever gained his confidence.

Two of the leading liberal opposition newspapers, *El Siglo XIX* and *El Monitor Republicano,* had closed their doors in 1896. Their complaints about dictatorship and foreign control of the mining industry and transportation system were intolerable to an economically dependent, increasingly authoritarian, narrowly based government and the irascible Díaz, who cut off their subventions. Between 1896 and 1900 *El Hijo del Ahuizote* and Filomeno Mata, the editor of *El Diario del Hogar,* who had been repeatedly arrested, carried the burden of press dissent.

By 1897 the intellectual-literary assault upon the regime became more encompassing. Frías published his book *El ultimo duelo* that year, portraying pervasive corruption through one-sided confrontations between rich and poor, powerful and powerless. José López Portillo y Rojas, in his *La parcela* published in 1898, echoed a nationalism provoked by foreign control of Mexico's natural resources. Two years later Porfirio Parra condemned the motives of the government as corrupt and cynical in *Pacotillas.* Using the presidential period of General González (1880–1884) for his setting, Parra pointed out the repression of popular forces and the need for radical far-reaching reforms in the face of corruption. The leading intellectual journal *Revista Postivista* hailed the book as an outstanding example of the new national literature.[27]

At the dawn of the twentieth century the discontented intellectuals found crucial new allies in their attacks on the regime among alienated elements of the provincial elites of the south and north. This new element presented a challenge to the regime that began with Camilo Arriaga's August 1900 "Invitation to the Liberal Party," which called for the creation of Liberal clubs throughout Mexico that would convene a national convention in San Luis Potosí in February 1901. Arriaga, the heir of an elite family in San Luis Potosí, started in motion a political resistance movement that comprised disparate Liberals, intelligentsia, radical students, and provincials. It culminated in the 1910 revolutionary movement headed by Francisco Madero of Coahuila.[28]

Arriaga's nationalistic pride and democratic political ideals, like others in his social group, were violated by what he saw going on in Mexico, but his economic experience hardened those convictions. His family owned mining enterprises in central Mexico and had prospered in the nineteenth century. During the 1890s, however, the economy in San Luis Potosí, where most of the family's mines were located, went into a recession. The family's holdings suffered greatly, and cave-ins, floods, and rising costs compounded the problem. Arriaga's attempts to recover by obtaining new concessions from the government ran afoul of American competition.

The state government, in conjunction with the Díaz regime, sought fresh economic life through foreign investment. By 1900 the Guggenheim-controlled Sociedad Metalúrgica Mexicana, a subsidiary of the American Smelting and Refining Company, achieved dominance over the mining industry of San Luis Potosí through preferential concessions issued to it by both the state and national government. A personal meeting in 1890 between Daniel Guggenheim and President Díaz solidified the position of the empresario in Mexico and shunted the provincial-elite interests of the Arriagas, Maderos, and others.

Foreign grants continued to be issued even after Arriaga mounted his political resistance and intensified his objections. In 1902 the Sociedad Metalúrgica Mexicana received a railroad concession linking Río Verde, a southern Potosino town, to the trunk line connecting the smelter construction sites in the state. The Guggenheims gained a virtual monopoly on the metallurgical industry in the region, which, combined with their railroad holdings and other American railway interests, placed Mexican mining entrepreneurs in a dependent position. Similar government-supported foreign intrusions into the economy and polity of Sonora during the Yaqui Wars alienated the provincial elite Maytorena family and others of that state's landholding oligarchy. Events in Coahuila, Nuevo León, and Tamaulipas paralleled those of San Luis Potosí and Sonora.[29]

Soon after Arriaga's appeal to the Liberals, attorney Antonio Díaz Soto y Gama created a Potosino Liberal club named Ponciano Arriaga, after Camilo's famous uncle and associate of Juárez. He recruited students. Arriaga served as club president, and journalist-poet Juan Sarabia headed its newspaper, *Renacimiento*. All three men were important revolutionary precursors. At the same time, the Flores Magón brothers in Mexico City, veteran student dissenters of the 1890s, welcomed the new movement as an opportunity to create a mass-based revolutionary organization. By February 1901 there were over fifty Liberal clubs affiliated with Arriaga's movement in thirteen states scattered over the northern half of Mexico. The club membership comprised shopkeepers, local manufacturers, artisans, industrial workers, and village elites. Its strength centered in the north, the area where foreign economic intervention was most overwhelming, and in the industrial areas of the south such as Puebla and Orizaba, where underground radicalism persisted among the working class.[30]

During the Liberal convention Ricardo Flores Magón delivered a violent speech diverting that conclave's attention from its pretense of preoccupation with anticlericalism by calling the government "a den of thieves." He became a national figure, a center of controversy. Already known among his Mexico City associates as a communist-anarchist of the Peter Kropotkin mold, Ricardo withheld his deepest political convictions from the public for another decade while conducting a "liberal" campaign to overthrow the government.

Ricardo, Enrique, and Jesús Flores Magón were the provincial sons of a moderately prosperous Oaxacan landowning family. Oaxaca had been a longtime center of provincial elite rebellion against the centrist regimes of the nineteenth century. Despite limited means, all three youths attended law school at the National University, but only Jesús completed the work required for the degree. After Ricardo's arrest in 1892 during the Mexico City student demonstrations, Jesús participated in the short-lived publication of *El Demócrata* in 1893. During the seven years following the government's closure of *El Demócrata,* Ricardo and Enrique adopted the anarchism of Mexico's artisans and syndicalists and of the Russians, Bakunin and Kropotkin, but remained out of public view. By 1900 the brothers had saved enough money to start another resistance newspaper, *Regeneración,* with Jesús as publisher and Ricardo and Enrique serving as writers. At first they maintained a temperate level of criticism against the government, but the situation began to change rapidly after Arriaga's call for a Liberal congress to convene in San Luis Potosí. The Flores Magón brothers responded by recruiting members for a Liberal club in Mexico City.[31]

The Potosino club, Ponciano Arriaga, followed the February congress by calling for the creation of a political party to oppose the dictatorship. In Mexico City Ricardo and Jesús headed the strengthening Asociación Liberal Reformista while other Liberal clubs also grew rapidly. At that point the Díaz regime closed them and jailed many of the leaders, including the two brothers. The Liberal cause, however, was not stopped. *Regeneración* succeeded in stirring up public opinion with a series of attacks on the government, including a promise by Antonio Díaz Soto y Gama to "wage unremitting war against the state," "arrogant foreigners," and the Church. *Regeneración* claimed that the foreign-owned railway system was stripping Mexico of profits that would otherwise accrue within the country for reinvestment and development. It gained wide public support with a nationalistic, democratic, consumer-oriented approach. In 1901 the government closed the newspaper, but newer and more militant publications replaced those that were shut down.

By the end of 1901 the fifty Liberal clubs created in February had increased to one hundred fifty with newspapers supporting them. The regime reacted by arresting leaders and newsmen. *El Diario del Hogar* was among the papers closed. Its editor, Filomeno Mata, whose resistance dated from the 1880s, was arrested again. When Arriaga tried to publish *El Diario* from San Luis Potosí, he was imprisoned. Dozens of newspaper writers and publishers joined the Flores Magóns in Belem prison.[32]

In the wake of the closings, the more zealous Liberals in San Luis Potosí published *El Demofilo* from April until July 1902, when the government confiscated the machinery. The reappearance of the opposition press despite arrests, closings, and equipment seizures demonstrated considerable financial support and depth of conviction. Army and police intervention in February 1902 prevented the convening of a second San Luis Potosí Liberal congress.

An overconfident government released the Flores Magóns from prison at the end of April. Jesús retired from revolutionary activities; Ricardo took over editorship of *El Hijo del Ahuizote* from Daniel Cabrera, who was still in prison. The radical attacks upon the government and foreigners that ensued provoked a prompt repression; the short-term jailings discouraged the less committed but had a radicalizing effect on the other dissidents. Their continued resistance electrified other young adults, who flocked to the Liberal banner and joined clubs. In February 1903 the Potosino club issued another manifesto calling for "reforms" in its title, but its message was clearly subversive.[33]

As the drama of Liberal political action was deepening, novelists gave the growing dissent another dimension. Simultaneous with the agitation before and after the Liberal convention, Manuel San Juan published *El señor gobernador* in 1901, and Rafael Delgado wrote *Los parientes ricos,* which appeared in 1903. Both novels described a repugnant political and economic elite collaborating with vulgar foreign interlopers in a system that exploited Mexican workers.[34] Data confirm the intelligentsia's estimate of foreign penetration and control of the economy.

Foreign interests dominated most sectors of commercial agriculture, owned over 120 million acres of land, and controlled 90 percent of Mexico's eighty largest capitalized business concerns, including nine of the top ten. The customary Mexican representation in these aggregations consisted of high-ranking politicians, including cabinet ministers who received stock in return for their aid in obtaining government licenses and approvals. The regional elites and pequeña burguesía felt not only excluded from the benefits of foreign enterprise but in direct competition with it. Meanwhile the plight of the industrial, village, and estate workers was growning more desperate. The police became increasingly active in strikes, arresting workers or expelling them from the vicinities of labor disputes.[35]

In April 1903 the Liberal movement reached a major turning point in which some leaders chose revolution. Demonstrations in Mexico City, Monterrey, and other state capitals protesting the arrests, the foreigners, and dictatorship, resulted in the shocking deaths of fifteen participants in the northern city when troops fired on the crowd. In Mexico City thousands gathered in front of the offices of *El Hijo del Ahuizote,* now published by Ricardo and Enrique Flores Magón, Juan Sarabia, and others. The editors, from families of the provincial pequeña burguesía, found support among professionals, intellectuals, and industrial workers. On 16 April the police raided the newspaper, which had a circulation of 24,000, and incarcerated its staff in Belem prison. Díaz Soto y Gama and Camilo Arriaga were already in exile in Texas. They fled after the police and army attack in Monterrey was followed by a roundup of political prisoners. While in Belem the Flores Magón brothers and their associates, faced with the choice of repeated arrests or the abandonment of their convictions, decided to continue the revolutionary movement from exile.

In February 1904 Ricardo and Enrique Flores Magón and Juan and Manuel Sarabia convened the Club Liberal Ponciano Arriaga in Laredo, Texas, and later that year *Regeneración,* financed by Arriaga, began publication in San Antonio. Local police and the Furlong Detective Agency, retained by the Mexican government, began a campaign of harassment that continued for years and caused the revolutionaries to move their operations from San Antonio to St. Louis in February 1905. They founded the PLM in St. Louis and in March 1906 moved to Toronto. They finally arrived in Los Angeles late in 1906. The U.S. government cooperated with Díaz's authorities in suppressing the PLM. U.S. Ambassador to Mexico David E. Thompson reflected official concern when he agreed with the Díaz government's pronouncement that the Flores Magóns were dangerous anarchists.

By September 1905 the party's supporters in Mexico as well as the government understood the PLM's revolutionary intentions. The organization's membership continued to grow, and *Regeneración*'s circulation reached 20,000. The monetary support available to the Liberal movement and the Magonistas dried up, however. The more narrowly nationalistic provincial elites and Arriaga dissociated themselves from the Magonistas, and Ricardo complained that Camilo had turned a previously sympathetic Francisco Madero against him.

The radicalizing PLM represented pequeña burguesa and lower social strata discontent. The organization received its financial support from small donations collected across central and northern Mexico and from American leftists, to whom the junta made frequent appeals. The provincial elites were faced with a choice between the radical PLM and the regime. Their opposition to the government floundered until Francisco Madero provided a regional elite-led reformist banner to which they could rally a few years later.

Meanwhile the PLM forged ahead. In 1906 it had over 350 underground clubs and guerrilla units operating in the five zones into which Mexico was divided. The PLM was sophisticated enough to avert serious compromise during the five years before the revolution. The national commander, Praxedis Guerrero, led the units in Mexico. He reported to the junta presided over by Ricardo in the United States. The five zone commanders, or *delegados,* served as Guerrero's direct contacts. In the north he also worked directly with the rank-and-file. Beneath the zone delegados were the individual unit leaders, *jefe de guerrilla,* and their aides, the *subjefes.* The PLM club and guerrilla unit members were town artisans and industrial workers and a lesser number of northern displaced farmers and rural workers. The groups ranged in size from 300 to no more than a dozen. The unit members elected the jefe and subjefe, thus providing anarchist self-management at the local level.[36]

In July 1906, shortly after the sensational workers' strike and rebellion at Cananea, the PLM promulgated a political platform that became famous. It called for sweeping economic, political, and social reforms. Attuned to the concerns of the disaffected, it advocated a minimum wage, Sunday rest, cash pay instead of script monies, a stable currency, abolition of company stores and child labor, industrial disability compensation, job safety standards, redistribution of unproductive lands held by haciendas, restoration of village political and law enforcement authority, federalism, an end to nationally imposed boss rule in the provincia, and more government control over productive enterprises, transportation, and communications.

Arrests at Douglas, Arizona, and Rio Grande City and El Paso in Texas, however, disrupted the PLM forces on the U.S. side of the border on the eve of an invasion designed to emulate Porfirio Díaz's feat in 1876 and trigger a general revolt in Mexico. A few of the uprisings scheduled in Mexico took place in spite of the fiasco on the border and resulted in a series of defeats near the border and in the Gulf coast zone south of Veracruz. Only the forces led by Donato Padua at Acayucán, Veracruz, survived. Numbering 300 men, they continued guerrilla activities until the revolution began in 1910.[37]

The PLM grew increasingly radical. In the spring of 1907 José Neira, one of many PLM *luchadores obreros* circulating among the workers in the textile factories of central Mexico, arrived in Río Blanco and began work there leading to the factory workers' rebellion of January 1907. By now labor unrest swept across Mexico, and most of it had no direct connection with the PLM. The same social, economic, and intellectual forces that brought about the revolutionary crisis created the PLM. The PLM did not start the revolution; it was a product of it. The worsening crisis radicalized the PLM and the intelligentsia.

The literature of 1906–1907 reflects growing nationalistic anger. In the wake of the Cananea and Río Blanco worker uprisings, the Mexican novel reached new heights of social protest, extolling the workers while decrying the foreigners and rich as corrupt. In Mariano Azuela's *Los fracasados,* which appeared in 1907, well-meaning, innocent, decent people were ruthlessly crushed, their lives ruined, by a vicious gangster-like government. In *Pajarito,* published in 1908, Gayetano Rodríguez Beltrán praised the virtues of the hard-working common man and angrily damned the powerful few as morally bankrupt. At the same time Heriberto Frías's *El amor de las sirenas* offered a revolutionary solution idealizing the nationalistic and once again protesting Mexico City pequeña burguesía and déclassé university students as the hope against the government and venal outsiders. In the same year Frias's *El triunfo de Sancho Panza* demonstrated the triumph of moral principle over powerful forces of evil, insisting that one must steadfastly adhere to one's higher ideals.

Reflective of the intellectual ferment but more removed from the social unrest and literary radicalism around them, a number of intellectuals founded the Ateneo de la Juventud in 1909. This group, composed of professors, artists, other professionals, and students, was important because its members rejected proregime positivism and speculated about social problems and possible reforms. Its wide-ranging membership included government supporters like Nemesio García Naranjo and nationalistic, liberal, and radical critics of the regime such as Isidro Fabela, José Vasconcelos, and Diego Rivera.[38]

As textile strikes continued to trouble central Mexico in 1907–1908 and the university students returned to the streets of Mexico City, the PLM prepared an uprising for June 1908. Coordinated U.S. and Mexican police efforts along the border averted it at the eleventh hour. The failure to link up with forces entering the country at border points once again isolated the PLM units that rebelled inside Mexico. Limited resources seriously impaired the PLM's efforts. Junta members, harassed by the authorities on both sides of the border since 1900, were in jail again and on the defensive when Francisco Madero emerged as a candidate for the presidency.

The economic disagreements between Madero and the intrusive national government, metropolitan elites, and foreign enterprises were typical of provincial elite revolutionism in the nineteenth century. Madero's father, Evaristo, owned the Compañia de Tierras de Sonora with 1,450,000 acres. Francisco served as president of the Negociación Agrícola y Ganadera de San Enrique of Nuevo León and Coahuila, which claimed 69,000 acres of commercial land. Evaristo and eight of his sons, including Francisco, also owned the 940,000-acre hacienda of the Compañia de Terrenos y Ganados de Coahuila. Madero believed in the modernization of agricultural practices, but he had no sympathy for the land redistribution programs associated with agrarian reform.

The border state of Coahuila served as the family's locus of power, but the Maderos owned vast properties in Sonora, Tamaulipas, and Durango. The provincial elites and pequeña burguesía in Durango, San Luis Potosí, Sonora, Chihuahua, Nuevo León, Tamaulipas, and Sinaloa interacted with the Maderos, and many of the them supported Francisco's candidacy. The pequeña burguesía proved especially important in Chihuahua, Sinaloa, Nuevo León, and Tamaulipas because the Díaz regime maintained strong elite ties in those states through clientelist political and economic cooperation dating from the 1870s. Removed from the national capital, the Maderos and Coahuilan elites had less influence with the government than did foreign investors. Lacking the connections in Mexico City needed for protection, the Maderos found their mining, industrial, banking, guayule-rubber, and agricultural enterprises in direct competition with foreigners who enjoyed vastly greater economic strength. The 1905 peso devaluation badly undercut the Maderos' ability to buy properties in competition with buyers using more powerful currencies such as the dollar. Compounding the problem was the fact that the foreigners enjoyed political advantages with the government.

The Compañia Metalúrgica de Torreón headed the Madero mining complex. Its assets totaled $5 million in 1907, but that amount was minuscule in contrast to the resources of the Guggenheim-controlled American Smelting and Refining Company, which the Mexican government allowed to open a smelter at nearby Valardina, Durango. ASARCO's intent was to "compete directly with the Torreon smelter which has long had a practical monopoly of the rich ores of this district." By 1906 ASARCO was the monopolist. It controlled most of the metallurgy in north-central and northeastern Mexico. Its hold on ore deposits was sufficient even to hamper an American competitor, the U.S. Smelting, Refining and Mining Company. That concern had planned to develop a smelter in the Chihuahua ore-producing zone at Jiménez.[39]

Another Madero mining concern beset by outside competition in 1907 was the Compañia Carbonífera de Sabinas, S.A. In 1876 Evaristo Madero and Patricio Milmo established a lucrative business selling coal to Colis Huntington for his International Railroad and to Lee Plumb of the National Railroad. In 1886 Madero and Huntington quarreled about the terms of the contract, including the price of the coal. George Brackenridge and Jean La Coste, bankers and merchants from San Antonio, Texas, served as negotiators in the dispute and were barely able to avert litigation.

The mines' daily output totaled one thousand tons when the metropolitan financier and descendant of capitaline colonial aristocracy Francisco Pimentel y Fagoada joined his wealthy Mexico City partners in purchasing the nearby and better-situated Compañia Carbonífera del Norte from the American-owned Monterrey Iron and Steel Company. The government approved the transaction and put well-placed metropolitan capitalists in competition with the Maderos. The intruders' relationship with the Americans ensured a market for their coal. The metropolitan-elite Martínez del Río family also placed a coal company in the region, and another coal-mining concern, the American International Land and Mining Company, purchased 1,200,000 acres for $600,000. It was a figure the Maderos and other *norteños* could no longer match. Pimentel y Fagoada and Martínez del Río developed financial and business partnerships with American and Texan oil companies and U.S. land development companies in Mexico.

Meanwhile the Monterrey Iron and Steel Company acquired 700,000 acres of coal-bearing lands from Nuevo León businessman Milmo. The Martínez del Río patriarch, Pablo, headed one of the U.S. Smelting Company's subsidiaries in the region. The Mexican-controlled Compañia Nacional Exploradora de Carbón y Coke, a coal exploration and development concern partly owned by the Maderos, suffered from outside competition, both foreign and capitaline. The government approved the interventions by foreign enterprise, and often its officials served as officers in the intruding companies.

The Maderos, whose coal enterprise at Sabinas prospered during the 1880s and 1890s because of contracts with Huntington and Plumb, found themselves and other northern elites in competition with an alliance of foreign enterprise and metropolitan elites for access to local resources and labor. Wages also became a source of friction between Mexican landowners and their American counterparts. An American employer in the Guadalajara-Colima area described the resentment toward the increasingly numerous American "boomers" on the part of the hacendados: "We paid them better wages and treated them better and housed them better than some of the Mexican ranchmen."

Elite and working-class hostility, however, had a wider basis than the economic dimension. The newspaper *La Libertad* described the Americans as "that swarm of ants which is invading . . . sending revolvers and establishing bar rooms everywhere." U. S. Consul General L. M. Gottechalk warned that "the lower class . . . might well direct their antagonisms toward Americans." Consul James Le Roy described the antagonisms that developed after 1906 in Durango:

> A very large part of the press in Mexico, and particularly the less important periodicals of the provincial towns, such newspapers as are rarely seen outside their immediate vicinity, are indulging in constant attacks upon the government of the United States, its people and everything American.[40]

American demand gave the Maderos unprecedented rubber profits in the late nineteenth and early twentieth century, but giant U.S. companies had the power to take those gains away. The Madero family rubber enterprises included the National Rubber Company, the Mexican Crude Rubber Company, the Compañia Coahuilense de Parras, and the Compañia Industrial de Guayule. The guayule shrub produced an inexpensive rubber over wide areas of northern Mexico. Its production boomed during the period 1905–1907. The value of Torreón guayule exports increased from $1,000 daily in 1905 to shipments ranging from $20,000 to $100,000 in 1907. In 1906, however, the Continental Rubber Company with a capitalization of $30 million entered into competition with Mexican producers. The company invested $4.5 million into factories at Saltillo, Torreón, and Ocampo, producing 250 tons monthly for the U.S. Rubber Company and others. Later that year U.S. Rubber agreed to make all of its purchases from Continental, reducing the Mexican producers' access to the American marketplace.

Continental expanded by purchasing guayule haciendas totaling more than 3,775,000 acres for $14.5 million and increased the Torreón plant's capacity to 800,000 tons monthly. In 1906 the increasing supply drove prices for guayule down from 65 cents to 25 cents per pound. The American company included John D. Rockefeller, Jr., Bernard Baruch, Senator Nelson A. Aldrich, and Daniel Guggenheim on its board of directors. Its parent corporation was financially allied with the National City Bank. Madero openly acknowledged the threat posed by Continental.[41]

Resourceful entrepreneurs, the Maderos found an outlet for their product in Germany. Because they controlled vast guayule properties and marketed in Europe, the Maderos survived Continental's challenge. Yet the role of the Díaz government in licensing the foreign competition and abetting its cost-inflating acquisitions and price-depressing trade practices deeply alienated the guayule producers among the northern provincial elites. By 1910 guayule prices had recovered to historic highs, but the heights of anger also had been reached. The Maderos were beyond reconciliation; they were organizing a political challenge to the regime.

Perhaps the most outraging experience the Maderos had with intrusive foreign competition aided by the Mexican government occurred in the realm of agriculture. The Maderos controlled sizable cotton-producing and processing facilities in the La Laguna region near Torreón. Those fields depended upon the Nazas River for irrigation. A British and American Company, with headquarters in New York, the Mexican Estates of Tlahualilo, Ltd., disputed the Maderos' access to the water, and spent $600,000 to divert the Nazas some eighteen kilometers. The courts ultimately decided the suit. A consortium of British investors headed by Lord Balfour and American shareholders headed by James Stillman, chairman of the board of the National City Bank, owned the Tlahualilo Estates company. Despite a decision ultimately favoring the Mexican farmers, the foreigners won de facto. They did so because they used the water for years while the government mediated and the case dragged on in the courts.

In 1905–1906 the Estates of Tlahualilo turned a small but adequate profit of nearly $49,000. The Maderos and other agriculturalists suffered devastating losses during the ensuing droughts of 1907–1910. Those droughts combined with economic depression to reduce freight by 16 percent on the International Railroad, which ran from Durango through the Laguna district and from Torreón to Eagle Pass. The Mexican commercial agriculturalists of the Laguna area protested the luring away of agricultural workers by the foreigners who paid as much as four pesos a day. The norm in the north was nearly 75 centavos, and the minimum wage for silver miners in central Mexico was 37 centavos per day. Labor costs and the results of the dispute over water rights provided compelling lessons for Mexican agriculturalists regarding their status within the Porfirian regime. An important segment of the provincial elites found itself in competition with foreigners and the government for access to material and labor resources.[42]

Madero's candidacy began in the aftermath of an interview granted by Díaz to James Creelman, a writer for *Pearson's Magazine,* a journal owned and used by Lord Cowdray to promote his multifaceted enterprises in Mexico. In the interview published in February 1908, Díaz declared his wish to retire from office and supported the creation of political parties to take part in the next presidential election. Later that year Madero published *La sucesión presidencial en 1910,* offering a legalistic but possible course of political action against the government. He appealed to a cross-section of alienated groups, especially the provincial elites and intelligentsia. Madero criticized reelection, not Díaz personally. He avoided criticism of the Americans; in fact, he quietly favored further foreign investment as long as it included broad-based Mexican participation. Simple and direct, the book was widely disseminated and conveyed a message of personal integrity, federalism, and political freedom. Translated in the minds of many listeners, his slogans "Effective suffrage, no reelection" connoted "one man, one vote" and "down with boss rule."[43]

Despite Díaz's subsequent decision to run for reelection, a number of independent political groups formed in 1909 in the hope of electing individuals like General Bernardo Reyes of Nuevo León to the vice-presidency, or for the adoption of various reforms. In May 1909 the Club Central Anti-reeleccionista of Mexico City made up a number of Liberals including newspaper publisher Mata, Madero, and Emilio Vazquez Gómez, a lawyer who served as its president. Later revolutionary intellectuals José Vasconcelos, Paulino Martínez, Felix R. Palavicini, and Toribio Esquivel Obregon joined the leadership.

At first the government focused its opposition against the campaign on behalf of Reyes because it attacked Ramón Corral, the incumbent vice-president. Reyes, a general and former minister of war, enjoyed support within both the army and elite and seemed to pose a serious threat. However, when Díaz announced his intention to run after all, Reyes gave up his quest. By then Madero's candidacy was well under way. It began with hard campaigning around Mexico City. Then he toured the eastern half of Mexico seeking support for the antireelectionist movement. His eastern trip included Progreso, Merida, and Campeche in Yucatán, Veracruz, Tampico, and Monterrey. He then returned home to Coahuila, where he worked on the local elections, which yielded mixed results.

In the meantime many Liberals, including Vasconcelos, became frustrated and advocated revolution. Madero assumed the burden of keeping them in line, urging the need to remain within the law. By his actions he assumed leadership of the antireelectionist movement. He toured the western states, receiving support from provincial elites and intellectuals there. The trip began in Querétaro and moved through Guadalajara, Colima, Sinaloa, and Sonora. José María Maytorena, a hacendado long excluded from power by the national government, and Benjamin C. Hill, another prominent Sonoran, supported him. Maytorena opposed Díaz and Corral, who was also Sonoran, over the long-fought Yaqui War in the state and the government's close alliance with American investors. The destruction caused by the Yaqui conflict contributed to the decline of Maytorena's agricultural enterprises, and the close cooperation of the national and state governments with the Americans diminished his political influence.[44]

Madero's campaign resulted in the formation of antireelectionist clubs across the nation and his enhancement as the principal leader of the movement. The leadership of the clubs devolved to local elites, landowners, intellectuals, and anarchist artisans. Aguiles Serdán took charge in Puebla and soon had over 300 groups, former PLM clubs and new adherents, consisting of several thousand members, many of them armed. The most important club leaders, all from state elites or the emergent pequeña burguesa, were María Pino Suárez and Delio Moreno Cantón in Yucatán, Maytorena and Hill in Sonora, Rafael Cepeda in San Luis Potosí, Heriberto Frías in Mazatlán, Manuel Bonilla in Culiacan, Manuel Ugarto in Guanajuato, Alberto Fuentes D. in Aguascalientes, and José Hinojosa in Veracruz.

The success of Díaz's economic programs had created a larger capitalist economy, but the government was truly a remnant of an ancien régime with a too-narrow political base originally created by an alliance established back in the 1870s. It maintained castelike ethnic limitations on vertical social mobility. Now frustrated elite and new pequeña burguesa forces created by a dynamic economic process found themselves excluded from an obsolescent government structure. They resorted to the only alternative to powerlessness: revolution. In the meantime, nationalistic provincial elite

Liberals like Arriaga were in flux, caught between the too-radical PLM and the too-conservative Madero movement with its narrow emphasis on political change.

Madero received the antireelectionists nomination for president on the first ballot taken at their convention, and his choice for vice-president, Francisco Vazquez Gómez, won over spirited competition. Francisco was veteran antireelectionist Emilio's brother and President Díaz's personal physician. One rationale for his selection was Madero's desire to discourage repression during the forthcoming campaign. A more likely explanation is that Madero wished to reach rapprochement with Díaz and establish transitional political ties with the Mexico City elite before open conflict developed.

On 16 April 1910, Madero and President Díaz met and the candidate was promised a free and honest election. The Madero-Vazquez Gómez combine then drafted a platform that promised an end to "boss rule," expanded public instruction, land reclamation and irrigation, and universal military training. Most of its provisions were actually modifications and enlargements upon proposals long considered by the government. Astutely, Madero avoided the mounting nationalistic anti-American clamor. Madero's convention declaration that government persecution or use of armed force "will be repelled with force by a resolute public" was his first uncompromising antireelectionist campaign statement.

In April and May Madero's presidential campaign set off wildly supportive street demonstrations in Mexico City. In Guadalajara and Puebla he witnessed massive demonstrations in his support. Then the repression began. The government arrested his partisans, denied them meeting places, and refused to grant parade permits. Still, thousands turned out at the scheduled places with the hope of hearing him speak or even of catching a glimpse of him.

On 4 June 1910 the authorities arrested Madero in Saltillo on charges of having assisted his colleague Roque Estrada to escape apprehension. The police sought to arrest Estrada, who was accompanying Madero on his northern campaign swing, for giving a public speech without a permit. Madero deceived the police and enabled Estrada to get away. Madero's arrest came as the government imprisoned thousands of his supporters. The campaign floundered, but he was a martyr in the eyes of the public. The primary election in late June resulted in fraud and victory for Díaz and Corral. The run-off election took place early in July but the primaries had sealed the antireelectionists' fate. The government confidently released

Madero on bail on 22 July but required him to remain under quasi-house arrest in San Luis Potosí.

Two distinct trends began to unfold during Madero's incarceration. First, moderates within the antireelectionist party, including vice-presidential candidate Vazquez Gómez, supported a rapprochement with the regime through the selection of a compromise vice-president. The accord was to be reached before Congress ratified the election results. Madero refused to cooperate and began to plan a revolution. Second, small-scale rebellions broke out across the country as unrest grew.

PLM-led peasants seized bottomlands on the 893,650-acre American-owned Corralitos hacienda in Chihuahua. Rebels burned American agricultural estates in Tehuantepec, Chiapas, Durango, Sonora, and San Luis Potosí. Rebels in Yucatán captured Valladolid. Troops restored order but only after a bloody battle. On 8 July antireelectionist Gabriel Leyva led an uprising in Sinaloa threatening the estates of Colonel Dan Burns of San Francisco, who controlled "the single largest interest in Mexico." Burn's Sinaloa-Durango properties netted him $800,000 per year in 1908–1910. In July Santana Rodríguez (Santanon), a pequeña burguesa agrarian, joined forces with the Veracruz PLM unit led by Donato Padua and launched their revolution in October. Their campaign endured until Madero unseated Díaz in 1911. A rebellion swept the San Luis Potosí Huasteca region in August and September. There were five revolts in the summer of 1910. Only one was *antireeleccionista*. The PLM led two. The others were made up of independent local elites, peasants, and agricultural workers. Revolutionists conducted widespread attacks against American properties. Emilio Madero led a destructive mob assault on the Continental Rubber Company complex at Torreón. Attacks on Americans and their property were a major part of the revolution.[45]

The violence that swept Mexico stemmed from central issues rather than diffuse minutia. The Mexican provincial elites and pequeña burguesía repeatedly expressed federalist, home rule, and other participatory demands. They appeared in political manifestos, novels, and in-house reform movements. They charged that the Mexican state had attempted to undergo a socioeconomic transformation in collusion with foreign capital without broad domestic political participation. Its economic program placed the provincial elites in open competition with much stronger foreign capital. The economic growth had created underrepresented social groups rendering the ancien régime politically archaic. Shaped and buffeted by external economic forces during the course of the Porfiriato, the regional elites lost in their efforts to participate in state largess and power. The pequeña burguesía, industrial and urban workers, and peasants were excluded altogether.

During Madero's campaign Undersecretary of Foreign Relations and writer Federico Gamboa captured the mystique of the times, echoing the candidate's concerns and the expectations of the public. In *La venganza de la gleba* he denounced the regime's shortcomings and called for reforms. But it was too late—reforms would no longer satisfy the bulk of the dissidents. Madero and his supporters among the alienated provincial elites and pequeña burgesía could not rely on the electoral process for redress of their grievances. In their struggle against the government, the rebellious elites now called upon the long restrained lower classes, which, as Porfirio Díaz pointed out upon his departure from Mexico a year later, once unleashed, would require years of struggle before they could be subdued and order restored.

FOUR

The Seizure of Power: Porfirio Díaz, American Expansion, and the Revolution of Tuxtepec

> If you will order Cortina to be removed from this frontier, Americans will loan you money.
>
> a prominent American[1]

In December 1875 Porfirio Díaz visited New York and New Orleans. In January 1876 he traveled to Brownsville, Texas, where he led a revolution to overthrow the government of President Lerdo. From the beginning the Mexican government charged that Díaz was preparing a revolution and using Brownsville as a base of operations and sanctuary. The American consul at Matamoros contradicted the Mexicans, describing Díaz as a political refugee, a man who would be unsafe in Mexico. The general was not innocent, however; the Lerdo regime was correct in its assessment. The Mexican government also feared American support for Díaz's revolution, a concern justified by the events that ensued.

The most powerful Americans in the Brownsville area were prominent New York merchant and National City Bank investor James Stillman, who controlled the Brownsville Town Company which was in charge of local real estate development, and Texas ranchers Richard King and Mifflin Kenedy. Stillman was also a half-owner of the ferry company that held the riparian rights to the Rio Grande River between the United States and Mexico from the Gulf coast inland toward Mier. King, Kenedy, and Stillman owned the shipping company whose vessels plied the river from Brownsville to Port Isabel on the Gulf coast providing the city its only contact with the outside world. Their support and that of the Brownsville business community was essential if Díaz was to have any chance of success.

The alliance between Díaz and the Americans set the stage for thirty-five years of U.S. economic expansion into Mexico. The American property holdings that resulted became prime targets of revolutionary attacks between 1910 and 1920.

Importantly, Stillman, the Brownsville merchants, and local landholders enjoyed extensive business contacts in New Orleans, the Lower Rio Grande Valley's principal trading partner. Stillman was a major stockholder in the Hibernia Bank and Trust Company, one of the city's largest banks. His friends included the Whitney family, owners of the Whitney Company and Bank, and the city's other leading merchants and bankers. Stillman sent his famous attorney and intimate friend, Charles Sterling of the law firm of Spearman and Sterling (located on the mezzanine of the National City Bank Building in New York City), to New Orleans and then to Brownsville at the same time Díaz made the journey "in order to represent his interests" in the Rio Grande area. Sterling remained there until late spring 1876, when the fighting in the Brownsville-Matamoros area ended and the combat shifted to central Mexico. During the five months of border fighting Stillman received reports from Sterling, employee Thomas Carson, and family friend Francisco Yturria. The latter two were prominent Lower Rio Grande Valley landowners and businessmen.[2]

On 15 January General Fidencio Hernández proclaimed the revolutionary Plan of Tuxtepec in Puebla, Mexico, naming Díaz leader of the insurrection. Díaz quickly endorsed the plan from his Brownsville sanctuary. During the winter and spring of 1876 he used Brownsville as a base of operations while amassing an impressive arsenal and an array of powerful American and Mexican supporters. The interest groups he brought together and the positions he took on the critical foreign investment, trade, and border issues between the United States and Mexico characterized the internal politics and the national and international economic alliances of the regime that ruled from Mexico City for the next thirty-five years. They also defined the parameters of the 1910 Mexican Revolution.

Between January and May 1876, while still in Brownsville, Díaz rallied an alliance inside Mexico of state governors, general officers, provincial commanders, and liberal professionals and intellectuals. He attracted men who wanted sweeping reforms in order to "modernize" Mexico along the pattern of the United States. Díaz and his allies sought foreign capital as the instrument of change. The Americans who supported his cause were equally impressive. They included Texas landholders, New York bankers, railroad tycoons, the state and national print media, U.S. congressmen and senators, officers of the Texas state government, and U.S. Army officers, including zone commander General Edward Otho Cresap Ord and Colonel Potter, the commanding officer at Fort Brown near Brownsville.

In his quest for national supremacy, which dated from uprisings in 1869 and 1871, Díaz now attached himself to expansive outside forces far more powerful than himself or Mexico. The success of the new regime's economic development program and his tenure in office required their continued goodwill. Díaz's appreciation of that necessity would dim as the years passed.

Díaz arrived in Brownsville amid undeclared range warfare between expansive American and recessive Mexican land claimants in the Nueces Strip, that portion of Texas between the Nueces and Río Bravo rivers that had been seized by the United States during the Mexican War. Border raids extended the length of the Texas-Mexico frontier, but they were most intense in the Nueces Strip area, where Mexicans headed by General Juan Nepomuceno "Cheno" Cortina, operating from the northeastern corner of Tamaulipas, raided as far north as Corpus Christi. The most frequent victims of the raids among the Americans in the area were Stillman, protégé of Moses Taylor, then chairman of the board of National City Bank, and son of the deceased Charles "Don Carlos" Stillman, and "Captains" King and Kenedy.

Stillman's Brownsville Town Company was created to sell town lots in the wake of his father's legally dubious acquisition of the *ejido* of Matamoros at the conclusion of the Mexican War. Unfortunately for the *ejidatarios* of Matamoros, their communal property was located on the north side of the Rio Grande, beyond the reach of Mexican authorities. Bills of sale from cooperative Mexican elites in Matamoros had seemingly transferred the inalienable property to the American when the U.S. Army occupied the area. Using the ejido of Matamoros site to promote a boomtown, Charles Stillman had added yet another fortune to an impressive real estate, mining, transportation, and mercantile empire in the Lower Rio Grande Valley and northeastern Mexico. He had also incurred the wrath of the community farmers of Matamoros.

U.S. Army troops at Fort Brown provided security for both Brownsville and Stillman's interests in the vicinity, but King and Kenedy were situated in the countryside and far more vulnerable. In their competition with dispossessed Mexican land claimants, King and Kenedy maintained private armies consisting of cowboys equipped with the latest Winchester and Remington rifles and even cannons. These forces supplemented the efforts of their state government allies in the region, the Texas Rangers.[3]

In January 1876 sentiment against President Lerdo ran strong in Texas.

The San Antonio Express reported with satisfaction that the American minister to Mexico, John W. Foster, had expressed the American view in a note to the Mexican government claiming the U.S. could

> end the border depredations [with] . . . permission for the regular troops of the United States to follow the raiders across the border when in close pursuit, or what would be still more efficacious, permission to temporarily occupy certain points on the Mexican side where the raiders are accustomed to cross the river.

The newspaper editor indignantly but accurately concluded, "the Mexicans refused."[4]

The locale of Díaz's insurrectionary effort, the Lower Rio Grande Valley, combined with his sources of support to place him firmly in the midst of an ongoing conflict between Mexico and American economic and political expansion. Competition between the two nations for control of polity and trade in what later became the southwestern United States had begun before the Mexican War. By the time of that conflict U.S. merchants had already gained control over more than 90 percent of the outside trade in what became New Mexico, Arizona, California, and Nevada. During the early 1850s Charles Stillman had provided a major source of financial support for the revolution led by General José María Carbajal in order to gain hegemony over northeastern Mexico for his allies in Monterrey and Matamoros-Brownsville. By the 1870s American economic and political growth was transforming the southwest through the introduction of railroads.[5]

In 1875 President Lerdo, recognizing the threat of American expansion and hegemonic policies such as the earlier Young America Movement of President Benjamin Franklin Pierce (a "kinsman" of the most important Texas railroad builder Thomas Wentworth Peirce) and Manifest Destiny, canceled a number of railroad concessions held by American promoters. Those contracts would have permitted the installation of railroads from the U.S. border to the Mexican interior.

Mexican nationalists charged that the proposed lines threatened Mexico's independence. Since the 1850s, however, an increasingly powerful faction of the Mexican Liberal movement had viewed economic and social integration with the United States as the way for Mexico to achieve a new prosperity. Earlier, the Conservatives had also recognized the problem of economic stagnation. To attract closer ties with Europe and its wealth they had sought a European-based monarchy at independence, a Spanish and British-supported monarchy aided by General Paredes in the late

1840s, and Hapsburg leadership backed by the French in the 1860s. Defeated and discredited for collaborating with foreigners, the Conservatives were displaced by the Liberals as the nation's rulers.

The Liberals, including the most radical among them such as Díaz and Ignacio Ramírez, favored American investment as the vehicle of progress. They were impatient with the tentative and cautious approach of the nationalistic and moderate variety of "liberalism" exercised by Presidents Juárez and Lerdo.

Lerdo's approach to railroad development between Mexico and the United States is exemplified by his probably apocryphal but famous quote, "It is preferable to maintain a desert between strength and weakness." This insight was astute in light of the alliance of forces that backed Díaz and the social disruption and loss of control over national resources that ensued during the Porfiriato. Lerdo backed his point of view with further action. In February 1876, fearing impending U.S. economic hegemony and an immediate loss of critically important customs revenues, the Mexican president refused to accept American Secretary of State Fish's proposal for a trade reciprocity convention between the two nations.[6]

Meanwhile Díaz sought and received the support of the leading American landholders and merchants of southwestern Texas—Stillman, King, and Kenedy. They offered not only local help but contact with financial, railroad, industrial, and political figures of the United States located in St. Louis, Kansas City, New Orleans, New York City, and Washington, D.C.

The manner in which American national power became linked with events in the Lower Rio Grande Valley and to the aspirations of large landholders there is central to understanding the rise of the Díaz regime, its essence, and the coming and process of the Mexican Revolution. Between the 1820s and 1910 the growth of American interests and power in the valley involved the rise of the world's largest bank, the career of one of the most important bankers in history, and the establishment of one of the United States' greatest railroads. The American bankers, railroad men, and other entrepreneurs negotiated their differences with Lerdo and then made new agreements with Díaz. The ultimate challenge to their ever-growing interests, however, came between 1910 and 1920, when lower-class-led revolutionaries attacked the vast holdings the Americans had established inside Mexico.

The effective beginning of U.S. economic penetration of Mexico got under way in 1828 when Charles Stillman, the scion of a Connecticut mercantile family claiming American ancestry to the seventeenth century, landed in Matamoros with a consignment of goods forwarded by his father's New York import-export firm for marketing in northern Mexico. In that era Matamoros served as the entrepôt for two-thirds of the imported goods consumed in Mexico from Querétaro and Guadalajara to the north. As the Yankee trader liked to put it to his New York business associates, "There's nothing down there but the Rio Grande. There's nothing across the Rio Grande but Matamoros. There's nothing in Matamoros but the gateway to all Mexico for cotton, hides and gold!" Stillman became one of northern Mexico's principal merchants exchanging raw materials for machinery and finished goods.[7]

Stillman opened a new era of American involvement in Mexico and, through his son James, for all of Latin America. He selected José Morell, a merchant in Monterrey, as a junior partner; Morell lent his name to Stillman's extensive properties along the frontier in order to help circumvent Mexico's 1840s legislation prohibiting foreign landownership near the borders and coasts. During the 1840s and 1850s Stillman invested in copper, iron, lead, and silver mines in Nuevo León and Tamaulipas. In the 1850s his Vallecillo mine midway between Monterrey and Nuevo Laredo produced over $4 million in silver and lead exports. Stillman sold shares in the Vallecillo mine on the New York Stock Exchange.[8]

During the Mexican War King and Kenedy joined Stillman in transporting American troops and provisioning them. Their principal occupation was the operation of a steamboat service along the Rio Grande from the Gulf coast inland past Matamoros. Kenedy and King ran the steamboat service while Stillman handled warehousing, off-loading, transshipping and marketing operations. It was Stillman who developed the wider range of marketing contacts as the three grew rich. In peacetime cotton was the principal agricultural product, and it brought a high rate of return. Stillman's network of cotton sellers and buyers reached from the interior of Texas and Mexico to New York and England. From the beginning all three men stressed land acquisitions from Mexican holders and refugees who had fled or were fleeing from Texas.

In the aftermath of Mexico's defeat, Stillman purchased the ejido of Matamoros, a large acreage directly across the river from Matamoros, from a faction of the deeply divided Cavazos family. As a municipal property or commons, the land was inalienable under Spanish and Mexican law. Stillman subdivided the land and began selling it as city lots. His specially created enterprise, the Brownsville Town Company, handled the sale of the properties. Some tracts sold for as much as $1,500. By 1850 the town of Brownsville claimed a population totaling between three and four thousand. Stillman began to amass even greater wealth.

By the 1850s the three men were consolidating enormous estates. In 1851 they bankrolled the attempted invasion of Mexico by José María Carbajal for the purpose of setting up their own Republic of the Sierra Madre extending south from Matamoros to Tampico, west from Tampico to Monterrey and Saltillo, and north from Saltillo to Nuevo Laredo. In 1892, they backed the De la Garza uprising. During the 1850s Stillman bought cotton properties alongside the river inland toward Laredo and placed tenant farmers, many of them Mexicans, on the land. King's first large "purchase" consisted of 15,500 acres of ranch grazing land for which he paid approximately $300. The dispossessed, intimidated, and refugee Mexican former landholders had little bargaining power.

In the wake of military defeat at the hands of the U.S. Army, the racially despised Mexican former landholders in the Lower Rio Grande Valley found no relief in the American courts against aggressive Texas land seekers. Court officers participated in the land grabbing. In 1854 King and Kenedy paid more than $12,000 for improvements on the Santa Gertrudis Ranch. Meanwhile Stillman consolidated the largest mercantile operation in northern Mexico and southwest Texas. He bought enormous properties to the north and east of Brownsville, much of which he later sold to Kenedy. Those lands became the main portions of what is now the Kenedy Ranch and constituted much of what is currently Kenedy County, Texas. Stillman also owned the Laureles Ranch of over 200,000 acres that became part of the King Ranch after the death of his son James.

By the late 1850s Charles Stillman, King, Kenedy, Jeremiah Galvan, Herbert Woodhouse, and Spaniard José San Roman dominated American finance, commerce, and landowning around Matamoros and Brownsville. In the wake of the failure of the Galveston Commercial and Agricultural Bank in 1859, they formed a banking consortium in the Lower Rio Grande Valley which controlled loans. They established economic and political hegemony over the Lower Rio Grande Valley.[9] Their major rivals, the European trading houses of Monterrey and Matamoros, were on the Mexican side of the Río Bravo. Then Stillman's business connections in New York and the advent of the Civil War thrust these aggressive men into the limelight of American wealth and power and into Mexican politics.

In 1862 the fall of New Orleans to Union forces turned Matamoros-Brownsville into a thriving boom area, the principal outlet for Confederate cotton and entrepôt for war materials. During the next three years the

Confederates shipped much of their cotton crop overland to Matamoros to get around the Union blockade on the Atlantic Ocean and the Gulf of Mexico. A number of Texas capitalists dominated and profited from the new trade nexus, drawing them into a closer relationship with Mexico.

Houston businessmen became prominent in the sale of cotton and its transportation to Mexico. T. W. House, founder of the Houston Cotton Exchange and the state's largest bank, led the way. He held cotton and other properties in Texas including the border area and developed a commercial relationship with Stillman. Later his son Edward Mandel House inherited much of his south Texas and border area landholdings. The House family's early experience in northern Mexico and the border area led to its ownership of silver mines in Guanajuato during the Porfiriato. The colonel's valuable properties there, the Mexican interests of other Texans in the cabinet of President Woodrow Wilson, and a virtual "Who's Who of American capitalists" deeply affected U.S. government actions during the Mexican Revolution.

Between 1862 and 1865, while Díaz and other Mexican Liberals resisted French intervention, King, Kenedy, and Stillman provided the Confederacy with transportation and shipping services for cotton moving to Matamoros from the east. The Buffalo Bayou, Brazos and Colorado Railroad, which had received early financing from the National City Bank, Moses Taylor, and Thomas Wentworth Peirce, hauled the produce to Alleytown about seventy miles west of Houston. Alleytown served as the railroad's western terminus and quartermaster's depot for the Confederacy for the duration of the Civil War.[10] Workers unloaded the cotton from the trains and ferried it across the Colorado River. Then they piled it on large four-wheeled wagons and high two-wheeled "Mexican" carts provided by Stillman, Kenedy, and King. The wagons traveled by mule, oxen, and horse power through Goliad and San Patricio to the Santa Gertrudis section of the King Ranch, where they were refitted with fresh animals and repairs were made. From the ranch they moved to the Río Bravo, where Stillman provided the warehousing and shipping services needed to market the cotton in Matamoros.

In order to avoid the Union gunboats at the mouth of the river, Stillman and Morell purchased the Gulf coast beach area just south of the Río Bravo. They aptly called it Bagdad and created a port of sorts. They also began to process some of the raw materials into cloth at textile factories they had constructed at Monterrey, beginning the city's industrialization. Freighters waited offshore while skiffs and small craft braved the surf to carry cargoes to them. Stillman bought much of T. W. House's cotton and then resold it through his merchandising network in New York, England, and Mexico.

The carts did not return empty to Alleyton from the border. The consortium of Stillman, Kenedy, and King hauled Confederate imports for loading onto the waiting trains. Merchandise included rifles, swords, medicine, alum, arrowroot, uniforms, and other military supplies.[11] Their contacts with ammunition suppliers gave them access to the Hartley family, arms merchants of New York, and the Remington Arms Company. That experience served them well a few years later, when they utilized those relationships to obtain weapons to support the 1876 Revolution of Tuxtepec conducted from Brownsville by General Díaz.

The Texas-Mexico trade route was by far the most important source of revenues and supplies that the south had after the fall of New Orleans in 1862. During the course of the war the Stillman-King-Kenedy triumvirate received 2.5 percent of the gross value of the goods they hauled to the Nueces Strip-Rio Grande Valley area and another 2.5 percent to deliver and store it in Matamoros prior to sale at public auction. Their payment was in gold. In addition, the three men, all born and raised in New York and Connecticut, earned income from supplies and services they offered the Confederates. King sold their armed forces cattle and salt. An 1863 contract signed by Stillman, Kenedy, and King rewarded them with a 15 percent profit above purchasing costs to provide supplies to Fort Brown to be paid in part by five hundred bales of cotton per month, which they could then market. Each man gained $60,000 per month from that arrangement without the bother of Confederate paper.

Stillman, however, did not settle for the mere transportation, warehousing, and local sale of cotton. He used his connections in Mexico, New York, Liverpool, and Manchester to capitalize on the cotton and hides market even further. He used José Morell as a "prestanombre" to buy cotton and hides at auction in Matamoros. He shipped them from "Bagdad," which had grown into a tent and shack community, to New York and Liverpool under Mexican, French, and British flags. In New York the "white gold" was marketed by another Stillman enterprise, the mercantile house of Smith and Dunning, known later as Stillman and Company. In one transaction "J. Morel" netted $18,851.30 on a sale in Manhattan of $21,504.18. Cotton bought by Stillman operatives, including future San Antonio banker Brackenridge, in Texas for 6 cents sold for 26 cents in New York. Brackenridge later served as a Mexican business agent for Huntington, Jay Gould, and James Stillman. In Liverpool and Manchester the profits were even greater, the price increasing to $1.26.

Stillman was a businessman and had few regrets when southern cotton was used for Union Army uniforms, especially when the undertaking was so lucrative. Based at Matamoros and Brownsville, Stillman continued to accumulate properties on both sides of the border.[12]

Accumulating ever greater wealth, Stillman, King, and Kenedy continued to buy the properties of displaced Mexicans in the Nueces Strip. King, Kenedy, and Stillman's brother Cornelius concentrated on grazing lands while Stillman emphasized cotton bottomlands, town development, commercial opportunities in Mexico, Texas, and New York, and banking opportunities on Wall Street. During the 1860s Stillman invested millions of dollars in the National City Bank. His profits in New York and Liverpool dwarfed the more limited operations of Cornelius, King, and Kenedy, who also owned large properties in the Rio Grande Valley.[13]

Between May 1861 and January 1863, before the Union blockade of Confederate shipping increased the tempo of Stillman's business, James T. Smith, a junior associate in New York, reported that he had received $500,000 in sales. Shipments of cotton purchased by Stillman agents in Texas sold in New York at over four times his total outlay. In 1864, when his profits reached their apogee, Stillman netted about $14,500 per cotton shipment to America's greatest market. Hides did even better: one cargo to New York in August 1864 gained a $26,070 profit. Net profits on a typical shipment of cotton to Manchester in 1864 totaled £3,875. Among his clients T. W. House, head of the Houston Cotton Exchange, was prominent.[14]

By the end of the Civil War Stillman was one of the world's richest men and his partners King and Kenedy had become two of its largest landholders. Stillman's interests in Texas and Mexico continued to grow. His former employee Brackenridge opened the San Antonio National Bank with a combination of personal assets and Stillman's outlay of $200,000, which fifty years later still totaled over 10 percent of the bank's ownership. After 1872, when Stillman fell seriously ill, Brackenridge became Stillman's son James's financial associate in Texas and Mexico. James extended his father's empire in Texas to include railroads and massive landholdings near Kerrville and farther west. His National City Bank and railroad investments brought him land development contacts with his father's associates in Texas. Those associations included the House family of Houston, Duval West of San Antonio, and William Jennings Bryan.[15]

By the late 1860s King had constructed five hundred miles of fences around his properties in the Lower Rio Grande Valley. He bought 350,000 acres of the San Juan de Carrecitos Grant, including El Sauz Ranch, a vast holding immediately northeast of Brownsville. He held 200,000 acres at Santa Gertrudis. In 1869, the year General Díaz attempted his Mexican revolution of La Noria against President Juárez, a census reported that King possessed 458,664 cattle. During one year in the 1870s, while Díaz sought allies for future attempts to gain power, King's profits totaled some $400,000 from the cattle trade with Kansas City. King established banking and financial connections there. Kenedy bought out Stillman's holdings south of Corpus Christi just inland from the Gulf coast, creating the Kenedy Ranch, and continued purchasing land, as did King through attorney Stephen Powers and later James Wells in Brownsville. Charles Stillman bought cotton acreage around Matamoros on the Mexican side of the border in addition to his Bagdad holdings. Dividing his time between his far-flung interests in Mexico, Texas, and New York and expanding his riches and power, Stillman associated with the most powerful financiers in the nation.

During the early 1870s, while Díaz built support in Mexico against Presidents Juárez and Lerdo, the continued resistance of rancheros in the Mexican northeast posed a critical problem for King, Kenedy, and Stillman. The fighting was directed from Matamoros by General Cortina, who the Texans labeled a "rustler." He was a dissenting heir of the Cavazos family, Tamaulipas hacendados, another faction of which had sold much of the family's Texas holdings to King, Kenedy, and Stillman under a cloud of illegality. The land transfers occurred amid charges of fraud and terrorism committed against Mexican ranchers north of the river.

Cortina was well positioned to lead a Mexican resistance to the American occupation of Nueces Strip properties. He was a general in the Mexican army; the populace recognized him as a social and military leader. He was descended from José Narciso Cavazos, who had bought 106.5 square leagues of cattle pasturelands of the San Juan de Carrecitos Grant at public auction on 15 August 1790. Narciso Cavazos had one surviving heir: José María Cavazos, who inherited the landholding. General Cortina was the second son of José María Cavazos's second wife. The children of the two wives, nine in all, developed a deep rivalry, which complicated the ensuing land disputations with the American intruders. Don Sabas Cavazos, a son of the first marriage, supported King, Kenedy, and Stillman and even joined Kenedy in leading armed men against his half brother "Cheno" Cortina.

The two sides of the family made conflicting claims to the land. Elements of both sold their inheritances piecemeal to King, Kenedy, and Stillman through the turbulent and insecure years following Mexico's defeat in the war with the United States. Meanwhile the local Mexican citizenry suffered duress, deceit, and armed violence. Their claims against King, Kenedy, Stillman, and their heirs occupied local, state, and federal courts for decades thereafter. Sometimes Cortina personally led the displaced ranchers, former ejidatarios, bandits, and cowboys in the raids against the Americans. The Mexican male populace was particularly able in warfare because of its ranching-cowboy background and experience with firearms gained during prolonged Indian wars. They joined local elites, such as the pro "Cheno" elements of the Cavazos family, against King, Kenedy, and Stillman, providing a consensus of Mexican support in the one-sided desperate struggle that local Mexicans conducted against the militarily stronger Americans.[16]

In 1872 King spent $50,000 on fences and purchased an arsenal of weapons, and Kenedy bought almost $3,000 in rifles from the Remington Arms Company. They established a working relationship with Remington through Stillman and the company's New York shipper, the Hartley Company. Stillman, King, and Kenedy sent agents to Mexico City to consult the Ramo de Tierras of the National Archives in an attempt to clear up the stream of land claims concerning their holdings. Their domination of politicians and sheriffs in the Rio Grande Valley made easier the task of defending their property against Mexican litigants.

Political aspirants in south Texas appealed to Stillman, King, and Kenedy for approval and active support. Lacking such endorsement, many chose not to run. Sheriffs and judges were allies of the two land barons. A contract drawn up by a candidate seeking the approval of Stillman was blunt in its purpose:

> I Jeremiah Gibson of the city of Brownsville, Texas, do hereby solemnly pledge my word of honor to the Rio Grande Railroad Company, that should I be elected a representative to the next legislature of the State of Texas from the 30th Senatorial District, I will not oppose directly or indirectly, but on the contrary, will favor and promote any legislation which may be sought at the hand of said body by the said company for its benefit on condition that the said company do not seek thereby to obtain wharf or ferry privileges at said city of Brownsville for the purpose of charging toll or will in any manner interfere in the rights of said city or messrs Stillman or Hale in regard to the ferry or wharf privileges aforesaid . . . [they are] the riparian proprietors of the Rio Grande.[17]

The railroad, owned by Brownsville merchants, was to run from Port Isabel on the Gulf coast inland to Laredo along the Río Bravo, where it was to join "at such point as the International Railroad may touch said river."[18] The International and Great Northern, running from northeast to south-southwest across central Texas, had backing from both Brackenridge and Stillman. In 1881, after the Rio Grande Railroad failed, King and Kenedy, with Stillman's assistance, found financial backing from a variety of eastern banks, including the National City Bank, in which Stillman's holdings were becoming ever more important, and completed the Tex-Mex narrow-gauge line from Corpus Christi to Laredo.[19] It became part of the Mexican National Railroad Company. By then James Stillman and Moses Taylor had joined a group of investors that included such national and state figures as Thomas Wentworth Peirce, House, and Huntington in financing the construction of several railroads in Texas.[20]

For magnates in the Nueces Strip and Texas and for Stillman in New York, Díaz served a dual purpose. He offered to stabilize the border, putting an end to the heavy losses to cattlemen such as King and Kenedy, and he shared the vision of an economically progressive Mexico linked to the United States by railroads, waxing with foreign investments, and selling her goods to the outside world. Díaz enthusiasts called themselves "Railroaders," and a pro-Díaz newspaper was named *The Railroader.* Díaz brought together Mexican laissez-faire Liberals, provincial elites who saw prosperity in the railroads, Texas entrepreneurs, New York bankers and merchants, and the Texas and United States governments. *The San Antonio Express* expressed their common vision:

> We need to have the two countries connected by railroads, and a large and profitable reciprocal trade developed. Therefore everything done on the frontier should be under the sanction and invested with the dignity and responsibility of the United States Government. A railroad would develop the trade in Mexican and draw it in this direction.[21]

Texas concerns with Mexico extended beyond mere interest in frontier peace. Railroad commerce with Mexico was a key factor in state and national planning. The Texas congressional delegation voted "as one man" on Mexican issues because

> our own prosperity in western Texas requires it not less than Mexico, to whom it is essential. . . . The extension of the International Railroad from San Antonio as the Peirce Railroad reaches our city . . . would restore all of our old commerce that brought in olden times such wealth and established general comity between the two neighboring peoples, but it would be increased a thousand fold. The urgent demands for sugar and coffee . . . we are necessarily compelled to look to Mexico for these staples. . . . With Saint Louis and other cities of the West opening up such an immense demand . . . it becomes the paramount duty of the government to [aid] . . . the International in its extension. . . . Trade from Mexico is already commanding the attention of the press of the whole country,

> and if sincerely friendly relations can be established between the two countries, the result commercially . . . would constitute the biggest bonanza that could possibly be conferred. . . . That country would take more millions of our products than it now uses thousands. . . . With free trade between Mexico and the United States, we should in a few years be able to draw . . . the sugar we need . . . and pay with . . . the products of our skilled mechanics.[22]

Three days later *The Express* added the production of precious metals to its list of Mexican exports that "on the west coast of Mexico showed an aggregate yield of $480,899,037 being an increase of $45,487,982 over 1874, the greatest previous annual yield." The newspaper went on: "Senator Hamilton of Texas and the Southern Pacific agree on the border route from San Diego through Texas via San Antonio and are mutually supporting." The American minister in Mexico City, John Foster, echoed hopes for enrichment when he claimed that Mexican coffee "is equal to the best known in any country . . . a far greater source of wealth and prosperity than her products of silver which averages about $426,000,000 annually."[23]

Along with the strong desire for expansion into Mexico on the part of U.S. capital, the American press continued to justify belligerency toward that country around the theme of "border outrages." *The New York Commercial Advocate* reported:

> Some time ago the American government asked permission for United States troops to follow the raiders into Mexican territory, but this was refused by the Mexican Secretary of State. . . . In the meantime the hapless frontiersmen are subjected to these outrages and no redress is offered them. The Mexican authorities exhibit no inclination to punish them and the bands murder, rob and destroy with impunity.[24]

Shortly thereafter Texas Congressman Gustave Schleicher's Mexican Border Committee in the U.S. House of Representatives requested the secretary of war to send "two full regiments of white cavalry and sufficient infantry to garrison important posts along the line."[25] The administration adopted Schleicher's proposal and dispatched the troops. Schleicher's concerns, however, reached far beyond mere border troubles. In February he proposed "the rapid coinage of the silver dollar." The Texas congressman's vision included Mexico: "It certainly cannot be the policy of the United States, having the richest silver mines in our own borders and in the adjoining provinces of Mexico, with which our dealings will steadily increase, to depreciate silver."[26]

Some in the Texas elite and U.S. government envisioned, as Charles

Stillman had, a new 300,000-square-mile Republic of the Sierra Madre encompassing the northeast of Mexico from the border between Nuevo Laredo and Matamoros, south along the Gulf coast to the Panuco River, and inland over the mountains to Monterrey. It would comprise the states of Tamaulipas and Nuevo León. The *San Antonio Express* eyed Mexico with hunger:

> The big bonanzas of the Comstock Lode are said to be inferior in yield to the possibilities of the silver mines north of the Sierra Madre. It is evident that if the committee [Schleicher's] can do anything it will do it. . . . Nationwide sentiment cited in favor.[27]

Schleicher's committee argued that "the Mexicans have violated the Treaty of Guadalupe Hidalgo a thousand times" and proposed "to go forward with a strong army and take forceable possession of the country lying between the Rio Grande and the Sierra Madre Mountains." While civilians focused on economic bonanzas, General Ord in San Antonio emphasized the need for border security while coveting the same region.[28] Ord and Schleicher reflected the political climate of February 1876. Possible war between the United States and Mexico caused Mexico's bond values to plummet to 1.5 cents on the U.S. dollar.

Problems between the United States and Mexico were much deeper than the border turmoil. In addition to canceling five of the six contracts for the construction of railroads between the U.S. border and the interior of Mexico, President Lerdo rejected the trade reciprocity agreement. He and other Mexican nationalists feared that the agreement would isolate Mexico from its European trading partners and make Mexico merely an economic appendage of the United States. The American government expressed its disappointment and continued to press for closer trade ties. Despite the problems, Lerdo and Ignacio Mariscal, his representative in Washington, maintained polite if not cordial relations with their expansive northern neighbor. Strong nationalistic concerns prevented concessions to the United States by an independent government, but the Lerdo regime repeatedly indicated its willingness to improve communications and transport between the two nations as long as guarantees protected Mexican interests. Mexico's isolation would not have endured long regardless of the results of Tuxtepec.

When Díaz issued his version of the Plan of Tuxtepec in mid-February, he discriminated between the renegade invasion of Tamaulipas by Texas Ranger Captain McNelly and the more careful position maintained by the U.S. Army and government. Signed by Díaz and General Guerra at Guanajuato, the Plan of Tuxtepec called for an end to the border troubles and indemnities from the United States for the Texas Ranger incursion. In return for the face-saving indemnity, Díaz promised to establish a new regime of law, order, and commerce in Mexico. The celebrated Porfirian Peace was thus anticipated in Brownsville in February 1876.

The Corpus Christi Daily Gazette expressed the hopes of King, Kenedy, and Stillman: "General Porfirio Díaz, one of the bravest and most distinguished soldiers of the Republic has, in order to defend himself from arrest, been forced to quit the country and is now a refugee in Brownsville where he is awaiting the expected outbreak." It added: "The governors of several of the northern states have entered into an understanding with each other and are only awaiting a favorable opportunity."[29] While Díaz built goodwill with the Americans, Mariscal, the Mexican minister in Washington, declared in a less conciliatory manner: "The Texans are known to be frequently at fault themselves and if occasionally a Mexican citizen is found in the wrong, his short-comings are magnified a thousand times."[30]

In late February, a few days after the proclamation of Tuxtepec, a group of prominent Texas railroad promoters and South Texas and Rio Grande Valley leaders met at Kingsbury, Texas, a town named for an intimate of Charles Stillman. The party consisted of Andrew Peirce, president of the Atlantic and Pacific Railroad and the International and Great Northern, which was building toward Laredo and connected San Antonio, Austin, and Dallas with northern cities; his brother, Thomas Wentworth Peirce, head of the Galveston, Houston and San Antonio Railroad (GH&SA); T. T. Buckley, banker of New York City and Texas; W. C. Fowler of Brooklyn; T. B. Edgar, a banker of St. Louis; A. W. Dickinson of Kansas City; and Texas and Missouri hotel owner and financier J. L. Griswold, whose properties included the Lindell Hotel in St. Louis. The controlling interests of the International and Great Northern Railroad later took part in construction of the Mexican National line from Laredo to Mexico City.

The Peirces' Texas experience reached back to the 1840s, when their Boston shipping firm Bacon and Peirce operated sixteen ships between Galveston and the northeast hauling cotton and dry goods. The closeness of King to some members of the investors' consortium is indicated by the fact that two years later his daughter Nettie was married at the Lindell Hotel: "Parlor seventeen had been transformed into a regular garden of flowers."[31] King then accepted a special offer to purchase $30,000 in International Railroad stock. Within four years Stillman, King, and Kenedy, along with New York City, Chicago, St. Louis, and Kansas City investors, helped finance the construction of the Tex-Mex Railroad from Corpus Christi to Laredo. The new transport system gave King and Kenedy rapid access to Kansas City and St. Louis by rail for the sale of their herds, eliminating the need for costly cattle drives.[32]

The new railroad network bypassed Matamoros-Brownsville, destroying the position of the large-scale, European dry goods merchants in the Mexican port who had formerly dominated northern Mexico's import-export trade in competition with Charles Stillman and the American merchants. James Stillman's control of the riparian rights to the river meant that no railroad crossing could be built at Brownsville without his permission. By building inland routes in the 1880s the Americans effectively eliminated European competition in northern Mexico while creating a new trade nexus between Monterrey and Texas. The cost was minimal: the drying up of business for Stillman's old associates in Brownsville. Matamoros and Brownsville lost their former prosperity and population. In 1894 Stillman listened to the desperate pleas of Brownsville political leader and personal employee Thomas Carson to construct the National Railroad line from the Gulf coast to Monterrey via Brownsville-Matamoros in order to end the border city's isolation and economic depression. Stillman refused but promised to let Carson "know when the time had come."[33]

At the time of the Tuxtepec rebellion and the February 1876 meeting at Kingsbury, King controlled over 550,000 acres of land and Kenedy owned much of the littoral between Corpus Christi and Brownsville. Meanwhile James Stillman, the ambitious son of their deceased partner "Don Carlos" Stillman, was already active in the leadership of the National City Bank. He later continued Moses Taylor's practice, when he was chairman of the board of the bank, by granting large outlays of cash to Texas railroad projects. In 1876 Stillman was actively managing his border cotton properties, marketing cotton, investing in Texas banks and railroads, purchasing land, operating a complex of mercantile, transportation, and land development companies in the region, and was the controlling owner of the ferry service across the river between Brownsville and Matamoros.

The coalescence at Kingsbury and Brownsville of these far-flung yet consistent interests between the finance capital of New York and the regional magnates of Chicago, St. Louis, Kansas City, and Texas in late February 1876 resulted in a large cash outlay to the Díaz revolution. Colonel John Salmon Ford, commander of the Texas Rangers, described one of the encounters with Díaz:

> Díaz asked if the Americans would loan him cash. He was told "You are no doubt fully aware of the trouble General Cortina is causing on this frontier. . . . If you will give your word that, if successful in the revolution you are to inaugurate, you will order Cortina to be removed from this frontier, Americans will loan you money." General Díaz gave his word. He obtained money from American citizens. . . . General Cortina has been under surveillance for nearly twenty years. Can any gentleman dare say President Díaz has not fully redeemed his pledge?[34]

The Galveston Weekly News reported, "General Díaz, having taken a look at the situation from this point for the last six weeks or more has determined, with the aid of his friends and some forty thousand dollars lately received to become a candidate for the Presidency of Mexico."[35]

Pro-Díaz sentiment spread throughout Texas. The expansionist *San Antonio Express* stated a Texan viewpoint: "The attempted assassination of Díaz last night created much indignation and increases the sympathies in his favor. . . . Díaz will soon have Matamoros. The people are in his favor."[36] As the fighting continued, Lerdo, who understood the forces at work, released Cortina from Mexico City detainment. Meanwhile Díaz publicly pledged greater trade between the United States and Mexico and to adopt "energetic measures" to prevent future raiding by Mexicans into Texas. A Texas newspaper owner, full of hope, exclaimed: "If he wins . . . he will do so as a matter of duty."[37]

In March 1876 Díaz received vast quantities of arms to combat the Mexican government. An initial supply of ordnance provided to Díaz by Brownsville merchants included 500 rifles, 250,000 rounds of ammunition, and 2,000,000 cartridges for recharging from the Remington Arms Company. The intimate relations of King, Kenedy, and Stillman with Remington and the Whitney Shipping Company in New Orleans facilitated the transactions and reduced the time needed for handling. By 17 April the Brownsville merchants had provided an additional 510 rifles, 350 carbines, and 382,000 rounds of ammunition plus horses, wagons, mules, uniforms, cattle, and forage.[38] King buttressed the donations of his borderlands, business, railroad, and banking associates with a grant of $20,000 to $30,000 and provisions for Díaz's forces.[39]

By spring 1876 Díaz had received sizable American contributions. They came from southwest Texas merchants and landowners; Don Sabas Cavazos, who gave $50,000; and the banking and railroad men. Sabas Cavazos, a half brother of Cortina, had accepted King's claim to the family's land grants in the Nueces Strip area over Cortina's protests, and members of his clique in the family accepted employment on the King Ranch. Cavazo's cash contribution could have come about through his services as an intermediary. The American donations on behalf of Díaz recorded in memorabilia and in the press totaled in excess of $130,000. Stillman's commitment to the cause is unknown, but his legal counsel Charles Sterling left New York at the same time as Díaz and remained in Brownsville during the conflict. Stillman's troubleshooter, attorney James R. Cox, was also on the scene. Stillman's Brownsville agent and later mayor, Thomas Carson, forwarded reports on the revolution.[40]

Stillman's Brownsville partners, import-export merchants and bankers José San Roman, Francisco Armendaiz, and Francisco Yturría, and his business associates inside Mexico, José Morell and the Milmo brothers of Monterrey, supported Díaz with arms and cash on a smaller scale than their American counterparts while keeping one another informed of the revolution's progress. Later Morell's orphaned daughter was adopted by Mifflin Kenedy. At the request of Milmo and Morell the arms were rushed to Brownsville by the Whitney Company. The Whitneys had close ties with the Brownsville merchants, but the family was especially intimate with Stillman. The two families merged through marriage. The merchants shipped the arms arriving in Brownsville to the Díaz forces. A typical consignment from New Orleans included 70 rifles, 20 pistols, 10,000 cartridges, 120 knives, and three barrels of hand grenades. On 4 April a case of pistols and three cases of cartridges arrived; on 1 April 10,197 pounds of mixed nitric and sulphuric acid was received. The total number of Americans involved in Díaz's forces that invaded Mexico from the U.S. side of the border are estimated as high as 50 percent. The arms traffic remained strong from February until May, when the Mexican government destabilized and revolutionary unrest developed to the south of Mexico City.[41]

Close relations between the American merchants and the leaders of the Tuxtepec Revolution reached from the professional level to the personal. Manuel González, rebel field commander in the Tamaulipas fighting, maintained open accounts with Stillman's dry goods agent Francisco Armendaiz. González's wife, who lived in Mexico City, contacted her husband through correspondence addressed to San Roman. The conservative merchants justified their support of revolution through complaints against Lerdo's "bad policies" of taxing imports and exports and the forced loans exacted by his commander in Matamoros. In April they celebrated: "Porfirio Díaz entered Matamoros on the 1st . . . you will no longer suffer forced loans and mortifications. The government forces surrendered and were taken into custody at Fort Brown."[42]

During the fighting Stillman bought out his ferry company partner and obtained the sole riparian or river crossing rights for the future railroad crossing the Rio Grande at Brownsville-Matamoros, which at that time was considered the gateway to Monterrey, the Sierra Madre, and central Mexico:

> the easements, rights; riparian, ferry and water rights, franchises and privileges . . . receipts of money . . . hereto arising or resulting from the foregoing described property . . . and all ferryboats, ferry fixtures and appurtenances thereto held by the Brownsville Town Proprietors or the Ferry Company of Brownsville . . . to have and hold forever.[43]

Stillman, however, realized the advantages of the inland railroad route via San Antonio and Laredo to Monterrey and supported it. On 18 March 1881, when he sold two-thirds of his riparian rights to cross the river between Brownsville and Matamoros to the Mexican National Railroad for $66,666.67, he did so while planning to connect south Texas with Mexico via Corpus Christi and Laredo in partnership with his longtime colleagues King and Kenedy and bypassing the European merchants at Matamoros.[44] The river crossing at Brownsville-Matamoros did not take place until the National City Bank-supported St. Louis, Brownsville and Mexico Railroad reached Monterrey in 1910. In the interim thirty-five years the once preeminent European mercantile competitors of the Americans who had presided in Matamoros had long since disappeared.

During his more than four months in the Brownsville area Díaz put his arms to good use, profiting from strong support among the Americans. When his forces took Matamoros on 2 April they numbered 1,500 and were well equipped.[45] During the revolt they crossed the border at will. The Lerdo government protested to the U.S. authorities in Washington. Generals Sherman at Chicago and Sheridan at St. Louis forwarded orders from Secretary of State Hamilton Fish instructing General Ord and the armed forces in Texas to intercept, detain, and remove the pro-Díaz forces from the border area.

General Ord in San Antonio and Colonel Potter in charge of Fort Brown at Brownsville explained that the action was impossible because it would "violate the civil rights of Mexicans." Sherman and Sheridan failed to press the orders upon their reluctant subordinates. Ord's daughter soon married General Geronimo Treviño of Monterrey, one of Díaz's leading commanders in the Tuxtepec Revolution. Ord later retired to Monterrey, living in the Treviño home with his son-in-law and daughter. A few years later Treviño received 880,000 acres in Coahuila as a reward for service to the nation. Treviño promptly rewarded Ord with a donation of over 90,000 acres from the gift tract. In 1888 the ungrateful Treviño anticipated fellow northern provincial elite leaders Alfonso Reyes and Francisco Madero by attempting a race against Díaz for the presidency.

Colonel Potter became infuriated when the U.S. naval commander of a gunship in the Rio Grande River turned over badly needed ammunition to the destitute and beleaguered Mexican federal army garrison at Matamoros. Both Potter and his immediate superior, General Ord, were intimate friends with and partisans of King and Kenedy. Potter disarmed and detained Lerdo's troops when they fled Matamoros and took refuge at Fort Brown in April.

The key to Díaz's victory was his ability to conduct a prolonged guerilla war against the financially bankrupt Lerdo government throughout the states of Tamaulipas and Nuevo León. The revolution's support from provincial and local elites such as the Longoria, Madero, Milmo, González, and Treviño families and the inability of the financially desperate Lerdo government to quickly suppress it encouraged local and provincial elite declarations of support across the nation. Beginning with local elites and commanders in the northeast who were readily influenced by American partners and by Díaz's closest associate, Manuel González, the revolt slowly gained supporters. The government's main problem in crushing it was the inability to acquire armaments.[46] Local levies on the merchants in Matamoros and Nuevo Laredo provoked resistance and refusals. English, Spanish, and American interests, including the principal New York City banking institutions, specifically refused to lend monetary support to the Lerdo government because of long-standing disputes.[47]

Díaz won his "revolution" despite a cool public reception. In Tamaulipas his weakness was manifested in an embarrassing way:

> General Díaz paraded the National Guard, about 800 strong and presented them with a battle flag. After making a stirring speech, he requested all who would volunteer to the interior to step to the front, only an officer and two men came forward. The whole regiment was then ordered to their barracks and there disarmed.[48]

"One hundred and ninety-nine men including 150 deserters and 49 citizens who did not wish to serve Díaz's cause fled across the river at Mier into the U.S."[49] Neither side in the fighting enjoyed widespread enthusiasm. Lerdo was regarded by the local and provincial elites and organized labor as both corrupt and attempting unconstitutionally to succeed himself in the presidency. Díaz relied on financial contributions from American land and business tycoons, Mexican merchants with close ties to Americans, and the personal influence of the Tamaulipas, Nuevo León, and Coahuila provincial elites. González's local personal prestige was sufficient to rally enough troops for the march to the south along the Gulf littoral.

González moved his column along the Gulf coast side of the Sierra Madre Mountains, thus avoiding interception by the federal troops on the *altiplano* to the west. When far enough south, he turned westward and crossed the mountains into the state of Puebla southeast of Mexico City, where he joined the powerful forces of Generals Treviño of Monterrey and Negrete of Puebla. The rebels counted contingents led by provincial elites from the states of Oaxaca, Mexico, and Puebla in addition to the troops that arrived with González. They dealt Lerdo's forces a stunning and decisive defeat at the battle of Tecoac.

That victory points to the strength of Díaz's overall stategy and to the financial weakness of the government. He had paralyzed the bankrupt government's efforts in the northeast, gaining nationwide support through the exposure of its weakness. Only one full division of the government's armed forces, the twelfth, was actually eliminated on the Tecoac battlefield, but the national treasury was empty. Attempts to obtain foreign loans were rebuffed. No replacements could take the field. The rebels were too weak to march directly against Mexico City, but they continued to gain strength because of the government's inability to conduct offensive operations.

The key to Lerdo's decision to step down was rooted in the government's lack of resources and Díaz's prolonged exploitation of that weakness during the campaign in the northeast. By spring 1876 the inability of the Lerdo government to stamp out the insurrection in the northeast gave added incentive to local garrison commanders to join the more radical generals such as Negrete and García de la Cadena of Zacatecas who were among the first in central Mexico to offer Díaz their support.[50]

Despite the fact that the fighting was in the remote northeast, it exacerbated the regional-metropolitan rivalries within the officer corps. The longer the revolt succeeded in sustaining itself in the field, the more likely it was to raise doubts in the minds of ambitious and alienated provincial officers regarding the government's ability to suppress it. Officers advanced their careers by the early identification of successful anbd unsuccessful *golpes de estado* (overthrows of the state). After Tecoac new garrisons joined the rebel fold. Just as important, the prolonged struggle enhanced opportunities for influential regional elite families such as the Díaz, González, Longoria, Madero, Milmo, and Treviño clans to recruit their counterparts elsewhere. By the end of the year, Porfirio Díaz was president of Mexico.

The new government quickly reversed the Lerdo regime's policies and sought greater U.S. participation in the Mexican economy through direct investments, trade, and bond purchases. Díaz's first important act was the payment of $300,000 due the U.S. by 31 January 1877 in accordance with the Claims Treaty of 1868. He obtained the funds for his destitute government from unnamed foreign banks at a high 12 percent interest rate.

Then the outstanding issue of border land disputes or, as the Americans phrased it, "disorders" had to be resolved. From the perspective of the U.S. government and Texas landholders, the problem revolved around foreign trade, investments, Indian raids, cattle rustling, and the rights of U.S. merchants in the north who claimed losses totaling $27,859,363. Díaz was able to solve the problem during his first term in office. He signed a trade agreement with the U.S. government. He repeated the invitation made to U.S. capitalists during the Tuxtepec Revolution to make financial commitments in Mexico. He ended the Cortina-led effort to sustain Mexican land claims north of the Río Bravo. He exiled General Cortina from the border area. He ended smuggling into south Texas from Matamoros by small operators. That form of free but illegal enterprise had long undercut the cartel set up by Stillman and his Brownsville associates. Díaz abrogated, de facto, the prohibitions on foreign landownership near the border and coast, opening northern Mexico and Tamaulipas to direct American economic penetration and control. Between 1877 and 1879 surveyors mapped the paths of railroads from the U.S. border at Matamoros, Nuevo Laredo, Piedras Negras, and Ciudad Juárez to central Mexico and to the mines and woodlands of the north.

During the first two years of his regime Díaz carried out an "anti-yanqui" propaganda campaign among the Mexican public while quietly working to improve relations with the Americans. Between 1877 and 1879 U.S. forces made several forays across the border in pursuit of Indians and "rustlers." At first Díaz protested, but the American government insisted, and Díaz tightened his control over the area. By the end of 1877 border friction was subsiding. On 15 March 1878 Díaz allowed "reciprocal" (i.e., U.S. military) crossings of the border. Nationalists accused Díaz and Treviño, his commander in Tamaulipas, of being "soft" on American invaders while diverse Americans complained that Díaz was harboring "bandits" and was no better than Lerdo. The border fighting continued for another two years, but the Mexican government now cooperated with U.S. authorities and south Texas private interests in suppressing the efforts of its Tamaulipas citizenry to recoup their lost property.

In January 1877 Díaz promptly paid the first installment on the U.S.

claims settlement despite his nearly bankrupt treasury. In February the U.S. government granted his regime de facto status; it never questioned his legitimacy. On 12 November 1877 the new government signed a concession with a consortium headed by General William Palmer, the Denver and Rio Grande Railroad interests, and others for a trunk railroad line to run from El Paso to Mexico City. Palmer sought funds for his project from James Stillman and the National City Bank and the Pennsylvania Railroad during lengthy negotiations.[51]

In April 1878 the U.S. government issued Díaz de jure recognition. Meanwhile Mexico came into virtually instant communications with the outside world through the opening of the Stillman-approved Brownsville-Veracruz Cable. By then plans were being developed for a new national railroad system and economic order in Mexico. The surveying and exploration by American companies seeking the most desirable railroad routes took most of Díaz's first presidency to complete. Then, late in his first term, Díaz and successor President Manuel González (1880–1884) began issuing railroad concessions and construction began.

FIVE

The Growth of the Porfirian Economy and the American Intrusion

> Commerce is the weapon . . . the all powerful arm with which we have entered in earnest, with every prospect of success, upon our conquest of Mexico.
>
> El Paso Bureau of Information, 1888

> The people of Mexico will have to be supplanted by another race, which is gradually being done, before any great development can be expected there.
>
> James Stillman, 1890

The Díaz regime began by quickly establishing a number of loyal generals as governors in outlying states noted for their autonomy from the national government. Tuxtepec revolutionary leader General Treviño received 880,000 acres of land in Coahuila for his service to the nation and became governor of Nuevo León. Díaz selected Tuxtepec participant Evaristo Madero as governor of Coahuila. The forces of some state oligarchies resisted, and the new president fought battles with them from Sonora to Yucatán. The government won but offered amnesties that rivaled the political advantages given its older allies among the provincial elites. It built a wide base of support through political rewards.

Díaz faced two challenges: to build a lasting government by resolving complex internal rivalries, and to satisfy American misgivings. He had moved quickly to quiet the Texas-Mexican border, but even more serious problems for the young regime loomed. President Rutherford B. Hayes came into office in 1877 and adopted a hostile attitude toward Díaz. Hayes's motivation stemmed from two directions; he faced internal political turmoil, and a Mexican crisis diverted the likelihood of violence in the United States; and he misunderstood Díaz's cancellation of Lerdo's remaining commercial and railroad concessions preparatory to making his own. The most important of those grants was held by Edward Lee Plumb, a twenty-year resident of Mexico, former chargé in Mexico City, and in 1876 both a representative of the International and Great Northern Railroad of Texas and secretary to the U.S. Legation in Mexico. Plumb had received the concession in May 1875 and proceeded to back Lerdo during Tuxtepec.

Díaz had received the backing of Peirce and Huntington, who were developing the Galveston, Houston, and San Antonio Railroad route across Texas to Piedras Negras, where it became the Mexican International. As a result of his pro-American policies, Díaz was able to placate Hayes while private U.S. loans and donations eased his difficult first year in office following the bankruptcy of the Lerdo government. Rival American railroad interests lined up offering support. His first year's budget counted 16,502,503 pesos in state income, only $4,500,000 fewer than his more established government garnered through taxes in 1880. Among those who pressured Díaz were Generals John B. Frisbie and M. G. Vallejo of California. At first they sought redress for the loss of their railroad concessions and the sale of Mexico's northern tier of states to the United States. Secretary of State Evarts endorsed their efforts and sent them to Mexico City to meet with Díaz. Frisbie established a lasting friendship with Díaz, becoming one of the president's closest advisers and a leading officer of the Mexican National Railway System.[1]

By the end of 1877 Díaz had placated the Hayes government by establishing peace on the Texas-Mexican frontier, an attractive tariff that invited American imports, and the opening of negotiations through General Frisbie for railroad construction with favored Americans, including Plumb and Huntington. Those negotiations gave the Plumb interests control of the future Mexican National routes running from Laredo to Mexico City, from Matamoros to Monterrey and Mexico City, and west from the national capital to Guadalajara and the port of Manzanillo; Huntington received the International concession from Piedras Negras to Mazatlán.

When Frisbie returned to the United States he worked with National City Bank's James Stillman, Huntington, and Senator Conkling of New York, who was able to achieve the convening of a special U.S. Senate committee to reconsider the hostile U.S. government position toward Mexico. Successful in his task as mediator, Frisbie served as Díaz's personal representative in railroad negotiations and with the National Railway System of Mexico for the next six years. King and Stillman were among the new line's largest stockholders. Kenedy and King then backed the construction of the line connecting Corpus Christi to the National at Laredo, completed in 1881.[2]

THE RAILROADS

In the eyes of Díaz and his associates, American and Mexican, railroads were the hope of a prosperous future. Before he came to power, however, railroad construction provoked a major public debate. The threat that foreign control of the railroads would result in dominance of the national economy and the government constituted the most serious objection. President Lerdo's congressional ally, Guillermo Prieto, had led the effort to establish domestically built and run railroads. The nationalistic perspective evolved from long-standing defensiveness regarding foreign intrusions.

Santa Anna had articulated populist concern regarding the disruption of working peoples' lives when he opposed the construction of a proposed railroad in the 1840s because of "the harm that would accrue to the raisers of mules, wagon owners, muleteers and drivers." Despite numerous grants issued to Mexicans by Presidents Santa Anna, Commonfort, Juárez, and Lerdo, little construction took place because of lack of capital and the high costs of foreign-made and imported retail-sold technology. These grants were issued to connect points within Mexico and to develop east-west passages from the Gulf to the Pacific. Before 1870 none was approved to connect American entrepôts along the border with the interior.[3]

Between 1867 and 1876 trackage increased from only 50 to 666 kilometers. From 1876 to 1884 the government committed between 130,000 and 270,000 pesos annually to railroad planning. In 1879 it agreed to contribute 32 million pesos for the construction of five railroads totaling 2,500 miles of tract. Preparations continued even during the 1883–1884 economic depression in the United States which dried up sources for new funds and foreign trade in Mexico and brought the interregnum government of Manuel González to the brink of collapse.

In order to foster railroad growth the regime resorted to land grants to compensate the builders. When the National finally completed construction of the line from Matamoros to Monterrey in 1910, it had received 819,000 acres of land as compensation for that relatively short route in lieu of cash payments. F. S. Pearson received over 3.5 million acres in Chihuahua for construction of the Northwestern Railroad in that state;

Captain James Eads and the Tehuantepec Ship Railroad received over 1.5 million acres reaching from north to south across the Isthmus of Tehuantepec. The Pearson railroad grant tied into the lands of the Peirce-owned Corralitos hacienda, Louis Booker, and Edwin Marshall in the north which reached to the U.S. border. To the south of the Pearson grant the Batopilas mining company, Cargill Lumber Company, and Hearst Babicora totaled over 2.2 million acres in a continuous mass of American-owned properties to the southern extremity of western Chihuahua. The Cargill holdings, acquired from Secretary of the Treasury Limantour, enveloped the town of Tomochic, which disputed the company's title, claiming the lands as community property. Twenty years earlier when the Northwestern Railroad surveyors laid out a proposed route to the immediate south of the town, its citizenry resorted to violent resistance, leading to the confrontation with the Mexican army in 1892. Between 1910 and 1920 these properties would be repeatedly raided by Mexican revolutionaries. The attackers were called "Villistas," but usually they were local citizenry who operated independent of outside authority.[4]

Trackage began to grow. By 1880, sixteen concessionaires had began construction. The trackage at the end of the year reached 1,052 kilometers. In 1881 it increased to 1,661 kilometers. In 1882 trackage reached 3,583 kilometers, and in 1883 the total was 5,328 kilometers. There were forty-nine concessionaires by 1884. Many were agents for the largest American railroad interests. In 1884 E. H. Harriman, Jay Gould, Russell Sage, J. P. Morgan, John D. and William Rockefeller, Meyer and Daniel Guggenheim, Grenville M. Dodge, Huntington, and Henry Clay Pierce, who represented the Rockefeller interests after his Waters Pierce oil company had been taken over by them in Missouri, began an intensive phase of railroad building. In 1884 the total national trackage reached 5,898 kilometers.

During the 1880s the four great trunk lines—the Southern Pacific-controlled road running from Nogales toward Mexico City, the Santa Fe-administered Mexican Central from El Paso to Mexico City, the Huntington-owned International from Durango to Eagle Pass, and the American-controlled National from Corpus Christi to Mexico City—made dramatic progress. Between 1880 and 1882 Huntington bought out Peirce's control of the GH&SA, which ran across Texas and Louisiana from New Orleans to El Paso via Eagle Pass. In 1883 he began construction of the Mexican International. By 1884 the National Line from Corpus Christi to Mexico City had over 700 miles of trackage completed, including the link between Saltillo, the capital of Coahuila, and Laredo.[5]

The Mexican Congress voted subsidies ranging from 7,500 to 15,000 pesos per kilometer to the promoters, and private funding controlled the projects. American banks, including the National City, Morgan, Brown Brothers, and First National of New York, and the Old Colony Trust of Boston, advanced funds to promoters to purchase equipment and loaned the Díaz regime the cash needed to pay the construction fees. The cash-short government made further land concessions to make up for its lack of capital. The Central completed its 1,970 kilometers from El Paso to Mexico City in 1884, but major problems arose immediately. The same contract called for a 1,000-kilometer east-west line from San Blas to Tampico. Only 40 kilometers were finished. The two ports—one Pacific, the other Gulf coast—were still not linked by steel rails in 1910 when the revolution began.

By 1896 the Mexican railroad system claimed 11,500 kilometers. In 1900, 14,573 kilometers connected the capital and the mineral-producing regions of the north with the major U.S. entrepôts at Nogales, El Paso, Eagle Pass, and Laredo. The tropical export crop zones of the south were also connected with their ports. The Tehuantepec Railroad, from Salina Cruz on the Pacific to Coatzalcoalcos on the Gulf of Mexico, carried tropical and industrial agricultural export products to both coasts. Transportation between state capitals and local agricultural and resource zones, however, was inadequate in the extreme. Freight rates on the British-controlled Interoceanic between Mexico City and Veracruz favored export-bound goods over identical items destined for the national interior.[6]

In 1860 U.S. trade with Mexico amounted to $7 million. In 1880 that trade still totaled only $15 million. By the end of the decade the railroad system had transformed economic relations between the two nations. In 1890 the volume of U.S.-Mexican trade reached $36 million and in 1900, $63 million. In 1910 the total foreign trade of Mexico had increased to $245,885,803. Imports valued $107,061,955 and exports, $138,823,848. "The share of the United States in the import and export trade was $61,029,681 and $105,357,236, respectively." Products from the U.S. constituted 57 percent of Mexico's imports. Exports from Mexico to the U.S. totaled 75.6 percent of the smaller nation's foreign sales. Both percentages dropped one point between 1909 and 1910, reflecting the U.S. economic crisis of those years and the increasing flow of petroleum and zinc to Great Britain. On the eve of the revolution the design of the nation's railroads had proved Guillermo Prieto and Lerdo's direst warnings about the dangers of foreign control.[7]

By 1908 the railroad system claimed 22,822 kilometers of track, of which the "minerales," adjuncts of foreign, mostly American, mining companies constituted 3,749 kilometers. Twenty-one of the nation's forty-four railroads were categorized as minerales and another three had extensive mineral business while hauling other extractive products. F. S. Pearson's Northwestern, for example, ran from El Paso through the timber and mining camps of the Chihuahua Sierra Madre. Mexican capital controlled only the Ferrocarriles Unidos de Yucatán.[8]

In the two years before the revolution railroad construction slacked off significantly to 869 kilometers per year after over a decade of new trackage totals averaging 1,030 kilometers. The 15 percent drop in construction between 1908 and 1910 reflected reduced American and European enthusiasm as a result of the 1907–1908 panic, the nationalization of most lines, and the maturity of the system from the point of view of foreign investors who had little interest in the development of internal marketing linkage.

By the time of the revolution the railroad system totaled 24,560 kilometers. The growth of mining, timber, and agricultural exports and the importation of finished goods constituted the railroad's principal impact upon the Mexican economy. Of the trunk lines, one traversed the Isthmus of Tehuantepec and five tied U.S. ports of entry on the border to the Mexican interior. Two lines connected Mexico City to Veracruz and the Gulf coast; on the West coast the route from the port of Manzanillo tied Colima and Guadalajara to Pacific trade.

In 1902 a remarkable consortium of U.S. capitalists held 80 percent of Mexico's railroad stock. That sum, over $350 million, constituted about 70 percent of the total U.S. investments in the country. The American-owned railroads in Mexico, however, were more narrowly held than indicated by nationality. During the 1870s and 1880s the major American railroad owners had formed an alliance in New York that consolidated control over roads in both the United States and Mexico. At that time Stillman, Gould, William Rockefeller, and the Kuhn and Loeb and Company held major interests in railroads in the South, middle Atlantic states, New England, Midwest, and Texas. Stillman and Rockefeller held one-third of the stock in the Union Pacific Railroad. They financed the Union Pacific Southern Branch into Texas. Then Stillman brought E. H. Harriman into their association, and with National City Bank financing, Harriman assumed control over the deceased Huntington's Southern Pacific empire. Bringing Jay Gould's son George into their effort, they established domination of the railroads in Texas, including Gould's International and Great Northern, which ran south to the border at Laredo.

Known in the United States as the "Big Four," the Stillman, Harriman, Rockefeller, and Gould syndicate then gained control of the Mexican National Road, the principal line of which ran from Corpus Christi to Laredo, where it intersected with the International and Great Northern and then to Mexico City. Later Jacob Schiff, a member of Kuhn, Loeb and Schiff and a director of the National City Bank, replaced Gould as a member of the Big Four. At the time of the Mexican Revolution in 1910, all members of the Big Four were directors of the National City Bank. Henry Clay Pierce managed the road for the consortium for many years.[9]

The Mexican National Railroad concession had been issued by Díaz to General William J. Palmer and James Sullivan, who then sold part of their interests to Stillman and the directors of the Pennsylvania Railroad. Those forces dwarfed Palmer and Sullivan, who became merely middlemen. Meanwhile the Union Pacific Southern Branch entered Texas from the north in 1880. It later gained control of the International and Great Northern when George Jay Gould, the only member of the Big Four who was not a member of the National City Bank board of directors, made a series of "enormous business errors." The latter road only reached Laredo in 1881. Gould's failure, and the caution of the Union Pacific Southern Branch's ruling combination of William Rockefeller and Stillman, caused construction of the road from Laredo to the interior of Mexico to lag.

During the late 1870s and early 1880s Sullivan served as the agent of Stillman and the Brownsville businessmen who had backed Díaz with arms and cash during the revolution of Tuxtepec. On 3 September 1880 he successfully obtained a government concession for the railroad to be constructed between Matamoros and Monterrey on behalf of James Stillman, Francisco Armendaiz, Thomas Carson, Simon Celaya, M. Belden, Lázaro Garza, Servando Canales, and G. M. Raphael, who joined incoming President González as partners in the enterprise. In 1886 Stillman and Rockefeller reorganized the Constructora Nacional inside Mexico, eliminating Palmer and Sullivan. Then they convinced Harriman to join their group. He accepted directorships in several of their companies and joined in the railroad construction venture.[10]

In 1892 Stillman had replaced his mentor Moses Taylor as chairman of the board of National City Bank, greatly increasing his already considerable power and influence in the American southwest. Taylor and the bank had been associated with T. W. House, Thomas Wentworth Peirce, and Huntington in several Texas railroad ventures. Stillman's background included railroad development throughout the East, Midwest, and Texas and the mercantile and mining businesses in Mexico, of which his father Charles was the most important American pioneer. Under Stillman's direction between 1892 and 1921 National City Bank became the largest bank in the world. In the 1890s it became "the financial arm of the Rockefeller Standard Oil Trust."

Stillman was one of the world's richest men and its most powerful banker until his death in 1921. He conceived the remarkable consolidation of banking and railroad trusts in the late nineteenth and early twentieth century that marked the rise of monopoly capitalism in the United States. He formed an alliance with J. Pierpont Morgan of the Morgan Guarantee Bank and Trust Company and George Baker of the First National Bank of New York. Known as the "Big Three," the bankers ensured stability for their operations by openly arranging joint participation in ventures such as the growing network of railroads and mining enterprises in the American southwest. In addition to the bankers, Stillman had led the way in organizing the railroaders Big Four. In the late 1890s this leading railroad consortium consisted of Stillman, George Jay Gould, Huntington, and Harriman. By the time of the revolution the Big Four was made up of Stillman, William Rockefeller, Harriman, and Jacob Schiff of Kuhn, Loeb and Schiff.[11]

Stillman used the National City Bank's enormous resources as a financial base for Gould, Huntington, Harriman, and Rockefeller operations. The bank and its chairman became part owners in an enormous range of enterprises. Their power was omnipotent in the southwest and in Mexico. As the National City Bank grew, its board chairman and president, who constantly reminded his associates of his "Mexican knowhow and experience," brought together in his board of directors the greatest concentration of Mexican wealthholders ever assembled. Among the directors were Cleveland Dodge, later chairman of the board of Phelps, Dodge and Company, and perhaps President Woodrow Wilson's closest and longest friend; Cyrus McCormick, president of International Harvester, which dominated the Yucatán henequen trade; J. P. Morgan, Jr., whose father's bank and the National City Bank were heavily involved in the formation of the emergent industrial complex at Monterrey; Joseph P. Grace of W. R. Grace and Company, which controlled the garbanzo industry of Sonora; and Jacob Schiff of Kuhn, Loeb and Schiff. Stillman, who owned 22 percent of National City Bank stock, and directors William Rockefeller, Harriman, and Schiff were the most powerful investors in the Mexican railroad system.

Harriman found the bank's resources and Stillman's help useful in expanding his railroad holdings. In 1903, following Huntington's death in

1900, Harriman, Stillman, Schiff, William Rockefeller, and their allies gained control of the Southern Pacific Railroad, including its Mexican and Texas affiliates. Stillman already owned some of the latter and a part of the National, and now he and the National City Bank were major partners in the lines running from Nogales down the West coast growing toward Mexico City, extending from Eagle Pass through La Laguna to Durango, and from the border to the Phelps Dodge copper fields at Nacozari. The Mexican railway commitments of the Big Four and the National City Bank were a logical extension of Benjamin Franklin Pierce's Young America Movement and Manifest Destiny.

By 1910 Stillman's businesses included the American Rio Grande Land and Irrigation Company, headquartered on the border at Mercedes. It held 90,000 acres in an expanse extending fifty miles along the international boundary from Brownsville inland. The president, Harry Seay, was a former National City Bank vice-president. John Closner's closest friend and fellow land purchaser at the site, William Jennings Bryan, was his summer-long house guest during two years in the period 1908–1910. Closner was one of the company's leading participants. Bryan bought some of the company's land in order to establish a fruit orchard and ranch. Bryan continued to hold land in Mexico that he had bought in the 1880s. Closner's property and Bryan's was attacked by Mexican insurgents who crossed the Rio Grande in 1912. Another investor in the company, James B. Wells, did so as part of his wide-ranging land investments in the Lower Rio Grande Valley. Bryan advocated Mexican investments for Americans in *The Commoner* for years, and Closner revealed intimate details of financing and construction of the Matamoros-Monterrey and Tampico-Monterrey railways.

Many of the other prominent stockholders in the American Rio Grande Land and Irrigation Company continued to extend their investments and land purchases beyond south Texas and the frontier into Mexico. For ten years their properties in Mexico were repeatedly assaulted by revolutionary bands usually calling themselves "Villistas" but actually operating without outside authority. Those prominent American owners in the American Rio Grande Land and Irrigation Company who extended their operations farther south into Mexico as part of a general wave of American expansion included Simon Guggenheim; Wilsonian envoy to Mexico Duval West of San Antonio; timber and paper magnate Ennis Cargill; James A. Baker, President of New York's First National Bank and a member with Stillman and Morgan of the Big Three banking trust; and B. F. Yoakum of the National City Bank-controlled Frisco Line, which built the St. Louis,

Brownsville and Mexico Railroad into the Lower Rio Grande Valley and whose contractor built the line onward to Monterrey.

The American Rio Grande Land and Irrigation Company also had important Mexican participants, men whose families had played leading roles in the 1876 revolution of Tuxtepec. They included Yreno Longoria of the nationally prominent banking family of Nuevo Laredo; Antonio Balli, an important Tamaulipas hacendado and land developer whose family intermarried with the family of Mifflin Kenedy; and members of the Cavazos family. Their properties, too, were singled out for attack and later confiscated by the Mexican revolutionaries.

John Shary, an officer of the National City Bank of Omaha, headed the smaller but also important International Land and Investment Company, and the Southwestern Land Company along the Rio Grande River. One of Shary's partners was Harry B. Seay, President of the American Rio Grande Land and Irrigation Company. A confidential credit rating assessed one of the company's officers as absolutely secure since he was in fact operating for the National City Bank.

> For over ten years the subject was a vice president of the National City Bank, in charge of their Branch Office at 250 Fifth Avenue, New York City. . . . He is the executor of a number of estates in trust with the National City Bank, and he is devoting his time to looking after these affairs.[12]

In Mexico the Stillman-Rockefeller group's original point of control had been the International and Great Northern's extension, the Constructora Nacional from Laredo to Mexico City. That government grant had given the railroad Big Four control of vast territories including the 819,000 acres between Matamoros and Monterrey as part of the Constructora Nacional concession. The lands combined with Stillman's water crossing riparian rights to the Rio Grande at Brownsville-Matamoros to create an empire in northeastern Mexico.

Stillman's ownership of the riparian rights to the Rio Grande and the Brownsville Ferry Company gave him the power to determine ownership of any railroad bridge crossing the Rio Grande between Laredo and the Gulf coast. The early construction of the railroad from Matamoros, which would have benefited the European merchants of that city, was delayed, however; instead, the American empresarios directed construction of the interior route, freezing out their European competitors in the Mexican north. In the early twentieth century, the National City Bank, the world's first "billion-dollar bank," played an important role through loans and the stock ownership of its directors in all of Mexico's major trunk lines running south from the U.S. border. The ultimate objective was a Pan American Railroad traversing North America linking Panama and the United States.

Between 1902 and 1908 Secretary of the Treasury Limantour, who had been an employee of Huntington in California, carried out a railroad stock purchase plan designed to reduce criticism of American power. The creation of the National Railroads of Mexico in 1908 resulted in the partial purchase of most of the American lines. The government acquired wildly overpriced stock, rolling equipment, roadways, and other facilities with loans from foreign banks at a low 5 percent interest. The rights of the American stockholders, now supposedly minority owners, and the European interests were guaranteed through the retention of an American staff, appointed by the New York-based railroad syndicate. The New York bankers continued directly to approve the director in charge of the railroad system's actual management and his duties until 1916.[13]

The Mexican negotiators carried out the 1908 purchase with diplomatic tact, but the American bankers and politicians realized that the transaction reduced their influence. In 1910 the American railroads, untouched by nationalization, were capitalized at only $60 million. The formerly smaller British railroad investment of $122 million more than doubled the American total. In addition, the Díaz regime invited representatives of the principal British interest group in Mexico, the Pearson Trust of Lord Cowdray, to serve on the "nationalized" railroad system's Mexico City-based board of directors. In 1910 the powerful U.S. investors and politicians saw clearly that the American position vis-à-vis their European competitors had deteriorated.

FINANCE CAPITAL

Banking came of age during the Porfiriato. Earlier in the nineteenth century Mexico had experimented with the idea of development banks for the promotion of industry and jobs. During the 1840s Lucas Alaman's Banco de Avío failed to create a nationally controlled textile industry. When the Díaz regime assumed power only two banks operated in the capital, the Monte de Piedad and the Banco de Londres, México y Sud América. In search of financial coordination for its economic program, the Díaz regime chartered the Mexican National Bank in 1882. Owned by the Franco Egyptian Bank of Paris, it served as the government's fiscal agent and creditor and joined the Monte de Piedad as one of the two institutions entitled to issued redeemable notes. Accused of being "Egyptian, French,

Jewish, anything but Mexican," it charged 4 to 6 percent interest, was endowed with a minimum capital of 6 million pesos, and was used by French retail and textile magnates.

Between 1880 and 1884 banking assets increased from 3 million to 30 million gold pesos despite the government's fiscal crisis. In 1884, in an effort to avert economic collapse, the government approved the merger of the National Bank and the Banco Mercantil Mexicano, creating the Banco Nacional de México. The new Banco Nacional served to coordinate and consolidate the regime's financial commitments and to serve the needs of industrial builders. It was French owned.[14]

The number of banks increased sharply, but by 1910 foreign interests claimed 80 percent of the capital in the financial system. The French, geographically removed, developed a plan that contrasted with American railway strategies. They concentrated their financial resources in banking, the domestic textile industry, and retail sales. In 1910 they claimed 45.7 percent of the capital committed to the largest fifty-two banks and controlled the nation's three leading financial institutions: the Banco Nacional de México, the Banco Central Mexicano, and the Banco de Londres y México. The government's financial agent, the Banco Nacional, secured foreign loans, serviced the debt, handled direct government transactions, and issued currency. French capital comprised 53.2 percent of the monies devoted to domestic industry, especially textiles, and controlled fourteen of the nation's largest twenty-six industrial enterprises and the six largest retail stores. The banking industry was crucial to economic diversification and social transformation. When the flow of French capital to Mexico became irregular during the 1899–1904 financial crisis in Europe, the Porfirian regime lost one of its essential supports: inexpensive foreign loans and investments. The rapid expansion of the European economy between 1899 and 1904 meant cash shortages for Mexico and rising interest rates, which tripled in the following decade, triggering fiscal crisis and economic instability.[15]

French and American investment strategies contrasted sharply. The French participated to an overwhelming degree in banking, commerce, and domestic industry. French capitalists committed over 98 percent of their assets in Mexico to those three sectors of the economy, establishing a close interaction between them. The French did not take part in railroad ownership, controlling only one sizable mining operation and one modest commercial agricultural enterprise.

In contrast, the immediate geographical proximity of the United States to Mexico produced the American strategy of railroad expansion from the southwest toward northern Mexico's natural resources. In 1902, 1,112 American companies and smaller businessmen totaling 40,000 U.S. citizens had invested $511,465,166 in Mexico. Railroad investments constituted 70 percent of the U.S. commitment. In 1910, after the nationalization of many American lines and their consolidation into the National Railroads of Mexico, while American railroad investments still totaled 520 million pesos; investments in mining, petroleum, and commercial agriculture dependent on the railroads totaled 340,100,000 pesos among the nation's 134 largest companies.[16]

The importation of foreign-produced and purchased railroad and mining technology with the exportation of ores, bars, timber, and cattle reduced the Americans' need for domestic banking resources. American banking investment totaled only 110,300,000 pesos, a small fraction of the total U.S. commitment. American railroad, mineral, and agricultural interests had their own banking resources in the adjacent United States. The result was financial operations independent of Mexican control or influence by the American companies. Banking, transportation, and raw materials production were often vertically integrated. This integration was reflected in the minerales lines and the Northwestern Railroad, which hauled its own timber and cattle to U.S. ports of entry. Even after Limantour's "scandalous nationalization" of the railroads by government stock purchases, and as late as 1916, active direction of the lines was maintained by the consortium of bankers in New York.

MINING

> Mexico will one day furnish the gold,
> silver and copper of the world . . .
> her subterranean treasure houses will
> build the empires of tomorrow.
>
> Cecil Rhodes

The completion of the American-controlled Mexican Central Railway in 1884 came in the same year as the regime's new mining code, which rescinded the colonial-era law mandating the state's ultimate ownership of the subsoil resources. Before 1884 the lack of railroad transportation services and legal assurances of ownership seriously inhibited American and other foreign investments in mining. The Mexican Central linked Chihuahua's mine fields to El Paso. The new transportation system made it possible to process Mexican ores in Colorado, Kansas, Missouri, Oklahoma, and El Paso. In addition, the Mexican government abolished state taxes and protective mining codes in 1887 and replaced them with a new law code and a national tax collected and administered from Mexico City.

The McKinley Tariff of 1890 placed higher exactions on lead content in ores, and the Sherman Silver Purchase Act provided for currency notes to be issued by the U.S. Treasury in payment for silver bullion. These laws further stimulated American interest in Mexico's high-grade silver ores and encouraged the building of smelters there to avoid the duty on lead. That year Daniel Guggenheim met with Díaz and received the assurances he needed in order to commit his resources to the Mexican mining industry. He obtained a concession dated 9 October 1890 to build three smelters. Guggenheim expanded on that beginning with other grants in 1891 and 1892 issued by the governor of Nuevo León, Bernardo Reyes, that outraged his native competition, the Madero family. It resulted in a deep enmity between the Maderos and Governor Reyes.[17]

An era of increasing American strength commensurate with the growth of the railroads began in the mining industry. In 1884 American companies were working only 40 concessions. By 1892 the total of mining properties had increased to 2,382. In that year a new mining law conferred "unquestioned title to whatever subsoil deposits there might be beneath the surface" upon the purchase of private property. By 1896 the number of mining properties totaled 6,939, with the great majority of them in American hands. Between 1896 and 1900 the number of mining titles leapt upward another 7,403; and 122,000 hectares of land were transferred as a result of the newly acquired mining grants. In 1904 the grand total of active mining concessions reached 13,696 involving 223,698 hectares, but the mining companies acquired many times more acreage than that by direct purchase.[18]

Of the thirty-one major mining companies operating in Mexico during the last years of the Porfiriato, United States capitalists owned seventeen and held 81 percent of the industry's total capital. Their British counterparts held ten of the companies and 14.5 percent the total capital. Mexican owners operated only a few concerns, of which the Torreón Metallurgical Company was the property of Evaristo Madero, Francisco's father. The Maderos were the only family of the Mexican elite to attempt mine through smelter competition with the broader-based larger American and British mining companies. In 1910 the Americans dominated the industry. The Guggenheim ASARCO operation was the largest privately owned enterprise in Mexico capitalized at 100 million pesos; its nearest competition, the Anaconda complex, owned, among other holdings, the 60 million pesos Greene Cananea Consolidated Copper Company, and the Phelps Dodge Company of President Wilson's friend Cleveland Dodge owned the Moctezuma Copper Company in Sonora capitalized at 3 million pesos. Few high-ranking national government officials held honorary directorships in the mining industry as was the custom in the railroads, banks, and other industrial concerns.[19]

The rise and fall of silver output reflected the Porfiriato's overall economic condition. In the late 1870s yearly production averaged about 26,500,000 pesos. In the early 1880s the annual output reached 31,565,000 pesos, growing to 39,840,000 pesos during the late 1880s. In the 1890s output boomed. After the mining law of 1892 took effect guaranteeing the foreign companies control in perpetuity over the rich ores, yearly production increased from 45,840,000 pesos during 1890–1893 to 70,000,000 pesos per year in the late 1890s. Between 1902 and 1905 it peaked at 80,055,000 pesos per year, but the value of exports inevitably dropped with silver's declining worth. Between fiscal 1901–1902 and 1904–1905 silver exports declined 9.5 percent from 72,420,883 pesos to 65,523,646 pesos. In 1908 Mexican silver production in ounces fell 6 percent from the total for 1905 according to Wall Street sources, while the value of silver declined 20 percent on the London and New York markets.

That reduction in value, accompanied by depression in the Colorado silver fields of the United states, caused a flood of returning unemployed miners to Chihuahua, where they joined their local out-of-work counterparts. Many of these men were veterans of the Cripple Creek strikes and Colorado mining wars between the company owners and the Western Federation of Miners. Relatively radical and sophisticated ex-miners joined the displaced rural workers who plagued Chihuahua's cities and towns. When silver went into eclipse, it was not alone. After 1905 copper, lead, and all other nonferrous mineral production stagnated and then declined.[20]

An erratic downturn prevailed in other sectors of mining. Copper production involving several of the nation's largest companies was one of the economy's key mineral industries. It boomed during the period 1890–1905, increasing output from 5,650 to 65,449 metric tons. Production then declined for the next three years, to 38,173 metric tons in 1908. The prominent Wall Street publication, *The Commercial and Financial Chronicle,* described the situation:

> Of course Mexico could not escape being affected by business depression in the United States. . . . An even more serious matter for Mexico was the drop

> in the price of silver and of other metals, more particularly copper. . . . The low prices are still affecting adversely many of the mines and some of the smelting plants along the lines of the National Railroad.[21]

A brief recovery to 57,230 metric tons of output in 1909 was followed by another slump to 48,160 metric tons in 1910.[22]

Lead production also enjoyed uninterrupted growth during the expansive 1890s. In 1891 national output totaled only 30,187 metric tons. In 1902 output peaked at 106,805 metric tons and then slumped, declining steadily to a low of 73,699 metric tons in 1906. During the next four years production improved but output levels continued to fluctuate. In 1909 lead production dropped to 118,186 metric tons from the previous year's level of 127,010 metric tons. During the last decade of the ancien régime yearly lead production was characterized by boom and bust volatility.[23]

Even coal, the nation's healthiest growth sector in mining, dropped off in total tonnage extracted during the gloomy economy of 1908. Coal production, like the output of other minerals, grew dramatically for more than a decade. Production increased from 200,000 metric tons in 1891 to 1,024,580 metric tons in 1907. In 1908, however, output slumped by 15 percent to 866,317 metric tons. The decline had been presaged between 1905 and 1906 when the coal industry's output dropped from 920,000 metric tons to 767,864.

The less important zinc industry was a disaster. The panic of 1907 and the 1909 American tariff on zinc demonstrated the Mexican mineral economy's dependence on the United States. After the tariff's enactment, zinc output, which had grown with Mexican mining in general, collapsed. Production, which totaled only 400 metric tons in 1893, reached a peak in 1907 of 23,197 metric tons. It then plummeted as a result of the panic to 15,650 metric tons in 1908. Following the enactment of the 1909 tariff, output sank to only 1,833 metric tons in 1910. The Díaz government reacted, restructuring freight rates to encourage export to Europe via Tampico.[24]

The railroads reflected the deepening crisis. While mines and smelting plants closed and curtailed operations along the lines of the National Railroad, the Interoceanic between Veracruz and Mexico City and the International also felt the impact of declining economic activity. In 1909 the Interoceanic hauled 9 percent less tonnage than the year before. As silver production fell 7 percent, the International Railroad, which ran from Durango through Torreón and Monclova to Eagle Pass, suffered a 16 percent decline in freight profits and a 9.3 percent reduction in freight tonnage. The silver-copper crisis combined with partial failures of the cotton and corn crops to deal the railroad, the Mexican economy, and ultimately political stability a hard blow.[25]

The erratic but clear pattern of declining mineral production in the last years of the ancien régime reflected growing employment uncertainty. Rising job insecurity accompanied an inflationary erosion of miner's real wages. The era of buoyant optimism regarding Porfirian economic growth ended with the fall of silver after 1905. The rising unemployment of 1906 brought strikes and worker unrest with it. After 1905 the Mexican mining industry was in deep trouble. In 1907 the former owner of the Cananea copper complex, William Greene, defaulted on his Sierra Madre Land and Lumber Company's obligations. In 1908 the Knickerbocker Trust, a New York institution active in foreign and Mexican mining investments, collapsed. Only the tiny iron industry, which increased production between 1901 and 1911 from 3,240 tons per year to 54,698 tons, prospered.[26] Given its need for revenues and social stability in order to continue to attract new foreign investment, the government of Mexico could not afford the mining industry's crisis.

PETROLEUM

Petroleum was the last mineral resource to be commercially developed. A capital-intensive industry, petroleum exploitation provoked a crisis between powerful American interests and Díaz. In 1876 Boston investors supported drilling near Tuxpan and achieved a modest flow, but local sales of kerosene were inadequate and the effort ended in failure. In 1887 California oilman Edward L. Doheny experimented in the Tampico region with maps originally developed by the W. A. Goodyear interests, but that endeavor too came to nothing. A more ambitious project during the 1890s involved Cecil Rhodes and Weetman Pearson of Great Britain. They gave up after losses totaling nearly a million dollars. Pearson continued his explorations to the south in the Isthmus of Tehuantepec, where he scored major successes a few years later before returning to Tampico to try again.

During the 1890s world market demand for petroleum increased drastically. During that decade the gasoline engine was perfected in Europe, and in 1895 Rudolph Diesel unveiled the more powerful internal combustion engine that bore his name. Lower-grade crude oil, used in those engines and for steam power, suddenly emerged as a critical resource. In 1900 American oilmen began to study Mexico seriously.

Surface evidence and earlier successes along the Gulf coast in Texas pointed favorably toward that region in Mexico. The Gulf afforded ready access, and the San Luis Potosí spur of the Mexican Central Railroad connected it with the interior. A. A. Robertson, president of the Mexican Central, contracted with Doheny, C. A. Canfield, A. P. Maginnis, and Herbert G. Wylie to develop fields near Tampico that could furnish fuel for his locomotives and transport for his trains. They formed the Mexican Petroleum Company. The Díaz government offered the consortium tax exemptions and land concessions including mineral rights as provided by the mineral laws of 1883, which surrendered subsoil resources. Doheny purchased a tract of over 549,000 acres south of Tampico, where he began operations.

On 14 May 1901 the first American-owned well blew in at El Ebano. As the field developed the gushers dwarfed per-well production in the United States. A well that was opened in 1904 initially produced 1,000 barrels per day. In 1905 the Mexican Petroleum Company provided the Central Railroad with 6,000 barrels a day. On the eve of the revolution national production approached 12 million barrels annually, but those figures would soon prove minuscule. In 1910 the Pearson interests at Juan Casiano near Tampico opened two wells, one producing 20,000 and the other 15,000 barrels per day. Mexican workers flocked to the ill-prepared coast littoral, creating population pressure that far outreached the capacity of local resources for employment, housing, sanitation, and human services.

A rush of foreign capital joined the earlier companies. By 1910 over 290 enterprises were active in the nation's oil industry. The Standard Oil Company had been well situated in Mexico before the boom. In 1904 its subsidiary, Waters-Pierce—60 percent owned by Standard but operated by its founder, Henry Clay Pierce, who still owned 40 percent of the company—claimed 90 percent of the national illuminating oil market and all gasoline consumption. In that year Pierce-Standard's profit margin reached 600 percent. Before the nationalization of the American-held railways Pierce had also provided the Mexican Central with fuel and the oil needed for 9,565 miles of rail service.

While exporting crude oil Mexico continued to import processed petroleum products, but the Pierce-Standard operation suffered a great loss of prestige by the revelation that lower-grade illuminating oils were being sold by the company as premium-quality fuel. President Díaz reacted by canceling Standard's railroad contracts in favor of the British Pearson Trust, offering the British inducements to develop new fields at Tampico and imposing new taxes on Standard's imports. Soon Pearson was providing two-thirds of the illuminating oil consumed on the Gulf coast. After 1903, when Doheny, the Texas Company, and Lord Cowdray entered the Mexican internal market, Standard's share of gasoline and illuminating oil sales fell from well over 90 percent to 40 percent. Its gasoline sales dropped to only a small fraction of the market. The company had lost control over petroleum marketing in Mexico. In 1910 company president William Rockefeller, his closest friend and business associate James Stillman, the company directors, and Mexican affiliate president Henry Clay Pierce were highly dissatisfied with Porfirio Díaz.[27]

In 1910 the Pearson interests and Doheny's Mexican Petroleum Company were the two principal oil exporters. When Doheny lost the Central Railroad oil contract he sold his predominantly heavy crude to the cities of Mexico, Puebla, Guadalajara, Tampico, Morelia, and Durango for street paving. The government intervened to ease his access to this internal market and offered him further concessions with the proviso that he not sell out to Standard Oil. Hence Díaz fought Standard and the Rockefeller interests in four ways: through nationalization of the Central Railroad, denial of exploration claims, cancellations of Standard distribution contracts, and the encouragement of Doheny and Pearson as competing producers and distributors. By 1910 the Pearson Mexican Eagle Company and its subsidiaries were capitalized at 59 million pesos. Doheny's Mexican Petroleum Company was capitalized at 38 million pesos. Despite the overwhelming economic presence of the Americans, following railroad nationalization the Pearson Trust, with its interests in petroleum, agriculture, and railroads, emerged as the largest economic entity in Mexico.[28]

The entry of the Houston-based Texas Oil Company into the Mexican petroleum industry had an even more important effect on U.S.-Mexican relations than Standard Oil, dramatically affecting U.S. government policies toward Mexico and the Mexican Revolution. The Texas company was the largest, most powerful, and fastest-growing business concern in Texas, the state most intimately involved, economically and politically, in Mexico. The composition of its ruling interests reflected the westward growth of the American economy and society across Texas and into Mexico. Like the forces at work in the earlier conflict at Brownsville-Matamoros, the Texas Company was a product of entrepreneurs located in Texas who utilized their East Coast connections to obtain financing. With declining production in its Texas and Louisiana fields, the concern's leaders saw their competition with Gulf Oil and Standard Oil in Mexico as decisive for the future. Using economic strength and technical and business know-how, they entered the Mexican marketplace and production zones. The company's efforts to advance its interests in Mexico through direct contacts and associates in the U.S. government and later among President Wilson's advisers had far-reaching effects upon Francisco Madero, Venustiano Carranza, and the company's revolutionary enemies General Lucio Blanco, Pascual Orozco, and the Villistas.

Some of Texas's most enterprising men controlled the Texas Company, but they depended on New York and Chicago capitalists for most of their financing. The company's largest investors were Arnold Schlaet and John W. "Bet a Million" Gates, a careful speculator in Rio Grande Valley and Mexican railroads and real estate. The National City Bank served as the company's major banker and source of institutional financial support. In the course of its operations the company linked an array of active financial magnates, including Stillman of National City Bank; Thomas Jefferson Coolidge, Jr., and George Abbot of Old Colony Trust in Boston; Gates, James Hopkins, and John Lamber, a banker, all of New York City; and two Chicago bankers, John A. Drake and John F. Harris.[29]

In addition to Tulsa and St. Louis interests, the company directors were closely linked with a cross-section of the Texas economic and political elite. Those individuals included Colonel Edward Mandel House, who dominated the Texas Democratic Party through his machine from 1892 to 1912, his brother T. W. House, Jr., his cousin, lifelong intimate, and Texas Company employee Henry C. House; Texas governors James S. Hogg, Joseph D. Sayers, Charles Culberson, and Samuel W. T. Lanham; the state attorney general Thomas Watt Gregory; lumber magnates William Marsh Rice, J. S. Rice, and John Henry Kirby; Walter B. Sharp, a cofounder of the Hughes Tool Company; attorney Duval West and cattleman John Blocker of San Antonio; and south Texas political boss and land speculator James B. Wells of Brownsville. The defeated Democratic presidential candidate Bryan participated in Rio Grande Valley land investments in which company president Joseph S. Cullinan, secretary Will Hogg, and treasurer Richard E. Brooks were active. The Texas Company directors were also associated with the Heywood-Jennings oil interests in their border investments. All of the above-named principals in these enterprises were Texas Democratic party activists. Brooks served as mayor of Houston. The Jennings oil interests bought a major share of the ownership of the 1,237,000-acre Piedras Blancas hacienda in Coahuila. John Blocker of San Antonio was co-owner of the Piedras Blancas and served as U.S. Consul at Parral during the revolution.[30]

The Texas Company operated in close association with the House machine that dominated the Texas Democratic party. It provided financial contributions to the political campaigns, and its directors enjoyed long-time business relations and friendships for twenty years prior to the ascension of House and his political associates to national power via the election of President Woodrow Wilson. By 1905 Texas Company president Cullinan had established the concern as the principal competition of the Standard Oil-controlled Waters Pierce Oil Company in Texas. The Texas Company actively supported the antitrust actions of Texas attorneys general including Thomas Watt Gregory, later attorney general of the United States in the Wilson administration, charging that Waters-Pierce was a front company for the Standard Oil Trust. These attorneys general were intimate friends of various company directors, including Cullinan, Brooks, Hogg, and the company's legal counsel and director, James Autry.

Frank Andrews, a key member of the House machine in statewide political campaigns, served as the company's principal representative in legal actions. Gregory, Andrews, and Judge Victor L. Brooks, who ruled against Waters-Pierce, were partners in 1910–1911 in the Missouri-Texas Land and Irrigation Company capitalized at $1 million with holdings on both sides of the Rio Grande River. In 1910 a consortium headed by Richard Brooks and Cullinan began to sell almost 5 million acres of land in Mexico including 600,000 acres of irrigated properties, some of them probably Stillman's, near Matamoros. Their holdings on the Mexican bank of the river comprised 2 million acres and was a cause of agrarian unrest in and around Matamoros.[31]

Before 1901, in addition to the Texas Company, Andrews also represented Huntington and his interests in the Southern Pacific Railroad (SP), and GH&SA, the Houston and Texas Central, the San Antonio and Aransas Pass Railroad, the Mexican International, and the major north-south Mexican trunk lines. The Huntington interests had bought Peirce's interest in the GH&SA in the early 1880s. That road, which spanned Texas from Houston to El Paso as the Sunset Route, connected with the Mexican International at Eagle Pass, while tie-ins with the International and Great Northern at San Antonio and the Texas and Pacific, and Denver and Rio Grande at El Paso gave it direct access to Chicago, St. Louis, and Kansas City. Headquartered in Houston, the GH&SA directors continued to work with Andrews after Huntington's death and W. H. Harriman's takeover of the SP. The Harriman-National City Bank interests that controlled the SP found that their association with Andrews served them well. It put them "in" with the House machine in the state's labyrinthine politics. The House family, through its bank, and the Andrews family had been financial supporters, with the National City Bank, of the GH&SA and the Houston and Texas Central after the Civil War.[32]

The House family entered this network in the 1840s when T. W. invested with Moses Taylor, chairman of the bank's board of directors, in the Brazoria Tap Railroad, a short line that connected the Thomas Wentworth Peirce cotton plantation and adjoining estates to the main railway between the port of Galveston and Houston. In the early 1870s House purchased the plantation from Peirce. His son Edward developed a political machine that grew from its Houston beginnings to encompass the state. Its most important ally around Brownsville, political boss Jim Wells, participated in Mexican investments and land speculations. Elected state officials from south Texas also tied into the process of railroad and land development as it passed their areas and then spread beyond into Mexico. The myriad associates included Wells, Judge Stephen Powers, the Texas Company officers, the Stillman-National City Bank interests, the King Ranch-Kleburg family, whose political scion, U.S. Congressman Rudolf Kleburg, was an ally of Colonel House, and an assortment of Brownsville and Rio Grande Valley irrigation and land company promoters. The many railroads that held properties in the lower Rio Grande Valley were the Harriman-controlled San Antonio and Aransas Pass, the Stillman-supported Texas and Pacific, and the St. Louis, Brownsville and Mexico built in 1903–1904 under the stewardship of B. F. Yoakum with Frisco Line-Harriman-Stillman control. Other railroads holding land at points on the Texas-Mexico border included the GH&SA, the Houston and Texas Central, the Denver and Rio Grande, the Southern Pacific, the Gulf Coast and San Francisco, the Texas and St. Louis, and the Denver and Western. Texas politicians, members of the House machine, participated with these railroads as attorneys, investors, and partners in land development schemes.

The House machine successfully supported the campaigns of governors Hogg (1891–1895), Culbertson, (1895–1899), Sayers (1899–1903), and Lanham (1903–1907). Texas Congressman Albert S. Burleson, who later served as postmaster general and political adviser to President Wilson, served as an important ally in Washington. These Texans, closely tied to the Hogg-Swayne Syndicate and the interests that came together to create the Texas Company after the bonanza of Spindletop, challenged the Standard Oil Trust in the 1890s and first decade of the twentieth century. They pushed for passage of antimonopoly legislation by the state government and for antitrust prosecutions by state attorneys general, especially Gregory, against Standard Oil and its local subsidiaries, the Waters-Pierce and Magnolia Oil companies. Colonel House, the most important figure in

Texas politics at the time and later the closest of President Wilson's advisers, counted Attorney General Gregory, Wells, Andrews, Governor James Hogg and his son Will Hogg, who was head of the Hogg-Swayne Syndicate and secretary of Texaco, and cousin Henry House, as his closest friends. Cousin Henry, a Houston investor and officer in the Kirby Lumber Company, which held 1 million acres in Mexican mining claims largely in the state of Guerrero, headed the Texas Company's operations in the booming oil zone of Tampico during those critical years of the revolution, 1913–1915.[33]

One of Cullinan's key successes in the creation of the Texas Company in 1902 was the merger of his Spindletop interests with the Hogg-Swayne Syndicate. Other participants included the Heywood-Jennings oil group. Both Jennings and Heywood joined the Texas Company directors in their Rio Grande Valley-Northern Mexico land speculations. Heywood and Jennings bought land along the American side of the international boundary and in Tamaulipas and Coahuila. Company secretary Will Hogg served an important role as the coordinator of the diverse associated interests. Company treasurer Brooks handled land investments and Mexican commitments via several operatives in Mexico, including William F. Buckley, Sr., W. B. Sharp, and Henry House. Ex-governor Hogg and Colonel House developed important liaisons with outside sources of capital for various Texas interests in New York, including their principal one with National City Bank, in Boston with the Old Colony Trust, and other institutions and friends in Massachusetts, London, and Chicago.[34]

Their close ties with the National City Bank coincided with that institution's long-standing domination of Texas economic expansion. James Stillman held $200,000 in stock in Brackenridge's San Antonio National Bank; a lien on the Chapman Ranch near Corpus Christi, a property that had been contested by Cortina; and stock in the Aransas Pass and San Antonio Railroad. Stillman was also a partner in a Swensen XIT Ranch acquisition in West Texas, owned development properties adjacent to several railroads in various parts of the state, and, as secretary and later president of the American Committee of the U.S. Guarantee and Trust Corporation, owned stock in fifteen other Texas banks, including institutions in or near Galveston, Houston, Dallas, San Antonio, Corpus Christi, Amarillo, Abilene, Brownsville, and El Paso.

In 1905 the formation of the Union Bank and Trust of Houston brought together the House family, the Texas Company, and some of the most powerful capitalists in the state in a jointly owned financial institution. The largest in Texas, it served as a key instrument in new investments.

The Union Bank counted among its directors the leaders of the Texas Oil Company, Cullinan, Will Hogg, and Brooks; Andrews, the House brothers, James Hogg, and other Houston bankers, lumber company owners, and railroad operators concerned with the Nueces Strip between the Nueces and Rio Grande rivers and northern Mexico. The bank served as an important source of funds as the Texas Company and its friends began to expand their operations southward. In 1905, when T. W., Jr., and Edward House became directors of the Union Bank, each inherited 50 percent of older brother John H. B. House's estate. John was a part-owner and director of a half-dozen silver mine companies in Guanajuato.[35]

The directors of the Union Bank and Trust (now known as Texas Commerce Bank), including the Texas Company representatives, had borrowed money from the T. W. House private bank of Houston in the early development of their lumber, railroad, cotton, and oil pursuits. In 1907 they supported the House family bank when it faced financial disaster. During the financial panic of 1907 the House Bank collapsed when 40 of Texas's 250 banks were forced to close. The same economic crisis and dearth of funds that staggered the Díaz regime also undermined the House family's fortunes. The family's old friends in Houston helped as much as they could. One of the major interests in Union Bank, John Henry Kirby, held on to $140,000 in House bank bonds even though he knew the bank was in trouble. He refused to apply for reimbursement as provided by the bankruptcy statutes. The Union Bank directors' loyalty also meant that they did not cash in their House Bank bonds. Colonel House was indebted to his lifelong friends and associates at the Texas Oil Company and the Union Bank and Trust. These men shared their social lives, efforts, and enterprises—both political and economic—in Houston, Texas, and Mexico.[36]

Kirby had a deep interest in Mexican mining. In addition to his one million acres of mining claims in the states of Guerrero, Jalisco, Aguascalientes, Mexico (El Oro), and San Luis Potosí, Kirby's Buena Fe silver mine in Jalisco served as a source of considerable profit. Kirby also owned oil claims near Tampico and a bank there. He was a longtime activist in the Texas Democratic party. A conservative, he worked closely with the House machine, attending state conventions and developing statewide political and business contacts. As a result he helped the later virulent anti-Villista Zach Cobb of El Paso gain an appointment with the new Wilson administration. When Colonel House made his patronage recommendations for the newly elected president, Cobb won the assignment of chief customs inspector at El Paso.[37]

Cobb's zealousness resulted in the repeated shutting off of arms and fuel supplies to Villa during the Mexican Revolution. His greatest successes in this regard came in the early summer of 1914, when Villa's coal-starved trains stalled near Aguascalientes while the pequeña burguesa- and upper-class-led forces of Alvaro Obregon Salido and Venustiano Carranza swept past him into Mexico City. Later, after Villa's defeats at Celaya and León in May and June 1915, Cobb's role was important in blunting the Mexican revolutionary's attempts to recover from his heavy losses and acquire new war material.

The Texas Company men entered Porfirian Mexico in 1898–1900, before the company was formed, because of momentarily declining production in Texas. Their competitive zeal drove them to participate in the wider expansion of the U.S. economy southward into Mexico. In 1901, while Texas oilmen still called their young firm the Texas Fuel Company, Walter B. Sharp, their drilling and exploration expert, anticipated problems:

> I will go to the City of Mexico soon to look into some deals. The Standard and Waters Pierce oil companies are fighting the oil business hard and it will take every energy and good business plans or they will own it all, this is why I am trying to get a start in old Mexico, before they get it all, as they will soon control the whole thing.[38]

In 1913 Sharp claimed $1 million as his share of the Texaco real estate holdings in Mexico. He was thinking in terms of millions of acres. Just three years earlier, before the revolution and after the oil boom began, land purchased by the company in Tamaulipas and the Gulf of Mexico area sold for twenty cents an acre.[39]

The Texas Company, created from an amalgam of diverse Texas Oil interests, faced a deepening crisis in the period after 1902. Production in its Texas and other domestic fields continued to decline, forcing it to move into foreign production. Between 1902 and 1905 output at the Spindletop field fell from 17,420,949 to 1,652,780 barrels. The situation in Texas looked grim. Between 1904 and 1909 Texas's share in U.S. production dropped from 21.52 to 5.94 percent. A company report in 1908 or 1909 summed up the situation:

> There have been no new discoveries of crude oil in South Texas in the past few years, and the supply has become quite low. The larger refineries have been compelled to go elsewhere for their crude supply. The United States government, three years ago, took the tariff off crude oil and put it on the free list, since which time the oil companies in Texas have found it necessary to go into

> Mexico to obtain their supplies of crude. They have encountered all sorts of difficulties with the Mexican government, and it has almost become necessary for them to organize separate companies in this republic, not being able to take out permits for the main company, as would be possible in this state.[40]

Between 1900 and 1910 per-well oil output in the Texas Company's area of operations in the southwest fell to an average of between 100 and 600 barrels a day. At the same time, the Mexican Cerro Azul well gushed forth 45,000 to 50,000 barrels per day. Survival dictated the Texas Company's entry into the Mexican fields as foreign producers hurried to exploit the new opportunity. The Texas Company's entry into Mexico deepened the commitment of the Texas state elite in Mexican affairs. It laid the basis for the Wilson administration's Mexican policies. The Texans stepped to the forefront of U.S. expansion and U.S.-Mexican relations, as they did in the 1830s, 1840s, and 1870s.[41]

In order to operate in Mexico in the face of what they regarded as hostility from Díaz and Limantour, the Texas Company directors created a series of separate companies including the Tamesi, Panuco, Tampico, Mexican Fuel Oil, Mexico, and Producers Oil companies. That maneuver also gave the Texans almost unimpeded control of the Mexican properties vis-à-vis their increasingly critical and financially more powerful New York investors headed by Arnold Schlaet.

The Texas Company entrusted operations in Mexico to three able men: Henry House, William Buckley, and Walter Sharp. House handled Texas Company headquarters operations at Tampico. His connections in Tampico were enhanced by his position as vice-president of the Kirby Lumber Company, whose president sat as a founding director of the Union Bank and owned a bank in Tampico.

Buckley, a University of Texas Law School graduate whose mansion stood a few blocks from the big home owned by his family friends, Colonel and Mrs. House, in Austin, administered the company's legal affairs in Mexico. He counted the Texas Company his most important among many clients that included the Gulf and Standard Oil companies. His father, John Buckley, former sheriff of Duval County in the Rio Grande Valley, had supported Díaz during the Revolution of Tuxtepec, giving William sympathetic access to the Mexican president, who remembered a favor. His brother, Edmund Buckley, served as a foreman on one of Colonel House's ranches before joining the family law firm in Mexico and handling some of the Texas Company's legal affairs. Edmund also participated in one of the land development ventures on the Rio Grande River promoted by Texas Company Treasurer Brooks.[42]

Sharp, the Hughes Tool Company cofounder, first made a fortune in oil drilling and land development, then took charge of Texas Company exploration, property leasing and purchases, and field development. Sharp helped the Texas Company develop important political ties in Tamaulipas and Monterrey. Taking advantage of Governor Hogg's contacts in Tamaulipas and Nuevo León, Sharp and Cullinan become friends and house guests of General Treviño and his wife, General E. O. C. Ord's daughter. Treviño received the Monterrey to Tampico railroad concession in 1887, a concession initially exploited by Italian Count Telfener, a participant with Kleberg, Kenedy, Stillman, Yoakum, and Rockefeller in the St. Louis, Brownsville and Mexico Railroad between 1900 and 1905. Cullinan and Sharp also cultivated a relationship with Cavazos family heirs who still held large properties in northeastern Mexico. The family was still allied with the King Ranch. Cullinan, Brooks, and Sharp purchased land and leases from the heirs of former President González. Texaco acquired vast acreage in Tamaulipas between Matamoros on the border and Ozuluama, fifty miles south of Tampico. The coordinated activities of Henry House, Buckley, Cullinan, Will Hogg, Sharp, and Brooks gave the Texas Company the over 4.5 million acres it came to control in northeastern Mexico through its subsidiaries.[43]

Cullinan and his confederates owned producing wells along the Panuco River and on the Chapacao Plantation near Ozuluama and, after acquiring vast expanses through purchase, lease, and concession, in association with James Stillman planned the irrigation and sale of 2 million acres immediately south of Matamoros. The National City Bank chairman of the board still controlled part of the riparian rights to the Rio Grande River at Brownsville-Matamoros, and he had extended his role through his bank's leadership, along with the Speyer Bank, in floating $25 million in gold bonds for irrigation projects on behalf of the Mexican government in 1909. The Texas Company and Sharp developed ties with Stillman. Sharp placed enormous quantities of cash in the National City Bank. When he died in 1916, Sharp's account totaled $326,715. In contrast, the total value of Sharp's largest savings account in his place of residence, Houston, amounted to only $4,670. The Texas Company concentrated its East Coast assets with Stillman's bank, which enjoyed great popularity with the directors because they believed that its enormous gold reserves, accumulated and publicized by Stillman, ensured them against financial collapse during the recurrent panics.[44]

In 1911 the Texas Company directors based in Houston offered to sell subdivided portions from their 4.5 million acres of land in Tamaulipas through their subsidiary concern, the Mexico Company. The Mexico Company was headquartered in Houston across the street from the Texas Company building. In addition to its Tamaulipas interests, the Texas Company and its directors owned hundreds of thousands of acres in Sonora, Chihuahua, Veracruz, and the Isthmus of Tehuantepec. In 1910 Edwin J. Marshall, the founding treasurer of the company, still a loyal and active Democrat living in California, was still owner of the 2.5 million-acre Las Palomas cattle hacienda opposite Columbus, New Mexico, in Chihuahua. It was "the largest fenced property in North America." He also controlled the Sinaloa Land and Water Company, which owned over 3 million acres of land in that Pacific coast state. The Mexico Company offered the 2 million acres just south of Brownsville as "ranchos" to American colonists with the promise of irrigation services provided by the Mexican government. The financially beleaguered Díaz regime had just received the $25 million that had been raised for irrigation by the National City Bank and the Speyer Banks in New York and London. The bond sale totaled an amount slightly more than half the size of the Mexican government's expenditures for a fiscal year.[45]

Despite growing government revenues as a result of increased petroleum production, the successes of that industry offered virtually no social or political benefits. Rather, as an enclave economy, the revenues it provided eased the need for reform in agriculture and industry that otherwise would have been necessary in order to generate an internally dynamic economy capable of providing the government with funds and power. Mexico exported crude oil and continued to import nearly all of the refined petroleum products consumed by the domestic market aside from the railroads.

The zones of economic growth were limited to the areas directly involved in production, and the surrounding territories were afflicted with displacement and dire poverty. The petroleum zones constituted capital-intensive economic enclaves whose greatest effect in outlying areas was inflation. The oil companies employed foreign technicians and foremen and paid them well. The crews of domestic laborers received extremely low pay considering the inflationary spiral. Aspiring Mexican capitalists could not compete with the power and know-how of the foreigners in the industry. The latter interests, meanwhile, pressured and tried to manipulate the Mexican government.

Díaz developed a strong antipathy to the assertive American oil companies despite the funds they provided his coffers. Mexican petroleum production was sizable, but it caused social, economic, and, eventually, political destabilization. It brought pressure on the Mexican state from the most powerful citizens of the United States. The growth of mining and petroleum enclaves was only part of the developing complexity of the Porfirian political economy. The expansion of commercial agriculture was one of the Porfiriato's most important aspects.

AGRICULTURE

The growth of the nation's railroad system brought the most isolated parts of the Mexican countryside into contact with the outside world. That single event caused agricultural, livestock, timber, and mining land values to skyrocket and brought about a transformation of the land tenure system through the foreclosures and seizures that resulted. For the 87 percent of the people who lived in the countryside, the opening up of their communities to the outside world meant a dramatic change in life-style and in their way of earning a living. For the campesinos, that 62 percent of the population that worked the land, it meant economic disenfranchisement, social dislocation, and violence.

Prior to the intervention of foreign capital into the Mexican economy, there were substantial barriers to horizontal mobility and the transition from village to hacienda or urban life. These included the sociocultural differences created by the sixteenth-century European conquest of Mesoamerica in which cities became the citadels of European life at one extreme while the Indian villages remained their cultural and economic opposites in the countryside. Rural culture, despite drastic changes in the sixteenth century, retained much of its pre-Columbian character, including the village land tenure system, milpa technology, and indigenous languages. The traditional haciendas acted as acculturating agents in the countryside, introducing the Spanish language and customs, religion, and European technology while providing commercial export crops consumed in the cities. The traditional great estates served regional markets for the most part, however, and were frequently undercapitalized. Except for the vast cattle ranches of the north, their operations were usually on a modest scale. They absorbed, acculturated, or displaced relatively few villagers through enclosure in comparison to their Porfirian counterparts.

A balanced distribution of labor formed over a period of centuries in which a majority of the population remained in its traditional self-sufficient though poor villages. A minority moved onto the estates as laborers or sharecroppers; others migrated to the European-oriented towns and cities, which assimilated them. As they made the transition to urban or town life a network of Spanish settlements gradually developed. The pueblo residents usually worked on the neighboring great estates for brief periods during the planting and harvesting seasons. The majority of the people of indigenous lineage found in the cities of the colonial era were urban in origin; some were even descendants of urbanites of pre-Columbian times. The majority of early nineteenth-century city dwellers likewise could claim descent from long-standing urban lineages, and many of those who migrated to the cities returned to the countryside later. In the nineteenth century, despite acculturation, fundamental differences remained between the expansive European economy and culture and the residual peasant countryside.

The introverted self-sufficiency of precapitalist peasant village property systems, with their cooperative forms of labor, constituted an overtly hostile block to the urban centers and commercially oriented elite. The latter group desired to gain access to workers and land for increased commercial productivity and profit-making "money" crops. Industrial labor recruitment was so difficult that intermittent shortages of workers existed in the urban areas and in some commercialized zones of the countryside during most of the nineteenth century. These labor shortages continued in the La Laguna region and elsewhere in the north until the onset of the revolution. Industrialists located their factories in countryside locales near main roads or major cities. In this way new factories combined ready access to rural labor with rapid transportation via carts and wagons to the urban centers. Later the search for reliable and sophisticated labor, and lower transportation costs, caused the factories to be located in the cities, creating an urban industrial working class. This could only happen, however, after masses of campesinos had been driven from the land and forced to the cities in search of survival.

The Porfirian land enclosure process was a necessary step in the country's capitalist economic transformation. During the late 1870s, the 1880s, and 1890s the peasantry lost most of its land and was driven increasingly to participate in new hacienda-based export-oriented commercial agriculture and industrial activity. Resistance to this process was magnified many times by foreign ownership of the great estates in the north and south and along the coasts.

About 130 million acres, more than 27 percent of Mexico's land surface, came into the possession of American owners. Their acquisitions were made in the offices of attorneys in New York, Chicago, San Francisco, Houston, San Antonio, Los Angeles, and Mexico City, remote from the masses of rural Mexico. At first the peasantry felt no direct impact from these transactions. Late in the 1890s, however, and especially after 1900, the new holders began to subdivide and sell their tracts to smaller, more active owners, "pioneers," and colonists. By 1910 15,000 American colonists had occupied properties in Chiapas, Oaxaca, Veracruz, Tamaulipas, San Luis Potosí, Jalisco, Sinaloa, Durango, Sonora, Chihuahua, Coahuila, and Baja California.[46]

Showing their property titles, the American colonists expelled Mexican "squatters" from the land, put up barbed-wire fences, and offered employment at what they considered attractive wages to those of the indigenous population they needed. The larger American corporate agricultural entities expelled tenant farmers and canceled rancho leases in order to produce cotton, henequen, ixtle, guayule, coffee, cacao, chicle, and tropical rubber for export.

The exclusion of Mexican peasants by American colonists and companies at Atascador and San Dieguito in San Luis Potosí, at the Blaylock Colony in Tamaulipas, on the properties of the Tezuitlan Estates in Puebla, in the secular, and Mormon colonies in Chihuahua and Sonora, on the Fortuna tract in Tehuantepec, and at Acuyucan in Veracruz led to riots, pillage, and killing within a few years. The expulsion of the Mexican peasantry from the land by the foreigners did not come at the time of sale; it came with the arrival of colonists and the commercial development of the land. Expulsion laid the groundwork for the nationwide campesino violence that exploded across the countryside beginning in 1909, devastating American properties and estates. The Europeans, who had not undertaken massive settlement projects, escaped with much smaller but by no means negligible losses. The foreigners, however, alienated far more than the peasants. The continued expansion of their holdings drove up real estate prices five and ten times, making it less feasible for Mexican local and provincial elites to compete, with their devalued currency, in the purchase of land and agricultural opportunity.

By 1910, despite the fact that the majority of agricultural landholdings were in the hands of Mexican entrepreneurs, American and, to a much lesser degree, British, French, and German companies and private owners possessed massive tracts, including most of the more desirable land used in industrial export agriculture with its invariably labor-intensive, labor-coercive methods. Foreign agriculture businesses controlled fourteen of the sixteen largest farming, processing, and marketing companies and between 95 and 96 percent of the total capital. American investors officially accounted for 46 percent of the foreign capital in the agricultural companies. American owners controlled 75 percent of the Culiacan Valley in

Sinaloa and were responsible for all of the commercial agricultural output in the Río Fuerte Basin. In reality the total American investment in agriculture was at least four times greater than the standard estimate of $50 million.[47]

The larger American landholdings were the 6,600,000 to 7,500,000-acre Hearst complexes in Chihuahua, Oaxaca, Tabasco, Chiapas, and Campeche; the 5,500,000 acres owned by Marshall in Chihuahua and Sinaloa; the 4,700,000 acre Texaco holdings; the Burns properties in Durango; the 3,500,000-acre Mengel timber concession in Quintana Roo and Yucatán; the 3,775,000 acres held by the Continental Rubber Company; Henry Burton's 1,800,000 acres in Baja California; the 1,500,000 acres owned by R. Vick in Sonora; the 1,450,000-acre Rascon Hacienda in San Luis Potosí and Tamaulipas; the 1,400,000-acre Wheeler property in Sonora; the 1,300,000-acre Laguna Corporation property in Campeche; the 1,256,000-acre T. O. Riverside Ranch and the 1,250,000 acres owned by the Henry Muller heirs in Chihuahua; the Jennings-Blocker 1,200,000-acre Piedra Blanca Ranch in Coahuila; the 1,200,000-acre San Antonio de las Rusias Hacienda and Annexes of Otto Brictson in Tamaulipas; the 1,200,000 acres of the American International Land and Mining Company; the 1,026,000 acres owned by Adolph Vietor in Chiapas; the 1,000,000 acres controlled by the Circle Bar Ranch in Baja California; Harry Chandler's over 1,000,000 acres in Baja California; the 993,650-acre Richardson Construction Company holdings in Sonora; the 893,650 acre Corralitos Hacienda in Chihuahua; the 750,000 acres pertaining to Senator William Langer and associates in Durango and Sinaloa; the 723,500 acres of the Guerrero Iron and Timber Company near Chilpancingo; the 700,000 acres of the Monterey Iron and Steel Company; and the 660,000 acres owned by the Gulf Coast Land and Lumber Company in Campeche.

Americans owned more than a hundred properties of between 100,000 and 500,000 acres. These included the Guerrero Trading Company's 1904 purchase of the Hacienda San Marcos south of Acapulco, a territory disputed through violence with the neighboring villages since the Yope wars of the 1520s and the Tecoanapa-Ayahualulco peasants' uprisings of the 1830s and 1840s. Hundreds of American landholders claimed between 10,000 and 100,000 acres each. In addition to the American landownership total of over 100 million acres, George H. Sisson claimed that 18 million acres were still held in Baja California by the International Company of Connecticut.[48]

The foreign marketplace had a momentous impact upon Mexican agricultural production during the Porfiriato. For years sugar output increased in response to foreign demand. During the era of economic growth it increased five times to an annual total of 2,503,825 tons. After 1907, however, despite increased production, foreign demand suddenly slumped, and by 1910 most of the sugar harvest had been consumed internally. Cuban and American competition and a new U.S. tariff combined to restrict Mexican opportunities in the United States and Europe. In 1909–1910 the entire Mexican crop shipped via Veracruz was destined for the United Kingdom. Reliance on outside marketing and distributors had once again left the Mexican economy vulnerable to foreign capital. The expectations of Mexican sugar that had brightened the eyes of San Antonio's dreamers in the 1870s went unfulfilled.[49]

Henequén output increased eleven-fold during the first thirty years of the Porfiriato to 128,849 tons per annum. Labor intensive and performed under forced work conditions, a joint consortium of local and foreign landholding monopolists in Yucatán, Campeche, and Quintana Roo controlled it. They were headed by Olegario Molina, Díaz's minister of development and Cyrus McCormack's chief agent in Yucatán. McCormack headed the consolidation of harvesting machine companies that became the International Harvester Company. McCormack served as a director in Stillman's National City Bank. The new company and longtime marketers such as the Henry Peabody trading company then joined with Molina to fix prices, giving established planters, buyers, and distributors their respective monopolies. The Americans gained marketing and distribution control of sisal hemp while the Yucatecan oligarchy "la Casta Divina" monopolized landownership and production in the state of Yucatán. The Americans made it clear, however, that the planters' power was limited even in the area of production. Four U.S. companies harvested over 3 million acres of hardwood forests in Campeche and planted vast tracts of henequén. Stillman, through McCormack, had coordinated the formation of yet another industrial "trust." The integration of the financial assets of his associates enabled Stillman to bring the trusts into his bank; henequén joined the wire, steel, copper, railroad, banking, and oil "trusts"; and the heads of each served on his board of directors.

Between 1877 and 1907 chile, cacao, coffee, peas, tobacco, and vanilla joined henequén in registering remarkable export increases. Vegetable production showed marginal increases. Accountable corn, wheat, rice, potato, celery, bean, and chile production all improved between an estimated 1.4 to 3.3 percent per year.[50] These figures are flawed, however, reflecting the greater accountability of commercial production versus the unrecorded crops of peasant minifundia. After 1907 redirected land use, population growth, drought, soil exhaustion, root rot, and irrigation shortfalls combined to wipe out the Porfiriato's modest gains in the output of domestic staples. Between 1907 and 1910 per capita production of corn dropped 2.3 percent; beans, 2.3 percent; chile, 1.5 percent; celery, 3 percent; and wheat, 1.9 percent. Only potatoes (.6 percent) and rice (1.2 percent) showed improved per capita output. The poorer less developed land still in the hands of the peasantry, lacking irrigation and chemicals, suffered far more severely.

After 1907 profoundly desperate conditions developed in agriculture, especially in the sugar-producing region of Morelos in the center-south, along the Gulf coast, and in wide areas of the drought-ridden center-north, and north of the country where export-oriented foreign investment dominated in the face of financially ruined and threatened provincial elites. In 1910, 90 percent of the Mexican campesino population was without land. Famine stalked the dispossessed peasants and working classes.[51]

SIX

The Crisis of the Porfirian Political Economy

The crisis in Mexico is . . . nothing more than the result of the terrible crisis in the United States and the world marketplace.

—Enrique Martínez Sobral
Porfirian Economist, 1909

1899, año culminante de la prosperidad porfirica

—Fernando Rosenzweig

In 1907 the H. W. Bennett companies, specialists in foreign and Mexican sugar production, and the Mexican National Sugar Company collapsed. A vice-president of the Carnegie Steel Company headed the Mexican National, which was capitalized in New York at $10 million. Despite improved irrigation and machinery, and a maximum of land taken from the villages, great estate sugar production in Morelos, the Mexican sugar nexus, dropped a disastrous 7 percent from 52,230,155 kilos in 1908–1909 to 48,547,600 kilos in 1909–1910. Production dropped even further in 1910–1911, to 48,531,600 kilos.

Mexican producers confronted a protective American tariff and new U.S. growers in Cuba. World sugar prices, over which the Morelos empresarios had no control, dropped sharply. The Morelos planters attempted to compensate for their losses by redirecting their product to Mexico City and domestic consumption. The leaner economy led estate owners to demand tougher land tenancy and water contracts with their campesinos. They resorted to layoffs and cutbacks in pay and working hours. The towns of Cuautla and Ayala filled with displaced workers, future recruits to the Zapatista revolution.[1]

Events in Morelos reflected a broader Mexican agricultural disaster.

Famine in the center and north of the country necessitated massive corn shipments from foreign sources totaling 200,000 tons annually between 1907 and 1910. Desperate conditions prevailed in the far northern states of Coahuila, Nuevo León, Chihuahua, and Tamaulipas. Adjacent commercial lands controlled by foreign and domestic producers exported livestock, guayule, and vegetables to the United States, and tens of thousands of tons of "Indian corn" came from the United States to feed Mexico's lower classes. Corn prices skyrocketed; in central Mexico they reached one peso per kilo. The mortality rate in Mazatlán reached an incredible 4.4 percent.[2]

In fiscal 1908–1909 the corn crop partially failed in the states of Durango, Chihuahua, and Coahuila because of drought compounded by inadequate irrigation for domestic food production. In fiscal 1909–1910 Indian corn imports valued $181,079 at Ciudad Porfirio Díaz. Shipments arrived at Mexican ports from Argentina, South Africa, Australia, and the United States. During September 1909 at Nuevo Laredo, tariff exemptions on corn exports from the United States enabled the shipment of 1,051,000 bushels via 1,051 boxcars. Nuevo Laredo received $115,200 worth of corn via the railroads in 1909. During a two-week period in 1910, 11,900 tons of corn arrived at Tampico on two ships from South Africa; three more ships were en route. Among the many shipments that ensued, the contents of one totaled 6,000 tons of Indian corn. Imports of U.S. corn at Tampico in 1909–1910 valued $349,084. Land reallocations for the raising of guayule and other commercial export crops, drought, and a lack of irrigation for the production of domestic staples combined to destroy the 1910 corn crop in Zacatecas and Aguascalientes. Famine spread from those states to adjacent areas.[3]

During the summer of 1910 the situation grew worse in the far north. In that climactic year, Ciudad Porfirio Díaz imported more corn than ever before, valuing $234,957. In Nuevo Laredo the desperate populace received corn at a cost of $118,000. The principal points of origin for emergency food shipments on the Gulf coast were Argentina, South Africa, and the United States. Australian and U.S. supplies arrived at the West coast ports. Massive quantities of U.S. corn passed through border points of entry for shipment to interior cities via the railroads. In 1908 the government imported 5 million pesos worth of corn. In 1909 the value of corn imports reached 15 million pesos, and in 1910 they totaled 12 million pesos. The remoteness of the rural population and distribution inefficiencies, however, rendered the effort fruitless.[4]

Devastating locust infestations and root rot in the center and south of the nation accompanied the drought in the north to speed the breakdown of the domestic agricultural regime. Mexican agriculture was vulnerable because the government failed to devote sufficient funds to irrigation and because of the displacement of peasant cultivators of staple foodstuffs by export-oriented commercial agriculturalists. Irrigation of medium and small plots in the north was rare.

In some areas east of the sierra in Chihuahua, after a "difficult year in 1909," lack of rainfall caused a 50 percent decline in agricultural output in 1910. Cattlemen at the American-owned Corralitos Hacienda between Janos and Casas Grandes slaughtered cattle for hides because the stockyards in El Paso were overcrowded. They sold at small fractions of their earlier value. In 1909 Chihuahua claimed only 330,035 acres of irrigated farmland; 589,035 acres were dry farmed. This condition prevailed despite the fact that millions of acres were irrigable. Chihuahua landowners used 24,314,311 acres of land for grazing, and 14,562,887 acres lay idle. Forests covered 10,218,421 acres. The Díaz government developed plans for irrigation, but peasant displacement in favor of cash export crop production on the farmlands had left the nation vulnerable to famine, unable to cope with drought and crop disease. The financially austere government was incapable of a meaningful response to the problem. Despite three years of agricultural disaster, famine, and corn imports, the state of Chihuahua reported that no irrigation projects of importance were initiated in 1910. Yet vast irrigation projects at La Laguna and between Matamoros and Reynosa were being carried out in conjunction with foreign agricultural empresarios, New York bankers and American land development companies. The situation provoked widespread outrage in Mexican society.[5]

The growth of agricultural exports and the penetration of the domestic economy by foreign capital transformed Mexican agricultural land tenure. First the Porfirian government subdued previously semiautonomous Indian societies—such as the Yaqui in Sonora, Mayo in Sinaloa, and Maya in Campeche, Chiapas, and Yucatán. The Yaqui and Maya had resisted intruders for almost four centuries. Technological advances such as the railroad and gatling gun made conquest possible in the remote areas. Then it converted former Indian lands to commercial use. Between 1877 and 1910 the commercialization of agriculture caused the number of great estates to increase from 5,869 to 8,431, while the greater part of the 57,778,102 hectares of land given out by the government between 1855 and 1911 were distributed after 1877 from terrain in the foreign-dominated far north. The powerful foreigners and their weaker Mexican counterparts, known as the "Younger Creoles" because in earlier times that caste had dominated landholding, joined in pushing agrarian labor productivity to new heights by a variety of means, including forced labor. Wanted posters sprinkled the northern state capitals offering rewards for the return of escaped debt peons who fled hoping to find work in the mines and cities.[6]

The dramatic growth of commercial agriculture, however, like industry, was superimposed upon a domestic economy unequipped to purchase its products. Nor were the foreigners interested in Mexican agriculture for the purposes of feeding the domestic population. Industry-related agriculture for the support of mines, railroad construction workers, and factory employees thrived briefly during the 1890s, but 1899 was "the last year of the Porfirian prosperity." Thereafter internal consumption slumped. Domestic consumption of unrefined sugar, *piloncillo,* fell from an earlier annual per capita growth rate of 2.1 percent between 1894 and 1901 to 1.5 percent in 1907 before the worst of the agricultural crisis struck. Domestic cotton underwent a similar decline in the rate of annual per capita growth, slipping from 2.4 to 1.4 percent; and sugar for export collapsed from 5.2 percent per annum to 1.8 percent. The cotton crop at the center of production, La Laguna, dropped from 300,000 bales in 1909 to 80,000 bales in 1910.

Between 1907 and 1911 per capita consumption of cotton fabrics contracted a disastrous 3.4 percent per capita each year and tobacco consumption declined a comparable 2.9 percent. Nineteen cotton factories manufacturing cloth and yarn were idle on 30 June 1910. National consumption of cotton dropped a full 6 percent from 37,000 tons in 1906–1907 to less than 35,000 in 1910–1911 despite significant population growth. Only sugar originally destined for export showed an improvement in domestic consumption. Sugar sales collapsed on the world market, forcing the growers to dump it in Mexico.[7]

The industrial sector, dependent on foreign investments for prosperity and growth, failed in its task of absorbing the peasantry displaced by the enclosures of commercial agriculture. Capital-intensive foreign industrial concerns created only 82,000 new jobs between 1895 and 1910. That total included the boom years of 1895–1899 and the surge of American investments in 1906 attracted by the low property values created by the 50 percent devaluation of 1905. Foreign investment, however, in addition to its higher cost through interest rates, caused severe inflation that hurt the working classes and pequeña burguesía severely while undermining the competitive position of the provincial elites for landownership.

The retrograde effect of foreign investment on domestic industrial, agricultural, and livestock employment manifested itself in the far north. Despite the fact that American capitalists committed 23 percent of their total investment in Mexico to Chihuahua, Sonora, and Coahuila, only 1.5 percent of the Mexican population resided there, and many of them continued in nonindustrial, traditional occupations. One of the Porfiriato's great failures was that foreign capitalization, raw materials exports, and increased productivity did not create more jobs. Dramatic testimony to this condition is found in the fact that during the thirty-five years of the Porfirian regime the percentage of the total population involved in industrial pursuits remained constant. Foreign capital displaced peasants, but the lack of a dynamic domestic economy meant that the enclaves of industry were too small to absorb them.

Foreign capitalization and increased per-worker productivity had reduced the total number of employed textile producers from 60,000 in 1895 to 40,000 before 1910. Between 1898 and 1907 the number of looms and spindles in the ever more centralized and streamlined textile factories increased from 13,944 to 23,507 and 469,547 to 693,842, respectively. Although the national population increased by one-third, foreign capitalization decreased the number of textile workers at the same time it diminished the number of peasant farmers. The restricted, foreign orientation of Mexican production failed to create the internal market demands needed to foster the growth of a dynamic wide-based domestic industrial complex after the limits of employment for infra-structure construction, mining, and the great estates had been reached.

Although railroads, communications, banking, mining, petroleum, and commercial farming output grew, Mexico became a grim setting for the "obsolete" artisans of the countryside towns. The arrival of the foreign-owned railroads and the accompanying abolition of protective tariffs compounded the problems presented by the new textile factories. Combined, they meant job displacement for the artisans through imports and factory production of industrial commodities. Import-export merchants prospered, but artisans faced proletarianization. Yet the 82,000 new jobs created between 1895 and 1910 were minuscule in the face of 30,000 displaced artisans, hundreds of thousands of displaced peasantry, and a population growth of more than 3 million.

During the last decade of the regime manufacturing real wages declined to somewhere between 42 and 36 centavos per day. This estimate, however, is based upon the unrealistically optimistic figure of 59 centavos per day as the average wage in 1910. Company records and the personal papers of American owners reveal significantly lower pay rates, averaging only 37 devalued centavos per day in central Mexico. In 1908 and 1909 the directors of the giant San Antonio de Abad textile plant in Mexico City, like other factories in central Mexico, were unable to pay dividends. Waves of strikes swept the textile factories in the center of the nation from 1907 through 1911.

Reflecting national trends, Veracruz, central Mexico's entrepôt for the North Atlantic nations, suffered volatile price increases. Foreigners—especially Spaniards, the French, and Germans—held over 95 percent of the city's private property, and the weakening peso contributed to a doubled cost of living between 1901 and 1911. Daily wages increased from 38 centavos in 1893 to only 62 centavos in 1911. The centavos, devalued by one-half in 1905 and facing steady inflation wrought by the silver basis of Mexican currency, did not go far in the port city.[8]

Like the mining support industries of the Bajío before the independence revolution, the new Porfirian enterprises found severely limited demand for their goods in the domestic marketplace. The mines and railroads were the principal consumers of manufactured products. Unlike the mining industry, whose smelters offered the advantage of escape from U.S. customs duties on imported ores, the Mexican manufacturing industry found little opportunity for exports. As mining slumped and the workforce dwindled, the Mexican support industries that depended on the mines for consumption of their products suffered. Mining, because of its sizable workforce, was the key to continued industrial prosperity in the north. Cattle ranch employment was limited because most hides left the country uncured while agricultural produce and fibers for industrial use could be shipped in raw bulk. Prepared tobacco exports suffered prolonged depression after 1899; sugar exports fell from over one-third of the national product in 1905 to only 3 percent of export earnings in 1909.

In the north—especially Chihuahua, which was the site of the greatest mining activity—the slumping silver, copper, lead, and zinc sectors of the Mexican mining industry compounded the agricultural disaster. The towns of the north, from Aguascalientes to Chihuahua, teemed with unemployed miners and industrial workers after 1908. Many of the unemployed workers in Chihuahua had returned from the closed mine fields and labor violence in Colorado. They confronted a grim combination of unemployment and food shortages. Meanwhile the owners of 19 of the 142 cotton factories and textile mills in central Mexico had closed down by 30 June 1910. Total exports shrank 4 percent in 1910, and the value of freight handled at Veracruz slid 23 percent between 1908 and 1909. The economy was traumatized.[9]

MONETARY AND FISCAL CRISIS

The imbalance between capital-intensive export enclaves and the less commercial labor-intensive modes of production rendered Porfirian development a social disaster. Foreign banks, located in cities with undercapitalized industries and technology, and mass underemployment, funded favored enterprises devoted to export production. Commercial agricultural estates in Morelos and elsewhere exported crops to cities and ports while villages disintegrated and peasants suffered privation. Foreign mine owners imported labor-saving technology, redoubling output for export, while unemployment grew around them. Railroads whisked mineral and tropical export crops away at shipping prices that forced the great majority to transport domestic consumables by cart and burro on the old roads.

Poverty and hardship were symptoms of a deeper malaise. The regime had artificially and suddenly imposed commercial agriculture, a factory system of industrial production, and a monetary exchange system that had taken centuries to develop in Europe upon a traditional prefactory artisan and peasant self-sufficiency-oriented society with minimal interregional trade. The centuries-long evolution of European trade routes and marketing relationships between city, town, and hamlet from the Middle Ages to the Industrial Revolution, with intermittent eras of growth in commercial farming and petite bourgeois enterprise, had taken on the appearance of sudden change in Europe upon the rise of empire in America, Asia, and Africa, the drama of the enclosure movement in England, and the violent rise to power of the national bourgeoisie in France. The resulting European institutions, banks, railroads, and multinational companies were superimposed on Mexico in their advanced form during the short span of thirty-five years.

Provincial elites, with their traditions of local economic hegemony and semiautonomous home rule, suddenly confronted powerful foreign companies and an intrusive central government. Peasants experienced enclosure without the industrial opportunities made available earlier to displaced Englishmen by the growing economic complexes and world markets of Birmingham and Liverpool. Imports and factory output saturated the limited consumption potential of an unprepared and in many ways still precapitalist system, displacing the industrial artisans. Meanwhile most of the technically trained—engineers, accountants, and lawyers—found advancement in society, government, and the foreign-owned and administered companies impossible. For twenty-five years, however, the economy and expectations grew. The foreign-owned and controlled apparatus for extracting the nation's resources expanded while its limited interest in the domestic market left it incapable of realizing more than a small part of Mexico's potential.

The government and metropolitan elites lacked the financial resources, will, or knowledge necessary to initiate the great hydraulic projects needed to develop domestic agriculture. They did not have the power to build the industrial complexes essential for interacting with a commercially successful countryside of small farmers. The intensity of commercial exchange within the domestic economy was insufficient to support the capitalism evident in Western Europe and the United States. The ruling laissez-faire ideology rendered the government intellectually incapable of treating the socioeconomic crisis that emerged on a national scale after 1899. Foreign capital was unwilling to venture support for enterprises where there were no markets, and the Mexican campesinaje lacked the capital required to become cash-earning urban-oriented truck farmers. Yet the system could have survived, as have other socioindustrial failures of the Third World, had it made the transition from peasant-artisan to farmer-factory production. Instead it suffered the simultaneous breakdown of domestic agricultural production, rising interest rates, fiscal crisis, the devaluation of silver, and the inflationary demise of the peso.

The weakness of Mexico's currency in the last years of the regime left the government afraid of insolvency, unwilling to meet the rising costs of infrastructure development and the needs of the populace. The problem was rooted in the long-term decline of silver and the increasing cost of indebtedness. The devaluation of silver caused inflation, weakened the peso, reduced real wages, drove up the costs of land improvements such as irrigation, provoked industrial layoffs and shutdowns, and enabled foreign investors to buy property at low prices.

During the 1890s the United States under the Sherman Silver Purchase Act of 1890, voraciously consumed the Mexican mineral. The Sherman Act provided for the purchase of 4 million ounces of silver per month, to be paid for by treasury notes redeemable in gold. U.S. gold reserves fell by 50 percent in only three years. As a result, in the late 1890s the U.S. government experienced increasing pressure from bankers, creditors, and international merchants who wanted to deflate currencies in order to safeguard the profitability of their domestic and foreign loans and investments. A liquidity crisis in the repayment of U.S. debts to Great Britain as a result of the loss of gold reserves reinforced their argument. The more valuable U.S. currency would enhance the ability of American institutional borrowers to repay their foreign indebtedness while offering advantages to

American domestic creditors by ensuring the real value of the internal debt.

America's return to the gold standard compounded the Porfirian regime's fatal economic problems. After 1900 the increased buying power of American currency in Mexico versus the declining peso offered tremendous advantages in the purchase of real property and material resources. Mexico was a principal focus of U.S. foreign investments at the time. In the 1900 U.S. presidential campaign William McKinley, a Republican gold standard advocate, defeated William Jennings Bryan, the Democratic leader who was supported by an important alliance of silver mining companies, landholders, land speculators, and individual debtors. The Currency Act of 1900 quickly followed, establishing the gold dollar as the national unit of value. That act alarmed the Mexican government and jeopardized its silver-dependent economy.

By 1904 Mexico's combined internal and external debt, conservatively estimated, had reached $250 million. Secretary of the Treasury Limantour described the roots of the situation as basically a crisis caused by the instability and the decline in the value of silver: "It is advisable that a clear and frank investigation be initiated . . . in order to arrive at an agreement with the concerned nations [establishing] stability in the price of silver." Limantour feared that Mexico's inflation would lead to political unrest and drive away foreign investment. An economic slowdown would bring about fiscal insolvency. He appointed a special committee to work out a series of international agreements. In 1903 Mexico and China jointly proposed a fixed ratio of gold to silver to the U.S. government. The objective was stability for the peso, a prerequisite for investor confidence. Limantour's committee recommended a four-point program: (1) establish a more stable system of international exchange; (2) create a new money system based on a fixed ratio between silver and gold; (3) encourage the Mexican government to purchase gold abroad to guarantee the value of its silver notes; and (4) the immediate cessation of free coinage by Mexican private banks and mints.[10]

Limantour's committee then visited Mexico's creditors in the United States, Brussels, Paris, and The Hague. It met with its fellow debtors in St. Petersburg and China. Mexico and China then joined in the multinational deliberations dominated by the governments and financiers of the North Atlantic powers. The U.S. government accepted Limantour's proposals but with a much lower value on silver than he had hoped. On 25 March 1905 the Mexican government promulgated the new currency system. It set the value of the silver peso at 75 centigrams of gold, or 50 cents (U.S.). At 50 cents valuation the weakening peso immediately declined 50 percent in purchasing power, but was temporarily stabilized. For the next two years wild fluctuations in the value of the peso were avoided, and foreign capital rushed into the economy to take advantage of lowered property costs for gold-based money. Mexican exports competed on better terms because they could now be bought at only 50 percent of their previous cost. Then, in order to ensure the continued reliability of the new peso, Limantour began purchasing and stockpiling gold in New York, maintaining a large balance there. Foreign exporters and investors heralded the deposits as security against devaluation.[11]

The drastic drop in value of the silver peso in Mexico adjusted the currency to the metal's declining worth in the United States, where Mexico conducted most of its foreign trade. The decrease in value could have created havoc in the U.S.-dominated mining industry of northern Mexico, but the government avoided that contingency by removing import taxes on the blasting powder and machinery needed by foreign companies in their operations. The savings totaled 4 million pesos per year for mine operators, compensating them for the reduced but stabilized value of their ore. American mining companies began exporting silver in rapidly increasing amounts, undermining the new peso valuation by flooding the U.S. silver market. The Guggenheim-controlled American Smelting and Refining Company flourished and quickly became the largest mining and smelting complex in the nation. Mexico was selling its metals cheaply and gained short-term liquidity.

The silver peso's lower value increased inflationary pressure. Limantour hoped for long-term stability by tying the value of silver to gold. The plan was to attract greater foreign investment, upon which the growth and continued vitality of the economy depended, but Limantour's actions had three immediately negative effects. First, the cost of imported consumer goods increased from 10 to 25 percent but much more in localities such as Cananea, which imported most necessities. Imports declined more than 50 percent in 1908–1909. Second, Mexican silver fled to foreign markets, where it had more value. The export of silver acted upon the masses like a tariff barrier, causing higher prices. It led to higher interest rates for the few domestic industrialists and pequeña burguesía. Third, it doubled the size of Mexico's foreign debt.

On 19 November 1906, in an attempt to recoup lost revenues and compensate for the erosion of the peso caused by the flood of silver moving to the United States, the government attached a 10 percent surcharge on silver exports. Until that time silver profits were leaving the Mexican economy directly, with minimal government or spin-off benefits. The new surcharge gave the regime additional income to service foreign debts, but the government's anti-social-services bias prevented the earnings from passing on as public works or relief.[12]

The agreement reached by the international commissions in their effort to solve the world trade and currency exchange problem offered only temporary relief to Mexico. Adopting the recommended austerity program, the government did momentarily attract more foreign capital investments in 1906 and 1907 because devaluation had made Mexican property and labor cheap, but it undermined domestic capital. The long-term decline of silver, with its undercutting effect on the national currency, hurt Mexico's artisan and working classes, small store owners, and shopkeepers. After 1905 they were increasingly joined by the provincial elites and domestic capitalists who lost heavily.

Despite the high cost of devaluation in order to achieve international solvency, the problem was not solved. The nation remained at a trade disadvantage because too many countries produced unessential silver, including Japan, which competed with Mexico in Asia, and the United States, whose domestic output greatly reduced Mexico's largest market. Porfirian economists feared free silver coinage because it destabilized prices and the currency; but when the problem came up again, it was more sudden and serious than they had anticipated. The economic panic of 1907–1908 swept Wall Street. Twenty percent of the banks in Texas closed. New investment funds for Mexico dried up. A Porfirian economist described the calamity and Mexico's reliance upon the U.S.: "The crisis in Mexico is . . . the result of the terrible crisis in the United States and the world marketplace."[13]

On 28 March 1908 the government inaugurated the National Railways of Mexico and assumed an indebtedness of $117 million pesos. During the fifteen months between the time the government announced partial nationalization plans and the consummation of those plans, its fiscal situation deteriorated. In 1905 government income reached a Porfirian apogee of 129,425,577 pesos. In 1907, the economic crisis reduced that total to 114,953,911 pesos, yet there was a 29 million-peso budget surplus. In 1908 total revenues dropped to 102,483,107 pesos, with millions diverted to emergency corn import purchases. Government income had declined 26 percent in two years.

Assumption of the railroad debt increased the already tremendous burden of public and private Mexican financial obligations. In 1886 the Díaz regime, in an effort to placate foreign creditors, recognized and gained consolidation of the debts of various nineteenth-century governments and even the empire of Maximilian. By 1910 Mexico's officially estimated foreign debt of 49,801,399 pounds sterling, or about $250 million in gold, was a disastrous five times the national budget. The large internal debt increased the burden. Much of the money used to buy out American railroad stockholders in 1908 came from loans from French banks headquartered in the capital. By 1910 the French held 33 million pounds sterling, or about 66 percent of the state's indebtednss. The British held 16.5 percent and the Americans, only 12 percent of Mexico's obligations. The Europeans held an 88 percent share. The official interest rate averaged to 5 percent; the real rate was 7 percent. The cost of servicing the debt, while within the government's ability to pay, grew rapidly to 25 percent of the budget and increased fiscal trepidation.[14]

The 1908–1909 government budget passed in the wake of rising social and political unrest. Uprisings at Cananea, Río Blanco, Casas Grandes, Corralitos, Janos, Las Vacas, and the rural areas of Veracruz, Tabasco, Campeche, and the Isthmus of Tehuantepec combined with a wave of strikes and factory closings in the Mexico City area. At the same time, "foreign bank capital was withdrawn in sizeable amounts owing to the economic crisis in the world markets." The crisis underlined the decline in imports from 322,000,000 pesos in 1907–1908 to 156,500,000 pesos in 1908–1909.

At the conjuncture when government spending was needed most, Díaz and Limantour concerned themselves with balanced budgets. Since 1884, when the González regime faced insolvency, Díaz had believed that government overspending was the greatest danger of all. Pressured by large increases in government indebtedness, Díaz tightened the purse strings just as the social crisis deepened. In 1908–1909, despite emergency corn purchases to avert mass famine and reduce food riots, the aging president and the minister of the treasury boasted that their government spent only 93 million of the 104 million pesos budgeted by Congress! In 1909–1910 the government expended 5 million pesos less than its income in a suicidal effort to remain solvent in the face of rising infrastructure costs.[15]

In 1909–1910, despite spending 15 million pesos on emergency corn imports, the government again refused to spend all of the money budgeted or received. It expended 97 million pesos in that year while collecting 104,275,854 in taxes and garnering a total income of 115,672,731. The ancien régime was saving money in the midst of an agricultural breakdown, silver devaluation, a 75 percent vacancy rate in mining claims, plant shutdowns, and strikes. It delayed hydraulic projects. Angry critics noted that water rights for native small-scale food producers had been canceled in favor of irrigation for foreign commercial exporters. During the last fifteen years of the regime's tenure, the era of most rapid railroad, mining, and latifundia growth, the government spent an average of only 4,250,000 pesos per year on public works. The refusal to begin public works projects in the midst of the crisis, caused by the regime's declining income and penchant for budgetary surpluses, constituted a political disaster. Fiscal conservatism removed a major source of social control, contributing to the coming of the revolution.[16]

The thrifty government of Díaz and Limantour claimed a treasury surplus of almost 83 million pesos in the midst of social crisis and an interest burden on its debt that totaled 25 percent of its budget. The government saved money, but public demand for services grew. The principal exploiter of those demands, Francisco Madero, had intimate experience with the problem. His holdings in the La Laguna, downstream from the Tlahualilo Estates owned by the Brown Brothers Bank, Lord Balfour, and Stillman, had been deprived of water because of government-authorized irrigation of foreign-owned lands upstream. Despite Díaz's vacillations in the matter and eventual de jure decisions in favor of the Mexican claimants, Madero was victimized along with the many Mexican ranchero or middle-sized farmers in the area. The Díaz government responded to the problem in the same manner that it had elsewhere in the nation. The foreign land developers not only continued to use the water, but the government refused to support alternative sources of water for Mexican farmers.

The regime's reluctance to expend funds for social services, while providing an infrastructure that benefited the foreigners, gave special meaning to the monetary crisis. The increasing costs of indebtedness provoked a sense of economic paranoia in the government's upper reaches. Díaz and Limantour, seeking to maintain the fiscal solvency of the government, withdrew funds from the already slowing domestic economy. They did so at the moment that a restless public demanded action. Mexican provincial elites complained that devaluation prejudiced their wealth. The state of the economy provided the basis from which the inevitable charges of corruption and special favors could be taken seriously. The crisis of the Porfirian economy was central to Madero's motivation and public acceptance.

THE DICTATORIAL STATE

The reorganization of agriculture as an export-oriented system of production, with growing colonies of American immigrants, and the growth of foreign-controlled railroads and extractive industries were the destabilizing features of Mexican capitalism in the late nineteenth and early twentieth centuries. To achieve those ends the Díaz regime applied force to the Mexican producing classes, deunionizing industrial workers and suppressing rural village autonomy. It temporarily achieved new levels of profit for foreign and domestic capital in all sectors of the economy. Foreign investors and domestic elites benefited from the cheap labor in the mines and industry that they dominated.

The resistance of the rural and industrial working classes created a need for the state to reach new levels of force. The foreign-dominated system of production thus had the effect of encouraging the use of government violence, not because foreign capital desired that result but because the contradictions between the Mexican working classes and the capitalist elites required it. The level of violence required resulted in the creation of large security forces.

Between 1900 and 1910 the rural police force, recruited largely from areas with high percentages of economically displaced peasants and workers, numbered about 2,400 men. The government positioned the rurales to protect textile factories, railroads, communications, mines, and commerce and to counteract those villages opposed to the intrusion of commercial enterprise. By 1905 the rise of industrial labor unrest caused the redeployment of rurales. In that year 80 percent of the rural police forces were stationed in factories for the sole purpose of keeping "the workers in line."[17] Located between two oceans, the United States, and Guatemala, Mexico had little potential for foreign warfare. The 2,400 rurales combined with a 14,000-man army, several thousand irregulars, and large numbers of local policemen to maintain social control. In that way the ruling class maintained "peace" during the enclosure process, enhanced its ability to exploit the impoverished masses, and provided the security needed to attract foreign capital.

By the twentieth century the Porfirian government was largely composed of an aged clique rendered increasingly obsolete by the creation and growth of new social and political groups that emerged as a result of overall economic growth. These middle classes—or, better stated, pequeña burguesía, because they were not "middle"—espoused a new nationalism, aspired to a share in polity, and wanted a government directly responsive to their interests. The narrowly based government, from which they were excluded, was immune to their increasing appeals. The governors of Puebla, Coahuila, and Guanajuato, surrounded by their extended families, had occupied their offices for fifteen years before the revolution broke out.

Luis Terrazas governed Chihuahua for twenty years. Several state governors claimed more than twenty-five years of tenure. The governor of Tlaxcala claimed the longevity record: he ruled for thirty-four years, the entire span of the Porfiriato.

The political structure prevented the participation of aspirants from newly important socioeconomic groups. The new pequeña burguesía and urban working class demanded social reforms and government services of a regime that ideologically never accepted that role as appropriate for the state to assume. The growing pequeña burguesía found important allies among the previously semiautonomous northern provincial elites, whose remoteness from Mexico City and accessibility to U.S. arms purchases made them particularly important. These two groups and the industrial workers separately demanded a greater degree of freedom and restoration of national integrity in the face of foreign economic domination. They reflected a changing moral consensus in the nation. Peasant demands to restore lands lost during the enclosure process and an end to outside intrusions into their pueblo economies and political life were now matched by the nationalism of the other groups.

Because of its narrow and obsolete political base, the government fell out of touch with the rising tide of dissent. The regime's political base was rooted in alliances made during the 1870s. It had failed to incorporate the new groups that came into being because of the economic growth that took place between 1876 and 1907, or to address their needs and aspirations. After developing an elaborate security structure and experiencing sustained economic and political success, the Porfirian political economy went into crisis.

AMERICANS AND OTHER FOREIGNERS

During the Porfiriato Mexico underwent a dramatic increase in foreign political influence and economic control. Between 1880 and 1900 the rate of profits in the United States dropped 30 percent. Between 1900 and 1910 the rate of profits declined another 15 percent. In the last twenty years of the nineteenth century, confronted with rising labor unrest and higher costs at home, American capitalists increasingly sought relief in foreign investments. In 1900 fully one-half of all U.S. foreign investments were in Mexico. The momentum of American economic expansion into the southwestern states continued on to the Pacific and into neighboring Mexico.

Massive quantities of American capital joined previously important British, French, Belgian, and German holdings, transferring the ownership of the means of industrial production, transportation, communications, banking, and natural resources from indigenous to foreign hands. The economic power of the Mexican bourgeoisie survived only in agriculture, and in that sector prosperity was measured largely in terms of access via foreign-owned railroads to urban markets, while American holdings reached the monumental total of over 100 million acres of the most profitable lands.

By 1910 foreign concerns exercised control over 130 of Mexico's largest 170 enterprises. The largest capitalized company was the partially nationalized Ferrocarriles Nacionales de México. With holdings purchased at high prices by the Mexican government, the primarily American and some European owners had not surrendered their active control of the railroads despite a new quasi-board of directors in Mexico City. Foreigners owned or controlled the remainder of the largest ten companies in the nation. Mexican representation as minority stockholders existed in only two concerns, the Banco Nacional de México and the Banco Central Mexicano, French-contolled institutions.

The foreign owners, with their overwhelming economic power and their respective embassies, demanded and received special police security and tax concessions, helping to shape Mexican polity. Their most serious problems came from their own rivalries. Beyond their central economic contributions, the government was deeply involved with foreign owners on a personal level. Porfirian cabinet officers and members of the president's family sat in their directorates as well-paid "counselors," and sometimes in even higher offices, but were not active in the management. The government did exploit the competitive differences between the United States and British oil companies and after 1900 increasingly favored the interests of Lord Cowdray over those of the more immediate and therefore more threatening Americans.

Among the high-ranking Porfirian officials who affiliated with the foreigners, Minister of Foreign Relations Enrique Creel served as president of the French-controlled Banco Central Mexicano. The minister of war and marine, General Manuel González, served as president of the French-controlled El Buen Tomo tobacco company. Olegario Molina, Minister of Development, acted as a director of several of Cyrus McCormack's International Harvester enterprises in Mexico. A wide range of Díaz government officials and family members, including the president's son, sat as officers or in honorary positions in dozens of companies. Mrs. Díaz's family shared in the operations of several of Lord Cowdray's companies. Strikes at these concerns' facilities by the closely watched industrial workers brought swift reprisals from the armed forces and police.[18]

A deepening liaison between the regime and the foreign companies accompanied the latters' takeover of the Mexican economy. Government officers granted formal business concessions in return for salaried and other remunerative positions. The alliance of foreign companies and government functionaries affected official decisions for the granting of new concessions, business regulation, taxes, and labor policy. This alliance presented formidable competition to nationalistic provincial elites and domestic businessmen in their search for opportunities.

The government-foreign enterprise alliances also competed with the industrial working class. At the invitation of Finance Minister Limantour, the predominantly French textile factory owners formed the Centro Industrial Mexicano in order to regulate and fix prices and formulate an aggressive labor policy in the face of rising unrest. Foreign ownership of industry and government complicity in the breaking of strikes blended working-class interests and nationalism leading to the uprisings at Río Blanco and Cananea.

Foreign domination of the economy and its subordination of the Mexican state outraged the emergent pequeña burguesía and the provincial elites. Large-scale giveaways of land in the northern tier of states—which included the sale, at token prices, of 10,500,000 hectares of land in Baja California Sur out of a land mass of 14,400,000 hectares—offended the national pride of the pequeña burguesía. It jeopardized the economic position, social status and political power of the provincial elites. Accustomed to semiautonomy through their geographic remoteness, they saw resources and opportunity passing to outsiders.

The enabling legislation passed in 1884 overturned a legal tradition giving the government ownership of the nation's subsoil resources, which dated from the Roman law established by the Spaniards. It passed because the government wanted these zones settled and developed by agricultural colonists. When the Americans first moved in, the nationalistic Mexican intelligentsia reacted with anguish, describing them as "that swarm of ants which is invading . . . which has begun sending revolvers and establishing barrooms everywhere."[19] By the end of the Porfiriato, U.S. consuls reported that "the lower class . . . might well direct their antagonisms toward Americans." James Le Roy, the Consul at Durango, reported:

> A very large part of the press in Mexico, and particularly of the less important periodicals of the provincial towns, . . . such newspapers as are rarely seen

> outside their immediate vicinity, are indulging in constant attacks upon the government of the United States, its people and everything American.[20]

The American colonists came as part of an empresario operation as old as the Spanish Reconquest, a tradition brought to America by the Conquistadores and used to expand the English holdings on the east coast of Indian America. The provincial elites and campesinos found little solace in historical precedent, however. Consortiums of powerful American investors that included the largest companies in the United States and thousands of colonists claiming small landholdings took over wide expanses of timber, farming, ranching, petroleum, and mining properties across the nation. By 1910 of the approximately 75,000 Americans residing in Mexico, 16,000 lived in agricultural colonies; 15,000 worked small holdings; and 5,000 were employed in the mines.

In the international context Mexico was only one of many nations in which factory-made commodities introduced at cheap prices by expansive industrialized countries broke down exclusionary resistance of traditional economies and their peasant and artisan-based production. One key phase in this process was the Porfirian government's abolition of the state and local tariffs known collectively as *alcabalas*. The removal of the alcabalas encouraged the increase of extractive enclave industries such as mining, export agriculture, and the textile factories, which transformed the Mexican economy.

The new commercial and industrial export agricultural complex moved Mexico from traditional peasant production toward a labor-intensive form of capitalist production. It was accomplished, however, through the extreme violence and repression of the rural masses needed to carry out land consolidation. It intensified the worst features of the feudal system of patriarchal and caste social relations associated with the great estates of earlier times.

A U.S. government report on the operation of the 300,000-acre San Pablo Hacienda by the San Pablo Company, owned by the International Development Company, a subsidiary of the United Security Life Insurance Company, described the labor system of the American management, a mode of operation that prevailed along the Gulf coast in Tabasco and Campeche:

> In practice, the workmen were in debt to an employer. He sold the laborers by assigning such accounts for a consideration. To the workmen's account of indebtedness was added the commission of a labor agent, transportation and other expenses, and a new contract for labor for that amount was executed.

> Most of the workmen signed such contracts by making their marks since they were illiterate. Such laborers were then compelled to work for the new employer, and apparently they could not even select such employer. The claimant is authority for the statement that some of their laborers had worked seven years, 1904–1911, and were still heavily in debt. When such workmen were no longer needed, the employer sold the accounts of indebtedness to another concern, who repeated the process. As a practical result, such laborers were never out of debt and therefore never able to offer their services on the open market.[21]

Foreign capital reinforced the imbalance of power between plantation owners and agrarian laborers, exacerbating the coercion associated with industrial export agriculture. The Porfirian hacienda created a subordinate labor force in the countryside and acted as the connecting link between Mexico's rural working class and the marketplace of North Atlantic capitalism. It provided the basis for metropolitan access to rural labor and the expropriation of agricultural production. Foreign capital intensified the repressive labor system over a wide area of central and southern Mexico.

Mexico's traditional class/caste structure exercised a key role in determining the characteristics of the growing Porfirian economy. Foreign capital, in its search for resources and profit, was not committed to the maintenance of underdevelopment and labor-intensive modes of production. Rather, the Mexican social environment provided the opportunity to take advantage of the low labor costs of an inequitable social structure. That opportunity attracted foreign capital, but unlike the colonization of Africa and Asia, investors in Mexico usually did not have to use their own force. They came at the invitation of a government in competition for investments with the states of Latin American and Europe's colonies in Asia and Africa. Foreign capital reinforced the Mexican state, inevitably aiding it in the maintenance of imbalanced class relations and national income distribution. With satisfaction American hacendados reported the docility of the "natives" in Oaxaca, Tehuantepec, San Luis Potosí, and Guanajuato, who stepped to the side, doffed their hats, and bowed their heads while the foreigners passed them on the road or trail.

The structure of world trade during the Porfirian era induced an international division of labor in which Mexico joined other underdeveloped nations in the production of raw materials such as rubber, sugar, henequén, minerals, and petroleum. Foreign investment in the Mexican economy leaned heavily toward access to and extraction of natural resources. During the Porfiriato more than 40 percent of the capital created ten railroad companies whose lines connected Mexico City with the port of Veracruz and several U.S. border points. The railroad system, designed and built by foreigners, provided for the direct transportation of products out of Mexico to the United States and Europe. It offered only limited east-west connections between the provincial cities, secondary ports, and industrial centers to assist in the autonomous development of the Mexican interior. In the south rubber, henequén, sugar, fruits, and hardwoods were shipped directly to the United States from the cities of Campeche, Carmen, Progresso, Salina Cruz, and Puerto Mexico. By 1910 the hardwood forests between the Gulf of Mexico and the Guatemalan border were almost entirely depleted; American owners replanted them with millions of rubber trees and henequén plants. The unprocessed hardwoods were shipped away after having been cut into crudely hewn planks.[22]

By 1910 foreign capitalists had amassed some 17 percent of their capital in fifty-two banks, giving them financial dominance over the Mexicans; another 17 percent of the foreign presence in the Mexican economy dominated the mining industry. Petroleum, a new and rapidly growing industry, exported crude oil directly to Texas, other American states, and England. Its share of the total of foreign-invested capital in 1910 was slightly less than 6 percent. Agriculture, livestock, and timber are traditionally reported to have received a little more than 16 percent of the total, but company records demonstrate that the figure is low.

Given a different Mexican social system, foreign capital would not necessarily have reinforced unbalanced growth and social backwardness in agriculture, mining, and industry. The products left Mexico in their crude, unprocessed forms, however. The owners achieved production and profits via labor-intensive great estate industrial export agriculture and enclave mining and labor-repressive industry. Foreign investment dominated the developing enclave capitalist system of production and technology. Foreign capitalists prevented the development of a dynamic entrepreneurial Mexican bourgeoisie in control of a diversified and balanced economy because of their overwhelming economic strength and control of international markets. The Maderos had to compete with Guggenheim, Stillman, Balfour, the Brown Brothers Bank, and the Rockefeller trust.

The growth of the new system of production created greater interaction with and reliance upon the international marketplace. The Mexican economic crisis of 1900–1910 demonstrated that the government was unable to defend Mexican interest groups from foreigners or to protect the national economy.

Diminution in the price of exported goods, combined with an American decision to restrict silver purchases in 1902, resulted in a serious decline in national income. The economy continued in crisis until 1905, when devaluation temporarily resolved the slowdown in foreign investments, but that step precipitated increases in the national debt, which by 1910 totaled over £50 million, more than ten times the amount owed less than 20 years earlier.[23] Real interest rates totaled 7 percent. Devaluation meant reduced income for the purchase of imported manufactures and higher prices for landowners, small and medium-sized merchants, and industrialists. These groups also lacked the cash liquidity needed to make large new investments and recoup their capital losses resulting from devaluation. The biggest losers in the fall of the peso, however, were the domestic-oriented small and middle-sized agriculturalists, the backbone of the provincial and local elites.

The economic crises between 1899 and 1910 in the industrialized countries caused the international companies located in Mexico to reduce the rate of growth in their new investments and loans while demanding higher prices for their manufactured goods. Inflation, brought about by higher textile price demands and food shortages after 1902 and compounded by devaluation in 1905, caused a dramatic reduction in the standard of living for the new urban pequeña burguesía. Inflation also meant diminished real wages and unemployment for the urban working class. World cotton prices rose 98 percent between 1900 and 1910 and drove up the price of finished domestic textile goods in underdeveloped countries. Reduced consumption, labor cutbacks, and wage reductions resulted.

The vast tracts of land used in the production of cash-earning industrial-agricultural export crops consumed in advanced economies of the North Atlantic nations meant fewer hectares available for the raising of domestic foodstuffs. During the first twenty-five years of the Porfiriato increased yields through fertilizers and technology more than compensated for the reduced lands in use for the production of these essentials. After 1903, however, successive crop blight, drought, and freezes reduced agricultural output, triggered food shortages, and aggravated working-class unrest. The relatively firm prices for domestic foodstuffs before 1900 suffered inflation between 1900 and 1910, and agricultural wages declined 17 percent between 1895 and 1910. The reduction in rural real wages was even greater considering the 50 percent devaluation of 1905.

During the first twenty-four years of the Porfiriato corn, beans, chile, and wheat costs rose at an acceptable average of 4 percent per year in the urban areas; per capita income also went up. After 1900, in ten years, chile costs rose 193 percent and beans, 64 percent. During the final three years the problem reached a crisis stage. Between 1907 and 1910 corn prices went up 38 percent and wheat, 20 percent. In the northern provinces, hit hard by corn shortages, the price of that basic commodity more than doubled in the last year before the revolution. Industrial workers, whose daily income in real wages declined from 1.92 pesos in 1897 to 1.40 pesos in 1907, faced an even steeper decline in their buying power.[24]

If the Porfirian social transformation was to succeed, it required the continued and growing presence of foreign capital. A diminution in the flow of that wealth threatened the nation's political and economic stability. Those interruptions came after 1899. The public blamed the state for Mexico's subordinate role in the world marketplace and the predominant position of foreigners in the domestic economy.

The Porfirian regime experienced two fundamentally distinct yet closely related phases. One, from the late 1870s to 1900, featured sustained rapid economic growth and political stability. The other, from 1900 to 1910, manifested an erratic economy and destabilized polity. The government, in what the nationalistic revolutionaries saw as a treasonous foreign-dominated program, intensified Mexico's economic and political relationship with the industrialized nations, especially the United States, to an extreme degree.

The ancien régime's emphasis on the development of mineral and agricultural exports with overwhelming American domination was rooted in Mexico's lack of finance capital and global economic and domestic labor relationships established during three centuries of Spanish colonialism and early nineteenth-century oligarchical rule. Although foreign-dominated railroads, communications, banking, mining, petroleum, and commercial farming output grew, the new Mexico was a grim setting for the "obsolete" artisans of the countryside towns. The arrival of the railroads, the abolition of protective tariffs, and the building of new textile factories meant job displacement for the artisans through imports and factory production of industrial commodities. Import-export merchants prospered, but Mexico's small industrial producers were destroyed. The new enterprises also displaced local entrepreneurs, peasants, and political officials. Foreign experts dominated the new technology, frustrating the hopes of native aspirants. Local politics were reshaped, overturning provincial and local regimes accustomed to varying degrees of self-defined political power and culture. Lucrative and much sought-after local public works contracts were disbursed on the same narrow excluding criteria.

Industrialization created a marketing system and commercial network that was not integrated with the bulk of public economic exchange. Not the product of a centuries-long pattern of balanced social and economic development, industrialization in Mexico was superimposed upon a minimally commercial society, which created a distorted pattern of social and economic islands. Mexico's revolution was caused by an economic system dependent on foreign capital imports that failed to absorb a displaced peasantry and reduced artisan class and then suffered destabilizing periodic contractions.

The destabilizing results of foreign penetration of the Mexican political economy were manifold, but the salient impacts were economic vulnerability through dependence on sometimes unavailable alien finance capital; an increasing rate of inflation characterized by wildly fluctuating food prices; peasant displacement as a result of agricultural commercialization; the proliferation of small industrial enclaves that failed to provide the employment opportunities needed for the economy successfully to complete enclosure; the defeat and exclusion of regional elites and pequeña burguesía in competition with foreigners for access to opportunity; the political exclusion of regional and local elites by the metropolitan regime; incipient famine in much of the country brought about by reduced acreage committed to domestic food production; and prolonged dictatorship made possible by an alliance with the foreigners, which upset the previous interregional balance of power.

Initially broad based in a Mexico of 9.5 million, the young Díaz regime maintained the general support of the provincial elites and pequeña burguesía until the end of the century. By then the pequeña burguesía was too large to be absorbed by a regime in which some state governors had served since 1876. Cut off from advancement and seeing the major profit-making opportunities passing into the hands of the hated Americans, the pequeña burguesía turned against the regime whose programs brought it into being.

This pattern of cause and effect in Porfirian Mexico reflected worldwide socioeconomic and political destabilization. The causes of the Mexican Revolution paralleled events in Iran, China, and Russia. The Mexican government, like its three counterparts in political-economic crisis, failed to withstand foreign competition and stressed fiscal conservatism in the face of acute social needs while building up enormous debts for infrastructure development in the face of rising interest rates. The new transportation and communications systems served the interests of the foreigners and the power of the national state vis-à-vis the autonomy-minded provincial elites better than they served the citizenry. All four governments failed in their attempt to duplicate the success of the North Atlantic economies by tying themselves to the enormous concentrations of capital that had been developed there. Undercapitalized and lacking the necessary socioeconomic diversity, they fell victim to fluctuations in the money supply and depressed markets.

SEVEN

Global Causation: Iran, China, Russia, and Mexico

INTRODUCTION

In the nineteenth century highly capitalized American and European industry achieved technological breakthroughs in the production of steel, copper, electricity, petroleum, synthetic chemicals, the internal combustion engine, and heavy machinery that resulted in large increases in industrial output and the work force. By the 1870s rising labor costs and working-class militancy combined with the need for more natural resources to stimulate an international search for massive quantities of raw materials, less expensive labor, and new consumers. The global and monopolistic industries that came into being sought access to the populations and resources of the less developed countries in order to meet the needs created by their high levels of investment and production.

Mexico became especially important to U.S. capital, industrial, and trade expansion. As Percy F. Martin put it, "The Anglo Saxon races have already cornered four-fifths of the gold producing mines of the world, and it is, therefore eminently fit that the magnificent mineral interests of Mexico should be likewise mainly in their hands."[1] Other North Atlantic financial and industrial powers had long-standing ties with the nation and continued to invest there, but Mexico was one among many for them. They were also busily expanding into Africa, Asia, and Latin America. For the United States, Mexico, with its common border, inexpensive labor, vast mineral wealth in the north, oil on the Gulf coast, tropical agriculture on the coasts and in the south, and the possible railroad and canal route through Tehuantepec, was central to the achievement of global power. By 1900 half of all U.S. foreign investments were in Mexico and the nation's most powerful capitalists were among the investors.

In 1867 Secretary of State Seward, like Thomas Wentworth Peirce and his kinsman, President Benjamin Franklin Pierce, envisioned a U.S.-controlled American empire embracing North and Central America. Mexico would become a mere state of the union, as would Canada. The business-oriented *Chicago Tribune* called Mexico an "almost virgin outlet for extension of the market of our overproducing civilization." Secretary of State James G. Blaine joined the chorus, informing the Mexican government that the United States desired no more Mexican territory; instead it wanted to invest the "large accumulation of capital, for which its own vast resources fail to give full scope." Blaine's visions had a practical side as well. He believed that American control over Mexico's budding railroad system was central to the establishment of U.S. economic hegemony.

The global expansion of the economies of Belgium, Britain, France, Germany, the United States, and even Russia in Iran provoked a worldwide pattern of revolutionary and nationalistic upheaval in the early twentieth century. At that time four especially strong autochthonous preindustrial societies that previously had been economically and demographically decentralized encountered the irregular but combined effects of industrialization, and the growing strength of national governments under the influence of foreign investors. In order to understand the Mexican Revolution, it must be placed in this global context.

The causes of the Mexican Revolution were duplicated in Iran, China, and Russia. Those countries underwent growing foreign influence and abuses; humiliating subordination to foreign regimes; state collaboration with international financiers while excluding domestic capitalists; and the social, political, cultural, and economic displacement of provincial and local elites, artisans, and peasants. Those factors, combined with the slow growth of employment in industry that failed to absorb displaced peasants and low wages, exacerbated social imbalances, creating endemic peasant and industrial worker unrest. Meanwhile the declining value of silver, fiscal crisis, and rising interest rates created an increasingly erratic cycle of inflation and depression. The result was cross-class dissent rooted in economic and political nationalism, followed by mass unrest and finally revolution.

THE 1905 IRANIAN REVOLUTION

—Ne'er may that evil-omened day befall
When Iran shall become the stranger's thrall!
Ne'er may I see that virgin fair and pure
Fall victim to some Russian gallant's lure!
And ne'er may Fate this angel-bride award
As serving-maiden to some English lord!
Mírza Áqá Khán

In Iran an era of expanding foreign trade and alien influence in the domestic economy began in the early nineteenth century. By the 1890s increasing outside control over the economy created alarm among regional elites, merchants, religious leaders, nationalists, artisans, and peasants. Growing foreign economic power complemented the aliens' increasing political influence in Tehran. The assertive cooperation of the foreigners with the increasingly powerful national government upset its long-standing, albeit strife-ridden, relationship with the Iranian provincial elites.

Before the nineteenth century Iran was a thinly populated amalgam of peoples with differing regional languages and customs tied together by a rich history and cultural pride. The central government had little direct control over those sectors lying beyond the vast stretches of arid lands in the center of the country. On the peripheries regional elites had competed for national power and influence for centuries. Civil war in the late eighteenth century devolved national military and political power on the Qajar shahs. Backed by the British, and under the watchful eye of the Russians, the Qajar shahs dominated Tehran and the nearby northern districts, but away from the center they shared power. The provincial elites of the east and south jealously guarded their own bases of economic and political prestige and ways of life. A royal governor's success in the provinces was measured to a considerable degree by his ability to work with the provincial ruling classes.

The core of the provincial elites were the Ulema, the Shiite clergy. They controlled local government and collected taxes. As high judges they legislated through the interpretation of law and defined the parameters of government. As local magistrates they decided right and wrong and civil and criminal cases. By invoking Shiite ideology they were moral teachers, the dominant ideological and cultural force. Their positions yielded them control over rich church properties, including vast agricultural lands. The Ulemas controlled the larger part of provincial export agriculture. Their families often owned the principal mercantile houses in the provinces.

They legitimized the national government through their recognition of it, and they gave it material support by collecting and paying taxes. They were bastions of stability in the towns of the far-flung provincial outreaches such as Fars, Kerman, Baluchistan, and Khurasan. The Ulemas' control of ideology, their predictable interpretation of the law, and the stable distribution of land, status, and wealth maintained a high degree of law and order at the local level. Linked by family ties to the merchant and landowning classes, they were an essential cog in the administration of government.[2]

During most of the nineteenth century the national government built up its military capacity. British assistance included military advisers, expensive armaments, and subsidies in return for trade concessions. In 1834 a new shah was installed with British and Russian troops on hand. He openly received financial backing from the British government. Russian traders gained strong positions in the Caspian provinces, and British merchants expanded their activities along the Persian Gulf. Meanwhile the Ulema continued successfully to define themselves to the public as the guardians of the Shiite religion and of national integrity. Some of them opposed the shah as a foreign-dominated usurper. After his death in 1848 provincial elite-led rebellions had to be put down in Khurasan.

The second half of the nineteenth century witnessed the beginning of an era of new foreign intrusions for Iran. In 1857 a series of British assaults launched from India forced a resistant Iranian government to concede special nation trading rights and exceptional legal status above those of mere Iranians to British businessmen. In 1869 the Suez Canal opened, sharply reducing the time and difficulty of travel between Western Europe and Iran. By 1889 a telegraphic communications network was in place that connected major towns with the capital and Iran with the world. By mid-century the key to the Iranian government's successful conduct of affairs in the international arena required the skillful balancing of interests between the increasingly more powerful and aggressive British and the ever-present Russians. In the domestic sphere the government was attempting to bring about greater centralized control, economic growth, and infrastructure development through the introduction of modern transport and communications.[3]

Beset with fiscal shortfalls in the midst of arms purchases and infrastructure development costs, the government needed ever greater revenues to maintain itself. The principal sources for those riches were new commercial concessions and higher tariffs. It sold concessions to foreigners for telegraph lines, metallic roads, railroad rights of way, urban streetcar lines, toll roads, port and warehousing facilities, fisheries, banks, mining, tobacco, and natural gas. It even sold archaeological sites.[4]

In 1891 British Baron Julius de Reuter received a concession to establish the Imperial Bank of Persia. The grant included mineral exploration and exploitation rights that eventually led to the formation of the Anglo-Persian Oil Company. By 1900 the bank claimed eight branches distributed in the larger cities. It displaced Iranian merchants as the principal source of banking services. The Imperial Bank of Persia's exclusive right to issue notes soon resulted in the notes becoming the principal form of legal tender in higher financial and commercial exchange. The competitive Russians opened their own Banque des Prêts de Perse in 1890 and soon had offices in their mercantile strongholds at Rasht and Tabriz. The bank quickly arranged some loans for the cash-starved Iranian government, further diminishing the role of Iranian merchants.[5]

The banks established the beginnings of a new national financial structure. Competing with each other, the banks joined with their respective British and Russian interests and quickly moved to develop and control the nation's transportation and communications systems. That move undermined the economic and political hegemonies of the local and provincial elites. Because of the Russian government's security concerns, however, railroads were not built in Iran before the 1905 revolution despite the efforts of Russian merchants to extend a line from Baku to the Iranian interior. The British threat still concerned the tsar's government. As a result the only railroad before 1906 was Belgian owned and ran eight miles from Tehran to the limestone quarries used in urban construction. The Russians, however, did build metallic roads from Rasht and Qazvin to the Caspian port of Enzeli and from Mashhad to the Transcaspian railway. Preferential Russian customs made lower-quality Iranian cotton competitive with Egyptian and American imports. Between 1870 and 1900 Russian imports of Iranian cotton increased from 27 to 12,700 tons. The British developed river navigation in the west running inland from the Persian Gulf toward Isfahan, but interior roads remained the major element in the Iranian commerce and transportation network. In 1905 there were four major improved roads in the country.

Unlike Mexico, Iran's mineral resources played only a small role in the development of the nation's transportation system. Foreign concessionaires did work turquoise, copper, lead, iron, bauxite, cobalt, and marble sites, but the location of labor resources, domestic markets, and carpet manufacturing and agricultural centers usually determined the placement of their endeavors.[6]

The growing road system reflected the fundamental nationwide socio-economic transformation that was under way and the foreigners' role in it. In 1890 the British-owned Imperial Bank of Persia inaugurated and then collected toll fees on the 160-mile highway running south from Tehran to Qum and Arak. That enterprise provided the needed transportation services for the British carpet manufacturers, Ziegler and Company of Manchester and J. C. P. Hotz and Son of London, who dominated the economy in the Arak district from the 1870s. British concerns, assisted by the toll road, established an extensive network of suppliers and operated large weaving factories and dye works in an elaborate areawide complex.

Russian entrepreneurs owned and operated the route from Rasht south and southeast to Qazvin and Tehran. The road opened in 1899, and because of the operators' fee structure it was highly restrictive for Iranian goods moving from the Caspian provinces toward Tehran. It connected the cotton, rice, and silk-rich province of Gilan with the Russian-controlled Caspian Sea traffic. Russian shippers and merchants conducted all of the import and export trade on the Caspian as a result of earlier concessions made in the wake of Russian military advances during the 1860s and 1870s. The Gilan peasantry resisted, both passively and violently, the substitution of silk for rice, their food staple. The favorable freight rates to the Caspian, in contrast to the fees imposed on goods moving toward Tehran, and the higher prices offered by Russian merchants encouraged rice exports to Russia. Annual rice exports to Russia increased from £25,000 in the 1870s to £234,000 in 1892–1893, a fourfold increase in real monetary terms and an even greater increase in terms of actual tonnage.[7]

The peasants continued to cultivate rice in lieu of cotton and silk because of the high costs of equipment needed for the latter two crops, their resentment of pricing and cost abuses resulting from foreign financial control of commercial export agriculture, and government taxes on silk. In the late nineteenth century Gilan produced about two-thirds of the nation's £400,000 in silk exports. Greek merchants had imported new silkworm eggs to Gilan from Japan after disease wrecked the Iranian industry during the mid-1860s and early 1870s. Most of the Gilan silk exports went to France and Italy. However, the social destabilization to be expected from the introduction of commercialized industrial export agriculture was minimized by the rise of Chinese and Japanese competition, which retarded the growth of the Iranian silk industry. Nonetheless Russian mercantile control of the Rasht road was a key element in the development of a northward flow of rice, silk, and cotton exports from Gilan.[8]

The Iranian government operated the third major highway, which ran 120 miles linking northeast Iran to Russian Turkmen through Ashkhabad to Mashhad. This road became the main entryway for oil imports from Baku. From Mashhad the oil was transported to the farthest reaches of the country. Before 1896 traffic consisted largely of crude oil. After that year the Russian government offered preferences on export duties for shipments of refined petroleum entering Iran. The result was a sharp rise in Russian kerosene exports, which quickly took over the Iranian market with an absolute monopoly over domestic consumption in Khorasan. In the south and west British and French capital began exploration for oil resources, but Russian control of the Ashkhabad-Mashhad road gave them an initial advantage.[9]

The fourth major road ran 280 miles from the Isfahan-Yazd tobacco, cotton, and opium-growing complex, west to Ahvaz where British-operated river navigation companies connected the interior Iranian marketplace with Western Europe and the world. The road was under the jurisdictional aegis of the Bakhtiar chiefs, who were able to improve and maintain it with formidable British financing. This road was a key link between the British-dominated Persian Gulf and the interior. The British handled 88 percent of the tonnage that passed through the four principal gulf ports. To their east the Bakhtiar chiefs controlled one of the nation's largest opium-producing zones. The chiefs' domination of the opium trade, both its production and transportation, provoked British claims of "discrimination," despite the fact that they marketed most of the drug for the Iranians. Although the British financiers provided the cash needed by the Bakhtiar provincial elites for one form of transportation, they provoked competition and open resentment from that group when they attempted to move in on opium production.[10]

British influence in the Isfahan area grew rapidly in the last decades of the nineteenth century. In 1890 the Iranian government sold a tobacco concession to the Imperial Tobacco Company of Persia, which, with its £650,000 capitalization, was enormous by Iranian standards.[11] Tobacco cultivation, legal and extralegal, provided a cash crop for peasants and local merchants nationwide. The tobacco concession provoked open hostilities between British entrepreneurs and provincial Iranian elites and peasants. The latter groups regarded the Iranian government's concession to the British concern an unwarranted and intolerable intrusion. Through its tobacco concession the company represented a challenge to local merchant hegemonies not only in the Isfahan-Yazd region but wherever tobacco was grown and sold. In 1891 the outcry against the company's attempts to restrain trade led to internal political turmoil, merchant and Ulema protests, and riots. The government was forced immediately to rescind the company's charter and restore the old system.[12]

Another indicator of the foreigners' influence upon the fundamental national socioeconomic transformation was foreign trade. Between the 1860s and 1905 total trade in real terms quadrupled. The growth in agricultural and manufacturing tonnage was even greater.[13] In 1900 exports totaled an estimated 5 percent of GNP, and imports constituted 8 percent. Then between 1900 and 1905 exports doubled. In 1900 Russia enjoyed 45 percent of the foreign exchange and Britain, 34 percent. Agriculture constituted one-half of the nation's exports. The largest export items in agriculture were dried fruits, opium, rice, and cotton. Manufactures constituted 25 percent of the exports, with carpets the leading manufactured product.[14]

Despite the growth of foreign-controlled economic enclaves very few Iranians benefited. When the 1905 revolution broke out, illiteracy afflicted 95 percent of Iran's estimated 10,200,000 population. Peasant displacement caused by the growth of export-oriented commercial agriculture had resulted in a rural-urban population shift. By the end of the century Tehran and Tabriz totaled 200,000 inhabitants each; their populations had doubled since 1860. Both suffered from extreme overcrowding, an almost total lack of social services, and underemployment. Isfahan claimed 100,000, and seven other centers had over 50,000 each. Those who left the countryside for the cities carried their rural allegiances to the Shiite clergy with them, whereas most of the 55 percent of the citizenry that remained in villages and hamlets hoped to sustain their traditional way of life.[15] Despite the fact that at the end of the century most of the populace still responded to provincial elite authority, urban migration alarmed the rural establishment because it threatened to end its economic and political power and way of life.

In most rural locales where the provincial and local elites sensed a threat to their control, their power was still very much intact. The rural elites held large arable properties amid caste-defined masses of landless peasants. Those elites were made up of merchants, clergy, political officeholders, and the descendants of military colonists who ruled dispossessed nationalities and now sedentary ex-nomads. During the course of the nineteenth century, however, the shahs' regimes had increased their national hegemony at the expense of their provincial rivals. One of the techniques used by the shahs' governments was the issuance of land grants to military colonists. As landowners the hierarchically organized and loyal ex-soldiers employed sharecroppers.

Usually the lands were underdeveloped regions similar to Mexico's northern frontier, and thus the ensuing disputes over proprietorship were between the newcomers and nomads or displaced occupants who lacked legitimacy. In one case 800 colonists at Solduz dominated 4,000 to 5,000 families of serflike sharecroppers and farm workers of various nationalities, including Kurds and Turks. The domination of the serflike peasants and agrarian workers was harsh; heavy taxes were imposed, and extreme force was used against dissenters.[16] Despite their initial differences with the traditional and ethnically distinct nationalities of the countryside, however, the colonists soon settled in and developed vested interests that were frequently at odds with the desires of the outside British and Russian investors who inevitably arrived on the scene endorsed by the national government.

During the thirty years before the 1905 revolution provincial and local elites strove to tighten their hold on the land, local resources, and commercial crops such as opium. They tried to maintain a strong share in the trade of all agricultural products. Despite the grim realities of rural lower-class life the provincial and local elites orchestrated their ideological control over the masses into a growing sense of unity against the central government and the foreigners. As the shah's regime issued concessions to the foreigners and moved closer to them at the expense of the provincial and local elites, it did so at its great peril.

The Iranian government's indebtedness grew rapidly in the 1890s, however, increasing pressure on the regime to open Iran to unprecedented levels of penetration by foreign capital. In 1892 the shah's regime borrowed half a million pounds from the Imperial Bank of Persia in order to pay compensation to the British tobacco monopoly that had been destroyed by provincial elite- and merchant-led nationwide protests in 1891. The loan required new concessions to British capitalists. By 1904 the government, which before 1890 had no debts, owed £4,050,000 to the Imperial Bank and Russian and Anglo-Indian creditors, and interest rates had tripled.

Iranian historians have not investigated the complications wrought by the European-Russian financial shortages and higher interest rates of 1899–1904, but they were severe. Nationalists complained about the exorbitant interest rates charged by the Russians and the Imperial Bank.[17] Contemporaries attributed the government's growing fiscal crisis to "corruption." Ever greater spending needs compounded that universal affliction. Caught between the British and the Russians and striving to control the provinces better, the shah increased military expenditures to one-half the national budget by the end of the century.

Costs incurred in the development of transportation and communications infrastructure constituted a growing drain on government revenues. These obligations included the construction of the Mashhad-Ashkhabad Road, built and then operated by the government; materials and support activities provided to the foreign telegraph concessionaires; various concessions bought back by the state because of public protests, such as the tobacco franchise; indemnities paid to foreigners, merchants, and manufacturers for losses incurred from highwaymen; the dredging of rivers; and port improvement. In the meantime local and provincial elites benefited from the archaic tax farming system, draining off local revenues while collecting much of the bloated bureaucratic pension system income, the costs of which absorbed 25 percent of the state's revenues.[18]

The new and greater role demanded of the state by national economic growth required financial outlays for infrastructure development from the already cash-depleted national government. One solution for the dilemma would have been to reduce the archaic practices of power and wealth sharing with the provincial elites that had maintained the ancient system of loyalties, but that challenge proved too much for the government. It dared not reduce the flow of benefits to the provinces. New outlays for infrastructure development compounded the fiscal problems presented by continuation of the old practices. Government debts mounted. The fiscal crisis deepened, tempting the government to sell yet more foreign concessions and to impose new taxes. The cost of these measures fell on Iranian peasants, workers, merchants, and the petite bourgeoisie and provoked open opposition.

Inflation, another familiar aspect of commercial-economic growth, compounded the crisis. At the turn of the century, in its efforts to attract foreign investment for banking, transport, and communications, the Iranian government linked its currency, the kran, to the West through adoption of the silver standard. That step, given the long-term decline in the value of silver, was clearly intended to create an internationally deflating currency and therefore lessened property values in the domestic market, making investments in Iran attractive to foreigners.[19]

The plan worked well. Foreign capital investment and trade increased rapidly in the 1890s. Between 1900 and 1905 exports leapt upward from 147.3 million krans to 293.0 million krans, compounding the already serious inflationary spiral experienced during the last quarter of the nineteenth century. Two sectors of the economy of strategic importance to the regime's stability were seriously hurt: the domestic dry goods business, controlled by local Iranian artisans and businessmen, and agricultural production in food staples.

The manner of Iran's increasing involvement in the world market at the beginning of the twentieth century contributed to the impoverishment and displacement of the peasantry, urban overcrowding, and unemployment. It immediately threatened the political power of the provincial elites and undermined the economic position of small and large domestic merchants. It also stimulated a commercial revolution in agriculture. Opium cultivation "encroached on the grounds available for cultivation owing to its yielding heavier profits to the cultivator than corn and other cereals."[20] The availability of staples diminished while population grew and prices rose. The highly commercialized northern provinces experienced declining barley production; wheat cultivation declined nationwide. The northern provinces moved from an area of food exports to an area of net food imports. At the turn of the century provincial food shortages and price hikes set off riots that spread to the cities. The crowds focused their protests against foreigners, wholesalers, and bankers. Demanding export controls and fixed food prices, they attacked the numerous British companies and banks. The government belatedly imposed price controls, and the unrest abated.[21]

The revolution of 1905 began when the governor of Tehran ordered some merchants whipped for cornering local sugar supplies. That action precipitated a confrontation between the government and an alliance of alienated elites. Businessmen and Ulema protested the governor's action against Iranian merchants and staged a sit-down strike at the shrine of Shah Abdul Azim. Urban unrest reached a new high in the spring of 1906, when soldiers fired upon crowds in Tehran. The outraged Mujtahid, Shiite clergy, and the merchants protested the soldiers' action, mobilizing even more public support. The government's response was another attempt to repress the unrest. Commercial activities were curtailed in much of the country. A group of bankers and larger merchants ironically sought sanctuary from arrest at the British Legation. They demanded government dismissals, a legal code restricting the power of the national government, and the return of the Mujtahid from Zum, where they had gone for sanctuary. The radicals in the protest were now demanding an elective parliament.

The shah agreed to a national assembly and exiled his ex-grand vizier

RUSSIA
USSR
TURKEY
CASPIAN SEA
WEST AZARBAYJAN
EAST AZARBAYJAN
GILAN
Aras R.
Atrek R.
Lake Urmia
Ahar
Tabriz
Ardebil
Dasht-i Mugan
Reza'iyeh
Hashtrud
Khalkhal
Miyaneh
Rasht
Pumin
Maraghen
Miandoab
Mahabad
Shahindizh
Tikab
Zanjan
Alburz Mountains
Qazvin
KURDISTAN
Karaj
Tehran
Shar-i-Rayy
Varamin
Damavand
MT. Damavand
Sari
Shahi
Gurgan
Bujunurd
Quchan
Darreh Gaz
KHURASAN
Nishapur
Mashhad
Sabzavar
Kashmar
Turbat-i Haydari
Turbat-i Jam
Sanandaj
Paveh
Hamadan
Qumm
DASHT-I KAVIR
Arak
Kermanshah
Borujerd
Kashan
Khorramabad
KERMANSHAHAN
Gonabad
AFGHANISTAN
Shar-i-Kord
Isfahan
ISFAHAN
Birjand
Dezful
Zagros Mountains
Karum R.
Yazd
DASHT-I LUT
IRAQ
SISTAN
Ahvaz
KHUZISTAN
Abadan
Kerman
KERMAN
Zahedan
PAKISTAN
KUWAIT
Shiraz
Bushehr
Jiroft
PERSIAN GULF
FARS
Bandar Abbas
BALUCHISTAN
SAUDI ARABIA
0 100 200 300 400
Km
QATAR
OMAN
Seymour

Iran in 1905

to Khurasan. On 30 December 1906 the broken and dying shah signed a constitution requiring the approval of the Majlis (assembly) for all contracts by the national government for foreign concessions, foreign loans, the sale of public lands, or the commitment of public revenues. The provisions created a constitutional monarchy with a highly restricted franchise that encompassed only the nobility, larger landowners, merchants, and artisan guild members. The peasantry, which constituted over 70 percent of the population, and the unskilled or unlicensed urban workers were excluded from voting.

The shah died on 4 January 1907 and his heir, Muhammed Ali, soon found allies in the fight against the growing power of the Majlis. He appointed as prime minister the pro-Russian Aminu's Sultan, Atabak, an action that outraged nationalists and provoked further nationwide disorders. Atabak was forced to aver loyalty to the new constitution when he arrived in the northern provinces upon his return from exile. Protest riots erupted at Tabriz and a rebellion at Isfahan.

The Russian and Turkish governments took advantage of the chaos by marshaling troops, provoking border incidents, and threatening intervention. Secret political societies involving members of the new national assembly took shape in Tehran. In August Atabak was assassinated. At that point the British and Russian governments signed a treaty, amid assurances of "Persian sovereignty," dividing Iran into three zones. The south became a British zone of influence, the north, Russian; and the center, "neutral."

Protest riots against the shah and the foreigners broke out in the nation's cities. A conflict ensued between the shah's forces, backed by the Anglo-Russo alliance, and the Assembly, supported by urban merchants, artisan guilds, and provincial elites. This leadership rallied the rural and urban masses. By 1908 the Constitutionalist revolutionaries were being called nationalists. The clashes were small, rarely counting more than a few hundred armed men on each side. The rebel forces concentrated on holding the provincial towns.

In April 1909, 4,000 Russian troops occupied Tabriz in the northwest. At the same time, two rebel columns numbering fewer than a thousand men each marched from the northern and southern provinces against the Tehran government. The small size of the rebel units reflected the provincial elites' tight control over the revolutionary movement. Unlike Mexico, China, and Russia, in the Iranian revolution no lower-class-led movements with a mass base took shape. The southern column of nationalist forces was led by the same Bakhliyari of the nation's center that in the 1890s had effectively combated the British tobacco concession and British attempts to penetrate the national merchants' hold on the opium trade. Russian troops moved into Tehran to defend the shah's government. Finally, on 16 July 1909, the shah reached a compromise with the nationalists. He stepped down, and his twelve-year-old-son replaced him.[22]

The Iranian conflict continued for years despite foreign interventions. Turkey, an ally of Germany and Austria, invaded the northwest during World War I; Russian troops continued to occupy other points in the north. The British remained in military control of the south. The provincial elite- and merchant-led Constitutional Revolution of 1905 failed in its objectives because of foreign intervention. The semiautonomous provincial elites, however, had served notice that they would not tolerate the divestment of their power or way of life by intruders or the central government.

The response of Iran's provincial and local elites, petite bourgeoisie, artisans, and peasants to foreign economic, political, and cultural penetration was comparable to that of Mexico despite the great differences in religion, economy, and culture between the two nations. In Iran, like Mexico, regional diversity and degrees of local autonomy, embodied in the Shiite clergy, stimulated regional and local elite opposition to the encroachments of the metropolitan regime and its foreign associates. In Iran the Ulema and provincial elites who controlled landholding and mercantile activity and dominated traditional export industries invoked Shiite and religious ideology. In Mexico local landowners and provincial elites asserted the tenets of liberalism and populism. In Chihuahua and northwestern Iran the descendants of military colonists used their special warfare skills to defend their hegemonies against rivals among local elites and outside intruders. Iranian provincial elites, led by the Ulema, exercised far greater control over the rural masses than their Mexican counterparts. They limited working-class participation in the movement and through controlled mobilization prevented the emergence of peasant demands and movements such as the Villistas and Zapatistas.

The Iranian government's foreign concessions outraged all but the few directly benefiting from the British and Russian entrepreneurial enclaves. Iranian historiography has not revealed data regarding a likely contraction or instability of new Belgian, British, and Russian investments after 1900. The destabilizing effects of cash shortages and higher interest rates on Mexico, China, and Russia are clear, however, and would have seriously undermined the Iranian economy and the shah's development program. The failure of the shah's government to ward off foreign interlopers successfully—indeed, its collaboration with and even submission to them—

provoked indignation, scorn, charges of "corruption," and popular demand for a more representative constitutional government.

In both Iran and Mexico the leaders of the provinces gained mass public support for initially moderate reforms. In both cases "constitutionalism" meant the guarantees of political power and representation enjoyed in the old order. In Iran the Ulema maintained authority over the revolutionary forces by virtue of their hegemonic cultural, economic, and political power over the rural and urban masses. They benefited from the fragmented nature of peasant society. In Mexico the tradition of the autonomous and free village with its collective landholding gave the peasantry an organizational basis that the Iranian peasantry lacked. In both cases direct foreign intervention prevented the revolution's further development. In Mexico the elites' social control over the lower classes was temporarily lost. A full-scale civil war took place, offering the public a wide range of choices before foreign intervention was deemed necessary, and again tipped the scales against the more extreme revolutionists.

THE 1911 CHINESE REVOLUTION

Between 1897 and 1911 recurrent waves of provincial-based unrest and uprisings swept China until the defeat of the Manchu dynasty and the imperial system. The insurrectionary leaders were composed of the bourgeois agricultural and commercial provincial elites and urban petite bourgeoisie, and students, those who succeeded in marshaling support from revolutionary peasants and gave focus to growing insurrectionism among industrial workers. In January 1912 the victorious revolutionaries formed a republican government with Sun Yat-sen at the head. The unrest that brought Sun Yat-sen to power developed during the last sixty years of the nineteenth century.

At the beginning of the nineteenth century China enjoyed a strong and unified culture with a proud historical consciousness that reached back thousands of years. A vast peasantry comprised the great majority of the population, which reached 430 million by mid-century. The great landowners, their middle-sized counterparts, and town merchants dominated the countryside and the peasantry. Village structures remained strong, with about half of the farm population still able to subsist by working its own land and by performing the usual sundry side enterprises practiced by the peasantry of all cultures. Of the peasantry, 20 percent worked varied balances of their own and rented land; 30 percent were wholly tenant farmers.

During the nineteenth century local exchange was the basis of Chinese agriculture to an overwhelming degree. Only 7 to 8 percent of agricultural output involved long-distance sales or urban consumption. Personal land cultivation, farm labor for others, and home industry took care of the peasants' nutritional needs, taxes, social commitments, and entertainment. Provincial elites and the rural bourgeoisie—especially local middle-sized commercial farmers—reinforced social stability through their intimate contact with the countryside population. They dominated the import-export trade, rented land to peasant cultivators, and served as primitive bankers.[23]

China's enormous size combined with the fragmented geography, economic localism, and underdeveloped transportation and communications systems to diffuse the 40,000 officials of the imperial state. The functionaries received special training after rigorous entrance examinations. That preparation included motivational indoctrination and career guidance. Then, as a matter of procedure, the government assigned them to duties far from their home localities. That tactic prevented the emergence of provincial elite political hegemonies via the consolidation of economic and political control. It eroded the local loyalties of the bureaucracy and replaced those sensitivities with a commitment to the state and career. The imperial bureaucracy that administered the provinces generally came from the top 2 percent of the wealthholders in an overwhelmingly rural social order. Their original family ties, deliberately broken in order to foster loyalty to the central government and emperor, were then refashioned. The state encouraged family visits to duty stations and family contact through paid vacations and trips home. These practices provided the family and relatives with special prestige, instilling loyalty to the regime among the most important local elites while preventing direct provincial and local elite family control over government administration.[24]

Each province had a governor, but eleven of the provinces that had strategic importance or records of unrest featured special military commanders who were immune to civilian interdiction. Magistrates administered the smaller divisions, subregions, circuits, and towns. The magistrates sometimes governed as many as 200,000 people with a staff and budget supported by local taxes. To ensure their success in administration local magistrates had to work well with the regional elites, landlords, and merchants. Local and provincial elites assisted in, and profited from, the collection of land and usage taxes; thus inevitably the cost of government fell to the lower peasantry. The magistrates further served the interests of the provincial and local elites. Their authority included the collection of debts and the maintenance of social order. Provincial and local elites depended upon the state for the legitimization and defense of their social standing, their material possessions, and the provision of suitable employment for their sons. The state in turn relied upon local and provincial elites for political support, political obedience from often far-removed peoples, and the commercial organization of agrarian property sufficient to supply the urban and industrial centers and provide exports and needed revenues.[25]

Chinese society enjoyed an equilibrium unparalleled in the world until massive foreign economic and political intrusions upset the sensitive internal balances. The state carefully regulated foreign economic penetration until Britain gained special trade concessions through victory in the Opium War of 1839–1842. As a result of that defeat Britain forced China to lower tariffs on imported goods and to open a number of treaty ports. The British and then the French, Germans, Japanese, and Russians established spheres of interest. A sphere of interest was a zone adjacent to a possessed property or ceded area. In those zones the foreign power claimed "the primary right of economic exploitation," which usually concerned railroads. In the 1840s the British gained extensive "interest" areas in the hinterlands of Canton. Significantly, the British abolished provincial transit tariffs, opening the southwestern Chinese interior. That step provided the underpinning of future unrest in the area.[26]

The unequal economic competition between British and Chinese producers soon created a massive trade imbalance. A vast outflow of Chinese silver resulted, causing a shift in currency ratios of silver to copper inside China from 1:2 to 1:3. The lessened value of copper to silver led to inflation for the Chinese working class and peasantry, who earned their incomes from crops and artisan goods using copper as their principal medium of exchange. Their products and copper currency had to be converted to silver in order to pay taxes and rents. Regional and local elites also suffered economic loss as a result of the lowered tariff barriers, inflation, and British merchant competition, but in the short term they were able to pass on most of the higher costs to local consumers through their hegemonies in local import-export commerce and village exchange.

The imperial state lost strength from the 1840s until the end of the century. Each defeat at the hands of foreigners forced further economic concessions, greatly damaging the state's ability to rule. The Opium War's outcome was only the first glaring episode in a series of debacles. The

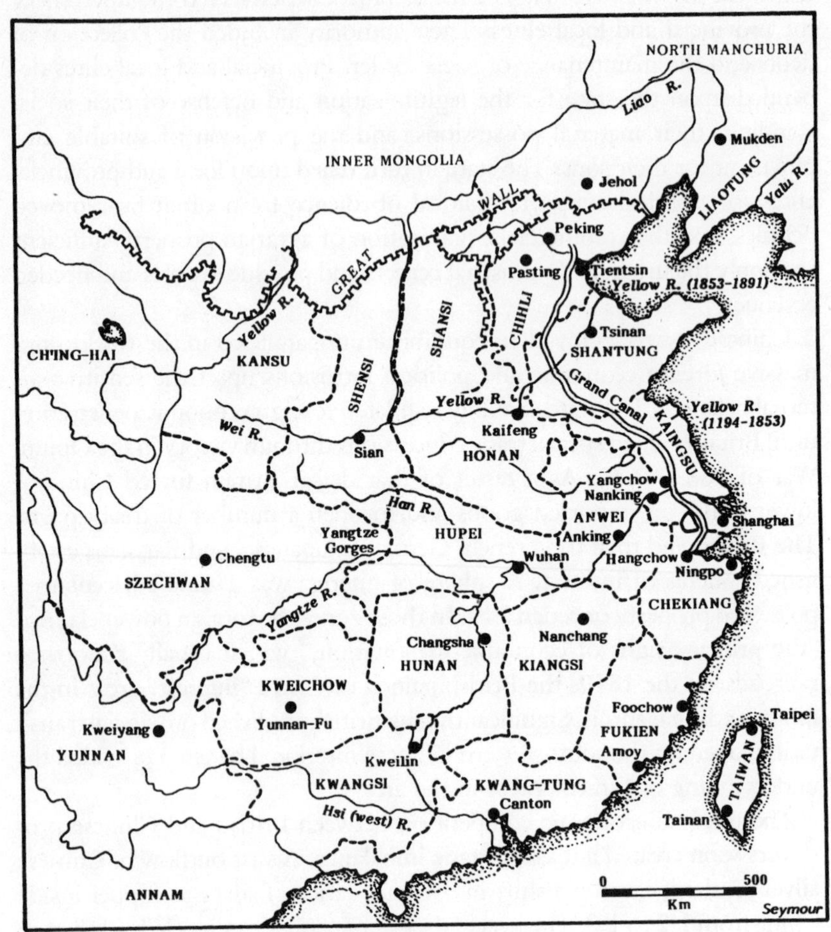

The provinces of revolutionary China

British aggressors successfully imposed a levy on the imperial government for fighting the war. They forced the Chinese state to pay Britain's war costs, drying up its treasury and rendering government and national defense ever more difficult. Other foreign invasions followed with France, Germany, Russia, and Japan, not only forcing economic concessions and further government-impoverishing indemnities but also appropriating Korea, Indochina, and parts of Mongolia and Manchuria. By the end of the nineteenth century special concessions in the principal port cities provided foreigners with bases of operation for control of special areas associated with railroads, mining, and river navigation. The large foreign enclaves in the cities featured autonomous police and military power and independent political jurisdiction. Foreign warships patrolled the navigable rivers. Missionaries with competitive cultural ideologies that challenged Chinese belief joined foreign capitalists in claiming large landholdings in the interior. The foreigners demanded and won tax and tariff reductions.[27]

The first of the great rebellions, the Taiping, swept across Kiangsi and Kwangtung provinces between 1850 and 1865. Those provinces, located inland from Canton, had been deeply affected by the earliest commercialization of agriculture inside the British concession. Indeed they had been earmarked before the Opium War for "conquest by railroad and bank."[28] An estimated 20 million Chinese died in the rebellion before its defeat. Rebels seized Nanking and made it their capital for eleven years. The rebellion was nationalist and strongly agrarian:

> Land shall be farmed by all; rice eaten by all; clothes worn by all; money, spent by all. There shall be no inequality, and no person shall be without food or fuel. No matter whether man or woman, everyone over sixteen years of age shall receive land.[29]

Similar to the Mexican Villistas and the teachings of the nineteenth-century French philosopher Charles Fourier, the living unit in China was to be based upon small militia-organized and equipped communes of twenty-five families each. Industrial work was to be organized in a similar manner around artisan battalions. The rebel ideology prohibited foot-binding, prostitution, white slavery, tobacco, opium, and alcohol. In addition to the economic and social issues, the rebels blamed the Manchu government for China's military weakness and foreign defeats.

As the rebellion wore on the leadership revealed a tendency to restore social stratification and taxes, decisions that the imperial government took advantage of in its propaganda. Once in Nanking, the rebel leaders quickly formed a bureaucracy; some formed harems. By doing so they allegedly dissipated petit bourgeois and peasant enthusiasm in the less commercially disrupted agricultural sectors of the nation, and the movement remained limited to the southwest, spreading only to Anhwei, Kiangsu, and Chekiang provinces in the previously commercialized Yangtzi Valley. The imperial government gradually gained strength and achieved victory with the help of French and British intervention. The foreign intruders provided officers and advisers, transport ships for troops and supplies, integrated units of European and imperial troops, and even entire combat units of indeterminate but not large size. Yet the rebels' spirit remained high. When Nanking fell in 1864 thousands of them committed suicide rather than surrender.[30]

The Nien Rebellion of 1852–1858 centered on Kiangsi Province just to the north of the Taiping revolt's point of origin. Kiangsi was a center of production of cereal and kaolin, a clay used in fired pottery. As in the Taiping revolt, Nien leaders were educated, many of them from the lower gentry. The movement was largely a peasant one, however, and less sophisticated than the Taiping. It did not seek to control the few cities in the area. The rebels directed much of their effort at highway robbery. One of their slogans read "Kill the officials, kill the rich, spare the poor!" The Nien rebels denounced the decadent weak Manchus and identified with the "Great Han Kingdom," a symbol of national strength. They were a localized spin-off movement of the larger Taiping Rebellion, the result of local socioeconomic disruption and of China's defeats in the Opium War of 1839–1842.

The weakening of national power allowed a series of smaller revolts to take place in areas affected by agricultural commercialization. The revolts were centered in market towns where traditional local elites took the lead. Thirty thousand peasants took part in the Red Band uprising of Szechwan in 1860. The Red Turban Rebellion of 1854, led by the Triads near Canton, seized market towns. The destruction wrought by the uprising and its repression reduced the population of Anhwei Province by 70 percent. The fighting devastated the cities of Nanking and Soochow. It is alleged that nearly a hundred years later the damage from the warfare of the Taiping Rebellion was still in evidence in those cities. Millions of farm workers and peasants relocated, staffing the commercialized estates and occupying the depopulated areas.[31]

For nearly thirty years after the Nien Rebellion China enjoyed a respite from large-scale insurrection and foreign wars. The rebellions continued but on a smaller scale. Between 1860 and 1870 all forty-two rebellions counted in one survey took place in the adjacent and commercially transforming agricultural regimes of the Hunan, Kiangsi, Hupei, and Honan provinces. Between 1870 and 1885, thirty-nine of fifty-one rebellions nationwide took place in those provinces, and nine of twenty-five between 1885 and 1895. In the last decade of the nineteenth century six revolts took place in Kwangsi, the heartland of the Taiping fighting and immediately south of Hunan. Throughout the last half of the nineteenth century peasant unrest was located in areas with relatively high tenancy rates where great landowners rented parcels and where peasants were maximally affected by devaluing currency, railroad and navigation projects, and an increasingly monetized agriculture.[32]

Agricultural commercialization destabilized Chinese rural society. As occurred in Mexico, displacement moved large numbers of people from their ancestoral homelands, but industrialization absorbed only a small percentage of the dispossessed. Foreign investment, rather than a dynamic process of internal economic growth and elaboration, was responsible for the growth of a system of commercial export agriculture and limited industry. The industrial sector and agricultural production were export rather than internally oriented. Increased tea, opium, silk, hemp, jute, flax, abutilon, and cotton production caused agricultural exports to soar and industrial and dry goods imports grew even more rapidly, causing a deficit balance in foreign trade. The emphasis on industrial-export agriculture led to grim social consequences, the creation of large-scale, low-income earning and coerced labor forces on the plantations. Reduced acreage in domestic foodstuff production, especially in the bottomlands given to foreigners as part of navigation and mining grants, drove up the cost of domestic staples and exacerbated the shortages in poor crop years.

The process of commercializing agriculture increased the Chinese government's need for transportation and communications infrastructure development. The formation of a native capitalist class could have been the result. Instead, like Mexico, in China foreign financial control undermined the potential development of an entrepreneurial national bourgeoisie. The international financial crisis of 1883 dealt a fatal blow to many native merchant bankers, "nipping in the bud . . . nascent Chinese industrial capitalism." Foreign concessions in lieu of nationally controlled development relieved the state's financial burden in the short run but led to domestic opposition and even violence against the regime. Loans strained the already threatened fiscal capacity of the state. After 1899 foreign investments and loans became more expensive as interest rates began to rise in the face of increased European demand for capital. By the end of the century the economic costs of infrastructure development, combined with a deficit balance of trade and devaluing currency, brought the Chinese government to the brink of bankruptcy.[33]

Faced with fiscal insolvency, the state was unable to update its already archaic war machine. Lessened repressive capacity coincided with the rise of peasant unrest in opposition to the spread of commercial agriculture. Responsibility for the control of peasant unrest was then delegated to the local and provincial elites, some of whom were among the first beneficiaries of agricultural commercialization. As the nineteenth century wore on, regional elites and provincial military commanders increased their powers vis-à-vis the Manchu dynasty.

Following each suppression of a peasant revolt the victorious provincial elites increasingly retained their military hegemonies in opposition to the national state. By 1900 they were in a position to reject the traditional rotational and mobile system of political officeholding. They continued to collect and hold taxes, with which they undertook the purchase of more powerful military technology. Like the Madero, Milmo, Garza, Sada, and Treviño families in the early years of Mexico's Porfiriato, they even drew up industrial development contracts with foreign entrepreneurs.[34]

As the provincial and local elites increased their effectiveness in the competition for revenues, the national government sought income ever more desperately through foreign trade. By the end of the century the Manchu dynasty garnered only 40 percent of the nation's tax revenues, including a mere 20 percent of the internal tariffs and sales taxes.[35] The most important and reliable source of income for the government had become the Imperial Customs Service, an agency administered by the foreign powers through the International Maritime Customs Service. After collecting payments on its credits, the Customs Service forwarded its net proceeds to Peking.[36] The Chinese government's credit was based upon foreign control and operation of the Customs Service. In the view of the conservative, nationalistic, angry element among the Chinese provincial elites, local producers, and artisans, this special relationship pointed to the government's corruption and weakness in cooperating with the foreign challenge to their economic, political, and cultural interests. In their view the government's debility and willingness to cooperate with the foreigners had already manifested in its treaty concessions and defeats in warfare.

The Boxer Rebellion swept China between 1899 and 1901. Rebel leader Yu Tung Chen wrote:

> These foreigners under pretext of trading and teaching Christianity, are in reality taking away the land, food and clothing of the people; . . . they seized our

> territory and cheated us out of our money; . . . piled up the public debt . . . burnt our palaces and overthrew our tributary states, . . . forcibly opened Kiaochau and now wish to divide up China like a melon.[37]

The Boxer Rebellion was an economic and nationalist movement led by provincial and local elites and artisans. It was preceded by a long era of violence against missionaries and missions and attacks on British consulates and officers of the Imperial Maritime Customs Service, many of whom were situated far from the sea.[38] The rebels acted against the burgeoning growth of foreign economic, political, and cultural power.

Famines in 1896–1898 preceded the uprising. As in Mexico, the devaluation of currency—copper, in the Chinese case—wreaked disaster among the peasants. In one province copper-based currency devalued from 2,000 per tael of silver to 8,000 per tael.[39] Peasant and worker rent and tax payments required silver. As the crisis grew worse, its effects touched a much wider populace than had the problems of 1850–1865. Over a wide area of China village artisan industries were succumbing to competition from foreign industrial imports. Repeated concessions had progressively eroded provincial tariffs. The interlude between 1865 and 1897 had been a time of peasant relocation and repopulation. The killings of the 1850s and 1860s had relieved the demographic pressure inland from Canton. Now the pressure built up again, and the foreign presence was greater than ever.

This was more than a peasant war; the Boxer rebels, led by the provincial elite petit bourgeoisie, opposed foreign penetration per se. Internal reforms were not the principal issues. In 1900 the Boxers seized Peking, put the Manchu government to flight, and attacked the foreign legations and trade offices. Intervention by the armed forces of the foreign intruders brought the affair to an end through the virtual occupation of large parts of the coastal zone and affected cities. The socioeconomic and political crisis, however, continued to deepen.

Each European nation planned its individual expansion into China; yet a remarkably similar pattern of four basic phases emerged. First, military force opened a certain number of Chinese treaty ports as points of trade exchange or contact. Second, railroaders and bankers seized territory for profits and ease of access to other foreigners. Third, the investors then developed their interests further with claims of extraterritoriality, spheres of interest, railway zones, and leased territories. These advances came about as the weakening Chinese government experienced increasing fiscal crisis and continued military defeats. It sold concessions to relieve the heavy foreign debt. Fourth, the American Open Door Policy merged the separate national strategies. It replaced the divided spheres of interest in order to avoid international rivalries, to ensure equal access to the Chinese marketplace and natural resources for the late-arriving U.S. investors, and to achieve unified foreign control of the chaotic finances of China. Henceforth large loans and bond issues could be consummated only with the full participation of the interested powers, avoiding undue competition and the resulting national frictions. The Open Door Policy replaced the practice of individual government intervention with joint "allied" invasions "to further national financial enterprise."[40]

Nationalistic unrest continued to grow in the Chinese interior. Provincial and local elite-led peasants numbering 150,000 formed "village leagues" in Chihli Province in 1902 to protest the indemnity forced upon the government by the foreign powers and to resist missionaries. At the same time, the Manchu government pleaded for and received loans from the foreigners for new armaments, social services, and railroads. By now the foreigners were appropriating virtually all of the revenues from customs for payment of accumulated debts. The Manchu government then shifted the burden of new revenues to the provinces and imposed new taxes on the peasants. Riots and small uprisings proliferated. In 1909, 113 recorded riots erupted and 285 more in 1910. Triad rebel leadership reappeared in Kwangsi, and the Boxers led a rising in Szechwan. In Kwangsi in 1904 rioters attacked the Catholic Church and destroyed the offices of the tax collector. On the eve of the republican revolution the entire district of Laiyang in Shantung Province revolted. Forty thousand people died in the course of its suppression.[41]

On 13 April 1910 rioting began at Changsha, Hunan Province. Changsha was an industrial town and railroad terminus. The causes of that unrest "resulted from the penetration into the area of Western economic forces which were steadily undermining the position of the scholarly elite. . . . Disturbances at this time resulted from similar causal factors; as the forces of Western capitalism gave a new impetus to the transformation of Chinese society."[42] The local elites in Hunan rose against "the foreigners for having brought the railway, and against the officials for having been hand in glove with the foreigners."[43]

The Changsha rioters of 13 and 14 April destroyed five foreign business establishments, four Chinese buildings utilized by foreigners, schools, and missions, among other properties. They looted the Japanese Consulate, the Customs Service office, an official's home, one hundred rice shops, twelve Japanese shops, and the missions of various religious denominations. Like the rurales who refused to act at Río Blanco, some of the

Chinese troops summoned to quell the uprising joined the 24,000 to 30,000 rioters. It "reached the height of its destructive powers that evening when it moved toward the American- and British-owned enterprises along the river. Gentry provided the leadership for the assault on the foreign companies."[44] The *North China Daily News* reported that the rising was part of a province-wide plot.[45]

International defeats in warfare and deepening economic desperation contributed greatly to the alienation of provincial elites and others among the upper social strata who had not participated in the endemic peasant-rural unrest plaguing China since the 1850s. Japan, an oriental former vassal state, attacked and defeated the Manchus in 1895. Critics of that loss could not be dismissed as readily as those who complained of abuse at the hands of the British, French, Germans, and Russians. Liberals in the court recognized the need for reforms, but their modest efforts were rebuffed by a coup d'état managed by the Dowager Empress, who was attempting to defend her hegemony. The Boxer Rebellion of 1899–1901, with its multiclass nature and regional elite leadership, demonstrated the extremity of the situation. Even the imperial upper classes in Peking produced factions sponsoring reforms. The reforms included study abroad, a national budgeting and accounting system, Western-style schools, and local and national elective assemblies, but a national parliament was not planned to convene until 1917.[46] The liberalization of the regime came far too late and was inadequate to defuse the crisis.

Rivalry between the government and provincial and local elites, who assumed greater responsibilities and powers during the recurrent waves of peasant unrest, had reached the breaking point. The provincial elites, merchants, and gentry tolerated their lack of prestige and authority during much of the nineteenth century in return for social stability and economic growth. Then they gained strength in the vacuum created by Manchu military and economic weakness.

By 1899 the rising cost of capital compounded the government's financial problems. In 1902–1903 and again in 1907–1908 China suffered in the wake of international economic crises characterized by bank failures in the United States. A binational conference of Mexican and Manchu administrators decided on a silver-based currency devaluation in 1905 that temporarily stabilized their currencies, relieved the first crisis, and reopened the countries to foreign investment and loans. The more serious Western economic crisis of 1907–1908, however, stopped the flow of investments and loans again. Banks could not help business or make loans to the government. The Chinese economy, like the Mexican, went into severe recession. Peripheral elite groups suffered economic disaster. They no longer had the incentive of economic growth to encourage their allegiances in the face of diminished national and personal pride, cultural and religious insults, ever larger zones of privation on the peripheries of the concessions, and lack of political representation. Provincial and class loyalties synthesized into demands for a "strong" federalist republican government. By now the loyalties of the "new army" officers were divided among their respective regions, extended elite family groups, and the government. In effect most of the old order had been replaced by macro-political-economic processes before the revolution brought down the political facade.[47]

Nationalization of the railroads, which eliminated local elite participation in their ownership, precipitated the great Szechwan rebellion of 1911 that immediately preceded the republican revolution. Provincial officials, intellectuals, shopkeepers, peasants, and industrial workers went on strike, marched in the streets, and then rioted. Their principal slogan was "Szechwan for the Szechwanese." The rioting grew into revolution. Next, the Wuchang garrison rebelled. Then provincial governors in charge of "new army" units rebelled. In Honan, where the local elites made no move, thousands of peasants rose up. Indicative of their radicalism was the slogan, "Kill the rich and help the poor."[48]

Powerful regional elites who dominated indigenous landholding and commerce in their respective localities steadily gained military power over a weakening national government. The Manchu state was unable to defend itself against foreign aggression and was exhausted by internal, largely provincial and local elite-mobilized lower-class revolts. In the wake of the Boxer Rebellion and the internal unrest of 1902–1908, the rebellious elites came to dominate the local and provincial assemblies elected between 1908–1910. In the view of the provincial upper classes, their interests were synonymous with national integrity and social control. As Sun Yat-sen put it: "It is my hope that . . . the class struggle between capital and labor can be avoided."[49] Initially foreign penetration engendered widespread but basically lower class unrest; but, combined with fiscal crisis and economic displacement, it fostered political revolution among previously prospering regional elites.

In the turn-of-the-century equation of national government military and fiscal decay vis-à-vis the foreigners, the military ascendancy of the economically, politically, and culturally embittered provincial elites was a potentially explosive development. Their role changed from that of detached individualized participation as migrant administrators or politically unassigned merchants and landowners in the centrist imperial regime to expectations of direct involvement in an emerging corporate structure. The provincial elites gained military strength while their localities were experiencing massive economic changes, social dislocation, and lower-class impoverishment. Their active local control provided the basis to confront the national government and the foreigners. By the time of the economic-financial crises of 1902–1908 they were ready to form the broader interregional alliances necessary to forge national rule.

Sun Yat-sen, a graduate of a medical school in Hong Kong who claimed a peasant background, led a multiclass alliance in the overthrow of the Manchus. His internal reform programs called for a parliament. He sought prodigious quantities of foreign capital but with the "nationalistic" proviso of direct participation by local elites through joint investments. He also advocated their power of approval of entrepreneurial projects by means of provincial and town assembly votes. Threatened by imperialist powers that many rebels thought planned "to slice China up like a melon," economic demise, and instability, the provincial and local elites asserted their nationalism and group interests. They moved to overthrow the weak centrist regime in favor of a decentralized constitutionalist government that would be more representative of their interests.

The 1911 Chinese Revolution, like Mexico in 1911 and again in 1920, gave victory not to the peasants and industrial workers but to multiclass alliances of officials, army officers, merchants, and landowners associated with provincial elites, "warlords," or military commanders. The various provincial and local elite alliances mobilized in the face of economic, social, and political chaos. Currency devaluation, mounting government debts, inflation and economic contractions, and peasant and local elite displacement reinforced their demands for greater political participation.

In the wake of the government's inability to defend their definition of national interests against foreign intruders, provincial and local elites, petite bourgeoisie, and artisans revolted in support of a decentralized, federalist, constitutionalist, parliamentary system of government. They rallied displaced peasants and radicalized industrial factory workers in their efforts. Unlike Mexico, because of China's enormous size and geographic remoteness, foreign intervention was unable to secure victory for one among many competing groups. The ensuing foreign invasion and warfare that continued until 1945 disrupted the development of local controls and stability, opening the way for a new revolution under more sophisticated leadership.

THE 1905 RUSSIAN REVOLUTION

All Russia is for sale isn't it?
—A Belgian lady

Between 1905 and 1907 social revolution swept the fifty provinces of European Russia. The causes of that upheaval, its suppression and short-lived political resolution, reveal important underlying global forces and national characteristics remarkably similar to those that simultaneously destabilized the three other pre-"modern" non-Western political economies under examination here. Those societies were among the world's most important centers of autochthonous civilization with strong indigenous cultures, polities, and social infrastructures that had evolved for centuries and even millennia.

During the forty-five years following 1861, when the serfs were made a relatively free or at least mobile labor force, Russia experienced an unprecedented influx of foreign capital. Those foreign investments stimulated rapid industrial growth, the creation of modernized communications and transportation networks, the emergence of large-scale banking and mining enterprises, and the commercialization of agriculture. North Atlantic financiers were attracted by a combination of cheap unorganized labor, a wealth of natural resources, generous guarantees, tax exemptions, government contracts, net profits on entrepreneurial capital four to five times as great as those available in Western Europe, and bank interest rates as much as 82 percent higher than those offered in the European market.

The tsar's government advisers, eager for new technology and accepting Western theories of economic development, participated in and encouraged foreign-controlled technological innovations, the commercialization of agriculture, and industrial projects. The state was searching for greater military power and increased control over the diverse peoples within the empire. The government attempted to rationalize the program for its own benefit, including the professionalization of the bureaucracy.

This preplanned industrial revolution reached its peak during the tenure of Sergei Witte, who served as finance minister from 1892 to 1903. The government's encouragement of economic growth through internal reforms and foreign investment antedated Witte, however. It prevailed throughout the forty-five-year period between the ending of serfdom and the 1905 revolution. Capital-intensive commercial agriculture and industrial production characterized the process as it displaced peasants, artisans, and provincial and local elites.

Russia. The 1905 revolution in the countryside

The program that seemed so successful during the early and mid-1890s collapsed after 1898, however, and failed to assimilate the displaced groups. That failure resulted from a Western European financial crisis that struck Russia especially hard because Western European investment funds, upon which the industrial-commercial expansion program depended, became more expensive and therefore less available. The inability to offer employment opportunities to the masses of displaced people compounded the usual social tensions associated with the Industrial Revolution and enclosure with a deep nationalistic resentment toward intrusive foreign capitalists. Rising unrest, riots, and general strikes resulted. Then the disastrous military defeats inflicted by Japan in 1904 and 1905 compounded the tension, resulting in over two years of revolutionary turmoil characterized by Leon Trotsky as a "dress rehearsal for 1917."

In the first half of the nineteenth century Russia emerged as a major European power through victorious participation in the defeat of Napoleon Bonaparte and the suppression of the revolutions of 1848. The tsarist government's autocratic foreign and domestic policy, however, which supported the violent repression of political liberalization in Europe, was an ominous reflection of a primitive economy, a coercive and intensive labor agricultural system, and a structure of severely limited political and social participation. That closed structure and primitive agriculture served the state poorly in its efforts to keep up with the rapidly advancing economies and technologies of Western Europe and Japan. The crushing defeats inflicted by the superior arms of the British and French expeditionary forces in the Crimean War (1853–1856) impressed upon the tsar the increasing obsolescence of his navy and army, the nation's lack of economic technical skills, and the deficiencies of its transportation and communications systems.

In the wake of Crimean defeat the government launched a program of state-supported and encouraged industrialization, commercialization of agriculture, and infrastructure development, virtually identical to that undertaken in Mexico, Iran, and China. Like those economies, Russia received massive quantities of foreign capital to help establish railroads, factories, electrical power systems, oil and mining production centers, banks, and export-oriented commercial agricultural enclaves. The publics of peasants, artisans, local elites, and provincial nobility, which bore the burdens created by the program, endured their burden with the hope of later benefits in the form of greater economic well-being and national strength.[50]

One of the first steps in the reorganization of Russian society was the commercialization of agriculture. To realize that objective a free enterprise-free labor system had to be created in the countryside. Relatively unproductive labor-intensive production had to be replaced by capital-intensive machinery. In its attempt to carry out this program the tsar's government tampered with the highly volatile Russian peasantry. Peasant unrest had been endemic since 1649, when a new law established serfdom by linking the lower agricultural working class to private estate properties. The edict of 1649 legitimized a de facto debt peonage system that had evolved during an era of rural and town population growth in the sixteenth century. In 1658 flight from the estates was made a criminal offense in order to curtail the peasantry's considerable geographic mobility.

By the 1760s the serfs constituted 52.4 percent of the rural populace, but the inefficiencies of the system, its labor-intensive methods in the face of rising land values and costs, and a multitude of owner obligations caused the total number of serfs to remain stagnant at 10,900,000 from 1800 until their liberation in 1861. The system no longer served the agricultural needs of an aspiring economic and military power. In the meantime peasant opposition to serfdom took other forms than mere flight. Sabotage, passive resistance, and rebellions became commonplace. Between the Pugachev revolt of 1773–1775 and 1800 about 300 violent episodes occurred across European Russia. Between 1826 and 1861 state officials recorded 1,186 incidents of rioting, looting, house burnings, and open revolts. The violence reached its apogee in the 1850s.

The long hoped-for freedom of the lower peasantry from serfdom, however, did not mean a qualitative improvement in their material conditions. Between 1861 and 1905 the peasantry became the most obvious and numerous victims of Russian industrial and commercial growth. In the immediate sense their freedom was achieved at considerable cost to themselves. The state required them to redeem the value of the lands they were given possession of in 1861. Of the former serfs, 69 percent were required to make long-term mortgage payments after their liberation. Many of the former serfs were paying for lands they had worked as tenant farmers during their bondage. Just as important as the land redemption payments, however, Russian village agriculturalists were caught in a complex of rising property taxes and operating costs, higher prices for manufactured goods provoked by a protective tariff, and a food price deflation in Western Europe.[51]

Between the 1860s and 1905 peasant property tax rates averaged seven times the valuations exacted from the nobility and commercial farmers for comparable acreage. Protective tariff rates, which ensured the tsar's government a favorable balance of trade and attracted foreign investment, also constituted a major factor in the peasants' demise. Prices for a wide range of originally low-cost industrial imports increased tremendously, causing the costs of their domestically produced alternatives to rise accordingly. The government initiated the problem in the late 1860s when it began to measure duty obligations in gold values. As a result the real tax rate increased 25 percent between 1868 and 1877. Then on 1 January 1877, the tariff levy climbed another 30 percent when the government required that foreign trade be conducted with gold-based notes in order to reduce the volume of devaluing rubles in the Berlin, Paris, Brussels, and London markets. Several more tariff increases ensued during the 1880s and 1890s. Then ruble devaluations and adoption of the gold standard in 1899, as part of the search for foreign investment capital, combined to drive the price of industrial goods beyond the ability of the peasantry to pay.[52]

By 1905 the peasantry's average holding had declined in size from 12.9 to 7.5 acres, and the total of peasant acreage declined by one-third. In the meantime their poverty, combined with the protective tariffs on fertilizers and machinery, made the costs of modernization prohibitive for them. Per-acre output on peasant holdings only increased from 400 to 520 pounds per acre during those traumatic forty-five years; Western European and North American yields more than doubled.

Growing impoverishment led to protests and caused the state to relieve the peasants of their redemption payments in 1894 and 1896. Yet despite the stop-gap measures taken by the government, tax arrears in 1898 reached dysfunctional heights. In Little Russia they totaled 27 percent; in the north, 30 percent; in the Baltic provinces, 64 percent; in the provinces near Moscow, 86 percent; and in the "black soil provinces" of the south-center, 177 percent. In some areas of the east tax delinquencies reached 232 percent. In 1899 the government again relieved the peasants of their redemption obligations but the situation was hopeless. Between 1870 and 1899 real estate indebtedness more than tripled from 353,700,000 to 1,246,400,000 rubles.[53]

By 1900 7 percent of the peasants in European Russia were landless and 20 percent held 2.7 acres or less. By then less than one-third of the peasants were self-sufficient. The mechanization under way in the commercial agricultural enclaves of Poland and the Ukraine demonstrated that four-fifths of the rural populace was not needed to work the land. Meanwhile improved neonatal survival rates and increased life expectancy added to the rural population. Survival and their self-sufficient orientation required peasant entry into cottage industries, Kustari, as the only alternative to emigration. They worked with dyes and made clothing, tools, kitchenware, and other artisan goods. In the 1890s half the male population was working at Kustari to supplement family income. Mass production by factories destroyed their markets, however, and forced most of them toward the manufacture of only their own necessities.[54]

Political unrest mirrored the economic demise of the peasantry. During the 1860s and 1870s despite their impoverishment, the *mirs* or village communes, practiced a degree of self-government under the watchful eyes of the tsar's police. Friction between the peasant mirs, intrusive commercial farmers, and the landed nobility, which was attempting to restore its greatly eroded power and affluence, caused the tsarist regime to appoint superintendents of the peasantry in 1889. The Zemstvos, rural elective bodies dominated by the local elites, and the mirs lost their independent powers. Local superintendents, modeled on the prerevolutionary French Intendancy system, tightened royal authority in the countryside, but they constituted a new form of outside interference. They became another source of alienation between the central government and the peasantry.

During the forty-five years preceding the 1905 revolution the village economies of rural Russia were progressively less able to support the people. Members of local elite, landowner, and lower peasant households began to migrate toward the industrial cities and the south, where burgeoning industrial expansion offered employment opportunity. Men were usually the first to go and constituted about 75 percent of the outflow. In some provinces, however, as many as 20 percent of the emigrants were children under sixteen years of age. In the wake of crop failures the percentage of women among those departing rose to 30 and 40 percent. Like Mexican campesinos, the Russian peasants brought their sense of community independence and equal sharing to the factories. In the beginning most of them hoped to return home with small savings intended to help the rural homestead meet its financial obligations. Some did return to the land, but the majority did not. The cities, the New South around Odessa and the Donets Basin, and Siberia were the principal destinations of the relocated.

By 1902 the capital city St. Petersburg counted 129,000 industrial workers from a population of slightly under 1.5 million. Moscow, a more industrial city, contained about 105,000 industrial workers of slightly more than 1 million citizens. The main indicator of urban industrial growth was found in the outlying towns and suburbs, where many of the factories were located. Near Moscow the number of industrial workers in these places reached upward of 23 percent of the populace. In 1902 the total of industrial workers reached 2.5 million. Their numbers had doubled in the previous ten years.

In 1902, at the height of the economic crisis and industrial slowdown that began in 1899, two of five peasants in Russia sought factory employment. By then fewer industrial workers than ever were attempting to return to their economically dysfunctional village homes. In the Moscow area 82 percent now claimed permanent residency. The economic depression increased the competition for jobs and left the majority without employment. The available jobs offered working conditions familiar to all students of the Industrial Revolution. The workday began between 4:00 A.M. and 5:30 A.M. and extended until noon. After a one and a half hour lunch break the laborers returned to work, from 1:30 P.M. to 7 or 8 P.M. Working-class housing reflected the high concentration of industrial ownership. Of the industrial concerns, 9 percent employed 78.5 percent of the industrial workers in European Russia, often housing them in enormous barracks complexes containing as many as 4,000 employees. Primitive living and working conditions characterized the workers' lives at the industrial centers in and around St. Petersburg, Moscow, Kharkov, Kiev, and Baku. The average industrial laborer's income of 249 rubles a year was barely more than the estimated 200 rubles per year minimum needed for the support of one person. As a result only 18 percent of the married male workers lived with their families, and only 8 percent of the families in common-law marriages lived together.[55]

The workers' difficult living conditions combined with a high degree of class consciousness and literacy. Radical literature proliferated. Sixty percent of male industrial workers read. In St. Petersburg the total reached 75 percent and in Moscow it was 56 percent. Women industrial workers, who constituted 40 percent of the textile labor force, claimed literacy rates of 41 percent in St. Petersburg. At one large foreign-owned factory near Moscow 66 percent of the work force was literate and 20 percent had completed grade school.[56]

By 1905 rioting and strikes had become endemic in the society of industrial Russia. General strikes swept Odessa and the southern metallurgical areas by 1903; urban centers to the north experienced outbreaks of violence in 1901 and 1902. Sixty percent of the industrial strikes evidenced advanced planning. Some of the unrest was characteristic of any successful industrial revolution: Luddite sabotage, discontent with the suddenly imposed regimented industrial-urban way of life, and miserable working and living conditions. But these industrial and urban grievances had one common denominator with the unhappiness in the countryside.

Economic transformation in Russia was being brought about to a large extent by foreign capital. By 1900 fully one-half of the active entrepreneurial capital was foreign, and control extended far beyond that. In their resentment of desperate working and living conditions in and around the factories and in the mirs, the industrial and agricultural working classes found upper-class Russian allies with their own hostilities toward foreign control and abuse. As a result of cross-class opposition, continued social stability required the successful transition of the economy from artisan-workshop industrial output and gentry-peasant agricultural production to factories and commercial farms. In that way occupational alternatives could be provided the displaced peoples.

One of the key problems in the disintegration of the old social order before 1905 was the decline of the landowning provincial and local elites. Their control of lands and a significant portion of agricultural output had traditionally been the basis for local political hegemonies. During the first half of the nineteenth century, however, they experienced growing indebtedness. The freedom of the serfs relieved the debt-ridden former owners of their social responsibilities and returned Russia to the basic system of agricultural self-sufficiency. Between 1860 and 1905 the reduced per-acre profits from agriculture because of lower market prices in Europe and at home, combined with rising costs for land and manufactured goods, undermined the traditional middle and large landholders' position. Most of the country gentry had their assets tied up in landholdings and were unable to make the expensive transition to mechanized agricultural operations. A few did succeed in joining that small but aggressive class of commercial farmers that was buying up peasants' and nobles' lands. The others watched their growing insolvency with bewilderment and anger. The gentry and noblemen who composed the majority of local and provincial elites lost 40 percent of their landholdings between 1862 and 1905.[57]

For those who lost, there might have been relief through employment in the bureaucracies of the local, provincial, and national governments. The financial shortages that began in 1899, however, combined with the costs of the Japanese War in 1904, to foreclose in its beginning a new revenue sharing program between the local and provincial governments and the tsar's central administration. In the meantime higher qualifying and educational standards excluded the provincial nobility from the positions in St. Petersburg and Moscow to which they traditionally aspired. In a doubly difficult situation, provincial and local elites saw their agricultural base eroding while political refinements excluded them in increasing numbers from high-level and lucrative government participation.[58]

Between 1876 and 1896 American grain exports to Western Europe and tariff imposts designed to protect the farmers of those nations reduced export grain profits in the extreme. In those twenty years the wholesale price of grain in Western Europe fell by 50 percent. Russian landowners had traditionally depended on that market for the cash sales that kept them solvent. Between 1877 and 1895 their landholdings in European Russia declined from 68,774,251 acres to 53,944,082. The decline continued until the upheavals of 1905 and the onset of world war. In 1905 the landholding provincial elites retained only 47,902,541 acres. The crisis deepened as Russia moved toward the 1917 revolution. By 1914 the provincial elites' position had deteriorated to a nadir of only 41,843,931 acres. The annual average loss totaled 832,898 acres during 1877–1895 and 604,154 acres between 1895 and 1905. In the interim between the "dress rehearsal of 1905" and the onset of World War I, the average annual loss of landholdings by the provincial elites was 673,178 acres.[59]

During the previous hundred years the nobility experienced a great loss of wealth, power, prestige, and political influence. In 1861 it lost much of its land through the emancipation of the serfs. The loss of assets could never be reimbursed properly through cash payments. That setback and the economic process that reduced the nobility's landholdings by 40 percent during the next forty-five years constituted what has been aptly called "the impoverishment of the nobility."

By the late 1890s the lower gentry were participating in a village-based opposition movement to the tsar's governmental professionalization and centralization program. The political forums of their efforts were the Zemstvos, the village and town councils. The higher provincial elites convened Assemblies of Nobility. Between 1900 and 1905 the Zemstvos called for greater revenue sharing with the national government in the face of a deepening economic crisis. They criticized the government bureaucracy. In 1902 Zemstvo veterans served on the tsar's hastily gathered Committees on the Needs of Agriculture, which were intended to help solve the agricultural crisis. As a solution they called for an elective parliament.[60]

In 1904 the Zemstvos openly demanded an elective legislature. Their own numbers now totaled several thousand and the employees of these local bodies numbered in the tens of thousands. In 1908 there were 10,229 elected Zemstvo representatives, and their own bureaucracy totaled about 70,000. They were a potentially powerful source of provincial and local elite discontent. Later in the year, when the initial patriotic fervor of the Japanese War had subsided and Zemstvo funds dried up, they became the focus of public criticism directed against the government. Large and unruly crowds often attended the meetings, urging the Liberal Kadets on, in complaints against rural poverty, corruption, and the subordination of Russia to foreigners.[61] Defeat by Japan in the Russo-Japanese War exacerbated the already overriding issue of national subservience to foreign capitalists. The nationalistic reaction to what were regarded as the foreigners' overwhelming power and selfish abuses temporarily united otherwise disparate elements of society: peasants, industrial workers, local and provincial elites, liberals among the commercial farmers, small businessmen, industrialists, bureaucrats, and conservative nobility.

Russian protests against foreign capital and Finance Minister Witte's aggressive efforts to recruit outside investment by offering the most lucrative terms possible paralleled conditions in China, Iran, and Mexico. Witte, like Mexico's Limantour, served as the focal point for complaints. Like those countries, public concern in Russia was rooted in recent military debacles; in the Russian case the Crimean War was the opening episode. In Mexico segments of the northern elites remained fearful after their losses in the middle of the nineteenth century and the ensuing American economic penetration. Russian concerns regarding foreign penetration and control, based on fact, were erroneously exaggerated by those who counted the most—the revolutionaries. They attributed every problem to foreign abuses and accused the government of collaboration with foreigners. The magnitude of foreign investment especially alarmed them.

Leon Trotsky estimated that foreign industrial capital alone increased by 1.5 billion rubles between 1890 and 1900, constituting almost 75 percent of the new funds. He claimed that it resulted in "an exceptional degree of concentration" in factory ownership. He was right about the concentration of ownership; 38.5 percent of the industrial work force performed in factories of over 1,000 employees in Russia whereas in Germany the concentration was only 10 percent.[62] A more recent estimate of foreign capital holds that it constituted only 55 percent of the capital that became active in Russia between 1893 and 1899, but that figure may not include the unrepatriated profits of foreign firms.[63] Trotsky's basic point was valid: in seven years during the 1890s the rate of growth of outside capital investments inside Russia reached a pre-1905 apogee.

By 1900 foreign investments constituted 72 percent of the total funds committed to mining, 71 percent of the capital in machine manufacturing, 44 percent of the cash outlay in the lumber industry, 31 percent of the funds active in the chemical sector, 35 percent of leather-processing capitalization, 20 percent of the capital committed to the paper industry, and 20 percent of monies in textiles. In 1905 total foreign investment had reached 1,037,400,000 rubles. Foreign capital in industry constituted 47.9

percent of the total. Foreign control over mining, manufacturing, lumber, banking, textiles, and commercial agriculture, however, was much greater than the percentage of capital committed.[64]

The capital of foreign company directors and their backers often totaled less than half of the stock in a company, yet they controlled companies at the request of less well organized, inexperienced, and not as well connected Russian capitalists with much larger cash commitments. The latter group sought out foreign control in order to assure itself of European market contacts, horizontal and vertical integration, access to fresh capital, managerial expertise, high technology, government favors in the form of special contracts and tax breaks, and foreign embassy representation in case of interference by tsarist officials. Often, out of concern for public outrage, foreign control was exercised in secrecy.

The more powerful foreign capitalists received favored treatment from the government. Witte worried about the foreigners' difficulties and "tribulations" in dealing with the primitive Russian work force, cumbersome governmental bureaucracy and inadequate system of communications, transportation, and other services. The state and foreign capitalists regarded their relationship as "mutually advantageous." Foreign capital constituted half of all investments made in Russian industry between 1885 and 1905. By the latter year the capital in control of banking came from French, British, Belgian, and German sources.[65]

Railroad construction was one of the key ingredients in the Russian government's program to attract foreign investment. Between 1861 and 1870, 5,833 miles of railroad were built. In the decade of the 1890s the figure rose to 13,920 miles. By 1905 a basic national infrastructure was in place with approximately 39,000 miles of track. The government controlled most of the rail system. Telegraphic communications connected the major cities and an extensive navigable river system allowed the transportation of Baku-area oil to the Moscow region and the interior of European Russia. Alfred Nobel dominated the Baku oil transportation effort by developing one of the world's first oil tanker fleets for that purpose.

For over thirty years Russian industrial output, like Mexico's, made striking gains. In 1866 only 342,950 tons of iron were produced. Impressive increases followed: in 1887 total production reached 648,000 tons, in 1895 it was 1,566,000 tons, and in 1904 it totaled 3,240,000 tons. Between 1887 and 1904 the southern region increased its share of industrial production from 11 to 62 percent of the national total. Foreigners were largely in control of the growing output. Sixteen of the eighteen steel companies in the south were in foreign hands. Their investments totaled 78 percent of the total capital involved. They also controlled 60 percent of the closely associated Russian coal industry. Fourteen of the new producers went into service during the boom between 1894 and 1900.[66] The number would have been greater but some halted work because of the financial contraction that struck Europe in 1898–1899. The South Russian Dnieper Metallurgical Company demonstrated the opportunities that Russian steel production offered. Between 1899 and 1903 its sales increased from 10,413,000 to 35,899,000 francs. The company's yearly profit between 1889 and 1902 was 26 percent of total investments.[67] By 1900 Russian iron production ranked fourth in the world and output had increased 190 percent in ten years.[68]

The allied Donets Basin coal industry was much smaller, but its central importance to metallurgy and profitability drew the attention of foreigners. Production increased from 2.2 million to 11 million tons between 1888 and 1900; metallurgy increased its consumption of the fuel from virtually nothing in 1888 to 35 to 40 percent of the total by 1905. The resulting coke industry was controlled by large foreign concerns, which accounted for a sevenfold increase in production during the six years between 1895 and 1900. An outstanding example of success in the industry was the Alamazonaia Coal Company, which was controlled by Credit Lyonnais. Its production increases and profits demonstrated the opportunity for abuse that Russia afforded foreign entrepreneurs. Between 1895 and 1900 coal output increased from 53,000 to 347,000 tons, and coke production leapt upward from 12,000 to 113,000 tons. Net profits paid as dividends were 95 percent in 1894–1895 and 74 percent in 1899–1900.[69]

The repatriation of profits from foreign enterprises grew until by the twentieth century they represented an overall loss to the Russian economy. Between 1891 and 1910 total foreign capital operating in Russia increased from 214,760,000 rubles to 1,358,000,000 rubles, an increase of 1,144,000,000. In the same twenty years 2,760,000,000 rubles in profits were repatriated to the North Atlantic economies, especially France, Belgium, Britain, and Germany. Banking interest rates were as much as 82 percent higher in St. Petersburg than the returns available in Western European markets. Exported profits depleted Russian economic strength at the very moment when foreign interest rates were rising and funds were needed for infrastructure development.[70]

After 1898, in the midst of declining real wages, deteriorating living conditions, rising interest rates, government fiscal crisis, and reduced profits, Russian nationalists and revolutionaries began to complain openly about the repatriation of profits, foreign competition with domestic producers, high operating costs for agriculturalists, and inequitable wage rates and preferential living practices that favored the foreigners. Critics claimed that the Western capitalists were plundering the country. A frank assessment of the privileged foreign employees described "far too many directors, commissioners, controllers, revisers, sales agents and secretaries who did little or nothing." Foreign wages averaged 50 percent more than those of Russians holding the same rank and performing the same tasks.[71]

In August 1900 antiforeign rioting broke out at the Konstantinovka Glass Company plant at Ekaterinoslav province just north of the Black Sea. Ekaterinoslav was the nation's second largest coal production center and the second largest population center near the Black Sea. An observer complained that life in the burgeoning city was "abnormal" and "expensive." The Russians were described as the downtrodden lower class in a place dominated by foreigners and characterized by labor unrest after 1899.[72] Two hundred Russian workers attacked their better-housed, fed, and paid Polish and Belgian counterparts, driving them from the premises and destroying their housing and property. The rioting spread to the nearby Konstantinovka Steel Plant, where the belongings of foreign workers were again destroyed. In 1904 criticism of the Belgian and Polish workers at these factories resurfaced because of their advantages.[73]

Nationalists and revolutionaries protested the collaboration of foreigners and government officials in bribery. Illegal inducements were given in exchange for special economic concessions not available to less powerful Russian competitors. Critics pointed out that foreign capitalists often violated the law and administrative rulings openly even though they already enjoyed special exemptions.

Foreign advantages were both economic and legal. The government allowed price-fixing and supply-allocating cartels in the foreign-dominated metallurgy and fuel industries. Fuel prices were allowed to go up 10 percent during the economic depression of 1901–1904 despite growing public hardship and unemployment. Another politically charged provision helped foreign steel company owners by abolishing the excise tax on pig iron in 1901 in the face of rising real import tariffs for Russian consumers. The state bank was notorious for the preferential consideration given foreigners in the issuance of business and industrial loans. A controversial decision to abolish the 5 percent sales tax on bonds sold in foreign markets angered Russian investors.[74] A cross-section of the Russian bourgeoisie, nobility, and provincial and local elites vigorously opposed these measures. The final straw came during the depression, when the government expanded its moratorium on all claims and interest except first mortgages to include what were regarded as the all-powerful foreign capitalists. The open praise of foreign capitalists by government officials like Witte further exacerbated the situation.

Odessa was symptomatic of the greater national crisis. In 1901 and 1902 growing urban unrest and industrial strikes set the stage for the more serious events at Odessa in 1903. The trouble began with a strike at the Odessa Tramway Company, a foreign-owned firm whose wages, working conditions, and performance of service had made it a center of controversy. The general position of foreigners at Odessa had become a burning issue.

The city had grown suddenly as an import-export center for Western Europe. Catherine the Great founded it in 1794 in order to consolidate her Black Sea conquests. By 1826 it counted a population of 33,000. In 1850 the figure reached 100,000 and in 1905 it was Russia's third largest city, excluding Warsaw, with 500,000 people. Unlike the industrial complexes of St. Petersburg, Moscow, and Warsaw, however, Odessa had only 20,000 workers employed in industry, and the surrounding territory of New Russia supported no large towns, only large estates. It was a commercial enclave economy linked to Europe by the grain export trade and, until 1857, as a free port for the introduction of manufactures and dry goods. Street signs were often in Western European languages.[75]

The volume of Odessa's exports led population growth and settlement patterns. Between 1798 and 1847 the value of goods passing outbound increased from 90,977 rubles to 44,000,000. Between 1824 and 1853 Russian wheat exports tripled, and Odessa handled more than half of them. By 1850 Odessa handled more than one-third of all Russian exports. Its speciality was staples produced by commercial farmers. Among them a group of Germans stood out, controlling 10,930,000 acres in the south largely devoted to corn export production. The land had previously supported a domestic wool industry; the original Russian owners had been displaced. Complaints about foreign control and influence surfaced among Odessa's Russian citizenry in the 1840s. The landed estates devoted to export trade minimized their costs by striving for utmost self-sufficiency after the import tariff was imposed in 1857. The manufacture of their own basic clothing and dry goods retarded the development of auxiliary towns and support industries in New Russia.[76] In a nation beset by food shortages, rye, the national staple, was a major export at Odessa.

The general hostility toward the foreign owners of the tramway company complicated a 1903 strike. Local officials shared the workers' animosity toward foreign influence and warned company officials that they might have to seize the franchise. The strike against the foreign-owned company quickly grew out of control. A general strike paralyzed Odessa. Widespread violence and antiforeign sentiment characterized the confrontation. In a prelude to the fighting at Odessa in 1905, the army and police quelled the unrest.

Upper-class rebellion complicated the extremes of urban and rural unrest in European Russia. Landed elites of the provinces and the nobility hated the social, economic, and political effects of foreign capital. Provincial elites, losers of 40 percent of their land in the previous forty-five years, launched public press and political attacks against the Western Europeans. The reactionary nobility warned of incipient socialism in the advanced Western industrial societies, and provincial and local elite-dominated Zemstvos called for the decentralization of government and local control of funds.

Russian industrialists, small businessmen, and nationalistic Liberals also became alarmed at the massive and growing government indebtedness, which increased from 4,905,000,000 rubles in 1892 to 6,679,000,000 in 1903. Large French loans obtained by the tsarist regime required arms purchases from French manufacturers and economic concessions. The critics' concerns were most evident in the greater Moscow industrial zone and in the Urals, where Russian capitalism had made a considerable start prior to the Westerners' arrival. In 1898 the Committee of the Moscow Stock Exchange complained against the foreign-controlled fuel cartel for unfairly raising the price of fuel oil. It then warned the government, which had authorized formation of the cartel and its price-fixing abilities, that foreign capital was interested in its own selfish aims and was therefore a threat to Russian independence. The petite bourgeoisie, nobility, and landowner organizations quickly endorsed that perspective.[77]

The complaint came for good reason. By 1900 the one billion rubles in foreign investment had resulted in 162 Belgian, 54 French, 30 German, 20 British, and four American concerns, of which the interests of the 146 largest companies totaled 2,075,000,000 francs. The value of these holdings by nations were as follows: France, 792 million francs; Belgium, 734 million francs; Germany, 261 million francs; and Britain, 231 million francs. Foreign power in the Russian political economy was much greater than this, however, because of the large amounts of passive capital contributed by domestic investors seeking the advantages offered by foreign operatives.[78]

The great majority of those Russians aware of the problems inherent in foreign capital were ambivalent about it during the expansive, prosperous pre-1899 phase. When Russian economic growth floundered because of overdependence on Western European investment sources that dried up in 1899, however, critics correctly identified the cause of the problem. The result was greatly exaggerated claims of outside control and denunciations of the state.

A cross-class alliance of critics presented ever more insistent demands for economic relief to the government. Urban marchers composed of government bureaucrats, businessmen, students, and industrial workers presented their complaints to the highest officials of the state. On Bloody Sunday, 22 January 1905, troops attacked gathering columns of petitioners, killing an estimated 4,600. Unaccustomed to dissent from within its own ranks and disgraced by defeats in the unpopular war with Japan, the government failed to slow the crisis. Strikes swept the cities, and naval mutinies revealed the disloyalty that was developing in the armed forces. Soviets competed with the government for power in the cities.

The deep class antagonisms between rural elites and the peasantry and massive foreign financial aid saved the bankrupt autocracy. The rural lower classes began to attack landowning elites in the provinces during two years of violence that was synchronized in its rise and fall with the needs of harvesting and sowing. In June 1905 there were 492 recorded outbreaks of peasant violence; in September, only 71. In November the figure climbed to 796. In May 1906 assaults on landlords' homes, land occupations, and burnings totaled 160; in June they surged to 739. In 1907 the violence tapered off, a reflection of agricultural needs.

Each social class responded to the violence according to its interests. The large landowners and nobility complained that the peasants were "taking away everything." The Assemblies of Nobles denounced the Zemstvos and disorder. The Zemstvos also had no taste for lower-class violence, however, and turned sharply to the right. As the unrest grew the liberal Kadets were increasingly outnumbered and outvoted in the assemblies. Landlords' associations formed private forces to protect their property and lives when the government was unable to help them. Industrialists and businessmen faced with strikes moved to the right. Landlords and nobles, long critics of the government, were hit hard by peasant uprisings and rushed to form an alliance with the tsar. After 1907 massive Rothschild and French loans refinanced the government, enabling it to restore order in the cities and countryside.[79]

Between 1907 and the outbreak of world war in 1914 an uneasy alliance between the still economically deteriorating rural elites and a temporarily recovered government ruled Russia. Parliamentary government was only a tenuous experiment. Massive lower-class unrest had thrown the quarreling upper classes together in an uneasy and short-lived alliance that fell apart in the disaster that began at Tannenburg in August 1914.

The transformation of land tenure in prerevolutionary Russia triggered rural mobilization on the part of hard-pressed nobility, local elites, and peasants. All three groups manifested extreme hostility toward commercial farmers and foreigners. Economic and social growth produced an enlargement of the professional and factory industrial working classes who demanded political participation and better government services ranging from effective economic management, education, and health care to national defense. They were disappointed on all counts. The economic depression that ended Count Sergei Witte's term as finance minister triggered cross-class urban and rural unrest. Defeats in war compounded by outside economic intervention revealed the government's weakness and infuriated nationalists. Foreign intervention in the form of financial support for the national government, combined with internal class rivalries, created a temporary alliance of rightist forces that ruled until the defeats of World War I broke their social control.

MEXICAN PARALLELS

Because worldwide social upheaval extending from Mexico to Russia, China, and Iran occurred simultaneous with and adjacent to expansive rival economic and national entities, an isolated explanation of revolutionary causation in one of these societies is no explanation at all. Those revolutions constitute local parts of global interactions.

Mexico, Iran, China, and Russia shared many salient characteristics at the beginning of the twentieth century. All four were sites of ancient civilizations with strong intact pre-Industrial Revolution social structures. Following disastrous nineteenth-century military defeats, they were all undergoing rapid economic penetration by the North Atlantic industrial powers. Their governments sought greater control over traditionally decentralized human geographies and stronger military power against other nations through foreign-provided communications and transportation infrastructures and armaments. All sought foreign investment for economic growth at the expense of their lower classes through protective tariffs, currencies linked to devaluing silver, and international loans paid for by taxes.

The contemporaneous opening of the transcontinental railroads of

North America and the Suez Canal in the second half of the nineteenth century provided new avenues of extranational economic access to Mexico and Iran. These countries joined China and Russia as centers of interest for North Atlantic investors. In the late nineteenth century technological breakthroughs in transportation and communications had strengthened the ability of entrepreneurs and government officials to extend their interests and authority to previously remote areas. As a result, in Mexico and Iran metropolitan authorities imposed state and local political appointments on previously remote semiautonomous areas while capitalists found new opportunities. Government functionaries in the provinces now sought their security and career advantages by pleasing the national administration rather than provincial and local elites.

In all four countries the alliance of government and foreign entrepreneurs engendered local and provincial elite hostility. Newly formed and foreign-controlled transportation systems served the needs of large foreign companies in preference to indigenous clientele and commerce. The intrusive process profoundly affected the rural working classes. It deprived self-governing "autonomous" towns and the peasant villages of their land, self-sufficiency, and authority structures while eroding their culture base. For the villagers, land occupations and local autonomy were the critical issues. Terrain seizures and rural deprivation became more intense during the economic boom. By the 1890s peasants in Russia, China, and Mexico had been displaced. Finally, paralytic elite crisis made town and village leader protest and peasant and industrial working-class rebellion ever more significant.

By the mid-1890s foreign bankers had established financial control over the new industrial and commercializing economies of all four countries, displacing traditional sources of financing. Railroads, river dredging, harbor improvements, and road construction provided access to national resources for extractive raw materials and agricultural export industries. Government leaders of all four countries linked their national currencies to silver in order to achieve deflating currency values and lower property costs for foreigners and thus to attract foreign investment. During the 1890s foreign investments flooded all four countries, and the rate of growth in commercial export agriculture, extractive industries, and infrastructure development peaked.

The growing foreign pressure displaced large numbers of provincial and local elite land and mine owners, artisans, and peasants. For the commercialization-industrialization process to be successful, the displaced rural sector had to be absorbed by new service or support industries as operators or employees. Any disruptions to the flow of new foreign investments, however, would leave these already alienated and displaced social groups with no prospects.

By 1900 all four countries were experiencing fiscal crisis because of the combined effect of rising infrastructure development costs, the declining value of their silver-based currencies, the rising interest rates demanded by the North Atlantic financiers upon whom they depended for loans, and increasingly erratic surges and lapses in new foreign investments. In Mexico the devaluation of 1905 exacerbated a land crisis similar to those that occurred in Russia and China, crushing Mexican abilities to buy land; American purchases compounded the problem by inflating prices. Brandishing their property titles, American colonists poured across the border, displacing tens of thousands of Mexican peasants and ranchers. They put up fences and hired campesino laborers and created a servile agrarian working class that replaced the formerly independent Mexican land users, who now became frustrated claimants. Beset with fiscal shortfalls, the Chinese, Iranian, Mexican, and Russian governments continued to sell exploitive concessions to foreigners even though these were often awarded in the face of competing offers from domestic provincial and local elites who were "undercapitalized."

The economic and fiscal crises led to the curtailment of public works projects, which constituted the cement holding together all four political regimes. The increasing fiscal insolvency and currency devaluations that resulted from the costs of infrastructure development, especially after 1890, became critical between 1899 and 1910, when the North Atlantic economies expanded rapidly at home, causing a period of rising interest rates and profound cash shortages in international finance. Foreign investment in capital-intensive areas of the economy became erratic, almost stopping at times. The shortage of capital in Europe was reflected in cutbacks by the French owners of textile factories in 1899, provoking statewide strikes in Puebla. Cutbacks continued during the American panic of 1902 and the economic contraction of 1907–1908. The economies of all four nations staggered despite increased raw materials production and an improved transportation network. Foreign influence grew greater as government officials visited the North Atlantic capitals in search of investors and massive, more expensive loans.

The result of this socioeconomic nexus was elite political crisis in which traditional provincial and local leaderships emerged that exercised their influence to mobilize restless peasants and workers against the metropolitan elites and their foreign allies.

In all four countries foreign economic dependency and fiscal crisis led to the governments' inability to carry out the needed massive projects in the development of domestic-oriented agriculture and industry. Only Russia, because of its navigable rivers, had a transportation system capable of contributing to internal economic diversification. After 1900, Mexico, unable to obtain sufficient foreign assistance despite the takeover of the nation's most critical industries by alien concerns, joined China, Iran, and Russia in facing rising unemployment, declining real wages, worsening labor conditions, lessened local profits and entrepreneurial opportunities, foreign preferences in the hiring of skilled industrial labor and supervisors, a massive loss of land to foreign commercial farmers, and no hope for relief for the displaced peasantry. Foreigners' increasing dominance exacerbated an already outraged sense of nationalism and failed to provide the steady, uninterrupted flow of investments into internal market opportunities that was necessary to save the economy. This situation contrasts sharply with the internally dynamic economic processes that characterized the successful industrial revolutions of North Atlantic societies. Denied electoral redress, the necessary number of provincial elites, pequeña burguesía, campesinos, and industrial workers then turned to armed insurrection.

The provincial elites, who had long opposed their loss of political and social importance, and the politically excluded petites bourgeoisies and intellectuals joined lower-class protests when their landholdings were threatened and their economies faltered. The provincial elites did so in defense of their economic base, semiautonomous political and social power, and definition of "national culture." The pequeña burguesía and intellectuals had grown greatly as a result of the social growth engendered by the economic programs, yet in all four nations they were excluded politically. Their eloquent nationalism, protests against corruption, and support of broader political participation had great public appeal.

Socioeconomic growth rendered the political foundations of all four governments obsolete. The political regimes were all based upon alliances formed in the preindustrial era. As the economic crisis deepened, their failure to include the upwardly mobile citizenry in the political process led to charges of corruption, national betrayal, and dictatorship. National political humiliation compounded economic frustration. China and Russia suffered further defeats in war; the governments of Iran and Mexico came to be regarded as mere pawns of the British and Russians and "yanquis," respectively. In all four nations upper-class-led constitutionalist, federalist, and parliamentary revolutionary movements emerged that demanded governmental representation in order to defend provincial elite and petit bourgeois interests.

In Russia, China, and Mexico pequeña burguesa, intellectual, and lower-class-led forces violently challenged their metropolitan elites and foreign capitalists. In Iran the powerful and all-encompassing cultural, economic, and political power of the provincial elites exercised by the Ulema precluded the development of an effective lower-class-led dimension within the revolutionary process. In each revolution foreign intervention competed with nationalist forces and violently opposed the insurgent lower-class leaders, becoming a major factor in the revolutionary outcomes. In the case of Mexico, American intervention proved decisive.

Part II

The Revolution

EIGHT

Elite Crisis and Mass Mobilization, 1910–1914

Madero has unleashed a tiger!
Let us see if he can control it!

—Porfirio Díaz

La Casa Grande?
La Tumbaron!

—A campesino at Rascon

The regionally based revolutionary movements that swept across most of Mexico between 1910 and 1917 laid bare, in their course of upheaval and competition, the nation's short-run and long-standing political, economic, and cultural contradictions. Its constituent elements paralleled those of Iran, China, and Russia. The revolution actually began in the spring of 1910 with the nationwide political crisis brought about by the challenge presented to the Porfirian government by the presidential candidacy of the Coahuilan provincial elite, landowner, industrialist, and banker, Francisco Madero. Peasant violence in Chihuahua and along the Gulf coast preceded Madero's candidacy. The popular Madero announced his own revolution in November 1910 following his electoral defeat that summer by what were widely regarded as fraudulent and repressive means.

Five areas of generalized unrest developed in late 1910 and early 1911: the Gulf and Pacific coasts, the southern and northern peripheries, and Morelos. By early 1911 two separate but relatively well-organized uprisings emerged from the wider violence. One encompassed the thinly populated northern periphery. There, in isolation, regional elites had ruled in a state of semiautonomy for centuries; and military colonists, at the urging of the national government earlier in the nineteenth century, had forged a ranchero economy on the uncharted expanses. The military colonies had created a demographic barrier between central Mexico and hostile Indians farther north. The far north was the area proximate to and most recently and deeply affected by the extension of railroads, mining technology, industry, and finance capital from the United States. Unlike their almost equally economically overwhelmed counterparts on the coasts and in the far south, the northerners still lived in intact locally ruled communities, were armed, enjoyed geographic remoteness, and had access to war materials from the United States. They could carry out protracted struggle.

The other relatively well-organized uprising emerged in the center-south state of Morelos and adjacent territories, where absentee estate owners, some of them Spaniards, from nearby Mexico City established metropolitan control over Mexico's most productive concentration of commercial sugar haciendas. The expansive sugar estate interests were in direct competition with local landholders, merchants, communally oriented village peasantry, and hacienda fieldworkers in the nation's most densely populated rural area. Twenty percent of the state's population still spoke Nahuatl. Pre-Columbian landholdings and traditions were still claimed by most of the village citizenry. Like the northerners, many of the Morelos citizenry lived in intact communities with their own leader. They too could be geographically remote because of the rugged topography in the region. Like the northerners, they were beleaguered by intrusive outside capitalists. Those specific zones of crisis, one to the far north and center and the other in the center-south, have received special attention in our examination of the pre-1910 breakdown of the Porfirian political economy.

By 1900 the economic success of the Díaz regime had far outgrown its older sociopolitical base by creating new entrepreneurial, intellectual, professional, and industrial workers' groups. The newly important economic and social groups shared the provincial and local elites' lack of representation in benefits through public works opportunities and in the higher councils of government. Meanwhile increasing agricultural exports made feasible a final assault on the now residual peasant village holdings by commercial farmers, land developers, and latifundia owners, many of whom lived in Mexico City and the United States.

The wealth and closeness to political power of these metropolitan elites contrasted with reduced real income for the great number of former peasants who had become *acasillados,* or residential agricultural workers, on the estates. Meanwhile the dynamic growth of the industrial, commercial, and banking sectors of the economy had concentrated unprecedented power in the hands of a relatively small group of foreign and metropolitan elite investors, to the competitive disadvantage of ambitious nationalistic Mexican businessmen.

Greater wealth accumulated by a small segment of the population contributed to a general rise in prices. Reduced acreage committed to the production of domestic staples after 1900 helped to drive up food prices for the newly created and increasingly sophisticated pequeña burguesía and the industrial working class. The majority of the industrial working class had lived in urban centers for less than twenty years. After 1905 the high expectations and real wages of these people were dashed by inflation and rising unemployment, creating an alienated citizenry. After 1900 the well-conceived and highly organized political structure that enabled Díaz to discipline the nation and create order before 1890 had become archaic and narrow. The regime politically excluded the newly affluent small merchants and industrialists, professionals, and intelligentsia, who were created by the growth of the economy before 1900, as well as provincial and local elites from representation or real power in the political process. Fiscal crisis narrowed the issuance of public works contracts to a privileged few.

After years of political meetings and shifting alliances, the alienated groups, beginning with the intellectuals, provincial elites, and pequeña burguesía, found a leader in Francisco I. Madero, heir to a Coahuila hacienda, banking, industrial, mercantile, and mining family empire. Unlike the radical pequeña burguesa Flores Magón, Madero was a socially acceptable wealthy man imbued with a traditional nineteenth-century laissez-faire Liberal-democratic political outlook.

Madero's role in opposition politics began in 1904, when he supported candidates among the provincial elites against those endorsed by the national government. He continued those efforts until his own presidential candidacy. He even contributed funds briefly to Flores Magón before discovering the latter's radicalism. In 1909 he published *La sucesión presidencial,* which set down the rationale for a reformist opposition party. The book contributed notably to his political status, helping to set the stage for the whirlwind of political tours later in the year during which he traversed much of the nation. In his unpretentious way Madero established valuable contacts during private meetings with discontented provincial and local elites. He addressed the concerns of hacendados, rancheros, and small industrialists and merchants. He broadened his support by organizing semipublic meetings, attended by artisans and workers, in Mazatlán, Hermosillo, Tampico, Monterrey, Campeche, and Merida. This exposure widened his already solid support in Coahuila and Chihuahua.[1]

Madero's organizing work paid off. In 1910 the future governor of Chihuahua, Abraham González, nominated him as the anti-reelectionist party's presidential candidate during its Mexico City national convention. Endorsement by the enthusiastic delegates was a mere formality. Madero and his vice-presidential candidate, Francisco Vasquez Gómez, campaigned on the narrowest of programs to avoid conflict with the government and the foreigners and because he did not envisage an activist government interfering with or otherwise upsetting the free enterprise economy, the prerogatives of private property owners, or the existing balance between social classes.

Madero assumed an antidictatorial, mildly nationalistic stance when he symbolically assured a campaign audience that the Mexican people did "not want bread, but liberty." Despite Madero's traditional laissez-faire liberalism and conservative approach to social change, the stakes were high not only for Díaz but for the bureaucracy and the consortium of metropolitan elites in Mexico City and the foreigners it served. Metropolitan elites exaggerated the fear that Madero intended to overhaul the bureaucracy by replacing Díaz government officials with "Maderistas" whenever possible. Those changes would have brought new recipients into the already tight competition for public works contracts.

The tension between the contestants provoked Madero's arrest, confirming Maderista charges of electoral harassment. The government's action enhanced Madero's image; he reappeared even more heroic. After the elections the authorities released him on the condition that he remain in San Luis Potosí. A few months later, however, on 5 October 1910, he escaped disguised as a railroad worker and fled to San Antonio, Texas. Madero took an apartment in the Hutchins boardinghouse. He maintained contact with San Antonio's leading businessmen and bankers, including the Frost brothers, owners of the Frost National Bank, and George Brackenridge, owner of the San Antonio National Bank, where Madero held meetings. His long association with the Frost brothers included a joint interest in the Banco de Coahuila at Saltillo. Brackenridge had negotiated the contract for the Madero family's Sabinas coal and coke mines with Colis Huntington and the International Railroad in the early 1880s.

Insulated from police harassment, Madero then issued his historic call for revolution, the Plan of San Luis Potosí, which rallied not only his followers but also PLM groups and formerly uncommitted people, including elements of the peasantry. He dated the plan 5 October 1910 to coincide with his last day in San Luis Potosí and thus avoided violation of the U.S. neutrality laws. The plan called for the Mexican Revolution to begin on 20 November.[2]

Madero created a revolutionary organization with a rudimentary infrastructure by which coordinated uprisings were to take place throughout the nation, with local elite-controlled insurrections in the central region planned for Puebla, Pachuca, and Mexico City. Madero planned to enter northern Mexico and lead an insurgency in Coahuila and Chihuahua. His organization, however, was not as well developed as the PLM's. The leadership of these rebellions was supposed to devolve upon men of local stature from among the alienated elites. However, the wealthy veterans of the anti-reelectionist movement failed to gain popular acceptance as leaders of a violent revolution. Madero needed to incorporate a diverse range of artisans, workers, and peasants if the movement was to succeed.

In his attempts to build a wide base of support, Madero offered incentives to both the workers and peasants which were not in evidence during his presidential campaign. These incentives were critical for the development of the revolution not only because they attracted elements of the lower classes into his movement but because they imbued them with expectations of change. Madero told the industrial and urban workers that they could organize in whatever manner fit their needs under a just and honest government. His legitimization of free unions and strikes won him widespread working-class support. The assurances given to the campesinos were explicit: Clause three of the Plan of San Luis Potosí promised to return peasant lands, "those who acquired them in such an immoral way, or their heirs, will be required to return them to the original owners." Madero stimulated lower-class idealism and support throughout Mexico.

In the south the combined defense committee of the village of Ayala and its adjunct pueblo Anenecuilco—led by ejido member, minifundia farmer, muleskinner, and horse trainer Emiliano Zapata—decided to make an independent revolution in concert with Madero. In the north previously unknown muleskinner Pascual Orozco and the rural worker-sometimes-bandit, Francisco Villa, openly declared their allegiance to Madero's revolution. Madero's promises and successful armed struggle encouraged the formation of the mass-based agrarian working-class and urban and industrial labor movements of the revolution. Madero's appeal to the working class and peasantry offered the opportunity and encouragement needed for mass mobilization. His elite-led confrontation with the Díaz government diverted its repressive apparatus and energies, providing the opportunity for the masses to act on a national rather than a local basis. The revolutionary participation of the working classes on a national scale provided the basis of conflict during the next ten years.

In Zapata's state of Morelos the sugar haciendas, initially carved out of Indian lands in the sixteenth century, were the central force in the economy. During the Porfiriato increasing foreign demand for sugar stimulated the conversion of the hacendado-controlled *trapiches* into technologically advanced *ingenios.* The estates expanded, supported by enabling legislation and the armed forces, at the expense of the pueblos. In 1888 Anenecuilco's resistance against land intrusion by the Hospital hacienda led to a violent outbreak and another setback for the pueblo.

As sugar profits soared and Mexican production increased fivefold, virtually every peasant community in the state suffered the same fate as Anenecuilco. Resistance flared at Yautepec in 1892 and 1904, and in Anenecuilco and Ayala in 1909. Zapata's area of operations—Morelos, the southern portions of the state of Mexico including Chalco and Sultepec, western Puebla, and much of Guerrero—resulted from the campesinos' long competitive struggle with outside intruders. Their forefathers had opposed the Aztecs in the fifteenth and sixteenth centuries, the Conquistadores, *encomenderos,* the growing strength of the hacendados in the eighteenth and nineteenth centuries, and the ultimate consolidation of elite landholding during the Porfiriato. In the last third of the nineteenth century they were introduced to revolutionary ideologies imported from Mexico City. The first mass-based Latin American agrarian revolution resulted.[3]

At the beginning, while Zapata's movement was still localized, much larger rural forces formed in the north under the leadership of Orozco and Villa. The Chihuahua, Durango, and southwestern Coahuila insurgency depended at first on the long restive miners, small farmers, and agricultural workers whose resistance against outside intrusion rivaled that of the southerners.[4]

The alienation of small farmers and village citizenry from the regime stemmed from multiple injustices. Their experience along the lower reaches of the Nazas River during the 1880s was typical. It united them with the alienated provincial elites. Together they had opposed water and land seizures by large metropolitan and foreign commercial operators such as the Tlahuallilo Estates of the Brown brothers bank, Balfour, and Stillman.

Between 1906 and 1910 most of the available water in southwestern Coahuila, Chihuahua, and Durango had been allocated to commercial operations as part of the Díaz regime's heightened commercial efforts, removing the very sustenence of life from the pueblos. By May 1911

Little is known of women in the revolution. The pictures that follow of fighters and participants, from the lower-class-led formations, tell their own story.

Maria Chavarria, Coronela Zapatista, with two of her officers.

Women factory workers were organized by anarchists beginning in the early 1870s. Women from factories like La Perfeccionaria were organized early, supported the Casa del Obrero Mundial, and took part in revolutionary efforts including the ácratas (those opposed to all authority), which was a nurses' formation 1,500 strong formed from the women factory workers of greater Mexico City to serve with the Red Battalions of the Casa.

The railroad provided the principal means of transporting military personnel and their supporters.

Federal troops under Huerta preparing to depart with their families for the north and the confrontation with the Villistas.

John Lind, President Wilson's emissary, meeting with Carranza's son-in-law General Candido Aguilar near Veracruz during the American arms buildup on behalf of the Carrancistas there. American intervention tipped the balance and enabled the right to defeat the lower-class-led forces.

Silver ingots at Alexander Shepherd's Batopilas mines in southwestern Chihuahua await shipment to the United States with the help of low-income Mexican guards.

In 1915 and 1916 the Carrancistas executed pro-Villista local leaders across the breadth of the Mexican north. The Villistas, such as the one above, were portrayed as bandits and renegades. A generation of Mexican working-class leaders was lost.

ZAPATISTAS

Madero had 5,000 armed supporters in the La Laguna region near Torreón, many of them displaced agriculturalists from the villages. Between November 1910 and May 1911 formidable rebel forces emerged in Durango. The rebels, many of whom were displaced village farmers ruined by the Díaz government's massive water reallocation program, had not participated in the anti-reelectionist movement. They supported the agrarian provisions in the Plan of San Luis Potosí.[5]

Considering that most of the waters of the north had been diverted since 1905, it seemed clear to the rebels that these acts violated constitutional law. Madero's revolution suffered setbacks elsewhere, but the dispersed units in the north under the indirect lower-class leadership of Villa and Orozco enjoyed growing countryside support and military successes.

In the north along the Gulf coast, in Campeche, the Isthmus of Tehuantepec, the Pacific coast of Chiapas, and Morelos, peasants and fieldworkers unattached to Orozco, Villa, Zapata, or Madero attacked and devastated commercial agricultural properties, including those of the foreigners. In all of these regions except Morelos the great majority of the alien landowners were Americans. In the north and south mass organizations formed that were based on the peasantry and agrarian working classes. These insurgents stood apart from the local elite-controlled revolutionary structure conceived by Madero and his circle of advisers. Madero's violent struggle for the presidency and his supporters' yen for access to political positions and government-funded construction contracts served as a rallying point for the campesinaje.

The revolutionaries in the north gained victories in Chihuahua, Coahuila, Durango, and San Luis Potosí. The Zapatistas and other units expanded their control in Morelos, Puebla, and Guerrero. The rebel forces in Zacatecas, Jalisco, Sonora, Sinaloa, Tamaulipas, Veracruz, Tabasco, Campeche, and the Isthmus of Tehuantepec also made advances. Locally led rural revolutionaries outside the control of Orozco, Villa, or Zapata took the lead in a growing wave of violence against domestic and foreign-owned (especially American) commercial estates. They dynamited American-owned mines, burned houses and rubber fields, tore down fences, and carried away livestock. Peasants occupied the hastily abandoned properties.[6]

PLM units contributed to the growing government military debacle with one of the most powerful columns in the Chihuahua campaign, headed by the party's military leader Prisciliano Silva. Other PLM units assaulted and occupied the vast Harry Chandler properties at Mexicali and

Tijuana from across the U.S. border. Their supporters also attacked the holdings of the McAleer interests and the 1 million-acre Circle Bar Ranch south of Ensenada and assaulted American and Mexican estate properties near Acayucan in Veracruz. Meanwhile the PLM leadership languished in prison, unable to capitalize upon the revolutionary opportunity. The Federal Army, tied to a static, garrison-type defense, gave rebels the freedom to choose the place and time of battle. The rebels advanced as governmental authority and unity degenerated. In fact victory came without Madero consolidating a chain of command. Madero's first serious conflict with his "followers" occurred on 13 May 1911 after rebel forces led by Orozco and Villa seized Ciudad Juárez on 10 May against his wishes.

Enjoying American tolerance, Madero crossed the border at El Paso to greet the revolutionary forces and establish his provisional government at the site of an important border entrepôt. On the thirteenth he announced his cabinet appointments. They included veteran Porfirian politicians, landowners, and Madero family members and excluded Villa and Orozco. The two men invaded Madero's headquarters and were only partly satisfied when Madero paid their men and promised them reforms. Madero rejected their demands to turn over the captured commander of the city's garrison, the distribution of farm- and ranchlands to the peasants who had done the fighting, and the selection of a new cabinet entirely from among the revolutionary forces. Madero's sense of capitalist and provincial elite hierarchy, and the clash of class-based economic interests between what his father called at the time "our 18 millionaire backers" vis-à-vis the northern revolutionary miners, rancheros, farmers, and agrarians, created an irreconcilable schism. The revolutionary participants had conflicting priorities.[7]

While Madero and his circle of advisers entered into what appeared to be the beginning of hard negotiations with government representatives sent to Ciudad Juárez, events elsewhere hurried the Díaz regime to capitulation. On 20 May Zapata led 4,000 campesinos into Cuautla, the road and rail hub of eastern Morelos. To the west federal forces fled Cuernavaca, the state capital, conceding Zapatista hegemony over the region immediately south of Mexico City. The strength of the Zapatista forces at Cuautla far exceeded their immediate numbers, however. By May Zapata's forces constituted a people in arms led by the elites of the remnant village society. The hacienda workers and village populations supported the revolution. Sugar plantation workers were especially discontented, in miserable rancherías, ill-paid, and without the land promised them in order to recruit them from afar. The alienation of the plantation workers led to the collectivization of the *ingenios* when the revolution matured.

The Zapatistas near Puebla and other revolutionaries nearer to Veracruz cut the crucial railroad transportation artery and escape route for the government between Mexico City and the port. In the north Durango, Torreón, and Hermosillo fell giving the rebels, very few of whom were controlled by Madero, power in much of the northwest. The fall of Tehuacán between Puebla and Veracruz further threatened Mexico City's Veracruz lifeline. In Jalisco and San Luis Potosí revolutionaries, including mine and hacienda employees, invaded American properties, blowing mines up and seizing arms and powder. Army desertions grew to alarming proportions, and local units disintegrated. Spontaneous land seizures took place in Chihuahua, Durango, Coahuila, Sonora, and throughout the center of the country.[8]

The rising tide of lower-class unrest spurred elites to end the turmoil. The negotiators in Ciudad Juárez representing the revolutionary provincial elites and the metropolitan Díaz regime reached a rapid accord. On 25 May 1911 Porfirio Díaz submitted his resignation to the Mexican Congress, although the agreement reached at Ciudad Juárez gave him until the end of the month to do so. Vice-president Ramon Corral resigned and Francisco León de la Barra, secretary of foreign relations and former ambassador to the United States, became interim president.

It is sometimes conjectured that Díaz resigned in such haste partly because American troops were massed along parts of the border with Mexico. Historians also note that both Japanese and American fleets were omnipresent offshore. These suggestions miss the mark, however. Although the United States expressed deep concern regarding events in Mexico, an invasion at that stage of the revolution was not seriously considered, and both sides in the revolutionary conflict understood this. Each represented itself well in Washington, and Madero achieved great success in obtaining local succor in the Texas border and San Antonio areas. Madero and his family had long-standing ties with the Texas financial and political elite, including Otto Wahrmund, head of the San Antonio Brewers Association, the Frost family, and other important members of the San Antonio International Club, whose penthouse meeting room occupied the top floor of Brackenridge's San Antonio National Bank building. Through his San Antonio associates, Madero enjoyed indirect connections with the Texas Oil Company directors in Houston. His New York contacts included railroad tycoon W. H. Harriman, a director of the National City Bank who owned the International Railroad and ran the Southern Pacific.

After Madero's revolutionary success Texas Company president Joseph

Cullinan and treasurer Richard Brooks immediately supported the entrepreneurial Madero family's venture in the production of oil at Tampico. The Houston oilmen bought the petroleum output from the family's fields and brought two of President Madero's brothers to Houston in 1912, where they were feted and given "gold keys to the city." Madero also struck a bargain with the Standard Oil Company. Madero's meetings with Standard began in San Antonio and continued in El Paso and Mexico City after he became president. On 5 June 1912 Madero and Standard celebrated one of the most one-sided business concessions imaginable. The company received ten years of tax-free operations, including imports, exports, and all domestic activities. In addition it obtained rights of eminent domain and denunciation for any properties, government or privately owned, it wished for pipelines, ports, roads, railroads, and refineries anywhere in the republic and for the support of its oil fields in Hidalgo, San Luis Potosí, Tamaulipas, and Veracruz.[9]

Through his association with Brackenridge and the attendance of Stillman and Madero family youth at the elite Culver Academy in Illinois, Madero had contact with America's leading capitalists. Brackenridge's long-standing ties with Charles Stillman, who had advanced him $200,000 in order to establish his bank, had continued via a close relationship with James Stillman, chairman of the board of the National City Bank. In 1910 Stillman held at least an 11 percent interest in Brackenridge's San Antonio National Bank. Those ties complemented Brackenridge's intimacy with Will Hogg, secretary of the Texas Company and lifelong close friend of Colonel Edward Mandel House, the political chieftain of the state who headed the Texas Democratic party machine and soon became President Wilson's chief adviser. Hogg maintained a home near Brackenridge's in San Antonio. The Texas Company controlled 4.5 million acres in Tamaulipas alone. Stillman and Brackenridge had large investments in Mexican bonds, the railroads, and land developments. They had also undertaken joint land speculations in Texas at Kerrville and the enormous Swenson XIT Ranch.

Stillman openly functioned as secretary of the American stockholders involved with Lord Balfour in such enterprises as the Tlahuallilo Estates. Stillman was also financial head of the Rockefeller-Standard Oil empire and the organizer of the Big Three banking trust with J. P. Morgan of the Morgan Bank and George Baker, chairman of the First National Bank. Stillman also coordinated the Big Four railroad consortium, which, until 1908 consisted of himself, W. H. Harriman, George Jay Gould, and William Rockefeller—all National City Bank directors—and which dominated the Union Pacific, Southern Pacific, and eastern U.S. and Mexican railroads. He and William Rockefeller also held 20 percent of the Atcheson, Topeka and Santa Fe Railroad, which had constructed the Mexican Central Railroad. When Jacob Schiff replaced Gould, each member of the Big Four along with J. P. Morgan, Jr., whose father had large Mexican railroad investments, sat as a director of the National City Bank. In 1910 the National City Bank was about to become the largest in the world; its operations in Mexico were that nation's largest.[10] The Madero family's business and social ties with the Stillmans helped maintain the goodwill of the American elites during the insurrection.

The Rockefeller, Kleburg (King Ranch), Stillman, and Brackenridge families were close at both the personal and the business level. Standard Oil was hostile toward Díaz. It would have been neglectful for William Rockefeller to stand aside while the Texas Company joined the expansive Texans, who in 1876 had financed the Revolution of Tuxtepec, in support of Madero. Madero made it clear that American capital would be welcome during his presidency. Despite openly violating the law, Madero experienced no problems from San Antonio, Texas, or U.S. authorities while he led the revolution from north of the border.

Madero's pro-American and pro-Texas policies were strategically important to his revolution. They did not engender U.S. government support, but they encouraged the ambivalent attitude of the American administration toward Díaz. American complaints included the following:

1. Díaz levied a preferential tax and set special railroad rates on zinc traveling to Europe instead of the United States. Díaz made that decision in retaliation to a U.S. tariff on the metal. Stillman's National City Bank was deeply involved with the zinc trust and included Stephen S. Palmer as trust representative on the bank board of directors.

2. Díaz nationalized most of the American-owned railroads and none of the British lines. He took that measure in order to forestall consolidation of the Mexican lines in one directorship located in New York and including the Stillman, Harriman, Rockefeller, Morgan, Vanderbilt, and Gould interests. The National City Bank already counted Schiff, Stillman, and Rockefeller from the Union Pacific, Robert Bacon and J. P. Morgan, Jr., of the Morgan Bank, Samuel Sloan, a directing member of several railroads, H. Walter Webb, and William D. Sloan among the railroad magnates on its board of directors. Sloan and Webb were both prominent in Vanderbilt enterprises. Webb served as a vice-president of the New York Central Railroad. They complained to the U.S. government about the Díaz administration's moves. Díaz then placed the British Pearson interests on the

new "Mexican" board of directors of the National Railway System, but the New York railroad consortium maintained dominance through selection of the head manager in Mexico. The Mexican government also demanded that American railroad employees learn to speak and read Spanish. It withdrew the request only after the U.S. government protested.

3. The Díaz government sought further European loans during and after the 1907–1908 banking crisis in the United States, a step that provoked outcries of anti-American discrimination from New York and Texas financial interests. The Mexican government's overtures to European financiers accompanied nationalistic demands for greater financial independence from the United States.

4. The American government became alarmed when Díaz opened negotiations with Japan for the development of a Japanese naval base at Magdalena Bay in Baja California and a possible secret mutual defense pact between the two countries.

5. Contracts with the Pearson and independent oil companies reduced Standard Oil's share of the Mexican domestic illuminating and machine oil market from 99.5 to 44 percent between 1904 and 1910.

6. The new National Railroad System broke its contract with the Standard Oil company's Mexican subsidiary and thereafter received its fuel from the Pearson-owned company.

7. The Díaz regime initiated a new tariff policy, spearheaded by Limantour, to develop stronger trade ties with Europe, lessening the nation's dependency on the U.S. market.

8. In 1909 Díaz canceled a large oil contract with American producer Edward Doheny, who had pioneered oil exploration in Mexico.

9. Díaz refused to accept U.S. military interference in Honduras and rejected a U.S. government invitation to endorse the American-imposed solution to that internal political dispute.

10. The Guggenheim-ASARCO interests complained when the Díaz government rejected their bid to buy the mines at Real del Monte near Pachuca and a British-Mexican consortium of the Pearson interests, the Díaz family, and Enrique Creel of the Terrazas family took them over.

11. Harriman, in charge of railroad operations of the Stillman-Rockefeller alliance, protested the diminution of his interests in the new National Railway System.

12. Standard Oil suffered exclusion from oil concessions in the richest Mexican fields, the Gulf areas of Veracruz, Tabasco, and the Isthmus of Tehuantepec, as well as Tamaulipas and San Luis Potosí. The independent

policies adopted by Díaz annoyed William Rockefeller, president of the Standard Oil Company.

13. The Texas Oil Company repeatedly complained that Díaz discriminated against American oil companies in favor of the British-owned Pearson interests.[11]

Despite the wide-ranging and deep problems that existed between Díaz and the government in Washington, there is still no evidence of active U.S. government support for Madero. No doubt the National City Bank board of directors pressured Taft on this matter. They claimed distinction in Republican party matters. The directors, apart from Democrats Stillman and Cleveland H. Dodge (who also belonged to the copper trust), had been the Republican party's largest presidential campaign financial contributor at the beginning of the century. The Taft administration accepted a representative of the Madero movement in Washington over Díaz's protests. It did nothing to intervene in Madero's revolutionary efforts in the United States. The U.S. government's attitude toward Madero contrasted with its hostility toward other Mexican revoltosos. Its reaction against Díaz and tolerance of Madero paralleled its 1876 reaction to Sebastián Lerdo de Tejada's nationalism and tolerance of Díaz's own efforts at Brownsville during the Revolution of Tuxtepec.

Although the Díaz regime distanced itself from the Americans in its later years and attempted to balance its dependence on the American economy with an association with British investors led by Lord Cowdray, it retained a solid reputation among American capitalists and government officials. They recognized Díaz's longtime maintenance of financial stability and social order in Mexico. In addition, he continued to enjoy the support of American ambassador Henry Lane Wilson and other rightists throughout the revolutionary crisis. The Japanese had no potential to act in Mexico, whatever their desires regarding a possible naval base at Magdalena Bay.

Díaz resigned when he recognized that continued fighting would only increase the threat posed by growing lower-class participation and radicalism in the revolutionary forces. He understood that the revolutionary process had to be terminated before mass participation went too far and could no longer be controlled by either his regime, the interim government, or Madero's narrowly based leadership circle. Díaz revealed his appreciation of the situation: "Madero has unleashed a tiger! Now let us see if he can control it!"

While revolutionary unrest was sweeping the countryside in 1910 and 1911, the industrial and urban working class began a mobilization that would be crucial to the ultimate outcome of the revolution. Just one week before Porfirio Díaz resigned, the typographic workers of Mexico City, led by Spanish anarchist Amadeo Ferrés, organized a *"sociedad de resistencia,"* the Confederación Tipográfica de México, to take the lead in the mobilization of the working class. As they put it, "A fresh wind is blowing." The hard-pressed Díaz government, which would have suppressed the workers as it did in the past when attempts were made to create labor organizations, now confronted widespread elite and agrarian violence and had no time to waste on the organization.[12]

Labor unrest continued to grow following the 1906 and 1907 uprisings at Cananea and Río Blanco, especially in the textile factories and mines. PLM organizers smuggled propaganda into Mexico City and adjacent states, including Puebla and Tlaxcala, via the party's newspapers *Revolución Social* and *Regeneración*, stimulating worker discontent. PLM clubs already existed in the capital city with many more in the pueblos and factories of Puebla and Tlaxcala. They popularized Ricardo Flores Magón as a revolutionary martyr who was harassed by the American and Mexican governments. They called for revolutionary action. However, with Flores Magón incarcerated in the United States, Madero inherited the mantle of revolutionary leadership.

Between 9 and 24 November 1910 riots swept downtown Mexico City. They began as anti-American demonstrations against the lynching of a Mexican at Rock Springs, Texas. Through the mix of crowd and police actions the violence grew and turned against the government. A badly organized insurrection based on more than three hundred groups headed by former PLM leader Aguiles Serdán in Puebla initiated the fighting. The police and army attacked and defeated the force at Serdán's home in the state capital one day before a planned insurrection involving hundreds of men and women broke out. Despite the defeat in Puebla, unrest grew. Shootings and attacks on private property and government buildings in Mexico City were commonplace for two weeks before order could be restored. In the spring of 1911 the most radical workers coalesced into small groups in their respective factories. Many of them supported Madero's revolutionary movement, but others formed more radical groups that would later form the core of the powerful revolutionary anarchosyndicalist labor organization, the Casa del Obrero Mundial.

When the announcement of the Treaty of Ciudad Juárez reached Mexico City, riots broke out again. Crowds marched through the streets calling for the president's immediate resignation. He did so the following day. While the crowds rioted, he slipped away via the Interoceanic Railway to

Veracruz. During his brief stay in the port city he enjoyed the hospitality of English merchants. The news of his departure spread quickly throughout the metropolis, and within hours the crowds of Mexico City, whose importance dates from the preindustrial uprisings of 1624 and 1692 and the overthrow of the viceroys, surged into the streets to celebrate. Church bells pealed the good news. A giant parade ensued. Freedom at last! Madero was coming to rule over a new Mexico in which everyone would get a fair deal. But as Díaz said, Madero had "unleashed a tiger."

The troubles began at once. The interim president, de la Barra, appointed a cabinet with a Porfirista majority, isolating the Maderistas to a grumbling minority. Madero accepted the arrangement after disarming the PLM units in Chihuahua or combining them under the authority of his own officers. He ordered most of his revolutionary forces, including those of Villa, to disband. He left the Porfirian army and its officer corps intact and incorporated only a few of his ill-received officers and units into its ranks. The government bureaucracy remained basically unscathed, although the forthcoming national elections portended changes at the higher levels and threatened the Porfiristas' sense of security. Madero tried to meld his following with the hierarchy but encountered resistance from all sides once he arrived in Mexico City. The continuing fiscal crisis did not permit budgetary expenditures to accommodate the expectations of the hierarchy and the demanding pequeña burguesa and provincial elite Maderistas for public works contracts and government employment.

In June Madero began a triumphant tour of the country between the border and Mexico City. Enormous crowds greeted him at the railroad stations and cities en route. He was the toast of the nation. People came to him for blessings, to touch him for good luck. Away from Madero and the center stage, however, the countryside was still in the throes of violence. The PLM held northern Baja California, where it occupied lands surrounding Tijuana and Mexicali that were owned by Harrison Gray Otis, Harry Chandler, and other Southern California investors. Armed peasant groups were seizing land and fighting with local authorities in traditional agrarian hot spots, including the Mezquital of San Luis Potosí, Chihuahua, Sinaloa, Tamaulipas, and the Isthmus of Tehuantepec. The peasants invariably invoked the name of the revolution and Madero to justify their actions. It was a chaotic situation. Madero called for calm and endorsed the shooting of "brigands." Meanwhile the Zapatistas continued to carry out land reforms.

A crisis developed between the provincial elite revolutionary leader and the peasant-agrarian worker Zapatistas in the south. The Maderistas were committed to political reform that included federalism and the incorporation of provincial and local elites into the regime. The Zapatistas' demand for redistribution of hacienda landholdings meant returning those lands to the pueblos which they claimed had been usurped by the great estate owners. They caused erosion of national elite cohesion and strength. Madero attempted to conciliate and bribe Zapata during the summer of 1911 through personal negotiations, a proffered hacienda, and promises of future court actions to satisfy village claims. In return he sought the disarming of the campesino forces and the evacuation of the occupied haciendas. The Porfirian elites were furious.

Zapata rejected the hacienda outright, as he would later do with bribes from Presidents Huerta and Carranza. He viewed the other conditions of the proposal as ridiculous while government forces under General Victoriano Huerta, who was anxious to defeat the peasant rebels, still advanced on Morelos, burning Zapatista towns and attacking residents. These attacks were carried out at the behest of the de la Barra government and frustrated Madero's attempt to placate the southerners. Madero wished to settle his differences in the south peacefully, although correspondence indicates this was because of a political motivation rather than a moral commitment to land redistribution. Madero, whose family controlled one of Mexico's larger latifundia complexes, had no sympathy for campesino communal desires. His priority was to seek peace and stability in order to establish a firm national government. He did not achieve this goal. The fighting continued, and Zapata denounced Madero as a traitor to the revolution. The border region of Baja California remained in hostile PLM hands. Elements of the Maderista left-wing intelligentsia and industrial labor were becoming increasingly dissatisfied with their former champion. Madero had not yet occupied the presidency.

The presidential campaign that began in August 1911 revealed further divisions in the popular front that originally supported Madero's cause. At his request the party dropped the more radical and well-known vice-presidential candidate Francisco Vasquez Gómez, who had run in the ill-fated 1910 campaign, in favor of a virtually unknown Yucatecan journalist, José María Pino Suárez. The latter's nomination resulted from Madero's desire to develop a basis for loyalty to the new government among Yucatecos. The election that followed was a virtual nonevent. Madero's only potential rival, the former governor of Nuevo León, Bernardo Reyes, gave up the race when his campaign failed to make headway and left a field of minor opposition candidates. Despite the disaffection of some of Madero's more important followers, he still enjoyed great general popularity. Elected president, he took the oath of office on 6 November 1911.

From the remote mountain poblado of Ayoxustla in southwestern Puebla state, Zapata and his officers signed the revolutionary Plan of Ayala on 25 November. They declared revolution against Madero for "inepti-tude" and "bloody treason." They recognized Pascual Orozco, the principal leader of the northern rural and town-based working-class insurgents, as their leader in an effort to create nationwide agrarian unity. Importantly, they called for redistribution of the holdings of all landlords who opposed them or who had taken properties that rightfully belonged to the pueblos. In rejecting Madero as a member of Mexico's landholding social elite, the anarchist Otilio E. Montaño, a rural schoolteacher from Ayala and the other déclassé intellectuals who helped in writing the Plan of Ayala, transcended the usual provincialism of peasant movements and reached across the nation seeking alliances. Throughout its ten-year history Zapatismo demonstrated the capacity to transcend the localism of the peasantry through alliances with the Villistas and repeated offers for the PLM to establish a national regime with Ricardo Flores Magon as president at Cuernavaca.

Zapatismo was much more significant than the man and his immediate following in the south-central area of the nation. His revolution reflected a wider grass-roots peasants' war. Lower-class unrest embraced two-thirds of the country from Sonora and Tamaulipas to Chiapas and Campeche. By mid-1912 a growing wave of violence and political instability swept the country. The American embassy, under Ambassador Henry Lane Wilson, which had been hostile toward Madero from the beginning, lost confidence in his ability to maintain law and order.

Strikes broke out among agricultural laborers on the estates of the American-owned Laguna Corporation and the Gulf Land and Timber Company in Campeche. Those properties, controlled by powerful New York, Philadelphia, and Chicago banking interests, were part of over 3 million acres of American-owned rubber and henequén plantations and hardwood forests in the state. As strikes and violence spread in the south, Bernardo Reyes and Emilio Vasquez Gómez attempted separate revolts in the north, entering Mexico from the United States and calling the people to arms. Both failed pathetically, not because they lacked ability but because they mistakenly attacked Madero at his principal point of strength, the northern tier of states where pro-Maderista provincial and local elites had taken power.[13]

Abraham González, who nominated Madero to challenge Díaz at the anti-reelectionist convention in Mexico City, served as governor of Chihuahua. Former Porfirian senator Venustiano Carranza, who attached himself to Madero's retinue during the president's tenure in San Antonio and accompanied him to Ciudad Juárez, became governor of Coahuila. The provincial elites and some of the alienated intelligentsia of the Díaz era proved to be the most steadfast of the president's supporters who remained from the revolutionary amalgam that had overthrown Díaz. Hopelessly isolated, neither Vasquez Gómez nor Reyes found it worthwhile to make an appeal to the material interests of the peasants in order to broaden their support.

After two weeks Reyes surrendered on Christmas Day to a detachment of rurales. He was court-martialed, and the government sentenced him to prison in the Federal District. Vasquez Gómez's attempt got off to a propitious beginning. His forces seized Ciudad Juárez, but Pascual Orozco, who was Madero's commander of rural police in Chihuahua, took command of the federal forces. Orozco still claimed rank-and-file support of the northern working class as a popular nationalist revolutionary. A peaceful meeting between Orozco and the Vasquez Gómez forces resulted in disarmament. A humiliated Vasquez Gómez demonstrated the distance between traditional politics and northern populist zeal. He retired from combat.

In the meantime a federal army entered Baja California and drove the anarchist Flores Magonista PLM from power and back across the U.S. border. The short-lived Anarchist Republic of Baja California had directly attacked and occupied the 35,000-acre San Isidro Rancho holdings of Southern California investors Harry Chandler, George Keller, George P. Griffith, and Edward Fletcher. The anarchists called on Mexico's revolutionaries to abolish capitalism and government, but their leadership was imprisoned in the United States. Geographically isolated, they were easily defeated.[14]

The most serious challenge to Madero in the north came not from right-wing elite figures or the PLM but from Orozco, who claimed a wide following among the agrarian population. Orozco rebelled in March 1912. The rift between provincial elite rule and northern lower-class nationalism was deep. It began in May 1911, when Orozco and Villa seized Ciudad Juárez against Madero's orders and then confronted him with their demands. Following Madero's failure to appoint Orozco to a position of responsibility, the revolutionary government promulgated its agreements with Díaz, which made no provision for peasant land allocations. The two military chiefs, Orozco and Villa, had then demanded land disbursements for the rank-and-file troops who served the revolution. The president's reply offered them little satisfaction. *Bienes nacionales,* national properties, would be bought by the new government at a later date and then dispensed to the men and their families. The plan infuriated Orozco and Villa. They believed the land reform would never come to pass, but they were not disposed to act because hope had not yet died amid the new government's popularity.

Both sides to this dispute recognized the deep social class and cultural contradictions between Madero and his inner circle of landowners, financiers, businessmen, and politicians on one side, and Villa and Orozco as working men leading agrarian working-class cohorts on the other. Peasant revolutionaries were already seizing and dividing up great estate holdings in Durango, western Chihuahua, and southwestern Coahuila.

Madero excluded Orozco and Villa from power in the new government. He made Villa an "honorary general" and ordered him to retire. He left Orozco, the key military leader in the northern revolution, with the command of rurales in Chihuahua. Villa excused Madero as "a victim of bad advice"; the ambitious Orozco was not so sanguine. Madero's refusal to grant meaningful land reform to either the northern or the southern peasant revolutionaries may be viewed as a strategic error, but it was consistent with his political and philosophical wisdom. It endorsed the class interests of his provincial elite backers. His refusal personally to accommodate Orozco was a major political blunder.

In the Pacto de la Empacadora Orozco issued a far-reaching reform package that equaled the 1906 PLM social program. It recognized the social reform principles of the Plans of San Luis Potosí, Ayala, and Tacubaya. Leftist Maderistas issued the latter plan from Mexico City in October 1911 and rebel Emilio Vasquez Gómez adopted it. It protested the merger of the Maderista revolution with the ancien régime, Madero's nepotism, and his acceptance of American financial aid in order to carry out his revolution. This American connection, Orozco claimed, reduced the president to a mere U.S. puppet.

Orozco's populist revolutionaries singled out American economic installations for attacks across the breadth of northern Mexico. He promised a ten-hour workday for urban and industrial labor, nationalization of the railroads, minimum wages, and far-reaching land reform. There is little doubt that Orozco sincerely believed in his program despite the fact that the rebellion, grasping an opportunity for financial support, soon received funds from the oligarchial Terrazas clan in Chihuahua. The Terrazas interests hoped to recover their political power and later control Orozco's rebellion.[15]

Although there is no indication that Orozco ever expropriated lands belonging to the oligarchy or the Americans, Orozquistas attacked American properties on both sides of the lower Rio Grande and American mines as far south as Jalisco, occupied the American-owned 1,400,000-acre Rascon hacienda in San Luis Potosí and the 1,200,000-acre San Jose de las Rusias Hacienda in Tamaulipas, and raided the American colonies from Tamaulipas to the Pacific shoreline and as far south as Colima. In the Isthmus of Tehuantepec rebels chased Americans off lands near Salina Cruz and the still partially Zapotec towns of Ixtepec and Ixtaltepec. The emmisary of President Taft, sent on board the *Buford,* an American transport, reported on the evacuation of Americans along the Pacific Coast:

> Twenty-eight refugees on board the Buford at Manzanillo. . . . In Colima . . . there is an anti-American sentiment . . . [even] more serious in its possible consequences . . . for the reason that it comes from the business and financial element of the state. It has been unconsciously engendered by the American investors and lumber companies in that state.[16]

In Salina Cruz another 130 desperate American refugees boarded the *Buford.* A total of 364 Americans fled Mexico on the *Buford,* leaving their property and possessions behind. The U.S. government watched the situation with deepening alarm.

Orozco's popular following and their countless attacks on American properties caused the American government to embargo the border and deny the rebels arms and ammunition. The Orozquistas were forced to fight major engagements while severely underarmed and undersupplied. Orozco's support in Sonora came from the Cananea workers and the oppressed Yaqui and Mayo Indians. In Chihuahua, Coahuila, and Sonora a multiclass front of supporters rallied to the revolt, but they were embargoed while Maderista commanders, including Alvaro Obregon Salido, received American arms. The Maderistas were able to defeat them while safeguarding American company properties. Finally General Huerta crushed the rebellion and restored order.[17]

Another rebellion against the Madero government followed. The revolt broke out in October 1912, led by the reactionary Felix Díaz, nephew of the deposed dictator. Díaz was a potential threat because despite his lack of a popular following, he appealed to the already disenchanted Porfirian officer corps, which still dominated the army. Progovernment forces quickly arrested, courtmartialed, and incarcerated Díaz in a federal district penitentiary.

The endemic rural unrest increased, however. Small bands of Zapatistas surfaced as far north as Sinaloa and Tamaulipas. Led by village elites, industrial workers, and rancheros, they attacked American-owned mines, *ingenios*, and landed properties, including the Rascon and San Jose de las Rusias haciendas in the northeast, and the United Sugar Company holdings along the Río Fuerte in Sinaloa.[18]

While the Madero government was struggling to control insurrections in outlying states, problems with the industrial and urban working classes developed to increasingly serious levels in Mexico City, Puebla, and other centers. The American chargé d'affairs reported that businessmen and foreign officials alike feared Madero's inability to deal with "the unintelligent demands of the proletariat."

Throughout 1912 the nuclei of industrial working-class groups hostile toward the Madero government multiplied. Railroad workers organized a new syndicate and staged several strikes; miners in Coahuila and Cananea and textile workers and craftsmen of Mexico City, Orizaba, Puebla, Guadalajara, Querétaro, Torreón, Tepic, Monterrey, Zacatecas, Oaxaca, and other cities formed new unions. Local groups initiated much of this activity, but nationwide working-class organizing attempts were also under way. Maderista workers and revolutionaries came into conflict with the regime because of the president's appointment of upper-class former Porfiristas and neutrals to high state offices, and because of his support of business during labor disputes. The most significant of these efforts, for the future, was that of the linotype-displaced typesetters who formed the Confederación Nacional de Artes Gráficas, headed by Spanish anarchist Amadeo Ferrés and his group, the Obreros Intellectuales. They strove to create a nationwide anarchosyndicalist workers' movement. By summer they had established a syndicate of publishing and printshop workers which disseminated revolutionary propaganda.

In June 1912 Juan Francisco Moncaleano, an anarchist former professor from Colombia, arrived in Mexico. His efforts prodded the Obreros Intellectuales and others into formating an active underground organizing group known as Luz. It was committed to the establishment of an anarchosyndicalist labor front along the lines of the Spanish Confederación Nacional del Trabajo. Luz intended to recruit the entire Mexican working class, including the peasantry.

The Madero government soon arrested Moncaleano for "subversive activity" and deported him as an undesirable alien. He ended up in Los Angeles. The Luz group, however, plunged ahead in its task of "uplifting the workers through group example and education" until labor could take over the economy and destroy the Church, state, and capitalism through strikes and armed self-defense. Luz created the Casa del Obrero in September 1912 as a workers' council in order to begin the uphill struggle. By the end of the year the Casa published its own newspaper and had recruited several thousand members in the Mexico City area in addition to groups in other industrial centers.

In January 1913 the Casa won a series of well publicized victories in direct action strikes and sit-ins in the Mexico City area. Crowds outside the struck establishments reached 2,000 and used such tactics as stoning windows and occupying the facilities.

The Madero government's response to the Casa and its anarchist control group, which changed its name from Luz to Lucha (struggle), was completely inadequate. Its attempt to create a trade union loyal to the government, La Gran Liga Obrera, was a miserable failure. Casa interlopers took over the Liga on one occasion when it held a public meeting for the election of its officers. Casa members promptly stood for Liga office, and when elected, they declared the group disbanded. The Liga, made a laughingstock, never recovered. It remained a paper organization with ties to Madero's Department of Labor. The use of force was the government's alternative, but the unintimidated Casa leadership noted the regime's growing weakness. A series of street battles ensued, fought between Casa militants and police in front of strike-closed establishments. The Casa emerged from these confrontations with the "*cosacos*" (Cossacks) with a heroic image among the industrial working class.[19]

In the view of many Mexico City area workers the Casa's struggle was their own against a discredited government that was at the service of foreign capital that dominated the nation's industrial production and much of the landholding. Ironically, the internationalist-minded revolutionary leadership of the Casa gained at the expense of the national government and industrialists because of the worker's nationalism. Madero's decision to wage war on the Zapatistas, for whom the workers had great sympathy, only compounded their alienation.

In 1912 the governing elite fully recognized Zapatismo as the ultimate threat to the regime's survival in a Mexico that was still 87 percent rural. The newspapers warned of its "communistic danger" to private property. Madero cited its "socialistic appeal to the ready intelligence of the Morlense campesinaje." While urging the government to act against the "rural savagery of the campesino masses," the landowning class concentrated in Mexico City blamed the president for having created the situation in the first place with his irresponsible promises of land repatriation in the Plan of San Luis Potosí.

On 27 June 1912 Madero defended himself in a newspaper article. Consistent with nineteenth-century Liberal ideology, he declared that he had never intended "despoiling the property of a terrateniente" but that he did favor the creation of small landholdings. Madero concluded that the great estate owners could not be deprived of properties to which they held titles. Although it was understood that a hacendado could obtain one form or another of legal entitlement, the president satisfied none of his wealthy critics and left the reformists demoralized and confused.

In the north campesino land seizures and risings in Coahuila, Chihuahua, Durango, Nuevo León, San Luis Potosí, Sonora, Tamaulipas, and Zacatecas discredited the government. In the south campesino revolutionaries raided foreign and domestically owned great estates from coast to coast while the armed forces unenthusiastically attempted to restore order. The nation was experiencing so much armed conflict that commerce and industry were at a near standstill. Uprisings and concomitant banditry, many of them directed against American holdings, were so widespread and numerous that the army's manpower was too thin to control them.

The countryside antagonisms were a crazy quilt of complexity: Mexican versus foreigner, ranchero against hacendado, Indian against mestizo, pueblo versus town, and hacienda workers seizing estate property. Peasant bands invaded towns and burned municipal archives. The basic antagonism was between village communalists and agricultural workers on the one side and hacendados and foreign landowners in defense of their commercial holdings on the other.

From Chiapas to Chihuahua the government controlled much of the countryside in the day but only the cities at night. The political and economic institutions of the Mexican ancien régime were on the verge of complete breakdown. Residents, general managers, and resident employees of American colonies and the most powerful companies in the United States looked on in disgust and amazement. They complained to their government and employers as campesino bands operating outside of any external authority invaded dozens of U.S.-owned establishments, among them the Corralitos hacienda near Casas Grandes; the Rascon hacienda, Atascador and San Dieguito colonies in San Luis Potosí; the Laguna Corporation and Gulf Coast Land and Lumber Company properties in Campeche; the San Jose de las Rusias hacienda and the Blaylock and La Palma colonies in Tamaulipas; the Piedra Blanca hacienda in Coahuila;

the Buena Fe mine in Jalisco; the Richardson Construction Company in Sonora; the Colima Lumber Company in Colima; the Motzorongo Plantation in Veracruz; the Medina Colony in Oaxaca; the Zacualapa-Hidalgo Rubber Plantation in Chiapas; the Mormon and secular colonies in the northwestern states; and the Cedros hacienda in Zacatecas. The American colonists recognized their assailants as former employees, neighboring "squatters" and villagers, and sometimes local rancheros and petty officials.[20]

By the end of 1912 the Madero government had entered a state of deep crisis. The president could not satisfy the aspirations of the campesino and industrial working classes without betraying himself and his closest associates. He lost the support of the leftist intellectuals who were at the forefront of the ideological debate with Díaz. He failed to maintain law and order in the countryside and city and therefore could satisfy neither investors, the industrial elite, nor the great landowners. His open investment policy and reassurances to foreign investors were blunted by his inability to protect their properties from attack. The army officer corps remained hostile toward what it regarded as his upstart and weak leadership.

Madero's idea of American-style democracy was out of touch with the realities of class contradictions in 1911–1913 Mexico. It is in this context that the otherwise weak revolutionary movement headed jointly by Bernardo Reyes and Felix Díaz in February 1913 had such far-reaching consequences. In the past Reyes, as governor of Nuevo León, had worked with the Standard Oil and Guggenheim interests. Díaz, as a landowner and partner of the Texas Oil Company board of directors, and Porfirian elites in the Tamaulipas Irrigation and Development Company enjoyed similar prestige. The consortium controlled 4,647,000 acres inside Mexico; most of the land was in Tamaulipas, but 147,000 acres were located near Guadalajara.[21]

Reyes and Díaz, incarcerated in separate prisons in the Mexico City area, established clandestine contact in late 1912 and planned a coup d'état. On 9 February, 1913 General Manual Mondragon, an accomplice, released them from prison. Supported by two thousand troops, including military cadets, the rebels marched on the National Palace. Reyes fell mortally wounded in the first moments of the ensuing exchange of fire with palace guards. The surviving rebels, led by Díaz, retreated to the old and weak citadel, the Cuidadela, on the southside of downtown. The so-called *decena tragica* was under way.

The loyal commander of Madero's forces, Lauro Villar, received wounds in the palace fighting, and Madero overrode the warnings of his aides and selected his enemy, Victoriano Huerta, to command his troops. Díaz and Huerta reached a tacit accord. The two sides fired artillery shells around the city at random for ten days, causing great privation and hundreds of civilian deaths. The city's populace was completely demoralized. Political faith in the Madero democracy waned among the city's pequeña burguesía and workers. Shells even fell near the British Embassy, causing its evacuation; observers noted that the U.S. establishment went unscathed.

Huerta neutralized troops loyal to Madero brought in from outside the city by sending them in hopeless frontal assaults straight into Díaz's fire. Huerta then moved to seize power. The Pacto de la Embajada was an agreement to overthrow Madero involving Huerta, Díaz, and American ambassador Henry Lane Wilson, who was acting, as he saw it, "to protect American interests." Wilson, who later denied participation in the planning, saw himself as the arbiter and judge of the "immature Mexicans" and the "emotional Latin race." Wilson expected Díaz to play a major role in the new government, perhaps to head it, but Huerta had other ideas.

On 18 February Huerta sent General Aureliano Blanquet to the National Palace to arrest Madero. Madero's brother, Gustavo, was murdered at lunch by his would-be captors. The vice-president, Pino Suárez, and some cabinet members were also seized. The conspirators, with the leading figures of the Madero government in custody, announced the Embassy Pact the following evening. The pact justified takeover of the government by pointing out the national unrest and Madero's shortcomings, both real and fanciful. The following day Secretary of Foreign Relations Pedro Lascurain Paredes, who participated in the conspiracy, succeeded to the presidency automatically, when, from their prison cells, both Madero and Pino Suárez renounced their offices. Lascurain immediately appointed Huerta secretary of the interior and then resigned after one hour in office, making Huerta the new head of state. By signing away their offices Madero and Pino Suárez made the scenario legal. They also facilitated their own murders. Despite Mrs. Madero's plea for her husband's well-being in an interview, Ambassador Wilson replied that he could not meddle in the affairs of a "sovereign nation."

On the evening of 21 February the escort ostensibly transferring Madero and Pino Suárez to a new place of confinement murdered them. Theories abound regarding the possible motives and circumstances of the assassinations. The two most plausible are based upon the assumption that alive, the former president presented the principal threat to the new government. One argues that individuals around Huerta recognized the instability of the new regime and attempted to ingratiate themselves with him through the elimination of Madero. The other posits that the military escort carried out the orders of the president himself and points to Huerta's bloody earlier counterinsurgency campaigns in Yucatán, Morelos, and the north and the killing of legislative critics a year later.

Madero failed to control growing unrest during his presidency despite the legitimacy he gained through the electoral process. Huerta's only chance lay in quickly forging alliances with some of the contending forces in the revolution. The strongest of Huerta's limited options was his close ties with the army officer corps and the old Porfirian elite of Mexico City. They rushed to accept his cabinet posts. The embarrassed foreign legations expressed sympathy, and the industrialists and landowners held their breath, hoping Huerta would restore law and order. Huerta's friends, however, brought with them the same ferocious combination of enemies that was the undoing of Díaz. His open ties with the American embassy earned the scorn of the nationalistic intelligentsia that had ridiculed Díaz, and peasants, industrial workers, and provincial and local elites once again formed a disparate but violent opposition.

The elite crisis that began with provincial liberalism in San Luis Potosí and the anti-reelectionist movement had precipitated the Madero-led overthrow of Díaz. It continued through the Madero period and Huerta's seizure of power. The elite crisis now entered another phase. Once again a member of the northern provincial elites, this time the governor of Coahuila, Venustiano Carranza, formally declared revolution. This time, however, the lower-class participants were better organized, stronger, and more experienced. The ensuing struggles laid bare the nation's social antagonisms. Lower-class and local elite attacks on American estates and properties intensified.

The Maderista governors of the northern states—Abraham González in Chihuahua, José Maytorena in Sonora, and Carranza—supported by their respective provincial elite, peasant, and industrial worker constituencies, opposed the new government. Huertista assassins promptly struck down González, but in March 1913 Carranza issued a revolutionary proclamation, the Plan of Guadalupe, which rejected the Huerta government and anointed Carranza the "first chief" of a "Constitutionalist" revolutionary army. The miners' militia of Coahuila, a workers' group that organized during the Madero era, formed the basis of his first military force.[22]

Carranza took some of his troops to Sonora, where he created a unified command of his forces with those of Governor Maytorena. In Sonora they enjoyed the benefit of arms acquisitions across the Arizona border. Maytorena, claiming illness, left Sonora to convalesce in the United States. Carranza's leadership was unchallenged. He attracted a following of young pequeña burguesa professionals, businessmen, and provincial elites, who later formed his conservative base of support within the revolution.

Obregon Salido, a marginalized member of one of Sonora's oligarchical families, headed the local rebel forces. Before 1910 he had filled a variety of pequeña burguesa occupations, such as shopkeeper, hotel manager, and ranchero. He actively commanded the troops and recruited several thousand previously domesticated Yaqui Indians to the cause. Some of the less acculturated "Bronco" Yaqui later became Villistas. They had militarily resisted Mexican land seizures and American land developers and railroad men during the previous thirty-five years. Those Yaqui enlisted by Obregon Salido with promises of land redistribution came from groups no longer violently resisting the loss of their homeland. Obregon Salido, working closely with W. R. Grace and Company, would later create one of Mexico's largest latifundia complexes while incurring a personal debt to the American company of $1.8 million in the early 1920s. After the revolution the Yaqui, who were so important in the origins of his military forces, would receive some of the most desolate, miserable terrain in Mexico in lieu of their former rich bottomlands.[23]

Huerta's most important allies besides the American government, whose arms support continued until September 1913, were the Church, army officer corps, Porfirian oligarchy, and Orozco, who bore the brunt of the government's efforts to stop the revolution's progress in Chihuahua. By supporting Huerta, Orozco ceased to be the hero and leader of the northern working classes. That mantle now fell upon Villa, who declared himself in revolt in Chihuahua and led coalescing rural groups that grew into the División del Norte, the largest military force produced by the revolution.

The División del Norte and its officers were initially peasant rural working-class, cowboys, artisans, and small-scale commercial farmers in origin and their following was a people in arms. They crisscrossed the northern steppes of Mexico on horses and, later, in trains, carrying informal and even extended family groups with them. The men, with some women and children, were the fighters. The bulk of the women, children, and aged performed logistical services. The División del Norte, like the great masses of Padre Hidalgo, marched toward the center against the government and the existing social order. Across the north thousands of lower-class rebels, without centralized direction but calling themselves Villistas, assaulted American- and Mexican-owned estates.

In the south the Zapatistas rejected Huerta when he attempted to recruit the southern campesino revolutionaries. Several Zapatista chiefs came close to accepting Huerta's offers of amnesty and land reform. As a result the Zapatista command tightened its discipline among the far-flung rebels in the field. Huerta's initial attraction for them seemed to stem from his promises of agrarian reform and humble origins; his mother was a Huichol Indian. Huerta reestablished order in southern Veracruz, Tabasco, and eastern Puebla, but the Zapatistas remembered Huerta's bloody campaign in Morelos during the de la Barra interim presidency which had frustrated the Madero-Zapata negotiations. They seized Huerta's emissaries and placed them on show trial. Pascual Orozco, Sr., father of the former revolutionary, was one of those tried. Zapata accused Orozco and Huerta of "assassinating the revolution" and removed Orozco's name from the Plan of Ayala, which had anointed him national leader of what constituted a rural lower-class revolution.

At this point, having secured most of the topographically easy Gulf coast, and while the northern revolution was still far removed from the center of the nation, Huerta decided to liquidate the Zapatistas and secure his rear to the southwest of Mexico City from Morelos to Acapulco. He planned then to send his army northward at full strength to crush the rebels in Chihuahua and Sonora. His standing forces and equipment were insufficient for the task. Morelos was surrounded by rugged mountains with a series of densely populated narrow valleys connected by deep canyons and good footpaths. It was perfect guerrilla country. Huerta lacked time and the necessary popular support in the southern countryside. In his first move he eliminated the reform-minded Liberals in the state government at Cuernavaca. In midnight raids he rounded up the governor and key legislators, transported them to Mexico City, and jailed them. He then appointed ruthless General Juvencio Robles interim governor of the state and charged him with the task of crushing the Zapatistas.

Huerta and Robles planned a scorched-earth counterinsurgency campaign against the campesinos of the south unmatched in Mexico since Viceroy Calleja's offensive against the Bajío villagers in 1811. Huerta explained his plan to the hacienda owners of Morelos during a gathering at the elite Jockey Club in Mexico City the day before launching the attack. John Womack reports that Huerta told the hacendados he would use "extreme measures, for the government is going, so to speak, to depopulate the state, and will send to your haciendas other workers [because the people of Morelos are] all Zapatistas. . . . It is necessary to clean out all such, and you must not be surprised." He promised a quick peace. The enthusiastic planters, composed largely of the nation's metropolitan elite in Mexico

City, offered to help any way they could in order to defeat the peasants and restore the security of their properties.[24]

Despite Robles's efforts, Huerta's plan failed. A few days after Robles seized the state capital the Zapatistas stormed Jonacatepec, an important district town, and captured the garrison and the general in charge. More important, the insurgent peasants seized the arms and ammunition in the armory. The Zapatistas then moved quickly to the offensive throughout the state, even harassing Robles's forces in Cuernavaca. Huerta reacted by pouring five thousand more troops into the state to carry out the Morelos phase of his plan and end the war on schedule. Successful counterinsurgency requires overwhelming forces, good intelligence, and a persuasive peasant political program. Huerta lacked all three.

On 9 May 1913 Robles ordered all of the state's citizenry to concentrate on the capitals of each municipio. Few obeyed, and the army then began a campaign to round up young men, sending them in boxcars to Mexico City as military inductees. The program failed. Only hundreds, not thousands of inductees could be found in the first few weeks. The reasoning behind the induction plan was that potential rebels and sympathizers, once removed from the state and trained like the "Foreign Indians" of the colonial era, could be converted into loyal federal troops prepared to fight in the north. Forced conscripts from Morelos and elsewhere, however, proved to be a disaster for the morale and fighting efficiency of the army. They deserted at the first opportunity, sometimes en masse, to the enemy.

The Huerta-Robles counterinsurgency plan proved to be a complete failure. In Cuba during the 1890s the concentration of a campesino population in special camps had worked. But Cuba was an island that could be swept clean by dedicated Spanish (i.e., foreign) troops. The Zapatista-campesino zone of insurgency in the south was surrounded by vast mountainous rugged terrain, and these insurgents were not the racially and nationally distinct rebels confronted by the Spanish Army in Cuba or the Yaqui and Mayo Indians whom the Mexican government had suppressed in the past. These people were neighbors of Mexico City, and many were acutely familiar with its way of life. Eighty percent of them spoke some Spanish. The army did its job, sometimes with relish, but for most of the men in the ranks it was a dirty, unpleasant task. The campesinos ensured the failure of the army's campaign by slipping into the bush whenever a military patrol approached. By the end of May Robles had caught and shipped about a thousand campesinos to Mexico City, only a small percentage of the planned manpower.

Robles's forces burned villages and crops, shot the old and infirm, and kidnapped women. The hacienda big houses and fields were destroyed. To their dismay the hacendados found that Robles, in carrying out Huerta's orders, was beyond all control or reason. They requested his removal, thus pressuring him to even greater efforts to conclude his military campaign with a quick victory.

Each Zapatista unit depended on its roots with the local people for support. For example, at Puente de Ixtla, in the vicinity of American General John Frisbie's Atlixtac hacienda, women and children banded together as a guerrilla force. Led by La China, a tortilla maker, they carried out raids throughout the district. The Atlixtac hacienda suffered heavy damages. The Zapatista forces tightened their discipline and instituted procedures that guaranteed the property and rights of the campesinos. For the peasants the choice of sides was made easier. Government forces raided and pillaged villages. Zapatistas exercised a program that carried out land reform, punishment of those soldiers who transgressed against campesinos, and support for the free and independent village, the *municipio libre,* as the basic economic and political unit of the nation. It was the same cause for which the Mexican campesino had fought during the previous two hundred years.

Finally realizing the impossibility of his task, Robles announced victory and withdrew. The result was a publicity event covered by Mexico City reporters in which the small town of Huautla, which had served for a time as Zapatista headquarters, was destroyed. All the troops found, however, was the executed Pascual Orozco Sr.'s body in the abandoned town. The government and press reported the "victory." The landowners believed it and staged celebrations in Mexico City and Cuernavaca. In reality the insurgent peasants had avoided conflict with Robles's main force in order to mount a counteroffensive.

Beginning in late 1913 and continuing into the spring of 1914, a campesino guerrilla war spread from Morelos toward the Isthmus of Tehuantepec in the south and to Michoacán and Hidalgo in the north. Villages that had participated in separate agrarian uprisings from 1707 to 1910 now joined under the banner of Zapatismo. The wave of unrest and growth of peasant forces spread out across Morelos and into adjoining states and then came crashing back against Cuernavaca, driving the army back to Mexico City. Some of the planters, alarmed by Villista victories in the north and growing Zapatista strength in the south, fled to Veracruz and even from the country.[25]

The loss of Chilpancingo and Iguala in Guerrero characterized the government's debacle. Using the insurgent peasant population of Guerrero as his base of support, Zapata first surrounded the cities and cut off their supplies. The Chilpancingo garrison fled, but the insurgents intercepted and destroyed it forty miles to the south at El Rincon, where campesinos in the great Guerrero peasant wars of 1842–1845 were mercilessly slaughtered by the forces of landowner Nicolas Bravo. The settling of old scores continued on 6 April 1914, when insurgents executed the captured garrison commander, General Carton. The cache of seized war material served as a basis for following Zapatista actions. At Iguala ranchero and local elite-led forces contested both the Zapatistas and the defeated government.

Huerta attempted to repair the government's deteriorating position by taking political advantage of the 21 April American invasion of Veracruz. He sent more emissaries to the south with a call for national unity against the Yanquis, but the Zapatistas rejected them. In early May they swept over Jojutla and its 1,200-man garrison and the main forces moved to the outskirts of Mexico City. The government's garrison defense of latifundia properties and urban centers in the south was a military and political disaster. The peasantry was mobilized. The Zapatistas occupied the countryside contiguous to the capital and prepared to negotiate its surrender. The government was not ready, however, to turn over the national center of culture, wealth, and political power to insurgent peasants.

Huerta held on until 15 July before turning over the reins of government to interim President Francisco Carbajal and fleeing the country. Carbajal then moved to surrender Mexico City to the forces of hacendado and former governor of Coahuila, Carranza. The government avoided negotiations with the Zapatistas for over two months in order to achieve that which they opposed, "a simple change in the personnel of government."

While the government officials stalled the Zapatistas and sought to surrender to Carranza, who was a member of their own social and cultural element, similar maneuvers by the first chief prevented the overwhelmingly lower-class-led División del Norte from reaching Mexico City before his own much weaker forces. During 1913 and 1914 the northern revolutionaries underwent a growing schism, which led to an open confrontation between Villa and Carranza with his provincial elite- and pequeña burguesa-led Constitutionalist forces.

The División del Norte formed from scattered groups of rebellious agrarian workers, miners, and artisans in the wake of the Madero assassination and Huerta coup. They occupied hacienda lands in Chihuahua, southern Coahuila, and Durango. Citizens of towns like Janos and Casas Grandes reclaimed lands lost to American and Mexican hacendados during the Porfiriato. Once in rebellion, most of the countryside rebel groups affiliated with the Villista forces. Most local rebel groups, however, operated without outside authority.

The Villista main forces congealed into an army. Formally conceived on 29 September 1913, the units of the División del Norte received arms and supplies through the confiscation and sale of livestock and crops seized from American and Mexican estates to American merchandisers along the border and by the seizure of armories. The higher-ranking Villistas attempted to maintain good relations with the Americans and their government by safeguarding their properties while pillaging Mexican holdings, but they could not control local units. The highly profitable arms trade with the Villistas attracted the largest American arms manufacturers to El Paso, and the insurgents established a working "cash on the line" relationship with them. The production of the commercial estates enabled the División del Norte to develop independently of Carranza.[26]

The División del Norte won a sensational string of victories. It gained strength until on 1 October 1913 it captured Torreón. Two weeks later it seized Chihuahua City, capital of the state. Then, using a train, the Villistas surprised the garrison at Ciudad Juárez. On 23 November they destroyed a government column sent to pacify them. On 11 January 1914 they eliminated the last important Huertista force in Chihuahua at Ojinaja. The División del Norte now controlled the vast state and resources of Chihuahua.

In January 1914 the Villistas garnered $100,000 for confiscated cattle hides from the Finnegan-Brown Company at Juárez. They quickly purchased arms. Another $50,000 shipment was awaited momentarily. They seized the Salazar hacienda adjoining the 2.5 million-acre Palomas hacienda owned by Edwin Marshal, the former treasurer of the Texas Company, and used it as their headquarters. They shot the Zalazar patriarch and threw him in the *casco* water well.[27]

From Sonora, Carranza and his pequeña burguesa, provincial elite, and hacendado advisers watched the events in Chihuahua with concern. The American administration of President Woodrow Wilson also looked on apprehensively. Carranza became preoccupied with the problem of controlling the División del Norte's largely rural working-class, artisan, and increasingly ranchero leadership. For him the Villistas represented a socially alien and geographically removed military force that fought under the Constitutionalist banner yet was stronger than his own forces. On several occasions Carranza attempted to wrest control of the División del Norte from Villa. Each time, the officers around Villa defended him and the political rivalry between the two men widened to parallel the extremely different social worlds from which they came. In his campaign against Villa, Carranza did succeed in one important way. He diverted attention from the profoundly contrasting goals of the two forces to the issue of Villa's character, a distraction that still sidetracks some historians.

The División del Norte moved south out of Chihuahua along the Central Mexican Railway, incorporating lower-class-led rebel bands as it advanced, preparing for the second battle of Torreón. In contrast, Carranza's forces under Obregon Salido moved carefully along the Pacific coast. They carefully sought to consolidate political control over the populace as they advanced. Rebellious elements were dealt with harshly. Rather than incorporating them, Obregon Salido's subordinate, Salvador Alvarado, suppressed an uprising among the Mayo Indians; and Plutarcho Elías Calles and Benjamin Hill secured order among the rebellious workers in and around the mine fields owned by Phelps Dodge at Nacozari and Anaconda at Cananea. Other protected properties included J. P. Morgan's La Quintana mine. Separated from the central campaign by the rugged Sierra Madre Occidental, the troops under Obregon Salido advanced in the wake of government withdrawals forced by Villa's victories. At the same time, Obregon Salido proved his tactical ability with rapid forced marches and modest successes.

Villista troops quickly took Saltillo in the east and then recaptured Torreón to the south against Carranza's orders. They had evacuated Torreón earlier in order to establish uncontested control over the north. With masses of new adherents, the División del Norte poured southward toward Zacatecas, the bastion of Huerta's defense line for central Mexico. In the Villistas' wake dozens of pueblos seized nearby estates and established collectives. The social revolution under way in the north center of the country worried Carranza almost as much as the División del Norte's victories concerned Huerta. The American government concluded that despite the Villistas' excesses, their leader still accepted Carranza's authority, and that no break between the revolutionary forces was imminent.

The government troops at Zacatecas had strong fortifications, good training, and abundant supplies. They were well led but lacked morale. Experienced fighters headed the assault forces of the División del Norte. The Villistas had an important advantage: a common desire to win land for their villages and end the political and economic power of the commercial intruders represented by the great estates and American mining, railroad, and timber companies. With thousands of women and children joining in, they became a people on the march with a common purpose, the destruction of the *terratenientes* and the national government and the seizure of the land.

In June the División del Norte took Zacatecas by storm. Carranza ordered the División del Norte to cease its advance. Instead the Villistas moved forward to Aguascalientes, where their coal-burning trains ran out of fuel. Carranza, in cooperation with the U.S. government and Zach Lamar Cobb, attorney and Texas Democratic party activist under Colonel Edward Mandel House, who served in El Paso as the zealous anti-Villista head of U.S. Customs, had cut off the Villista coal supplies. Cobb, like Bryan and the Texans in Wilson's cabinet, supported Carranza and regarded Villa as a "bandit, hypocrite, thief and murderer." To avoid an open break between the infuriated Villistas and the Carrancistas, a development which the weaker Carranza men did not want, they held a meeting in Torreón.

The resulting Pact of Torreón of 8 July 1914 recognized the División del Norte as a formal part of the Constitutionalist armed forces. It legitimized Villa as its head and promised that a convention of all the revolutionary armed forces would be held to agree upon a revolutionary program and regime after final victory. The pact contained an agrarian clause insisted upon by the Villistas that threatened the owners of great properties "to economically emancipate the campesinos, making an equitable distribution of land and resolving the agrarian problem."[28]

The leadership of the División del Norte did not have a precise agrarian plan as did the Zapatistas, but one of their first acts in Durango was to promulgate a land redistribution program. They also called for the "well-being of workers" and condemned "militarism, the Church and plutocracy." Carranza had no sympathy for lower-class radicalism. He did not want to see Mexico fall to an amalgam of Zapatista and Villista peasants and pequeña burguesía. The pact revealed considerable variance among his own forces because the officers under Obregon Salido endorsed it. The Pact of Torreón exposed Carranza's political weakness, but the railroad between Zacatecas and Aguascalientes had to be repaired before the División del Norte's main forces could move forward. Meanwhile, the attention directed toward Torreón and the American denial of rails and fuel neutralized Villista opposition to a strategically important Carranza-Obregon Salido military advance.

When Zacatecas fell, Huerta's forces began to disintegrate. Constitutionalists under Obregon Salido occupied Guadalajara and then moved eastward, past the División del Norte's stalled trains to Querétaro. The lack of rails and coal helped stay the División del Norte's hand long enough for the Constitutionalists to pass by within otherwise close striking distance and advance into central Mexico. At Querétaro, ten days after Huerta's resignation, the Carbajal government arranged to surrender his troops to the Carranzistas.

Obregon Salido guaranteed the safety of persons and private property in Mexico City to the Carbajal government while the Villista leadership watched in frustration. The government surrendered to the provincial elite-led military forces of Carranza and Obregon Salido, not the lower-class-led cohorts of the north under Villa or of the south under Zapata. The major contestants all demonstrated awareness that the revolution was a struggle between distinct interest groups for control of the nation.[29]

Under Huerta urban working-class organizations made important advances before being suppressed. The Casa del Obrero benefited from the government's attempt to maintain a base of support in central Mexico against the Constitutionalist rebellion in the north. In addition to seeking the help of Orozco, Zapata, and other rebels in the countryside, Huerta also appointed some reformers to government posts. They made tentative labor, educational, and agrarian reform proposals that never reached fruition. Tolerance of the working-class organizations was part of Huerta's strategy for political stability. The working-class organizations, strategically located in the nation's largest cities, built up large memberships.

In March and April 1913 the Lucha directorate of the Casa del Obrero coordinated successful strike and organizing efforts among restaurant workers, retail clerks, and weavers of greater Mexico City. On 1 May they held the largest May Day rally Mexico City had seen to that time. The Huerta government allowed the event despite skirmishes with the police. The Casa stressed "safe" issues such as the eight-hour day and the six-day work week and not working-class control over industrial production. That month Lucha affiliated the Casa with the anarchist International Association of Workers (AIT) in Amsterdam and changed its name to the Casa del Obrero Mundial (World) in recognition of its new international ties.

The Huerta regime and the Casa came into conflict during May when police intervened strikes. Near the end of the month Lucha confronted the government openly by joining with Liberals hostile toward Huerta in a large demonstration on 25 May. Eight thousand marched and heard speeches by anarchists, trade unionists, and Liberal politicians denouncing "military dictatorship" and "usurpation" of the free government. Without mentioning Huerta by name, the speakers condemned him and called for a return to "democracy."

Huerta's intolerance would not have allowed urban civil disorders regardless of the status of his government elsewhere in the country. With his steel and fire campaign against the Zapatistas bogged down, however, and his alarming failure to contain the northern rebellion, he moved to destroy the Casa and restore order to Mexico City. Two days after the 25 May demonstrations the government rounded up a dozen Lucha leaders and deported three as undesirable aliens. The prisoners were not treated harshly, perhaps because of their popularity. Their treatment contrasted with the fate of Liberal Mexico City politicians arrested and murdered in February and later in the year. The murder of popular labor leaders meant certain rioting and strikes.

The arrests disrupted efforts by Lucha to organize further the working class until the late summer of 1913, when Amadeo Ferrés and the Obreros Intellectuales brought the resources of the Confederación de Artes Gráficas into the Casa. The typesetters and printers had their own newspaper and considerable cash at hand. The move gave the labor movement new life. The organizers necessarily kept their efforts secretive and underground. The Casa leadership constructed a skeletal national organization that could be fleshed out with memberships when the opportunity arose. That chance came a year later.

The Casa adopted a new tactic. Rather than invite the reactions of plant owners, police, and government through strikes and open factory organizing, Casa leaders began a propaganda campaign. Radical newspapers addressed to the working class supplemented the efforts of street orators. A group of skilled speakers known as the Tribuna Roja addressed crowds, urging syndicate membership, unity, and the need to develop class consciousness. Antonio Díaz Soto y Gama and others addressed increasingly large crowds and recruited several thousand workers to the Casa during the next six months. They held meetings and issued polemics against the state in general, not the Huerta regime in particular, the Church, and capitalism. The crowds grew larger, into the thousands, and as defeats for the Huerta government mounted on the battlefields they became unruly.

Finally, with the Tribuna Roja talking revolution and the city filled with tension, the government raided Casa headquarters, razed the interior, and arrested between fifteen and twenty leaders. The police set the ransacked building on fire. Several leaders were detained and others deported. Importantly, a few of the most radical, including Díaz Soto y Gama, fled the city and joined Zapata in the south. Other Casa fugitives hid in Mexico City until Huerta resigned on 15 July. There was barely enough time in the interim to reform the Casa as Mexico's central workers' council and to find suitable facilities and finances before the arrival of the Constitutionalist forces led by Obregon Salido on 20 August. Rioting against the government and its business supporters greeted the arrival of what effective propaganda had convinced the workers were the pro-Casa Constitutionalists.

Obregon Salido attended one of the Casa's public meetings celebrating Huerta's flight and the city's "liberation." He astutely recognized the importance of cultivating urban worker support for the forthcoming struggle against the basically peasant agrarian-oriented Villistas and Zapatistas. In his speeches he sounded all the right phrases about "proletarian Mexico," a Mexico for the workers, and a revolution that would harness the "capitalists." Carranza, despite his contempt for working-class revolutionaries, allowed the charade to go on because of its political importance. He would not tolerate discussion of the "reds" in his presence.

The Casa received meeting places and the authority to organize workers in those territories where the Carranza-Obregon Salido forces were in charge. The organizing effort was intense, anticapitalist in its rhetoric, and highly successful. The Casa found worker recruitment an easy task when accompanied by government tolerance, but its leadership remained linked to Lucha and was vociferous in its opposition to any official ties to the Constitutionalists.

During the fall of 1914 the Casa reconstructed its organization based on self-governing syndicates. Their locals were connected at the national level by leaders who sat on twenty-three administrative committees that handled armed defense, education, health care, strikes, organizing drives, international affairs, relations with the AIT, and general policy. A Casa member affiliated with three organizations: the syndicate, the municipal Casa, and the national Casa. Membership also involved health, education, and workers' militia activities depending upon the stage of local Casa development. The formation of militias was more advanced in Morelia and Monterrey than in Mexico City, probably because of the earlier breakdown of government controls in the north, greater vigilance in central Mexico, and Carranza's refusal to tolerate an armed workers' force in the capital. The Casa created armories wherever it could marshal the resources.

Obregon Salido understood in the fall of 1914 that it was premature to attempt any kind of formal or open government-Casa relationship while anarchosyndicalist leaders still dominated the syndicates. Instead he gave the Casa food, clothing, buildings—all the help he could—and asked for nothing in return. He spoke of the peasant leaders as the "reaction" and alleged that they represented the interests of the Church and oligarchy.

Nothing could have been further from the truth, but to many of the workers of Mexico City the Zapatistas and Villistas seemed regressive because of their religiosity and adherence to a rural way of life long since left behind. Hostility toward possible rural political hegemony was not new to Mexico City's working classes. The capitaline populace had rejected the rural forces of Hidalgo and Allende during the Independence Revolution a century earlier.[30]

While Obregon Salido was building bridges between the Constitutionalists and the revolutionary labor movement, relations between the Zapatistas and Villistas and the provincial elite leader Carranza continued to deteriorate. Meanwhile the businessmen of Mexico City and the Americans increasingly recognized that Carranza was their only viable choice. Villa and Carranza demanded each other's resignation while Zapata rejected Madero-like agrarian compromises offered by Carranza's representatives, Luis Cabrera and Antonio Villareal. Through myriad village, pueblo, and agrarian worker land seizures, the people of the center-south, like the grassroots movement under way in the Villista north, were moving toward the agrarian transformation that Adolfo Gilly has aptly called the Morelos Commune.

In Chihuahua, Jalisco, Morelos, San Luis Potosí, Zacatecas, the Isthmus of Tehuantepec, along the Pacific coast from Sonora to Chiapas, and along the Gulf coast from Tamaulipas to Campeche, agrarian rebels sacked commercial estates. Campesinos attacked the properties of large American companies and U.S. "pioneer" colonists. The George Blaylock-owned colonies in Tamaulipas and San Luis Potosí, the Motzorango Plantation in Veracruz, the Jantha Plantation, and others in Tehuantepec and Chiapas were ravaged in a new wave of assaults. The giant American properties in Campeche were again attacked by field hands "who had rebellion in their eyes."[31]

Unlike the Villista leadership, who delayed land redistribution and suffered an erosion of peasant support and even armed resistance, the Zapatista leadership continued to take the initiative. They insisted that the Constitutionalists accept a revised Plan of Ayala with stiff agrarian terms. Carranza defended the hacendados, insisting that they had property rights that could not be violated in order "to give land to those who had no rights." Both sides hardened their positions as the Zapatistas moved to wholesale land redistributions throughout the territory under their control.

In the north the Villistas nationalized the great estates in order to support the war effort. Meanwhile campesinos carried out unauthorized land seizures against the American-owned great estates. They called themselves "Villistas" despite no authority to act from the División del Norte high command. Villa's failure to act on agrarian reform brought him into conflict with his uncontrollable countryside supporters. In some cases Villista troops evicted campesino "squatters" from nationalized and American estates.

In September 1914 Villa finally demanded that Carranza immediately "approve measures for the redistribution of the land." He announced that the División del Norte would not attend any general convention of the revolutionary forces that did not include the basic demands of the campesinaje. The following day Villa rejected Carranza as leader of the revolution because Carranza failed to support his agrarian plan and was unrepresentative of the people's will. Villa's actions outraged John Lind, President Wilson's emissary to Mexico and a Carranza supporter. Lind called Villa a "traitor."[32]

Obregon Salido assumed the task of finding a middle way, a compromise that would allow the revolutionaries to talk before fighting among themselves. A number of generals had expressed interest in a general meeting to discuss their differences and agree upon a program. It was not difficult for Obregon Salido to arrange a convention. The problem would be to reconcile the conflicting social and class interests that propelled them toward drastically different goals. The historic meeting convened at Aguascalientes on 10 October 1914.

NINE

Class Confrontation, American Intervention, and Workers' Defeat, 1914–1916

Since . . . the manufacturer insists on having the world as a market, the flag of his nation must follow him, and the doors of nations which are closed against him must be battered down. Concessions obtained by financiers must be safeguarded by ministers of state even if the sovereignty of unwilling nations be outraged in the process.

Woodrow Wilson, 1907

It is not our purpose to annex your country or any part of it. . . . But in the future our flag is to be your flag, and you are to be directly under the protection of the United States.

—Philip Dru to the Mexican President, in *Philip Dru Administrator,* by Colonel Edward Mandel House

Between 1914 and 1916 the peasants, industrial and urban workers, provincial and local elites, pequeña burguesía, and the intelligentsia, constituting the popular front that brought down the Díaz regime and the Huerta government, asserted their antagonistic economic, political, and cultural interests. They confronted one another in a climatic and intense struggle for power. In a last-ditch effort to avert even more intense warfare than that which unseated Huerta, the revolutionary amalgam convened the Convention of Aguascalientes on 10 October 1914.

Mexico moved toward what some historians have misunderstood as personalistic strife. In reality the fighting resulted from pursuit of the specific interests of antagonistic social groups. The pattern of factional and class alignments and foreign intervention paralleled the major world revolutions of the twentieth century.

When the delegates from the larger revolutionary groups convened at Aguascalientes, only the campesino-led Zapatista agrarians were absent. They did not belong to the Constitutionalist movement and had never accepted the hacendado and Porfirian politician Carranza as their first chief. The Zapatistas already referred to the upper-class and pequeña burguesa officials around Carranza as the enemy. On the other side, the Carrancistas recognized the Zapatistas' demands for an end to the great estates as a continuation of the centuries-old struggle between peasants and what they believed to be progressive commercial agriculture. The hundreds of small revolutionary bands composed of local campesinos that constituted much of Mexico's chaos in 1914 were not directly represented.

The hacendado provincial elites and pequeña burguesa Carrancistas regarded Zapatista demands as irreconcilable with their program in support of the laissez-faire yet caste-based social order legitimized by the Constitution of 1857. From the beginning, however, despite the ideological appeal of Zapatismo, the Carrancistas and Obregonistas recognized the Villistas as the greater danger. Although their agrarianism appeared to be less developed than the Zapatistas', the Villistas possessed the strongest armed force in Mexico. That capacity, coupled with their demands during the negotiations at Torreón for local control over the agrarian program, clearly made them the more dangerous enemy.

While the Zapatistas were issuing a new agrarian plan calling for pueblo control over uncompensated hacienda expropriations and the inalienability of peasant holdings, the campesinos of the north, without a formal ideology or program, continued seizing estate properties in the wake of Villista victories. Myriad local units claiming Villista affiliation but actually controlled by no one raided mines and set up squatter communities on American and northern elite-owned estates. Meanwhile the Villista high command seized Mexican-owned haciendas and used them to support its war machine.[1]

Villa wanted to establish self-governing agrarian colonies federated in a national union and protected by workers' militias controlled by the communities. His plan duplicated the ideas of nineteenth-century French socialist Charles Fourier. The defenders of private property around Carranza could tolerate neither the Zapatista nor the Villista peasant revolution, but the first chief and his followers were politically isolated. Most of the nationalistic and socially upward-bound officers and intellectuals among the Constitutionalists sympathized with the plight of the campesinos. They rallied around Obregonista reformism.

The politics of Obregonismo included populist sympathy for peasant and urban worker aspirations, national elite-controlled but more open political participation for the masses, nationalism, anticlericalism, and "just rewards" for the victorious revolutionary leadership within the parameters of a capitalist economy and private property. They represented the pequeña burguesía's search for a better Mexico consistent with its rising class power. Yet they could not bring themselves to accept the communalist working-class revolutionary goals of the Zapatistas, Villistas, or the Casa.[2]

Obregonistas had the aggressiveness and flexibility that the provincial elite-led Carrancistas lacked. They represented a subclass of middle-echelon technicians, businessmen, and intelligentsia created by the economic revolution of the Porfiriato. Obregon Salido and Elías Calles were less nationalistic and hostile toward the Americans than was Carranza; they personified the marginalized elements of the provinical elites that had learned to function and survive in the hectic pequeña burguesa world of small business and low-level politics. They, like their class, demanded wider public participation in politics and government services, consistent with the economic and cultural power they had achieved under the ancien régime.

The pequeña burguesía identified with both mass aspirations and private property. They responded to the demands of both sides in the revolutionary struggle. Obregon Salido, a novice to military strategy but quick to learn it, as well as a cynical politician, was typical of his class. His mother's membership in the Sonoran oligarchy, combined with his wide-ranging and socially mobile pequeña burguesa background, business experience, intelligence, aggressiveness, and practical education, served him well. His varied family connections and work and business experience, including his close relationship with W. R. Grace and Company, to which he owed $1,800,000 in 1920, enabled him to interact successfully with revolutionary workers and peasants, middle-echelon intelligentsia, urban radicals and businessmen, foreigners, and the autocratic Carranza.

After a late-September parley between Obregon Salido and Villa in Torreón, the break between the División del Norte and the Constitutionalist bloc led by Carranza and Obregon Salido became irreparable. Villa caught Obregon Salido trying to lure some of his officers away and almost had him shot. After the close call at Torreón, Obregon Salido decided to isolate Villa's outnumbered representatives at Aguascalientes and gain the convention's official endorsement for his own "middle way" while maintaining political stability under the titular leadership of Carranza.[3]

The Carrancista alliance with Obregon Salido was a sensible unity of provincial elite and pequeña burguesa forces that shared the same "civilized" values vis-à-vis the indigenous folk of the countryside. The Carrancistas and Obregonistas consciously identified with values, language, economic aspirations, and jargon that were European and American in origin. When they forged alliances with the unpalatable peasants and workers, they did not intend to grant concessions to the rank-and-file but to their leadership. That leadership identified with Obregonismo and differed with the Carrancistas about the degree of social reform needed in terms of both their own sociopolitical future and the degree of succor due the masses. There was no way for the provincial elite Carrancistas to avoid accepting the powerful Obregon Salido-led pequeña burguesa revolutionaries into the sociopolitical hierarchy. The only question was how high they would rise.

The Convention of Aguascalientes reflected all of the social contradictions of the revolution. Attended by leading Constitutionalist officers, the Convention claimed the power to decide the nation's fate. It soon turned into a debate of irreconcilable factions. The Carrancista leaders showed up in pressed uniforms with shiny buttons, shaven, powdered, and perfumed. The Obregonistas were somewhat less formal. The less articulate Villistas presented a cross-section of dirty, sloppy countryside attire. The Villistas strove for the adoption of an agrarian plan that they could neither draw up nor fully explain. They lost every vote of substance until 27 October, when the even more ill-clad nonvoting Zapatistas arrived and presented the Plan of Ayala. They were the only group with a clear program, and it was steeped in the aspirations of Mexico's countryside masses, including the norteños. The Zapatista demand for locally controlled land redistribution put the previously dominant Obregonistas, with their hodgepodge of reform measures to be carried out by the national state, on the defensive.

By means of oratory, Zapatistas Paulino Martínez and Antonio Díaz Soto y Gama turned the convention into a confrontation over what the Mexican Revolution was about. Martínez argued that Villa and Zapata, with the leadership of their movements taken right out of the rural working class, were the leaders of the Mexican masses. Díaz Soto y Gama rejected European prejudices and values of the noncampesino leaders by denouncing the governments ushered in after Iturbide's coup as "criollo" and "heirs of the conquerors who infamously continue to cheat and abuse the oppressed Indian."[4]

The convention became a tumultuous assemblage that moved steadily to the left. Despite the nonvoting status of the Zapatistas, and Carrancista-Obregonista efforts to stop the slippage, previously unaligned officers increasingly identified with the agrarians. Finally the convention broke with Carranza and chose agrarian General Eulalio Gutiérrez of San Luis Potosí as provisional president of Mexico. Because of his revolutionary program as governor of San Luis Potosí that abolished debt peonage and established minimum wages, Gutiérrez stood out as a leading radical. Carranza rejected the Convention's decision; his followers fled Aguascalientes and regrouped in Mexico City. Obregon joined them.

On 10 November 1914 President Gutiérrez declared Carranza to be in rebellion and open fighting began. General Pablo González conducted a rearguard action for the Constitutionalists along the Aguascalientes-Querétaro road against the advancing División del Norte, which was now part of the official armed forces of the convention government. Despite what appeared to be their imminent defeat at the hands of the overwhelming División del Norte, now closing in on Mexico City, the Constitutionalists had one chance left: the Americans.

Carranza and Obregon Salido made an alliance with the U.S. government. Over the protests of the Villistas and Flores Magón, who demanded the appointment of a bipartisan commission, the Americans turned over invaluable Veracruz and its environs to the retreating Constitutionalists as a provisional capital. From there the seemingly hopeless Obregon Salido- and Carranza-led factions had access to foreign commerce and assistance and could regroup, recruit, and train a new army while the Villista and Zapatista rural and basically lower-class-led revolutionaries controlled the Mexican heartland from the Isthmus of Tehuantepec to the American border. Treasury resources, loans from both national and foreign sources, and port income became essentials for the desperate Constitutionalists, who had to find armaments quickly. The Americans had turned the Veracruz port into a marshaling yard for an enormous stockpile of arms. That equipment, combined with military training for the thousands of raw Casa recruits from greater Mexico City, forged a new army 20,000 strong.

The arms came from confiscated property seized when the Americans occupied the port, cargoes intended for the Huerta government that arrived in port after the American intervention, consignments addressed to the U.S. forces in Mexico, and private shipments to Carranza's government. American and Carrancista officers worked side by side in the storage and allocation of weapons. The military effort complemented the advisers who were sent soon afterward by Samuel Gompers of the American Federation of Labor and President Wilson and who established liaison with the Casa del Obrero recruits in the Constitutionalist marshaling and training areas between Veracruz and Orizaba.

The Americans, operating out of their base at Veracruz and led by presidential emissary John Lind and General Frederick Funston, dealt with the labor leaders of the Casa and Constitutionalist officers. Lind orchestrated the American efforts on behalf of Carranza at Veracruz. He regarded Carranza as Mexico's most responsible leader, despised Villa as a treasonous renegade, and viewed the Convention of Aguascalientes as a captive fraud:

> Villa acted with wanton disloyalty against the Carranza government . . . as early as the month of May of last year, when Villa was professing loyalty to Carranza in the public press, his agents, Consul Carothers and Felix Sommerfield, were surreptitiously negotiating for arms and ammunition for Villa's account. . . . The much heralded Aguascalientes Convention was backed by Villa and dominated by his army surrounding it. Carranza showed much patience in his efforts to placate Villa. He made him governor of the state of Chihuahua, in addition to his military position, but to no purpose.[5]

In 1914 the Wilson administration carried out a concerted policy toward Mexico. Its highest priorities were the preservation of U.S. economic interests and the protection of its 75,000 nationals residing there. Key Wilsonian cabinet members, presidential advisers, and congressional leaders combined their concerns for the welfare of American investors in Mexico and the border region with their own financial commitments. Their investments coincided with the much larger interests of their friends, associates, Democratic party supporters, and the leading financiers and businessmen of the United States.

The intervention of Carranza in August and September 1913 against the redistribution of landholdings on the border in Tamaulipas by General Lucio Blanco gained the Constitutionalist leader the sympathy and support of Secretary of State Bryan, Colonel House, Thomas Watt Gregory, David Houston, Sidney Mezes, Charles Culbertson, Albert Burleson, and the bulk of the leadership of the Texas Democratic party. That group had been instrumental in the nomination and election of President Wilson in 1912. Wilson's withdrawal of arms aid to Huerta occurred immediately after Carranza's action in defense of the 2 million-acre Sautema land tract near Matamoros dominated by the directors of the Texas Oil Company, their Mexican elite partners, and James Stillman. Stillman also held irrigation bonds committed to the Sautema tract and the Mexican side of the Rio

Grande. Stillman and Cleveland Dodge helped to arouse pro-Carranza sentiment. Dodge's valuable holdings were largely centered in Sonora. Both men were financially crucial to President Wilson's political support.[6]

In California, Democratic party landowners in Mexico led by Colonel Dan Burns of San Francisco, identified as the "largest single American interest in Mexico," Gould Harrold, and W. M. Kent supported the administration's policies of aid for the first chief and opposed the invasion of Mexico for the establishment of a protectorate or possible annexation. Later, in 1916, they led the Mexican Property Owners Non-Interventionalist League of Oakland, a Democratic party front group supporting President Wilson's renomination and election. Another California Democrat was also pleased. Edwin Jessup Marshall, the original treasurer of the Texas Company in Houston and an old friend of Cullinan and the Hogg and House families, owned "the largest fenced property in North America," the 2.5 million-acre Las Palomas hacienda on the border between New Mexico and Chihuahua. In addition, he served as president of the Sinaloa Land and Irrigation Company, which held 3 million acres in that state in Mexico. A longtime Democratic party activist in Texas, Marshall supported Wilson.[7]

In Louisiana two major Mexican interest groups were avidly pro-Wilson. Their business connections in Mexico and the Rio Grande Valley intermeshed directly with the House group in Texas. The Minor family, which owned the Hibernia Bank of New Orleans jointly with James Stillman, the second-largest financial institution in the state, was part owner of the $2 million Rascon hacienda of San Luis Potosí and Tamaulipas. The Rascon complex included railroads, *ingenios,* dams, and a hydroelectric plant on its 1.4 million acres. The Hibernia Bank had a line of credit with the National City Bank. The Minor family supported President Wilson offering him the hospitality of their home on several occasions and supporting his reelection. Dr. George Lee of the University of Texas Medical Branch at Galveston, an earnest supporter of the House machine candidates and the Texas Democratic party, owned the controlling interest in the Rascon enterprises. Tom Lee, his son, was a University of Texas-educated attorney and represented the Gulf Oil Company and Rascon Manufacturing in Mexico. Later he joined Attorney General Gregory in lawsuits on behalf of Gulf against the Mexican government.[8]

Another consortium of Louisiana-Texas capitalists in Mexico with longstanding links to the Texan cabinet secretaries and advisers to the president was the Jennings-Heywood Syndicate. Alba Heywood and William Jennings purchased land on both sides of the Rio Grande. They participated with the Texas Company in joint investments. They joined in Rio Grande Valley Land and Irrigation Company promotions with Stillman, Gregory, Bryan, Lind, Duval West, the National City Bank, and the Texas Company directors. Jennings joined John Blocker, owner of the Lytle Ranch near San Antonio and the U.S. consul at Parral, and purchased the 1,250,000-acre Piedra Blanca hacienda of Coahuila.[9]

These Californa, Louisiana, New York, and Texas Democrats more than offset the protests of Democrat William Randolph Hearst, who owned between 6,600,000 and 7,500,000 acres in Chihuahua, Sonora, and Tehuantepec, in addition to other properties. Hearst demanded the annexation of Mexico. In pursuit of its pro-Carranza policy the U.S. government instituted embargoes and arms aid and resorted to armed intervention on two occasions. In doing so, Wilson and his cabinet secretaries from Texas, supported by Texas, New York, California, and Louisiana Democratic mine owners and landowners in Mexico, largely determined the winners of the Mexican Revolution.[10]

In many respects Wilson administration policies toward the Mexican Revolution continued the defense initiated by President Taft and the state government of Texas of American property and commercial interests inside Mexico and along the border. Those policies defended the holdings of the National City Bank, Stillman, Bryan, the T. O. Riverside Ranch, the Texas Oil Company, and the Texans who became members of President Wilson's cabinet. Other investors included presidential envoys Duval West and John Lind and Secretary of the Navy Josephus Daniels.

Between 1910 and 1912 American strategies included use of the U.S. Army Maneuver Division and the Texas state militia along the border, totaling almost 24,000 troops. That effort to protect the border and enforce the embargo against the overwhelmingly anti-American Orozco rebellion resulted in the defeat of that uprising. The Taft administration used reinforcements on the border to guard the crossings at Ciudad Juárez, Nuevo Laredo, Reynosa, and Matamoros, preventing those towns from serving as sources of supply for the Orozquista forces. Meanwhile President Taft authorized the passage of military equipment including guns, ammunition, and even two observation airplanes for General Huerta's column of government forces that ultimately defeated the uprising.

Pro-Orozco uprisings among the workers at Cananea, the rural populace of Chihuahua, the Yaqui Indians in Sonora, and the Mayo Indians in Sinaloa alarmed American officials. The U.S. Army monitored the fighting as rebels gained control of most of western Chihuahua. During the wave of unrest, concerned representatives of 205 American companies and private investors in Sonora noted the protection of their properties by the state government militia commander Obregon Salido. The U.S. consul at Hermosillo identified Obregon Salido as the "most reliable commander in Sonora."[11]

During the Constitutionalist revolution that followed General Huerta's *golpe de estado,* the rebels ran guns and ammunition across the border on an unprecedented scale. Despite U.S. government attempts to stop the traffic, the Constitutionalists enjoyed support from regional and local elites in Texas, New Mexico, and Arizona on behalf of their provincial elite counterparts in Tamaulipas, Coahuila, Chihuahua, and Sonora. Between March and September 1913 the U.S. government could not prevent the growth of the Constitutionalist movement despite enormous shipments of armaments to Huerta by Wilson. The Department of Justice was unable to obtain convictions of American businessmen for violations of the Neutrality Acts in El Paso, the greatest center of smuggling activity.[12]

President Wilson supported Huerta until mid-September 1913. During his first six months in office Wilson repeatedly signed exceptions to President Taft's embargo on arms and ammunition which had been imposed during the suppression of the Orozco revolt. The president approved dozens of arms shipments, many of them massive, as the U.S. and Mexican governments tried to crush the Constitutionalists and restore order and stability. Wilson abandoned and denounced Huerta as a dictator in isolation from other Latin American despots, whom he continued to support, only when Wilson's personal representative indicated that the Mexican leader would not be able to restore order. The president reached his decision with the support of Colonel House and the Texans in the administration who unanimously supported Carranza.[13]

In September 1913 Wilson finally embargoed further shipments of arms to Huerta; and after four months of ambivalence, in the winter of 1914, the American government opted to open the border to legitimate arms purchases by the rebels.[14] The increased flow of armaments made the conquest of central Mexico possible and resulted in the southward march of the Constitutionalists. The large-scale flow of arms across the border allowed the insurgents to overthrow Huerta, but the American government's intervention at Veracruz proved equally critical to the outcome of the revolution.

The Wilson administration and Mexico were deeply intertwined because of the shared economic interests on the part of key figures in the cabinet, congressional leaders, presidential advisers, and Democratic party financiers. Dodge, one of the president's closest friends, soon became chairman of the board of Phelps-Dodge Company, which controlled the fabulously rich copper fields at Nacozari, Sonora. He was one of Wilson's key fund raisers on the East coast. Colonel House held part ownership in six silver mines in Guanajuato, which, in conjunction with the Mexican railroad, mining, and hacienda holdings of his family and Texas, New York, and Boston business associates, strongly influenced his staunch support of Carranza and military interventions in 1914 and 1916.

The revolution directly touched Colonel House in the winter of 1914, when uncontrolled local revolutionists pillaged the home of his cousin and lifelong best friend Henry House. Cousin Henry headed the Texas Company's operations at critically important Tampico. The colonel was further tied to Mexican events through his wife, who, prior to their marriage had befriended the Texas Oil Company's chief representative in Mexico, William F. Buckley, when she lived in Mexico City. Buckley was a former Austin neighbor of House's. Their mansions were only a few blocks apart in the neighborhood just south of the University of Texas. "Mr. House's contacts on the border, and with Americans in Mexico, inclined him to lend a sympathetic ear to suggestions of intervention."[15]

James Stillman was the Democratic party's wealthiest supporter. His board of directors comprised most of the leading figures in Mexican capitalism, including W. R. Grace, who was involved with Alvaro Obregon in Sonora. Postmaster General Burleson, who as a Texas congressman served as a key figure in Wilson's National Democratic Convention struggle in 1912, was a northern Mexico land and mine owner. Secretary of Agriculture David S. Houston and Sidney Mezes, presidential adviser, were both former presidents of the University of Texas and had befriended House when he, Hogg, Brackenridge (Stillman's frequent representative in Texas and Mexico), and Gregory sat on the university's board of regents. Mezes was House's brother-in-law. Gregory, Houston, and Mezes speculated in Mexican property and mining claims. Gregory's entanglements in Mexico caused him to fight hard for the Mexican ambassadorship, a quest he gave up only to accept the post of attorney general of the United States.

Two of President Wilson's key representatives in Mexico—John Lind of Minnesota and Duval West of San Antonio—owned properties in Mexico, where they enjoyed long-standing ties with the major American landholders there. Both men were interested in the Mexico Land Company, which complained that it suffered $750,000 in damages to its properties in 1914. The company moved its headquarters during the revolution from Houston to St. Paul, Minnesota. Lind coordinated American relations with the Constitutionalist forces at Veracruz in 1914. He despised Villa, and West denounced Villa to President Wilson as a "socialist." The Wilson administration appointed anti-Villa John Blocker of San Antonio as U.S. consul at Parral. Blocker's and William Jennings's 1,250,000-acre Piedra Blanca hacienda had suffered heavily from Orozquista and Villista raids. Blocker was an old friend of House, Robert Lansing, and the Texas Democratic party leadership. The president's Texas men enjoyed friendship with the Lees of Galveston, Alba Heywood, Jennings, and Edwin Marshall.[16]

Events in Mexico loomed large among the president's supporters in Texas, who included the Texas Oil Company directors Joseph Cullinan, president, Will Hogg, secretary, Richard Brooks, treasurer, James Autry, legal counsel, and W. B. Sharp, who headed their Mexican explorations and field development for fifteen years. These men were staunch pro-House conservative "gold" Democratic party activists in the state and business associates of both Colonel House and James Stillman. They all carried large balances in accounts with the National City Bank, which was the most powerful financial force in the state.

Stillman was the most powerful investor in Texas. He held shares and bonds in fifteen banks in the state, natural gas company and railroad stocks, as well as ranching and real estate development properties. His personal holdings in George Brackenridge's San Antonio National Bank still totaled over $200,000.

Brooks's political clout enabled him later to become mayor of Houston. The Texas Company directors were joined in their delight over Wilson's victory by John Henry Kirby, president of the Kirby Lumber Company, who held one million acres in mineral claims in Guerrero. His company vice-president, Henry House, the colonel's closest family friend, soon changed executive positions, joining Texaco. The Texas Company directors and Kirby enjoyed several joint ventures, including co-ownership of the Union Bank of Houston, of which both Colonel House and his brother, T. W. House, Jr., were directors. Kirby's Buena Fe silver mine in Jalisco was not far from the House-owned silver mines in Aguascalientes. Kirby helped anti-Villista Zack Cobb to obtain his post as customs chief at El Paso from President Wilson via Colonel House, who handled presidential patronage. Henry House gave up his position with Kirby when he accepted the assignment to serve during the next few years with the Texas Company as its chief representative in Tampico. Texaco president Cullinan expressed his frustration with Presidents Díaz and Taft and the pleasure of Wilson's Texas supporters after the 1912 presidential elections:

> With the new administration in Washington . . . we are now in a much stronger position than ever before. . . . From now on we may devote our time and undivided attention to our affairs without the constant nightmare of being sandbagged at every turn of the road.[17]

Wilson's Texas Company supporters despised Orozco, Villa, and Lucio Blanco. Company treasurer Brooks viewed them as property violators. The oil men—Zack Cobb, Duval West, George Lee, and the Minor family—regarded Villa as a bandit and a killer. The company directors and W. B. Sharp worked closely with General E. O. C. Ord's son-in-law, General Jacinto Treviño of Monterrey, in the development of oil leases and railroads. After 1910 they established a business relationship with two Madero brothers and feted them in Houston in 1912, where Raoul Madero was given the key to the city.

Carranza became the Texaco directors' favorite when he returned the 2 million-acre Sautema property near Matamoros to them and their agents, H. C. Swanson and E. T. Rowson, after Lucio Blanco seized and distributed the acreage to the campesinos.[18] The American capitalists had taken possession of the land through purchase and renewable long-term leases from some of Mexico City's wealthiest men: Fernando Pimentel y Fagoada, Iñigo Noriega, Luis Barroso Arias, Francisco Garza, Vicente Barrienchea, Luis García Barballa, Felix Díaz, and Manuel González, Jr. The Texas Company directors had taken a major risk when they gained control of their 4.5 million acres in Tamaulipas.

Brooks, Cullinan, Rowson, and Swanson held the larger part of the acreage as well as the development contract for the Sautema tract. That contract called for European, Canadian, and U.S. immigrants to occupy 400,000 acres of property to be irrigated by the government using the bonds issued by Stillman, the National City Bank, and Speyer Bank in New York in 1909. Mexican farmers were not included in the plans for settlement. The lands extended from Stillman's property at Bagdad on the Gulf coast along the Big Four-controlled Constructora Nacional's railroad line to Reynosa. Among the property owners whose holdings were seized by Blanco, only Felix Díaz, nephew of the deposed dictator, lost out. Díaz held over 1,500,000 acres in the state, with most of it concentrated in the north. His El Borrego hacienda between Bagdad and Matamoros remained in campesino hands.[19]

In California the pro-Wilson Democratic party landowners in Mexico shared their Texas and eastern counterparts' distaste for Lucio Blanco and Orozco and their enthusiasm for Carranza. Marshall, with control of 5.5

million acres, and Burns, whose mining, timber, and cattle income in Sinaloa and Durango exceeded even that of Marshall, consistently supported President Wilson's pro-Carranza stand. The Democrats adopted this strategy in the face of demands from Democratic and Republican rightists for invasion and the creation of a satellite state similar to that King and Stillman envisioned (Republic of the Sierra Madre) in the nineteenth century. Hearst, Kirby, Buckley, and outspoken Republicans favored outright annexation or at least a protectorate over Mexico.[20]

The financial backers of the Texas Democratic party and most of its leaders shared deep concerns about Mexico because of the large investments there. For several years the Texas Company directors had viewed the Díaz regime as unfairly partial to the interests of the Pearson Oil Trust in Mexico and complained about it to their East Coast investors and government officials. During Madero's presidency they attempted to circumvent Mexican hostility by forming an alliance that included sponsorship of the Madero-owned oil company at Tampico. Through Sharp and Henry House the Texas Company purchased Madero's oil at Tampico. The family was courted with receptions in Houston. Texas Company directors were angered by the Huerta regime's seemingly pro-British policies. Colonel House joined them in their anguish, attributing the conflict between British and U.S. capital to "the intransigence of the Cowdray oil interests there."

The Texas Company directors, who supported both Madero and Carranza, continued buying large properties in northeastern Mexico between 1911 and 1914. As the revolution continued the Texas Company's commitments to the Gulf coast oil zones and land speculation opportunities resulted in ever larger cash outlays to its Mexican subsidiaries: the Panuco, Tamesi, Tampico, Mexico Fuel, Producers Oil, and the Mexico Companies. These subsidiaries served to hide the dimensions of the Texas Company's operations inside Mexico from the Houston management's increasingly interventionist and hostile New York investors, the competition, and the Mexican government. When the New Yorkers finally took over the company in November 1913, the Texas directors, W. B. Sharp, in charge of the company's exploration effort in Mexico, and the deceased John W. "Bet a Million" Gates of New York, one of Cullinan's most important financial supporters, had already made massive personal and corporate commitments to Mexican landholding. Earlier Gates had backed William C. Greene's Cananea Copper Company and then Arthur Stilwell's Kansas City, Mexico and Orient Railroad. Meanwhile the principal accounts of the company, its Texas-based directors, and Colonel House were all with Stillman's National City Bank. The company enjoyed a line of credit with the bank, which held many of its outstanding loans.

The pressure on the U.S. government to intervene continued to mount. Demands came from U.S. investors with several hundred million dollars committed to over 100 million acres of holdings in Mexico's finest railroad, timber, mining, rubber, and agricultural lands. The preparation for U.S. intervention at Veracruz began in November 1913, when William F. Buckley, Sr., wrote to House as the chief legal counsel for the Texas Company in Mexico and as an old friend. His sixteen-page letter explained the developing threat to American interests. During 1913 and 1914 American interests suffered terrible losses as campesinos and mine workers blew up sugar mills and mines and burned fields. Rioters sacked Tampico and threatened Campeche. In 1914 the Texas Company suffered heavy property damage at Topila, Veracruz. The company estimated its losses at $10 million. Buckley's argument described the situation of America's principal international entrepreneurs including Dodge, Stillman, and other New York financiers who also demanded intervention. The cumulative concerns of prominent party leaders across the nation reinforced the demands of Stillman and Dodge and the advice of the president's Texan cabinet secretaries and advisers.[21]

Wilson's association with National City Bank Chairman of the Board Stillman carried special significance. After his election the president-elect met with Stillman, bank director William Rockefeller, and bank president Frank Vanderlip at the latter's home on the Hudson River. Rockefeller dominated the conversation while the taciturn Stillman looked on and listened. The bankers explained the need to alter the U.S. Currency Act in order to allow U.S. banks to make direct investments in foreign countries. In lieu of that opportunity Stillman had been forced to bend the law, forming the City Company as an illegal conduit for National City Bank funds into foreign investments. The extent of that commitment to Porfirian Mexico is unknown, although Stillman often bragged that he was an expert on Mexico.

In addition to the riparian rights to the Rio Grande River extending inland from Matamoros, Stillman had pioneered the Big Four's interest in Mexico, where they held a dominant position in the Central, National, and Southern Pacific Railroad lines. In addition to his land development companies on the border and in the interior, he had joined Speyer in floating the gold-based $50 million (U.S.) water and irrigation bonds in

New York and London in 1909 and 1910. Those funds made possible the development of the lands of the Mexico Company and National Railroad in the strip of land between Matamoros and Reynosa.

Wilson and the bankers reached an agreement. Accordingly, the Federal Reserve Act of 1914 legalized both direct investments by U.S. banks abroad and the opening of foreign branches. The National City Bank quickly became the nation's foremost investor in foreign economies, including Mexico. After their meeting, Stillman when asked for his impression, replied that the incoming president seemed a "weak man."[22]

Despite Wilson's reservations, the argument in favor of intervention was carried by the Texans in the cabinet, Colonel House, and the president's New York supporters. The Wilson government adopted a strategy in contrast to Republican demands for annexation, a protectorate, or the severing of northern Mexico from the center for inclusion in the United States. Beginning in September 1913 the Democrats strove to topple Huerta and install the northern provincial elite leader Carranza as president. They did so despite concern for his nationalism. The Wilson cabinet's decision contrasted with the position of Republican Senator Albert Bacon Fall of New Mexico, who led the Republican and Democratic campaign in favor of the occupation of Mexico. A mine and ranch owner in northern Mexico, Fall joined Harry Chandler, Hearst, and a number of Republican financiers in demanding the outright seizure of Mexico.[23]

In early January 1914 the cabinet met and agreed upon an armed invasion of Mexico and initiated a series of secret U.S. government actions that profoundly affected the outcome of the revolution. Secretary of War Lindley Garrison and Secretary of the Navy Josephus Daniels (another Mexican property owner) conferred for the greater part of a day. The topic of conversation was the forthcoming attack on Mexico: "Intervention had already been agreed upon . . . [it was] only a question of an opportune time and sufficient arrangements."[24]

The War Department, Army, and Navy surveyed the artillery, naval resources, and logistics of the American and Mexican armed forces. Supplies were stockpiled at Galveston and Philadelphia for a naval operation and troop transfers were carried out. Three months later, in the midst of Admiral Fletcher's intrusions at Tampico, word of the *Ypiranga*'s course toward Veracruz arrived. That report accentuated another message to the president on 18 April informing him that a consignment of Colt machine guns had already left New York on 17 April aboard the steamship *Monterrey*.[25]

When the American forces struck at Veracruz a week later, they found extensive armaments in the arsenal and fort at San Juan de Ulloa, at the Vivac arsenal in the Palacio Municipal, in the full square-block Benito Juárez lighthouse building, and at the Baluarte of Veracruz, a fortified two-square-block complex used to garrison Mexican troops. In addition the U.S. forces seized three steamships in the port—the *Monterrey, Esperanza,* and *Mexico*—that were carrying military gear as cargo. The Americans also encountered arms unloaded from the *Morro Castle* and other backlogged shipments stockpiled in the warehouses and offices of the Aduana (Customs). All four ships were owned by the U.S. and Cuba Steamship Company of New York, which had informed the U.S. government of the cargos, including the twenty-five Colt machine guns aboard the *Monterrey.* After securing the city the American commanders set out to safeguard the armaments now under their control. These included 239 bultos (crates) from the *Monterrey,* 12 from the *Dania,* 44 from the *Hornby Castle,* 142 from the *Mexico,* and 12 from the *Patapasco.*[26]

The Americans determined that the best course of action to ensure control over the large quantities of arms in the harbor area was to concentrate them in the Aduana's large stone-walled warehouses with their steel-reinforced roofs. Other secure buildings were also utilized, including the Vivac storage quarters in the Municipal Palace, the fortified Baluarte de Santiago, and the storeroom of the enormous Benito Juárez lighthouse. They ordered immediate inventories of the arms caches in the various storage points and estimates of the manpower needed to move them to more secure points. The situation was urgent because of overcrowding from backlogged materials in the warehouses of various shippers, including the Veracruz Terminal Warehouse Company, waiting shipment to Mexico City: "The capacity of the Terminal Warehouses [of which buildings one, two, and three each measured 57½ yards square by 21 feet in height plus other buildings] has been taxed to the utmost to accommodate both private merchandise and military stores." One consignment of arms from the Companía Terminal Veracruz S.A. required thirty-four man-days in order to complete the transfer to warehouse number one. Another weapons consignment required a half-day for six crews using two rail-mounted wagons to move it 410 meters. The Terminal Warehouse Company had 291 crates of arms. The backed-up stores of arms dated from July 1913.[27]

The accumulated war materials in the port included artillery, machine guns, rifles, shotguns, carbines, revolvers, pistols, grenades, bayonets, sabers, primed shells, cartridges, ammunition, wads, parafine, poison gas, barbed wire, dynamite sticks, and blasting powder. The cargos from the *Monterrey* and the *Mexico,* which had arrived on 7 March and 18 April respectively, included several thousand pistols, revolvers, and rounds of ammunition. The 2,000 confiscated Remington pistols from the *Monterrey* appear to have been shipped by the world's largest arms dealer at that time, Bannerman and Sons of New York. Bannerman had purchased all of Remington's pistols when the company discontinued production.[28]

The concentration of weapons in the more secure warehouses continued throughout the summer. This included not only those arms already in the harbor at the time of the American invasion but those war materials that arrived in the ensuing months. As the arms accumulated the Constitutionalist leadership pressed the U.S. government to release some of them. Major Blanton Winship, civil affairs officer of the military government of Veracruz, explained the U.S. position: "The arms in question seem to be of a purely military character. Absolutely no arms of a military nature will be dispatched without the special authorization of the Military Governor." Others accepted the inevitable: "A. Combaluzier, arms dealer, Mexico City, would like his arms held at warehouses since he knows they cannot be brought to Mexico City."[29]

Ships bearing armaments in their cargos continued to arrive during the following months. The French cruiser *Descartes* unloaded seven tons of arms, of which only three and a half tons consisted of 500 Mauser rifles and 45,000 rounds of rifle ammunition. Heavy weapons such as machine guns and artillery were not identified in the *Descartes* shipments to discourage theft and probably account for the unitemized contents among the other three and a half tons. "Military machinery" arrived in 380 boxes aboard the *SS Andyk;* it, too, was impounded. State Department files show that the military cargo of the *Krownprincessen Cecile,* which arrived on 9 May, was returned to Germany. On 23 November, however, the date on which Americans departed, there were 467 crates of arms from the *Krownprincessen Cecile* in warehouse number 2, including one bulto weighing 6,300 kilos.[30]

The steamship *Tabasco* landed arms on 17 July. Another ship docked at pier 5 carrying a consignment of 125 rifles and 7,000 rounds intended for the Italian Legation in Mexico City. Some were late shipments ordered by Huerta; others were intended for foreign enterprises and embassies. A typical smaller consignment included two crates of rifles and eighty boxes of shotguns. The American authorities released a cargo of shotguns and rifles to "the police forces and planters of Yucatán in order to put down rioting." Another shipment included a load of cartridge-making machines. Meanwhile ammunition and dynamite sticks came in bulk. One load of ammunition totaled 200,000 rounds. A shipment of dynamite totaled

12,000 cases. As the arms arrived the Americans impounded them. On 1 August, 291 crates of weapons were transferred from various *bodegas* on the pier to warehouses 1 and 2. A consignment of six crates weighing 520 kilos each consisted of shotguns, sabers and swords, and heavier weapons. Weight analysis indicates 900 kilos of probable machine guns and artillery in the inventory total.[31]

The shippers of arms to Veracruz included Hartley (Remington Arms), H. K. White, Bannerman, and Stone and Company of New York (who specialized in Colt machine guns and gatlings); Joachimson of Paris; Genelot of France; Adolf Frank of Kiel and Hamburg, Germany; I. W. Stokes Kirk of Philadelphia; Ancion Marx of Liege; M. Duering and J. H. Krupp of Germany; Wexell and De Gress of New York and Mexico City; and A. Combaluzier and the Gómez Hermanos of Mexico City. The last three were Mexico's largest arms dealers. Shippers did not include machine guns and artillery listings on shipping manifests because of pilfering.

On 16 October the *San Marcos,* an army transport ship, returned 1,297 cases of ammunition weighing 158,977 pounds to Veracruz that had been recorded as sent to the San Antonio Arsenal. A note had been attached to the shipment when it was sent to Galveston: "This ammunition not to be taken off ship. See letter D.Q.M. Vera Cruz, [sic] Oct. 1, 1914." It also returned 186 additional cases that had been sent to the San Antonio Arsenal containing 174,000 30-caliber cartridges and 770 rifles. The "laundering" of arms in the cases of the *San Marcos* and *Krownprincessen Cecile* is even more notable considering that the ships' manifests and other records of military shipments to Veracruz are in the National Archives.[32]

In mid-November the *Morro Castle* unloaded 354 rolls of barbed wire, which was impounded. H. O. Stickney, administration of customs and captain of the port, explained the procedure: "The Aduana has orders not to dispatch this merchandise during our occupation. We are to clear the arms through customs and then turn them over to the military government for disposition." By 1 November, the identifiable armaments among the mass of military cargo in Veracruz would equip an army of 13,000 men with the most modern weapons.[33]

All inventories specifying the storage of military arms are missing from the records of the Military Government at Veracruz. However, warehousemen's transmittal slips and vouchers for the special handling of damaged articles escaped the censor's eye. Crucial documents depict the unloading of arms during the Americans' final week at Veracruz. On 18 November, six days before the U.S. forces departed, the steamship *Monserrat*'s hasty 24-hour per day unloading effort resulted in cargo damages.

The damage required special paperwork by the warehousemen, who identified all thirty-two crates involved as military equipment, arms, and ammunition. The *Monserrat* was one of five ships being unloaded at the piers adjacent to *cobertizos* 1, 2, and 3 simultaneously on a 24-hour per day basis between 18 November and 22 November 1914.[34]

To understand the critical importance of the 1914 Veracruz episode, it must be placed in the broader context of the choices available to the American government between the revolutionary factions in 1914. Despite their desirability, General Felix Díaz and Governor Teodoro Dehesa of Veracruz lacked public support and armed force. By early summer five principal leaders—Villa, Eulalio Gutiérrez, Zapata, Obregon Salido, and Carranza—had made strong impressions on the U.S. government, the first three highly negative and the last two relatively favorable. Generals Bliss, Pershing, and Funston repeatedly labeled Villa and his lower-class fellow leaders of the División del Norte with epithets such as "devilish," "ambitious," "irresponsible" and "murderous." President Wilson, Secretary of State Bryan, and presidential emissaries John C. Lind and Duval West saw Villa as "treasonous," "socialist," and a "brigand." Despite allegations that General Hugh Scott supported Villa and sympathetic comments regarding the Mexican in a letter to his wife, Scott vehemently denied suggestions of Villista sympathies. American officials opposed the Villistas, Zapatistas, and Convention government.

Villa's official agent in Washington, D.C., Felix Sommerfeld, had discovered in early July 1914 that Bryan and Wilson were secretly approving arms shipments to Carranza via Tampico, lifting the embargo instituted in the wake of the Veracruz invasion while stalling approval of the same for Villa. In August the Justice Department prosecuted the owners of the ship *Sunshine,* who tried to support Villa through that port after the United States alerted the Carranzistas regarding the cargo. American officials happily reported that the embargo on fuel and munitions to the División del Norte asked for by Carranza in the early summer of 1914 was a success. It was carried out through the cooperation of the Constitutionalist leaders and the Americans, including anti-Villista customs inspector Zach Lamar Cobb at El Paso. Through American control of border points the flow of supplies had been stopped. The Villistas would not be able to interfere with Obregon Salido's advance on Mexico City.[35]

At the Convention of Aguascalientes the alliance of Villa, with Eulalio Gutiérrez of San Luis Potosí, and Zapata generated intense hostility from American leaders. Gutiérrez was ill-regarded because he led guerrilla attacks on American-owned mines as an insurrectionist and then, as soon as he gained control of San Luis Potosí in October 1914, threatened nationalization of foreign-owned properties, abolished debt peonage and indebtedness, established minimum wages, and prohibited food exports by the commercial estates. The American Consul regarded Gutiérrez as a dangerous agrarian radical who was distributing land to the peons and threatening to nationalize the great estates. Among the properties damaged in San Luis Potosí during 1913–1914 was the Villista and Zapatista-ransacked 1,400,000-acre Rascon hacienda of George Lee and the Minor family of New Orleans. In Jalisco the Buena Fe silver mine, the most prosperous Mexican enterprise owned by Colonel House's old family friend and benefactor, John Henry Kirby, was attacked, captured, and dynamited by Villista rebels, including former workers from the mine. Kirby claimed $562,000 in damages inflicted at the Buena Fe; the Lees and Minors reported $302,835 in damages at Rascon.[36]

In November, as the U.S. government prepared to depart Veracruz, its officials considered Eulalio Gutiérrez, president of the Convention government, one of the most radical leaders of the revolution. The U.S. consul at San Luis Potosí reported:

> A decree issued under date of September 15, 1914, by Governor Eulalio Gutiérrez, fixes the minimum wage in the State of San Luis Potosí at 75 centavos per day, to be paid in cash, which at the ruling rate of exchange is equivalent to about 21 cents United States currency. In mines the minimum wage is fixed at 1.25 pesos, or about 35 cents in United States currency. The 9-hour day is also decreed. Employers who have been paying more than the minimum are forbidden to reduce wages to the minimum. Workers on farms must be supplied free water, wood, and shelter. By the same decree company stores are abolished. All debts contracted by laborers to employers expire by limitation in one year. Employers are prohibited from placing any obstacle in the way of laborers who desire to change their place of employment or to accept other employment. The wages of laborers are exempted from garnishment.
>
> The decree provides that a landowner who furnishes to the tenant land, implements, animals, and seed shall not collect more than 25% of the crop for rent and reimbursement, but in cases where he makes these advances and also furnishes water for irrigation he may collect 50% of the crop. All advances to the tenant must be in cash and must be returned in cash or in grain at the price current in the nearest market.
>
> Probably the most important article of the decree provides that in view of the exceedingly low wages heretofore prevailing all loans and advances heretofore made and now outstanding against the laborers, must be considered as a voluntary supplement to the inadequate wages and are therefore declared liquidated and canceled.[37]

The Wilson administration regarded the third element of the Conventionalist triumvirate, the Zapatistas, as the ultimate threat not only to American interests but to civilization itself. Zapata was seen as the murderous head of a peasant rabble bent on pillage and rape. The metropolitan elite Escandon and Noriega families, refugees in Veracruz, whose family heads were issued special permits to carry sidearms, confirmed American fears. General Funston, head of the Veracruz expeditionary force, expressed American military thinking:

> Have just been informed foreigners and citizens in Mexico City will unite in request that United States troops occupy city to prevent massacre and pillage by Zapata. . . . If consent refused [by the Mexican government] we can go anyhow and overcome any likely opposing force. . . . For several days there has been firing in the city. . . . Zapatistas are very active in the suburbs. Principal fear is that mob will get control. . . . Troops are not considered reliable. . . . Zapatistas would probably enter to take part in sacking if mob should prevail.[38]

On 5 August Alfredo Breceda, Carranza's representative in Veracruz, candidly described the Constitutionalists' supporters:

> Representative Lord Cowdray places at our disposal railroad from Alvarado here, will help temporarily forces Alvarado. . . . Leaders commanding forces south and center present themselves to me daily recognizing plan Guadalupe, also capitalists, manufacturers, bankers, merchants, representatives large foreign enterprises.[39]

The American leadership in Washington respected "the wily old fox" Carranza, a man of high standing in Mexican society and a hacendado, ex-senator, and governor. He represented the only viable elite leadership left in Mexico. As the leader of the Coahuila oligarchy he had forged a successful alliance with a Sonoran provincial elite faction headed by the Pesquiera, Salido, and Elías families.

In Chihuahua the oligarchy for the most part had stood and fallen with Díaz. Huerta supporters murdered the Maderista governor, Abraham González, in the early hours of the golpe de estado. As a result the working-class Villista leadership dominated the revolution there. The Villista leadership defined the revolution in Fourier-like terms. Villa's own position duplicated the phalangism of Charles Fourier: a society of democratic local governments in control of production and consumer services, with armed defense based upon a locally recruited and directed militia acting in concert with its neighbors. Fourier's ideas had permeated Mexican radical thinking since the 1840s. In 1912 anarchist and Zapatista Otilio Magaña deeply influenced Villa when he taught the northern revolutionary Mexican history and politics while they were incarcerated in adjacent cells in Mexico City.[40]

In Sonora the Maytorena family, oligarchical rivals of the Pesquiera, Elías, and Salido families, joined forces with Villa, and the state became an early testing ground of U.S. policy in support of Carranza. A U.S. Army intelligence report described the situation:

> The real facts of the controversy [are] . . . two political factions striving for . . . supremacy in the state, for the honors, appointments and patronage. . . . For years the state of Sonora has had two political machines, that headed by Maytorena having until recent time held the power. With the beginning of the [Constitutionalist] revolution the other machine saw opportunity. Charges and counter charges are made by each faction against the other, while the real issue is who will control the patronage. . . . The military headed by Colonel P. Elías Calles heading the Pesquiera faction has at the present time the upperhand . . . has ordered the arrest of the various civil authorities one by one. . . . The Cananea situation may turn grave at any time, the laborers there being strong followers of Maytorena.[41]

The Americans might also have noted Obregon Salido's past ties with the Phelps Dodge of President Wilson's "dear friend" Cleveland Dodge, the Southern Pacific, the H. E. Richardson Company, and his massive debts to W. R. Grace. Maytorena's support from the Yaqui Indians "probably originating with his father's generous treatment of them during the Indian Wars of 1890s," alienated the American company and government officials. The Yaqui wars of the previous twenty-five years had prevented completion of the railroad from El Paso to Guaymas and had threatened the properties of the Richardson Construction and the Wheeler Land companies and the Pacific coast route of the Southern Pacific Railroad. During the summer of 1914 the U.S. government allowed shipments of military supplies to Salvador Alvarado to assist in a campaign against the Yaqui and, through Naco, to Elías Calles's column, which then seized Cananea from pro-Villista workers. That policy stands in sharp contrast to the simultaneous refusal by Secretary of War Garrison to approve the petition of the Hirsch Brothers arms dealers in St. Louis to sell arms to Maytorena.[42]

In the meantime the American government developed closer ties to the Constitutionalists. Carranza gave his son-in-law, Candido Aguilar, "the youngest general in the Mexican army," a noncombat but important task in September: "This government has decided to designate General Candido Aguilar, Governor of the State of Veracruz . . . to receive the port

[and] to appoint the federal and local authorities to take charge."[43] Seven Constitutionalist officers including Aguilar and Alejo González, Obregon Salido's cavalry commander at the critical battle of Celaya, had been in Veracruz for two months. They had worked alongside the Americans in charge of the arms buildup before the formal order to evacuate the city was given. Cavalry officer González received a consignment of cavalry gear for 1,500 men that had been stored in Veracruz. The shipment he received outfitted 2,000 cavalrymen, with whom he outflanked and routed Villa at the battle of León.[44]

Frank Rabb, whose father had been killed in the 1870s border violence and a rabid Villa hater, prevailed as President Wilson's chief customs inspector at the Brownsville-Matamoros crossing point. His role was central to Carranza's Veracruz success. One Brownsville merchant openly shipped over $600,000 in armaments to the Carranza forces at Matamoros during the summer of 1914 border embargo that shut off supplies to the Villistas. Marciano Moreno, Jefe de Telégrafos in Veracruz, intercepted most of the Americans' and Constitutionalists' incoming and outgoing messages. He learned that Constitutionalist arms shipments were coming from Matamoros to Veracruz by sea:

> Venustiano Carranza received the arms in Veracruz via Matamoros. These arms were stockpiled and guarded here. The chief intermediary with the Americans in this trade was General Pablo González. The machine guns were taken to the Baluarte de Santiago for the utmost security.[45]

Secretary of War Garrison directed Funston: "surrender . . . all physical property excepting money to the designated successor." On 31 October W. W. Wright, adjutant general of the army, informed his officers at Veracruz of the ultimate disposition of the arms buildup: "In the event of the withdrawal of the United States troops from Veracruz, the arms, munitions and gun implements referred to will be turned over to the Mexican authorities."[46]

The Conventionalist forces controlled most of the central plateau of Mexico from the Isthmus of Tehuantepec to the American border, but they were unable to crush the Constitutionalist forces backed up against Guaymas, Mazatlán, Manzanillo, Acapulco, Salina Cruz, Naco, Matamoros, Tampico, Veracruz, and Campeche. The latter received supplies from the United States in late 1914 and early 1915, carried by American ships while the border remained closed to land-based shipments to the Villistas.

The forces of Elías Calles at Naco received reinforcements in addition to supplies from the Americans. Arms flowed across the border at Matamoros; meantime the Constitutionalists backed up at Manzanillo counterattacked with devastating effects upon the Villistas. The repairs of the lighthouses at Manzanillo, Acapulco, Mazatlán, and Tampico enabled night deliveries that went undetected by the Villistas.

An exception to the land-frontier embargo against Villa was made in September-October 1914, when Carranza refused to give the Wilson government assurances regarding the Mexicans in Veracruz who had collaborated with the occupation authorities. Carranza quickly backed down in a secret message to Wilson reinforced by assurances from U.S. Vice-Consul John R. Silliman from Mexico City. The Americans restored the anti-Villista embargo. The U.S. Navy repaired the lighthouses on both coasts to ensure the safe passage of supplies from San Francisco, New York, and other ports to the Constitutionalist forces. In the meantime John Lind, the president's emissary to Mexico, met with Aguilar in Veracruz, and Constitutionalist officers were introduced to their jobs preparatory to the Americans' departure.

On the evening of 23 November 1914 the American authorities withdrew their guards from the warehouses and the Constitutionalist officers with whom they had been working took over. They left the keys to the storage facilities at the Veracruz Chamber of Commerce offices. Foreign concerns dominated the city's business and the chamber, which was overwhelmingly foreign. Of Veracruz properties, 98 percent were held by absentee owners and foreigners. The Americans deposited 2,604,051.20 pesos of customs revenues and other funds in New Orleans with the understanding that Carranza's government would be given a line of credit if it "acceded to our desires," including the safeguarding of the refugees and Mexican nationals who had worked for the United States in Veracruz.[47]

The armaments turned over to the Constitutionalists at Veracruz and the forces backed up to the ports on the two coasts, as well as the embargoes on supplies to the Convention forces, shifted the balance of power among the revolutionary factions. The "massive" arms cache in the Vivac described by General Funston occupied a storage facility 47 yards long, 18 yards deep, and 15 feet high. It was constructed by the Spanish government as a storage facility for grains and corn, and the Díaz government converted it to a military arsenal. The Americans placed the weapons taken from the Mexican armed forces installations around the city, including the arsenal and fort at San Juan de Ulloa, in the Vivac, the Baluarte de Santiago, and the Juárez Lighthouse. The Duering Company had just completed the rearming of San Juan de Ulloa, which it labeled "the Gibraltar of America."

The U.S. forces stacked the arms in the Vivac in "large heaps" and kept them under lock and key until they withdrew. The Duering Company, the largest of forty-eight German commercial houses in Veracruz, complained to the Americans that it had not received payment for its shipments of artillery. Duering demanded $19,751 from the U.S. government because it had turned over the state-of-the-art guns to the Constitutionalists. Among the otherwise immaculate records of the U.S. Military Government of Veracruz, the Vivac weapons inventory by Captain J. T. Watson and the inventories of arms stored at the Baluarte de Santiago or the Juárez Lighthouse, each of which occupied a full square city block, have not been found among the "screened" records available in the U.S. National Archives.[48]

Warehousemen's receipts did record part of the massive arms buildup at the wharves. Filled to capacity in 1914, warehouses 1 and 2 still stand as they did in 1914 with the exception of new floors. Thick stone walls, heavily timbered floors, and peaked reinforced metal roofs offered excellent security. Rails from the Terminal Company warehouses at the north end of the dock area reached the wide-sloped access ramps leading to the heavy wooden sliding doors. The weapons came from the world's largest arms dealers.[49]

In November 1914 warehouse number 1 contained 3,877 crates of arms and ammunition. The bultos varied in size from 6 to 1,300 kilos. Warehouse number 2 was filled to capacity with 639 crates of military equipment. The other warehouse inventories showed over 30,000 other parcels of both military and nonwar materials. For example, the contents of warehouse number 3 included 278 rolls of barbed wire, three armorers tables, and nine radio transmitters among 1,995 total bultos. Warehouse number 4 contained 1,776 bultos including arms consignments to the Duering Company, the arsenal, and the Mexican army. The Bodega Norte held 11,571 bultos including 173 bags of parafine, 200 rolls of barbed wire, and enormous crates containing unknown goods. In October the port's warehouses contained a total of 37,190 bultos. Of those, 18 percent were located in warehouses 1, 2, and 3 which had been set aside by the American forces for the storage of military materials originally intended for shipment inside Mexico. On 13 November crews unloaded the 354 rolls of barbed wire on board the *Morro Castle*. Explosive materials in the ship's cargo were stored apart from the guns, in the *plazuela* of the customs complex.[50]

Sixty percent of the contents of warehouses 1, 2, and 3 shows 25 machine guns; 8,458 rifles; 3,550 carbines; 1,650 shotguns; 3,375,000 rounds of ammunition including dumdum bullets; 632 rolls of barbed wire; 380

crates of military machinery ordered by the artillery division of the Mexican army, three armorers tables; nine shortwave radio sets; 2,034 pistols; six boxes of hand grenades; 1,250 boxes of sodium cyanide, which, combined with nitric or sulpheric acid, created poison gas; 1,500 sabers; 619 bags of parafine; three Benz trucks; and nine sedans. But there was much more.

Artillery that was supposed to return to the United States with the American forces on 23 November did not arrive. Quartermaster Sergeant George H. Hahn at Fort Monroe, Virginia, complained that he received only a casket from the hold of the *San Marcos*. He estimated the cargo that was to have been loaded at Veracruz:

> Approximately 140 cu. tons miscellaneous equipment
> Approximately 4 cu. tons baggage
> 6 Guns—(3″ landing guns)
> Approximately 75 cu. tons ammunition.[51]

On 23 November the warehouseman at cobertizo 1 summed up a new level of intensity in the stockpiling of arms during those last few days in Veracruz when he wrote the captain of the port regarding arriving and uninventoried material: "Need men in order to put armaments in order. Four steamships have unloaded here at this warehouse in the last three days creating mass confusion."[52]

These weapons arrived at the last moment and were not included in the inventories. The last ship to arrive, the *City of Mexico,* unloaded all night on 22 November. The *Monterrey* unloaded a cargo consigned to the arms importers Duering and Company and Gustavo Struck. The *Morro Castle* began its stay at the pier on 18 November, joining the *Imperator* and *San Bernardo*.[53]

The Carranza government then accepted U.S. terms in order to receive the 2,604,051.20 pesos deposited at New Orleans. During the occupation Lt. Colonel James Biddle Porter explained U.S. strategy:

> The revenue of this customhouse is greatly desired by the Mexican government. The amounts [sic] to many millions of pesos a year. Granting permission that merchandise should pass through in bond and the tariffs collected at some interior customhouse by Mexican authorities might please the Mexican government greatly, but it would certainly weaken one of the arguments which might induce the Mexican government to accede to our desires.[54]

Carranza considered it "inexpedient" to compromise himself in the eyes of Mexican public opinion by acceding to American demands regarding the Veracruz collaborators during the Americans' continued controversial presence in the port city. Vice Consul Silliman, an avid supporter of Carranza and an old friend of President Wilson from their Princeton days, was serving as one of the American leader's special representatives in Mexico. He explained the first chief's sensitive political position to Robert Lansing, acting secretary of state:

> No one will be molested on account of service rendered Americans and no back duties or taxes will be collected. . . . Cabrera in conversation this afternoon suggests that such proclamation might follow soon after evacuation.[55]

The Zapatistas and División del Norte occupied Mexico City in early December 1914 while the Constitutionalists evacuated central Mexico in apparent defeat. On 4 December Zapata and Villa held their famous meeting at Xochimilco on the outskirts of the capital. Their conversation symbolized the violent social antagonism that divided the nation. Villa described the Obregonista pequeña burguesía as "men who have always slept on soft pillows. How could they ever be friends of the people who have spent their lives with nothing but suffering?" Zapata summed up the attitudes resulting from two centuries of campesino struggle against the European-oriented men of property: "they have always been the scourge of the people." He shared Villa's contempt for the Obregonista pequeña burguesía: "Those cabrones as soon as they see a little chance, well, they want to take advantage of it and line their pockets!"

The rural working-class leaders, aware of the failures of the past, pronounced their historic distrust of bourgeois government. Villa: "No más vamos a encargales que no den quehacer." Zapata: "Por eso yo los advierto a todo los amigos que mucho cuidado, si no, les cae el machete." They rejected the presidency, entrusting the chief administrative role of the Convention government to Gutiérrez, who was radical, relatively cosmopolitan, and educated. Villa and Zapata, unable to control the hundreds of autonomous campesino rebel groups that operated in the countryside in their name, realized that their central task lay in the defeat of the Constitutionalists and not in the presidency. Despite their knowledge of past betrayals, the peasant leaders turned over the reins of government to Gutiérrez and a cohort of contradictory pequeña burguesa administrators.[56]

The new Conventionalist administrators, while sympathetic to the need for social reform to benefit the lower classes, were openly hostile toward the campesino extremes of Villismo and Zapatismo. One of them, Martín Luis Guzmán, immortalized his cultural contempt for Villista and Zapatista "bestiality" and "savagery," criticizing the crudeness and brutality of

Villa and his lieutenants and mocking the "simplicity" and "humility" of the Zapatistas. In his books *The Eagle and the Serpent* and *The Memoirs of Pancho Villa,* he repeated the exaggerated atrocity stories invented by the Constitutionalists for use against the Villistas without any mention of the thermidorean annihilation of peasant communities carried out by the Constitutionalists in wide areas of the nation after 1914.

In the exercise of their government positions Guzmán and other pequeña burguesa functionaries sabotaged the peasant war effort by sequestering Zapatista calls for war materials, canceling messages between peasant leaders, delaying the issuance of orders, and sidetracking supplies. An exception was Heriberto Frías, who published the Convention newspaper and remained loyal to the lessons of his Porfirian protest novel *Tomochic,* and to the Villista forces, long after the defeats of 1915 rendered Villismo unchíc for men of fashion. The interjection of the hostile Convention government bureaucracy between the peasant armies of the north and those of the south crucially frustrated their plans. The provincial perspectives of the peasantry, combined with the antipeasant bias of the pequeña burguesía contributed to the Convention's eventual defeat. The perspectives of many Gutiérrez government officials had much in common with Obregonismo, whereas Carrancismo was intolerable for them.

While the revolutionary armies were maneuvering for position during the fall of 1914, the Casa del Obrero Mundial began an intense organizing effort. Despite the departure of anarchist leaders Jacinto Huitrón and Antonio Díaz Soto y Gama to join the Zapatistas during Huerta's repression, Lucha representatives continued an energetic organizing campaign. They visited workers in factories and artisan shops throughout the nation's industrial centers. The Casa prepared for its resurgence during the months of suppression after May 1914 by means of underground committees and emissaries that reached out from Mexico City to towns all over central Mexico. National leaders came together in the Casa directorate for syndicate and militia organizing, mutual aid during strikes, and ideological instruction and education, including hygienic and nutritional information.

The syndicates and Casa leadership group grew rapidly until twenty-three committees of unpaid secretaries in the national directorate were running the organization. The Casa grew with extreme rapidity. By late 1914 the number of national secretaries surpassed seventy-five. The greater diversity of the directorate caused the rubric Lucha to fall into disuse. Leaders worked without pay in the name of working-class equality.[57]

In late 1914 and 1915 the economic and political instability caused by the revolutionary fighting meant government weakness in the control of labor, extreme inflation, and high unemployment. A series of strikes manifesting an urban version of the revolution's deep working-class nationalism resulted. They shut down the foreign-owned Mexico City rail transit system, the electrical power company, the telephone and telegraph companies, and textile factories. The Casa's rhetoric was class oriented and internationalist in tone, but its tactics were nationalistic. Strike targets were often foreign companies. The syndicates possessed a strong sense of working-class unity, and because of the crucial public service nature of their industries, they exercised unusual strength. The Convention government did little to encourage or deter Casa activities. Its position was compatible with the anarchists' tenet of independence from government but did nothing to encourage those leaders who sought advantage, income, or position with the government. Meanwhile the New York-based electrical power company managers protested the strikes and the Convention government's failure to protect foreign property.

During its short stay in Mexico City during the late summer of 1914, the Carranza government found a valuable contact within the urban labor movement and a solution for the power company strikes. In order to restore service it gave the union and its leader, Luis N. Morones, a partial management role. The anarchosyndicalists in the Casa initially applauded these developments because, to them, it represented workers' control of industry. Morones, despite earlier ultraradicalism, had already developed close relations with Obregonista and Carrancista officers. He suddenly emerged with enormous influence and prestige within the labor movement. Antianarchist, Morones espoused a blend of trade unionism and corporatism. He avoided conflicts with idealistic working-class leaders while working to establish Constitutionalist control over labor. He maintained regular contacts with the Carranza government and the companies while developing an especially close alliance with Obregon Salido.

Morones's successful work with the companies and his close ties with Constitutionalist officials prepared the way for his future rise to power under President Obregon Salido as head of the government's Department of Labor and the government-sponsored Confederación Regional Obrera Mexicana (CROM), which replaced the Casa as the principal workers' organization. During the twenties the CROM, with radical rhetoric, would recruit tens of thousands of deceived rank-and-file working-class radicals, who thought they were joining a revolutionary labor movement. Even the anarchist international did not understand or denounce the CROM until the late 1920s. Morones's rise to power reflected a developing alliance between the working class, despite its strong propensities toward anarchosyndicalism and independence, and the reform-minded Obregonista pequeña burguesía, who sought a powerful government responsive to its needs for social order, stability, and viable relations with the United States.[58]

The Obregonistas developed a good relationship with the Casa before the advance of the División del Norte forced them to withdraw from Mexico City. In response to Casa demands, the Constitutionalists made the most of their stay in the capital by donating meeting halls to it, contributing radical speakers such as Gerardo Murillo (Dr. Atl) to labor meetings, permitting syndicate organizing, and even helping achieve favorable strike settlements via arbitration. Emergency monetary policies, such as paper centavo bills, helped to alleviate desperate conditions for the lower-echelon workers of Mexico City. Compared to the goodwill created among labor leaders by the Obregonistas and sincere radicals affiliated with the Carranza government such as Dr. Atl, the Villista and Zapatista revolutionaries of rural Mexico seemed almost alien. The labor leaders' sympathy for the peasants' difficult living conditions should not be confused with respect. When Zapata and Villa met at the National Palace in December 1914 in what was the high point of the rural lower-class revolutionary tide, urban labor leaders objected with complaints that Villa was a "personalist" and that the Zapatistas were "Catholic."

The Casa's unrealistic assessment of Villa and agreement with the pequeña burguesa cadres of Obregon Salido that the peasant revolution represented "the reaction" was the result of the cultural and economic differences between urban and rural Mexico at that time. Twenty percent of the Zapatistas spoke Nahuatl. Those who spoke Spanish did so in a manner vulgar to urban listeners. Villa and Zapata were unknown and threatening outsiders who offered scant reassurance to industrial workers who were accustomed to the European conveniences of urban Mexico.

There was sympathy for the plight of the campesino, especially for the articulate Zapatistas; but urban workers, as proud citizens of Mexico City, considered themselves more sophisticated than the seemingly primitive campesinaje. As constituents of Mexico City they enjoyed the wealth of the metropolis even if an unbalanced distribution of income gave them only peripheral advantages, such as public transportation and parks, paved streets, a few schools, sewage disposal, and other public services. The Zapatistas reinforced the patronizing attitude of most urban labor leaders when they "begged food" from the Mexico City "bourgeoisie" during their occupation of the city. They also exhibited seemingly subservient "humility," religious devotion, and acceptance of the clergy. Religious arm patches and banners, such as the Zapatista Virgin de Guadalupe, reflected the close relationship of countryside clergy with the peasants of Morelos. In some cases the priests had served as longtime defenders of the pueblos. Village clergy had led the Independence Revolution, the Yautepec revolution of 1832, and the Huastecan uprisings of the early 1880s. The religious aspect of the rural working-class forces especially galled uncomprehending Casa "rationalists."

The urban and industrial workers' hostility toward the clergy derived from the Church hierarchy's nineteenth-century right-wing political activism. The anarchosyndicalist leaders of urban and industrial labor believed that they had more in common with the "Jacobin" urban pequeña burguesía of Obregon Salido than with the working class of the countryside. The economic polarity between countryside and city and cultural differences between the rural and urban sectors made the syndicate leaders' attitude toward the campesinos predictable.

Mexico's political left had not yet developed the ideological theory that later in the twentieth century would bridge the vast differences between the indigenous countryside and the European-oriented cities. The differences that rendered the urban industrial working class silent during Mexico's version of the Tupac Amaru uprising in Puebla in 1780, during the peasant war that accompanied Hidalgo's move for independence in 1810, and during the myriad waves of campesino violence that swept across central Mexico throughout the nineteenth century were still present.

Given the economic and cultural contradictions that existed between the periphery and the metropolis and between the rural and urban working classes, it is difficult to conceive of a political force capable of a cross-class and multicultural alliance that could have bridged the vast material differences and enlisted the support of both sides. Those differences were not bridged in China in 1911, in Iran from 1905 to 1911, or in Russia until after October 1917. In Russia the Zemstvos were divorced from the peasantry during the Revolution of 1905. In the Ukraine the peasant movement grew under anarchist leadership while factions of the Social Revolutionary party commanded the loyalty of most peasantry. The Bolsheviks' base of strength lay with the workers. In 1917, however, the rural and urban working-class formations cooperated with each other until the defeat of their enemies. It was only after the elimination of the rightist forces in the civil war that the anarchist and Social Revolutionary (peasant-based) forces and the Bolshevik forces (urban and industrial working class) turned against each other.

In February 1915 a Casa delegation traveled to Veracruz and met with

Carranza and Obregon Salido representatives. Their results committed the manpower of organized labor to the Constitutionalist military effort. The delegation's explanation for this commitment went beyond the condemnation of the campesino Villistas and Zapatistas as "the reaction" or the bizarre allegations of "Church and banker" support for the peasants. The Casa leadership had no illusions about the "bourgeois alliances" of President Carranza but reasoned that the Constitutionalist movement, which had received Veracruz from the American government and masses of armaments through that port and Tampico as well as Pacific ports, was a likely winner.

The Casa leaders reasoned that their participation ushered in a new era of syndicate organizing and working-class power. They provided the Constitutionalists with the personnel needed to operate the newly acquired American weapons, the Veracruz origins of which they may have known about. The anarchosyndicalists interpreted the pact as a contract giving them authority to organize workers throughout the country. The Casa intended to organize the working class and then to confront the divided Constitutionalist movement with its mutually antagonistic Obregonista radical pequeña burguesía and the conservative Carrancistas. In that confrontation the Casa leaders counted on "Jacobin" support, including that of Obregon Salido.

Casa delegates to Veracruz, representing 50,000 workers in the cities, correctly assessed the disaffection between the bureaucracy of the Convention government and the campesino armies of Villa and Zapata as indicative of their eventual defeat. They recognized their own importance to the weak Constitutionalist movement and clearly felt in control of the situation. An agrarista minority of the Casa leadership dissented but with minimal impact because the leadership clearly expressed its intent to incorporate agrarian reform and the militant peasantry to its ranks after victory, and because the important figures Huitrón and Díaz Soto y Gama, who favored alliance with the rural working class instead of the Jacobin and radical pequeña burguesía of Obregon Salido, had already left Mexico City during labor's confrontation with the ruthless Huerta regime in order to join in the creation of the Zapatista Comuna de Morelos.

During the winter of 1915 between 7,000 and 10,000 workers—9,000 according to Obregon Salido's own estimate—departed for the Constitutionalist military training center in Orizaba. They escaped from the Convention government's territory aided by the treasonous complicity of the alienated pequeña burguesa Conventionalist bureaucracy in the capital city. Military commanders organized them into six "Red Battalions." The role of the Americans in the training of the new Constitutionalist army is not known, but foreign military advisers and soldiers have been credited with providing the Constitutionalists their margin of victory. The Constitutionalist forces were re-equipped with the arms at Veracruz, and American "consultants" from the American Federation of Labor, including John C. Murray, a U.S. government agent, posing as a reporter lived in the camp, establishing daily contact with Casa leaders.

Nationwide at least 15,000 industrial and urban labor militiamen participated in the revolution. These forces included metropolitan and provincial Casa members, and independent units, such as the miners' militias from Coahuila and Sonora, which joined the Constitutionalist movement in the beginning, and industrial workers from Monterrey, Tampico, Guadalajara, and Veracruz. The number does not include those workers at Cananea who supported Villa. The urban and industrial labor forces constituted a massive augmentation of the Constitutionalist armies.

While the Constitutionalists regrouped in Veracruz and recruited the bulk of the urban workers, the peasant revolution, faced with the enmity of all other social classes except a handful of leftist déclassé intellectuals, reached its most radical and powerful stage. The Americans had embargoed the Villistas by sea, but the border was permeated with smuggling routes. The Villistas were geographically well positioned to purchase an abundance of contraband arms, for which they paid the merchants in gold, cattle, and crops obtained from the confiscated haciendas of the north.[59]

Yet the Villistas suffered from a chronic shortage of cash and U.S. Customs interdictions at El Paso. Their representatives rarely had enough money to purchase all the arms they needed. Zach Cobb zealously sought their shipments. In 1915 Lazaro de la Garza, the Conventionalist purchasing agent at the border city, rarely had more than $15,000 for purchases. Bought at the border at inflated prices from America's largest arms manufacturers and dealers, the weapons and ammunition sometimes did not match. Defective shipments also plagued the Villistas. The northern rebels seized more estates and used those assets to avert bankruptcy as their military strength waned. The Fourier-like Villistas planned to partition the estates among the soldiers of the División del Norte and their families into ejidos and cooperative properties defended by autonomous militias after the fighting concluded. Despite delays in their program that even provoked campesino rebellion, their aims threatened American and provincial-elite landholdings in the north.[60]

At the same time, the Zapatistas demonstrated a capacity to replace the state with decentralized self-government but did not have the power to correct the imbalance of forces created by foreign intervention. As the villages communalized the lands of the south, they moved toward a new society based upon the fundamental peasant sociopolitical and economic unit, the municipio libre. This independent pueblo was held together in voluntary federation with the other communities under the loosely structured Zapatista high command.

The Zapatista federation of municipios libres seemed archaic, but it was based on countryside reality. The Zapatista campaign to forge a united nationwise peasant force based on the municipios libres and the communalized property of the nation floundered at this stage because of the resistance of the administrators of the hopelessly divided Convention government and the foreign assistance that bailed out the scattered Constitutionalists.

The communalism of the lowest-status workers, the campesinos, alienated most of the radicals of the more affluent working classes, including factory workers, artisans, and déclassé intellectuals, first in the Constitutionalist movement and then within the Conventionalist government. Guzmán described the bureaucratic pequeña burguesía's hostility toward Zapatismo, objecting to the campesinos' bare feet on the carpets in the National Palace and averring, "we were working more as allies of Obregon." The rural revolution, with its insistence on local control of property in the face of massive foreign ownership representing about 25 percent of the nation's surface and a much higher percentage of the productive land, constituted economic nationalism in its most extreme form. American authorities recognized the threat.[61]

The alienated pequeña burguesía never admitted their conservatism in the face of agrarian and industrial working-class revolution. Instead they labeled the lower-class-led rural forces "the reaction" and attacked the anarchosyndicalists. They gave the revolution a definition of purpose consistent with their own interests. The cornerstone of the preservation of those interests was the elaboration of the nation-state. They initiated the revolution's complex nationalist, pro-burguesía "problem solving" state within both the Conventionalist and Constitutionalist movements.

With a series of pro-working-class manifestos in early 1915, the Constitutionalist pequeña burguesía gained momentum against their Conventionalist counterparts who could not overcome the taint of their association with lower-class campesino ideology and military power. Structured and controlled, Constitutionalist "radicalism" was the safe road for those who benefited from social hierarchy. They justified their anti-campesino stance with effective sniping at Villa's character and Zapata's education. Conventionalist bureaucrats and Constitutionalist leaders with multiple mistresses and bastard children hypocritically complained about Villa's wives. Villa did not take marriage rites seriously. He gave his mistresses status in their communities through marriage, while Obregon Salido ignored formalities.

In early 1915, while the Conventionalist bureaucracy was sabotaging coordination between the Zapatistas in the south and the Villistas in the north and delaying Villista agrarian reforms that could have secured an even greater surge of rural lower-class support, the Constitutionalist forces under Obregon Salido launched their critical invasion of central Mexico from Veracruz. His unified command and well-equipped forces gave him a better-than-even chance against the Conventionalist forces, which were divided into three geographic zones, with Zapata south of Mexico City, Villa north of the central valley and in the west, and Villista general Felipe Angeles, the finest military strategist and tactician of the revolution, in the northeast.

The Constitutionalists enjoyed an abundance of arms and ammunition, but Villista supplies trickled across the border past Cobb, the vigilant U.S. customs authority at El Paso. Cobb was an appointee of Colonel House. An El Paso lawyer, Cobb was a political ally of John Henry Kirby, a Texas Democratic party activist and Mexican investor who had posted $140,000 to help keep the House Bank in Houston afloat before it collapsed in the U.S. financial panic of 1907. Cobb was also an ally of West Texas and New Mexico investors in Mexico. Anti-Villista, Cobb diligently enforced the U.S. anti-Villa customs effort. With Secretary of State Bryan's approval, the Constitutionalists bought shiploads of arms and unloaded them at Tampico. Meanwhile Bryan denied Sommerfeld permission to export arms to the Villistas. Sommerfeld, who was the Villista representative in Washington, D.C., discovered that Bryan was secretly allowing arms shipments to the Carrancistas while embargoing the Villistas. De la Garza, the chief purchasing agent for the División del Norte at El Paso, made acquisitions with the limited funds in his accounts and then struggled to get them across the border past Cobb.[62]

The Constitutionalist resurgence was profoundly political, promising a national government that would recognize foreign property rights, carry out land reform on behalf of the peasants, and support the industrial labor movement. This stance appealed to peasants and workers, but it was especially attractive to the pequeña burguesía of both Constitutionalism and the Convention. It retained the national government's control over the reform programs, rejecting both the self-governing anarchist syndicates of the urban workers and the equally autonomous municipios libres of peasant radicalism.

Government control of these programs removed power from the masses and retained the social and political hierarchy from which the pequeña burguesía received its special status vis-à-vis 90 percent of the population. In every revolutionary process the radical pequeña burguesía groups reflect this egoism in relation to working-class power. The structures they invent in order to control the revolutionary process are a product of an economic system that stresses individualism, cultural pride based upon upper-class values, and an intellectual contempt for the masses, especially the latter's capacity for self-government.

Before the campaign between the Obregonistas and the División del Norte moved toward its inevitable showdowns at Celaya and León, the Gutiérrez government had already fled Mexico City in early 1915 because of the deteriorating military situation and the conflict between its bureaucracy and the antigovernment campesino radicalism of the Zapatistas. There is no evidence of conflict between Gutiérrez and Villa. Gutiérrez established an independent government in Nuevo León. Roque González Garza became the new Convention president in Mexico City and was recognized by the Zapatistas, but by now the Constitutionalists had gained a threatening position north of Mexico City and forced the Villistas to challenge their advance at Celaya.

The battles of Celaya, León, and Aguascalientes, which took place between April and July 1915, decided the revolution. Obregon Salido used elaborate, sophisticated, and expensive barbed-wire networks and machine-gun placements with crossed fields of fire for use against the División del Norte's cavalry charges, and indirect artillery fire with weapons far superior to the Villistas' mix of brass cannons and up-to-date weapons. The tactics learned from the German successes of 1914–1915 are indicative not of the neophyte Obregon Salido's military genius but of alien advisers in addition to the earlier equipping of his army by American advisers at Veracruz.

U.S. military intelligence described Obregon Salido as "a former small farmer and storekeeper of common school education, without technical military training." American support was central to the victory of the Constitutionalist forces. When word of the Constitutionalists' victory at Celaya was received at Veracruz, John R. Silliman, President Wilson's special envoy to the Carrancistas, gloated to the German Consul, "We have taken León, we have defeated Villa, and we will soon occupy the City of Mexico."[63]

U.S. emissaries described the Villistas and Zapatistas as "dangerous socialists." The Americans' transfer of the arms stored at Veracruz to the Constitutionalists in November 1914 turned the tide of the revolution. The Wilson government quickly made its support of the Constitutionalists official. In October 1915 the United States extended diplomatic recognition to Carranza, although the Constitutionalists controlled only a little more than half the country.

Mexico's development as a mixed caste and class society divided between elites and workers and European urban versus indigenous rural sectors characterized the struggle of the revolutionary forces. In 1914 and 1915 the main forces of the urban and rural sectors, divided by ancestry, culture, and class interests, turned on each other. American intervention eliminated any possibility of victory for the rural working class. At this point, with continuing but no longer immediately critical countryside resistance, the victorious, more commercial and industrial Europeanized classes faced each other. The industrial and urban workers, Jacobin pequeña burguesía, and the mostly Carrancista provincial elites, who quickly solidified the support of the metropolitan and foreign bourgeoisies, moved into a new phase of conflict.

In the late spring of 1915, the industrial working class under Casa leadership constituted a formidable force. Its mobilization began when the Casa directorate created a Comité de Propaganda, numbering about eighty members divided into fourteen committees, to organize workers in the wake of the advancing Constitutionalist armies. After the defeat of the División del Norte the Constitutionalist unity of upper-class elements, pequeña burguesa, and industrial workers' groups began to unravel. Casa anarchism, workers' militias, and strikes provoked the concern of industrialists and Constitutionalist officials.

Urban food shortages, runaway inflation, unemployment, public demonstrations by angry workers, script monies for factory payrolls, wildcat strikes, and armed workers calling themselves "red" created a volatile situation. The Constitutionalist elites and Obregonista Jacobins had armed the urban workers in order to defeat the agrarians. Now they faced the spector of a working-class revolution. Yet they could not crush the Casa at this early point in the revolutionary process without seriously damaging unity needed while the Villistas and Zapatistas remained a force to be reckoned with.

The economic crisis in the cities continued to deepen. Hundreds of small shops and businesses closed in the Mexico City area, and the same occurred in the provincial cities in about the same proportions. Large industrial concerns cut back production and reduced their work forces. Nationwide poverty reduced tens of thousands of workers to charity; with a heavy concentration of them living in the urban areas in the center of the nation. Beggars were omnipresent. Counterfeiting, scrip money, and a loosely managed flow of paper currency contributed to an inflation that further exacerbated the situation. Middlemen, many of them partisans of the Constitutionalist government, and Spanish merchandisers came under fire from organized labor for profit levels that reached 900 percent on some items and 150 percent on beef. Meat was in short supply because of the continuing warfare in the countryside, widespread hoarding, and an uneven distribution of foodstuffs in the urban areas that favored allocations to the upper-class residential zones.

The government responded to mounting working-class violence, sabotage, arson, and even rioting with fines for businessmen that overcharged in violation of profit guidelines. The governors of Veracruz and Puebla, confronted with hunger and food riots, resorted to the distribution of food and clothing and to price controls.

Urban and industrial workers in the provinces who had been organized by the Casa committees that followed in the wake of the Constitutionalist armies flocked into syndicates. During the first six months of 1915 dozens of new syndicates and tens of thousands of new members swelled the Casa's ranks. Thousands of workers in the American-owned mines joined the syndicates. Most of the newcomers had little ideological understanding. They were affiliated with the anarchist international and were members of an anarchist regional organization, but there had not been time to teach the concepts of anarchosyndicalism, antigovernmentalism, and "class struggle."

Marxism was weak because Mexico's transitional working classes were still more concerned about the loss of artisan freedoms than holding state power. Except for a small group of German glassworkers in Toluca and Mexico City, Mexican workers still opposed a strengthening central goverment. They exhibited strong antitechnology-Luddite tendencies. Cement, linotype, and textile technological changes created radicalized and anarchist Mexican workers from among the former stonecutters, typesetters, and tailors.

Syndicate leaders and members were susceptible to appeals for cooperation with the revolutionary government. "Bread-and-butter" concessions obtained by nonanarchist leaders including Dr. Atl and Morones attracted them. Despite the eroded purity of anarchosyndicalist ideology, the great bulk of organized workers in the center of the nation and the

Gulf coast had the most radical leadership imaginable in Latin America at that time. That radicalism propelled them into a fatal conflict with the government.

In late summer 1915 the Casa established its headquarters in the formerly posh Mexico City salon, the House of Tiles, and workers flocked there for protest meetings and revolutionary speeches that denounced their "betrayal" by the Constitutionalist government. The crowds overflowed into the streets, and thousands marched on government buildings and strike-closed factories to express their demands forcefully. The House of Tiles was a facility of two stories, a mezzanine, and numerous rooms, well suited to the Casa's needs. On 13 October 1915 the Casa inaugurated a full-fledged Escuela Racionalista, the goal of its former leaders Ferrés and Moncaleano. Speakers denounced "burguesa" and clerical "brainwashing" in the government and Church-run schools. To the anarchists the Escuela Racionalista represented workers' instead of state "control of the learning process" and complimented the anarchosyndicalist newspapers in disseminating "libertarian socialist" ideals.

In mid-1915 the ultimate outcome of the conflict between the rural lower-class-led and the urban bourgeois-led revolutionary factions came into focus. The Carrancista provincial elite and Obregonista pequeña burguesa-led forces had won. Now the anarchosyndicalist urban working class moved into violent confrontation with the Constitutionalist elite and its capitalist allies. The Lucha leaders survived the fighting with the Villistas and Zapatistas and returned to Mexico City along with the assertive Red Battalion veterans ready to claim their "rights." They led the ever larger and more threatening crowds at the House of Tiles. They published a Casa newspaper, *Ariete,* which called for the restructuring of society and the economy around the growing Casa syndicates.[64]

Through *Ariete* the Casa promulgated working-class definitions of the revolution that competed with the Constitutionalist view, including workers' control of the factories and the expulsion and nationalization of foreign capital. These doctrines were completely unacceptable to the Carrancista elite and Obregonista Jacobins in charge of the government. *Ariete* also carried essays by European anarchists, including Proudhon, Bakunin, Kropotkin, and a plethora of Spaniards denouncing "burguesa government" and calling for a "final working-class revolution." Working-class radicalism, which had devastated American properties across the nation since 1910, now threatened its pequeña burguesa and provincial elite counterparts as much as it did the foreigners.

The recruitment of workers into the Casa continued through the second half or 1915 while labor unrest deepened as a result of devalued scrip monies, persistent inflation, unemployment, food shortages, and the efforts of Casa organizers who did their work in the slums and factories. The first wave of strikes began in the early summer, giving impetus to an urban working-class upsurge that threatened the survival of the capitalist economy and Constitutionalist state.

The late spring walkouts of 1915 by schoolteachers and carriage drivers presaged the showdown between labor and capital. On 30 July the Bread Bakers Syndicate shut down the important bakery industry and bakery owners were forced to grant large wage increases, guarantee the quality of their products, and lower prices, which had been raised 900 percent in just a few months. In October petroleum workers closed down Lord Cowdray's Compañia Mexicana de Petroleo "El Aguila" S.A., and turned to the Casa for support in the name of working-class solidarity. They became a Casa syndicate during the ensuing violence between the strikers and their Casa allies against strikebreakers and police. In October and November the Textile Workers Syndicate struck and shut down the textile factories of central Mexico. The largely French owners promptly granted a 100 percent increase in wages, an eight-hour workday, and a six-day work week. Almost two dozen new syndicates joined the Casa in November and December.

The Mexican working class had never before acted with such audacity in industrial disputes or experienced so much success. As these gains were being won the foreign industrialists and leading capitalists of Mexico had no choice but to seek asylum from the militant workers in a close alliance with the Constitutionalist government. The regime continued to purchase American arms for whatever contingency while the embargo held fast against the Villistas in the north.

In December 1915 the strikes became even more serious and threatening to the elite. The Casa Carpenters' Syndicate struck, paralyzed construction in central Mexico, and gained a 150 percent wage increase. The buttonmakers and barbers followed suit and achieved immediate gains. A mining strike spread rapidly, with the center of action at the American, French, and British-owned silver mines of El Oro in the northwestern corner of the state of Mexico. The mines closed amid violence, sabotage, and assassinations between strikebreakers and syndicate members. The attacks by Casa labor against foreign holdings paralleled a new wave of assaults on American-owned mines carried out by Villistas in the far north.

The anarchosyndicalist Casa leaders demanded workers' control of production, wages, and prices. They had the support of the membership and they knew how to use it. They challenged the power of capital and a government that had just come to power by force of arms. Their confidence stemmed from the conviction that the power of the working class expressed through strikes and militias was capable of toppling any capitalist state. They underestimated the capacity of the capitalist and Constitutionalist leadership to merge their interests—and soon after their membership—into what was becoming the new state and to maintain the lifeline of foreign military supplies needed to remain in power.

No era in the history of Mexican labor has witnessed the working-class solidarity and belligerence that the Casa members, now over 100,000 in number and moving toward 150,000, demonstrated in 1915 and 1916. The confrontation of the working class with its capitalist rivals moved toward the general strikes of 1916. The affection for labor of even the most radical pequeña burguesía Jacobins in the government had already disappeared.

On 13 January 1916, faced with increasing syndicate unrest, Carranza ordered the last elements of the Red Battalions dissolved. When the contingents of discharged soldiers returned to their homes, they found scrip currencies and inflation driving the urban working classes back toward a subsistence level of living, and rising unemployment. They felt that all of these problems could be immediately alleviated by workers' control via workers' councils and coordinating committees.

During the winter of 1916 the final phase of the working-class confrontation with the government and businessmen began when impoverished and angry veterans of the Red Battalions marched in the streets of Mexico City and Casa leaders attacked the government in speeches and through the working-class press. The Red Battalions' veterans demanded jobs, the nationalization of industry, and government compensation in the form of public services for their contribution to the Constitutionalist fighting effort. Smaller but equally violent demonstrations took place in Veracruz and Tampico.

In reaction the government carried out almost simultaneous raids on Casa centers throughout the nation. Rightist general Pablo González ordered his troops to raid the Mexico City Casa headquarters at the House of Tiles and to arrest those found on the premises. A number of Casa leaders, jailed and badly treated, remained in custody for nearly four months.

In response the leaders of the Casa planned a general strike. Intended to paralyze commerce, industry, and public services in the greater Mexico City area, the strike was to be carried out by the Federation of Federal

District Syndicates, an amalgam of Casa unions located in the area that surrounded Mexico City. Including some of the most militant and powerful syndicates in the nation, the federation counted some 90,000 members in the spring of 1916. In the meantime in the provinces—especially in the centers of foreign economic hegemony, Veracruz and Tampico—radical urban-industrial workers staged demonstrations and strikes. State governors, including Jeriberto Jara of Veracruz, declared a state of siege in order to regain control.

The struggle between the urban working class and the state-building elite in the Constitutionalist government moved toward a climax. The emergent state-building elite composed of the former provincial hacendados and pequeña burguesa Jacobins faced a major crisis when the first general strike of 1916 paralyzed Mexico City and its environs in the early morning of 22 May. The Casa leadership demanded a redress of grievances that included the government's return of its House of Tiles headquarters, the release of the arrested Casa leaders, and economic reforms such as the abolition of scrip money, fixed price ceilings to stop inflation, and work projects to solve unemployment problems.

The strike closed public utilities and services in the Mexico City area, and thousands of workers marched on the Alameda plaza in the heart of downtown. The government, caught by surprise, agreed to meet with the Casa leaders. General Benjamin Hill, Commander of the Federal District, accepted the syndicates' demands. Hill, an ally of Obregon and Morones, pleased the workers by expressing personal agreement with their point of view and issuing an ultimatum forcing businessmen and industrialists to attend a meeting over which he presided. He dictated the terms of their settlement with the workers. The Casa restored electrical power and other vital services to the city when Hill promulgated the accord. They should have known that their victory came too easily; Hill was Obregon Salido's selection to suppress the pro-Villista Cananea workers in Sonora in 1914.[65]

The general strike of May 1916 seemed a notable success for the Casa. It demonstrated the power of working-class solidarity and the degree of discipline that the anarchosyndicalists had achieved in a brief span of time. Rather than heralding the demise of government and capitalism, however, as the anarchist leaders had predicted during the previous fifty years, the general strike encouraged anarchosyndicalist labor's enemies to cooperate. The Constitutionalist regime demonstrated considerable acumen in settling the affair rather than risking the economic chaos that would have resulted from a prolonged confrontation with the industrial working class, especially with the Villista and Zapatista armies still in the countryside.

The anarchosyndicalist leaders of the Casa celebrated the outcome of the strike. It affirmed, to them, the existence of a powerful and independent labor movement. For a growing number of labor leaders such as Morones, however, the outcome confirmed the advantages of working with the government and enjoying its patronage. The Constitutionalist government was building a bridge of confidence between itself and a rising generation of pragmatic, career-oriented pequeña burguesa labor leaders. At the same time, the government incorporated the more flexible members of the Porfirian intelligentsia into its ranks and continued to merge its interests and programs with those of the Porfirian banking, industrial, and landowning elite. The end result of this inexorable economic and political process was polarization along class lines of the formerly allied urban sector of the revolutionary forces. The Constitutionalist government recognized the growing threat of a powerful revolutionary working-class movement dedicated to the destruction of the state and capitalism. It responded decisively and confronted the Casa "reds" in a showdown during the second general strike of 1916.

In less than three months following the May general strike the paper currency pesos guaranteed to workers by General Hill had been devalued by the banking houses of Mexico City to only two gold centavos in purchasing power, and the government's inaction signaled approval of the situation. Industrialists and businessmen still routinely issued scrip money to the workers, and the government ignored syndicate complaints about the situation. Once again the Federal District syndicates, through a series of surreptitious leadership meetings, prepared and then declared a general strike for the greater Mexico City area. Once again the workers demonstrated their solidarity. The walkout began on the morning of 31 July. It was the largest strike Mexico has ever seen. The entire economy of the greater Mexico City area closed down. Once again thousands of workers converged on the center of the city.

The police intelligence services that had survived the collapse of the Díaz regime and had been incorporated by the new regime, as well as sympathizers in the syndicates, warned the government of the Casa's plans in advance. The government responded energetically; troops brought into the city under the cover of darkness attacked the working-class crowds, scattering them into small groups. They also raided the Casa's headquarters, arresting leaders. At the same time, Dr. Atl, Carranza's emissary to a workers' meeting in a downtown theater, invited the first strike committee, a group in charge of negotiating workers' demands, to a meeting with the president in the National Palace. Carranza immediately placed the committee under arrest, charging the hapless delegates with treason, a capital offense. On 2 August the government declared martial law to help quell the rioting crowds.

Casa electricians' syndicate leader, Ernesto Velasco, threatened with death by his army captors who held a gun to his head, showed them how to restore the city's electrical power service. The government declared the Casa subversive and outlawed. Troops seized the regional offices and armories of the Casa. Obregon Salido, the Casa's erstwhile friend who had used its men and women against Villa, denied the urban working-class leaders' appeal for assistance against Carranza; instead, he suggested that the Casa disband.

With electricity restored and troops patrolling the streets, the stores and factories of Mexico City gradually reopened. By 3 August the city began to resume normalcy. The Constitutionalist army, working in concert with the foreign and wealthiest owners and managers of private enterprise, broke the Casa. In so doing they defeated the working-class revolution and destroyed the independence of the industrial and urban labor movement. Workers and their anarchosyndicalist leaders were defeated by a dynamic combination of elite elements, the Constitutionalist movement, and the Obregonista pequeña burguesía, blended with the most sophisticated and durable capitalists of the ancien régime, including the foreigners who had quickly learned to cooperate when necessary with the new government. After the Casa's August 1916 defeat the state rescinded the workers' earlier gains and used force to crush further working-class mobilizations that year. The political and economic elite amalgam that emerged from the revolution was terminating working-class initiatives in the countryside and cities.

The victorious forces were forging a Mexico that allowed upward mobility and participation for the pequeña burguesía and the nearly complete integration of the regional elites into a new ruling class. To the defeated groups, the workers and campesinos, it looked like the old system. While small groups of workers attempted to form new mass organizations, dozens of independent campesino insurgencies and hundreds of localized rural rebel groups continued to occupy estates. The peasants still under the aegis of Zapatismo in the south and Villismo in the north also continued to resist.[66]

After the defeats at Celaya, Aguascalientes, and León, the División del Norte lost its cohesion, and massive desertions combined with the arms embargo and ever more assertive American hostility rendered its attempts to retain control of northern Mexico hopeless. By October the Villistas controlled only Chihuahua and parts of Durango and Sonora, but they had plans to consolidate their control along the American-Sonoran border by taking the important supply entrepôt of Agua Prieta. Guarded by an isolated Constitutionalist garrison and dominated by hills on the Mexican side, Agua Prieta should have been easy prey.

In November Villa's forces attacked Agua Prieta in a bold stroke that seemed destined for success. Villa still commanded 6,500 loyal remnants of the División del Norte that had crossed the rugged Sierra Madre Occidental in a rapid forced march. What should have been a quick and strategically important victory giving him access to the American arms blackmarket for further Sonoran campaigns turned into a military disaster because American trains carried Constitutionalist troop reinforcements to the battle site via tracks on the U.S. side of the border. These forces launched a surprise counterattack that routed the Villistas, who left their heavy equipment on the battlefield. The defeat eradicated the División del Norte and reduced the Villistas to guerrilla warfare, which frustrated the Constitutionalists and outraged the Americans. The defeat caused Villa to turn violently against the Americans.

The U.S. government had opposed Villismo after the fall of Huerta, despite the Villistas' courting of American support and Carraza's nationalism. Wilson and Bryan succored the Carrancista and Obregonista forces, with only a few lapses, from the beginning of their conflict with the peasant-led forces. They began their aid to the Constitutionalists by embargoing Villista coal supplies following the overwhelming victory against Huerta at Zacatecas. Then the Wilson administration turned over the key port city of Veracruz and a vast store of arms to the Constitutionalists in their hour of retreat.

The Mexican investments of Wilson administration officials reflected the wider involvement of U.S. capitalism in Mexico. The property holders were a virtual "Who's Who in America," including the leading contributors to the Democratic and Republican parties. The overwhelming commitment of American capital to Mexico and the subordinate origins of the Díaz regime underscore the deeper significance of the Mexican Revolution: a war of national liberation against the United States.

Samuel Gompers, an antiradical trade unionist, shared Wilson's dream of a free enterprise American empire. The leadership of the American Federation of Labor (AFL) lent advisers to both labor and government during the Constitutionalist alliance with the Casa. The Americans helped facilitate the recruitment of about 9,000 troops for the undermanned Obregon Salido-led army, the main force of which numbered less than

20,000 when it defeated the División del Norte during the spring of 1915.[67]

The American government's recognition of Carranza and enforcement of the arms embargo along the border compounded the Villistas' anger. Using their government's diplomatic recognition of Carranza as justification, American merchants supplying war munitions to the Villistas refused to complete transactions for which advance payments had been made. The merchants took this step despite their refusal to comply with government demands during the Madero-Díaz elite crisis of 1911. One of the border towns where the merchants closed their doors to Villista contraband despite cash advances for goods yet undelivered was Columbus, New Mexico.

The Villistas reacted to what they considered American outrages by killing sixteen American mining employees in a train ambush in January 1916 at Santa Isabel, Chihuahua. The Americans carried safe conduct passes from the Constitutionalists, but they had made no attempt to obtain permission from the Villistas. The Villistas considered the Americans' entry into contested territory with Constitutionalist endorsements a hostile act. The murders outraged public opinion in the United States and reduced the Villistas' image to that of renegades.

Two months later the Villistas sought revenge against some of the merchants who had cheated them out of their supplies. Their selection of Columbus, a U.S. Army garrison town, indicates a political motive equal in importance to revenge. They ravaged the town, killing eighteen Americans; the U.S. Army killed over one hundred Villistas. Their attack was intended to accomplish more than revenge against unscrupulous merchants, however; it invited American intervention. The Villistas wanted to expose to the Mexican public the Carranza government's weakness and its relationship with the Wilson administration. In the Villista scenario the government would have to compromise itself in the eyes of Mexican nationalists by tolerating a Yanqui invasion or face military disaster if it resisted. In either case the Villistas would gain versus the government.

The Villistas' ploy did not work. Carranza handled the situation with the same adroitness used to bring military victory over the agrarian and workers' revolution while at the same time promulgating programs on their behalf. He denounced the Americans to beguiled Mexican nationalists while diplomatically clearing the road for the invaders to pursue Villa for hundreds of miles inside Mexican territory without armed resistance.

The Americans entered Mexico with 12,000 soldiers under the command of General John J. "Blackjack" Pershing, whose previous personal claim to fame was the defeat and near annihilation of the Apache Indians during their hopeless defense of their homelands. The size of the invasion force alarmed the Mexicans because it seemed to be far in excess of the number needed to punish the small groups of Villistas. In actuality it was not large considering the long supply lines and rear areas that had to be secured.

The Americans' pursuit turned into a farcical search across trackless deserts during which they underwent harassing attacks from Villistas once they were deep inside Mexico. The folly of the mission was brought home to the Americans and the Carranza government when pro-Villa rioting broke out in Parral after U.S. troops violated an agreement and entered the city. The Constitutionalist government, spurred on by Jacobin nationalists, became concerned about American intentions. It was obvious that the Americans' slow-moving columns were not going to catch Villa, and they were already four hundred miles inside Mexico. In May the Constitutionalist government began preparing a highly publicized defensive line deep inside Mexico. In June the Constitutionalists won a battle with the invaders at El Carrizal. Meanwhile Villa recovered politically, seen as the defender of the nation against the Yanqui invaders. His military forces gained strength.

In the fall of 1916 the Villistas seized Chihuahua City from Constitutionalist defenders. The Villista forces were growing as a result of their nationally popular combat with the Americans. In December the invaders finally recognized the hopelessness of the situation and withdrew from Mexico. When they left, Villa was still in Chihuahua with widespread campesino and working-class support in the north, and Zapata still held on in the south-center of the nation.

These lower-class rural leaders were becoming legendary figures in the eyes of the nation's campesino masses because of their dedicated resistance against all odds. Zapata's mystique came from both his social program and his military exploits. In the north the Villista high command had not carried out agrarian reforms on behalf of the pueblos, only nationalizations in order to mobilize economic support for the military effort. Even during the period of their hegemony over much of Chihuahua, where Villa exercised great power, the Villista high command had not endorsed the land occupations carried out by campesino groups. The property seizures carried out by the insurgent citizenry of Janos and Casas Grandes against American colonists and hacendados and similar episodes in Sonora were not suppressed by the Villistas, but they did nothing to support them.

While the Obregonista army was driving the Villistas from central Mexico during the spring and summer of 1915, the Zapatistas, ignored as the lesser threat by the Constitutionalist military, continued developing their municipio-based Commune of Morelos in the south. Directed by Manuel Palafox serving as the Zapatista secretary of agriculture, radical students from the National School of Agriculture assisted in laying out new economically intelligent property boundaries between villages. The properties of the great estates that were not divided between the pueblos as communes or cooperative ejidos were placed under the administration of the Zapatista general headquarters. Hacienda income helped offset the costs of the war and paid pensions to the families of fallen soldiers.

In October 1915 Palafox, one of the most radical of the Zapatista agrarians, composed a new agrarian law. It provided that the hacendados were to receive no compensation for their properties, nor was anything to be left for them. The law reflected the agrarian ideology that had evolved during two centuries of struggle: "The nation recognizes the irrefutable right of all Mexicans to possess and cultivate a piece of land the products of which permit him to meet his needs and those of his family."[68]

About 87 percent of the Mexican population still lived in the countryside. This law and many other ordinances demonstrated the peasant movement's capacity to address the great majority of the Mexican public. Zapatista ideology had evolved through more than two centuries of struggle and agrarian plans.

The agrarians' problem was threefold: alienation of the property-owning middle peasants and rancheros, the combined opposition of the culturally and economically antagonistic urban classes, and competition with foreign capitalists over the ownership of land. These groups had much to lose in a nation ruled by peasant equalitarianism and a balanced exchange of product values between the countryside, city, and foreign enterprise. The opposition of the rancheros and local elites hurt the Zapatistas around Iguala in Guerrero, but their resistance was to be expected. The Zapatistas had tremendous appeal to the Mexican masses and the allegiance of the lower-class Morlense and outlying populations. Their peasant-led militias, however, with their provincialism and tendency to return home when crops needed planting or harvesting, and circumscribed by the American embargo imposed against them on both coasts, lacked the military capacity to combat the provincial elite- and pequeña burguesa-led Constitutionalist forces. At the end of 1915 the Constitutionalists began a military buildup along the northern edge of Morelos while simultaneously conducting a political war with the Zapatistas by protesting their own desire for "agrarian reform."

When the Constitutionalists invaded Morelos, a familiar scenario unfolded. The pequeña burguesa elements in the Convention government once again exhibited their hostility toward Zapatismo. The Convention government officer in charge of the defense of Cuernavaca, General Pacheco, betrayed the Zapatistas by allowing the invading Constitutionalist forces of General González to approach the city without resistance. The peasant forces of Genevevo de la O had to intervene. The invasion and occupation of Morelos followed the bloody pattern earlier conceived by Huerta. For two years the population of Morelos experienced horrible violence against civilians. When the Constitutionalist troops withdrew in defeat two years later, half the population of the state had been displaced or killed.

The Constitutionalists captured the cities and towns of the state. They razed pueblo lands, stole cattle, and seized collectivized estates. Generals claimed the haciendas as their own while sometimes carrying out mass executions of campesinos caught in their villages. The Zapatista resistance, not militarily strong at first, was intelligent. It avoided open combat with Constitutionalist main forces, which invited heavy losses and expenditures and even more retaliations against peasants. Instead the Zapatistas attacked haciendas, ingenios, road convoys, and trains in small-scale surprise raids. Their tactics rendered them virtually indestructible while their choice of targets—the occupied haciendas and ingenios—marked them once again as defenders of the campesino population and guaranteed continuing popular support.

By the end of 1916, 5,000 Zapatista guerrillas had 30,000 Constitutionalist troops on the defensive. González's failure stemmed from his inability to stimulate popular support. It was a failure inherent in the struggle between Mexico's insurgent peasantry and the Constitutionalist defense of rural capitalism. The Constitutionalists demanded campesino subordination to foreign and domestic owners of property and the new urban-based nation-state dominated by the provincial elite Carrancistas and the Obregonista pequeña burguesía.

Zapatista raiders blew up trains on the mountain slopes between Mexico City and nearby Ajusco. The train disasters, which inflicted heavy civilian casualties, discredited González among Constitutionalist officers, although it is unlikely that any of them could have done better. Tremendous propaganda successes, the attacks helped to break the government's will to continue the expensive and embarrassing campaign against the majority of the people of Morelos. In late 1916 and early 1917 Constitutionalist troop withdrawals accompanied disastrous Zapatista ambushes and a statewide offensive against the remaining government garrisons. By January 1917 González's heavy-handed efforts to occupy Morelos collapsed. Obregon Salido and the other leaders of the Constitutionalist general staff refused to help him while entire garrisons were overrun or surrendered. When the Zapatistas surrounded Cuernavaca government forces fled the state in disarray, suffering heavy losses. For a time the Zapatistas' wishful thinking got the best of them. Remembering Huerta's collapse, they thought the revolution was won, that Mexico City would soon be theirs, but the Constitutionalists were not fazed.[69]

Meanwhile, during 1914–1916 thousands of campesinos had occupied hacienda and American development company lands from Chiapas to Baja California, along the Gulf coast from Tamaulipas to Campeche, and in Durango, San Luis Potosí, Chihuahua, and Zacatecas. They attacked the properties of the largest corporations in Mexico and the United States and the colonies of American farmers. They settled on the best lands on the estates. They acted on their own initiative around Batopilas, Casas Grandes, Janos, and Jiménez, in Chihuahua; at Rascon, Agua Buena, and the Atascador Colony in San Luis Potosí; and at the Medina Colony in Oaxaca, Pijijiapan, Juchtepec, Izúcar, Ixtepec, Almoloya, and Atlixtac across the south; and hundreds of other places.

The Constitutionalist government rarely displaced the campesinos by force. Rather, they stalled the complaining American and Mexican landholders. The Constitutionalists negotiated agrarian compromises giving the insurgent country people portions of the land they claimed.

From 1913 through 1916 the Constitutionalist movement forged and learned to control a strong nationwide alliance of provincial and metropolitan elites, pequeña burguesa radicals, and revolutionary urban workers and peasants. They learned how to deal with American capitalists and government officials. In December 1916, with American invaders in the north and Zapatista victories in the south, a constitutional convention convened in Querétaro. Once again the Constitutionalists proved their political mettle, the strength of the interclass solidarity between the provincial elites and pequeña burguesía, and how that combination of classes reflected the realities of economic and political power in Mexico during 1916–1917.

The Constitution of Querétaro confronted the Americans with a strong but limited nationalism. It presented the Church with government control of health, education, and welfare. It gave the peasants agrarian reform controlled by the government, and the industrial and urban workers a "magna carta," once again controlled by the government, the Constitutionalist elite. The Zapatistas and still resisting anarchist working-class leaders called it a farce. But it was a framework that addressed Mexico's political realities, that made concessions to all social classes, that called for national unity against the foreign intruder, and that gave control over all things to the national government and the emergent state-building elite.

TEN

Elite Synthesis and Sociopolitical Reorganization, 1916–1924

> There was a very deep conviction that the natural resources of the country had been taken away from them, and that the people were not sharing in the profits of development.
>
> —Josephus Daniels

> La Revolución Mexicana Vencerá
> con nosotros
> contra nosotros
> o sin nosotros
>
> —Grafitti of Cuernavaca

By late 1916 the revolutionary factions led by Jacobin pequeña burguesía and the provincial elites, which had incorporated the most flexible elements of the Porfirian political and economic hierarchy, had defeated the equalitarian tendencies of the rural and urban worker-led groups by force of arms. The remaining challenge for the new rulers was to establish a broad-based regime that, by politically adjusting to new socioeconomic realities and incorporating all important groups into the political process, would have stability and be able to work out a new relationship with the foreigners.

Stabilization required the meshing of liberalism and nationalism in order to reconcile and balance the differences between the dynamic, powerful, and upwardly mobile forces of the pequeña burguesía and those of Carrancismo, which already claimed "revolutionary" adherence from the scions of Mexico's oldest, most prestigious and wealthy families. The ideological pacification of the militarily defeated but still rebellious workers and peasants was important, but the contradictions between the Jacobin pequeña burguesía and the Carrancista elites, which included the Molina, Terrazas, Martínez del Río, Rabasa, and López Portillo families were acute.

The upwardly mobile pequeña burguesía expected to share fully in the economic and political benefits to be derived from industrialization. They had fought to alter the caste-ridden hierarchical nature of Porfirian society and to facilitate the rise to power of representatives from their class. This relationship between the elites and upwardly mobile pequeña burguesía had to be achieved within normal sociopolitical processes without precipitating an elite crisis such as the one that had brought down the Porfirian regime and unleashed the "uncivilized" campesinos and workers. At Querétaro Mexico's new leaders applied the political lessons learned during the previous years of struggle with Villismo, Zapatismo, and the Casa.

Obregonismo, or Jacobinism, symbolized the pequeña burguesa doctrine of the "open society" in which newly potent economic and social groups participated directly in the leadership of an increasingly powerful national government. Educated, articulate, and energetic, this dynamic new group, fostered by the economic successes of the Díaz regime, demanded full representation in national polity, including access to the presidency via party elections. The more far-sighted elements of Carrancismo and Porfirian elite families finally accepted this difficult turn of events. It was well for them that they did because the period 1916–1924 served as a transitional stage leading to the merger of the newly powerful pequeña burguesa revolutionary leaders with elite society and its economy.

In the years that followed, intermarriage between the new and old elite families would create a broader-based and more secure ruling class. In the elite families of long standing, political, economic, and social survival meant the emergence to family leadership of the scion best adapted to the peculiar revolutionary situation. This versatility allowed them to survive the Conservative, Liberal, Spanish, and French struggles of the nineteenth century, and it functioned throughout the Mexican Revolution.

Elite adaptability to pequeña burguesa Jacobin demands did not, however, come easily at Querétaro or in the years that followed. Don Venustiano Carranza found the Obregonista scenario hard to accept and resisted it, even while yielding to the forced promulgation of the Constitution of 1917 as the new body of law. The unyielding Carranza paid with his life when he resisted the culminating stage of the pequeña burguesa state-building elite's rise to power by attempting to retain the presidency against the Obregonista upsurge of 1920.

With high ideals and pragmatic intent, the writers of the Constitution of 1917 aspired to something better, but theirs was also a preconceived and cynical attempt to coopt the defeated peasants and workers into a political and economic system controlled by a new ruling class and an already resurgent capitalist-owned export economy. Heríberto Jara, who posed as a delegate for labor, was in fact a leading figure in the opposition to the Veracruz workers during the 1916 confrontations with the Constitutionalist government before and after the demise of the Casa. Several "agrarian" delegates took part in the fighting against the Zapatistas and Villistas. The delegates did not reflect the composition of social groups that participated in the revolution; rather, they were overwhelmingly from the upper strata of the pequeña burguesía: lawyers, medical practitioners, engineers, military leaders, and various Constitutionalist functionaries. The electoral process that sent them to Querétaro was dubious at best. Despite the delegates' unrepresentative makeup they aspired to achieve ideals that had permeated all social sectors of the revolutionary movement during the previous seven years. As one delegate put it,

> This revolution that we are engaged in is not for political objectives alone, as you well know, and as we the citizens of the country perceive it; it also involves very deep social needs; this revolution that was made to regenerate the people, to lift up the needy, and to redeem the indigenous race, has been received with open arms, as a blessing from Heaven, by all those who wear on their forehead the shame of not having enough to live like human beings and who must dwell in a filthy hovel because of the greed of the evil Mexican capitalists.[1]

Many of the pequeña burguesía in the Obregonista faction accepted these concepts during the course of the revolutionary struggles and gave them self-righteous and nationalistic interpretation at Querétaro. With their pan-national vision they wrote a constitution that promised land reform and the final resolution of "the agrarian problem" in Article 27 while asserting the supremacy of the national government over the *patria chica* of the campesinos.

They declared the municipio libre to be the basic political unit in the nation but denied it any real power. They formalized governmental hegemony over labor organizations and industrial disputes. With honest intent, however, the delegates guaranteed the working class a wide-ranging collection of assurances that included minimum wages, working hours and conditions, and fringe benefits that were advanced in comparison to the rest of the Western Hemisphere. The failure to apply those constitutional provisions later in order to better the condition of the working class resulted from the underdeveloped structure of the economy of which polity is an administrative reflection.

The debates of the Congreso Constituyente frequently projected revolutionary romanticism and fancy, but articles 3, 5, 15, 27, 123, and 130 of the new Constitution demonstrated that the delegates were capable of hard-headed realpolitik. They reflected the influence of the intelligentsia that the politically unrepresented and therefore alienated pequeña burguesía had produced in the last half of the Porfiriato. Nationalistic, they wanted an activist government involved in social programs that reached the masses.

The delegates reflected a nineteenth-century liberal bias in their hostility toward the Church. The lower-class-led rural and campesino revolutionaries had minimal conflict with that institution; indeed, its roots in the countryside gave it a close intimacy with the workers there. However, the provincial elites and the pequeña burguesa Obregonistas had a long-standing history of hostility toward the Church dating from the first Liberal governments of the nineteenth century. Articles 3, 5, and 130 banned clerical participation in primary education, required attendance in secular primary schools, ordered divestiture of most Church-owned income properties, and provided sweeping regulations that included restrictions on foreign clergymen and professionals. The government took power over public functions dominated by the Church.

Indicative of the delegates' realpolitik, the Constitution of 1917, unlike its 1857 predecessor, offered the proviso for the municipio libre as the fundamental basis of government. The ideology of the agrarian movement throughout the campesino uprisings of the previous two centuries centered upon the idea of the independent village. The municipio libre, popularized by the working-class press during the previous fifty years as the basis of a cooperative agrarian social order, and championed by the Zapatistas, was incorporated into the new Constitution as Article 15. Carranza pledged to give the municipio libre his full support as the "political and economic basis of free government." Nothing was ever done to bring about this utopian outcome, but it was effective anti-Villista, anti-Zapatista propaganda at the time of the Constitution's promulgation.[2]

When they promulgated Article 27 the delegates demonstrated the nationalism and depth of pequeña burguesía resentment that had developed against foreign domination in the mining and petroleum industries. They declared that all subsoil resources belonged to the nation—that is, the government. The article asserted the right to nationalize any mining or petroleum property. Foreign companies and embassies protested to Carranza. The president responded by playing down the confiscatory aspect of the article. President Wilson rewarded him with de jure recognition.

In 1919 Carranza came into conflict with the American oil companies over the ownership of natural resources. In 1923 Obregon Salido conceded that the confiscatory proviso in Article 27 could not be applied to subsoil rights already held when the Constitution was promulgated.[3]

The domestic reforms contained in Article 27 reveal the political needs of a government still in conflict with the peasant-led Zapatistas and largely lower-class Villistas. It also reflects the changes in Mexican sociopolitical ideals between the Constitutions of 1857 and 1917. As a response to the demand for agrarian reform, it provided for the breakup of the great estates. It promised to restore to the villages those lands illegally taken from them, to grant the campesinos additional lands and waters whenever necessary, and to establish new rural population centers endowed with needed resources.

The municipio government gained recognition with the proviso that "local laws shall govern the extent of family patrimony and determine what shall properly constitute the same on the basis of its inalienability." By such action the delegates granted to the agrarians a degree of self-government for which the Zapatistas continued to fight even as the Constitution was being prepared. But this provision also established the right to hold "small properties," providing the basis for the defense of large private holdings wherever local elites still held or had regained power. The latter condition prevailed in most of the nation.

The comparable article in the 1857 Constitution, a document that legitimized the Mexican enclosure movement during the last half of the nineteenth century, was also written in the midst of widespread agrarian violence. Drafted by professionals and large landowners, it was a product of nineteenth-century laissez-faire thought. Its authors felt no pressure from the rural masses and made no concessions to them.[4]

The delegates, with the memories of Casa-led working-class riots and general strikes and the armed workers of the Red Battalions still fresh in their minds, approved Article 123 of the Constitution, the "Magna Carta of Mexican Labor." Heriberto Jara headed the subcommittee that wrote the article. An upwardly mobile former artisan who had become a revolutionary general, the antisyndicalist Jara worked hard to harness industrial and urban working-class support for the new government. Literally a social program for labor, the article established state control over labor relations. It laid a legal foundation for workers' rights and the limits of those rights in a capitalist economy. The workers' new rights and privileges included the restriction of nocturnal labor to seven hours, the eight-hour workday, double pay for overtime, the protection of children under twelve years of age from employment, and the prohibition of women and minors over twelve years of age from hazardous conditions and night work. The prohibition of children under twelve years of age from labor raised by one year the cynical eleven-year-old limit decreed by President Díaz during the Río Blanco labor dispute ten years earlier.

Enforcement has been a national scandal ever since. Small enterprises continue to ignore the provisions with impunity. The pequeña burguesía imposed labor rules for large-scale industry that did not affect small shops and stores. The article limited the workers' right to organize without government supervision. It forbade the right to strike without government approval.

Article 123 granted most of the "bread-and-butter" demands expressed in the labor manifestos issued since the 1870s. The article's social program reflected the aspirations of the Mexican industrial and urban labor movement since the 1860s, when radical and anarchist artisans and students stepped out of their social class and began organizing factory and service workers. The Flores Magonistas and anarchosyndicalists of the Casa carried forward the same ideas.

The differences between the long-held goals of the workers and what was granted them in the Constitution were their failure to gain control over production through workers' self-management and the loss of their highly valued freedom. The delegates empowered the new government to arbitrate strikes and industrial disputes. They also gave it sweeping powers to enact labor legislation, a Ley del Trabajo—the ability to legalize and even create unions or declare them renegade and their leaders subject to imprisonment without trial. The Constitution of 1857, enacted before the emergence of the industrial and urban working-class movement, included no workers in the deliberations that created it and gave no consideration to industrial labor. By 1917 the growth of the economy and the corollary development of industrial production made control of the working class one of the major concerns of the new elite.

During the debate on Article 9, which treated civil liberties, one delegate raised the question of the right to strike, demonstrate, and picket. Nicolás Cano, a miner from Guanajuato and one of the few delegates with a working-class background, cited the shooting of strikers in Mexico City during the July-August general strike called by the Casa a few months earlier. He demanded to know if Article 9 guaranteed strikers the right to assemble freely. Cano declared: "There are those of us who came here with no illusions, we have none because we know that the government, the Church and the capitalists are born enemies of the worker."[5]

General Jara, who headed the First Committee on Reforms, responsible for the preparation of Article 9 and an ardent opponent of the uncontrolled labor syndicates of the revolution, assured the Convention that striking workers were included in the provision. In reality the article did not mention workers or industrial disputes, and provisos elsewhere in the Constitution made it clear they were to be controlled. Satisfied, the predominantly pequeña burguesa delegates overwhelmingly approved the article.[6]

The new state building elite achieved legitimized control, to supplement their victories on the battlefields and in the streets, over the historic demands of the working classes, urban and rural, through the Constitution of 1917. The pequeña burguesa majority in the Constitutional Convention combined revolutionary idealism, an appreciation of the problems of the working classes, and nationalism with realpolitik to achieve legitimized political stability. Their program appealed to the working classes with a peaceful alternative to what now seemed, to the disorganized workers and the isolated campesinos, a fruitless confrontation with the preponderant Constitutionalist armed forces. The Constitution became the framework for the new state and social order of the postrevolutionary era.

In the wake of the Constitutional Convention the government began rebuilding the national economy. Foreign-owned enterprise hired nonunion workers in the cities, and Carrancista generals took over agricultural estates and restored production of labor-intensive industrial export agriculture. The peasants' resistance to the takeovers in Morelos maintained the Zapatistas' hopes while Villista raiders exposed the government's inability to guarantee order in the north. The nation returned to the production of colonial exports. The mines reopened, with the largest deposits of industrially important ores still under the control of foreign corporations. The petroleum industry continued to thrive. Foreign financiers and industrialists continued to dominate the Mexican economy. The new regime, despite a nationalistic bombast from Carranza, administered to the process. The Church, despite its opposition to the Constitution, found little in the government's actions to complain about. The revolution was over. The search for a stable regime continued.

Stability had eluded Madero in the north and south. Now it was the Constitutionalists' turn. Following the 1916 Zapatista victory over General González, the campesinos of the center-south politically reorganized into local Associations for the Defense of Revolutionary Principles under the remote direction of the Zapatista high command in Tlaltizapán. Economic recovery was slow; privation gripped the area. Hacienda fields no longer functioned, the livestock were destroyed, and poultry were lacking. During the winter schools opened and town and municipal governments assumed authority, and in the spring the campesinos planted a new crop. Morelos was destitute, however, and the strategic military situation remained hopeless. The Zapatista leadership's sense of isolation increased and defections continued. Late in 1918 General González launched a new campaign against the *surianos*. The army captured the main towns and closed the roads.

The Zapatistas continued to look for new alliances. They remained a threat to the new regime. González prepared a trap. On 10 April 1919 the men of Colonel Jesús Guajardo assassinated Zapata during negotiations for a promised turnover of men and equipment. Carranza abetted the killing. Zapata's publicized death reduced the military threat of Zapatismo, but not the regime's basic political problems. The campesinos now seemed ennobled to the urban pequeña burguesía and reformist elements, and Carranza was discredited.

The Jacobins, who had come to admire Zapata's honesty and courage, were insulted by the Carranza government's public bragging about the murderous deception. They also disliked the Carrancistas' support of the continuance of the labor-intensive, labor-repressive great estates, which in effect meant the perpetuation of the caste system. One of the pequeña burguesía's great accomplishments in the revolution was to abolish the caste-based social system that had plagued Mexico and continues to hold down social progress in those Latin American nations under oligarchical rule.

In the north the Villistas continued the guerrilla war after the American withdrawal, but the government forces were too strong. U.S. arms came to the government in abundance while the Villista embargo still held. Morale was low. Exile groups in the United States formed alliances with the Villistas, but they were militarily weak.

In 1919 Felipe Angeles returned from exile in New York and attempted to forge a new Villista offensive. He was now an avowed democratic socialist, interested in remaking Mexican society. His strategy included the formation of one formidable strike force out of the scattered Villista units that would be capable of taking cities and confronting the government army once sufficient logistical materials were assembled from the captured towns and from across the border. Villa agreed to the plan. First they captured Parral and then withdrew to attack Ciudad Juárez, the scene of so many turning points during the revolution. Just as the assault troops were taking the city, however, the Americans across the border opened fire with their artillery with devastating results, and American infantry reinforced the garrison for one critical day. After that defeat Villa recognized the fact that the military supplies needed for their campaign would never be forthcoming and rejected Angeles's plan. Angeles left Villa but remained in Chihuahua. He was captured on 15 November 1919, and Carrancista officials executed him on 26 November.

While Villista and Zapatista efforts to keep the revolution alive flagged, the industrial and urban workers fared no better. The new government banned syndicate meetings for several months after the suppression that took place in the wake of the general strike of July-August 1916. During the Carranza years government-endorsed labor meetings headed by Morones competed with regional gatherings called by the anarchosyndicalists who were trying to reorganize. Morones, a friend of Samuel Gompers and John C. Murray, attended AFL meetings in the United States and received AFL delegates and U.S. government support for his labor meetings in Mexico. In May 1918 a majority of one hundred delegates who had assembled at Saltillo approved the creation of the Morones-led Regional Confederation of Mexican Workers (CROM). The few radicals in attendance walked out and the following year formed the General Confederation of Workers (CGT).

During the 1920s the state-dominated CROM gradually gained ground against the independent CGT and attracted many workers. The precedence established by the CROM carried over into the creation of the state-dominated Mexican Confederation of Labor (CTM) during the 1930s. The CTM came to dominate the Mexican labor movement during the late 1930s after the large labor centrals were brought under control of the increasingly powerful government in 1931.[7]

The Carranza government, however, did not possess the flexibility demonstrated by the Mexican state during the 1920s and 1930s. Between 1917 and 1920 the Carranza government made the same crucial mistake that the Díaz and Madero regimes before it had committed. Basing its leadership upon a narrow stratum of upper burguesía and provincial elites, it failed to establish a wide enough basis of support in an economy that contained too many sophisticated groups that were excluded from political power. In early 1920 Carranza announced his choice of Ignacio Bonillas, one of his personal advisers and confidants, as his successor. According to the Obregonistas, Bonillas had not participated in the revolution beyond a mere presence in Carranza headquarters. They called him a "classic Pocho," pointing out that he had been educated in the United States since adolesence and was a former student at the Massachusetts Institute of Technology. The labeled him "timid," "completely dominated" by the first chief.

In mid-1919 Obregon Salido announced his presidential candidacy to succeed Carranza with the backing of the Sonoran oligarchs, governor Adolfo de la Huerta, military commander Plutarcho Elías Calles, and a number of American companies in the north. He interpreted Carranza's moves as an assurance that he could not be elected. Obregon Salido's popularity stemmed from his victories during the revolution and his timely retirement from Carranza's government. He served as minister of war in 1917 after the Constitution was promulgated and resigned before the repression and assassination of Zapata took place. He returned to Sonora and outside of the public eye quietly constructed a latifundia. Much of it was based upon the land he had earlier promised to return to the Yaqui Indians who had supported him against Huerta in 1913. His presidential campaign of 1919 was a careful one. Obregon Salido's plan of Agua Prieta stressed the security of private property and foreign investments while promising agrarian reform. At the time of his campaign he owed W. R. Grace and Company $1.8 million.[8] He was able to reduce that obligation to only $400,000 by 1924, when he left office. He satisfied Grace by transferring title to valuable Yaqui River bottomlands from the defunct Richardson Company. Obregon Salido gained control over much of the Richardson property before and during his presidency.

Where Obregon Salido functioned as the ultimate compromiser capable of negotiating with Carrancistas, Villistas, workers, Zapatistas, and Americans, Carranza was "hard-headed." On domestic issues Carranza was the most reactionary major leader during the revolutionary epoch, but he was more capable of nationalistic outrage than the compromised and insincere Obregon Salido.

Huerta, despite deep cynicism, perhaps because of his Indian lineage and humble origins, had far more appreciation for the needs of the common man than either Carranza or Obregon Salido. During his brief and reactionary regime he created an Indian institute and even planned an agrarian reform program. Huerta was an alcoholic brute capable of outright murder, however, and he served as a tool of Porfirian reactionaries, foreign and domestic, that wanted to crush mounting unrest. Carranza filled his government with provincial elites and administrators of the obsolete Madero administration. Some of his supporters had served in Congress after Huerta's bloody coup d'état. He refused to consider reform demands for three years, opposed the agrarian revolution, and treated

Zapata as a bandit. His critics claimed he favored the clergy, hacendados, and "ricos." Carranza's ultimate mistake after the defeat of the peasants and workers was his arrogance toward and refusal to coopt the powerful pequeña burguesía, which dominated the new army and had defined the revolution during the Constitutional Convention at Querétaro.

In the spring of 1920 the differences between the Carrancistas and Obregonistas reached the breaking point. The younger officers in the army supported Obregon Salido en masse. From their perspective Carranza had violated the mandate of the revolution and Constitution. Obregon Salido forged an alliance with Gildardo Magaña, the bureaucratically ambitious new leader of the Zapatistas. Obregon Salido did not have to accept the Plan of Ayala, as Zapata had insisted; rather, he proclaimed revolt under his own Plan of Agua Prieta, which stressed private property. The industrial and urban workers' groups, including those headed by Morones, joined a popular front in favor of Obregon Salido. Even conservative general Pablo González supported the insurgents. Obregon Salido made his revolutionary headquarters in the south and in early May began a symbolic march on Mexico City with Zapatista troops. The bulk of the regular army supported him.

Carranza could not rely on the army units in the capital, and on 7 May he fled the city with millions of dollars in an attempt to reach Veracruz and continue the fight from there. Obregonista and Zapatista troops chased him. On 9 May Obregon Salido entered Mexico City with one of Zapatismo's most loyal generals, Genevevo de la O, at his side. De la O's honesty caused him to die, like Zapata, a poor man. On 21 May members of Carranza's escort killed the fleeing president at Tlaxcalantongo. On 24 May Congress declared Obregon Salido's confidant, Adolfo de la Huerta, provisional president pending elections.

Carranza, from the time he first challenged Huerta, recognized the aggressive pequeña burguesa Obregon Salido as a threat. He counted on Pablo González, who was in charge of the revolutionary forces of the northeast, including Monterrey and Tampico, to serve as a military counterpoise. González, however, turned out to be a disaster on the battlefield and in politics, where his arrogant provincial elite attitudes set him apart from the pequeña burguesa revolutionaries while his anti-working-class and anti-campesino biases alienated workers and agrarians. Obregon Salido, through his battlefield victories and diplomacy with groups ranging from Casa radicals and elements of the Yaqui Indians to intellectuals and aspiring government functionaries, advanced to a position that Carranza could not deny.

Later in 1920, before Obregon Salido took office, Villa accepted a peace offering from de la Huerta that included the sizable but broken-down hacienda of Canutillo, which he occupied, rebuilt, and operated as a cooperative with his personal escort of about fifty men. The Zapatistas threw out the Carrancista generals who had occupied their lands and a few temporarily went back to the raising of corn and beans before the economic values of the new state brought pressures for the return of sugar production. Some of the old Zapatista leadership, including Magaña and Díaz Soto y Gama, became active in the government. They called for agrarian reform but accepted gradualist offerings of land, which came very slowly.

Obregon Salido's four-year reign took Mexico a long way toward the political and economic structure that prevails in the nation today, but not without aftershocks. In 1922 elements of the army rebelled and were crushed. In 1923 de la Huerta led an alliance of left- and right-wing groups against the regime when Obregon Salido passed him over in favor of Elías Calles as presidential successor.

Promulgated in 1920, the Plan of Agua Prieta denounced Carranza while praising both private landownership in "small" parcels and agrarian reform. It rallied the pro-Obregonista forces throughout Mexico. The support of Adolfo de la Huerta and especially Generals Elías Calles and Fortunato Maycotte assured the plan's success. In addition to most of the Army, Obregon Salido attracted a wide range of groups opposed to Carranza. The alliance that resulted included compromising elements of the Zapatista leadership, antisyndicalists from organized labor, and pequeña burguesa intellectuals, low-level government functionaries, and small businessmen who disliked Carranza's nineteenth-century upper-class-oriented politics. The support given Obregon Salido by the overwhelming majority of the army officers proved decisive.[9]

The demoralized acceptance of Obregon Salido by the defeated working-class-led forces of Zapatismo, Villismo, and the Casa followed the classical pattern for the seizure of power exhibited in the Bonapartist coup d'état of Louis Napoleon in France following the revolution of 1848. By accepting Obregon Salido, these leaders surrendered their demand for working-class autonomy from the emergent nation-state via village governments and labor syndicates.[10]

Carranza exercised virtually no power over the army commanders in remote garrisons despite bribing them. The officers depended on their own resources to pay and maintain the men. The soldiery possessed nearly autonomous power in many localities. Their basic loyalty was to the victorious army and its leaders, many of whom were local rancheros. Often they despised the traditional landed elites, conservative generals, and high functionaries allied with the president. Many of Carranza's supporters had seized property in central Mexico, including lands claimed by the Zapatista villages. They were viewed by their adversaries as reactionary and corrupt. Similar practices by Obregon Salido and his allies in Sonora escaped their attention. Carranza's attempts to buy loyalty through bribes had minimal effect in relation to the appeal of the powerful military commanders Obregon Salido and Elías Calles, who invited their cohorts to share power and wealth.

In Sonora the pro-Obregon Salido alliance paralleled the new hegemonies of other outlying areas, especially the north. There Elías Calles achieved supremacy while pursuing Villa by placing Obregonistas in charge of the important commands. Obregon Salido, Elías Calles, de la Huerta, and allied army officers including Obregon Salido's old friend, Porfirian governor Luis Torres, carved out new empires with close ties with W. R. Grace and Company in the export of agricultural produce, including garbanzo crops. The Yaqui Indians suffered military attacks by this cabal in 1916, 1920, 1923, and again in 1926.

Carranza attempted to take advantage of the state's unrest and sent in outside troop commanders. The most important among these appointees were generals Juan José Ríos, a former commander of the Red Battalions, and Manuel Diéguez, who had negotiated the capitulation of the workers during the 1906 Cananea uprising. Ríos, alienated from Carranza, soon threw his support to Obregon Salido in the competition between the Sonorans and the president.

In the meantime the Sonorans began to buy arms through American intermediaries, including Phelps Dodge, which eased the way in gaining presidential embargo exemptions. President Wilson's old friend, Cleveland Dodge, served on the company's board of directors and was chairman of the board for three years between 1924 and 1926 during the national hegemony of Obregon Salido and Elías Calles.[11]

During his presidential term Obregon Salido made giant strides toward the creation of a new governing structure. He synthesized personal, presidential, and party loyalties. Under his direction and his minister of war, Elías Calles, the army was largely brought under control. The process was not completed during his tenure, but the defeat of major military revolts in 1921 and 1923 laid the basis for tightening the reins of control on behalf of centralized government.

The triumph of the Obregonista alliance over the Carrancistas established the basis for the new Mexican state. Formerly antagonistic social groups were amalgamated under the authority of a state-building elite that came to power through armed force and thereafter imposed order by the same means. The new regime quickly set about establishing a stable basis for rule. The victorious elite emerged as state builders, creating political institutions that incorporated the subordinate participation of the defeated peasants, workers, metropolitan bourgeoisie, and Carrancista provincial elites.[12]

The government, after years of struggle with radical and independent labor groups, encouraged and controlled the new CROM. Morones, who deserted the Casa during the general strike crisis of July-August 1916, became head of the Mexican Labor Party and served simultaneously as minister of labor in the Obregon Salido government while also leading the CROM. His men, many of them naïve workers who thought they served a revolutionary cause, joined specialized gangs of thugs, police, and soldiers attacking CGT strikers in Tampico, Veracruz, and the Mexico City area. The deceived rank-and-file of the CROM inadvertently opposed independent labor organizing through corrupt leadership. Morones's moral turpitude became public knowledge a few years later.

The struggle spread throughout the nation. The CROM claimed devout working-class radicals in its ranks who were attracted by the organization's stunning successes. Depite the CROM's wildly exaggerated membership list, its probable 80,000 adherents nonetheless outnumbered their independent anarchosyndicalist competitor, the CGT. Numbering about 40,000, the CGT operated virtually without financial assets. The government did not destroy it during the 1920s because it suffered challenges to its authority from the Church, the remaining Porfirian right, army dissidents, continuing campesino unrest, and the foreign companies that actively defended their concessions. In addition, the Obregon Salido regime needed a "revolutionary" image in order to maintain its uneasy alliance with the lower classes. By the mid-1920s the corruption of the CROM leadership was public knowledge. After Morones resigned from the cabinet of Elías Calles in 1928 in a dispute over the presidential succession, the CROM disintegrated in a fortnight.

The Agrarian party, led by former PLM, Casa, and Zapatista activist Díaz Soto y Gama, spearheaded the Obregonista rapprochement with the campesinos. Like the CROM, the Agrarian party contained a large number of faithful adherents. In this case, however, the leadership expected a revolution in land tenure on behalf of the lower peasants. The Obregon Salido regime approved only a handful of land transfers for legally petitioning peasants betwen 1920 and 1924 despite great fanfare in the Senate by the party's colorful leader. The majority of land allocations made during Obregon Salido's presidency, like those of Carranza, consisted of legalizing previous locally initiated peasant land seizures. Most of the land occupations that he sanctioned took place between 1913 and 1916. The government's search for social stability called for the settlement of disputes between countryside antagonists as quickly as possible. Obregon Salido's actions, although limited in the extreme, alarmed hacendados and gave the land-hungry peasantry hope.

One of the regime's most important decisions regarding the land question made the National Agrarian Commission a working entity. The commission was started by the Carranza regime, and the Obregon Salido government intensified the efforts of the commission's idealistic and highly motivated agronomists and anthropologists who began to survey Mexico's countryside. They assembled an inventory of the rural populace that included community size, age and gender groupings, language distributions, economic, sanitary, and health conditions, and ecological and land resource summaries. They submitted reports on land tenure over wide regions.

The surveys included analyses of the capacity of the local population to defend its interests, what parcels of land they wanted, and what acreages would do the populace the most good. The commission's investigators also reported on the neighboring great estates, the nationality of their owners, and the crops harvested. American landholders not connected with large companies and Spanish large landholders fared badly in contrast to Mexicans in the redistribution of acreage. The agrarian commission investigators analyzed the legality of land titles and their viability under the provisions of the Plan of Agua Prieta and the Carrancista Seis de Enero agrarian proclamation of 1915.

The enthusiastic employees of the National Agrarian Commission of the period 1916–1924 laid the basis for the agrarian reforms carried out by President Lázaro Cárdenas between 1934 and 1940. No intelligent agrarian reform program could have been effected until this project was completed. It defined the nation's agricultural and human problems and potential. Begun during the period 1916–1920 on a limited basis, it grew enormously between 1920 and 1924. Interest diminished between 1924 and 1934 when the conservative Elías Calles regime slowed the process. It reached a maximum of activity during the reforms of the Cárdenas regime. The agrarian land grants of the Cárdenas era frequently carried out to the letter the recommendations made by agrarian investigators during the Obregon Salido years.[13]

The army became a more tightly controlled force under Generals Obregon Salido and Elías Calles than the loose amalgam of revolutionaries that prevailed when they seized power. Elías Calles served as minister of war and prosecuted conflicts with dissident elements, defeating disgruntled rightists and leftists in a series of skirmishes. In 1923 the assassination of Villa ended the threat of a lower-class-led countryside insurgency in the far north. Villa's elimination undermined the potential of Adolfo de la Huerta's challenge to Obregon Salido. Villa and de la Huerta had enjoyed excellent relations. The Obregon Salido government has frequently been charged with planning Villa's assassination. The defeat of the de la Huerta revolution in 1923 removed some of the powerful dissident army officers in the provinces, enabling Obregon Salido and Elías Calles to tighten their discipline over the armed forces while moving toward open conflict with the Church.

The Obregon Salido government struck a compromise between the economic nationalists of the revolution and foreign businessmen. His conciliation of these forces established the basis of Mexico's future relationship with foreign enterprise. Unlike Carranza, who had challenged the American oil companies' claim to unlimited rights over their properties in Mexico, Obregon Salido sought to reconcile differences. Carranza had stood fast in the face of American pressure resulting from incidents such as the kidnapping and release by unknown persons and later arrest by officials in Puebla of prominent American businessman and U.S. Consul William O. Jenkins.[14]

In 1919 Carranza refused to reassure American banking, mining, and oil concession holders regarding their rights in the future. In doing so he provoked the wrath and indignation of Secretary of State Robert Lansing and Senator Albert Bacon Fall. The senator had worked with U.S. firms in Mexico including the Doheny, Standard, and Texas Oil companies, the Richardson Construction Company, and the big banking and railroad interests. The Association for the Protection of American Rights in Mexico developed an anti-Carranza interventionist policy that included demands for annexation of the northern Mexican states or the invasion and establishment of a protectorate over the entire country. Their demands represented a strong current within the Republican party during Wilson's last five years in office. In 1916 Democratic party landowners in Mexico had formed a Non-Interventionist League in conjunction with Wilson's tactic of tough negotiations with Carranza.

Obregon Salido quickly reassured the multinational finance and advanced technology companies of their place in Mexico's economy. Foreign investors committed to endeavors that Mexican capitalists could perform or those such as the Corralitos Company, which had become the object of local public outrage, no longer had a place. American and other foreigners who held agricultural and cattle lands and who were not extremely powerful stood to lose in the widespread land occupations by peasants extending from the Isthmus of Tehuantepec to northern Chihuahua.[15]

The petroleum companies, Cargill, Phelps Dodge, W. R. Grace, ASARCO, Anderson-Clayton, National City Bank, Morgan Bank, The Chase Bank, Anaconda, and other corporations, which were linked closely to the Mexican search for favorable export earnings, received reassurance and some even prospered. The Obregon Salido regime's redefined role for foreign capital in the Mexican economy established the basis for Mexico's future relations with foreign capital. That policy declared Mexican preeminence in those sectors of the economy where Mexican capital functioned effectively. It encouraged foreign investment to move into avant-garde technologies and export marketing in which Mexican capital lacked expertise or the necessary international linkages.[16]

The Obregon Salido government quickly responded to oil company and U.S. pressures, reassuring them regarding the security of foreign investments. The Mexican Supreme Court ruled in September 1921 that the oil companies had rights under the law to subsoil resources acquired prior to 1 May 1917, when the Constitution had gone into effect. A codicil of the 1923 Bucareli Treaty between the Mexican government and the leaders of America's largest banks and mineral and petroleum companies advised that Article 27 of the Constitution would not be applied retroactively. It declared that the rights to subsoil resources purchased prior to 1917 were not subject to seizure. Since 1917 this issue had been central to U.S. government and Mexican relations. The oil companies and the U.S. government worked together to pressure the Mexicans. Company representatives frequently received access to State Department memorandums, and on several occasions company declarations were presented to the Mexican government as official missives from its American counterpart.

With Obregon Salido's presidency, relations between U.S. businessmen and the Mexican government began to improve. A campaign on both sides of the border reconciled the differences between the nationalism of the revolution and the American business community. Members of the San Antonio Chamber of Commerce, including many investors in the Mexican economy, conducted a presidentially sponsored tour of the country. They visited the northern mining regions, where San Antonio's pioneer investors George Brackenridge and Jean La Coste had made commitments during the Porfiriato; Guadalajara, where Charles Stillman and the Brownsville-

Matamoros merchants had dominated trade in the nineteenth century; and Mexico City. Local and national officials feted them throughout the trip.

In 1920, shortly after the overthrow of Carranza, Governor William P. Hobby of Texas, an important oilman and landowner in Mexico and supporter of Senator Fall's anti-Carranza policies, urged President Wilson to recognize the Obregon Salido regime. At a reception in El Paso, Hobby praised President-elect Obregon Salido and concluded, "as far as Texas is concerned General Obregon is already recognized."[17] By the end of the year six state governors had urged U.S. recognition of the new regime. Obregon Salido enjoyed strong support from elites of the American border states and American industrialists. One of them claimed that Obregon Salido was "by far the best ruler Mexico had had since Díaz . . . and in some respects is superior to Díaz." American investors still had not given up. In 1932 Senator Edwin Ladd of North Dakota echoed the San Antonio newspapers of the 1870s and Cecil Rhodes when he claimed that Mexico was "still the treasure chest of the World." Governor Hobby sat at Obregon Salido's right hand during his presidential inauguration in Mexico City and was praised in the Mexican press on that occasion as "our most distinguished visitor, the governor of Texas."[18]

In June 1922 Adolfo de la Huerta and Thomas W. Lamont of the Morgan Bank and chairman of the International Committee of Bankers agreed to a contract in which Mexico rescheduled its debts for forty years of payments. After a five-year recovery period during which Mexico would have a moratorium on some payments and reestablish credit ties with the United States, the Mexican government promised to repay all obligations. Following the rescheduling, the governments negotiated the sensitive oil-mineral rights issue. The oil and mining companies received guarantees before recognition of the Obregon Salido government was granted. Their anguish revolved around nationalistic Article 27 of the Constitution. The companies also objected to Mexico's claimed taxing powers over their properties, which contradicted the escape clauses they had negotiated with earlier regimes.

The companies' position was strongly represented by Secretary of the Treasury Andrew Mellon, whose family controlled the Gulf Oil Company. Their adamancy resulted in the dismissal of General J. A. Ryan as head of a special commission designated to negotiate with the Mexicans; he was found to be sympathetic to Obregon Salido, recognition, and even taxes. The Gulf Oil Company leadership claimed it distrusted Ryan because he had previously represented the Texas Company and was close to Governor Hobby. While sharing a common resentment of Standard Oil, the directors of the Gulf and Texas companies harbored a long-standing distrust rooted in the Texas Company's early use of the Texas state government against outside competitors during the years of the House machine. Governor Hogg and his successors had used "trust busting" to restrain the Texas Company's rivals. The 1923 Bucareli Accords balmed petroleum and mining company worries enough so that the United States recognized the Obregon government. In September United States ambassador Charles Beecher Warren took office in Mexico City.[19]

In 1923 the de la Huerta rebellion threatened the survival of the Mexican government. De la Huerta had hoped to succeed Obregon Salido in the presidency until the selection of Elías Calles ended that dream. Defined by the Plan of Veracruz, the revolt opposed the Bucareli Accords with the American companies and government as a national capitulation. The revolution, which has not been adequately studied, was dismissed as interested only in the "pocketbook." A seeker of bribes, personal estate enhancement, and payola could not have hoped for better opportunity than the blatant corruption of latifundistas Obregon Salido and Elías Calles. The latter's mode of governance seemed to be derived from his experience as chief of police in a border town with a "tolerance zone."

De la Huerta's Plan of Veracruz sounded the same grievances against centralized *caciquismo* (bossism) as Obregon Salido four years earlier. He reunited rebellious elements of the provincial elites and pequeña burguesía. Reportedly more than half of the army generals joined the insurrectos. The de la Huerta movement brought together former CGT anarchosyndicalist opponents of the government, Zapatistas, anti-American Huertistas, and provincial-elite hacendados including those of Yucatán. Many of those who supported de la Huerta agreed with him that the Bucareli Accords were a "sellout." Local grievances provided the basis for much of the fighting. Yucatecan henequén planters used the uprising to attack Felipe Carrillo Puerto, the "socialist" governor of Yucatán. Carrillo Puerto's civilian working-class militias were no match for the planters and military allied against him.[20]

The U.S. government granted Obregon Salido the arms and ammunition he needed to suppress the revolt. The anti-American nature of the de la Huerta rebellion was threatening to the mining and timber companies in the north, the agricultural export firms of Sonora, Coahuila, and Tamaulipas, the oil companies on the Gulf coast, and the McCormick interests of the National City Bank and International Harvestor Company in Yucatán. American police and intelligence services reported meetings, strategies, and arms movements near the border to the Mexican authorities. Once again, as in the cases of the PLM, Orozquista, Huertista, and Villista revolts, the United States imposed scrutiny and an arms embargo upon Mexican revolutionaries from the American side of the border. Once again the strategic nature of U.S. involvement proved critical despite abundant military expertise on the side of the uprising. The revolt lasted less than a year.[21]

After the monumental struggle for power between 1910 and 1920 and the resurgence of the Mexican state between 1916 and 1924, the position of the Church in the new order remained uncertain. As an aftermath to the revolution, The Cristero War, 1926–1929, settled the smoldering dispute between the Church and the new state. The dispute combined with campesino resistance to government-sponsored outside intrusions into the distinct cultures, economies, and polities of the pueblos to create a complex civil disturbance. Parts of three states in an area bordered by Zacatecas, Morelia, and Guadalajara were in the hands of Cristero guerrillas for a time, and the Archbishop fled to San Antonio. The Church, deeply rooted in the way of life of the countryside since the first century after the Spanish conquest, had no real hope of victory, nor did the campesino villagers who did the fighting. The rebellion was a complex mix of Church hierarchy and ranchero and peasant opposition to government attempts to replace the clergy in education and other local functions; government appointees and educators intruded upon traditional village life. The fighting officially ended in 1929, although sporadic violence continued through most of the 1930s.

Despite the religious devotion of a cross-section of the public, the Church no longer enjoys the political support or importance it once possessed. During the Porfiriato, with the growing power of the national state, it became a superfluous instrument of social control. From the standpoint of Mexico's postrevolutionary state-building elite, the Church was a reactionary vestige of the ancien régime. If the clergy had retained the strength it held during its mid-nineteenth-century confrontations with the Liberals, the Church-state struggle of the postrevolutionary era would have been critical.

The Cristero War concluded a conflict begun during the Bourbon reforms and Spanish Enlightenment. At that time rising government activism challenged the central role of the Church in society and economy. During the nineteenth century that process continued with the Church suffering heavy blows from successive Liberal regimes. The fighting of the 1920s and its residual aftermath in the 1930s resulted from the intrusion by the socially active state into what was previously the purview of the Church and the religious orders. The Cristero War was the last serious challenge to the consolidation of the new regime. The result completed the government's long struggle for hegemony over rural economic, social, and political affairs.[22]

Conclusion

THE REVOLUTIONARY CRISIS

The Mexican Revolution came about as part of a wave of nationalistic political unrest linked to socioeconomic crisis that swept the world in the early twentieth century. Economically and politically estranged pequeña burguesía, provincial and local elites, urban and industrial workers, and peasants joined forces in a nationalistic uprising. Provincial elites and pequeña burguesía participated in order to overthrow a dictatorial polity. Urban and industrial workers fought to end the labor-repressive productive system. Campesinos rebelled to regain municipal autonomy and lost property, their means of production. This cross-section of society unified around nationalism to regain control of the nation's basic resources and economic infrastructure from foreign domination. They gathered around provincial elite leaders Madero and Carranza until mutual antagonisms became overwhelmingly evident and led to civil war.

The 1876 insurrectionists of Tuxtepec benefited greatly from American financial support, which enabled them to continue until the government of Sebastián Lerdo de Tejada destabilized. The new government promoted an expansive economy emphasizing the use of foreign capital in the development of export-oriented mining and commercialized industrial export agriculture. The foreigners also controlled the banking, transportation, and communications infrastructure. Like so many states with industrializing economies overthrown in the twentieth century, the Porfirian government allowed a politically intolerable degree of foreign domination of the new enterprises. It failed to establish controls on the foreigners adequate to satisfy the growing ambitions of the citizenry. It denied political expression and was unable to provide economic stability to newly created businessmen, intelligentsia, professionals, and industrial workers or alternative opportunity to displaced campesinos.

During the 1880s and 1890s the expansive regime intruded upon the provincial elites' semiautonomous rule. After 1900, however, the increasingly erratic inflow of foreign investment, plant shutdowns, and layoffs and economic stagnation reduced general well-being. The loss of economic prosperity removed the only source of satisfaction that the politically and socially displaced provincial and local elites could claim. In addition to the aggrieved upper classes, the economic crisis reduced employment opportunities and real wages. That situation, coupled with the industrial workers' long-standing competitiveness with capital, unleashed an increasingly tumultuous working-class movement. The economic crisis and devaluation of the peso intensified an American-dominated revolution in land tenure, even leading to colonization.

After 1900 the emphasis placed on the cash crops tobacco, henequén, and sugar and development of the railroads and the mining industry cut into the resources available for the production of domestic staples. Redirected land, labor, and capital efforts combined with drought and crop blight to reduce Mexican cereal consumption. Labor shortages as a result of the extremely low wages paid to agricultural workers reduced production by 50 percent in some areas. New agricultural projects floundered because the government panicked over the cash flow crisis brought on by an overextended infrastructure development program, growing interest payments on the foreign debt to international banks, and the repatriation of profits by foreign companies. Shortages and higher prices for basic foodstuffs resulted, spurring the political unrest. By 1908 the failure to meet the public's nutritional needs had reached catastrophic proportions. The Porfirian political economy, like those of Iran, Russia, and China, failed because of its dependence upon the economies of the North Atlantic industrial powers as they entered a period of financial crisis in the early twentieth century.

Through deunionization, tax incentives, land grants, and political stability, the Porfirian government opened Mexico and attracted the expansive economies of the North Atlantic. It recruited foreign investments and non-Mexican financial, administrative, and technological experts. In the Guanajuato mining complex, where Colonel House held a large interest, foreign elitism was so pervasive that one investigator could not find a single Mexican employee in a management position with the alien-owned mines. On the Gulf coast foreign capital reinforced coercive labor and the imbalance of wealth. The regime promoted open marketing and political centralization through the abolition of state taxes that protected native-owned domestic industry and the development of a rail and telegraph system.

In 1906 and 1907, when industrial workers began the violence at the American-owned Cananea and French-owned Río Blanco sites, the 12 largest industrial concerns in the country were foreign controlled. That condition applied to over 130 of the 170 principal companies in the nation, or 77 percent of the total. Foreign investment constituted 88 percent of the capitalization of those 170 enterprises.

After twenty-five years of economic growth, foreign investment, had it followed the pattern of the Industrial Revolution in Western Europe, should have been moving ahead into an ever more advanced, eventually self-sustaining Mexican technology. That second stage in the European and U.S. industrialization process, however, was never reached in Mexico. Instead of establishing ever larger manufacturing complexes based upon advanced technology increasingly devoted to the needs of a growing domestic marketplace, foreign investors balked. Despite the fact that it entered the country between 1900 and 1910 at a pace three times as great as that between 1876 and 1900, foreign capital, now primarily American, continued to concentrate in competition with fledgling Mexican businesses and struggling landowners in raw materials exploitation. The foreigners focused upon landholding for commercial export production, driving up the cost of land ten times over in some places while the currency of their Mexican competitors devalued, by 50 percent on one occasion. Foreigners also took over transport and communications, banking, and basic industries.

The development of Mexican technology was not the reason for the foreigners' risk. All that Mexican industrial development would have meant to them were higher labor costs and a larger domestic market in one insignificant economy. As a result the foreigners came into competition with local elites, which they quickly overwhelmed in the race to exploit the nation's natural resources. Instead of stimulating avant-guarde industrial and economic development, with an increasingly prosperous working class and an enriching ripple effect in the growth of new industries and prospering national entrepreneurs, foreign capital, especially American, defeated native competition.

The first crisis for the Mexican economy came about because of its relationship with European investors. Europe entered a period of financial contractions in 1899–1904 and 1906–1907 that caused a dramatic slowdown in French capital investments in foreign textiles. That industry was the largest domestic manufacturing sector in the Mexican economy. Several years of shutdowns, layoffs, and wage reductions contributed to labor unrest in the mills of Puebla, Tlaxcala, and the greater Mexico City area.

An overwhelming influx of American capital penetrated the Mexican economy, competing with Mexicans. The ensuing discriminatory labor relations and land displacements provoked a nationalistic reaction from provincial elites, pequeña burguesía, industrial workers, and peasantry. The devaluation of 1905 deeply weakened Mexican capitalists in relation to foreigners. Some of the confrontations spurred elite revolutionary activity. First, in mining, the successful Guggenheim-ASARCO bids for mineral and rail concessions over the Arriaga family's opposition in San Luis Potosí and the Guggenheim concessions in Nuevo León in competition with the Garza, Sada, and Madero interests challenged Mexican provincial and local elites. Second, the government removed the Madero bank at Monterrey as the federal depository. Third, after bidding up the price of land many times over, outstripping Mexican production, and driving up the product's price by over two-thirds, the Continental Rubber Company attempted a U.S. boycott of the Madero guayule enterprise at Torreón. Fourth, diversion of the waters of the Nazas River from ranchero and Madero-owned properties at La Laguna near Torreón continued for many years despite court decisions and government assurances of support for the Mexican litigants. Fifth, the government damaged the Maytorena interests in Sonora by displacing the family from state leadership and suppressing its labor force, the Yaqui Indians. Sixth, the Yaqui and Mayo were resisting the combined land intrusions of American developers, including the Richardson, Huntington, Harriman, Stillman, Wheeler-Hyer, Burns, Marshall, United Sugar Company, and Los Angeles Times interests and their allied metropolitan Mexican intruders in Sonora and Sinaloa. Nearby labor and peasant unrest at Durango challenged the same interests. Seventh, in Chihuahua, the reorganization of range land on behalf of the state elites and American cattle, timber, and mining companies, including the Cargill, Palmer, Fred Pearson, Edwin Morgan, Marshall, Hearst, and Peirce interests, combined with a stagnating economy after 1902 to provoke multiclass ranchero and local elite-led town and rural rebellions. Eighth, a general inflation caused by the reduced supply of food and textiles eroded the real wages and well-being of workers, who witnessed open foreign control of production, supply, and prices. Ninth, beginning in the late 1890s over 7,000 American colonists bought and occupied small tracts of land from large U.S.-controlled development companies, erected fences, and drove the unlegitimized Mexican peasantry off long-occupied lands.

In the ensuing years further slowing of domestic trade and consumption led directly to curtailments of new investment and lower production in the French-controlled textile industry. The success of the anarchist Serdán family in spearheading the formation of over 300 PLM clubs in Puebla and Tlaxcala, ranging in size from 25 in the smaller pueblos to 300 in some of the textile factories, resulted from the effects of the foreign-engendered economic crisis in that area.

Foreign export-oriented enterprises created increased needs for government-supported infrastructure, streets, highways, and ports. The increasing cost of public indebtedness, however, seriously curtailed the regime's ability to maintain services. The inevitable tax increases fell on the native businessmen, industrial workers, and peasants; the foreign companies were exempt. In March 1905 the government reduced taxes on the foreign-owned mines by over 40 percent from a total of $9.5 million to $5.5 million yearly. The tax relief enjoyed by alien concerns, coupled with higher Mexican levies, led to multiclass indignation. As most of the capital came from the United States, Mexico's economy was more closely tied to the American marketplace and its business cycle. The cessation of American silver purchases in 1902 and the recession of 1907 revealed heightened vulnerability.

During the ten years prior to the revolution the intelligentsia in the press, novels, and political cartoons increasingly protested the alien hegemony. These protests reflected the changing national moral consensus. Guadalupe Posada's lithography portrayed a government in league with foreigners oppressing an agonized people. *El Hijo del Ahuizote,* published by intellectual Daniel Cabrera, pushed opposition to the regime. The front-page banner of each edition announced the root cause of its alienation: "Mexico para los Mexicanos."

Industrial workers, shopkeepers, and provincial elites shared the intellectuals' frustration and adopted their description of events. The slogans and definitions of issues used in the revolution were already in vogue several years before provincial and local elite political opposition emerged. Between 1906 and 1910 workers at Cananea, Río Blanco, and the textile factories of central Mexico demonstrated a new moral community when they militated against foreign ownership of production and ethnic discrimination.

The Porfirian regime, founded in 1876, was rooted in the political structure of the past. Acting in conformity with nineteenth-century Mexican government precedences of special concessions, enclaves of privilege, and monopolies for the well-born, the regime failed to adjust to changing conditions after its early years. It began dynamically, establishing a broad base of support among the local pequeña burguesía. The overthrow of pro-Lerdo and pro-Iglesias state oligarchies after the Revolution of Tuxtepec allowed pro-Porfirian officers and local elites the opportunity to replace them. The young regime created a temporary and narrow upward mobility and lasting loyalties. Thereafter it established an impressive record for longevity in office for its members from the president, cabinet officers, and governors down to bureaucratic functionaries and local jefes políticos. By 1910 most cabinet officers were in their seventies and had served for many years. Local allies of the national government seemed anchored to their offices, and younger rivals were denied all opportunity for political advancement. In one generation the regime moved from flexible expansive youth to ancien rigidity.

Declining vertical political mobility paralleled the problem of growing economic centralization and inelasticity. The national and metropolitan government in Mexico City insisted upon control over the granting of major concessions for the development of national raw materials resources and labor. Enormous multinational companies joined other foreign concerns to dominate Mexican capitalism.

They brought in high-ranking government officials as junior partners. Native and provincial elite competition had no chance. The need for effective guidance of the burgeoning economy and marketplace, combined with the historic pattern of external economic control created centralization. The domestic focal point in this nexus of power and wealth was a foregone economic and political conclusion—Mexico City. The center of foreign power for Mexico was equally predictable: New York City. Continued U.S. economic expansion increasingly came into conflict with the hegemonies of Mexican provincial and local elites and shut off the aspirations of ambitious pequeña burguesía. Continued foreign economic penetration in provincial export-oriented enclaves deepened the paralytic elite crisis between Mexico's center and periphery.

A government that stressed decentralization and states' rights when it came to power imposed its control from the capital. Members of the semiautonomous provincial elites, pequeña burguesía, and artisans chafed during the 1880s and 1890s. They protested the preponderance of Mexico City and the successes of those privileged financial elements closest to the regime, but they were placated by economic growth that seemed to have no limits. Some were left out, but success was everywhere. During the prosperity dissatisfied elements in the upper classes were relatively isolated among their own kind. That situation began to change in the late 1890s when widespread industrial layoffs signaled a slowdown in economic growth. The slowdown and the rising economic competition of foreigners with the provincial elites splintered the upper classes.

The staggering economy after 1900 caused by the same global financial crisis that triggered unrest in Iran, China, and Russia compounded the political tensions between the overly centralized and too-narrow power structure of the government elites and the bypassed state and local elites on the periphery. Successful commercial agriculturalists and businessmen of the provincia who had resented the foreigners' power and the government's closed nature in an era of prosperity now confronted hard times. Closed off from public works contracts by favoritism, they were joined in their alienation by the recently created businessmen, intelligentsia, professionals, and industrial workers with their frustrated expectations. These powerful groups had no peaceful means of expressing their needs. Slowly the peripheral elites were forced to demand political participation. Their demands for local autonomy and free elections became ever more urgent as their economic situation worsened. Reluctant rebels, the provincial elites, and their pequeña burguesa allies forged political alliances that ran local candidates against those promoted by the national government. New worker and peasant groups supported them. In demanding a more open society, the varied groups acted in their own class self-interests.

With time running out on the aged president and regime, a struggle over the presidential succession broke out. Madero forged a nationwide political movement, then a party. A cross-section of society except for the metropolitan Porfirian elite backed his electoral bid to end "boss rule." When the government fraudulently terminated that effort with Madero's arrest and an unfree election, the dissident leadership turned to political rather than social revolution. In search of greater revolutionary appeal, Madero deepened his offerings.

Utilizing the popular principles of the 1906 PLM political plan, Madero sought worker and peasant backing through promises of reform. He gained support, but with the belief on the part of many of his lower-class and radical adherents that campesino land tenure complaints and industrial labor controversies would be settled in favor of the working classes. In their call to arms the alienated hacendados, rancheros, and businessmen of the provinces looked for allies, as did their late nineteenth-century predecessors Miguel Negrete and Trinidad García de la Cadena, among the industrial workers and the peasantry while their nationalistic rhetoric sowed consternation among the foreign governments and companies.

THE INDUSTRIAL WORKERS AND PEQUEÑA BURGUESÍA

During the revolution pequeña burguesa Jacobins such as Baca Calderon and Dr. Atl struck a responsive chord when they called for an end to boss rule, one man-one vote, wage equity with foreigners, income sufficient for a decent living, women's rights, more civil liberties, secular education, opportunity for all, and, in Dr. Atl's case, workers' control over the means of production. Mexican industrial workers had fought for those ideals since the founding of the labor movement nearly a half-century earlier. Their democratic impulse caused Mexican workers to support claims for greater political freedom postulated by liberalism in the nineteenth century and succeeding progressive antidictatorial movements, including those of the PLM and Madero.

In the nineteenth century two rival tendencies dominated the labor movement; both were receptive to Madero's revolutionism. In the 1860s and 1870s a leftist movement developed among the artisans that challenged the elitist organizing that had been limited to the guilds and artisan shops. It challenged the hierarchical structure of artisan industry and the leadership of the master craftsmen. It opposed those who favored close cooperation with, and subordination to, successive Liberal governments under Juárez, Lerdo de Tejada, and Díaz.

The labor tradition from which the Madero adherents emerged was anarchist, Fourierist, nationalistic, and antigovernment. It supported independent syndicates in control of production. It organized industrial workers in the 1860s and 1870s despite government opposition. In 1880 the Mexican Congress of Workers joined the anarchist "Black" International headquartered in Amsterdam. This, too, was done over the heated opposition of those who favored the more conservative trade union or mutualist approaches.

The Díaz government smashed them as an organized force in the early 1880s. Deunionization created a more attractive investment climate for foreign and domestic capitalists. The Mexican government was competing with Eastern Europe and the African, Asian, and American colonies of the North Atlantic powers for western investments. For twenty years prior to the revolution workers' groups in the textile mills and mining centers espoused various anarchist and socialist ideologies and shared a common hostility toward the regime.

Revolutionary anarchism remained a strong current in the workers' movement, reemerged during the 1906–1907 unrest, and contributed to Madero's public support. In the years preceding the revolution there were two main tendencies of anarchism that strengthened Madero's cause. One was the communist anarchist, antigovernment, and equalitarian "liberalism" of the PLM. The PLM established links with the industrial workers of central Mexico through a radical underground made up of anarchist and other workers' protest groups, intellectuals, and even Protestant evangelists. Flores Magón and other members of the PLM Junta were members of that underground in the 1890s. In 1910 the PLM had revolutionary plans of its own and opposed Madero. Many former PLM leaders, however, such as Aguiles Serdán, with his enormous organization of 300 clubs in Puebla and Tlaxcala, joined Flores Magón because of his greater chance of success against the regime.

The other tendency in the organized labor force that initially served Madero's cause, anarchosyndicalism, came from the industrial workers and pequeña burguesía of central Mexico. Before Madero they backed government critics, including Filomeno Mata, the often imprisoned editor of *El Hijo del Ahuizote*. His newspaper repeatedly attacked the abuses of government, foreigners, and big capital. Flores Magón was a popular hero among the anarchosyndicalists, and they appreciated Madero as an idealist who might bring democracy and greater freedom. When Madero's forces captured Ciudad Juárez, working-class crowds filled the streets of Mexico City, surrounded the president's palace, demanding his resignation, and rioted. Similar unrest in provincial capitals required the imposition of martial law. To prevent the spread unrest, the president resigned and left the country; the American authorities gave Madero polite treatment in Texas and continued to suppress the PLM.

Radical workers identified Madero's nonconformist spiritualism as progressive. In addition to demands for a better economic life, workers' self-management, freedom of the press, womens' rights, universal suffrage, and individual liberties, organized labor was long a center of Protestant challenge to religious orthodoxy and the Church's power and wealth. Protestant tabernacles and centers thrived in the prerevolutionary industrial sites of Río Blanco-Orizaba, San Angel, Mexico City, Querétaro, Guadalajara, Veracruz, and the mining camps, including Cananea. They served as workers' and community meeting places while the government made its peace with a conservative, hierarchical, and monopolistic Church.

In the late 1890s deepening workers' unrest led to increasingly frequent strikes, sometimes linked to radical Protestantism. The violence of 1906–1907 at Cananea and Río Blanco began with Protestant anti-Catholicism, secular humanism, and PLM anarchism in the same meeting halls. The humanist Liberal club at Cananea and the evangelical tabernacle at Río Blanco were essential preparation for the uprisings that were rooted in the economic setbacks of the workers. Madero's visionary hallucinations were appreciated among some progressive workers because some of them were millennarians who shared Madero's ability to see past and future.

THE RURAL CLASSES

Simultaneous with their appeal to the industrial working class, the rebellious elites of the periphery called upon the long-oppressed peasantry of the nation. They were sought in every area of the countryside through the Plan of San Luis Potosí and found by Jacobin radicals and local rancheros in what often constituted "controlled mobilization." Hundreds of small bands soon got out of control, however, and attacks against American properties became prevalent in late 1912 and continued for years. The local elite leaders of the insurrection attempted to control the situation, calling for restoration of usurped lands, municipal autonomy, local control of banks, and abolition of the jefes políticos.

In making their revolutionary appeal the rebellious periphery and local elites, village leaders, and rancheros touched a peasantry that had revolted on a regional basis throughout the eighteenth and nineteenth centuries against seizures of village properties. The landholding pueblos and their wishful emulators, the rancherías and *cuadrillas,* were the source of countryside discontent before and during the revolution. The roots of their alienation were long standing. Colonial charters granted the pueblos possession of land in perpetuity. During three centuries of Spanish rule the only viable means of alienating those holdings was through denunciation of untitled properties, or lands not in use. This procedure developed as a result of countryside depopulation in the sixteenth and seventeenth centuries. In the eighteenth century the process continued but on the basis of growing commercialized agriculture and localized migrations, because the countryside population began to increase.

During the eighteenth century the pattern of later land disputes was firmly established. The economic and trading pulse of Mexico quickened. In the south export agricultural estates took shape while mining boomed across the colony. Many pueblos failed, and their lands were sold for nominal fees to those who could prove their ability to make them agriculturally productive. This practice provided ample opportunity for land developers and hacendados desiring property near towns and roads to bribe local and crown officials. They often obtained perjured testimony regarding the status of desired properties. The economic and commercial growth under way lent urgency to the process, provoking "Indian" uprisings in Tehuantepec, Puebla, and Sonora. Jesuit properties were also seized by the government and bought by commercial entrepreneurs. The Crown's "Indian Courts" and the official government policy, however, which had originally granted the pueblos land titles in order to gain Indian loyalties, mitigated the most excessive abuses. The government merely surrendered the lands piecemeal to the ambitious new claimants.

With independence in 1821, a new regime came to power that was controlled by the elite classes so long restrained by Spanish Indian policy. Between the 1820s and 1850s new head and crop taxes imposed by the national government joined with local ordinances to commercialize village produce as much as possible. State laws were passed that facilitated the denunciation of *terrenos baldíos*. The result was the occupation by estate owners of disputed lands. The hacendados often controlled the courts with jurisdiction in the disputes. By the 1840s the villages in southern Mexico had lost most of their croplands and were paying rents to estate owners and working for them part-time.

In 1856 the Ley Lerdo, a land law constitutionalized the following year, provided for the reorganization of all village properties. They were to be divided into individual plots. Failure to comply laid the holdings open to denunciation and seizure by individuals who could prove noncompliance and indicate their ability to make the land productive. The purposes of the edict were twofold: first, to develop a strong commercial agriculture in order to provide the export earnings and surpluses needed for industrialization; second, to facilitate the removal of the peasantry from the countryside to the cities and textile towns, where industrial workers were acutely needed. The Liberal landholding elites of the provincia were the direct beneficiaries of the land enclosure edict and the process that followed it until the 1890s.

The results were manifold. Rural population density in central and southern Mexico was too great to allow self-support on the small plots that resulted. As a consequence the newly created miniholders in those villages that obeyed the law either sold or rented their properties. Frequently villages refused to obey the decree or sought to evade its effect through only pro forma compliance. In those cases outside denunciation and foreclosure were carried out by court and police action. Many pueblos lost their legal status along with their lands. They became rancherías and cuadrillas, settled places on great estates without the legal right to elect their own municipal officials or to litigate as a unit. The pueblos and those that had recently lost their legal status combined with the older extralegal localities to provide the basis for resistance to the spread of capitalist agriculture and the power of the private property owners.

Hacendados and rancheros emerged stronger as a result of the Ley Lerdo's application. The spread of private ownership of what had been the property of the pueblos spread northward from central Mexico beginning in the late 1860s when the Liberals reoccupied the seat of power in the wake of Maximilian and the French. Between 1877 and 1910 the number of haciendas increased from 5,869 to 8,341 and ranchos from 11,000 to 45,000.

The hacendados developed estates that enveloped the once semiautonomous pueblos, turning their citizens into part- and full-time workers on the haciendas. The owners of the larger estates often lived in Mexico City and turned over day-to-day operations to professional administrators. Many of these hacendados envisioned themselves as patriarchs of both a family and an estate. They regarded workers as retainers and vassals. The hacendados often self-identified as European. They frequently referred to their subjects as *"morenos"* and *"gente sin razón."*

The rancho owners represented both a qualitative and quantitative increase in local countryside leadership. Overwhelmingly mestizo, they shared the pretensions and values of the hacendados but were less well off and generally less educated. Many of them came from towns whose corporate holdings had been broken up. Using their wits, local status, and personal means, they bought out and even intervened against their insolvent neighbors in Indian and mestizo towns to forge functionally sized properties. The rancheros greatly increased commercial agricultural activity. They constituted a rural pequeña burguesía.

The rancheros often lived in their villages of origin. In difficult times these owners of modest properties were frequently on bad terms with both the hacendados and the government. They often lost properties, rights of way, and access to water in litigations with the more powerful hacendados. Unlike the hacendados, the rancheros lived among their employees, spoke the same dialects, and wore the same clothes. Ranchero hegemonies maintained much more effective social control than the absentee owners of the great estates with their alienated workers. When rancheros established good relations with their own or neighboring pueblos, they became political forces to be reckoned with in their localities. In the nineteenth century and during the revolution the ranchero owners provided insurrectionary leadership. Those leaders strove to defend their interests against Zapatismo and Villismo, and most of them worked in favor of Obregon Salido against Carranza.

Throughout the nineteenth century villages violently resisted the land consolidations that were under way. In 1832–1833 and 1842–1845 the southwestern pueblos from Tehuantepec to Michoacán rose up in hard-fought battles against land seizures carried out by the giant haciendas La Marquesana in Tehuantepec and San Marcos in Guerrero. They fought against the new coffee fincas in Oaxaca and the sugar estates in southwestern Puebla and southern Morelos. They resisted the growing holdings of the Mexico City-based owners of the mines at Sultepec between Morelos and Michoacán and the expansive citrus growers of the Balsas River basin between Guerrero and Michoacán.

In 1856 the fighting generalized throughout central Mexico as the development of commercial export agriculture moved northward. The peasant villages and campesino settlements took advantage of state and national-level elite crises and even civil war to prosecute their demands. Each time ranchero leadership was critical in organizing and sustaining the fight. The government often exploited ranchero leadership by negotiations that resulted in the loss of village communal lands and the survival of "small" private properties.

In 1848–1849, 1868–1869, 1878–1883, 1892, 1896, and 1906 important village and campesino insurrections took place in the center and far north of the nation among almost continuous smaller revolts extending from Yucatán to the American frontier. Peasant tenure was being overwhelmed by the same commercialization of land that had occurred in the south during the previous century and a half. Agriculture, livestock, timbering, mining, and railroads were the stimulants. The last three rebellions—Tomochic, Chihuahua in 1892 and Papantla, Veracruz in 1896 and 1906—involved the immediate intrusion of surveyors, railroads, and land developers, precipitating a revolution in property values with resultant denunciations and seizures. The Tomochic rebellion also resulted from the imposition of greatly increased taxes. Local crises reached the rebellious stage because macropolitical rivalries came into play. At Tomochic rival state elites sought to exploit the tension with arms and financial aid while in Papantla the PLM intervened to make the rising a part of the national challenge to the Díaz regime.

When Porfirio Díaz became president, the process of land aggrandizement and village dispossession reached to the north. Land expropriations, which totaled 127,111,824 acres between 1876 and 1910, demonstrate the ruthless application of the Ley Lerdo and its supporting legislation. Those denunciations, however, reflected only part of the consolidation of landownership. The more powerful foreign capitalists purchased the lands of the increasingly economically hard-pressed provincial elites as well as those of the villages. Most of the land seizures were in the far north, where access to American markets provided incentives. Land developers encountered a corporate village in the north that differed from those of the south and center of the country.

The mestizo villages of the northern frontier had been established by the Spanish Crown and succeeding Mexican governments as a military and demographic buffer against incursions of Comanche, Apache, and other Indians. Land grants induced migration to the remote frontier outposts from the settled areas of Mexico. The villages resembled those of the south and center of the country in the respect that they enjoyed autonomous rights to litigate as municipal entities and to elect their own governments. Alone in the steppes or mountain valleys, they developed internal solidarity. They differed from the southerners, however, in several important respects. They were not originally wards of the Church-state, as were the sedentary Indian pueblos of the south and center. They were well armed, experienced in military self-defense, and, equipped with horses, they were highly mobile. Finally, many freely sold and bought property. They were far more functional in the outside commercial economy than their campesino village counterparts of the south.

In the twenty-five years before the revolution the states of Sonora, Chihuahua, and Coahuila underwent commercial transformation. Largely American-owned railroads, timber, mining, livestock, and agricultural companies turned the remote frontier into a border region indivisibly linked by economy to the United States. By 1902 over 23 percent of all U.S. capital in Mexico was invested in those three states.

The mestizo communities of the north lost their lands and municipal autonomy just as those to the south had earlier. Left to face their more powerful adversaries on an individual basis, the private property-owning citizens of the northern communities lost heavily. The biggest losers were those nearest the railroads or fertile watered zones. In Chihuahua the massive property acquisitions by the foreign Booker, Cargill, Hearst, Marshall, Morgan-Peirce, Northwestern Railroad, Pine King Lumber, and Riverside Ranch interests confronted the pueblos and smallholders with landlessness.

In Sonora the Mexican government drove the Yaqui and Mayo Indians from their river valley farming enclaves and from pueblos with land use rights and protective provisions similar to those of the villages of central and southern Mexico. Local elites watched as the Compañia Constructora Richardson acquired 993,650 acres extending eighty miles inland. The company's holdings south of the Yaqui River extended to the Mayo River. The railroad holdings of E. H. Harriman and his associates Stillman and William Rockefeller, who controlled the Southern Pacific Railroad, extended the length of the state. In the timber and mining regions of the Sierra Madre fewer people were involved, but the same process prevailed. In the Sonoran interior the Wheeler Land Company, owned by Chicago capitalists, held 1,450,000 acres extending from the Richardson properties eastward to those of Hearst and the others in Chihuahua.

In Tamaulipas the Texas Company controlled over 4,500,000 acres and planned to irrigate 800,000 of them; the National Railroad held 819,000 acres between Matamoros and Monterrey. The Rascon Company, owned by Galveston and New Orleans investors, claimed 1,400,000 acres in Tamaulipas and San Luis Potosí. In Coahuila William Jennings and John Blocker owned over 1,237,000 acres, and Chase Manhattan Bank, 80,000 acres. Continental Rubber and the International Railroad, which was controlled by the Southern Pacific Railroad after 1903, owned vast tracts. In Durango and Sinaloa over one-third of the land area was in the hands of American companies. In the north over a dozen colonies of Americans who called themselves "pioneers" occupied 500,000 more acres and expelled the Mexican occupants, sometimes offering them employment later. Their self-image as "pioneers" alarmed Mexican elites who remembered the loss of Texas in 1836 and the American southwest in 1848. In 1900 Mexico was host to half of all American foreign investments. The Mexican Revolution constituted the first great Third World uprising against American economic, cultural, and political expansion.

Prior to 1900 in the north, the villages were alone in violent opposition to the regime. Real wages for miners, lumberjacks, and railway workers rose throughout the northern economy causing agricultural labor shortages. Small support businesses owned by Mexicans sprang up alongside the foreign-owned giants. The railroads afforded access to American markets for provincial elite landowners.

Then, after 1900, economic setbacks in the United States sent thousands of unemployed Mexican workers back to their homeland, flooding the northern labor market. Most of them rejected agricultural labor and crowded the northern towns looking for work. Curtailed silver purchases in the United States devastated the silver mining industry. U.S. investments continued to poor into raw materials extraction instead of advancing industrialism, thus driving up land and mine prices and lowering market values for raw materials exports. They were competing with and overwhelming native capital.

Industrial unemployment denied opportunity to displaced peasants. Arbitrary closures and cutbacks depressed local economies, bankrupting Mexican businessmen in support industries and shopkeepers and impoverishing the artisans. Skilled American machinists, engineers, miners, agriculturalists, administrators, and timbermen precluded the hiring and advancement of Mexican industrial personnel in the midst of growing unemployment. American small businesses often displaced Mexican entrepreneurs.

Within a few years after 1900 the angry campesinos of the north had allies and new leadership. Rancheros and artisans led revolutionary gangs in attacks on the massive American-owned properties in the northern states. The fighting soon included raids across the border. The violence threatened the lower Rio Grande Valley and borderland properties of an impressive array of American capitalists and politicians and thousands of "pioneer" colonists.

THE REVOLUTION

Across the north, except in Chihuahua, the economic crisis was a unifying impulse that brought together the state elites. The pequeña burguesía, rancheros, miners, and even Indians joined them. Townsfolk, peasants, and miners in Sonora, Chihuahua, and Coahuila rallied to Madero's call. In Chihuahua the Terrazas family dominated and enjoyed a close working relationship with the national government. It shared the wealth of the state with the empresarios of American enterprise.

With the oligarchical Terrazas clan supporting Díaz, revolutionary leadership in Chihuahua fell upon the working-class leaders Orozco, Silva, and Villa, creating a basis for future conflict between them and the provincial elites of other states. In Sonora the recruitment of Yaqui Indians and miners under the leadership of the rival Pesqueira and Maytorena families created armies with hierarchical authority that reflected society at large.

The pequeña burguesa leaders Alvarado and Hill, and the marginalized members of the oligarchy, Obregon Salido and Elías Calles, actively headed those armies. An alliance of provincial and local elites controlled events. A similar pattern prevailed in Coahuila.

In Morelos, where a more demographically dense and peasant society existed side by side with haciendas held by absentee owners, a contest over land possession emerged. Metropolitan elite landholders in the state overshadowed the reform-inclined provincial elites. The Morelos elite was too close to the metropolis to enjoy the northern elite's tradition of semiautonomy derived from remoteness. Like Chihuahua, the dissenting reformist administrators in the state elite were eliminated during the Huertista golpe de estado. Huerta removed the Morelos political administration to Mexico City to ensure the state's political allegiance. That action left revolutionary leadership to the pueblo elites and working classes.

Village peasants forged their own leadership to confront the landowners and with anarchists from the Casa del Obrero and radical rural schoolteacher ideological support, formulated their program. Lower peasants from virtually landless pueblos, displaced workers from the depressed sugar haciendas, poor townsmen, and a sprinkling of slightly more prosperous but hardly "middle" peasant leaders, constituted the Zapatistas and their leadership. The rapid growth of the insurrection created an almost chaotic mix of local risings and land occupations over which the Zapatista high command had no control.

The composition of other peasant movements in the south, including Guerrero, Oaxaca, Puebla, and Tlaxcala, resembled the Zapatistas. Rancheros, artisans, and even state elites were prominent among rival rebel groups in the area. Outside influences upon the Zapatistas in the beginning came from rural schoolteachers and radical intellectuals such as Manuel Palafox, Otilio Magaña, and Huitrón and Díaz Soto y Gama from the Casa, who tried to develop an organized approach to pueblo communalism. The southern movement was incompatible with Madero's political revolution. The Díaz regime lost control of the countryside and its forces fell back to the state capitals before Madero and the government agreed on a truce.

Madero's inability to satisfy the Zapatistas or reassure interim President de la Barra and the Porfirian functionaries before taking office presaged the failure to reconcile the goals of his supporters with the interests of the ancien régime elite. Peasant land occupations had already taken place across the nation. His refusal to carry out land reforms was compounded by the exclusion of his lower-class backers from power including Orozco and

Villa in Chihuahua. In Durango, Morelos, Puebla, and Tlaxcala, Madero's appointees had been noncombatants and even active supporters of the ancien régime. In Puebla and Tlaxcala they suppressed industrial strikes by former PLM and pro-Madero workers. The more radical Maderistas abandoned him first, but by 1913 the president stood alone.

Despite his efforts to placate the right, Madero allowed the labor movement in central Mexico to grow, especially in the Valley of Anahuac, even when it fell into the hands of anarchosyndicalist leadership. The uncertainties of labor organizing and strikes, inflation, unemployment, and a general business slowdown alarmed the foreigners and men of property. A massive attack against American-owned properties spread along the Gulf and Pacific coasts from Campeche to Tamaulipas and Chiapas to Sonora, jeopardizing rubber, oil, timber, and sugar holdings, while fieldworkers devastated the orchards in Tehuantepec, Chiapas, and Oaxaca.

On the Pacific coast the uprisings were so widespread that the U.S. government dispatched a transport from San Diego to pick up American refugees in Sinaloa, Colima, and Oaxaca-Chiapas. The presidential emissary on board considered the Colima debacle the most serious because the local and provincial elites had openly manifested their hostility toward the American holdings there. The anti-American character of the Orozco revolt in the north, the Zapatista debacle, Mayan uprisings in Quintana Roo and Yucatán, rising unrest in Puebla and Tlaxcala, and growing labor militancy in the greater Mexico City area gave elements of the ancien régime their chance to overthrow Madero.

General Huerta was backed by President Wilson with unlimited military provisions until mid-September 1913. The Americans abandoned Huerta only after he demonstrated his inability to maintain order. With American arms and supplies the northerners marched southward in the winter of 1914 while Zapata's communalist movement continued to grow and radicalize in the south-center. At that point differences involving power, class, and caste arose between the Villista forces and the Carrancistas.

The differences between the two groups stemmed from the fact that the Chihuahua revolution lacked upper-class leadership. At first the Villistas had no hacendados among their directors. The state's oligarchy had been pro-Díaz, eliminating it from the transition to the Madero regime. Then, unlike Sonora and Coahuila, Huerta's troops killed the Maderista governor Abraham González. That left the ensuing insurrection in the state to develop without direction from above. A populist movement emerged led by dynamic elements from among the displaced and still-intact rancheros, agrarian workers, shopkeepers, and artisans. Displaced campesinos selected the enormous American-owned haciendas for invasion and occupation. Strikers and ex-mine workers attacked the largely American mineral properties. A notable element among the developing División del Norte in Chihuahua were the displaced or marginalized peasants and ranch workers, labeled "bandits" by their upper-class rivals.

In contrast with Chihuahua, the Sonora and Coahuila transitions from Porfirian to Maderista politics had been better controlled. Regional and local elites long excluded from political power by Díaz occupied political offices. The new governor of Coahuila, Carranza, had been a Porfirian senator before joining the state's elite revolutionaries who backed Madero. In Sonora, Maytorena became governor while Obregon Salido, who refused to break with the Porfirian elite Pesqueira family and General Torres in order to support Madero during the revolution, became the hacendado and businessmen-supported mayor of Huatabampo in the south of the state. The Sonoran elite was divided between two equally conservative antiagrarian reform families who shared power after Madero's success, with the Maytorena group enjoying a short-lived advantage over the Pesqueira.

When Huerta seized the government Carranza was able to call upon a cross-section of Coahuila supporters, including elite Maderistas, miners who had armed during the 1911 fighting and now constituted a rudimentary "militia," and policemen. Governor Maytorena in Sonora joined Carranza in revolt but absented himself, allowing the Pesqueira clan and its allies to gain control of the emergent military. During the 1913–1914 civil war with Huerta the Sonorans avoided open warfare at home, but when victory in central Mexico was assured, the two elite-led groups turned on each other.

Understanding the basis of the Sonoran fight and the American role in it provides insight regarding the revolution's contending forces. During the latter part of 1914 and 1915 the Maytorena faction fought as Villa's allies against the Pesqueira forces who had taken over the military leadership of Carranza's army in the person of Obregon Salido. Throughout that time the U.S. government surreptitiously backed the Pesqueira forces, especially those of Elías Calles, with arms while maintaining a facade of neutrality and even sympathy toward Villa for many months. Villa courted the U.S. government assiduously throughout that time, not fully realizing President Wilson's deep contempt or the hostility in the American cabinet toward him as a bandit.

In December 1913 the American government, under enormous political pressure from American property owners, including many of the administration's most important Democrats, secretly began to plan a Mexican intervention. Occupation of Veracruz offered several advantages over its alternatives. First, it enabled the seizure of Huerta's arms buildup in the port, although the *Ypiranga* escaped and delivered its shipment at Puerto México. Second, it sealed off Huerta's most important port, lengthening his supply lines and forcing new troop developments in order to cross long stretches of guerrilla-held terrain between Puerto México and the center of the country. Third, it afforded the Americans a quick invasion route to Mexico City if, as was feared, the Zapatista attack on the capital triggered an urban lower-class uprising inside the city. Fourth, the port city was optimally suited for the storage of arms and their distribution to revolutionaries whose success the Americans wanted.

The intervention was crucial to the outcome of the revolution. It deeply eroded Huerta's military supplies. The arms Carranza's retreating troops received when they occupied Veracruz enabled Obregon Salido to recruit, train, and equip new forces, with which he counterattacked the Villistas and Zapatistas. The victors returned to central and northern Mexico, strategically defeating Villa and Zapata by late 1915. Then they set about the arduous task of restoring order to the countryside, a high priority with the Americans. U.S. cabinet-level support for Carranza had strengthened after he intervened in August 1913 to suppress Lucio Blanco's move to distribute the American-owned lands south and west of Matamoros.

The key leaders of the Constitutionalist armed forces were Sonoran pequeña burguesía tied to the Pesqueira family and American companies in that state. Obregon Salido, Hill, Alvarado, and Elías Calles played key roles in the creation of the new regime. Between 1913 and 1920 Obregon Salido rose from a colonel in the Sonoran militia to commander of the forces that defeated the División del Norte and then to leader of a political amalgam of provincial elites and pequeña burguesía with subordinate worker and peasant formations that deposed conservative, but insistently nationalist, President Carranza.

In 1912, Obregon Salido, after refusing to participate in the revolution against Díaz, entered politics winning the mayor's post in Huatabampo with the support of hacendados and businessmen over the opposition of the local union men. Later that year he earned the admiration of Governor Maytorena and the American businessmen in the state by leading his own militia unit to victory over the anti-American Orozco forces in southern Sonora. Because of that success and the unpopularity of his confederates he became leader of the Sonoran armed forces who fought Huerta. Alvarado's popularity was limited by his suppression of Mayo and Yaqui

Indians, who were later recruited for the revolutionary army. Elías Calles, former police chief of the bordertown Agua Prieta, already had a reputation for corruption when he joined Hill in the suppression of workers at Cananea and the imprisonment of elected officials at Cananea and Naco.

Hill, Elías Calles, and Alvarado repeated their early local functions in Sonora at the national level later in the revolution. Hill led the military suppression of the urban workers during the July-August 1916 general strike in Mexico City. As military commander of the Federal District, he established a law and order in favor of the government and the industrialists over the workers of the nation's most industrialized area. Alvarado's campaign against the insurgent Indians in southern Sonora presaged his suppression of the rebellious Maya and the reorganization carried out by the Constitutionalists in Yucatán. Elías Calles prosecuted the northern campaign against Villa, which included the imposition of Constitutionalist military officers in place of elected pro-Villista officials whom he imprisoned. Then, as defense secretary and president, he led the fight to remove the Church from education and public service. As president and strongman, he headed a regime noted for corruption and dictatorship.

Obregon Salido proved himself the master Sonoran politician upon whose success the others depended. He escaped public blame for the Casa's defeat by remaining aloof despite earlier promises of support. The tactic paid dividends once more when he stood by while Carranza's armies devastated the Zapatistas. When Obregon Salido rode from Cuernavaca to Mexico City to become president, he did so with compromised and future bureaucrat Gildardo Magaña, one of Zapata's longtime aides, at his side. In 1912, at the beginning of his career, he enjoyed the endorsement of the 205 American companies in Sonora. He was their "benefactor" in a time of lower-class violence and Indian insurgency. They appealed for and received exemptions from President Wilson in order to import military supplies to Sonora during the Orozco revolt despite the American embargo.

During the early fighting Obregon Salido protected the Phelps-Dodge holdings at Nacozari of Cleveland Dodge, President Wilson's "dear friend" from Princeton. Between 1917 and 1919 the victorious soldier established business ties with W. R. Grace and Company in Sonora, resulting in an enormous debt. At the same time, he laid the basis for one of the largest latifundia complexes to survive the Mexican Revolution and Lázaro Cárdenas's reforms of the 1930s. Many of the properties were former Yaqui Indian lands. His family holdings most recently survived challenge during the Echevarría government between 1970 and 1976.

Obregon Salido's defeat of Villa and eventual seizure of power coincides with the victory of pequeña burguesa interests, the American companies, and a new state building elite over the lower-class tendencies toward egalitarian localism of the Villistas, Zapatistas, and the Casa. Obregon Salido's victory preserved capitalist property relations against the working-class extremes of violent attacks on foreign property, anarchosyndicalism, and village communalism. Pequeña burguesa demands for wider economic and political participation deeply eroded the castelike social structure but safeguarded foreign interests from the extremes of lower-class nationalism. It moved foreign investments away from raw materials exploitation that competed with Mexican capitalists. It encouraged foreign participation in joint ventures with the Mexican elite in avant-garde technology, industrial advancement, and the quick profits of tourism.

Obregon Salido's rise to power was inextricably linked to Mexico's geographical proximity to the United States. That juxtaposition determined American control of late nineteenth-century economic growth and the development of the railroads. The resultant political instability led to a revolution that was decided by a compromise between Mexican nationalism and American intervention. The U.S. government first opposed the revolution because of the anti-private property stance manifested by Flores Magonistas and Zapatistas and the spontaneous working-class anti-Americanism evidenced by the lower-class rebels of the north, including the supporters of Orozco. Huerta's inability to control events and his continuation of the European sympathies manifested by Díaz in his last years alienated the Wilson administration. The U.S. government then gave strength to the elite revolutionaries most capable of ending the strife and who best served "American interests."

In 1920, when Obregon Salido came to power, both the president and the Mexican government reached a rapprochement with U.S. interests. Obregon Salido reduced his personal debt to W. R. Grace from $1,800,000 to $400,000 in just three years and then fulfilled the rest of his obligation by transferring a large piece of Yaqui Valley lands to the American concern. In 1922 the Obregon Salido government successfully negotiated an agreement with the U.S. banking houses providing a forty-year installment plan for the payment of Mexico's debt. In 1923 his government signed the Bucareli Accords, agreeing not to apply retroactively the Constitution of 1917 against the foreign oil companies. In return the U.S. recognized the Mexican government.

THE POSTREVOLUTIONARY REGIME

The Mexican regime that emerged after ten years of fighting was broad-based and viable. It came to power by a force of arms headed by provincial elites with pequeña burguesía field commanders. The exclusivist Porfirian oligarchy, rival provincial elites, industrial and urban workers, and peasants were all defeated at various points in the struggle and reincorporated into the new regime through subordinate organizations that recognized the supremacy of the new state. Even the Americans were forced to negotiate.

Each defeated group—peasants, industrial workers, and capitalists, and later the Church—renegotiated its status from a disadvantageous position, forced to concede ultimate power to the state-building elite. Even the foreign capitalists ceded the right to subsoil resources to the state. In return these groups gained a variety of constantly revised concessions. For the Porfirian industrialists and foreigners, beginning with the Carranza government of 1915–1920, recognition of the new regime's authority meant protection from the workers of the Casa and participation in the capitalist postrevolutionary economy. This involvement was later extended to polity, demonstrated by the prominence of the Rabasa and López Portillo families in recent times and the intermarriage of pre- and post-revolutionary elites. The provincial elites and Porfirian elements that rallied around Carranza surrendered to Obregon Salido but then joined the open polity that balances political appointments, power, and grievances far more lucidly than the Porfirian anachronism.

By winning the war, the pequeña burguesía kept its economic and social individualism and gained a state-directed hierarchically organized industrialization program, commercial expansion, and a growing problem-solving bureaucracy composed of its members. According to some estimates the government now controls about 70 percent of the national economy. Whatever its share, the government's role in the economy continues to grow.

Through partnerships with business, professionals and technical functionaries in institutions such as Nacional Financiera and the government-operated banking system provided capital, expertise, stability, and even bankruptcy insurance to businessmen. Some of the largest hotel chains are owned by the government and leased to management consortiums of multinational companies and wealthy Mexican partners. The government-owned Petroleos Mexicanos provided refinery products and the crude oil for a still largely foreign-owned petrochemical industry for conversion into plastics and other finished products and energy for domestic industry.

Pemex is attempting to develop its own advanced petrochemical complex. The expansion of Pemex's operations contributed greatly to the enormous indebtedness officially placed at about $111 billion; unofficial estimates that include private debt soar past $140 billion.

The dilemma of servicing a massive debt with badly needed surplus value illustrates the problems inherent in the development of Third World economies even when adequate wealth appears to be available. An austerity program and higher gasoline and consumer product prices have placed the burden of Mexico's indebtedness squarely on the pequeña burguesía and working classes. Meanwhile the native economic elites and multinational companies, while enjoying the stability offered by government participation in their industries, object strenuously to new regulations. Increasing government control of the economy progressively limits the ability of the "crisis-solving" PRI bureaucracy in its traditional intervention in culpable sectors of the economy in times of national stress. The more the government controls, the more likely it is that the public will view it as the problem rather than the solution. The mutual hostility and cooperation between the economic elites and the pequeña burguesa functionaries now running the government's institutions, while normal fare in all of the Western industrialized nations, is historically rooted in the divisions that appeared during the revolution.

The U.S. government and American investors strove mightily to maintain stability and therefore control over Mexico during the early phases of the revolution. They failed and were forced to choose between the lower-class revolutionaries and the nationalism of Carranza. They chose Carranza as the lesser of two evils, because of his respect for private holdings. Their relations with the present regime are based upon an American role in the high profit sectors of advanced technology and the Mexican government's acceptance of a place within hegemonic American global "security interests." As Colonel House put it, "our flag is to be your flag." The weight of American investments is heavily committed to the cutting edge of industrial advancement. Repatriation of profits is a dead letter because of the lucrative opportunities available in the Mexican marketplace. The present fifty-fifty arrangement in terms of foreign ownership of companies, profits, and opportunity would please both the Porfirians and the revolutionary nationalist critics.

The urban and industrial working class and peasantry gained the least in postrevolutionary Mexico. Since the 1930s strikes and unions have been carefully regulated and workers' organizations licensed in order to maintain a balance between the need for social control and the highest possible profit margins. Real wages have not increased over the last thirty years and the standard of living is about average for workers in Latin America's larger countries, none of which has undergone a revolution. Unemployment stands at around 40 percent.

The revolution swept away most of the caste barriers that still plagued much of the Latin American countryside. The majority of the countryside population, however, has fared even worse than the urban and industrial workers. The overabundance of economically unassimilated city dwellers results from the backwardness of rural technology, the focus of government services toward the urban sector, and the imbalance of power in the marketplace, which assigns greater value to industrial products than agricultural. These factors produce rural hardship, rural-urban migration, and high rural birthrates.

In the 1930s an agrarian reform program eased growing social unrest. A majority of the nation's peasants received land before 1940. A doubling of the rural population between 1940 and the 1960s, however, left most campesinos landless by the 1970s despite another agrarian reform effort between 1958 and 1964. Those who received land now comprise a middle peasantry composed of ejido cooperative members and "small farmers" engaged in commercial agriculture. Loyalty to the regime of those who have received land appears boundless. The *jornaleros,* or landless rural day laborers who produce the nation's foodstuffs, are its poorest group.

All of the social strata in the countryside are "represented" by official and extraofficial organizations linked to the government. One of the principal groups representing the middle peasants is the National Confederation of Small Propertyholders, which works hard in opposing further land distribution. The National Confederation of Campesinos (CNC) is composed of both ejidatarios and landless farm laborers. It lobbies for more land *dotaciones* on behalf of the ejidos but often opposes grants for landless workers who cannot qualify for citizenship in an eligible pueblo. The CNC supports the original land law proposal set forth by Carranza in January 1915 and insists that all land disputes be handled through the administrative channels of the Secretariat of Agrarian Reform (SRA). This approach has left many peasant and rural settlements in perpetual litigation since the 1920s. The destitute campesinos and peasants are tied to the government through the SRA, local agrarian committees of the CNC, public service attorneys, and local administrators. All of the agrarian organizations have pequeña burguesa and bureaucratic leadership at the top and oppose extralegal peasant land actions and the formation of independent campesino unions. These institutions function as mechanisms of social control.

The Mexican Revolution was part of the first wave of worldwide political and social upheavals that has made the twentieth century an era of revolution. The processes leading to social conflict and the competition between the participating groups between 1910 and 1920 are complicated but classic. The forces at work in Mexico were remarkably consistent with contemporary revolutions and those Third World upheavals that followed. Social classes, global economic crisis, foreign intervention and ideologies, individual events, and the pursuit of personal self-interest interacted with geography to create definable parts in the process.

The Mexican Revolution stands as the first successful Third World uprising of the twentieth century. Because the peasant and worker-led formations were defeated, their original demands for autonomous local working-class control over production and government have not been realized. The nation, however, regained ownership of its real estate and natural resources from the foreign intruders. The major portion of the 150 million acres that have been seized and redistributed went to the social group that caused most of the disturbance: the peasantry.

The pequeña burguesía was the principal military victor, and the achievement of its goals radically changed Mexico in ways that both benefited and damaged the interests of its rivals. Mexico changed from a caste-closed society to an open one that stresses individual competition and social mobility. It moved from an almost totally foreign-controlled economy in the hands of private holders to a mixed one in which the still powerful foreign element prospers through the global financial structure and a commitment to advanced technology, a role for it that pequeña burguesa nationalists have felt appropriate since the 1890s.

The victorious Obregonistas achieved their goals. Among the results, a new and experienced elite group has emerged that is composed of a blend of the most successful pequeña burguesa revolutionaries and the more sagacious provincial and Porfirian elites, creating a genuine national burguesía. The broad-based elite synthesis that forged the new burguesía reaches into virtually every community. It has demonstrated an astute sensitivity to mass unrest in a perpetually troubled economy, resolving sociopolitical contradiction with a mixture of violence and cooptive concessions to peasants, workers, foreign capital, the Church, and intellectuals. It directs an advanced and growing state capitalist economy fully incorporated with the industrialized West through its transnational corporations in a pattern aptly called "dependent development."

In 1910 alien capitalists held a 77.7 percent participatory share in Mexico's largest 170 companies. In 1970 foreign investors held 24.1 percent of the capital commitments to Mexico's 500 largest companies. The totals, 170 companies for 1910 and 500 corporations for 1970, represent the principal business institutions in the nation in those years. The percentages of domestic and foreign ownership in Mexico's largest capitalist enterprises reflect both the successful advancement of the economic interests of the Mexican national burguesía in the nation and its continued relationship with foreign capital.

Until now the new regime has bestowed sufficient opportunity and rewards for its up-and-coming pequeña burguesía, at least in comparison to the relatively small amount of vertical social mobility in the more powerful capitalist economies of the industrialized West. The cornerstone of that effort is the impressive state-supported system of higher education that presides over a million undergraduate students, providing them with university experience. Unfortunately, the great majority are untouched by these institutions. The already enormous gap between rich and poor increased between 1950 and 1970 and now is increasing at an unprecedented rate. Of Mexico's wage earners, 80 percent receive less than $9 per day and 95 percent receive less than $18 per day. In effect there is no "middle class" of wage earners.

Characteristic of national bourgeois regimes, contemporary Mexican society, through industrial growth and a variety of social programs, including rural education that emphasizes European language and culture, is highly integrative. Overcentralized development and human services continue the process of urbanization, concentrating masses of unprepared rural migrants on the fringes of a few large cities, where they are used to perform low-paid marginal tasks. The Mexican government, after 450 years of trying, finally is capable of absorbing the indigenous culture into a dominant Hispanic one while offering empty homages to the indigenous heritage.

Epilogue

Until the mid-1890s Mexico achieved a political stability unique in twentieth-century Latin America. This was done by maintaining a steadily increasing rate of per-capita production and the long-term development of a complex matrix of social controls. The Mexican army and police have acted with energetic violence against dissent. The government is one of the world's most sophisticated political systems reaching into every locality through a network of official and semiofficial business, peasant, and worker organizational hierarchies. Today the clientelist government and official party, the PRI, dominate appointments and opportunity, maintaining political stability in the face of growing socioeconomic inequity and massive exploitation of the working classes.

The process of consolidation that followed the revolution brought a new ruling elite synthesis into being which incorporated defeated elements such as the Church, big businessmen, the agrarians, and the industrial and urban workers into subordinate units of the new regime. From the beginning the winning pequeña burguesa elements linked their political success with economic opportunity. The old economic elites that survived welcomed the newly powerful political rulers into a new symbiotic relationship of joint state and private enterprises. The agrarian and labor parties of the early 1920s abided by rules laid down in the Constitution. The government interpreted those rules, assuring it of domination of popular political movements for the next sixty years. The leaders of the latter-day agrarian and labor groups, the CNC and the CTM, formed during the reformist government of Lázaro Cárdenas (1934–1940), have incorporated millions of members and are closely associated with the ruling PRI.

Broad-based political participation is the basis of the modern regime.

The reforms of the Cárdenas era now provide the ideological basis of a "revolutionary" nationalism. Those reforms, in addition to the creation of new urban labor organizations and the issuance of many land grants to the peasantry, included governmental purchase of that portion of the nation's railroads still in foreign hands, the seizure of tens of millions of acres of American-owned lands, and the nationalization of the oil industry. Mexico regained control of its natural resources and infrastructure during the 1930s.

Despite those efforts foreign-based multinational corporations and foreign investors still controlled 70 percent of the modern oil-made synthetics industries in the late 1970s. Now the interest payments on Mexico's over $111 billion debt passes the profit gained from petroleum exports to U.S. banks. Americans acquire most of the exported oil. The international financial structure has re-created the colonial outflow of material resources and profits, a condition that prevailed with silver in the Spanish era and during the Porfiriato.

U.S.-based multinational corporations and banks are increasingly focusing on the most avant-garde technology and high-profit sectors of the economy. U.S. investments in Mexican high technology have been estimated at over $5 billion. Despite a powerful foreign presence, the domestic entrepreneurial elite and government continue a nationalistic defense of their economic interests. Since the revolution the Mexican share in the larger capitalized enterprises has increased from 10 percent to an estimate of nearly 70 percent. State capital is a major factor in Mexican participation.

The balance between state-owned private Mexican and foreign-held enterprises provides a clear picture of the results after fifty years of economic transformation and nationalist ideology. None of the largest ten corporations in the nation is foreign owned, and only two, Celanese Mexicana and Fértil Fosfátados, are foreign dominated. The Mexican government, principally through its economic development corporation, Nacional Financiera, is in control or strong in 70 of the largest 500 companies, while private Mexican capital controls or is strong in 282. Direct foreign capital controls or is strong in only 174. Despite indigenous control over the steel and petroleum sectors, however, when Mexican industry is broken down into precise categories, foreign control looms large in some of the most important.

The two largest automotive concerns are Ford and Chrysler. The latter is purported to be 40 percent American-owned and has active foreign direction. The principal machine and equipment manufacturer is the American-controlled John Deere Company. Italian-controlled Olivetti-Under-wood leads the computer and office equipment industry. B. F. Goodrich, the largest automobile tire and rubber producer, is completely foreign owned. Syntex, S.A., controlled by Ogden, Abott, and Lilly, occupies first place among the chemical and pharmaceutical firms. Brown and Williamson are the outright owners of the largest Mexican cigarette producer, the Compañia Cigarrera La Moderna. Unilever of Great Britain owns all of Lever de México, S.A., the largest manufacturer of household goods.

Anaconda still dominates the mining industry. It remains a part-owner in Cananea, where it developed large operations before the revolution, contributing to the anguish of both local elites and workers at the time. Anaconda of Mexico is a wholly American-owned and controlled subsidiary of the parent company in the United States. ASARCO is said to be 49 percent American owned with active administration by American "experts." The parent American company of Sears and Roebuck of Mexico totally owns and controls the largest privately held retail chain. Anderson Clayton is the largest food producer and distributor. Despite the widespread nationalizations of American farm properties during the Cárdenas era, foreign-owned agricultural production accounted for 37 percent of the total value of Mexican farm produce in 1978. Despite frequent listings of foreign interests in a given concern at 49 percent, the practice of using *prestanombres* (name lenders) of Mexican nationality continues extranational control in many corporations.

The nationalistic propensities of the urban working classes and pequeña burguesía are best satisfied by the overwhelmingly Mexican ownership of the lesser capitalized enterprises. In addition, the three leading construction materials producers are Mexican owned. This condition marks an improvement from the foreign and monopoly domination of such industries during the Porfiriato. Similar to the petroleum monopoly and the biggest steel producer, the largest retailing concern, Conasupo, is owned by the government and serves as a constant reminder that this regime is active both in public services and in the marketplace. The government nationalized the banks in 1982 during the difficult financial crisis and corruption scandals of that year which touched President José López Portillo, who now lives in elegant exile, and sent the director of Petroleos Mexicanos and other officials in that enterprise to prison.

The modern political success of the Mexican regime is based on a combination of four factors: (1) broad-based public political participation that provides social control over previously resistant elites and revolutionary working-class groups through parastate organizations; (2) continued economic growth through foreign investment and government cooperation with investors; (3) a unifying cross-class nationalistic revolutionary ideology that argues for the interests of the pequeña burguesía, the elite entrepreneurial classes, and the state bureaucracy; and (4) the illusion of hope and opportunity offered by economic growth to the masses of unemployed workers and landless peasants, of which only a small percentage can be accommodated.

By almost any humane measure, Mexico in 1987 constitutes an economic and social disaster characterized by massive unemployment and deficits in foreign exchange, a steadily weakening peso, sustained high rates of inflation, and declining real wages. Officially reported indebtedness has reached $111 billion. Unofficially, financial experts concede another $30 billion in uncounted private indebtedness. Payments on the interest alone exceed all of the nation's export and foreign exchange earnings. The international lenders that dominate Mexico blame Mexican "corruption" for the nation's inability to pay. But they demand payments and "austerity programs" (which mean the removal of government subsidies on staples such as meat, eggs, corn, and beans) from a nation where an estimated 70 percent of the children suffer from malnutrition. "Corruption" has many faces. Because of population growth and the maldistribution of resources, more people are illiterate and suffering from malnutrition than before the revolution.

The government has now entered the General Agreement on Tariffs and Trade (GATT), which will allow drastically lower duties on imports and exports. After over sixty years of trying to create a vital domestically controlled industrial plant, the government has been forced to recognize that the economy is stalled because of the oil and financial crisis. Through entry into GATT it has placed the heaviest burden upon the pequeña burguesía and working classes in accordance with the directives of the international banking consortiums, including the International Monetary Fund, and old adversaries Citibank, Morgan, and Chase.

The lack of public services in the midst of a population explosion has delivered a devastating blow to the quality of life experienced by the great majority. Untreated sewage, polluted drinking water and food, and flies cause approximately 90 percent of the nation's incidence of communicable sickness. The fecal bacteria from untreated waste saturate the nation's air, water, and food, causing inestimable illnesses, decreased productivity, and misery. The World Health Organization estimates that 107,000 Mexican children died in 1983 from only three of the diseases for which immunization is available: neonatal tetanus, 31,000; measles, 57,000; and whooping cough, 19,000.[1]

The currency devaluations of the 1980s are virtually identical in their causes and are more extreme in their effects than the 50 percent reduction in the value of the peso in 1905. In 1986 over 80 percent of Mexico's wage earners gain less than $9 per day. Slowed foreign investments, a deteriorating foreign exchange, government indebtedness, and fiscal crisis provoked the devaluations of 1905 and the 1980s.

The consequences of the nation's social and economic crisis will take several years to become clear, but they will be extreme and unprecedented since 1920. Despite the broad-based nature of the regime, it is difficult to imagine the delay of those consequences by traditional government maneuvers for more than a decade. No political system, not even the sophisticated PRI, can withstand the setbacks of recent years without severe repercussions.

THE UNRESOLVED CONTRADICTIONS

And the raven, never flitting, still is sitting, *still* is sitting
On the pallid bust of Pallas just above my chamber door;
And his eyes have all the seeming of a demon that is dreaming,
And the lamp-light o'er him streaming throws his shadow on the floor;

Notes

Introduction

1. *Peasants* are defined for the purposes of this study as rural households that, with an orientation toward self-sufficiency, have the power to determine the product of a relatively small parcel of land. *Campesino* is a more general term applied in Mexico to both agrarian workers and peasants. The *pequeña burguesía* included ranchero owners of commercially oriented middle-sized ranching and farming properties and those figures familiar to the industrialized West, the small entrepreneurs, shopkeepers, bookkeepers, technicians, and educators of the cities and towns, and the middle-level administrators of large companies and the government. The regional or provincial elites with whom we are concerned were those people whose economic power and high social standing caused them to aspire to rule in the periphery, especially in states geographically far removed from the center of the nation where they were accustomed through long practice to semiautonomous power.

2. A ranchería is a small rural residential concentration of agricultural workers, usually located on an estate and lacking the juridical rights to land, water, self-support, and de jure autonomous government granted to pueblos, towns, and villas.

One: The Peasantry

1. For the survival of Indian customs and society in the colonial era, see Robert Wasserstrom, *Class and Society in Central Chiapas* (Berkeley, Los Angeles, London: University of California Press, 1983); Gonzalo Aguirre Beltrán, *Regiones de refugio* (Mexico City: Instituto Indigenista Interamericano, 1967); Murdo J. McLeod and Robert Wasserstrom, eds., *Spaniards and Indians in Southeastern Mesoamerica: Essays on the History of Ethnic Relations* (Lincoln: University of Nebraska Press, 1983); and Grant D. Jones, ed., *Anthropology and History in Yucatán* (Austin: University of Texas Press, 1977).

2. For discussion of this phenomenon in the south, see John Mason Hart, "The 1840s Southwestern Peasants War," in Friedrich Katz, ed., *Riot, Rebellion, and*

Revolution: Rural Social Conflict in Mexico (Princeton: Princeton University Press, forthcoming); and John Tutino, "Indian Rebellion at the Isthmus of Tehuantepec: A Socio-Historical Perspective," *Actes du XLIIe International Congress des Americanistes,* II (Paris, 1976): 198–214.

3. See the Sala Estatal, Archivo Historico de la Secretaría de Reforma Agraria, Oaxaca: Ixtaltepec, municipio same, communal, 276.1/776, 5 bundles; Almoloya, municipio same, communal, 276.1/298, 5 bundles; Ixtepec, municipio same, communal, 276.1/298 (723.7), 2 bundles; Santiago Ixtaltepec, Municipio Ixtaltepec, communal, 276.1/215, 1 bundle; Santo Domingo Tomaltepec, communal and ejidal, 276.1/216, 8 bundles; and San Pedro Pochuitla, Municipio Putla de Guerrero, communal, 276.1/2398, 9 bundles. See also Tutino, "Indian Rebellion."

4. Ibid.

5. Ibid.; also see Hart, "Southwestern Peasants War."

6. For Yaqui social life and unrest caused in part by Jesuit abuses, see Evelyn Hu-DeHart, "Peasant Rebellion in the Northwest: The Yaqui Indians of Sonora, 1740–1976," in Katz, *Riot, Rebellion, and Revolution;* and idem, *The Yaquis: A Cultural History* (Tucson: University of Arizona Press, 1980).

7. Evelyn Hu-DeHart, *Missions, Mines and Indians: The History of Spanish Contact with the Yaqui Nation of Northwestern New Spain, 1533–1820* (Tucson: University of Arizona Press, 1983).

8. See Beltrán, *Regiones de refugio;* Magnus Morner, ed., *The Expulsion of the Jesuits from Latin America* (New York: Knopf, 1965); Robert Ricard, *The Spiritual Conquest of Mexico* (Berkeley and Los Angeles: University of California Press, 1967); and Nancy Farriss, *Crown and Clergy in Colonial Mexico* (London: University of London Press, 1968).

9. Colin M. Maclachlan, *Criminal Justice in Eighteenth Century Mexico: A Study of the Tribunal of the Acordada* (Berkeley, Los Angeles, London: University of California Press, 1974).

10. The Ramo de Infidencias, vol. I, Archivo General de La Nación (hereafter cited as AGN), contains valuable documents regarding the Izúcar uprising and even earlier *"sublevaciones"* at Tultepec and Tulancingo in 1771. See also José Antonio Calderon Quijano, *Los virreyes de Nueva España en el reinado de Carlos III,* vol. II (Seville: Escuela de Estudios Hispano-Americanos de Sevilla, 1968), pp. 163–175.

11. The Ramos de Tierras and Indios of the AGN and the Archivo Historico, Seis de Enero de 1915, de la Secretaría de Reforma Agraria (hereafter cited as AHSRA) contain countless examples of the gradual loss of Indian land and water claims despite many favorable court decisions. For an excellent discussion of the litigation process, see Cheryl Martin, "Crucible of Zapatismo: Hacienda Hospital in the Seventeenth Century," *The Americas* (July 1981): 31–44.

12. For the best explanation of the clergy in village life, see Jean Meyer, *La Cristiada,* 3 vols. (Mexico City: Siglo XXI, 1973).

13. The rise of lower-class rural unrest is reflected in the reports of pueblo and town homicides and rioting between 1790 and 1810 found in the Ramo Criminal, AGN. Reported murders increased from 139 during the decade of the 1790s to 285 between 1800 and 16 September 1810. Thirty-six homicides occurred in the first nine months of 1810, 20 percent more than the twelve-month total for 1809.

Between 1790 and 1810 the character of homicides and assaults also changed. Group assaults by Indios against men of property with "purses" resulting in the theft of money pouches and the victims' deaths became increasingly common. For more on rural violence in the colonial era, see William B. Taylor, *Drinking, Homicide and Rebellion in Colonial Mexican Villages* (Stanford: Stanford University Press, 1979). For an intensive analysis of millennial Indian revolts, see Wasserstrom, *Class and Society.*

14. This process will be examined in depth in Hart, *A Social History of the Mexican Peasant Wars, 1810–1910* (forthcoming). The bulk of the data is available in the Archivo Judicial del Tribunal Superior de Justicia del Distrito y Territorios Federales (hereafter cited as AJTS) and the AHSRA. The Ramos of Tierras, Indios, and Criminal of the AGN provide important background materials pertaining to the villages.

15. For a comprehensive study of the social causes of the Bajío revolt, see Tutino, "Agrarian Insurrection: The Hidalgo Revolt and the Origins of Agrarian Violence in Modern Mexico" (unpublished); and David Brading, *Haciendas and Ranchos in the Mexican Bajío, León 1700–1860* (Cambridge: Cambridge University Press, 1978).

16. For superb analyses of the independence struggle in Jalisco and Michoacán, see William B. Taylor, "Rural Unrest in Central Jalisco, 1790–1816," and Eric Van Young, "Moving Towards Revolt: Agrarian Origins of the Hidalgo Rebellion in the Guadalajara Region," in Katz, *Riot, Rebellion, and Revolution.*

17. Fanny Calderon de la Barca, *Life in Mexico: The Letters of Fanny Calderon de la Barca,* eds. Howard T. Fisher and Marion Hall Fisher (Garden City, N.Y.: Doubleday and Company, 1970), offers vivid commentaries in our best available report on countryside conditions in the aftermath of the widespread unrest and destruction that took place during the eleven-year struggle for independence.

18. The Liberal and Conservative movements and ideology have been examined by a number of scholars. See Jesús Reyes Heroles, *El Liberalismo Mexicano,* 3 vol. (Mexico City: Fondo de Cultura Económica, 1974); Charles A. Hale, *Mexican Liberalism in the Age of Mora, 1821–1853* (New Haven: Yale University Press, 1968); and John S. Brushwood, *Mexico in Its Novel: A Nation's Search for Identity* (Austin: University of Texas Press, 1966). See also Romeo Flores Caballero, *Counterrevolution: The Role of the Spaniards in the Independence of Mexico* (Lincoln: University of Nebraska Press, 1974).

19. See Katz, *Riot, Rebellion, and Revolution;* Leticia Reina, *Las luchas populares en México en el siglo XIX* (Mexico City: Casa Chata, 1983); and idem, *Las rebeliones campesinas en México (1819–1906)* (Mexico City: Siglo XXI, 1980).

20. See Hart, "Southwestern Peasants War," and Reina, *Las luchas populares,* pp. 13–60.

21. Volumes 1212–1213, Ramo de Tierras, AGN; and San Marcos, Municipio San Marcos, ejidal, 23:1226 (723.6), 4 bundles; San Juan Colotlipa, Municipio Quechultenango, ejidal, 25:1206 (723.6), 8 bundles; Nazintla, Municipio Quechultenango, communal, 276.1/35 (723.6), 7 bundles; Tecoanapa, municipio same, ejidal, 23:13772 (723.6), 3 bundles; and Lamatzintla, Municipio Chilapa, ejidal, 23:10228 (723.6), 6 bundles; ASHRA. See also *Noticias Históricas sobre los Pueblos de Ajuchitán, Coyuca, Cutzmala, Coahuayutla, Petatlán, Tecpán, y Atoyac*

(Mexico City: ed. Vargas Rea, 1947), pp. 1–34; Miguel Domínguez, *La erección del estado de Guerrero, antecedentes históricos* (Mexico City, 1949), pp. 20–47. For background on Tehuantepec see Ixtaltepec, municipio same, communal, 276.1/776, 5 bundles; Ixtepec, municipio same, communal, 276.1/298 (723.7), 2 bundles; Santiago Ixtaltepec, Municipio Ixtaltepec, communal 276.1/215, 1 bundle; Santo Domingo Tomaltepec, Municipio Tomaltepec, communal and ejidal, 276.1/216, 8 bundles; Almoloya, Municipio El Barrio de la Soledad, communal, 276.1/1959, 2 bundles; Santo Domingo Chihuitan, municipio same, communal, 276.1/2328, 9 bundles; ASHRA—Oaxaca, Oaxaca. See also Tutino, "Indian Rebellion," pp. 198–214.

22. Domínguez, *La Erección del estado,* pp. 20–47; *Noticias históricas sobre los Pueblos,* pp. 1–34; and Luis Guevara Ramírez, *Síntesis historicas del estado de Guerrero* (Colección de Estudios Históricos Guerrerenses, 1959), pp. 70–113.

23. Interview Hart with Ignacio Mendoza, Comisario y Presidente de varios trabajos en el pueblo, Ayahualulco, Guerrero, 2 August 1980. Ayahualulco, Municipio Chilapa, ejidal, 21:702 (723.6), 6 bundles; Nazintla, Municipio Quechultenango, communal, 276.1/35 (723.6); San Juan Colotlipa, Municipio Quechultenango, ejidal, 25:1206 (723.6), 6 bundles; and Lamatzintla, Municipio Chilapa, ejidal, 23:10228 (723.6), 6 bundles; ASHRA. José María Tornel, Secretario de Guerra y Marina, *Memoria del Ministerio,* Mexico, 11 de Enero de 1844, pp. 54–55; Domínguez, *Erección del estado,* pp. 22–30, 47; and Guevara Ramírez, *Síntesis históricas del estado,* pp. 70–113.

24. Tornel, *Memoria,* pp. 56–59; *Documentos históricos de Guerrero,* vol. 7: 295; Juzgado de Letras de Tlapa, 24 April 1843, packet 3, Archivo Judicial de Puebla, cited in Reina Cruz Valdés, "Levantamientos Populares en Tlapa en los años 1842–1849" (unpublished). Interview Hart with Eric M. A. Jasso Herrera, Consejero Agrario, Secretaría de Reforma Agraria, Oaxaca, 7–8 August 1980; and interview Hart with Mendoza, Ayahualulco, 2 August 1980. San Bartolome Atlacholoya, fojas 147–149, Tomo 4, Junta Protectora de las Clases Menesterosas, AGN. Copantoyac, municipio same, communal, 276.1/2346, 1 bundle; Tlapa, municipio same, ejidal, 23:18593 (723.6), 4 bundles; Tlaxiaco, municipio same, communal, 276.1/1149 (723.7), 11 bundles; San Agustín Tlacotepec (for San Bartolo, San Mateo Penasco, and other centers of unrest), municipio same, communal, 276.1/544 (723.7), 14 bundles; Santiago Ixtaltepec, Municipio Ixtaltepec, communal, 276.1/215, 1 bundle; Ixtaltepec, municipio same, communal, 276.1/776, 5 bundles; and Almoloya, Municipio El Barrio de la Soledad, communal, 276.1/1959, 2 bundles; AHSRA. For further sources on the course of campesino rebellion in the 1830s and 1840s, see Hart, "Southwestern Peasants War."

25. For the background of and disputes surrounding the 1849 uprisings, see Acambay, municipio same, ejidal, 23:2502 (725.2), 5 bundles; AHSRA. For background to the revolt at Xico, Coatepec, Guadalupe Hidalgo, Hueypostla Tianguistengo, Las Cuevas, Santa María Ajoloapan, Amecameca, and San Juan Tlatilco in the eastern part of the central valley of Mexico, San Lucas Nextitelco near Cholula in Puebla, and Tuitepec, San Agustín Tetlama, Tecaxeque, and Huasulco in Morelos, see Expedientes 19–37, Legajo 1786, Ramo de Gobernación, Tranquilidad Pública, AGN. These were centers of unrest and government concern between 1868 and 1872. For the land grants and petitions of the rural settlements

in the zone of revolt, see the Junta Protectora de las Clases Menesterosas, AGN; and the Ramos of Terrenos, Pueblos, and Haciendas, AJTS. The Junta Protectora archive contains numerous examples of village support for Maximilian; see also Charles Berry, *The Reform in Oaxaca, 1856–76* (Lincoln: University of Nebraska Press, 1981), pp. 94–96.

26. For the economic causes of the revolt see Tlalmanalco-Tepetlixpa versus the possessor of the Rancho del Jardín, and the petition of San Vicente Chicoloapan in 1854, Ramo de Terrenos, AJTS. For a full discussion of the political background of this revolt, see Hart, *Los anarquistas Mexicanos, 1860–1900* (Mexico City: SepSetentas, 1974), pp. 49–71. Tutino, "Agrarian Transformation and Peasant Rebellion in Nineteenth-Century Mexico: Chalco, 1840–1870," in Katz, *Riot, Rebellion, and Revolution,* offers a superb analysis of long-term trends in the area based on the Mariano Riva Palacio papers in the Nettie Lee Benson Latin American Collection, University of Texas, Austin (hereafter cited as BLAC). For countless episodes of water and land rights losses by the pueblos in the area to metropolitan land speculators, see the Ramos of Pueblos, Haciendas, Potreros, and Aguas of the AJTS.

27. For military and political strategy against the revolt, see Legajo 1546, Ramo de Gobernación, Tranquilidad Pública, 1868, AGN. For military summaries of the places and times of revolt, see Reina, *Las rebeliones campesinas,* pp. 64–82 and 132–135; and idem, *Las luchas populares,* pp. 119–121.

28. Sale of the hacienda La Tenería, Jurisdicción Tenancingo, by the government to José Iwes Limantour in 1861, Ramo of Haciendas "T," AJTS; San Bartolo, 1869, San Juan Juxtepec contra la hacienda de Doncuaz, 1860, and Lic. Mariano Parres contra los naturales de San Francisco Xocotitlan de las Salinas, 1869, Ramo Pueblos, AJTS; and San Juan Huisnahuac, Departmento del Valle, 1864, Ramo Terrenos, AJTS.

For socioeconomic data regarding the pueblos in these revolts, the following are useful: Coahuixtla, Morelos, and Hacienda de Bocas, Ramo of Haciendas "T," AJTS. Nochistlán, Municipio same, Zacatecas, ejidal, 23:5768 (724.2), 3 bundles; San Miguel Acambay, Municipio Acambay, Mexico, ejidal, 23:2502 (725.2), 5 bundles; Amealco, Municipio same, Querétaro, ejidal, 23:4134 (724.6), 3 bundles; San Juan Dehedó, Municipio Amealco, Querétaro, ejidal, 23:4128 (724.6), 6 bundles; San Martín, Municipio Río Verde, San Luis Potosí, 23:4349 (724.3), 3 bundles; Tizayuca, Municipio same, Hidalgo, ejidal, 23:1588 (724.7), 4 bundles; Tultepec, Municipio same, Mexico, ejidal, 23:2148, 11 bundles, and 21:5148, 2 bundles; Mixquiahuala, Municipio same, Hidalgo, ejidal, 25:1503, 12 bundles; and Tarejo, Municipio Zacapu, Michoacán, ejidal, 25:2740 (723.5), 8 bundles; AHSRA. For reports on the revolts see Antonio Díaz Soto y Gama, *La revolución agraria del sur y Emiliano Zapata su caudillo* (Mexico City, 1961), pp. 27–32; Reina, *Las luchas populares,* pp. 119–126; idem, *Las rebeliones campesinas,* pp. 132–135; and Miguel Mejía Fernández, *Política agraria en México en el siglo XIX* (Mexico City: Siglo XXI, 1979), pp. 88–94.

29. See Hart, *Anarchism and the Mexican Working Class, 1860–1931* (Austin: University of Texas Press, 1978), pp. 69–78.

30. Ibid.; also see "Los socialistas," *La Voz de Mexico,* 24 June 1879; and Reina, *Las rebeliones campesinas,* pp. 291–321.

31. Paul Vanderwood, *Los rurales mexicanos* (Mexico City: Fondo de Cultura Económica, 1982), pp. 49–50.

32. Hart, *Anarchism,* pp. 69–70.

33. John H. Coatsworth, "Railroads and the Concentration of Land Ownership in the Early Porfiriato," *Hispanic American Historical Review* 54 (February 1974): 48–71. The records of the AJTS and AHSRA extensively document the land enclosure process and resulting zones of unrest extending north from Mexico City, across the Mezquital, San Luis Potosí, the Huasteca, and Tamaulipas.

34. Anenecuilco, Municipio Ayala, Morelos, ejidal, 25:2961 (724.10), 9 bundles; and Ayala, municipio same, ejidal, 23:2960 (724.10), 10 bundles; AHSRA.

35. For Francisco Franco's letter to President Cárdenas, see Anenecuilco, Municipio Ayala, ejidal, 25:2961 (724.10), 3 bundles; AHSRA. John Womack, *Zapata and the Mexican Revolution* (New York: Vintage, 1970) remains the best treatment of the background to the Zapatista revolt.

36. The records of Tomochic and neighboring pueblos were stored in the now dispersed AHSRA. The records of the principal landholder at Tomochic-Cusihuiriachic repose in Box 26, "Cargill Lumber Company," Archive of the Agrarian Claims Commission (U.S. Section), Washington National Records Center, Suitland, Maryland (hereafter cited as WNRC).

37. For a description of the fighting and the millennarian aspect of the Indo-peasant unrest that swept the Sierra Madre Occidental and Mexican northwest, see Heriberto Frías, *Tomochic* (Mexico City: Valadés y Cía., 1906).

38. Hacienda de Corralitos Archive, Papers of Jack Wentworth Peirce, Topsfield, Massachusetts (private collection); and interviews: Hart with Billy Marshall III, owner of the Hacienda de Corralitos, Corralitos, Chihuahua, 23 February 1984; and Oliver Scott Bluth, local historian, Casas Grandes Viejo, Chihuahua, 23 February 1984.

39. Interviews, Hart with Franz Schryer, Houston, Texas, 16 April 1984, and Leticia Reina, Austin, Texas, 17 July 1984.

40. Ibid. For a general description of the tropical export agricultural complex around Papantla, see Luis Nicolau D'Olwer et al., *El Porfiriato, la vida económica,* in Daniel Cosio Villegas, ed., *Historia moderna de México* (Mexico City: Editorial Hermes, 1965), pp. 104–106. For an excellent analysis of the Indian-Mexican social nexus in Hidalgo and the Huasteca, see Schryer, "Ethnicity and Political Conflict in Northern Hidalgo" (Agrarian Conflict in a Nahuatl Region), Working Paper No. 5 (Ontario: Centre for Research on Latin America and the Caribbean, York University, 1983), 56 pages.

41. Folders 13, 20, and 31, Box 106, Senator Albert Bacon Fall Papers, The Huntington Library, San Marino, California.

42. "Testimony of Peter Kritzberger," March 1920, Document 285, vol. 2, *Fall Committee Reports, Investigation of Mexican Affairs: Preliminary Reports and Surveys,* 66th Cong., 2d sess. (Washington, D.C.: Government Printing Office, 1921), pp. 1978–1979.

43. See Leafar Agetro [pseud. Rafael C. Ortega], *Las luchas proletarias en Veracruz: Historia y autocrítica* (Jalapa: Editorial "Barricada," 1942); and James Cockcroft, *Intellectual Precursors of the Mexican Revolution* (Austin: University of Texas

Press, 1968), pp. 124 and 146–149. The extensive American holdings at Acayucan are discussed as part of a larger context in chapters 6 and 9.

44. The peasant occupation and Guerrero-led PLM invasions of the estate are described in detail by the hacienda foreman in a lengthy letter to the management of the company. See George A. Laird, San Pedro, Chihuahua, to Edwin D. Morgan, New York City, 28 December 1910 (typecopy, 14 pages), Hacienda de Corralitos Archive. The Corralitos owners included many important American capitalists. Among them were Levi P. Morton, Edward Shearson, Charles A. Dana, Thomas Wentworth Peirce, Jr., and Morgan.

45. The compilation of acreage is derived from archival sources in Mexico City, Casas Grandes, Ciudad Victoria, Texas, California, Massachusetts, New Orleans, Washington D.C., and Suitland, Maryland. Extensive records of most American companies and the others with large holdings in Mexico are available in Records Group 76, Archives of the Special Claims Commission, the Mixed Claims Commission, the Agrarian Claims Commission (U.S. Section), and American Mexican Claims Commission of the United States and Mexico (over 1850 feet), WNRC.

Two: The Industrial and Urban Workers

1. See Chester Lyle Guthrie, "Riots in Seventeenth-Century Mexico City: A Study of Social and Economic Conditions," in Adele Ogden and Engel Sluiter, eds., *Greater America: Essays in Honor of Herbert Eugene Bolton* (Berkeley and Los Angeles: University of California Press, 1945), pp. 243–254.

2. Ibid.; and Noel Stowe, "The Tumulto of 1629: Turmoil at Mexico City" (Ph.D. diss., University of Southern California, 1970), pp. 58, 382–383.

3. On the nature of insurrectionist ideology and social composition, see Gastón García Cantú, *Utopías Mexicanas* (Mexico City: Fondo de Cultura Económica, 1978), pp. 41–49; Hugh Hamill, *The Hidalgo Revolt: Prelude to Mexican Independence* (Gainesville: University of Florida Press, 1966); and Tutino, "Agrarian Insurrection," chaps. 4, 5, 7, 8, and 9.

4. For the limits of artisan leadership in labor movements, see Shulamit Volkov, *The Rise of Popular Anti-Modernism in Germany: The Urban Master Artisans* (Princeton: Princeton University Press, 1978), 399 pages; Zachary Lockman, "Class and Nation: The Emergence of the Egyptian Workers' Movement" (Ph.D. diss., Harvard University, 1983), chaps. 1 and 2; Philip S. Foner, *History of the Labor Movement in the United States* (New York: International Publishers, 1955) 2:75–92, 132–144, and 157–170; and Gerald Grob, *Workers and Utopia: A Study of Ideological Conflicts in the American Labor Movement 1865–1900* (Chicago: Quadrangle, 1969).

5. For the effects of artisan and working-class proletarianization on working-class organizations, see Michael Mann, *Consciousness and Action among the Western Working Class* (London and New York: Macmillan, 1973); Robert Michaels, *Political Parties* (New York: Free Press, 1962); Edward Shorter and Charles Tilly, *Strikes in France, 1830–1968* (London and New York: Cambridge University Press, 1974), pp. 42–88; George F. E. Rudé, *Ideology and Popular Protest* (New York: Pantheon, 1980); Bernard Moss, *The Origins of the French Labor Movement* (Berke-

ley, Los Angeles, London: University of California Press, 1976); Albert Soboul, *The Sans Culottes: The Popular Movement and Revolutionary Government, 1793–1794,* trans. Remy Inglis Hall (New York: Doubleday/Anchor, 1972); and Louise Tilly, "Paths of Proletarianization: Organization of Production, Sexual Division of Labor, and Women's Collective Action," *Signs* 7, no. 2 (Winter 1981): 400–418.

6. Hart, *Anarchism,* pp. 11, 17, 21, 47–48, 86–87, and 108–114; and Manuel Díaz Ramírez, *Apuntes históricos del movimiento obrero y campesino de México, 1844–1880* (Mexico City: Fondo de Cultura Popular, 1938), pp. 32–33. For artisan ideology and activist biographies, see García Cantú, *El socialismo en México siglo XIX* (Mexico City: Ediciones Era, 1969), pt. 3, Documentos, and pt. 4, Biografías, pp. 265–426.

For artisan data see Fernando Rosenzweig, "El desarollo económico de México de 1877 a 1911," *Trimestre Económico* 37 (Julio-Septiembre 1965): 444. For the most encompassing description of the growth of the textile factory system and its attendant problems, see Dawn Keremitsis, *La industria textil Mexicana en el siglo XIX* (Mexico City: SepSetentas, 1973), p. 247.

7. Hart, *Anarchism,* pp. 30–31, 44–49; and *Diario del Imperio,* 19 June 1865.

8. Hart, *Anarchism,* pp. 46–50; Díaz Ramírez, *Apuntes históricos,* pp. 33–38; and *El Socialista,* 9 July, 15 October, and 12 November 1871.

9. For the struggle for independent unions, see Hart, *Anarchism,* pp. 48–54; and idem, "Los obreros y el estado 1860–1931," *Nexos* 37 (Enero 1981): 21–27.

10. Cuauhtemoc Camarena Ocampo, "Las luchas de los trabajadores textiles: 1850–1907," in Reina, *Las luchas populares,* pp. 217–228; Jorge Basurto, *El proletariado industrial en México (1850–1930)* (Mexico City: Instituto de Investigaciones Sociales, Universidad Nacional Autonoma de México, 1975), pp. 37 and 97; and Jorge Villaseñor Cornejo, "Origines del movimiento obrero Mexicano, 1870–1880" (thesis, 1980), 39–57.

11. José C. Valades, "El 50 aniversario del Primer Congreso Obrero en América," *La Protesta* (Buenos Aires), April 1926. For examples of the newspaper articles, see *El Socialista* and *El Hijo del Trabajo* (Mexico City).

12. "Manifiesto," *El Socialista,* 23 April 1876.

13. The best description of the Mexican elements in the revolution of Tuxtepec is Laurens Ballard Perry, *Juárez and Díaz: Machine Politics in Mexico,* in *The Origins of Modern Mexico* (DeKalb: Northern Illinois University Press, 1978), 451 pages. For Negrete see Hart, "Miguel Negrete: La epopeya de un revolucionario," *Historia Mexicana* 24, no. 1 (Julio-Septiembre 1974): 70–93.

14. See José María González, "La cuestion indigeña (Hacienda de Bocas)," a series of articles published in *El Hijo del Trabajo* in 1877 and 1878. For an extended discussion of the involvement of urban radicals in the agrarian unrest of 1878–1883, see Hart, *Anarchism,* pp. 60–73.

15. *El Hijo del Trabajo,* 6 and 13 April 1879.

16. *El Socialista,* 26 September 1882.

17. *El Socialista* 30 June 1881, 7 December 1884, and 28 June 1885.

18. Camarena Ocampo, "Trabajadores textiles," pp. 252–255.

19. Ibid., pp. 262–277; Moisés González Navarro, *Las huelgas textiles en el*

porfiriato (Puebla: Editorial José Cajica, 1971), pp. 36–40; and David Walker, "Porfirian Labor Politics: Working-Class Organizations in Mexico City and Porfirio Díaz, 1876–1902," *The Americas* 37, no. 3 (January 1981): 257–290.

20. By 1903 Gates and his associates held at least seven directorships, which they sold to the Amalgamated Copper Company interests actively headed by John D. Ryan and Thomas F. Cole. The funding made available by the Gates-Hawley group and then the Rockefellers' Anaconda Company enabled Greene to run the Cananea site actively until 1907, when Ryan and Cole removed him. See Susan Friesell, "John W. Gates: A Study of Railroad and Industrial Consolidation 1900–1911" (University of Houston, 1984, unpublished); the *Commercial and Financial Chronicle,* 3 October 1903, p. 826; 31 October 1903, p. 1535; 30 January 1904, p. 345; 13 February 1904, p. 705; 2 April 1904, p. 1277; 16 April 1904, p. 1448; and 7 May 1904, p. 1785; and *The Wall Street Journal,* 21 February, 27 July, 8 August, 15 August, and 19 August, 1903. The quote is from Friesell. The Anaconda Company archive at Duluth, Minnesota, contains telegraph communications relaying instructions to Greene from Ryan antedating the 1906 strike-uprising by the Mexican workers, who were challenging not merely a flamboyant Arizona character but the most powerful consortium of capitalists in America.

21. For an excellent summation of events at Cananea, see W. Dirk Raat, *Revoltosos, Mexico's Rebels in the United States, 1913–1923* (College Station: Texas A&M University Press, 1981), pp. 80–91. For data on Cananea's dependence on trade with Arizona, see the *Daily Consular and Trade Reports,* Bureau of Manufactures, Department of Commerce and Labor, 27 October 1910, pp. 323–324; and Hu-DeHart, "Indians and Immigrants: Rebellion and Assimilation in Sonora" (Paper delivered at the annual meeting of the American Historical Association, Washington, D.C., 29 December 1982).

22. For the most detailed treatments among the many sources on Río Blanco, see Luis Araiza, *Historia del Movimiento Obrero Mexicano,* Tomo II (Mexico City, 1964–1966), pp. 99–117; and González Navarro, "La huelga de Río Blanco," *Historia Mexicana* 6 (April-June 1957):510–533.

23. For an overview of the Cananea-Río Blanco era and its aftermath, see Rodney D. Anderson, *Outcasts in Their Own Land: Mexican Industrial Workers, 1906–1911* (DeKalb: Northern Illinois University Press, 1976); González Navarro, "Las huelgas textiles en el Porfiriato," *Historia Mexicana* 6 (October-December 1956):201–216; idem, *Las huelgas textiles en el Porfiriato,* p. 409; Lawrence J. Rohlfes, "The Porfirian Church and the Social Question: *Rerum Novarum* and Mexico" (Paper delivered to the Southwest Social Science Association, San Antonio, Texas, March 1982); and Camarena Ocampo, "Trabajadores textiles," pp. 292–297. For the strikes at La Colmena, Hercules, and so on, see González Navarro, *Las huelgas textiles,* pp. 29–47.

24. Henry Lane Wilson to Philander Knox, 24 May 1911, State Department File 812:00, Mexican Despatches, VII (File Number 812:00/1943), quoted in Jules Davids, *American Political and Economic Penetration of Mexico, 1877–1920* (New York: Arno Press, 1976), pp. 267–269.

Three: The Pequeña Burguesía and Provincial Elites

1. For the Crown's tactics see John Leddy Phelan, "Authority and Flexibility in the Spanish Imperial Bureaucracy," *Administrative Science Quarterly* 5 (June 1960):47–65, an essay "in terms of a thought-provoking hypothesis recently advanced by Andrew [sic] Gunder Frank." Phelan's study is based on the seminal work by André Gunder Frank, "Goal Ambiguity and Conflicting Standards: An Approach to the Study of Organization," *Human Organization* (Published by the Society for Applied Anthropology) 17 (Winter 1958–1959):8–13. See also Gunder Frank, "Growth and Productivity in Ukranian Agriculture and Industry from 1928–1955" (Ph.D. diss., University of Chicago, 1958); Phelan, *The Kingdom of Quito in the Seventeenth Century: Bureaucratic Politics and the Spanish Empire* (Madison: University of Wisconsin Press, 1967), 432 pages; idem, *The People and the King: The Comunero Revolution in Colombia, 1781* (Madison: University of Wisconsin Press, 1977), 309 pages; idem, "The Rise and Fall of the Creoles in the Audiencia of New Granada 1700–1781," *Boletín de Historia y Antiguidades* (Bogotá) 59, nos. 697/698 (1972):597–618; idem, "Similarities and Contrasts of the Comuneros in New Granada and the Revolution of Independence," *Boletín de Historia y Antiguidades* 63, no. 714 (1976):329–351; and Colin M. Maclachlan, *Spain's Empire in America: The Effect of Ideas on Social and Political Change* (Berkeley, Los Angeles, London: University of California Press, forthcoming).

2. Tutino, "Agrarian Insurrection," offers an extended analysis of the social crisis in the Bajío; see also Brading, *Haciendas and Ranchos.* For data on alcoholism and crime, see Taylor, *Drinking, Homicide and Rebellion;* and the Ramo Criminal, AGN.

3. See Hamill, *The Hidalgo Revolt,* for details of the revolt. Tutino, "Agrarian Insurrection," treats the socioeconomic crisis and the condition of local elites.

4. For treatment of the rural crisis on the western periphery of the Bajío, see William B. Taylor, "Rural Unrest in Central Jalisco" and Van Young, "Moving Towards Revolt."

5. For analysis of the Conservatives and Liberals at Independence, see Lucas Alaman, *Historia de Méjico desde los primeros movimientos que preparon su independencia en el año de 1808, hasta la época presente,* 5 vol. (Mexico City, 1849–1852); Reyes Heroles, *El liberalismo mexicano;* José María Tornel y Mendivil, *Breve reseña histórica de los acontecimientos más notables de la nación Mexicana desde el año de 1821 hasta nuestras días* (Mexico City, 1852); Hale, *Mexican Liberalism;* and José María Luis Mora, *Obras Sueltas,* vol. 1, CCLXXIII (Paris, 1837).

6. Reyes Heroles, *El liberalismo mexicano,* II:222.

7. Ibid., p. 233.

8. For an analysis of metropolitan-peripheral elite crisis, see Hart, "Southwestern Peasants War." The late nineteenth-century rivalries are treated by Mark Wasserman, "Oligarquía é intereses extranjeros en Chihuahua durante el Porfiriato," *Historia Mexicana* 22, no. 3 (Enero-Marzo 1973):279–319; and idem, "Chihuahua: Family Power, Foreign Enterprise, and National Control," in Thomas Benjamin and William McNellie, eds., *Other Mexicos: Essays on Regional Mexican History, 1876–1911* (Albuquerque: University of New Mexico Press, 1984), pp. 33–54; Frans J. Schryer, "A Ranchero Economy in Northwestern Hidalgo, 1880–

1920," *Hispanic American Historical Review* 59 (August 1979):418–443; William Stanley Langston, "Coahuila: Centralization against State Autonomy," in Benjamin and McNellie, eds., *Other Mexicos,* pp. 55–76; David LaFrance, "Puebla: Breakdown of the Old Order," in Benjamin and McNellie, eds., *Other Mexicos,* pp. 77–118; Dudley Ankerson, "Saurnino Cedillo: A Traditional Caudillo in San Luis Potosí, 1890–1938," in Brading, eds., *Caudillo and Peasant,* pp. 140–168; and Ian Jacobs, *Ranchero Revolt: The Mexican Revolution in Guerrero* (Austin: University of Texas Press, 1982), pp. 3–77; Romana Falcon, "Los orígines populares de la Revolución de 1910? El Caso de San Luis Potosí," *Historia Mexicana* 29, no. 2 (Octubre-Diciembre 1979):197–240; Hart, "Miguel Negrete"; Hu-DeHart, "Development and Rural Rebellion: Pacification of the Yaquis in the Late Porfiriato," *Hispanic American Historical Review* 54, no. 1 (February 1974):72–93; and Perry, *Juárez and Díaz.*

9. Domínguez, *La erección del estado de Guerrero,* pp. 20–47; *Notícias históricas sobre los Pueblos,* pp. 1–34; Guevara Ramírez, *Síntesis histórica del estado de Guerrero,* pp. 70–113; and Hart, "Southwestern Peasants War."

10. For details, see Hart, "Southwestern Peasants War."

11. Ibid. For the massive documentation regarding the San Marcos hacienda, see Tierras, vols. 1212–1213, AGN.

12. Richard Sinkin, "The Mexican Constitutional Congress, 1856–1857: A Statistical Analysis," *Hispanic American Historical Review* 53 (1973):1–26.

13. The archive of the Secretaría de Transportes y Comunicaciones, Mexico City, contains detailed and indexed records of the imperial government's effort to develop the nation's economic infrastructure. These materials include survey reports on the resources and economic potential of various regions; great estate inventories and descriptions; analyses of the population's skills; geographic route feasibility studies for telegraph, road, and rail systems; and recommendations for governmental reorganization and efficiency.

14. For García de la Cadena, see the Archivo Histórico de la Defensa Nacional, Departmento de Archivo Correspondencia É Historia (Pensionistas), pp. 15–395 (hereafter cited as AHDN). For Negrete, see ibid., Expediente X/111.2/15–709; and Hart, "Miguel Negrete." For the fiscal crisis between the states and national government, see Francisco R. Calderon, *La república restaurada, la vida económica,* in Cosio Villegas, ed., *Historia moderna,* pp. 129, 166, and 295–306.

15. For an extended analysis of the Tuxtepec Revolution, see Perry, *Juárez and Díaz,* pp. 203–306.

16. See García de la Cadena, article in *El Socialista,* 2 June 1879; idem, *Discursos,* 16 September 1877, 16 September 1880, and 14 March 1881 (Mexico City: Impresa Irenio Ruiz, 1881); idem, "Memoria en que el ejecutivo del estado de Zacatecas da cuenta a la honorable legislatura de los actos de su administración" (Zacatecas, Mariano Mariscal y Juan Lujan Impresores, 8 September 1870); and Trinidad García de la Cadena, 15–395, AHDN. For the abolition of debt peonage in Zacatecas, see *El Siglo XIX,* 20 January 1868, 16 September 1871, and 18 September 1880, and for the quote on the liberation of the peons, see Calderon, *La república restaurada,* p. 60. For the Treviño land grant, see Edward Otho Cresaps Ord III et al., Claim 328, Box 11, the American Mexican Claims Commission, Approved Agrarian Claims, 1936–1947, WNRC. On Negrete, see Hart, "Miguel

Negrete"; Negrete, "Municipio Libre," *El Hijo del Trabajo,* 23 May 1880; Negrete, "El Plan de Loma Alta" (Loma Alta, Puebla, 26 June 1886), Expediente X/111.2/15–709, Tomo II, Documento 00342, AHDN; and Negrete to Porfirio Díaz, 30 January 1893, Expediente X/111.2/15–709, Tomo II, Documento 499.

17. See Negrete, article in *El Socialista,* 9 June 1879; idem, "Municipio Libre"; and Hart, "Miguel Negrete."

18. Notable events in the García de la Cadena presidential campaign were reported in *El Hijo del Trabajo,* 6 and 13 April 1879, 14 and 20 December 1879, and 16 May 1880; and in *El Socialista,* 18 December 1879.

19. For the González government, see Don M. Coerver, *The Porfirian Interregnum: The Presidency of Manual González of Mexico, 1880–1884* (Fort Worth: Texas Christian University Press, 1979), 321 pages.

20. On García de la Cadena's execution, see Pedro Hinojosa, reports of July, August, September, and October 1866, Expediente X/111.2/15–709, Tomo II, AHDN; Roman Suastegui, Zacatecas, to Pedro Hinojosa, Ministro de Guerra y Marina, 19 October 1886, Expediente 15–395, Documento 204; Hinojosa, directive to apprehend García de la Cadena, Mexico City, 20 October 1886, Expediente 15–395, Documento 214; General Carlos Lueso, Zacatecas, reports concerning the death of García de la Cadena, 25 October and 11 November 1886, Expediente 15–395, Documentos 218 and 220; and Hinojosa, report, Mexico City, 16 November 1886, Documento 219, AHDN. See also *El Siglo XIX,* 3 November 1866. For the 1892 Negrete-led uprising, see the report by Luis Carballada, 20 October 1886, Expediente X/112.2/15–709, Tomo II, Documentos 00359 and 00360, AHDN; and Hart, *Anarchism,* pp. 81–82.

21. The emergent revolutionary nationalism of Mexico has been measured among the nation's authors by Juan Gómez Quiñones, "Social Change and Intellectual Discontent: The Growth of Mexican Nationalism, 1890–1911" (Ph.D. diss., University of California, Los Angeles, 1972), 319 pages.

22. See Frías, *Tomochic,* especially the last two chapters, "Tenia que ser!" and "Chapultepec, Chapultepec!"; and Gómez Quiñones, "Intellectual Discontent," pp. 78–82.

23. Barrington Moore, Jr., *Social Origins of Dictatorship and Democracy: Lord and Peasant in the Making of the Modern World* (Boston: Beacon, 1966). For dissent in the press, see Gómez Quiñones, "Intellectual Discontent," pp. 155–193. For the arrests, see Cockcroft, *Intellectual Precursors,* pp. 81–82 and 102.

24. See Gómez Quiñones, *Sembradores: Ricardo Flores Magon y El Partido Liberal Mexicano: A Eulogy and Critique* (Los Angeles: Atzlan Publications, 1973), pp. 1–18; and Cockcroft, *Intellectual Precursors,* pp. 86–87.

25. "Manifiesto de la Convención Nacional Liberal," in Manuel González Ramírez, *Fuentes para la historia de la revolución mexicana,* Tomo IV, *Manifiestos políticos* (1892–1912) (Mexico City: Fondo de Cultura Económica, 1957), pp. 3–8; and Gómez Quiñones, "Intellectual Discontent," pp. 200–206. For the alcabalas, see Luis Nicolau D'Olwer et al., *El Porfiriato,* 1:314 and 2:913. For a defense of the abolition of the alcabalas and a denial that this move opened the Mexican economy to foreign penetration, see ibid., 1:314 and 2:904–918. See also Joaquin Ramírez Cabañas C., "Los Ingresos Federales de México durante los años de 1876 a 1930," *Revista de Hacienda* (Mexico City), no. 1 (Abril 1938):3–25.

26. "Manifesto de la Convención Nacional Liberal," in Manuel González Ramírez, *Fuentes para la historia,* pp. 3–8; and Gómez Quiñones, "Intellectual Discontent," pp. 200–206.

27. Gómez Quiñones, "Intellectual Discontent," pp. 82–85.

28. Cockcroft, *Intellectual Precursors,* pp. 56–116.

29. On the meeting between Díaz and Guggenheim, see Marvin Bernstein, *The Mexican Mining Industry, 1890–1950* (Albany: State University of New York Press, 1964), p. 51; and Fernando Rosenzweig et al., *El Porfiriato: la vida económica,* in Cosio Villegas, ed., *Historia moderna,* 1:283, 1:493–544, and 2:1092, 1155, 1184. See also Cockcroft, *Intellectual Precursors,* pp. 18–19, 22, 26–28. For the Guggenheim concessions in Nuevo León, see Permisos y Concessiones 1890–1912, Memorias del General Bernardo Reyes, MDR 1891–1899, Daniel Guggenheim for the "Compañia de la Gran Fundición Nacional Mexicana"; and MDR 1895–1942, Solomon Guggenheim; Archivo General del Estado, Nuevo León (hereafter cited as AGNL). For Maytorena, see Hector Aguilar Camin, *La revolución nomada: sonora y la revolución Mexicana* (Mexico City: Siglo XXI, 1977), pp. 19–163.

30. On PLM organizing in Puebla and the crisis of the ancien régime in that state, see David LaFrance, "A People Betrayed: Francisco I. Madero and the Mexican Revolution in Puebla" (Ph.D. diss., Indiana University, 1982), chaps. 1 and 2. On the PLM guerrilla movement, see Armando Bartra, "Ricardo Flores Magon en el cincuentenario de su muerte," *Supplemento de Siempre,* 6 December 1972.

31. See Gómez Quiñones, *Sembradores,* pp. 1–18; and Cockcroft, *Intellectual Precursors,* pp. 72, 80, 86–87.

32. Cockcroft, *Intellectual Precursors,* p. 102.

33. Ibid., pp. 104–112.

34. Gómez Quiñones, "Intellectual Discontent," pp. 85–87.

35. See González Navarro, *Las huelgas textiles,* p. 409; Hart, *Anarchism,* pp. 90–99; and Camarena Ocampo, "La luchas de los trabajadores," pp. 299, 301; Teresa Morales Lersch, "Las luchas de los trabajadores mineros: 1825–1907," pp. 358–361; and Marcelo Abramo Lauff, "Las luchas de los trabajadores ferrovarios: 1870–1908," pp. 415–418 in Reina, ed., *Las luchas populares.*

36. Bartra, "Ricardo Flores Magon," *Supplemento de Siempre,* 6 December 1972.

37. Cockcroft, *Intellectual Precursors,* pp. 154–155.

38. Gómez Quiñones, "Intellectual Discontent," pp. 88–92.

39. For the most comprehensive list of the Madero family's holdings, see Mario Cerutti, *Burguesía y capitalismo en Monterrey 1850–1910* (Mexico City: Claves Latinoamericanas, 1983), pp. 57–106. See also Walker, "The Martínez del Río Family: An Elite Mexican Family: 1839–1963" (unpublished, University of Chicago), pp. 51–54. For the most useful discussion of the Guggenheim holdings and operations, see Bernstein, *The Mexican Mining Industry,* pp. 36–39, 50–53, 55–56, 60, 66, 158.

40. For the Evaristo Madero-Colis Huntington contract of 10 May 1876, see Box 2E311, Jean B. La Coste Papers, Barker Texas History Collection, Austin (hereafter cited as BTHC). For the disputes, see William L. Purcell, Saltillo, to Patricio Milmo, Monterrey, 30 January 1884, in William L. Purcell, *Frontier Mexico 1875–1894: Letters of William L. Purcell* (San Antonio: Naylor Company, 1963),

pp. 83–84; Evaristo Madero, Hacienda del Rosario, Parras to W. N. Navarro, Los Angeles, California, 12 March 1886; L. M. Johnson, San Antonio, Texas, to M. M. Gonzalez, Piedras Negras, 28 March 1886; and the document dated 2 May 1876, Box 2E311, La Coste Papers, BTHC. For the Martínez del Río data, see Walker, "The Martínez del Río Family." For the other facts, see James Le Roy, *Diplomatic and Consular Reports,* Numbered File 1906–1910, Case 100, p. 56, cited by Kenneth Cott, "Porfirian Investment Policies 1876–1910" (Ph.D. diss., University of New Mexico, 1979), p. 67. For the quotes from *La Libertad* and Gottechalk, see Cott, "Porfirian Investment Policy," p. 287.

41. The archive of the Intercontinental Rubber Company is found in Records Group 76, Special Claims Commission, United States and Mexico, Entry 125 (Case Files for U.S. Claimants), Agency File 5820, WNRC. The Continental Rubber Company of New York (Mexico) was a division of International Rubber Products Corporation of New York. It enjoyed National City Bank financing.

42. See Walker, "The Martínez del Río Family," p. 54. The Laguna agricultural complex included both Mexican and American entrepreneurial "pioneers." The prominent Mexicans included Evaristo Madero and the Treviño family of Monterrey. The earliest American was William L. Purcell. See Purcell, *Frontier Mexico 1875–1894,* and Cerutti, *Burguesía y capitalismo* pp. 74–75 and 94–95; and José Vasconcelos, *Don Evaristo Madero: Biografía de un Patricio* (Mexico City: Impresores Modernas, 1958), pp. 110–193. The Tlahualilo Company directors were almost entirely Americans with headquarters in New York. For the consortium of British investors headed by Lord Balfour and American investors headed by James Stillman, Chairman of the Board of National City Bank, which controlled the Tlahualilo Company, see Mary H. Potter, Claim 347, Box 11, American Mexican Claims Commission, Approved Agrarian Claims, WNRC, and the Balfour Letterbook, Box 5, James Stillman Papers, Butler Library, Rare Book and Manuscript Library, Columbia University (hereafter cited as BL). Purcell's archive is found in Records Group 76, Special Claims Commission, United States and Mexico, Case 125, Docket 140; and Records Group 76, Agrarian Claims Commission (U.S. Section), Case 125, Docket 93, Box 19, WNRC.

43. Francisco Madero, *La sucesión presidencial* (San Pedro, Coahuila: El Partido Nacional Democratico, 1908), 357 pages.

44. For studies of Madero and his career, see Stanley R. Ross, *Francisco I. Madero, Apostle of Mexican Democracy* (New York: Columbia University Press, 1955); and Charles C. Cumberland, *Mexican Revolution: Genesis under Madero* (Austin: University of Texas Press, 1952).

45. On the Burns's interests in Sinaloa and Durango, see Folder 14, Box 100, The Albert Bacon Fall Papers, Huntington Library, San Marino, California. On the revolts in Chihuahua, see the reports of the foreman, Corralitos Hacienda Archive, Peirce Papers, Topsfield, Massachusetts; and "Villista attacks causing the cessation of business" on the 60,000-acre Louis Booker estate east of Pearson in 1910, Records Group 76, Special Claims Commission, Entry 125, Agency 943, Docket 83, WNRC. On the destruction of Alexander Burleson's twenty-four-room hotel at Temosachic in early 1911, see Records Group 76, Special Claims Commission, Agency 216, Docket 81, WNRC. On the 11 May 1911 report on the protection of the American Tlahualilo holdings against Villistas, see 312.115T541/

1 Department of State Decimal File. On the Huasteca, the Maderista attacks against the Rascon Hacienda on 6 May 1911, and the ensuing strikes, see the Townsend-Stanton Family Papers, Box 5, Folder 1, Howard-Tilton Memorial Library, Tulane University (herafter cited as HTML). On the attacks on the Continental Rubber Company on 11 May 1911 by forces led by Emilio Madero, see Records Group 76, Special Claims Commission, Box 318, Document 1733, WNRC. On Jalisco, see the assaults on the Buena Fe Mine, Letters, 15 February and 18 May 1911, from Walter Estes, Ojuelos, Jalisco, to John Henry Kirby, Houston, Box 32, John Henry Kirby Papers, Houston Metropolitan Research Center (hereafter cited as HMRC). Insurgents forced American bankers to abandon the 18,200-acre Rock Island Tropical Plantation in Oaxaca during the winter-spring of 1911, Records Group 76, Special Claims Commission, Entry 125, Agency 2417, WNRC. On 1911 attacks against the Palos Blancos Land Company in Sinaloa, see Records Group 76, Special Claims Commission, Entry 125, Agency 5442, WNRC. In the state of Mexico Zapatistas prevented the harvesting of lumber by an American-owned company, Records Group 76, Special Claims Commission, Entry 125, Agency 1313, WNRC. For the March 1912 attacks by forces claiming Zapatista affiliation against the American-owned United Sugar Company's installations at Las Mochis, Sinaloa, see Hector R. Olea, *Los asentamientos humanos en Sinaloa* (Mazatlán: Universidad Autónoma de Sinaloa, 1980), pp. 148–152. Attacks against the large American Blaylock Colony in Tamaulipas are recorded in 812.152/3892, Department of State Decimal Files, National Archives and Records Administration (hereafter cited as NARA). On attacks in Sonora, see the Richardson Construction Company, Box 106, The Fall Papers, Huntington Library.

Four: The Seizure of Power: Porfirio Díaz, American Expansion, and the Revolution of Tuxtepec

1. John Salmon Ford, "Memoirs," Typescript, p. 1237, BTHC.

2. For Díaz's itinerary, which the consul regarded as significant, see Consul Thomas F. Wilson, Matamoros, to William Hunter, Department of State, Washington, D.C., 8 January 1876, Roll 7, Despatches Received by the Department of State from U.S. Consuls in Matamoros, 1826–1906. At the same time Wilson violently criticized President Lerdo de Tejada and expressed sympathy for General Díaz, who "no longer felt safe within the limits of Mexico." On Sterling looking after Stillman's interests in Brownsville during an 1876 "maze of Mexican intrigue," see Anna R. Burr, *The Portrait of a Banker: James Stillman 1850–1918* (New York: Duffield Press, 1927), p. 51.

3. For descriptions of the fighting and expansion of U.S. business interests in the Nueces Strip, see Tom Lea, *The King Ranch,* vol. 1 (Boston: Little, Brown, 1957), 467 pages; John Salmon Ford, "Memoirs," especially Box VII, Volume 7, BTHC; and L. E. Graf, "The Economic History of the Lower Rio Grande Valley 1820–1875" (Ph.D. diss., Harvard University, 1942). The original status of the Brownsville townsite as the ejido of Matamoros, known as Refugioito, is described in the *Brownsville Herald,* 1 January 1947, p. 2.

4. *The San Antonio Press,* 1 January 1876.

5. For U.S. trade penetration of the northern Mexican states that became the American southwest after the Mexican War and its implications for political and cultural hegemony, see Raúl A. Fernández, *The United States-Mexico Border: A Politico-Economic Profile* (Notre Dame, Ind.: Notre Dame University Press, 1977). On efforts to attack Mexico from Texas along the Lower Rio Grande, see Graf, "Economic History," pp. 303–309; and Ford, "Memoirs," chap. 4, p. 644. Stillman's support of the 1852 Carbajal invasion of Mexico is described by Graf, "Economic History," p. 303; and documented in Ralph Crane, New York City, to Charles Stillman, Brownsville, 8 February 1852, Letter Book 1850–1852, Box 1, James Stillman Papers, BL; and in Charles Stillman, Letters, 16 December 1850 and 7 February 1851, in James Stillman, Diaries and Personal Accounts, 1855–1876, 48 Volumes, Folder 1859, Houghton Library, Rare Books and Manuscripts Room, Harvard University (hereafter cited as HL).

6. Vicente Fuentes Díaz, *El problema ferrocarrilero de México* (Mexico City: Edición del autor, 1951), p. 21.

7. See John Kennedy Winkler, *The First Billion: The Stillmans and the National City Bank* (New York: Vanguard Press, 1934), 272 pages. For the quote regarding cotton, hides, and gold, see ibid., p. 23.

8. For references to the Vallecillo mines, see Chauncey Devereux Stillman, *Charles Stillman 1810–1875* (New York: Chauncey D. Stillman, 1956), p. 15, Rare Books Room, Arnulfo L. Olevira Memorial Library, Texas Southmost College, Brownsville, Texas; Colonel J. R. Reynolds, Vallecillo, to Charles Stillman, Brownsville, 5 June 1852; and José María G. Villareal, China, Mexico, to Charles Stillman, Brownsville, 25 December 1852; both in Box 3, and José Morell, Monterrey, to Charles Stillman, Brownsville, 4 July 1861, Boxes 7–8; and Morell, Monterrey, to Charles Stillman, Brownsville, 8 February and 9 June 1862, Letters, Letterbooks, Accounts, Bills, and Other Business Papers of Charles and James Stillman, 1850–1879, HL; and Patricio Flores, Vallecillo (Mina de Jesus), to Charles Stillman, Brownsville, Box 1, 18 April 1853; and José Antonio Elizondo (Mina de Teresa), to Charles Stillman, Brownsville, Box 1; and N. Jarvis to Charles Stillman, Corpus Christi, 29 July 1853, Box 2, BL.

9. See Lea, *The King Ranch,* 1:179, 405–407, 418; William Broyles, Jr., "The Last Empire," *Texas Monthly* (October 1980):159–161; and Graf, "Economic History," pp. 198–697. See also Ford, "Memoirs."

10. Alleyton Historical Marker, Alleyton, Texas.

11. Lea, *The King Ranch,* 1:179, 200, 405–407.

12. For specifics on their Civil War contracts, see Charles Stillman 1860 Account Book, 1863 Account Book, 1861 Receipt of Francisco R. Rendon, Bills of Lading, Clients 1859–1861, and letters, Morell, Monterrey, to Stillman, Brownsville, 8 and 16 February 1862, and the 1865 diary, in James Stillman, Diaries and Personal Account Books, 1860–1918, HL. The story of their Civil War enterprises is told by Graf, "Economic History," pp. 496–607; Lea, *The King Ranch,* 1:179–214; Broyles, "The Last Empire," p. 238; and Winkler, *The First Billion,* pp. 25–31.

13. For profit margins and receipts for sales in England and New York via Smith and Dunning, see James Stillman, Diaries and Personal Account Books, 1860–1918, HL. For dates and prices of land purchases, see the James B. Wells Papers, BTHC. For growth of Stillman's estate during the immediate postwar era,

see Winkler, *The First Billion,* pp. 48–60. The Houghton collection is especially rich in Civil War era receipts and bills of sale from New York and Liverpool. See also Ford, "Memoirs," pp. 1207–1208, BTHC.

14. For the T. W. House accounts via Matamoros, see Charles Stillman, Account Book, 1860, 1 July, 8 July, and 30 July 1860, in James Stillman, Diaries and Personal Account Books, 1860–1918, HL; and Frederick Huth, Liverpool, to T. W. House, Houston, 1 December 1864; Huth, Liverpool, to House, Houston, 1 February 1865; Huth, Liverpool, to Droge, Oetling and Company, Matamoros, 14 February 1865; Huth, Liverpool, to House, Houston, 22 March 1865; Huth, Liverpool, to House, Houston, 12 August 1865; Volume II, the T. W. House Papers, BTHC.

15. The Stillmans held an enormous $200,000 interest in George Brackenridge's San Antonio National Bank from the 1870s. See Brackenridge, San Antonio, to James Stillman, New York, regarding $770 interest payment as Receiver of the Bank, 1 December 1876, Diaries and Personal Account Books, Box 11, 1860–1918, HL. James Stillman, New York, to Brackenridge, San Antonio, 15 December 1890, Letterbook, 15 March 1890–11 February 1891, Box 4; James Stillman, New York, to Brackenridge, San Antonio, 4 January 1907, Box 6, regarding $12,000 payment as 6 percent dividend on his San Antonio National Bank stock; and a massive Swenson-Stillman Texas ranch land transaction involving Lord Balfour and Brackenridge, 20 January 1908, Box 3, BL. Marilyn McAdams Sibley, *George W. Brackenridge: Maverick Philanthropist* (Austin: University of Texas Press, 1973), pp. 91–93, discusses the Stillmans' support of Brackenridge over several decades but was unaware of their powerful position in the San Antonio National Bank.

16. The story of Cortina as hero or bandit has been told repeatedly by scholars with different ideological slants. For his background as a Mexican hacendado and provincial elite defending absolutely valid personal land claims usurped north of the Rio Grande, see the bill of sale José María Cavazos, sole surviving heir of Narciso Cavazos, 15 August 1790, 106.5 leagues of cattle pasturelands sold at public auction to José Narciso Cavazos, and the ensuing estate history, Box 3E 136, San Juan Carrecitos Grant, Camargo Archives, BTHC. See ibid., p. 8, for the land purchases from questionable "owners" by Richard King. For the most authoritative account of the Cortina heritage and conflict, see Ford, "Memoirs," 5:880–885, 905–907. For the most complete record of King, Kenedy, and Stillman land purchases and titles, see the James B. Wells Papers, 1837–1927 and Stephen F. Powers Papers, 1777–1885, BTHC. The latter two collections contain over forty boxes containing land documents, claims, deeds, and counterclaims. For the Cavazos claims, see Box 2H 207, Wells Papers, BTHC.

17. For Kenedy's purchase of arms, see Box 2H 202, Wells Papers, BTHC. Gibson's compromising note is found in Box 2H 349, ibid.

18. Box 2H 181, ibid.

19. Ibid.

20. The Peirce holdings in Texas are detailed in his will dated 25 February 1882, Essex County Courthouse, Salem, Massachusetts, and Schedules A and B, and in the personal archives of the author. Correspondence and related material between Peirce and Huntington were found in the Colis P. Huntington Papers,

1856–1901, "Introduction," pp. 10–16, Series III, "Legal and Financial Records 1797–1901," Reel 1, 14–33, Film Z–G 1, Tampico-Panuco Valley Railroad Company Ltd. 1913–1931, Reel 361, Part 5, and Reel 251, Part 2, Western Railroad Company of Mexico Ltd., 1890–1951 "to construct and operate"; Series III, Reel 1, Items 14–31, Correspondence with Peirce and Converse; The Bancroft Library, University of California, Berkeley. The combinations of investors committed to the development of the railroads in Texas, including House, Huntington, Taylor, Stillman, and Peirce, are described in many secondary works. See S. G. Reed, *A History of the Texas Railroads* (Houston: St. Clair Publishing Company, 1941); James L. Allhands, *Gringo Builders* (Dallas: Privately published, 1931); and idem, *Railroads to the Rio Salado* (Texas: Anson Jones Press, 1960). House's railroad investments in partnership with Peirce and Huntington are mentioned in the secondary sources. Stillman's extensive investments in Texas are found in his papers at the BL. Box 5, p. 461 is exceptional (this page lists seven railroads, banks, and other enterprises), while the Letterbook 6 April 1893–28 February 1897 lists fifteen Texas banks. Other larger investments in the state's most important institutions are scattered throughout the collection.

21. *The San Antonio Express,* 7 March 1876.

22. "Our Relations with Mexico," *The San Antonio Herald,* 13 January 1876.

23. *The San Antonio Herald,* 22 January 1876; and John W. Foster as quoted in Robert B. Gorsuch, *The Mexican Southern Railway to Be Completed under a Charter from the Mexican Government through the States of Veracruz and Oaxaca* (New York: Hosford and Sons, 1881), p. 7.

24. "More Mexican Outrages," *The San Antonio Herald,* 19 January 1876.

25. *The San Antonio Herald,* 22 January 1876.

26. Schleicher as quoted in *The San Antonio Herald,* 8 February 1876.

27. *The San Antonio Express,* 7 March 1876.

28. Ibid., and *The San Antonio Herald,* 19 February 1876.

29. *The San Antonio Express,* 9 March 1876; and *The Corpus Christi Gazette,* 5 March 1876.

30. *The San Antonio Herald,* 19 February, 1876; quoting the *Courier Journal.*

31. *The San Antonio Herald,* 21 February 1876.

32. Lea, *The King Ranch,* 1:343.

33. See the 18 March 1881 agreement between James Stillman and the Mexican National Railroad, in which he was a stockholder, regarding the sale of two-thirds of the Brownsville Ferry Company for $66,667. Subsidies to be paid by the Mexican government to the Matamoros and Monterrey Construction Company, Box 10, James Stillman Papers, BL. For the description of Stillman's strategy to bypass Matamoros with the railroads until the European merchants there were ruined through isolation, see the letter Thomas Carson, Brownsville, to Stillman, New York, 23 December 1894, Box 1, Stillman Papers, BL.

34. Ford, "Memoirs," Volume 7, Box VII, pp. 1237–1238.

35. "Expecting a Revolution in Mexico Instigated by Díaz," *The Galveston Weekly News,* 26 February 1876.

36. *The San Antonio Express,* 19 March 1876.

37. *The Galveston Weekly News,* 20 March 1876.

38. Perry, *Juárez and Díaz,* pp. 215–216.

39. Lea, *The King Ranch,* 1:292; and Broyles, "The Last Empire," p. 161.

40. Box 2H 207, Wells Papers; and Ford, "Memoirs," p. 1238; BTHC.

41. José (illegible) to Francisco Armendaiz complained of forced contributions of $910 by Daniel Milmo and Company, 1,046 by Luis Peltispaint, $1,000 by J. Eversman, $500 by Adolfo Marks and Hermanos, and "ustedes" of $329 "totaling 4,000 pesos collected by coronel Juan A. Arocha, the District Rent Collector for the State." Letters 1875–1876, Box 2G 102, San Roman Papers, BTHC. For San Roman as intermediary for General González, see Laura M. de González to San Roman, 19 February 1876; ibid. Charles A. Whitney and Company, Agents Shipping on the Morgan Line, New Orleans, to San Roman, Brownsville, February 1876, ibid. The arms shipments are described in the Francisco Armendaiz Receipt, March 1876, Samuel Baker and Company, Liverpool, to Francisco Armendaiz, Brownsville (on board the San Marcos), and various inventory documents listing arms in Box 2G 102, San Roman Papers, BTHC. See also Perry, *Juárez and Díaz,* pp. 215–216. For the Treviño and Ord land bequests, see Edward Otho Cresap Ord III et al., Claim 328, Box 11, American Mexican Claims Commission, Approved Agrarian Claims, WNRC.

42. Matías Ibañez, to San Roman, Santander, Spain, 19 April 1876, ibid. The surrender and its effects are described in Perry, *Juárez and Díaz,* pp. 215, 220–231.

43. See the contract, Box 2H 207, Wells Papers. See also the reaffirmation obtained by Stillman, 2 March 1877, ibid.

44. See the contract, 18 March 1881, the Brownsville Ferry Company with the Mexican National Railroad, Box 10, Stillman Papers, BL.

45. *The Galveston Weekly News,* 7 February and 31 March 1876; and *The San Antonio Herald,* 25 April, 5 May, and 6 May 1876.

46. Perry, *Juárez and Díaz,* pp. 221–231, 284.

47. On Lerdo's financial crisis, see Perry, *Juárez and Díaz,* pp. 237–238, 273–276; Calderon, *La república restaurada,* pp. 470–480, 484–488; and Jan Bazant, *Historia de la deuda exterior de México* (*1823–1946*) (Mexico City: El Colegio de México, 1946), pp. 102–105.

48. *The San Antonio Herald,* 25 April 1876.

49. *The San Antonio Herald,* 5 and 6 May 1876.

50. For a detailed discussion of Díaz's guerrilla war strategy and the recruitment of provincial elites, see Perry, *Juárez and Díaz,* pp. 215–284.

51. David Pletcher, "Mexico Opens the Door to American Capital, 1877–1880," *The Americas* XVI (July 1959):1–14; and Karl M. Schmitt, *Mexico and the United States 1821–1973: Conflict and Coexistence* (New York: John Wiley and Sons, 1974), pp. 90–97.

Five: The Growth of the Porfirian Economy and the American Intrusion

1. Interview, Hubert Howe Bancroft with General John B. Frisbee, n.d., Manuscript 351, 40 pages, Bancroft Library, Berkeley. Frisbie served as an important adviser to Díaz during his meetings held in the United States between 1881 and 1883 with Huntington, U. S. Grant, Jay Gould, T. W. Peirce, H. Sanford, and

Plumb, among others; Box 1, Folder 1, Townsend-Stanton Family Papers, HTML. At that time Díaz was minister of development in the González government. Frisbie became a man of means in Mexico. On his valuable 40,000-acre Atlixtac hacienda on the edge of the Morelos sugar complex and Taxco area and its enormous losses during the revolution, see Records Group 76, Special Claims Commission, Entry 125, Agency Number 4486, WNRC.

2. Interview, Frisbie-Bancroft. The details of the International concession, including landholdings and the actual building of the railroad, are available in the Colis P. Huntington Papers, 1856–1901, Microfilm, Bancroft Library, especially Series III, Reel 1, correspondence with T. W. Peirce and James Converse.

3. For a detailed report on the construction of Mexico's first important railroad, see John Gresham Chapman, *La construcción del ferrocarril Mexicano (1857–1880)* (Mexico City: SepSetentas, 1975), 197 pages. For an analysis of the socioeconomic impact of the railroad system, see John H. Coatsworth, *Growth against Development: The Economic Impact of Railroads in Porfirian Mexico* (DeKalb: Northern Illinois University Press, 1981), 249 pages.

4. On the Tehuantepec Ship Railroad, its plans, concessions, and contracts, see the Elmer Lawrence Corthell Papers (1840–1916), John Hays Library, Brown University, Providence, Rhode Island. Fifty linear feet stored in 135 boxes, this previously unexamined collection details the Tehuantepec project and contains contracts between Captain James B. Eads and the Díaz government, including the names of U.S. participants. See the scrapbooks for references to 1.5 million acres of land in the Isthmus of Tehuantepec granted by the Mexican government as part of the railroad concession, other lands in Quintana Roo and Durango, and the names of recipients. On the González regime's bankruptcy, see Coerver, *Porfirian Interregnum,* pp. 230–270, especially pp. 240–247. On the Pearson landholdings, see the Northwestern Railroad Collection, Nettie Lee Benson Latin American Collection, University of Texas, Austin (BLAC). Pearson also obtained 400,000 acres from the Arizona Lumber and Investment Company.

5. See the Huntington correspondence with Peirce and Converse, Series III, Reel 1, Huntington Papers, Microfilm, Bancroft Library; and the Peirce Papers, Topsfield, Massachusetts. For railroad kilometerage, see Francisco Calderon, "Los ferrocarriles," in *El Porfiriato,* pp. 517, 533–542, 566–568, and 625–628. For the González-era construction, see Coerver, *Porfirian Interregnum,* p. 205. Discriminatory rates against corn shipped toward Mexico City from Cordoba as opposed to corn shipped to the port of Veracruz for export from Cordoba is discussed by Arthur P. Schmidt, Jr., "The Railroad and the Economy of Puebla and Veracruz, 1877–1911: A Look at Agriculture" (Paper delivered to the Southwestern Social Science Association, Dallas, 1973).

6. Interview Bancroft with D. Sanchez, 1883, Mexican Manuscript 356, Bancroft Library. Sanchez "operated" the Tehuantepec Railroad from Salina Cruz to Coatzalcoalcos. For foreign control of agricultural production in Soconusco, see the Graham M. Ker Papers, La Zacualapa-Hidalgo Rubber Company of San Francisco, 1915–1920, BLAC; Curlis L. Gómez to Otto F. Brant, Harry Chandler, Lycurus Lindsay, and Moses H. Sherman, 27 July 1914, Box 71, The Esperanza Timber Company 1914–1935, Otto F. Brant Papers, Sherman Library, Corona del Mar, California; and Daniela Spenser, "Soconusco: The Formation of a Coffee

Economy in Chiapas." The Soconusco land promotion was originally undertaken by a combine that at first included Thomas Wentworth Peirce, the Rockefeller-Iron Mountain Company, and Stillman and that owned the Pan American railroad. For passing references to the Pan American and its board of directors, see the Allhands Papers, JECM and the Kirby Papers, HMRC. The road was to run from Houston to Panama. The company held its meetings in Corpus Christi and Chattanooga, Tennessee. See Thomas W. Howard to Kirby, Houston, and the enclosed unidentified newspaper clipping, Folder H-17, Box 22, Kirby Papers, HMRC. Eventually the road was constructed only from Tehuantepec to Guatemala.

7. For the quote see Consul General Arnold Shanklin, "Commercial Conditions in Mexico," *Daily Consular and Trade Reports,* No. 252, 27 October 1911, p. 469. For 1907–1911 see ibid., 18 January 1913, pp. 305–323, and 25 October 1911, pp. 417–437; and Rosenzweig, "El Comercio Exterior," in *El Porfiriato,* pp. 710–729.

8. For the Ferrocarriles Unidos de Yucatán, see D'Olwer, "Las Inversiones Extranjeras," in *El Porfiriato,* p. 1079. The railroad "minerales" are described by Bernstein, *Mexican Mining Industry,* p. 33.

9. Winkler, *The First Billion,* pp. 61, 67–69, 74, 82–83, 91–92, 94, 98, 101, 104, 123–124, and 201–209.

10. Ibid. See also the Stillman Diaries, Stillman Papers, Houghton Library.

11. Ibid., pp. 98–101 and 123–124. Stillman's son James married "Fifi" Potter, daughter of James Potter of the Tlahualilo Estates Management.

12. For some of the principal owners of the enormous complex of American interests that coalesced on the border before continuing into Mexico, and their holdings, see the American Rio Grande Land and Irrigation Company (a concern that operated virtually as a confidential subsidiary of National City Bank, hereafter cited as ARGLI), *Reference Book* and the *Abstract of Lands* prepared by company officer Duval West, Rio Grande Valley Historical Collection (hereafter cited as RGVHC), Pan American University, Edinburg, Texas; and the James L. Allhands Papers, John E. Connor Museum, Texas A and I University, Kingsville, Texas (hereafter cited as JECM). On the transfer of the Yrenio Longoria and Juan José Hinojosa family holdings, see West, *Reference Book,* vol. I, p. 4, RGVHC. For the original Stillman contract see West, *Reference Book,* vol. II, p. 60, RGVHC. The lists of stockholders are included in the Minute Books of the ARGL and in the Allhands interview notebooks at the JECM.

For this phase in the development of Stillman's New York business affairs, see ibid., pp. 208–210. For the Rio Grande quote, see A. L. Burns, New York, to B. C. Greene, Mercedes, 7 February 1930, Reference Book, Section I, ARGLI, RGVHC. For the owners of the company, see the List of Proxies as of 11 November 1913, Minute Book, ARGLI, RGVHC; and Lists of Stockholders as of 12 November 1912 and 1 March 1915, Reference Book, Section I, ARGLI, RGVHC. For original Stillman landownership, see the abstracts of lands, Section I, p. 114, ARGLI, RGVHC. For warranty deeds with references to Stillman, Longoria, Matías Cavazos, the Balli family, and Wells, see Section II, pp. 46–52, 60, 181, ARGLI, RGVHC. For additional mention of the stockholders in 1912 including Guggenheim and Yoakum, see vol. I, p. 4, ARGLI, RGVHC; and for the St. Louis Union Trust Company, the Minute Book, 2 February 1920, p. 108,

ARGLI, RGVHC.

For the network and interplay between Texas and New York interests in the land development projects of the Lower Rio Grande Valley, see the ARGLI proxy and stockholders lists, the credit report, Burns to Greene, 7 February 1930; and especially James Grover, Vice-President, St. Louis Union Trust Company to H. B. Seay, Mercedes, Texas, 16 October 1922, ARGLI, RGVHC. See also Scrapbook XI, article from *The Houston Chronicle,* 11 April 1915, John H. Shary Papers, RGVHC. For tomato catsup processor J. Augustus Heinz's interest and Shary's "ownership" of the Southwestern Land and Investment Company, see Scrapbook X, p. 7, Shary Collection; for his "ownership" of the International Land and Investment Company and role as a vice-president of the National City Bank of Omaha, see Scrapbook XIV, Number 176, article from the *Omaha Daily News,* 2 April 1913, Shary Papers, RGVHC. For Shary's role in the sale of Stillman lands just west of Corpus Christi, see Scrapbook XI, p. 41, article from *The Omaha World Herald,* n.d., and article from *The Omaha World Herald,* 22 March 1913, Shary Papers, RGVHC.

The formation of the intricate network of entrepreneurs that moved directly across Texas and Mexico and their political representatives will be examined in book-length detail in my forthcoming study, *Empire and Revolution: The United States and Mexico, 1876–1940*.

For the most easily obtainable data on foreign investment in Chihuahua, Sonora, and Coahuila, see D'Olwer, "Las Inversiones Extranjeras," in *El Porfiriato,* p. 1134. However, D'Olwer's investment data are in error, Tamaulipas being one of the leading centers of American and other foreign investment.

13. The partial nationalization of Mexican railroads allowed two directorates, one of them national, but a second tier of directors in New York continued to hold a large equity on a long-term buy-out. The company's articles of confederation called for the New York board of directors to approve changes made in Mexico. This control at the highest level included the power to approve appointment of the railroad's active director. See Rafael L. Hernández, New York, to Alberto Madero, El Paso, 28 October 1914, Wallet II, Folder H, Letter 3, Lazaro de la Garza Papers, BLAC. Other letters from Hernández expand on this arrangement. For the plans to construct the Pan American Railroad, see Thomas W. Howard to Kirby, Houston, MSS 148; and "Pan American Directors Meeting, Chattanooga, Tennessee," unidentified newspaper clipping, both in Folder H-17, Box 22, Kirby Papers, HMRC.

14. For the Banco Mercantil Mexicano-National Bank merger, see Coerver, *Porfirian Interregnum,* pp. 225 and 255. For the growth of banking assets, see ibid., p. 229.

15. The statistical data are treated by José Luis Ceceña, *México en la órbita imperial: las empresas transnacionales* (Mexico City: Ediciones El Caballito, 1979), pp. 57, 72–75. The effects of the rising costs of foreign loans and investments will be discussed in chapter 6. Among the many studies that examine their impact elsewhere, see Charles Issawi, *The Economic History of Iran 1800–1914* (Chicago: University of Chicago Press, 1971); and T. W. Overlach, *Foreign Financial Control in China* (New York: Macmillan, 1919).

16. For the American investment pattern, see Ceceña, *México en la órbita,* pp. 55–68.

17. Permisos y Concesiones, 1890–1912, Memorias del General Bernardo Reyes (hereafter cited as MBR); 1891–1899, 20 January 1891, pp. 480–481; and MBR, 1895–1942, pp. 1085–1089, AGNL; Bernstein, *Mexican Mining Industry,* pp. 51–56; Cockcroft, *Intellectual Precursors,* pp. 18–19; and Cerutti, *Burguesía y capitalismo,* pp. 68–172.

18. Bernstein, *Mexican Mining Industry,* pp. 29 and 72–77; and Ceceña, *México en la órbita,* pp. 55–56.

19. Ceceña, *México en la órbita,* p. 66; and Bernstein, *Mexican Mining Industry,* pp. 72–74.

20. Silver output during the Restored Republic (1867–1876) is treated by Calderon, *La república restaurada,* p. 134. Silver production for the Porfiriato is summarized by Percy F. Martin, *Mexico's Treasure House,* (*Guanajuato*): *An Illustrated and Descriptive Account of the Mines* (New York: The Cheltenham Press, 1906), p. 13; and *The Commercial and Financial Chronicle* (New York), 24 October 1908, p. 1063, and 20 February 1909, p. 480. For analysis of the economic effects of declining silver values, see Enrique Martínez Sobral, *La reforma monetaria* (Mexico City: Tipografía de la Oficina Impresora de Estampillas, 1909), pp. 109–118; Ceceña, *México en la órbita,* pp. 95–101; Miguel A. Quintana, *Los ensayos monetarios como consequencia de la baja de la plata. El problema de la plata y el de la moneda de la plata en el mundo y en México* (Mexico City: Universidad Autonoma Nacional de México, 1931), pp. 79–130; and David M. Pletcher, "The Fall of Silver in Mexico, 1876–1910, and Its Effect on American Investments," *Journal of Economic History* 18 (March 1958):33–55. See also Edgar Turlington, *Mexico and Her Foreign Creditors* (New York: Columbia University Press, 1930), pp. 239–241; Bernstein, *Mexican Mining Industry,* pp. 29, 51, and 128; and Rosenzweig, "Moneda y Bancos," *El Porfiriato* pp. 794–795.

21. *The Commercial and Financial Chronicle,* 31 October 1908, p. 1130. The mining crisis is described by Pletcher, "The Fall of Silver," pp. 33–55; and Bernstein, *Mexican Mining Industry,* p. 51.

22. Bernstein, *Mexican Mining Industry,* pp. 51 and 128–129.

23. Ibid., pp. 128–129. See also Guadalupe Nava Oteo, "La minera," *El Porfiriato* pp. 190–191 and 215.

24. Bernstein, *Mexican Mining Industry,* pp. 128–129.

25. *The Commercial and Financial Chronicle,* 18 December 1909, p. 1594.

26. Ibid., 29 August 1908; and Nava Oteo, "La Minera," *El Porfiriato,* pp. 189, 244–245, and 379–381.

27. For the Standard Oil Company's Mexican operations, see *Report of the Commissioner of Corporations on the Petroleum Industry, Part III: Foreign Trade* (Washington, D.C.: U.S. Department of Commerce and Labor, 1912. New York: Arno Press, 1976), p. 83. This report, which analyzed Standard's foreign operations including its sponsorship of a coup d'état in Peru and interference in the affairs of foreign states, was "buried by the government [in 1912] for some fifty years"; see Paul A. Weinstein, "Introduction," p. 1.

28. For a full discussion of Standard's demise in Mexico, see Richey Barron

Campbell, "Taft, Díaz and Oil: You Can't Always Get What You Want" (unpublished, University of Houston, 1981), 15 pages. For the capitalization of the oil companies, see Ceceña, *México en la órbita,* pp. 66 and 69.

29. The best treatment of the Texas Oil Company in its formative years is John O. King, *Joseph Stephen Cullinan: A Study of Leadership in the Texas Petroleum Industry 1857–1937* (Nashville: Vanderbilt University Press, 1970), 229 pages.

30. For the borderlands investments of these men, see the Allhands Papers, Notebook 5, pp. 51, 56, 66, and 70, JECM. Allhands interviewed the leading land developers and politicians of the Rio Grande Valley over a period of years, taking shorthand notes and later transcribing part of their testimony. For Bryan see the Allhands Papers, Notebook 1, JECM.

31. The Missouri-Texas Land Company was one of several land development companies with overlapping ownership whose operations extended for several hundred miles on either side of the Rio Grande River. Its major officers included R. L. Batts of Austin, an attorney for the Gulf Oil Company; V. L. Brooks of Austin, the judge who ruled against Standard Oil in its attempts to operate in Texas; and Thomas Watt Gregory, attorney general of Texas, a close associate and friend of the Texas Company directors and member of the House political machine in the state, and attorney general of the United States during the Mexican interventions. The Missouri-Texas Land Company's holdings extended along the route of the St. Louis, Brownsville and Mexico Railroad controlled by the Frisco Lines of B. F. Yoakum and E. H. Harriman, National City Bank director in charge of railroad operations. Stillman "donated" a roundhouse and terminal to the railroad at Brownsville. E. F. Rowson of the closely related Indiana-Texas Land and Improvement Company was Secretary of the Mexico Company, the land development company in Tamaulipas owned by the Texas Company directors. The network continued. The Blaylock Company of Tamaulipas was financed by many of the border investors. Incorporated in Texas as the Blaylock Town and Improvement Company at $100,000 on 11 November 1904, it sponsored American colonization in Mexico by American "boomers" and "pioneers." On the Blaylock Colony at Atascador and its 500 American colonists, see Allhands, Notebook 5, p. 68, JECM; the Mexico Company map, Kile Papers, BLAC; Records Group 76, Special Claims Commission, Entry 125, Agency 2618, WNRC; *Fall Committee Report,* vol. 2, p. 1035; and the State Department Decimal File 812.152/3882.

Meanwhile border penetration continued via the railroad. On 3 July 1903 Captain W. M. Scott contracted to build the Matamoros-Monterrey extension of the National Lines of Mexico with 500 men and 1,000 wheelbarrows. The land concession by the Mexican government to the railroad for construction between Matamoros and Monterrey totaling 819,000 acres. See the Allhands interview with John Closner, Looseleaf Notebook, Allhands Papers, JECM.

32. For the consolidation of the rail network, see Reed, *A History of the Land Grants and Other Aids to the Texas Railroads by the State of Texas* (Kingsport, Tenn.: Kingsport Press, 1942), 187 pages; and Reed, *Texas Railroads,* pp. 188–205. See also the annual reports of the Southern Pacific Company, 1885, 1897, and 1905, Southern Pacific Building, Houston. By 1905 the Southern Pacific board of directors, which dominated the Texas rail network to the Mexican border, featured Stillman, Thomas Jefferson Coolidge, Jr., founder of the Old Colony Trust of

Boston, Jacob Schiff, and E. H. Harriman. Schiff and Harriman along with William Rockefeller were the National City Bank directors most concerned with railroad investments. Both Coolidge and Stillman had a special relationship with Colonel House and his family by virtue of early investments by the fathers of all three men in the Houston and Texas Central Railroad, the Brazoria Tap, and the Trinity and Brazos Valley Railroad. See Allhands, *Boll Weevil: Recollections of the Trinity and Brazos Valley Railway* (Houston: Anson Jones Press, 1946), p. 5; and Rupert Richardson, *Colonel Edward M. House: The Texas Years* (Abilene: Hardin Simmons University Press, 1964), pp. 202–203.

33. For the interrelations among the Texas Company directors, Texas politicians, and the House machine between 1892 and 1912, see the James B. Autry Papers, Box 13, Folder 579A, Box 16, File 612, Box 27, and Box 35, File 932, WRC. See also the W. B. Sharp Papers, ibid. In addition to the various economic relationships between the businessmen and the House machine loyalists, the Autry Papers also outline the formation of the Union Bank. The bank's directors and principal participants are listed in Box 13, Folder 579A, Autry Papers, WRC. They are also listed in the House Papers, BTHC; and the Kirby and Cullinan Papers in the HMRC. Andrews receives excellent treatment in Evan Anders, *Boss Rule in South Texas: The Progressive Era* (Austin: University of Texas Press, 1982), pp. 71–75, 86–95, 201–202, and 249–262. Secondary sources on Texas politics that reflect the economic ties with eastern capital during the expansion of railroad and land investments across Texas toward Mexico, during the Progressive Era, abound; see Robert C. Cotner, *James Stephen Hogg: A Biography* (Austin: University of Texas Press, 1959); and Richardson, *Colonel House*. The James Stephen Hogg, Albert Sidney Burleson, Edward M. House, and James B. Wells Papers, all in the BTHC, are invaluable for reconstructing the network of interests. For Kirby's holdings in Mexico see the Reports of Walter S. Estes (in Mexico) to Kirby, Houston, 15 February 1911 and 18 May 1911; Kirby, Houston to Senator J. W. Bailey, Washington, D.C., 17 May 1911; Kirby, Houston, to Estes, Joplin, Missouri, 3 April 1914; Captain J. W. Flanagan to Kirby, Houston, 3 February 1915; and assorted documents from 1908, Box 132, The Buena Fe Mine Folder, Kirby Papers, HMRC. The Buena Fe and Chihuahua Mine folders in the Kirby Papers are being reclassified and the box numbers will be changed.

34. For William Hogg's titles and shareownership in the Hogg-Swayne Syndicate, see Box HC 5/35, William Clifford Hogg Papers, BTHC. For the move into Mexico see ibid., and the interview of Wilson Mathis Hudson by W. M. H., Jr., 16 September 1952, Austin, "Pioneers in Texas Oil," Oral History Library, BTHC; the Autry Papers, WRC; and the Cullinan Papers, HMRC. For example, Cullinan, Houston, to Al Casterline, Findlay, Ohio, MSS 69, and associated documents in Box 8, Folder 12, Cullinan Papers. The Autry and Cullinan papers include ownership lists of subsidiaries which indicate a cooperative overlap of the Texas Company directors, the Frisco Line-National City Bank directors'-controlled St. Louis, Brownsville and Mexico Railroad, and land development in the Rio Grande Valley and northeastern Mexico as far south as Monterrey and Tampico.

For the directors of the Mexico Company, which controlled sales and development and owned the minimal rights to over 4.5 million acres in Tamaulipas, see the Houston City Directory, 1911. For their contracts see the Mexico-Texas

Petroleum and Asphalt Company, 311,450 hectares, Libro Number 5, Fojas 1–9; The Mexican Gulf Land and Development Company, 75,000 acres, Legajo 163, Number 4; La Sautema Company, 810,000 hectares, Libro 2, San Fernando, Tercer Distrito, Documento 10, Folio 115; Registro de la Propiedad, Registro Pública, Ciudad Victoria, Tamaulipas; and *Tamaulipas, reseña geográfica y estadística* (Mexico City: Viuda de C. Bouret, 1910), pp. 55–65. See also the Cullinan Papers, Box 7, Folder 24; Will Hogg, New York, to R. E. Brooks, Houston, 28 April 1913; and the report to Cullinan on the prospective sale or lease of the Treviño lands, Box 11, Folder 4, "Producers Oil-Mexican Properties," Cullinan Papers, HMRC. For more Texas Company holdings in Mexico, see Boxes 1, 6, 11, 40, 59, and 67, ibid. For the relationship between Cullinan and Colonel House, see Box 6, Folder 22, Cullinan Papers, HMRC.

35. For Stillman's interest in the San Antonio National Bank, Chapman Ranch, Swenson Ranch, Texas railroads, fifteen Texas banks, and the U.S. Guarantee and Trust Corporation Ltd., with its myriad Texas holdings, see Box 4, Letterbook, 7 November 1888 to 14 March 1896; Stillman, New York, to Brackenridge, San Antonio, 15 and 24 December 1890; Stillman, New York, to A. Balfour, London, 30 December 1890, p. 366; Stillman, New York, to A. Balfour, London, 9 January 1891, p. 383, 9 January 1891, p. 387; Letterbook, 11 February 1891 to 31 August 1891; Stillman, New York, to A. Balfour, London, 16 February 1891, pp. 13–14. Box 5, Letterbook, 1 September 1891–20 April 1892; Stillman, New York, to A. J. Sewell, President, First National Bank, McGregor, Texas, pp. 140–141; the A. Balfour Letterbook, 14 February 1893 to 8 February 1894; Box 6, Stillman, New York, to Brackenridge, San Antonio, 4 January 1907; and Box 10, Letterbook, 6 April 1893 to 8 February 1897, Arkansas and Texas Land Company. For the John H. B. House will, see the Probate Minutes, Volume 20, Number 381, Probate Court of Harris County, Harris County Records, Houston.

36. For the House Bank, see John Henry Kirby to N. D. Silsbee, Cohasset, Massachusetts, 1 November 1907, Box 158, Kirby Papers, HMRC.

37. Cobb cultivated his relationship with Kirby for years before his appointment as chief customs collector at El Paso during the Mexican Revolution. See Zach Lamar Cobb, El Paso, to Kirby, Houston, 7 December 1907 and 2 July 1908, Folder 395, Box 6, Kirby Papers, HMRC.

38. Walter B. Sharp, San Antonio, to the Texas Company Directors, Houston, 21 September 1901, Box 1, Walter B. Sharp Papers, WRC.

39. For Sharp's claim see the correspondence of 17 November 1913, File 619, Box 16, Sharp Papers, WRC. Sharp bought the contested land while representing two Texas Company subsidiaries in Mexico: the Industrial Securities Company and Producers Oil Company. For land prices, see George Harmon's purchase of 50,000 acres at one peso per hectare, J. R. Sharp to Joseph Cullinan, Houston, 14 March 1913, Folder 4, Box 11, Cullinan Papers, HMRC.

40. Report to the Texas Company Directors, Box 13, File 579a, Autry Papers, WRC. For a description of the declining production in the Texas oil fields and the threat it presented to the company's survival, see King, *Cullinan,* p. 177.

41. For massive documentation, see the Cullinan Papers, Boxes 8, 11, 40, and 67, HMRC; and the Autry Papers, Boxes 7, 13, 16, 18, and 20.

42. Buckley's role is discussed by R. E. Brooks, Houston, to H. H. Jones, 29

March 1913, Box 11, Folder 4; and W. O. Thompson, Jr., New York City, to Autry, Houston, 30 June 1913, Box 11, Folder 4, Cullinan Papers, HMRC. For House, see Cullinan, Houston, to T. J. Donoghue, 31 July 1913, Box 11, Folder 4, HMRC; and Henry House, Records Group 76, Special Claims Commission, Entry 125, Agency Number 128, WNRC.

43. For Treviño see Cullinan to J. R. Sharp, Tampico, 8 February 1913, Box 11, Folder 4, Cullinan Papers, HMRC. For references to the other individuals and land purchases, see note 36 and Box 16, File 612, Autry Papers, WRC.

44. For Sharp's National City Bank account, see Box 20, File 785, Autry Papers, WRC. The New York investors headed by Arnold Schlaet controlled most of the Texas Company's stock after the death of John W. Gates in 1911. Gates also had long if tempestuous dealings with Stillman in several railroad ventures, including the Kansas City, Pittsburg and Gulf Railroad. See Keith L. Bryant, Jr., *Arthur E. Stillwell—Promoter with a Hunch* (Nashville: Vanderbilt University Press, 1971), pp. 160–162, cited by Friesell in "John W. Gates," p. 11.

45. Edwin Marshall and the Las Palomas Ranch are treated in Record Group 76, Special Claims Commission, Entry 125, Agency 1850, WNRC; and in the interview of Lois Archer by Hart, Pacific Palisades, California, 8 January 1984. Marshall and the Sinaloa Land and Water Company are discussed in U.S. Department of State Decimal file 312.114W/171, NARA. For the National City Bank and Speyer Bank Mexican water bond issue, see *The Commercial and Financial Chronicle,* 17 October 1908, p. 1013, 24 October 1908, p. 1090, and 31 October 1908, p. 1162.

46. Lists of the colonists are contained in the records of the Special Claims Commission—for example, for the Blaylock Colony, see Entry 156, Case Number 80. See also the *Daily Consular and Trade Reports;* for example, William L. Bonney, "Commerce of Central Mexico," Number 265, 11 November 1911, pp. 738–739.

47. The percentage of American participation in Mexican agriculture is treated by Ceceña, *México en la órbita,* p. 61; and Records Group 76, Special Claims Commission, WNRC. For U.S. agricultural ownership in Sinaloa and the Culiacan Valley and Río Fuerte Basin, see William E. Alger, "Mazatlán," *Daily Consular and Trade Reports,* Number 265, 11 November 1911, pp. 746–748; and the United Sugar Company, Entry 125, Claim 185, Docket 137; Records Group 76, Special Claims Commission, "The Sinaloa Land and Fruit Company," Entry 125, Agency 1624, WNRC; and the Sinaloa Land and Water Company, Department of State Decimal File 312.114W/171, NARA.

48. The named properties are all contained in Records Group 76, Special Claims Commission and the Agrarian Claims Commission (U.S. Section), WNRC.

49. Despite serious crises, technological innovation, irrigation, and the growth of acreage committed to production, Mexican sugar output grew dramatically until 1907. See Roberto Melville, *Crecimiento y rebelión: el desarrollo económico de las Haciendas Azucareras en Morelos (1880–1910)* (Mexico City: Nueva Imagen, 1979), 113 pages. After 1907 growing Cuban output and the U.S. tariff combined to force Mexican production onto the domestic market if it could not be sold to the United Kingdom. For the disastrous results, see the report by consul Arnold Shanklin, *Daily Consular and Trade Reports,* Number 265, 11 November 1911, p. 752. See also *The Commercial and Financial Chronicle,* 29 August 1908 and 14

November 1908. Sugar exports via Veracruz in 1909–1910 totaled $601,479. All sugar went to the United Kingdom; see William W. Canada, "Commerce of Southern Mexico," *Daily Consular and Trade Reports,* Number 250, 25 October 1911, p. 420.

50. For a quantitative analysis of the increases in Porfirian agricultural output, see Coatsworth, "Anotaciones sobre la producción de alimentos durante el Porfiriato," *Historia Mexicana* XXVI, no. 2 (octubre-diciembre 1976):167–187. For the data on output, see p. 184. For 1910 data, see *Seminario de historia de México, estadísticas económicas del Porfiriato: fuerza de trabajo y actividad económica por sectores,* introduction by Rosenzweig (Mexico City: El Colegio de México, 1965), pp. 67–82. For Yucatán, see Allen Wells, "Henequén and Yucatán: An Analysis in Regional Economic Development, 1876–1915" (Ph.D. diss., State University of New York at Stony Brook, 1979); and Gil Joseph, *Revolution from Without: Yucatán, Mexico, and the United States, 1880–1924* (London: Cambridge University Press, 1982), pp. 37–69; and the Henry W. Peabody Papers, MSS D-5 GC-A, 1890; and HG-1, 1915–1923, Baker Library, Harvard University School of Business.

51. The post-1907 agricultural crisis is treated by Luis Cossio Silva, "La agricultura," *El Porfiriato,* pp. 8–133. For detailed reports on the agricultural disaster that actually took place, see the *Daily Consular and Trade Reports,* 1908–1913.

Six: The Crisis of the Porfirian Political Economy

1. See the announcements of the Mexican National Sugar Company's collapse in *The Financial Chronicle,* no. 2253, 29 August 1908 and no. 1302, 14 November 1908. For the data on Morelos sugar production, see Melville, *Crecimiento y rebelión,* pp. 90–94. On prerevolutionary conditions in Morelos, see Womack, *Zapata,* pp. 3–66; and Andres Chieu, "Peones y campesinos Zapatistas," in *Emiliano Zapata y el movimiento Zapatista: Cinco ensayos* (Mexico City: Instituto Nacional de Antropología é Historia, 1980), pp. 102–178.

2. For the mortality rates, see William E Alger, "Mazatlán," *Daily Consular and Trade Reports,* no. 265, 11 November 1911, p. 746.

3. The food crisis, corn shipments, and rising prices are described in Harold G. Bretherton, "Aguascalientes," in ibid., p. 750; ibid., no. 121, 23 November 1910, p. 720; Edward S. Cunningham, "Production of Indian Corn in South Africa," in ibid., no. 115, 16 November 1910, p. 643; Clarence A. Miller, "Mexican Importations of Grain," in ibid., no. 98, 27 October 1910, p. 359; and G. B. McGoogan, "Progreso" (in which the district corn crop was a total loss), in ibid., no. 250, 25 October 1911, p. 437.

4. Luther T. Ellsworth, "Ciudad Porfirio Díaz," in ibid., no. 15, 18 January 1913, pp. 309–310; Alonzo B. Garret, "Nuevo Laredo" in ibid., no. 13, 18 January 1913, p. 310; idem, "Heavy American Exports to Mexico," in ibid., no. 107, 7 November 1910, p. 504; Miller, "Import Trade of Mexico," in ibid., no. 209, 22 December 1911, p. 1484; Thomas Edwards, "Ciudad Juárez," in ibid., no. 256, 1 November 1911, p. 559; Garret, "Nuevo Laredo," in ibid., no. 256, 1 November 1911, p. 548; Ellsworth, "Ciudad Porfirio Díaz," in ibid., no. 256, 1 November 1911, p. 551; C. M. Leonard, "Chihuahua," in ibid., no. 256, 1 November 1911, p. 554.

5. For locusts see McGoogan, "Progreso," p. 437. For Chihuahua see Edwards, "Ciudad Juárez," in ibid., no. 256, 1 November 1911, pp. 559–560; and especially Leonard, "Chihuahua" (a report on conditions in 1910), pp. 553–557.

6. Some of the "wanted " posters are stored at the Coahuila state archives in Saltillo, according to Professor William H. Beezley. For a discussion of the "Younger Creoles" see William D. Raat, "Ideas and Society in Don Porfirio's Mexico," *The Americas* 30 (1973):32–53.

7. See the La Laguna figures in Charles Freeman, "Mexican Cotton Crop," *Daily Consular and Trade Reports,* no. 109, 9 November 1910, p. 528. Production figures for piloncillo, cotton, and sugar, in addition to the domestic dumping of the sugar crop, are available in Rosenzweig, "La industria," pp. 337–342. The sugar problem is also pointed out by Arnold Shanklin, *Daily Consular and Trade Reports,* no. 252, 27 October 1911, p. 443. For cotton manufacturing, see Shanklin, "Commercial Conditions in Mexico," in ibid., no. 256, 1 November 1911, p. 471. For additional data on production and consumption, see *Seminario, Estadísticas económicas.*

8. The estimate of foreign investments in the north is made by Katz, *The Secret War in Mexico: Europe, the United States and the Mexican Revolution* (Chicago: University of Chicago Press, 1981), p. 7. For the volume of foreign investment, see D'Olwer, "Las inversiones extranjeras," in *El Porfiriato,* pp. 1154–1161. For the best analysis of the debt crisis linking it to the devaluation of silver, see Martínez Sobral, *La reforma monetaria,* esp. pp. 109–113. The cost of the debt is also treated by Ceceña, *México en la órbita,* pp. 95–101. Minister of the Treasury Limantour noted that over 25 percent of the national budget had been paid to service the government's debt; see Quintana, *Los ensayos monetarios,* pp. 105–106; and Cott, "Porfirian Investment Policies," p. 301. The conditions in Veracruz are described in Octavio García Mundo, *El movimiento inquilinario de Veracruz* (Mexico City: SepSetentas, 1976), pp. 19–35. For the number of jobs created by capital between 1895 and 1910, see Rosenzweig, "La industria," pp. 338–339.

9. Trade in Veracruz declined 15 percent between 1907–1908 and 1909–1910. At Tampico it declined 8 percent. See Miller, "Commerce of Northern Mexico," *Consular and Trade Reports,* no. 15, 18 January 1913, p. 305.

10. Limantour's four-point program is discussed in Joaquin Ramírez Cabañas C., "Los ingresos federales de México durante los años de 1876 a 1936," *Revista de Hacienda,* no. 1 (Mexico City, 1938):11–12.

11. For the multinational negotiations, see Quintana, *Los ensayos monetarios,* pp. 87–93.

12. For analysis of the effects of the silver crisis on agriculture, entrepreneurs, the working classes, and consumers, see ibid., pp. 109–117; and Edgar Turlington, *Mexico and Her Foreign Creditors,* pp. 239–241.

13. Martínez Sobral, *La reforma monetaria,* p. 203.

14. The new debts are treated by Ceceña, *México en la órbita,* pp. 97–101; Martínez Sobral, *La reforma monetaria,* pp. 109–113; Quintana, *Los ensayos monetarios,* pp. 109–117; Turlington, *Mexico and Her Foreign Creditors,* pp. 240–242. On Díaz, see Felipe de la Garma, "Resumen de los egresos efectuados por el gobierno federal desde el año de 1876 hasta 1936," *Revista de Hacienda,* no. 3 (November 1937):4.

15. For the quote, see Martínez Sobral, *La Reforma Monetaria,* p. 202. Ramírez Cabañas C., "Los ingresos federales," pp. 12–13. For Díaz's fiscal conservatism, see Coerver, *The Porfirian Interregnum,* p. 270.

16. On the regime's savings, see Turlington, *Mexico and Her Foreign Creditors,* p. 212; Cott, "Porfirian Investment Policies," 301; and the *Consular and Trade Reports,* no. 47, 1 September 1906, cited by Gilberto Valles, "Crop Failures in Mexico 1900–1910" (unpublished, University of Houston), p. 6.

17. Interview Hart with Paul Vanderwood, Las Cruces, New Mexico, 27 July 1985. For the definitive work on the rurales, see Vanderwood, *Los rurales Mexicanos,* p. 246.

18. Ceceña, *México en la órbita,* pp. 81–85.

19. *La Libertad,* cited by Cott, "Porfirian Investment Policies," p. 287.

20. James LeRoy, *Diplomatic and Consular Reports,* Department of State Numbered File 1906–1910, Case 100. p. 67, cited by Cott, "Porfirian Investment Policies," p. 287.

21. Investigative Report, Special Claims Commission, Entry 125, Agency 1396, WNRC.

22. Ibid.; and the Laguna Corporation file, Entry 125, Agency 1391, WNRC.

23. The debt total is available in Ceceña, *México en la órbita,* pp. 97–101. The effects of devaluation are discussed by Martínez Sobral, *La reforma monetaria;* Quintana, *Los ensayos monetarios,* pp. 79–121; and D'Olwer, "Las Inversiones Extranjeras," pp. 1029–1053.

24. Rosenzweig, "El Desarrollo Económico," p. 418. The wages of industrial workers in mines and factories recorded in the Kirby Papers, Fall Papers, Special Claims Commission files, the *Consular and Trade Reports,* and the Archivo del Tribunal Superior consistently show Rosenzweig's estimates to be overly optimistic by between 10 and 25 percent.

Seven: Global Causation: Iran, China, Russia, and Mexico

1. Martin, *Mexico's Treasure House,* p. 8.

2. For a perceptive assessment of the Ulemas as regional elites, see Gad G. Gilbar, "Persian Agriculture in the Late Qajar Period, 1860–1906: Some Economic and Social Aspects," *Asian and African Studies* 12, no. 3 (1978):312–365; and Gene R. Garthwaite, "Khans and Kings: The Dialectics of Power in Bakhtiyari History," in Michael E. Bonine and Nikki Keddie, eds., *Modern Iran: The Dialectics of Continuity and Change* (Albany: State University of New York Press, 1981), pp. 159–172. On provincial society and economy, see Gilbar, "The Persian Economy in the Mid-19th Century," *Die Welt des Islams* 19, nos. 1–4 (1979):177–211; Robert T. Olson, "Persian Gulf Trade and the Agricultural Economy of Southern Iran in the Nineteenth Century," in Bonine and Keddie, *Modern Iran,* pp. 173–190; and Charles Issawi, *The Economic History of Iran, 1800–1914* (Chicago: University of Chicago Press, 1971), p. 405.

3. See Issawi, *Economic History,* pp. 70–164, 224–246, and 266–296; and Gilbar, "The Persian Economy." For a discussion of foreign intervention, see Joseph

M. Upton, *The History of Modern Iran: An Interpretation* (Cambridge: Harvard University Press, 1960), p. 163; and W. Morgan Shuster, *The Strangling of Persia* (New York: The Century Company, 1912), p. 423.

4. Julian Bharier, *Economic Development in Iran 1900–1970* (London: Oxford University Press, 1971), pp. 9–11; and Issawi, *Economic History,* pp. 248–251, 314–318, and 356–361.

5. Issawi, *Economic History,* pp. 346–356; Bharier, *Economic Development,* pp. 18–19; and Upton, *Modern Iran,* p. 9.

6. Issawi, *Economic History,* pp. 136, 143–144, 155–159; Gilbar, "Persian Agriculture," pp. 312–365; and idem, "Trends in the Development of Prices in Late Qajar Iran, 1870–1906," *Iranian Studies* 16, nos. 3–4 (Summer-Autumn 1983):177–198.

7. Issawi, *Economic History,* p. 243.

8. Gilbar, "Persian Agriculture," pp. 315–323; and Issawi, *Economic History,* pp. 225–226.

9. Bharier, *Economic Development,* pp. 13–16; and Issawi, *Economic History,* pp. 326–334.

10. Bharier, *Economic Development,* pp. 13–16; Issawi, *Economic History,* pp. 238–240; and Gilbar, "Persian Agriculture," pp. 314, 323–346.

11. Issawi, *Economic History,* pp. 247–251.

12. Ibid.; also see Upton, *The History of Modern Iran,* pp. 8–9; and Keddie, "Religion, Society and Revolution in Modern Iran," in Bonine and Keddie, eds., *Modern Iran,* pp. 25, 27.

13. Issawi, *Economic History,* pp. 70–75, 130–131.

14. Gilbar, "Persian Agriculture," pp. 186–188; and Issawi, *Economic History,* pp. 206–212.

15. See Gilbar, "The Persian Economy in the Mid-19th Century," pp. 177–211; and "Persian Agriculture"; also Issawi, *Economic History,* pp. 206–212.

16. Gilbar, "The Persian Economy in the Mid-19th Century," p. 190.

17. Issawi, *Economic History,* p. 371.

18. Issawi, *Economic History,* pp. 152–205 and 361–372; Gilbar, "Persian Agriculture," pp. 334–335; Edward Granville Browne, *The Persian Revolution of 1905–1909* (Cambridge: Cambridge University Press, 1910), p. 136; and Upton, *Modern Iran,* pp. 13–14.

19. Issawi, *Economic History,* p. 350; and Gilbar, "Trends in the Development of Prices."

20. "Report by Arthur J. Herbert on the Trade and Industries of Persia [for the year 1886–7]," UK Foreign Office, *Diplomatic and Consular Reports,* Annual Series, 5, cited in Gilbar, "Persian Agriculture," p. 315.

21. Upton, *Modern Iran,* pp. 13–16.

22. See Browne, *The Persian Revolution;* and Shuster, *The Strangling of Persia,* pp. xviii–lvi.

23. Dwight H. Perkins, *Agricultural Development in China, 1368–1968* (Chicago: Aldine, 1969), pp. 172, 184; and G. William Skinner, "Marketing and Social Structure in Rural China (Part 1)," *Journal of Asian Studies* 24, no. 1 (November 1964):32.

24. Michael Franz, "State and Society in Nineteenth-Century China," in Albert Feuerwerker, ed., *Modern China* (Englewood Cliffs, N.J.: Prentice-Hall, 1964), p. 58.

25. Theda Skocpol, *States and Social Revolutions* (Cambridge: Cambridge University Press, 1979), p. 72.

26. T. W. Overlach, *Foreign Financial Control in China* (New York: Macmillan, 1919), pp. 1–14.

27. Ibid. For an illuminating discussion of foreign expansion in China, see Overlach, *Foreign Financial Control*. On abolition of internal tariffs and the treaty of Nanking, which settled the Opium War, see ibid., pp. 7–14. For a useful examination of the process and effects of nineteenth-century British financial and economic expansion elsewhere, see David S. Landes, *Bankers and Pashas: International Finance and Economic Imperialism in Egypt* (New York: Harper, 1958), 354 pages.

28. Overlach, *Foreign Financial Control,* p. 271.

29. Jean Chesneaux, *Peasant Revolts in China, 1840–1949* (New York: W. W. Norton, 1973), p. 28.

30. Ibid., pp. 24–32.

31. Ibid., pp. 32–39.

32. Ibid., pp. 40–51.

33. Han-sheng Chuan, "The Economic Crisis of 1883 as Seen in the Failure of Hsu Jun's Real Estate Business in Shanghai," in Hou Chi-ming and Yu Tzong-shian, eds., *Modern Chinese History* (Taipei: Institute of Economics, Academic Sinica, 1979), p. 499. For a book-length treatment of this subject, see Overlach, *Foreign Financial Control.* See also L. L. T'ang (Thung Liang Lee) and M. S. Miller, "The Political Aspect of International Finance in Russia and China," *Economica,* 1st Series, 5 (March 1925):69–88.

34. Feuerwerker, *China's Early Industrialization: Sheng Hsuan-huai (1844–1916) and Mandarin Enterprise* (Cambridge: Harvard University Press, 1958), pp. 12–16; Ralph L. Powell, *The Rise of Chinese Military Power, 1895–1912* (Princeton: Princeton University Press, 1955); and Philip Kuhn, *Rebellion and Its Enemies in Late Imperial China* (Cambridge: Harvard University Press, 1970).

35. Feuerwerker, *The Chinese Economy 1870–1911* (Ann Arbor: Michigan Center for Chinese Studies, 1969), pp. 64–72.

36. Overlach, *Foreign Financial Control,* pp. 268–269.

37. Lancelot Lawton, *The Empires of the Far East,* vol. 1 (Boston, 1912), p. 2.

38. Chesneaux, *Peasant Revolts,* pp. 51–56.

39. Ibid., p. 42.

40. Overlach, *Foreign Financial Control,* pp. 272–278.

41. Chesneaux, *Peasant Revolts,* p. 56.

42. Thomas F. O'Brien Jr., "Anti-Commercialism in China: The Changsha Riot of 1910" (unpublished, University of Connecticut, Storrs, 1970), p. 25.

43. *South China Daily Post,* 6 May 1910, cited in O'Brien, "Anti-Commercialism in China," p. 5.

44. O'Brien, "Anti-Commercialism in China," p. 13.

45. *North China Daily News,* 25 April 1910, cited in ibid., p. 17.

46. Frederic Wakeman, Jr., *The Fall of Imperial China* (New York: Free Press,

1975), chap. 10; John K. Fairbank, Edwin O. Reischauer, and Albert M. Craig, *East Asia: Tradition and Transformation* (Boston: Houghton Mifflin, 1973), pp. 726–737; and Mary C. Wright, ed., *China in Revolution: The First Phase, 1910–1913* (New Haven: Yale University Press, 1968), introduction.

47. Sun Yat-sen, *The International Development of China* (London: Hutchinson and Company, 1921), p. 176. See also Ernest P. Young, "Nationalism, Reform and Republican Revolution: China in the Early Twentieth Century," in James B. Crowley, ed., *Modern East Asia: Essays in Interpretation* (New York: Harcourt, Brace and World, 1970), p. 166.

48. Chesneaux, *Peasant Revolts,* p. 63.

49. Sun Yat-sen, *The International Development of China* (London: Hutchinson and Company, 1921), p. 6.

50. The Russian economic development program and crisis of the ancien régime have been examined in a number of recent works: Roberta Thompson Manning, *The Crisis of the Old Order in Russia: Gentry and Government* (Princeton: Princeton University Press, 1982), 555 pages; Theodore H. Von Laue, *Sergei Witte and the Industrialization of Russia* (New York: Columbia University Press, 1963), 360 pages; John P. McKay, *Pioneers for Profit: Foreign Entrepreneurship and Russian Industrialization 1885–1913* (Chicago: University of Chicago Press, 1970), 442 pages; Olga Crisp, *Studies in the Russian Economy before 1914* (London: Macmillan, 1976), 278 pages; and Pavel Alexeyevich Kromov, *The Economic Development of Russia in the Nineteenth and Twentieth Centuries,* trans. Fabian Vaksman (forthcoming). For the first Russian edition, see *Ekonomicheskoye Razitiye Rossii V XIX–XX vekakh* (Moscow: Institute of Economics, Academy of Science, 1950), 545 pages (hereafter cited as *Ekonomicheskoye Razitiye*).

51. Peter I. Lyashchenko, *History of the National Economy of Russia to the 1917 Revolution* (New York: Macmillan, 1949), pp. 280 and 370. See also Paul Avrich, *Russian Rebels, 1600–1800* (New York: Schocken, 1972). For an excellent discussion of the peasant condition, see Wayne S. Vucinich, *The Peasant in Nineteenth-Century Russia* (Stanford: Stanford University Press, 1968), 314 pages. For the peasant in social transition after 1861 see Von Laue, "Russian Labor Between Field and Factory 1892–1903," *California Slavic Studies* 3 (1964):33–65.

52. Kromov, *Ekonomicheskoye Razitiye,* p. 270; and Von Laue, "The High Cost and the Gamble of the Witte System: A Chapter in the Industrialization of Russia," *Journal of Economic History* 13, no. 4 (1953):443; and Von Laue, *Witte,* pp. 145.

53. Von Laue, "Russian Labor," p. 36. A useful source for agricultural output and trends is Raymond W. Goldsmith, "The Economic Growth of Tsarist Russia 1860–1913," *Economic Development and Cultural Change* 9, no. 3 (April 1961):441–475.

54. Von Laue, "Russian Labor," pp. 38–46.

55. Ibid., pp. 47–65.

56. Von Laue, "Russian Peasants in the Factory 1892–1904," *Journal of Economic History* 21 (1961):68.

57. Manning, *The Crisis of the Old Order,* pp. 3–24.

58. Ibid., pp. 25–64; and Geroid Tanquary Robinson, *Rural Russia under the Old Regime* (New York: Macmillan, 1957), pp. 129–137.

59. Manning, *The Crisis of the Old Order,* pp. 373–374; and Leon Trotsky,

1905 (London: Penquin, 1971), pp. 61–64. For a statistical breakdown of "large," "commercial," and "middle peasant" landholdings in 1900, see Kromov, *Ekonomicheskoye Razitiye,* p. 160.

60. Manning, *The Crisis of the Old Order,* pp. 45–64.

61. Ibid., pp. 67–88.

62. Trotsky, *1905,* pp. 38–40; and A. F. Yakovlev, *Ekonomischeskie Krizisy v Rossii* (Moscow, 1947), p. 217.

63. McKay, *Pioneers for Profit,* pp. 26–27.

64. Ibid., pp. 216–220.

65. Ibid., pp. 25–36, 380; Lyashchenko, *National Economy,* pp. 704–711; George Sherman Queen, *The United States and the Material Advance in Russia 1881–1906* (New York: Arno Press, 1976), pp. 20–25; and Kromov, *Ekonomicheskoye Razitiye,* pp. 381–382.

66. Kromov, *Ekonomicheskoye Razitiye,* pp. 452–453, 462; M. W. Kovalevsky, ed., *La Russie à la fin du 19e siècle* (Paris, 1900), p. 291; and McKay, *Pioneers for Profit,* pp. 4, 28, 297.

67. McKay, *Pioneers for Profit,* p. 297.

68. Kromov, *Ekonomicheskoye Razitiye,* pp. 453–454.

69. McKay, *Pioneers for Profit,* p. 310.

70. Ibid., p. 27; L. Eventov, *Innostrannye Kapitaly v Russkoi Promyshlennosti* (Moscow, 1931), pp. 20–23; and Kromov, *Ekonomicheskoye Razitiye,* pp. 382–385.

71. Cited in McKay, *Pioneers for Profit,* p. 189. See also Von Laue, *Witte,* pp. 167–193; and Manning, *The Crisis of the Old Order,* pp. 67–131.

72. McKay, *Pioneers for Profit,* pp. 192–257.

73. Ibid.

74. Ibid., pp. 283–285; and Queen, *The United States and Material Advance,* pp. 176–221.

75. Patricia Herlihy, "Odessa: Staple Trade and Urbanization in New Russia," *Jahrbucher für Geschichte Ostreuropas* 21, no. 2 (1973):184–195.

76. Ibid.; also see Margaret Miller, "The Trade Balance of Russia," *Slavonic Review* 1, no. 2 (1922):414–415; McKay, *Pioneers for Profit,* p. 281; and Jacob Walkin, *The Rise of Democracy in Pre-Revolutionary Russia* (New York: Praeger, 1962), pp. 188–191.

77. Miller, *The Economic Development of Russia,* p. 121; and Kromov, *Ekonomicheskoye Razitiye,* pp. 382–387.

78. Kromov, *Ekonomicheskoye Razitiye,* p. 384; and Teodore Shanin, "Russia as a Developing Society" (Washington, D.C., Unpublished, Woodrow Wilson Institution, 1984).

79. Kromov, *Ekonomicheskoye Razitiye,* p. 384.

Eight: Elite Crisis and Mass Mobilization, 1910–1914

1. For an assessment of the extent of support for Madero among the industrial workers see Anderson, *Outcasts in Their Own Land,* pp. 257–267.

2. Madero's campaign and rise to power are treated by Charles C. Cumberland,

Mexican Revolution: Genesis under Madero (Austin: University of Texas Press, 1952); and Stanley R. Ross, *Francisco I. Madero, Apostle of Mexican Democracy* (New York: Columbia University Press, 1955).

3. The developing tensions in Morelos are described in Anenecuilco, Municipio Ayala, ejidal, 25:2961 (724.10), 9 bundles, and Ayala, Municipio Ayala, ejidal, 23:2960 (724.10), 10 bundles, AHSRA; and Womack, *Zapata,* pp. 3–96.

4. For background on the northern revolutionaries, see Aguilar Camin, *La revolución nomada,* pp. 19–163; Katz, *The Secret War in Mexico,* pp. 7–21; and William K. Meyers, "Interest Conflicts and Popular Discontent: The Origins of the Revolution in the Laguna, 1880–1910" (Ph.D. diss., University of Chicago, 1979), chap. 3.

5. On Durango, see Meyers, "La Comarca Lagunera: Work, Protest, and Popular Mobilization in North Central Mexico," in Benjamin and McNellie, eds., *Other Mexicos,* pp. 243–274; and idem, "Politics, Vested Rights, and Economic Growth in Porfirian Mexico," *Hispanic American Historical Review* (August 1977):425–454.

6. The papers of the Mixed Claims Commission record dozens of assaults by armed revolutionaries against American properties from 1910 until May 1911. For examples, see Agency Numbers 216, 289, 1399, 1426, 1524, 1553, 1703, 1733, 1922, 2346, 2603, 3497, and 5820; and Docket Number 83, Entry Number 125, Records Group 76, The Mixed Claims Commission, WNRC. For other assaults against American properties, see the lengthy report on the attack on and occupation of the Corralitos hacienda, the Corralitos Archive, Peirce Family Papers, Topsfield, or the duplicates in possession of the author. See also the Rascon hacienda records, Townsend-Stanton Family Papers, HTML; and the Northwestern Railroad Archive, BLAC.

7. An insightful analysis of the competing interests in the revolution is Adolfo Gilly, *La revolución interrumpida* (Mexico City: Ediciones "El Caballito," 1973), pp. 41–93.

8. The land seizures are described in the Mixed Claims Commission Records; of special interest are the reports of the American land companies along the lower Gulf coast and in Campeche. See Markly and Miller, Contractors, to Henry Lane Wilson, Mexico City, 22 November 1911, Agency Number 1396, Entry 125, and the Laguna Corporation Papers, Agency 1391, Entry 125, Records Group 76, The Mixed Claims Commission, WNRC. For Tabasco see Agency Number 1703, Entry 125, The Mixed Claims Commission, Records Group 76, WNRC.

9. The Madero-Standard Oil Contract is found in Transcontinental Petroleum Company, Agency 5049, Boxes 184–185, General Claims Commission, Extended Claims, Records Group 76, WNRC. See also *Diario Oficial,* 5 June 1912, pp. 436–438. The Standard Oil Company owned 99.975 percent of Transcontinental's stock. For Madero's dealings with Standard Oil, see Kenneth Grieb, "Standard Oil and the Financing of the Mexican Revolution," *California Historical Quarterly* 49 (March 1971):59–71; Campbell, "Taft, Díaz and Oil," pp. 1–15; and Chief, Bureau of Investigation, Washington, D.C. to the Attorney General, Washington, D.C., 26 April 1911, and other documents, in Gene Hanrahan, ed., *Documents on the Mexican Revolution,* vol. I, pt. II (Salisbury, N.C.: Documentary Publications, 1976), pp. 411–423. The Francisco Madero-Frost brothers link via the

Banco de Coahuila is established in Fred Leber and Guadalupe Garcia Leber, Agency 5247, Box 187, The Mexican American General Claims Commission, Deferred Miscellaneous Claims Approved after 1935, Records Group 76, WNRC.

10. See Winkler, *The First Billion,* for construction of the National City Bank into the giant of international finance.

11. For the roles of the National City bank directors, see ibid. For an example of the Texas Company leadership's complaints, see Cullinan, Houston, to Arnold Schlaet, New York, 11 March 1913, File 619, Box 16, Autry Papers, WRC. Ludwell Denny, *We Fight for Oil* (Westport, Conn.: Hyperion Press, 1976), pp. 46–52, describes the grievances of American oil producers in Mexico, especially Doheny and the Rockefellers.

12. Hart, *Anarchism,* pp. 104–111.

13. The nature of Madero's support in Chihuahua is explained by William H. Beezley, *Insurgent Governor: Abraham González and the Mexican Revolution in Chihuahua* (Lincoln: University of Nebraska Press, 1973). For background, see Mark Wasserman, *Capitalists, Caciques, and Revolution: The Native Elite and Foreign Enterprise in Chihuahua, Mexico, 1854–1911* (Chapel Hill: University of North Carolina Press, 1984), p. 232.

The Reyes revolution is explained by Anthony Bryan, "The Career of General Bernardo Reyes: Continuity and Change in Mexican Politics, 1905–1913" (Master's thesis, University of Nebraska, 1967); and Victor Niemeyer, "Frustrated Invasion: The Revolutionary Attempt of General Bernardo Reyes from San Antonio in 1911," *Southwestern Historical Quarterly* 67 (1963–1964):213–225. Henry Lane Wilson and Madero are treated in Lowell L. Blaisdell, "Henry Lane Wilson and the Overthrow of Madero," *Southwestern Social Science Quarterly* 45 (1962):126–135.

For examples of the assaults on American properties in Campeche, see Agency Numbers 1391 and 1396, Entry 125, Records Group 76, The Mixed Claims Commission, WNRC.

14. The Baja California conflict is described in Blaisdell, *The Desert Revolution: Baja California, 1911* (Madison: University of Wisconsin Press, 1962). The properties of Chandler, Griffith, and Fletcher of Los Angeles and three of California's richest citizens are described in Folder 9, Box 19, the Henry W. Keller Collection, the Huntington Library.

15. The dispute between Orozco, Villa, and Madero at Ciudad Juárez over agrarian reform is treated in Gilly, *La revolución interrumpida,* pp. 73–75. The best treatment of the Orozco revolt is Michael Meyer, *Mexican Rebel: Pascual Orozco and the Mexican Revolution, 1910–1915* (Lincoln: University of Nebraska Press, 1967).

16. Claude E. Guyant, Consul on Special Detail, on Board the *Buford,* to Secretary of State, Washington, D.C., 14 June 1912, Department of State Decimal File 312.11/635.

17. Huerta's campaign and ensuing political career are treated in Michael Meyer, *Huerta: A Political Portrait* (Lincoln: University of Nebraska Press, 1972); idem, "The Militarization of Mexico, 1913–1914," *The Americas* 27 (1971):293–306; and Grieb, *The United States and Huerta* (Lincoln: University of Nebraska Press, 1969).

18. Violent attacks against American properties by Mexican revolutionaries

grew dramatically in size and scope during 1912. These innumerable assaults, which parallel the attacks against Mexican elite-owned estates, are recorded in the archives of the Mixed Claims Commission. For examples see Agency Numbers 218, 227, 239, 289, 331, 436, 525, 527, 531, 536, 562, 595, 624, 1316, 1343, 1391, 1396, 1703, 1733, 1737, 1921, 2336, 2381, 2452, 4486, 4976, and 5855, Entries 119, 125, and 152, Records Group 76, The Mixed Claims Commission, WNRC. See also the Department of State Decimal Files, especially the 312.11 collection. For examples, see the report of Guyant, Consul on Special Detail, 14 June 1912, 312.11/635; or the reports numbered 312.115M574/3 and 312.115T541/1. The latter file treats the armed invasion of the Tlahualilo Estates on the Nazas River by armed rebels calling themselves Maderistas on 15 February 1912.

19. Jacinto Huitrón, *Orígenes e historia del movimiento obrero en México* (Mexico City: Editores Mexicanos Unidos, 1975), p. 227; "Un boicót, un jurado y una manifestación," *Lucha* (Mexico City), 5 February 1913; "La Gran Confederación del Trabajo," *El Obrero Liberal* (Mexico City), 1 February 1913; and "La Gran Liga Obrera y la sesión tormentosa de la confederación," in ibid.

20. The Mixed Claims Commission records contain the complaints of over 3,200 American companies and individuals who suffered losses as a result of violence between 20 November 1910 and 31 May 1920. Other complaints for the period 1912–February 1913 can be found in myriad company archives and the Department of State Decimal Files, some of which were cited earlier. A book-length study of the Mexican confrontation with American capital in the countryside is forthcoming.

21. For the Texas Oil Company's holdings, see the Mexico-Texas Petroleum and Asphalt Company, 311,450 hectares, Fojas 1–9, Libro Number 5; The Mexican Gulf Land and Development Company, 75,000 acres, Legajo 163, Number 4; La Sautema Company, 810,000 hectares, Folio 115, Documento 10, Libro 2, Soto la Marina, San Fernando, Tercer Distrito; Registro de la Propiedad, Registro Pública, Ciudad Victoria, Tamaulipas. See also John R. Southworth and Percy G. Holms, *Tamaulipas, reseña geográfica y estadística* (Paris and Mexico City: Librería de la Viuda de C. Bouret, 1910), pp. 55–65; and the map of Mexico Company holdings, The Kile Papers, BLAC.

22. The complex makeup of the northern revolutionaries is studied by Aguilar Camin, *La revolución nomada*, pp. 265–359; Wasserman, *Capitalists, Caciques, and Revolution,* p. 232; Linda Hall, *Alvaro Obregon, Power and Revolution in Mexico, 1911–1920* (College Station: Texas A&M University Press, 1981), pp. 38–58; Douglas Richmond, *Venustiano Carranza's Nationalist Struggle, 1893–1920* (Lincoln: University of Nebraska Press, 1983), pp. 22–58; Meyers, "La Comarca Lagunera," pp. 243–274; and Beezley, *Insurgent Governor,* pp. 139–162.

23. The relationship between Obregon Salido and W. R. Grace and Company is revealed in the company's files. See W. R. Grace and Company, Case 306, Docket 136, Box 30, Agrarian Claims Commission (U.S. Section), Records Group 76, WNRC.

24. Womack, *Zapata,* pp. 165–166.

25. For the La China episode see ibid., p. 170. The Zapatista offensive is described in ibid., pp. 159–190.

26. Details of the relationship between American arms dealers and manufac-

turers and the División del Norte are contained in the Lazaro de la Garza Papers, BLAC.

27. The events at the Marshall and Salazar haciendas were related in the Archer interview, Pacific Palisades, California, 6 January 1984.

28. See Gilly, *La revolución interrumpida,* pp. 106–109; and Katz, *The Secret War in Mexico,* pp. 260–267.

29. For the best analysis of the situation in Mexico City and the strategies of the Carbajal government, Carranza, and Obregon Salido, see Gilly, *La revolución interrumpida,* pp. 106–118. His argument is borne out by the documents of the U.S. military. For the Carbajal-Carranza accord to surrender the remnants of the Federal Army to the Carrancista forces, see the intercepted wire from Carranza to Carbajal forwarded by General Frederick Funston, Veracruz, to the Adjutant General, Washington, D.C., 7 August 1914, Document Number 114, Box 7477, Collection Number 2149991, Mexican Intervention, NARA.

The general conflict between the convention forces and the Constitutionalists, the denial of fuel for the Villista forces, and Obregon Salido's entry into Mexico City is treated by Robert E. Quirk, *The Mexican Revolution, 1914–1915: The Convention of Aguascalientes* (New York: Citadel Press, 1963). Anti-Villista chief customs inspector at El Paso, Zack Lamar Cobb, was anxious to stop the Villistas. Cobb repeatedly denounced Villa and the Villistas during 1913–1915. For example, see Cobb, El Paso, to Secretary of the Treasury, Washington, D.C., "request to refuse transportation and entry," 14 January 1914, Folder 4, Box 106, Fall Papers, Huntington Library.

Cobb was charged with the oversight and approval of all materials crossing the border from El Paso to Chihuahua. His law firm partners, attorneys Walthall and Gamble, worked for Luis Terrazas, the Chihuahua oligarch. Cobb frequently accused Villa of stealing cattle hides from Terrazas and Baird, another Chihuahua hacendado. See Cobb, El Paso, to Secretary of the Treasury, Washington, D.C., 18 January 1914, Folder 1, Box 106, Fall Papers, Huntington Library. American concern regarding the possible repair of the railroad tracks between Zacatecas and Aguascalientes is expressed by the Commander of the 17th Infantry (name illegible), Camp Eagle Pass, Texas, to the Commanding General, Southern Department, 7 August 1914, Number 1072, Box 7477, Collection Number 2149991, Mexican Intervention, NARA.

For American plans to occupy Mexico City in case of a Zapatista or urban working-class takeover, see Funston, Veracruz, to Adjutant General, Washington, D.C., 7 May 1914, Number 1, Box 7473, Collection Number 2149991, Mexican Intervention, NARA.

30. The "betrayal" by Obregon was described in the interview of Rosendo Salazar by Hart, Tlalnepantla, 10 August 1969. Studies of the Casa del Obrero Mundial abound. For those written by participants, see Huitrón, *Orígenes e historia;* Luis Araiza, *Historia del Movimiento Obrero Mexicano,* Tomo III (Mexico City: 1964–1966); Salazar and José G. Escobedo, *Las pugnas de la gleba, 1907–1922,* vol. 1 (Mexico City: Editorial Avante, 1923); and Salazar, *La Casa del Obrero Mundial* (Mexico City: Costa-Amic, Editor, 1962). For an examination of Casa strategy during the revolution, see Hart, "The Urban Working Class and the Mexican Revolution: The Case of the Casa del Obrero Mundial," *Hispanic American Historical Review* 58 (February 1978):1–20.

31. For examples of the myriad land seizures and violent attacks against American-owned commercial estates by lower-class groups outside the authority of the revolutionary elites, see Docket Number 78 and Agency Numbers 90, 136, 226, 236, 296, 1391, 1396, 1568, 1804, 1914, 1921, 1922, 2350, 2605, 2607, 2691, 4978, 5104, and 5830, Entries 118, 119, and 125, Records Group 76, The Mixed Claims Commission, WNRC. See also the Department of State, Decimal Files 312.115M5712/2 and 312.1150C3/6, NARA. At this time the Rascon hacienda was devastated, as was John Henry Kirby's Buena Fe mine, the Corralitos hacienda, and many properties of the Northwestern Railroad. See the Townsend-Stanton Family Papers, HTML; the Kirby Papers, HMRC; the Corralitos Archive, Peirce Family Papers; and the Northwestern Railroad Papers, BLAC, respectively.

32. For Villa's agrarian reform plans, see Katz, *The Secret War in Mexico,* pp. 280–287; and Arnaldo Cordoba, *La ideología de la Revolución Mexicana,* 2d ed. (Mexico City: Ediciones Era, 1973), pp. 155–172 and 465–470. Both Lind and chargé to Mexico Silliman despised Villa and jubilantly followed reports regarding the progress of what Silliman labeled "our" forces at Celaya. Lind's analysis of the Villa-Carranza dispute is presented fully in chapter 9. "Villa acted with wanton disloyalty against the Carranza government . . . as early as the month of May of last year. Carranza showed much patience in his efforts to placate Villa." See the report of John Lind to Robert Lansing, Washington, D.C., Folder 2321, Box 70, House Papers, Yale University Library. On 4 August 1915 Lind denied charges that he had served as Carranza's attorney; see ibid.

Nine: Class Confrontation, American Intervention, and Workers' Defeat, 1914–1916

1. For hundreds of reports of peasant land occupations and attacks against commercial estate properties by groups outside external authority but claiming Villista and Zapatista allegiances, see the Mixed Claims Commission Papers, WNRC. In addition, see the Corralitos hacienda archive, Peirce Family Papers, Topsfield, or the copies in my possession; the Rascon hacienda records, Townsend-Stanton Family papers, HTML; the Northwestern Railroad Papers, BLAC; the Santa Fe mine folder, Kirby Papers, HMRC; the Richardson Construction Company documents, Fall Papers, Huntington Library; and the Allhands Papers, JECM.

2. For a view of Carrancista nationalism, see Richmond, *Venustiano Carranza's Nationalist Struggle*. The rapport between the Americans and Obregon Salido and Elías Calles is heavily documented in the Mexican Intervention Files, Collection Number 2149991, Records Group 92, NARA. See also W. R. Grace and Company, Case Number 306, Docket Number 136, Box 30, Agrarian Claims Commission (U.S. Section), Records Group 76, WNRC.

3. The most complete treatment of the convention is Quirk, *The Mexican Revolution*. See also Gilly, *La revolución interrumpida,* pp. 120–138.

4. Quirk, *The Mexican Revolution,* pp. 109–111.

5. Lind to House, Washington, D.C., 23 July 1915, Folder 2321, Box 70, House Papers, Yale University Library.

6. For a description of Carranza's action, see Gilly, *La revolución interrumpida,* p. 93. Land descriptions of the Texas Company's holdings in Tamaulipas are found

in the Sherman Kile Papers, One Box, Uncatalogued, BLAC; and in Southworth and Holms, *Tamaulipas: reseña geográfica y estadística,* pp. 56–63. The sales and development contracts are recorded in the offices of the Registro de la Propiedad de Tamaulipas, Ciudad Victoria (311,450 hectares), Fojas 1–9 and 24, Legajo Number 122, Sección 1, Ciudad Victoria, 1944; Libro 5, Propiedad 1896–1900, Aldama (1,000,000 acres); Fojas 3, 14, and 15, Legajo 163 (75,000 or 87,000 acres); and Folio 115, Documento 10, Libro 2, Soto la Marina, 1907 (for $8,830,000 capitalization, and 810,000 hectares), San Fernando, Tercer Distrito.

The jointly held lands of development companies on the American side of the Rio Grande involving Frank Andrews, James B. Wells, Thomas Watt Gregory, William Jennings Bryan, and James Stillman are shown, with the companies' names, in the "New Development Map of the Lower Rio Grande Valley of Texas," 1 September 1928, Geography and Map Division, Library of Congress. Stillman's separately owned properties are listed on the same map.

7. Interview, Archer, Pacific Palisades, 8 January 1984. For more on Marshall's property holdings in Mexico, see Agency Number 1850, Entry 125, Special Claims Commission, Records Group 76, WNRC; and the Department of State, Decimal Files 312.114W/171 and 312.115P181/51, Records Group 59, NARA.

8. The Rascon hacienda papers involving the Lee, Townsend, and Stanton families of Galveston and New Orleans are found in Boxes 1, 2, 5, 6, and 7, Townsend-Stanton Family Papers, HTML. For Tom Lee and Attorney General Gregory, see Box 19, the Thomas Watt Gregory Papers, Manuscripts Division, Library of Congress. Gregory's oldest son served as an administrator in the bonds department of Stillman's National City bank. In the years that followed Tom Lee served as a legal counsel for the Gulf Oil Corporation specializing in Mexican problems.

9. Heywood and Jennings had landholding partnerships near the Mexican border with the Houston-based Texas Company directors, businessmen Duval West and George Brackenridge of San Antonio, the National City Bank, and numerous Democratic party officials in Texas. For repeated citations see Notebooks 1, 4, 5, and 15, the Looseleaf Notebook, and Folder 7, Box "35" or "46," Allhands Papers, JECM; and the Reference Books, and the Abstract of Lands prepared by Duval West, ARGLI, RGVHC.

10. For the sequence of embargoes and the alternating opening and closing of Mexican border points and ports for shipments from the United States by the American government, see Roll 167, 1910–1944, 812.10/–812.345/17, Records Group 59, Purport Lists for the Decimal File, Department of State, NARA (hereafter cited as Purport Lists, Roll 167). For the executive order of 9 June 1914, inaugurating the embargo policy in favor of Carranza during the Carrancista-Villista dispute, see Box 7476, Mexican Intervention, Collection Number 2149991, Records Group 92, NARA.

While allowing imports of arms at Tampico and other ports William G. McAdoo issued the following order on 22 July 1914 to General Tasker H. Bliss, army commander at El Paso and anti-Villista Chief Customs Inspector Zack Cobb at El Paso: "Inspect thoroughly all coal cars, oil tanks, and dynamite boxes passing through El Paso into Mexico to prevent smuggling of arms and munitions of war." McAdoo, Washington, D.C., to Bliss, El Paso, 22 July 1914, Box 7477, Mexican Intervention, Collection Number 2149991, Records Group 92, NARA.

11. Consul Louis Hostetter, Hermosillo, to Secretary of State Bryan, Washington, D.C., 28 April 1913, Box 7473, Collection Number 2149991, Mexican Intervention, Records Group 92, NARA.

12. For gun running from El Paso into Mexico during the early years of the revolution, see Charles H. Harris and Louis R. Sadler, "The Underside of the Mexican Revolution: El Paso, 1912," *The Americas* 39 (July 1982):69–84.

13. The role of the Texans in the cabinet and the influence of Texas investors in Mexico upon Colonel House are described by Arthur D. Howden Smith, *Mr. House of Texas* (New York and London: Funk and Wagnalls, 1940), pp. 81–83. The network of Texas investors in Mexico and their support of Carranza and then Obregon Salido will be developed in greater detail in my forthcoming book, *Empire and Revolution: The United States and Mexico, 1876–1920*.

President Wilson's support for Huerta is demonstrated by his exemptions from the Mexican arms embargo on the dictator's behalf. For examples, see 812.113, Subjects 2108, 8 March 1913; 2120, 3 April 1913; 439, 440, 2215, and 2216, 19 April 1913; 2204, 30 April 1913; 2271, 1 May 1913; 2556 and 2528, 8 July 1913; 2670, 12 August 1913; and 2643, 15 August 1913; the Purport Lists, Roll 167.

14. The arms shipments were halted in late August after the Wilson administration decided that Huerta could not maintain order; see 812.113, William Jennings Bryan, Subjects 2717a and 2717b, 27 August 1913; the Treasury Department announcement, Subject 2729, 29 August 1913; and President Wilson, Subject 2750, 27 August 1913; Purport Lists, Roll 167.

The Constitutionalists began to obtain arms legally via border shipments on 3 February 1913 when the American president revoked the embargo proclaimed on 14 March 1912. See 812.113, Subject 3105a, 3 February 1914, Purport Lists, Roll 167. Obregon Salido thanked the president on 4 February 1914; see 812.113, Subject 3114, Purport Lists, Roll 167.

15. Smith, *Mr. House of Texas,* p. 81. For the attacks on the home of Henry House, see Henry Houze (*sic*), Entry 125, Agency Number 4674, The Mixed Claims Commission, Records Group 76, WNRC.

16. For Lind on Villa, see Lind to House, Washington, D.C., 23 July 1915, Folder 2321, Box 70, House Papers, Yale University Library. For insight regarding House's network of associates in Texas see Anders, *Boss Rule in South Texas;* and the array of House's fellow founding directors in 1905 at the Union Bank and Trust of Houston, File 579A, Box 13, Autry Papers, WRC; and the list of his partners at the bank in 1920, File 932, Box 25, ibid. See also Folder 22, Box 6, Cullinan Papers, HMRC.

17. Cullinan, Houston to Schlaet, New York, 11 March 1913, File 619, Box 16, Autry Papers, WRC.

18. In order to re-create the interrelationships among the leadership of the Mexican Company, which was the land development concern for the Texas Company directors in Mexico, first see the Houston City Directory, the Mexico Company, 1910–1912. Mexico Company officers Swanson and Rowson associated with Texas Company directors Cullinan, Brooks, Hogg, and Autry in a variety of land development projects near Houston and in the Lower Rio Grande Valley; see Folder 24, Box 7, Folder 12, Box 8, and Folder 4, Box 11, Cullinan Papers, HMRC; and Box 7, and File 619, Box 16, Autry Papers, WRC. Brooks bought

350,000 acres in Tamaulipas. For the acquisitions in Mexico, see Cullinan, Houston, to J. R. Sharp, Tampico, 8 February 1913; Cullinan, Houston, to Coke K. Burns, Houston, 19 October 1910, Folder 24, Box 7, Cullinan Papers, HMRC; The Mexico-Texas Petroleum and Asphalt Company, Fojas 1–9, Libro Number 5; The Mexican Gulf Land and Development Company, Legajo 163, Number 4; and La Sautema Company, Folio 115, Documento 10, Libro 2, San Fernando, Tercer Distrito, Registro de la Propiedad, Registro Pública, Ciudad Victoria, Tamaulipas. See also Southworth and Holms, *Tamaulipas: reseña geográfica y estadística,* pp. 55–65; and the map of Mexico Company holdings, the Kile Papers, BLAC.

19. For the irrigation bonds, see the *Commercial and Financial Chronicle,* Number 1013, 17 October 1908. A detailed description of the properties and contracts of sale and colonization by Americans is contained in Southworth and Holms, *Tamaulipas: reseña geográfica y estadística,* pp. 53–65.

20. On the Democrats, see "Mexican Property Owners Non-Interventionist League," Folder 14, Box 108 and Folder 2, Box 109, Fall Papers, Huntington Library. For interventionist strategies, see the Fall Papers, especially Box 106, and the Buckley Papers, BLAC.

21. Buckley, Tampico, to House, Washington, D.C., 3 November 1913, Folder 664, Box 20, House Papers, Yale University Library.

22. For the meeting of Wilson, Stillman, Rockefeller, and Vanderlip, see Winkler, *The First Billion,* p. 210. On 18 March 1881 Stillman sold two-thirds of his riparian rights to the Rio Grande that he had purchased during the Brownsville phase of the Revolution of Tuxtepec to the National Railroad of Mexico; see the contract, Box 10, the Stillman Papers, BL.

23. See Boxes 106, 108, and 109, the Fall Papers, Huntington Library, and the Buckley Papers, BLAC.

24. Thomas P. Littlepage, Washington, D.C., to A. M. Trueb, New York City, 9 January 1914, Northwestern Railroad Collection, BLAC.

25. See Lindley Garrison, Washington, D.C., to Hon. Swagar Sherley, House of Representatives, Washington, D.C., 20 April 1914, Box 7473, Mexican Intervention, NARA. For the machine gun shipment aboard the *Monterrey* and confiscated at Veracruz by the U.S. armed forces, see File 91, Entry 1, Records group 141, Military Government of Veracruz (hereafter cited as MGV), WNRC.

26. See the General Correspondence, Files of the Secretary's Office, Fiscal Year 1915, Entry 19, Record Group 141, MGV, WNRC.

27. Files 64, 150, 156, 162, 165, 217, 227, 231, 235, 236, 243, 257, and 272, Entry 12, Correspondence of the Administrator of Customs and Captain of the Port, April-November 1914, Records Group 141, MGV, WNRC.

28. File 64, Entry 12; Audit of 9 July 1914, Entry 19; and File 129, Entry 1, Records Group 141, MGV, WNRC. The Bannerman information was made possible through the interview of James B. Hughes, Jr., by Hart, 3 August 1982, Houston. Hughes is one of the world's leading experts on Mexican arms and is an authority on the history of U.S. and European arms dealers. His book, *Mexican Military Arms: The Cartridge Period, 1866–1967* (Houston: Deep River Armory, 1968), has been used in classes at the Colegio Militar, Estado Mayor, Secretaría de la Defensa Nacional, México D.F., since its publication.

29. File 120, Entry 1, Records Group 141, MGV, WNRC.

30. Files 64, 156, and 257, Entry 12, ibid. Hughes provided the cargo and weight analysis for the *Descartes* armaments; Hughes, Interview, 3 August 1982. For the *Krownprincessen Cecile* inventories, see Files 249 and 272, Entry 12, and the warehouse inventory, 1 August 1914, Cobertizo number 2 and the succeeding inventories, including that of 21 November 1914, Entry 19, ibid.

31. Files 64, 132, 165, 214, 227, 228, and 235, Entry 12, ibid. For the *Tabasco,* see File 229, Entry 12, and File 120, Entry 1, ibid.

32. Weight analysis via interview, Hart with Hughes, 3 August 1982. The known weight of the cargo confirmed Hughes's analysis. For the shipments of arms to the "police and planters" of Campeche at the request of the "Constitutionalist Government of Mexico," see the audit of 9 July 1914, Secretary of the Custom House, Arms and Ammunition Transferred to Cobertizo number 1, Entry 19, ibid. For the *San Marcos* cargos secretly returned to Veracruz, see the Shipping Manifest, Number 17, 11 October 1914, the Bill of Lading, and the memorandum, "Ammunition Not Unloaded," Number 18, 1 October 1914, U.S.A.C.T. San Marcos, Box 1449, Entry 2023, Office of the Quartermaster General, Army Transport Service, General File, 1914–1940 (Declassified), Records Group 92, WNRC. For machine guns, see Shipping Manifest Number 17, Box 1449, 22 October 1914, ibid. See also Box 1450, ibid., regarding orders "not to unload" at Galveston and to return the arms to Veracruz.

33. Files 80 and 165, Entry 12, Records Group 141, MGV, WNRC.

34. See "Vapor Monserrat" and "Vapor Tabasco," "Armamento y Parque," Warehouseman's Report, Cobertizo number 2, 18 November 1914, Entry 19, ibid.

35. Felix Sommerfeld, Washington, D.C., to Lazaro De La Garza, El Paso, 4 June 1914, Wallet V. Folder B, Document 23, De La Garza Papers, BLAC. Bryan's hostility toward Villa deepened when raiders calling themselves "Villistas" crossed the border and attacked the secretary of state's and other estates near Mercedes, Texas. His hacienda inside Mexico also suffered attacks, but its whereabouts and the identity of the assailants is not known at this time. The papers pursuant to his estate's claim against the Mexican government have been removed from the Claims Commission's files. For the background on the arms shipment and prosecution of the *Sunshine*'s owners, see 812.113, Subject Number 3399, 23 June 1914; Subject Number 3401, 16–23 June 1914; Subject Number 3492, 13–20 July 1914; Subject Number 3464, 20 July 1914; Subject Number 3463, 20 July 1914; Purport Lists, Roll 167. For shipments to Carranza forces during the arms embargo following the Veracruz intervention on 23 April 1914 and against Villa during the late spring and early summer of 1914, both from across the border at Brownsville to Matamoros and to Tampico from Galveston, see M. J. García, 412.11G164, Box 4752L, Records Group 59, NARA. In July 1914 García moved arms and ammunition valued at $59,250 from Brownsville to General Luis Caballero at Ciudad Victoria, including 1,500 carbines and 1,500,000 cartridges. On 28 July 1914 he delivered $94,000 in arms and ammunition to Carranza's son-in-law, General Candido Aguilar, at Tampico consisting of 2,000 rifles and 1,000,000 cartridges. Garcia shipped similar amounts to Generals Lucio Blanco at Matamoros, Jesus Carranza, and De Los Santos, while customs authorities opposite

Chihuahua and Sonora continued to harass the Villistas; see ibid. Joseph Besteiro and Brothers, Brownsville, also supplied the pro-Carranza Constitutionalists in May 1914, Box 7473, Mexican Intervention, Collection Number 2149991, Records Group 92, NARA.

On 9 June 1914 President Wilson approved the continued shipment of arms via Carancista-controlled Tampico and other seaports under the supervision of the Department of Commerce. Correctly, the Department of the Treasury was given jurisdiction over the border crossing points. On 20 July 1914, the president ordered all munitions shipments into Chihuahua halted. The Treasury Department issued the following order to Cobb: "Inspect thoroughly all coal cars, oil tanks and dynamite boxes passing through El Paso into Mexico to prevent smuggling of arms and munitions of war"; William G. McAdoo, Washington, D.C., to General Tasker H. Bliss, El Paso, 22 July 1914, Box 7477, ibid.

For Secretary of State Bryan's arrangements for the transportation of Constitutionalist General Benjamin Hill and his staff from Ciudad Porfirio Díaz to Naco by train on American territory in order to oppose the Villistas there, a decision which was seconded by the governors of Texas, New Mexico, and Arizona, see Secretary of State Bryan, Washington, D.C., to the Secretary of War, Washington, D.C., 21 August 1914, Box 7477, ibid.

The army generals consistently expressed the anti-Villa and pro-Carranza actions and sentiments of the administration; for examples, see General Tasker Bliss, El Paso, to Witherspoon, Washington, D.C., 18 July 1914, ibid. For Villa's "deviltry," see Funston, Veracruz, to Witherspoon, Washington, D.C., 15 August 1914, ibid. For the working-class alignment at Cananea in favor of Maytorena, his Yaqui support, and Constitutionalist hostility toward the workers at Cananea, and U.S. military concern, see Colonel Hatfield, Douglas, Arizona, to the Brigade Commander, Fort Sam Houston, San Antonio, 15 August 1914, ibid. For the order to General Bliss and reference to the Treasury Department's order to "the custom house collectors along the Mexican border" to embargo Villa, see Judge Advocate General, Washington, D.C., to General Witherspoon, Washington, D.C., 15 August 1914, ibid. For the transportation by the Americans via trains of the defeated forces of Elías Calles at Nogales to reinforce the Constitutionalists at Naco, see Bliss, El Paso, to Adjutant General, Washington, D.C., 19 August 1914, ibid. Witherspoon, Washington, D.C., to Secretary of War, Washington, D.C., 7 September 1914, suggested "deployment of Funston's troops along Bliss' border" to enforce the embargoes against Villa after withdrawing from Veracruz; see ibid.

General Pershing's apology and embarrassment in being trapped by circumstance and etiquette into a meeting with Villa are described by Cobb, El Paso, to G. C. Carothers, Washington, D.C., 27 August 1914, ibid. After four days of hesitation and evasions, arrangements were made for Pershing to meet also with Obregon Salido; Acting Secretary of State Robert Lansing finally approved of the meeting on 1 September 1914; see ibid.

Characteristic of the anti-Villa sentiment of Bryan that Sommerfeld discovered, Cobb's partner Walthall's warning to his friend Senator Fall that "Pancho Villa" was preparing a looting attack against El Paso scheduled for May 1914 was given credence; Walthall, El Paso, to Fall, Washington, D.C., 28 April 1914, Folder 1, Box 106, Fall Papers, Huntington Library. Alongside the murder of businessman

William Benton, perhaps the most important among the myriad complaints against Villa's personal "brigandage" came from the Balfour-Stillman-Brown brothers-controlled Tlahualilo Estates: "Troops . . . under command of General Francisco Villa, at once began ransacking and looting the houses on the hacienda"; Company Report, 7 May 1912, 312.11/100/W, Box 3698, Records Group 59, NARA.

Complaints poured in to the Department of State about looting by troops of the División del Norte during Villa's march on Torreón and Zacatecas in late spring 1914. See James D. Sheahan, Richmond, to Bryan, Washington, D.C., 9 March 1914, 312.115In8/8, Box 3698D, Records Group 59, NARA. Meanwhile Carranza offered to protect the large American-owned Cinco Minas Company in Jalisco from local revolutionaries. See Carranza to George C. Carothers, El Paso, 5 June 1914, 312.1151C49/22, Box 3812, Records Group 59, NARA.

36. For the basis of U.S. government hostility toward Gutiérrez and the question of food exports by commercial estates, see W. L. Bonney, "Decree Prohibiting Exportation of Food Products from the State," *Consular and Trade Reports,* no. 238, 10 October 1914, p. 181. For the labor law abolishing both the debts and debt peonage, see Bonney, "New Labor Decree in Mexico" in ibid., p. 171. For the Rascon attacks, see Folder 1, Box 5, and Folder 1, Box 6, Minor Family Papers, HTML; and the Rascon Manufacturing Company, Docket Number 222, Claim 38, Box 109, Agrarian Claims Commission (U.S. Section), Records Group 76, WNRC. See also the Buena Fe Mining Company, Agency Number 959, Entry 125, Special Claims Commission, Records Group 76, WNRC; and the Rascon Manufacturing Company, Agency 4444, ibid.

37. Bonney, "Labor Decree," no. 238, 10 October 1914, *Consular and Trade Reports,* p. 171.

38. General Frederick Funston, Veracruz, to Adjutant General, Washington, D.C., 7 May 1914, Box 7473, Mexican Intervention, Collection Number 2149991, Records Group 92, NARA.

39. For the first quote, see Alfredo Breceda, Veracruz, to Venustiano Carranza, c/o M. García, Laredo, Texas, 5 August 1914, Headquarters U.S. Expeditionary Forces, p. 4; and Breceda, Veracruz, to Rafael Zubarán, Washington, D.C., 5 August 1914, ibid.

40. Magaña's "anarchist" influence on Villa during their stay in prison together in 1912 was explained by Frederich Katz in "Francisco Villa and the Mexican Revolution," the Woodrow Wilson Center, Smithsonian Institution, Washington, D.C., April 1984.

41. Colonel Charles Hatfield, Douglas, Arizona, to Commanding Officer, Fort Sam Houston, 8 June 1914, ibid.

42. For denial of permission to ship weapons to Maytorena, see the curt letter of Secretary of War Lindley Garrison, Washington, D.C., to B. J. Hirsch, Washington, D.C., 16 September 1914, Box 7477, Mexican Intervention, Collection Number 2149991, Records Group 92, NARA; and Major General W. W. Witherspoon, Chief of Staff, Washington, D.C., to Hirsch, Washington, D.C., 24 September 1914, ibid. For Alvarado's supplies in order to restore order against the Yaqui and workers at Cananea, see Subject Number 3408, 26 June 1914; Subject Number 3428, 15 July 1914; Subject Number 3441, 9 July 1914; and Subject Number 3446, 17 July 1914; Purport Lists, Roll 167.

For a description of the situation in which the Constitutionalist forces acquired arms legally and openly with the cooperation of U.S. military authorities, customs officials, the president, and cabinet officers, see Commanding General, Southern Department, 29 July 1914, in Garrison, Washington, D.C., to Secretary of State Bryan, Washington, D.C., 4 August 1914, Box 7473, Mexican Intervention, Collection Number 2149991, Records Group 92, NARA. For countless reports on supplies to the Villistas being halted and Carranza allies routinely receiving shipments via Tampico and Mazatlán in June, July, and August 1914, see Boxes 7473–7480, ibid. For an example of impounding Villista supplies, including 515,000 rounds of ammunition, see Cobb, El Paso, to Secretary of the Treasury, Washington, D.C., 8 August 1914, Box 7477, ibid.

43. Carranza to Vice Consul Silliman, Mexico City, 17 September 1914, quote forwarded in Cardos de Oliveira, Brazilian minister, Mexico City, to Secretary of State, Washington, D.C., 17 September 1914, Box 7478, ibid. For a study of the relationship between Carranza and Wilson, see Mark T. Gilderhus, *Diplomacy and Revolution: U.S.-Mexican Relations under Wilson and Carranza* (Tucson: University of Arizona Press, 1977).

44. For one of the many references to the Constitutionalist officers working with the Americans at the port and their names, see File 222, Entry 12, Correspondence of the Administrator of Customs and Captain of the Port, April-November 1914, Records Group 141, MGV, WNRC. For the shipment of cavalry equipment received by Alejo González, see his receipt for same titled "INFORME DE LAS REMESAS DE CAJAS DE PARQUE PERTENECIENTES A VARIOS VAPORES ALMACENADAS EN BODEGAS C.T.V.C., S.A. Y LLEVADOS AL COBERTIZO NO 1 Y 2 DE LA ADUANA MARITIMA DE VERACRUZ, POR ORDEN DE LA MISMA [*sic*], Entry 19, ibid. For the inventory of the boxes and their contents, see File 249, 9 May 1914, Entry 12, ibid. The military gear came from the *Kronprinzessen Cecile,* which the State Department incorrectly claimed had returned to Germany without unloading its cargo.

45. Inteview, Hart, with Antonio Salazar Páez, Professor, Cronista de la Ciudad y Director del Museo de la Ciudad, Veracruz, 28 July 1983.

46. Adjutant General W. M. Wright, War Department, Washington, D.C., to the Remington Arms, U.M.C. Company, New York, 31 October 1914, Document 227, File 23/11, Entry 12, Records Group 141, MGV, WNRC.

47. For the security of the "arms, munitions and gun implements," the procedure for replacing U.S. with Constitutionalist guards, and the deposit of the keys at the chamber of commerce, see File 400, Entry 1, ibid. The cash deposit of customs revenues is reported in "Balance of Customs Deposited with Assistant Treasurer of U.S. at New Orleans," Box 7479, Mexican Intervention, Collection Number 2149991, Records Group 92, NARA. For one of the many letters regarding American policy on the safeguarding of Mexicans who worked for them, see Captain of the Port H. O. Stickney, Veracruz, to Gabriel Remes, Veracruz, 29 April 1914, File 169, Entry 12, MGV, Records Group 141, WNRC.

48. For Duering see Provost Marshall General E. H. Plummer, Veracruz, to the Military Governor, Veracruz, 18 November 1914, transmitted in Assistant Secretary of War Henry Breckinridge, Washington, D.C., to the Secretary of State,

Washington, D.C., 3 December 1914, Box 7478, Mexican Intervention, Collection Number 2149991, Records Group 92, NARA.

49. The markings on the crates were cross-checked via references to the cargo in correspondence between customs officials and the captain of the port and in the interview, Hart with Hughes, 3 August 1982. The warehouses were measured by the author. The construction data and methods of transportation and storage were obtained in the interview, Hart with Manuel García Rodríguez, Supervisor de Servicios Portuarios, Veracruz, 17 August 1983.

50. To locate and itemize the armaments in the warehouses, see the arms claims, handling reports, and inventories in Entries 12, 19, and 28, Records Group 141, MGV, WNRC. The inventories of 19–21 November 1914 are found in Entry 19, ibid. There is no useful listing of armaments in the index to Records Group 141.

51. Quartermaster Sergeant George H. Hahn, Fort Monroe, Virginia, to Quartermaster, Fort Monroe, 24 December 1914, Box 7479, Mexican Intervention, Collection Number 2149991, Records Group 92, NARA. For the manifests, see U.S.A.C.T. San Marcos, Box 1450, Entry 2023, Office of the Quartermaster General, Army Transport Service, General File, 1914–1940, Records Group 92, WNRC.

52. Ygnacio H. Moncada, Head Warehouseman, Cobertizo number 2, Veracruz, to Captain of the Port, Veracruz, 23 November 1914, Entry 19, Records Group 141, MGV, WNRC.

53. Ibid.

54. Judge Advocate Lieutenant Colonel James Biddle Porter, to Captain of the Port, Veracruz, 6 August 1914, File 120, Entry 1, ibid.

55. Vice Consul Silliman, Mexico City, to Secretary of State, Washington, D.C., 22 October 1914, Box 7477, Mexican Intervention, Collection Number 2149991, Records Group 92, NARA.

56. Gilly, *La revolución interrumpida,* p. 147.

57. Hart, *Anarchism,* pp. 115–131; Fernando Córdoba Pérez, "El movimiento anarquista en México (1911–1921)" (Licenciado thesis, Facultad de Ciencias Políticas y Sociales, Universidad Nacional Autonoma de México, Mexico City, 1971), pp. 134–141; and Rosendo Salazar and José G. Escobedo, *Las pugnas de la gleba, 1907–1922,* pp. 93–95.

58. Obregon Salido's alliance with the Casa and Morones's rise to power were treated in the interviews, Hart with Salazar, Tlalnepantla, 10 August 1969; and Hart with José C. Valadés, Oaxtepec, 6 November 1969, and Mexico City, 13 August 1971. See Hart, *Anarchism, pp. 128–129;* and Córdoba Pérez, "Movimiento anarquista," p. 134.

59. For estimates of the number of volunteers sent from the Mexico City area to join the Constitutionalist ranks as members of the Red Battalions, see Jacinto Huitrón, *Orígenes e historia del Movimiento Obrero en México* (Mexico City: Ediciones Mexicanos Unidos, 1975), p. 274; and Salazar and Escobedo, *Las pugnas de la gleba,* p. 85. For the role of foreign soldiers making the "difference in victory," see Lawrence D. Taylor, "The Great Adventure: Mercenaries in the Mexican Revolution, 1910–1915," *The Americas* (July 1986):39. Villista arms purchases were

carried out by operatives inside the United States, including Lazaro de la Garza, who was Villa's principal financial agent. To understand the Villistas' operations and problems, see the De la Garza Collection, BLAC.

60. The delays were cited by Katz in "Francisco Villa in the Mexican Revolution," Wilson Center, Washington, D.C., April 1984.

61. The extreme hostility toward Zapata is clearly expressed in U.S. military dispatches. For example, see the concern to "prevent massacre and pillage by Zapata" in Mexico City; Funston, Veracruz, to Adjutant General, Washington, D.C., 7 May 1914, Box 7473, Mexican Intervention, Document Collection 2149991, Records Group 92, NARA.

62. Sommerfeld, New York, to De La Garza, El Paso, 4 June 1914, Wallet V, Folder B, Document 23, De la Garza Collection, BLAC.

63. For the U.S. Army's assessment of Obregon Salido, see "Intelligence Report on Constitutionalist Army Officers," p. 3, Kile Papers, BLAC. For Silliman's statement regarding the battle of León, see his conversation with Cornelio Gertz, the German consul at Veracruz in 1915, Priscilla Buckley et al., *WFB—An Appreciation by His Family and Friends* (Private Printing, 1979), p. 99, BLAC. For John Lind's support of the North versus the South (Zapata and the Casa), see ibid., p. 97. William F. Buckley served as an adviser to Bryan "while he remained Secretary of State," ibid., pp. 154–155.

64. See "Por que la carne cuesta cara," *La Vanguardia* (Mexico City), 2 June 1915; "La critica situación de la ex-capital," ibid., 3 June 1915; "Movimiento obrero local: Huelga de panaderos," *Ariete* (Mexico City), 7 November 1915; "Movimiento obrero local: Sindicato de Zapateros," ibid., 21 November 1915; "Movimiento obrero local: Las obreras se sindican," ibid.; "Movimiento obrero local: Los companeros tejidores," ibid., 12 December 1915; "Movimiento obrero local: Sindicato de carpinteros y similares," ibid.; "Movimiento obrero local: sindicato de costureros," ibid.; Juan Tudó, "Desde la Atalaya," ibid., 31 October 1915; Leonardo P. Castro, "Nuestros mejores auxiliares," ibid., 24 October and 7 November 1915; Adalbero Concha, "Maquinaciones del alto comercio de México para aumentar el costo de la vida del pueblo," *Acción Mundial,* 5 February 1916.

65. For the organization of labor in the second half of 1915 and 1916, see the labor newspapers cited earlier. For the developing crisis that led to the general strikes of 22 May and 31 July–2 August 1916, see Hart, *Anarchism,* pp. 138–155.

66. The records of the Special Claims Commission indicate that violence against American-held properties abated somewhat in 1916–1917 but remained intense enough to render most of them commercially inoperative. Their operators, after returning from exile, were often forced to flee once again.

67. John C. Murray served as an American government agent in Mexico during 1914–1916. For his anti-Villista role in 1914 among the recruits for the Red Battalions and the Casa leadership as a registered "news reporter" for the *New York Call,* his reports to President Wilson, and his anti-anarchist efforts in 1916 along with Samuel Gompers to develop a closer relationship via Luis Morones between the American and Mexican labor movements, see Salazar and Escobedo, *Las pugnas de la gleba,* pp. 95, 155–162; Huitrón, *Orígenes e historia del Movimiento Obrero en México,* pp. 275, 296; and Araiza, *Historia del Movimiento Obrero Mex-*

icano, p. 85. Araiza describes Murray as "a very important factor in the relationship between the Confederación Regional Obrera Mexicana and the American Federation of Labor, between Luis N. Morones and Samuel Gompers . . . which has grown into the [American and CIA dominated] Organización Regional Interamericana de Trabajadores (ORIT)."

68. Womack, *Zapata,* p. 406.

69. See Womack for the best history of the lower-class revolutions, not only of the Zapatistas but for the overall sense of events. His depiction of Morelos elite dissent led by the Leyva family, the economic crisis, the alienation of the intellectuals, workers, and peasants, written more than a decade before the publication of the facts related earlier, capture the sense of events throughout Mexico. Unfortunately a traditionalist historical viewpoint has attempted to minimize this contribution by arguing that Morelos was an "exception." It is hoped that this study has shown that the mass unrest demonstrated in Morelos was the rule nationwide, although demographic and topographical factors limited the growth and coalescence of the myriad local revolutions of the coasts and isthmus into the more organized movements seen in Morelos and Chihuahua.

Ten: Elite Synthesis and Sociopolitical Reorganization, 1916–1924

1. *Diario de los Debates del Congreso Constituyente,* Tomo 1 (Mexico City, 1922), p. 9.

2. For Carranza on the municipio libre, see ibid., p. 266.

3. The 1923 Bucareli Accords are treated by Robert Freeman Smith, *The United States and Revolutionary Nationalism in Mexico, 1916–1932* (Chicago: University of Chicago Press, 1972), pp. 213–228. See also the Buckley Papers, BLAC; the correspondence of Thomas Lamont in the Fall Papers, Huntington Library; and John W. F. Dulles, *Yesterday in Mexico: A Chronicle of the Revolution, 1919–1936* (Austin: University of Texas Press, 1961).

4. For a comparison of the 1857 and 1917 constitutions, see H. N. Branch, "The Mexican Constitution of 1917 Compared with the Constitution of 1857," supplement of the *Annals of the American Academy of Political and Social Science* (May 1917). For an analysis of the Liberals who wrote the 1857 Constitution, see Richard Sinkin, *The Mexican Reform, 1855–1876: A Study in Liberal Nation-Building* (Austin: University of Texas Press, 1979), 263 pages. The 1917 Constitutional Convention is analyzed by E. Victor Niemeyer, *Revolution at Querétaro: The Mexican Constitutional Convention of 1916–1917* (Austin: University of Texas Press, 1974), 297 pages.

5. *Diario de los Debates,* Tomo 1, p. 610.

6. Ibid., p. 617.

7. The CGT is treated in Hart, *Anarchism,* pp. 156–177. The most complete assessment of the early CTM is Joe C. Ashby, *Organized Labor and the Mexican Revolution under Cárdenas* (Chapel Hill: University of North Carolina Press, 1967).

8. W. R. Grace and Company, Case Number 306, Docket 136, Box 30, Agrarian Claims Commission (U.S. Section), Records Group 76, WNRC.

9. See the Plan of Agua Prieta, 25 April 1920, Box 7478, Mexican Intervention,

Collection Number 2149991, Records Group 92, NARA, or the Kile Papers, BLAC. For the Obregon Salido-led military golpe de estado, see Hall, *Alvaro Obregon,* pp. 233–248.

10. For a description of the Zapatista leadership's "uncritical spirit" in accepting Obregon Salido, see Hall, *Alvaro Obregon,* p. 240. For an analysis of how demoralized revolutionary groups can be maneuvered into passive acceptance of military takeovers, see Karl Marx, *The Eighteenth Brumaire of Louis Bonaparte* (Beijing: Foreign Language Press, 1978).

11. Carrancista behavior in Morelos is described by Arturo Warman, *We Come to Object* (Baltimore: The Johns Hopkins University Press, 1980), pp. 109–110; and Womack, *Zapata,* pp. 256–287. For a defense of the Carranzistas, see Richmond, *Venustiano Carranza's Nationalist Struggle,* pp. 83–203. For the corruption and their treatment of the Yaqui, see Ruiz, *The Great Rebellion, Mexico 1905–1924* (New York: Norton, 1980), pp. 321–322; Alvaro Obregon, *Ocho mil kilómetros en campaña* (Mexico City: Fondo de Cultura Económica, 1970), p. 471; and Barry Carr, "The Peculiarities of the Mexican North, 1880–1928: An Essay in Interpretation" (Glasgow: Institute of Latin American Studies, University of Glasgow, 1971), pp. 16–17. For the Sonoran political struggle between the Carranza government and the Obregonistas, see Collection Number 2149991, Mexican Intervention, NARA; for example, the report of Colonel Charles Hatfield, Douglas, Arizona, to General Bliss, Fort Sam Houston, San Antonio, 8 June 1914, Box 7473. See also Hall, *Alvaro Obregon,* pp. 203–245.

12. For an excellent analysis of the postrevolutionary state-building process, see Skocpol, *States and Social Revolutions.* For Obregon Salido in this process, see Manuel González Ramírez, "Alvaro Obregon, Estadista," Appendix in Obregon, *Ocho mil kilómetros en campaña,* pp. 513–549.

13. The role of the CROM and Agrarian party as mechanisms of social control is examined in Hart, *Anarchism,* pp. 156–177. The CROM is also analyzed by Ruiz, *The Great Rebellion,* pp. 295–303.

14. Katz, *The Secret War in Mexico,* pp. 511–549; and Richmond, *Venustiano Carranza's Nationalist Struggle,* pp. 189–218.

15. The records of the Claims Commissions reveal the demise of concerns that focused their efforts in agriculture and mining. For Corralitos see the hacienda records in the Peirce Family Papers, Topsfield, or in the possession of the author. For Obregon Salido's attitudes and policies, see Ruiz, *The Great Rebellion,* pp. 387–388, 398–405.

16. For data, see Ceceña, *México en la órbita imperial,* pp. 103–271.

17. James A. Clark with Weldon Hart, *The Tactful Texan: A Biography of Governor William Hobby* (New York: Random House, 1958), p. 141.

18. Ibid., pp. 139–142.

19. Smith, *The United States and Revolutionary Nationalism in Mexico,* pp. 216–223.

20. The arms shipments to the Obregon Salido government and the 7 January 1924 embargo against the de la Huerta forces are detailed in 812.113/9367, 15 November 1923 to 812.113/9606, 4 August 1924, Records Group 59, Purport Lists for the Decimal File, Department of State, NARA. For the de la Huerta

affair, see Ruiz, *The Great Rebellion,* pp. 377–378, 394; and Smith, *The United States and Revolutionary Nationalism in Mexico,* pp. 222–225.

21. The 312 and 412 series, Department of State Decimal Files, Records Group 59, NARA, contain multitudinous reports of the companies to the U.S. government regarding the de la Huerta rebellion. Arms shipments to the American companies for their defense against marauding workers and local citizenry are noted as exceptions to the arms embargo in the 812.113 series, Records Group 59, NARA.

22. For the Cristero war, see David C. Bailey, *Viva Cristo Rey!: The Cristero Rebellion and the Church-State Conflict in Mexico* (Austin: University of Texas Press, 1974); and Jean Meyer, *La Cristiada.*

Epilogue

1. The World Health Organization, cited in *The New York Times,* 20 December 1984. For the best defense of the postrevolutionary political economy, see James Wilkie, *The Mexican Revolution: Federal Expenditure and Social Change Since 1910* (Berkeley and Los Angeles: University of California Press, 1967).

Notes on Archival Sources

This book is based on a multiplicity of archives in the United States and Mexico. Important papers of many of the large American corporations active in Mexico before and during the revolution are available in the Archives of the United States because they submitted crucial data from their records as part of the Bucareli Accords, which established a procedure for the payment of claims. The local archives in the United States contain the papers of many important American entrepreneurs. In Mexico government records that include those held in the Archivo General de la Nación, the central and local archives of the Secretariat of Agrarian Reform, the Tribunal Superior de la Nación, and local sources, provided a wide-ranging picture of changing sociopolitical conditions in the countryside before, during, and after the revolution.

The problems were manifold. The United States government, its officials, and American businesses and entrepreneurs have lost or kept secret many of the data regarding their activities in Mexico. The papers of Wilson administration officials in private collections and in the Library of Congress have been carefully culled to remove damaging or embarrassing material. The Military Government of Veracruz archive (Records Group 141) and related papers in the National Archives were too complex for the censors to control. They left behind sufficient evidence to reveal the significance of that intervention. The complexity of these documents was also a tangle for this researcher, however, who spent six months over a period of five years sorting them out.

Fortunately the voluminous American sources for the Mexican Revolution are well ordered and relatively accessible. The most important U.S. records used in this study were the Department of State documents on Mexico, Series 312, 412, 512, 612, 712, and 812 (Records Group 59).

The 812 Series is already well known to Mexican historians. The others, especially Series 312 and 412, are more important because they provide detailed insights regarding the protection of U.S. property and citizens in Mexico.

Records Group 141 in the Washington National Records Center in Suitland, Maryland, is an invaluable resource for understanding the activities of the U.S. Military Government of Veracruz. Carefully censored, the index for the mass of documents offers no hint of the enormous military buildup and political intrigue that went on in Veracruz between April and November 1914. The warehousemen's invoices, however, which described damaged armaments and arms transfers by the respective shippers' and receivers' markings, provided the basis for locating these items among the tens of thousands of shipping crates in the harbor. The Villa's Revolution and Mexican Intervention collections at the National Archives in Washington, D.C. complement Records Group 141 and are available through the Old Army and Navy Office.

The records of the various claims commissions (Records Group 76) are also located at Suitland. They provide the best imaginable picture of what went on during the revolution as more than a thousand small groups of local Mexican citizenry attacked American properties and those of other landholders in what constituted a massive countryside revolution. This archive documents the chaos of the Mexican Revolution, its grass-roots nationalism, and American responses with great detail.

University and local libraries in the United States also contain invaluable resources. The Barker Texas History Collection in Austin, Texas, is invaluable for its data on the support of Brownsville merchants for the Tuxtepec Revolution, the growth of the oil industry, the economic and political backgrounds of entrepreneurs who ventured into Mexico, and politicians who exercised national influence during the Wilson administration. The Benson Latin American Collection Rare Books Room contains the Northwestern Railroad Records, the W. F. Buckley Papers, the Lazaro de la Garza Papers, the Graham Ker Papers, and the S. Kile Papers, all of which include valuable intelligence information or other data on conditions inside revolutionary Mexico.

In Houston the Metropolitan Research Center holds the valuable John Henry Kirby and Joseph Cullinan Papers. These documents, when combined with the James Autry and W. B. Sharp Papers at the Woodson Research Center at Rice University, offer an insider's view of the intricacies of the oil business and the motives of the Texans who entered Mexico and who were longtime supporters of Colonel House and then the Wilson presidential campaign. They also reveal their deep and long-standing relationships with the Stillmans and the National City Bank.

In the Rio Grande Valley the James L. Allhands Papers found in the John E. Conner Museum, Texas A&I University in Kingsville, Texas, proved invaluable in reconstructing the manner in which U.S. enterprises connected with New York capital expanded across Texas and into Mexico. Allhands recorded in shorthand interviews with the leading developers and settlers of the Lower Rio Grande Valley. They are stored in two boxes. The Rio Grande Valley Historical Collection at Pan American University, Edinburg, Texas, provided some of the links between the land development companies along the boundaryline, the rest of Texas, and the National City Bank.

The Bancroft Library at the University of California at Berkeley contains a microfilmed set of the Colis F. Huntington Papers, the William Randolph Hearst Collection, and the interviews of Mexican industrial and political leaders by Hubert Howe Bancroft. The Huntington Papers are helpful in conjunction with the Allhands and Peirce papers in piecing together that entrepreneur's endeavors to build a railroad network across the American southwest and into Mexico. The Huntington Library, San Marino, California, holds the Albert Bacon Fall Papers, within which the Franklin Lane Papers are an unusually rich source of information regarding American economic interests in Mexico, especially Sonora. The Tulane University Library, New Orleans, Louisiana, houses the Stanton-Townsend Family Papers, with the rich files of the Rascon sugar hacienda at San Luis Potosí.

The Houghton Library at Harvard University and the Butler Library of Columbia University contain the papers of Charles and James Stillman, which, combined with the sources available in the Rio Grande Valley and Barker collections, demonstrate the Stillman's deep commitment and manner of operation as investors and the National City Bank as a source of finance capital for land development and railroad construction in Texas and Mexico. The Butler Library also holds the W. R. Grace Papers, which complement the Grace files in the Claims Commission Records at Suitland. The Sterling Library Rare Books and Manuscripts collection at Yale University holds the papers of Colonel Edward Mandel House and John Lind. Although the House papers reveal virtually nothing of his economic life, they do have the letter by William F. Buckley urging U.S. intervention in Veracruz and an array of correspondents, including cousin Henry House, which allows the researcher to piece together at least some of his nonpublic life. The Lind papers are useful in their depiction of his hostility toward Villa and sympathy for Carranza.

The Mexican archives offer evidence of peasant, working class, pequeña burguesía, and provincial elite conditions before, during, and after the revolution. The political economic background of peasant displacement and violence is found in the Archivo Seis de Enero of the Agrarian Reform Secretariat and its local archives. I was able to use the Secretariat of Agrarian Reform local archives in Oaxaca and Chilpancingo to great advantage. The Archivo Judicial del Tribunal Superior de Justicia del Distrito y Territoriales Federales offers a wide range of data on agrarian litigation and rural unrest through its ramos of pueblos, haciendas, potreros, aguas, and trabajo.

The Archivo General de la Nación is essential to understanding the background of conflicting land claims posited by the villagers and their opponents. In addition to the colonial-era documents held in the ramos Indios, Tierras, and Criminal, I found the ramo of Gobernación with its presidential concessions and the Junta Protectora de las Clases Menesterosas important. The most informative records of the advances made by foreign investors are available in the offices of Registros Públicos. I found the Public Registry office in the state capital building at Ciudad Victoria instrumental in establishing actual landownership beyond the mere status of sales agent or lessor for the Texas Oil Company in Tamaulipas.

The intrigues of American business interests and the Wilson administration are shrouded by the closed archives of the corporations involved; however, the personal papers of most public officials in the U.S. government housed in the Library of Congress are of only secondary importance because of their "cleaned" nature. However, the records contained in the four series of documents associated with the claims commissions and the State Department 312 and 412 series go a long way toward correcting these shortcomings. A better understanding of the linkages between U.S. businessmen and government officials and the interests of both groups in Mexico is possible through examination of the relatively unculled private papers of leading corporate figures. For example, the papers of Thomas Wentworth Peirce, Joseph Cullinan, W. B. Sharp, James Autry, James Stillman, the Brownsville merchants, and the Allhands interviews provide a surprising degree of otherwise confidential information.

Bibliography

List of Archival Abbreviations

AGN	Archivo General de la Nación, Mexico City
AGNL	Archivo General del Estado, Monterrey, Nuevo León
AHSRA	Archivo Histórico de la Secretaría de la Reforma Agraria
AJTS	Archivo Judicial del Tribunal Superior de Justicia del Distrito y Territorios Federales, Mexico City
ARGLI	American Rio Grande Land and Irrigation Company Papers, Pan American University, Edinburg, Texas
ASHRA	Archivo Historico, Seis de Enero de 1915, de la Secretaría de la Reforma Agraria, Mexico City
BL	Butler Library, Rare Book and Manuscript Library, Columbia University, New York
BLAC	Nettie Lee Benson Latin American Collection, University of Texas, Austin
BTHC	Barker Texas History Collection, University of Texas
HL	Houghton Library, Rare Books and Manuscripts Room, Harvard University, Cambridge
HMRC	Houston Metropolitan Research Center, Houston
HTML	Howard-Tilton Memorial Library, Tulane University, New Orleans
JECM	John E. Connor Museum, Texas A&I University, Kingsville, Texas
MBR	Memorias del General Bernardo Reyes
MGV	Military Government of Veracruz
NARA	National Archives and Records Administration, Washington, D.C.
RGVHC	Rio Grande Valley Historical Collection, Pan-American University

UNAM Universidad Nacional Autónoma de México, Mexico City

WNRC Washington National Records Center, Suitland, Maryland

WRC Woodson Research Center, Rice University, Houston

List of Sources Cited

Archivo General de la Nación, Mexico City
Ramo Criminal
Ramo Ferrocarriles
Ramo de Gobernación, Tranquilidad Pública
Ramo de Indios
Ramo de Infidencias
Ramo de Tierras
Ramo Junta Protectora de las Clases Menesterosas

Archivo General del Estado, Monterrey, Nuevo León
Memorias del General Bernardo Reyes

Archivo Histórico de la Defensa Nacional, Mexico City
Departmento de Archivo Correspondencia E Historia (Pensionistas)

Archivo Histórico de la Secretaría de Reforma Agraria, Chilpancingo, Guerrero

Archivo Histórico de la Secretaría de Reforma Agraria, Oaxaca, Oaxaca

Archivo Histórico de la Secretaría de Transportes y Comunicaciones, Mexico City

Archivo Histórico, Seis de Enero de 1915, de la Secretaría de la Reforma Agraria, Mexico City
Ramo Comunal
Ramo Ejidal

Archivo Judicial del Tribunal Superior de Justicia del Distrito y Territorios Federales, Mexico City
Ramo de Aguas
Ramo de Haciendas
Ramo de Potreros
Ramo de Pueblos
Ramo de Terrenos

Archivo Judicial de Puebla, Puebla.
Juzgado de Letras de Tlapa

Arnulfo L. Olevira Memorial Library, Rare Books Room, Texas Southmost College, Brownsville, Texas

Baker Library, Harvard University School of Business
Henry W. Peabody Papers

Bancroft Library Rare Books and Manuscripts Room, University of California at Berkeley
Bancroft Interviews
Colis P. Huntington Papers (microfilm)

Barker Texas History Collection, University of Texas
Albert Sidney Burleson Papers
Camargo Archives
Edward M. House Papers
James B. Wells Papers
James Stephen Hogg Papers
Jean B. La Coste Papers
John Salmon Ford Papers
Pioneers in Texas Oil, Oral History Library
San Roman Papers
Steven F. Powers Papers
T. W. House Papers
William Clifford Hogg Papers

Butler Library, Rare Book and Manuscript Library, Columbia University
James Stillman Papers

Essex County Courthouse, Salem, Massachusetts
Thomas Wentworth Peirce Probate Will

Harris County Records, Houston
Probate Court of Harris County

Houston Metropolitan Research Center
John Henry Kirby Papers
Joseph S. Cullinan Papers

Houghton Library, Rare Books and Manuscripts Room, Harvard University
James Stillman Diaries and Personal Accounts
Charles and James Stillman Letters, Letterbooks, Accounts, Bills, and Other Business Papers, 1850–1879

Howard-Tilton Memorial Library, Tulane
Townsend-Stanton Family Papers

Huntington Library, San Marino, California
Albert Bacon Fall Collection
Henry W. Keller Collection

John E. Connor Museum, Texas A&I University, Kingsville, Texas
James L. Allhands Papers

John Hays Library, Brown University, Providence, Rhode Island
Elmer Lawrence Corthell Papers (1840–1916)

Library of Congress
Geography and Map Division
Thomas Watt Gregory Papers

National Archives and Records Administration, Washington, D.C.
Department of State Decimal Files, Series 312, 412, 512, 612, 712 and 812, Records Group 59
Department of State Purport Lists for the Decimal File, 812.10–812.345/17, 1910–1929, Records Group 59

Despatches Received by the Department of State from U.S. Consuls, 1826–1906
U.S. Adjutant General, Mexican Intervention, Collection Number 2149991, Records Group 92
U.S. Adjutant General, Villa's Revolution, Collection Number 2212358, Records Group 92

Nettie Lee Benson Latin American Collection, University of Texas, Austin
Graham M. Ker Papers
Lazaro de la Garza Papers
Northwestern Railroad Collection
William F. Buckley Papers
Sherman Kile Papers

Registro Público, Ciudad Victoria, Tamaulipas
Registro de la Propiedad

Rio Grande Valley Historical Collection, Pan-American University, Edinburg
American Rio Grande Land and Irrigation Company (ARGLI) Shary Collection

Sherman Library, Corona del Mar, California
Otto F. Brant Papers

Southern Pacific Railroad, Southern Pacific Building, Houston

Sterling Library, Yale University
Edward Mandel House Papers

Thomas Wentworth Peirce Papers, Topsfield, Massachusetts
Hacienda de Corralitos Archive

Washington National Records Center, Suitland, Maryland
Agrarian Claims Commission (U.S. Section), Records Group 76
American Mexican Claims Commission, Approved Agrarian
Claims, 1936–1947, Records Group 76
Mexican American General Claims Commission, Deferred
Miscellaneous Claims Approved after 1935 (Declassified), Records Group 76
Military Government of Veracruz, Records Group 141
Mixed Claims Commission, Records Group 76
Office of the Quartermaster General, Army Transport Service General File, 1914–1940 (Declassified), Records Group 92
Special Claims Commission, Records Group 76

Woodson Research Center, Rice University, Houston
James B. Autry Papers
Walter B. Sharp Papers

Newspapers

Brownsville Herald
Corpus Christi Gazette
Galveston Weekly News

New York Times
North China Daily News
Omaha Daily News
Omaha World Herald
San Antonio Herald
San Antonio Press
The Commercial and Financial Chronicle (New York)
The South China Daily Post

Mexico City

Acción Mundial
Ariete
Diario del Imperio
Diario Oficial
El Hijo del Trabajo
El Obrero Liberal
El Socialista
La Vanguardia
Lucha
Siglo XIX

Books

Agetro, Leafar [pseud. Rafael C. Ortega]. *Las Luchas Proletarias en Veracruz: Historia y Autocrítica*. Jalapa: Editorial "Barricada," 1942.

Aguilar Camin, Hector. *La revolución nomada: sonora y la revolución mexicana*. Mexico City: Siglo XXI, 1977.

Aguirre Beltrán, Gonzalo. *Regiones de refugio*. Mexico City: Instituto Indigenista Interamericano, 1967.

Alaman, Lucas. *Historia de Méjico desde los primeros movimientos que preparon su independencia en el año de 1808, hasta la época presente*, 5 vol. Mexico City, 1849–1852.

Allhands, James L. *Gringo Builders*. Dallas: Privately published, 1931.

———. *Boll Weevil: Recollections of the Trinity and Brazos Valley Railway*. Houston: Anson Jones Press, 1946.

———. *Railroads to the Rio Salado*. Texas: Anson Jones Press, 1960.

Anders, Evan. *Boss Rule in South Texas: The Progressive Era*. Austin: University of Texas Press, 1982.

Anderson, Rodney D. *Outcasts in Their Own Land: Mexican Industrial Workers, 1906–1911*. DeKalb: Northern Illinois University Press, 1976.

Araiza, Luis. *Historia del Movimiento Obrero Mexicano*, Tomos II and III. Mexico City, 1964–1966.

Ashby, Joe C. *Organized Labor and the Mexican Revolution under Cárdenas*. Chapel Hill: University of North Carolina Press, 1967.

Avrich, Paul. *Russian Rebels, 1600–1800*. New York: Schocken, 1972.

Bailey, David. *Viva Cristo Rey! The Cristero Rebellion and the Church-State Conflict in Mexico*. Austin: University of Texas Press, 1974.

Basurto, Jorge. *El proletariado industrial en México (1850–1930)*. Mexico City: Instituto de Investigaciones Sociales, UNAM, 1975.

Bazant, Jan. *Historia de la deuda exterior de México (1823–1946)*. Mexico City: El Colegio de México, 1946.

Beezley, William H. *Insurgent Governor: Abraham González and the Mexican Revolution in Chihuahua*. Lincoln: University of Nebraska Press, 1973.

Benjamin, Thomas, and William McNellie, eds. *Other Mexicos: Essays on Regional Mexican History, 1876–1911*. Albuquerque: University of New Mexico Press, 1984.

Bernstein, Marvin. *The Mexican Mining Industry, 1890–1950*. Albany: State University of New York Press, 1964.

Berry, Charles. *The Reform in Oaxaca, 1856–76*. Lincoln: University of Nebraska Press, 1981.

Bharier, Julian. *Economic Development in Iran 1900–1970*. London: Oxford University Press, 1971.

Blaisdell, Lowell. *The Desert Revolution: Baja California, 1911*. Madison: University of Wisconsin Press, 1962.

Bonine, Michael E., and Nikki Keddie, eds. *Modern Iran: The Dialectics of Continuity and Change*. Albany: State University of New York Press, 1981.

Brading, David. *Haciendas and Ranchos in the Mexican Bajío, León 1700–1860*. Cambridge: Cambridge University Press, 1978.

Brading, David, ed. *Caudillo and Peasant in the Mexican Revolution*. Cambridge: Cambridge University Press, 1980.

Browne, Edward Granville. *The Persian Revolution of 1905–1909*. Cambridge: Cambridge University Press, 1910.

Brushwood, John S. *Mexico in Its Novel: A Nation's Search for Identity*. Austin: University of Texas Press, 1966.

Bryant, Keith L., Jr. *Arthur E. Stillwell--Promoter with a Hunch*. Nashville: Vanderbilt University Press, 1971.

Buckley, Priscilla, et al. *WFB: An Appreciation*. Private printing, 1979.

Burr, Anna R. *The Portrait of a Banker: James Stillman 1850–1918*. (New York: Duffield Press, 1927.

Calderon, Francisco R. *La república restaurada, la vida económica*. In *Historia moderna, de México,* ed. Daniel Cosio Villegas. Mexico City: Editorial Hermes, 1965.

Calderon de la Barca, Fannie. *Life in Mexico: The Letters of Fanny Calderon de la Barca,* Howard T. Fisher and Marion Hall Fisher, eds. Garden City, N.Y.: Doubleday and Company, 1970.

Calderon Quijano, José Antonio. *Los virreyes de Nueva España en el reinado de Carlos III,* vol. II. Seville: Escuela de Estudios Hispano-Americanos de Seville, 1968.

Ceceña, José Luis. *México en la órbita imperial: las empresas transnacionales*. Mexico City: Ediciones El Caballito, 1979.

Cerutti, Mario. *Burguesía y capitalismo en Monterrey 1850–1910*. Mexico City: Claves Latinoamericanas, 1983.

Chapman, James Gresham. *La construcción del ferrocarril Mexicano (1857–1880)*. Mexico City: SepSetentas, 1975.

Chesneaux, Jean. *Peasant Revolts in China, 1840–1949*. New York: W. W. Norton, 1973.

Clark, James A., with Weldon Hart. *The Tactful Texan: A Biography of Governor William Hobby*. New York: Random House, 1958.

Coatsworth, John H. *Growth against Development: The Economic Impact of Railroads in Porfirian Mexico*. DeKalb: Northern Illinois University Press, 1981.

Cockcroft, James D. *Intellectual Precursors of the Mexican Revolution* Austin: University of Texas Press, 1968.

Coerver, Don M. *The Porfirian Interregnum: The Presidency of Manuel González of Mexico, 1880–1884*. Fort Worth: Texas Christian University Press, 1979.

Cordoba, Arnaldo. *La ideología de la Revolución Mexicana,* 2d ed. Mexico City: Ediciones Era, 1973.

Cotner, Robert C. *James Steven Hogg: A Biography*. Austin: University of Texas Press, 1959.

Crisp, Olga. *Studies in the Russian Economy before 1914*. London: Macmillan, 1976.

Crowley, James B., ed. *Modern East Asia: Essays in Interpretation*. New York: Harcourt, Brace and World, 1970.

Cumberland, Charles C. *Mexican Revolution: Genesis under Madero*. Austin: University of Texas Press, 1952.

Davids, Jules. *American Political and Economic Penetration of Mexico, 1877–1920*. New York: Arno Press, 1976.

Denny, Ludwell. *We Fight for Oil*. Westport, Conn.: Hyperion Press, 1976.

Díaz Ramírez, Manuel. *Apuntes históricos del movimiento obrero y campesino de México, 1844–1880*. Mexico City: Fondo de Cultura Popular, 1938.

Díaz Soto y Gama, Antonio. *La revolución agraria del sur y Emiliano Zapata su caudillo*. Mexico City, 1961.

D'Olwer, Luis Nicolau et al. *El Porfiriato, la vida económica*. In *Historia moderna de México,* ed. Daniel Cosio Villegas. Mexico City: Editorial Hermes, 1965.

Domínguez, Miguel. *La erección del estado de Guerrero, antecedentes históricos*. Mexico City, 1949.

Dulles, John W. F. *Yesterday in Mexico: A Chronicle of the Revolution, 1919–1936*. Austin: University of Texas Press, 1961.

Eventov, L. *Innostrannye Kapitaly v Russkoi Promyshlennosti*. Moscow, 1931.

Fairbank, John K., Edwin O. Reischauer, and Albert M. Craig. *East Asia: Tradition and Transformation*. Boston: Houghton Mifflin, 1973.

Farriss, Nancy. *Crown and Clergy in Colonial Mexico*. London: University of London Press, 1968.

Fernández, Raúl A. *The United States-Mexico Border: A Politico-Economic Profile*. Notre Dame, Ind.: Notre Dame University Press, 1977.

Feuerwerker, Albert, ed. *China's Early Industrialization: Sheng Hsuan-huai (1844–1916) and Mandarin Enterprise*. Cambridge: Harvard University Press, 1958.

———. *Modern China*. Englewood Cliffs, N.J.: Prentice-Hall, 1964.

Flores Caballero, Romeo. *Counterrevolution: The Role of the Spaniards in the Independence of Mexico*. Lincoln: University of Nebraska Press, 1974.

Foner, Philip S. *History of the Labor Movement in the United States*. New York: International Publishers, 1955.

Frías, Heriberto. *Tomochic*. Mexico City: Valadés y Cía., 1906.

Fuentes Díaz, Vicente. *El problema ferrocarrilero de México*. Mexico City: Edición del autor, 1951).

García Cantú, Gastón. *El socialismo en México siglo XIX*. Mexico City: Ediciones Era, 1969.

———. *Utopías Mexicanas*. Mexico City: Fondo de Cultura Económica, 1978.

García de la Cadena, Trinidad. *Discursos*. Mexico City: Impresa Irenio Ruiz, 1881.

García Mundo, Octavio. *El movimiento inquilinario de Veracruz*. Mexico City: SepSetentas, 1976.

Gilderhus, Mark T. *Diplomacy and Revolution: U.S.-Mexican Relations under Wilson and Carranza*. Tucson: University of Arizona Press, 1977.

González Navarro, Moisés. *Las huelgas textiles en el Porfiriato*. Puebla: Editorial José Cajica, 1971.

Gómez Quiñones, Juan. *Sembradores: Ricardo Flores Magon y El Partido Liberal Mexicano: A Eulogy and Critique*. Los Angeles: Atzlan Publications, 1973.

Gorsuch, Robert B. *The Mexican Southern Railway to Be Completed under a Charter from the Mexican Government through the States of Veracruz and Oaxaca*. New York: Hosford and Sons, 1881.

Grieb, Kenneth. *The United States and Huerta*. Lincoln: University of Nebraska Press, 1969.

Grob, Gerald. *Workers and Utopia: A Study of Ideological Conflicts in the American Labor Movement 1865–1900*. Chicago: Quadrangle, 1969.

Guevara Ramírez, Luis. *Síntesis histórica del estado de Guerrero*. Colección de Estudios Guerrerenses, 1959.

Hale, Charles A. *Mexican Liberalism in the Age of Mora, 1821–1853*. New Haven: Yale University Press, 1968.

Hall, Linda. *Alvaro Obregon, Power and Revolution in Mexico, 1911–1920*. College Station: Texas A&M University Press, 1981.

Hamill, Hugh. *The Hidalgo Revolt: Prelude to Mexican Independence*. Gainesville: University of Florida Press, 1966.

Hart, John Mason. *Los anarquistas Mexicanos, 1860–1900*. Mexico City: SepSetentas, 1974.

———. *Anarchism and the Mexican Working Class, 1860–1931*. Austin: University of Texas Press, 1978.

Hou Chi-ming, and Yu Tzong-shian, eds. *Modern Chinese History*. Taipei: Institute of Economics, Academic Sinica, 1979.

Hu-DeHart, Evelyn. *The Yaquis: A Cultural History*. Tucson: University of Arizona Press, 1980.

———. *Missions, Mines and Indians: The History of Spanish Contact with the Yaqui Nation of Northwestern New Spain, 1583–1820*. Tucson: University of Arizona Press, 1983.

Hughes, James B., Jr. *Mexican Military Arms: The Cartridge Period, 1866–1967*. Houston: Deep River Armory, 1968.

Huitrón, Jacinto. *Orígenes e historia del movimiento obrero en México*. Mexico City: Editores Mexicanos Unidos, 1975.

Issawi, Charles. *The Economic History of Iran 1800–1914*. Chicago: University of Chicago Press, 1971.

Jones, Grant D., ed. *Anthropology and History in Yucatán*. Austin: University of Texas Press, 1977.

Joseph, Gil. *Revolution from Without: Yucatán, Mexico, and the United States, 1880–1924*. London: Cambridge University Press, 1982.

Katz, Friedrich, ed. *Riot, Rebellion, and Revolution: Rural Social Conflict in Mexico.* Princeton: Princeton University Press, 1987.

———. *The Secret War in Mexico: Europe, the United States and the Mexican Revolution*. Chicago: University of Chicago Press, 1981.

Keremitsis, Dawn. *La industria textil Mexicana en el siglo XIX*. Mexico City: SepSetentas, 1973.

King, John O. *Joseph Steven Cullinan: A Study of Leadership in the Texas Petroleum Industry 1857–1937*. Nashville: Vanderbilt University Press, 1970.

Knight, Alan. *The Mexican Revolution*. 2 vols. London: Cambridge University Press, 1986.

Kovalevsky, M. W., ed. *La Russie à la fin du 19e siècle*. Paris, 1900.

Kromov, Pavel Alexeyevich. *Ekonomicheskoye Razitiye Rossii V XIX–XX vekakh*. Moscow: Institute of Economics, Academy of Science, 1950.

Kuhn, Philip. *Rebellion and Its Enemies in Late Imperial China*. Cambridge: Harvard University Press, 1970.

Landes, David S. *Bankers and Pashas: International Finance and Economic Imperialism in Egypt*. New York: Harper, 1958.

Lawton, Lancelot. *The Empires of the Far East,* vol. 1. Boston, 1912.

Lea, Tom. *The King Ranch*. Boston: Little, Brown, 1957.

Lyashchenko, Peter I. *History of the National Economy of Russia to the 1917 Revolution*. New York: Macmillan, 1949.

Maclachlan, Colin M. *Criminal Justice in Eighteenth-Century Mexico: A Study of the Tribunal of the Acordada*. Berkeley, Los Angeles, London: University of California Press, 1974.

Madero, Francisco. *La sucesión presidencial*. San Pedro, Coahuila: El Partido Nacional Democratico, 1908.

Mann, Michael. *Consciousness and Action among the Western Working Class*. London and New York: Macmillan, 1973.

Manning, Roberta Thompson. *The Crisis of the Old Order in Russia: Gentry and Government*. Princeton: Princeton University Press, 1982.

Martin, Percy F. *Mexico's Treasure House (Guanajuato): An Illustrated and Descriptive Account of the Mines*. New York: Cheltenham Press, 1906.

Martínez Sobral, Enrique. *La reforma monetaria*. Mexico City: Tipografía de la Oficina Impresora de Estamillas, 1909.

Marx, Karl. *The Eighteenth Brumaire of Louis Bonaparte*. Beijing: Foreign Language Press, 1978.

McKay, John P. *Pioneers for Profit: Foreign Entrepreneurship and Russian Industrialization 1885–1913*. Chicago: University of Chicago Press, 1970.

McLeod, Murdo J., and Robert Wasserstrom, eds. *Spaniards and Indians in Southeastern Mesoamerica: Essays on the History of Ethnic Relations*. Lincoln: University of Nebraska Press, 1983.

Mejía Fernández, Miguel. *Política agraria en México en el siglo XIX*. Mexico City: Siglo XXI, 1979.

Melville, Roberto. *Crecimiento y rebelión: el desarrollo económico de las haciendas azucareras en Morelos (1880–1910)*. Mexico City: Nueva Imagen, 1979.

Meyer, Jean. *La Cristiada,* 3 vols. Mexico City: Siglo XXI, 1973.

Meyer, Michael. *Mexican Rebel: Pascual Orozco and the Mexican Revolution, 1910–1915*. Lincoln: University of Nebraska Press, 1967.

———. *Huerta: A Political Portrait*. Lincoln: University of Nebraska Press, 1972.
Michaels, Robert. *Political Parties*. New York: Free Press, 1962.
Moore, Barrington, Jr. *Social Origins of Dictatorship and Democracy: Lord and Peasant in the Making of the Modern World*. Boston: Beacon, 1966.
Mora, José María Luis. *Obras sueltas,* vol. 1, CCLXXIII. Paris, 1837.
Morner, Magnus, ed. *The Expulsion of the Jesuits from Latin America*. New York: Knopf, 1965.
Moss, Bernard. *The Origins of the French Labor Movement*. Berkeley, Los Angeles, London: University of California Press, 1976.
Niemeyer, Victor E. *Revolution at Querétaro: The Mexican Constitutional Convention of 1916–1917*. Austin: University of Texas Press, 1974.
Noticias históricas sobre los pueblos de Ajuchitán, Coyuca, Cutzmala, Coahuayutla, Petatlán, Tecpán, y Atoyac. Mexico City: Editorial Vargas Rea, 1947.
Obregon, Alvaro. *Ocho mil kilómetros en campaña*. Mexico City: Fondo de Cultura Económica, 1970.
Olea, Hector R. *Los asentamientos humanos en Sinaloa*. Mazatlán: Universidad Autonoma de Sinaloa, 1980.
Overlach, T. W. *Foreign Financial Control in China*. New York: Macmillan, 1919.
Perkins, Dwight H. *Agricultural Development in China, 1368–1968*. Chicago: Aldine, 1969.
Perry, Laurens Ballard. *Juárez and Díaz: Machine Politics in Mexico*. In *The Origins of Modern Mexico,* Laurens Ballard Perry. DeKalb: Northern Illinois University Press, 1978.
Phelan, John Leddy. *The Kingdom of Quito in the Seventeenth Century: Bureaucratic Politics and the Spanish Empire*. Madison: University of Wisconsin Press, 1967.
———. *The People and the King: The Comunero Revolution in Colombia, 1781*. Madison: University of Wisconsin Press, 1977.
Powell, Ralph L. *The Rise of Chinese Military Power, 1895–1912*. Princeton: Princeton University Press, 1955.
Purcell, William L. *Frontier Mexico 1875–1894: Letters of William L. Purcell*. San Antonio: The Naylor Company, 1963.
Queen, George Sherman. *The United States and the Material Advance in Russia 1881–1906*. New York: Arno Press, 1976.
Quintana, Miguel A. *Los ensayos monetarios como consequencia de la Baja de la plata. El problema de la plata y el de la moneda de la plata en el mundo y en México*. Mexico City: Universidad Autonoma Nacional de México, 1931.
Quirk, Robert E. *The Mexican Revolution, 1914–1915: The Convention of Aguascalientes*. New York: Citadel Press, 1963.
Raat, W. Dirk. *Revoltosos, Mexico's Rebels in the United States, 1913–1923*. College Station: Texas A&M University Press, 1981.
Reed, S. G. *A History of the Texas Railroads*. Houston: St. Clair Publishing Company, 1941.
———. *A History of the Land Grants and Other Aids to the Texas Railroads by the State of Texas*. Kingsport, Tenn.: Kingsport Press, 1942.
Reina, Leticia. *Las luchas populares en México en el siglo XIX*. Mexico City: Casa Chata, 1983.
———. *Las rebeliones campesinas en México (1819–1906)*. Mexico City: Siglo XXI, 1980.

Reyes Heroles, Jesus. *El liberalismo Mexicano,* 3 vol. Mexico City: Fondo de Cultura Económica, 1974.

Ricard, Robert. *The Spiritual Conquest of Mexico.* Berkeley and Los Angeles: University of California Press, 1967.

Richardson, Rupert. *Colonel Edward M. House: The Texas Years.* Abilene: Hardin Simmons University Press, 1964.

Richmond, Douglas. *Venustiano Carranza's Nationalist Struggle, 1893–1920.* Lincoln: University of Nebraska Press, 1983.

Robinson, Geroid Tanquary. *Rural Russia under the Old Regime.* New York: Macmillan, 1957.

Rosenzweig, Fernando et al. *El Porfiriato: la vida económica.* In *Historia moderna, de México,* Volume 1, Daniel Cosio Villegas. Mexico City: Editorial Hermes, 1965.

Ross, Stanley R. *Francisco I. Madero, Apostle of Mexican Democracy.* New York: Columbia University Press, 1955.

Rudé, George F. E. *Ideology and Popular Protest.* New York: Pantheon, 1980.

Ruiz, Ramón E. *The Great Rebellion, Mexico 1905–1924.* New York: W. W. Norton, 1980.

Salazar, Rosendo. *La Casa del Obrero Mundial.* Mexico City: Costa-Amic, Editor, 1962.

Salazar, Rosendo, and José G. Escobedo. *Las pugnas de la gleba, 1907–1922,* vol. 1. Mexico City: Editorial Avante, 1923.

Schmitt, Karl M. *Mexico and the United States 1821–1973: Conflict and Coexistence.* New York: John Wiley and Sons, 1974.

Seminario de historia de México, estadísticas económicas del Porfiriato: fuerza de trabajo y actividad económica por sectores, Fernando Rosenzweig, trans. Mexico City: El Colegio de México, 1965.

Shorter, Edward, and Charles Tilly. *Strikes in France, 1830–1968.* London and New York: Cambridge University Press, 1974.

Shuster, W. Morgan. *The Strangling of Persia.* New York: The Century Company, 1912.

Sibley, Marilyn McAdams. *George W. Brackenridge: Maverick Philanthropist.* Austin: University of Texas Press, 1973.

Sinkin, Richard. *The Mexican Reform, 1855–1876: A Study in Liberal Nation-Building.* Austin: University of Texas Press, 1979.

Skocpol, Theda. *States and Social Revolutions.* Cambridge: Cambridge University Press, 1979.

Smith, Arthur D. Howden. *Mr. House of Texas.* New York and London: Funk and Wagnalls, 1940.

Smith, Robert Freeman. *The United States and Revolutionary Nationalism in Mexico, 1916–1932.* Chicago: University of Chicago Press, 1972.

Soboul, Albert. *The Sans Culottes: The Popular Movement and Revolutionary Government, 1793–1794,* Remy Inglis Hall, trans., New York: Doubleday/Anchor, 1972.

Southworth, John R., and Percy G. Holms. *Tamaulipas, Reseña geográfica y estadística.* Paris and Mexico City: Librería de la Viuda de C. Bouret, 1910.

Stillman, Chauncey Devereux. *Charles Stillman 1810–1875.* New York: Chauncey Devereux Stillman, 1956.

Sun Yat-sen. *The International Development of China*. London: Hutchinson and Company, 1921.

Taylor, William B. *Drinking, Homicide and Rebellion in Colonial Mexican Villages*. Stanford: Stanford University Press, 1979.

Tornel y Mendivil, José María, Secretarío de Guerra y Marina. *Memoria del ministerio*. Mexico City: 11 Enero 1844.

———. *Breve reseña histórica de los acontecimientos más notables de la nación Mexicana desde el año de 1821 hasta nuestras días*. Mexico City, 1852.

Trotsky, Leon. *1905*. London: Penguin, 1971.

Turlington, Edgar. *Mexico and Her Foreign Creditors*. New York: Columbia University Press, 1930.

Upton, Joseph M. *The History of Modern Iran: An Interpretation*. Cambridge: Harvard University Press, 1960.

Vanderwood, Paul. *Bandits, Police and Mexican Development*. Lincoln: University of Nebraska Press, 1981.

———. *Los rurales Mexicanos*. Mexico City: Fondo de Cultura Económica, 1982.

Vasconcelos, José. *Don Evaristo Madero: Biografía de un patricio*. Mexico City: Impresores Modernas, 1958.

Volkov, Shulamit. *The Rise of Popular Anti-Modernism in Germany: The Urban Master Artisans*. Princeton: Princeton University Press, 1978.

Von Laue, Theodore H. *Sergei Witte and the Industrialization of Russia*. New York: Columbia University Press, 1963.

Vucinich, Wayne S. *The Peasant in Nineteenth-Century Russia*. Stanford: Stanford University Press, 1968.

Wakeman, Frederic, Jr. *The Fall of Imperial China*. New York: Free Press, 1975.

Walkin, Jacob. *The Rise of Democracy in Pre-Revolutionary Russia*. New York: Praeger, 1962.

Warman, Arturo. *We Come to Object*. Baltimore: Johns Hopkins University Press, 1980.

Wasserman, Mark. *Capitalists, Caciques, and Revolution: The Native Elites and Foreign Enterprise in Chihuahua, Mexico, 1854–1911*. Chapel Hill: University of North Carolina Press, 1984.

Wasserstrom, Robert. *Class and Society in Central Chiapas*. Berkeley, Los Angeles, London: University of California Press, 1983.

Wilkie, James. *The Mexican Revolution: Federal Expenditure and Social Change Since 1910*. Berkeley and Los Angeles: University of California Press, 1967.

Winkler, John Kennedy. *The First Billion: The Stillmans and the National City Bank*. New York: Vanguard Press, 1934.

Womack, John. *Zapata and the Mexican Revolution*. New York: Vintage, 1970.

Wright, Mary C., ed. *China in Revolution: The First Phase, 1900–1913*. New Haven: Yale University Press, 1968.

Yakovlev, A. F. *Ekonomischeskie Krizisy v Rossii*. Moscow, 1947.

Articles

Alger, William E. "Mazatlán." *Daily Consular and Trade Reports,* Number 265 (11 November, 1911).

Ankerson, Dudley. "Saurnino Cedillo: A Traditional Caudillo in San Luis Potosí, 1890–1938." In *Caudillo and Peasant in the Mexican Revolution,* David Brading, ed., Cambridge: Cambridge University Press, 1980.

Bartra, Armando. "Ricardo Flores Magón en el cincuentenario de su muerte." *Supplemento de Siempre,* 6 December 1972.

Blaisdell, Lowell L. "Henry Lane Wilson and the Overthrow of Madero." *Southwestern Social Science Quarterly* 45 (1962).

Bonney, William L. "Commerce of Central Mexico." *Daily Consular and Trade Reports,* Number 265 (11 November 1911).

———. "New Labor Decree in Mexico." *Daily Consular and Trade Reports,* Number 238 (10 October 1914).

———. "Decree Prohibiting Exportation of Food Products from the State." *Daily Consular and Trade Reports,* Number 238 (10 October 1914).

Branch, H. N. "The Mexican Constitution of 1917 Compared with the Constitution of 1857." Supplement of the *Annals of the American Academy of Political and Social Science* (May 1917).

Bretherton, Harold G. "Aguascalientes." *Daily Consular and Trade Reports,* Numbers 121 (23 November 1910) and 265 (11 November 1911).

Broyles, William, Jr. "The Last Empire." *Texas Monthly,* October 1980.

Camarena Ocampo, Cuauhtemoc. "Las luchas de los trabajadores textiles: 1850–1907." In *Las luchas populares en México en el siglo XIX,* Leticia Reina, ed. Mexico City: Casa Chata, 1983.

Canada, William W. "Commerce of Southern Mexico." *Daily Consular and Trade Reports,* Number 250 (25 October 1911).

Carr, Barry. "The Peculiarities of the Mexican North, 1880–1928: An Essay in Interpretation." Glasgow, 1971.

Chieu, Andres. "Peones y campesinos zapatistas," in *Emiliano Zapata y el movimiento Zapatista: cinco ensayos.* Mexico City: Instituto Nacional de Antropología e Historia, 1980.

Chuan, Han-sheng. "The Economic Crisis of 1883 as Seen in the Failure of Hsu Jun's Real Estate Business in Shanghai." In *Modern Chinese History,* eds. Hou Chi-ming and Yu Tzong-Shian. Taipei: Institute of Economics, Academic Sinica, 1979.

Coatsworth, John H. "Anotaciones sobre la producción de alimentos durante el porfiriato." *Historia Mexicana* 26, no. 2 (October-December 1976).

———. "Railroads and the Concentration of Land Ownership in the Early Porfiriato." *Hispanic American Historical Review* 54 (February 1974).

Cossio Silva, Luis. "La agricultura." In *El Porfiriato, Vida Económica; Historia moderna de México,* Volume 1, ed. Daniel Cosio Villegas. Mexico City: Editorial Hermes, 1965.

Cunningham, Edward S. "Production of Indian Corn in South Africa." *Daily Consular and Trade Reports,* Number 115 (16 November 1910).

De la Garma, Felipe. "Resumen de los egresos efectuados por el gobierno federal desde el año de 1876 hasta 1936." *Revista de Hacienda,* no. 3 (November 1937).

Edwards, Thomas. "Ciudad Juárez." *Daily Consular and Trade Reports,* Number 256 (1 November 1911).

Ellsworth, Luther T. "Ciudad Porfirio Díaz." *Daily Consular and Trade Reports,* Numbers 15 (18 January 1913) and 256 (1 November 1911).

Falcon, Romana. "Los orígines populares de la Revolución de 1910? El caso de San Luis Potosí." *Historia Mexicana* 29, no. 2 (Octubre-Diciembre 1979).

Franz, Michael. "State and Society in Nineteenth-Century China." In *Modern China,* Albert Feuerwerker, ed. Englewood Cliffs, N.J.: Prentice-Hall, 1964.

Freeman, Charles. "Mexican Cotton Crop." *Daily Consular and Trade Reports,* Number 109 (9 November 1910).

García de la Cadena, Trinidad. "Memoria en que El Ejecutivo del Estado de Zacatecas da cuenta a la honorable legislatura de los actos de su administración." Zacatecas: Mariano Mariscal y Juan Lujan Impresores, 8 September 1870.

Garret, Alonzo B. "Heavy American Exports to Mexico." *Daily Consular and Trade Reports,* Number 107 (7 November 1910).

———. "Nuevo Laredo." *Daily Consular and Trade Reports,* Number 256 (1 November 1911).

———. "Nuevo Laredo." *Daily Consular and Trade Reports,* Number 15 (18 January 1913).

Garthwaite, Gene R. "Khans and Kings: The Dialectics of Power in Bakhtiyari History." In *Modern Iran: The Dialectics of Continuity and Change,* eds. Michael E. Bonine and Nikki Keddie. Albany: State University of New York Press, 1981.

Gilbar, Gad G. "Persian Agriculture in the Late Qajar Period, 1860–1906: Some Economic and Social Aspects." *Asian and African Studies* 12, no. 3 (1978).

———. "The Persian Economy in the Mid-19th Century." *Die Welt des Islams* 19 (1979): 1–4.

———. "Trends in the Development of Prices in Late Qajar Iran, 1870–1906." *Iranian Studies* 16, nos. 3–4 (Summer-Autumn 1983).

Goldsmith, Raymond W. "The Economic Growth of Tsarist Russia 1860–1913." *Economic Development and Cultural Change* 9, no. 3 (April 1961).

González, José María. "La cuestión indigeña (Hacienda de Bocas)." *El Hijo del Trabajo,* various dates 1877 and 1878.

González Navarro, Moisés. "Las huelgas textiles en el Porfiriato." *Historia Mexicana* 6 (October-December 1956).

———. "La huelga de Rio Blanco." *Historia Mexicana* 6 (April-June 1957).

González Ramírez, Manuel. "Alvaro Obregon, estadista." In *Ocho mil kilómetros en campaña,* ed. Alvaro Obregon. Mexico City: Fondo de Cultura Económica, 1970.

Grieb, Kenneth. "Standard Oil and the Financing of the Mexican Revolution." *California Historical Quarterly* 49 (March 1971).

Gunder Frank, André. "Goal Ambiguity and Conflicting Standards: An Approach to the Study of Organization." *Human Organization* (Published by the Society for Applied Anthropology) 17 (1958–1959).

Guthrie, Chester Lyle. "Riots in Seventeenth-Century Mexico City: A Study of Social and Economic Conditions." In *Greater America: Essays in Honor of Herbert Eugene Bolton,* eds. Adele Ogden and Engel Sluiter. Berkeley and Los Angeles: University of California Press, 1945.

Harris, Charles H., and Louis R. Sadler. "The Underside of the Mexican Revolution: El Paso, 1912." *The Americas* 39 (July 1982).

Hart, John Mason. "Miguel Negrete: la epopeya de un revolucionario." *Historia Mexicana* 24, no. 1 (Julio-Septiembre 1974).

———. "The Urban Working Class and the Mexican Revolution: The Case of the Casa del Obrero Mundial." *Hispanic American Historical Review* 58 (February 1978).

———. "Los obreros y el estado 1860–1931." *Nexos,* 37 (Enero 1981).

———. "The 1840s Southwestern Peasants War," in *Riot, Rebellion, and Revolution: Rural Social Conflict in Mexico,* ed. Friedrich Katz. Princeton: Princeton University Press, 1987.

Herlihy, Patricia. "Odessa: Staple Trade and Urbanization in New Russia." *Jahrbucher für Geschichte Ostreuropas* 21, no. 2 (1973).

Hu-DeHart, Evelyn. "Peasant Rebellion in the Northwest: The Yaqui Indians of Sonora, 1740–1976." In *Riot, Rebellion, and Revolution: Rural Social Conflict in Mexico,* Friedrich Katz, ed. Princeton: Princeton University Press, 1987.

———. "Development and Rural Rebellion: Pacification of the Yaquis in the Late Porfiriato." *Hispanic American Historical Review* 54, no. 1 (February 1974).

Keddie, Nikki, "Religion, Society and Revolution in Modern Iran." In *Modern Iran: The Dialectics of Continuity and Change,* eds. Michael Bonine and Nikki Keddie. Albany: State University of New York Press, 1981.

La France, David. "Puebla, Breakdown of the Old Order." In *Other Mexicos: Essays on Regional Mexican History, 1876–1911,* eds. Thomas Benjamin and William McNellie. Albuquerque: University of New Mexico Press, 1984.

Langston, William Stanley. "Coahuila: Centralization against State Autonomy." In *Other Mexicos: Essays on Regional Mexican History, 1876–1911,* eds. Thomas Benjamin and William McNellie. Albuquerque: University of New Mexico Press, 1984.

Lauff, Marcelo Abramo. "Las luchas de los trabajadores ferrovarios: 1870–1908." In *Las luchas populares en México en el siglo XIX,* ed. Leticia Reina. Mexico City: Casa Chata, 1983.

Leonard, C. M. "Chihuahua." *Daily Consular and Trade Reports,* Number 256 (1 November 1911).

Martin, Cheryl. "Crucible of Zapatismo: Hacienda Hospital in the Seventeenth Century." *The Americas* 38 (July 1981).

McGoogan, G. B. "Progreso." *Daily Consular and Trade Reports,* Number 250 (25 October 1911).

Meyer, Michael. "The Militarization of Mexico, 1913–1914." *The Americas* 27 (1971).

Meyers, William K. "Politics, Vested Rights, and Economic Growth in Porfirian Mexico." *Hispanic American Historical Review* 57 (August 1977).

———. "La Comarca Lagunera: Work, Protest, and Popular Mobilization in North Central Mexico." In *Other Mexicos: Essays on Regional Mexican History, 1876–1911,* eds. Thomas Benjamin and William McNellie. Albuquerque: University of New Mexico Press, 1984.

Miller, Clarence A. "Mexican Importations of Grain." *Daily Consular and Trade Reports,* Number 115 (27 October 1910).

———. "Import Trade of Mexico." *Daily Consular and Trade Reports,* Number 209 (22 December 1911).

———. "Commerce of Northern Mexico." *Daily Consular and Trade Reports,* Number 15 (18 January 1913).

Miller, Margaret. "The Trade Balance of Russia." *Slavonic Review* 1, no. 2 (1922).

Morales Lersch, Teresa. "Las luchas de los trabajadores mineros: 1825–1907." In *Las luchas populares en México en el siglo XIX,* ed. Leticia Reina. Mexico City: Casa Chata, 1983.

Negrete, Miguel. Article in *El Socialista* (9 June 1879).

———. "Municipio Libre." *El Hijo del Trabajo* (23 May 1880).

Niemeyer, Victor. "Frustrated Invasion: The Revolutionary Attempt of General Bernardo Reyes from San Antonio in 1911." *Southwestern Historical Quarterly* 67 (1964–1964).

Olson, Roger T. "Persian Gulf Trade and the Agricultural Economy of Southern Iran in the Nineteenth Century." In *Modern Iran: The Dialectics of Continuity and Change,* eds. Michael E. Bonine and Nikki Keddie. Albany: State University of New York Press, 1981.

Phelen, John Leddy. "Authority and Flexibility in the Spanish Imperial Bureaucracy." *Administrative Science Quarterly* 5 (June 1960).

———. "The Rise and Fall of the Creoles in the Audiencia of New Granada 1700–1781." *Boletín de Historia y Antiguidades* (Bogotá) 59, nos. 697/698 (1972).

———. "Similarities and Contrasts of the Comuneros in New Granada and the Revolution of Independence." *Boletín de Historia y Antiguidades* 63, no. 714 (1976).

Pletcher, David. "The Fall of Silver in Mexico, 1876–1910, and Its Effect on American Investments." *Journal of Economic History* 18 (March 1958).

———. "Mexico Opens the Door to American Capital, 1877–1880." *The Americas* 16 (July 1959).

Raat, William D. "Ideas and Society in Don Porfirio's Mexico." *The Americas* 30 (1973).

Ramírez Cabañas C., Joaquin. "Los ingresos federales de México durante los años de 1876 a 1930." *Revista de Hacienda* (Mexico City), no. 1 (Abril 1938).

Rohlfes, Lawrence J. "The Porfirian Church and the Social Question: *Rerum Novarum* and Mexico." Paper presented at the Southwestern Social Science Association, San Antonio, March 1982.

Rosenzweig, Fernando. "El desarrollo económico de México de 1877 a 1911." *Trimestre Económico* 37 (Julio-Septiembre 1965).

Schryer, Franz. "A Ranchero Economy in Northwestern Hidalgo, 1880–1920." *Hispanic American Historical Review* (August 1979).

———. "Ethnicity and Political Conflict in Northern Hidalgo" (Agrarian Conflict in a Nahuatl Region). Working Paper Number 5. Ontario: Centre for Research on Latin America and the Caribbean, York University, 1983.

Shanklin, Arnold. "Commercial Conditions in Mexico." *Daily Consular and Trade Reports,* Numbers 250 (25 October 1911) and 256 (1 November 1911).

Sinkin, Richard. "The Mexican Constitutional Congress, 1856–1857: A Statistical Analysis." *Hispanic American Historical Review* 53 (1973).

Skinner, G. William. "Marketing and Social Structure in Rural China (Part 1)." *Journal of Asian Studies* 24, no. 1 (November 1964).

T'ang, L. L. (Thung Liang Lee) and M. S. Miller. "The Political Aspect of International Finance in Russia and China." *Economica,* 1st Series, 5 (March 1925).

Taylor, Lawrence D. "The Great Adventure: Mercenaries in the Mexican Revolution, 1910–1915." *The Americas* (July 1986).

Taylor, William B. "Rural Unrest in Central Jalisco, 1790–1816." *Riot, Rebellion, and Revolution: Rural Social Conflict in Mexico,* Friedrich Katz, ed. Princeton: Princeton University Press, 1987.

Tilly, Louise. "Paths of Proletarianization: Organization of Production, Sexual Division of Labor, and Women's Collective Action," *Signs* 7, no. 2 (Winter 1981).

Tutino, John. "Indian Rebellion at the Isthmus of Tehuantepec: A Socio-Historical Perspective." *Actes du XLIIe International Congress des Americanistes* (Paris) II (1976):198–214.

———. "Agrarian Transformation and Peasant Rebellion in Nineteenth-Century Mexico: Chalco, 1840–1870." *Riot, Rebellion, and Revolution: Rural Social Conflict in Mexico,* Friedrich Katz, ed. Princeton: Princeton University Press, 1987.

Valadés, José C. "El 50 aniversario del Primer Congreso Obrero en America." *La Protesta* (Buenos Aires, April 1926).

Van Young, Eric. "Moving Towards Revolt: The Agrarian Origins of the Hidalgo Rebellion in the Guadalajara Region." *Riot, Rebellion, and Revolution: Rural Social Conflict in Mexico,* Friedrich Katz, ed. Princeton: Princeton University Press, 1987.

Von Laue, Theodore H. "The High Cost and the Gamble of the Witte System: A Chapter in the Industrialization of Russia." *Journal of Economic History* 13, no. 4 (1953).

———. "Russian Peasants in the Factory 1892–1904." *Journal of Economic History* 21 (1961).

———. "Russian Labor Between Field and Factory 1892–1903." *California Slavic Studies* 3 (1964).

Walker, David. "Porfirian Labor Politics: Working Class Organizations in Mexico City and Porfirio Díaz, 1876–1902." *The Americas* 37, no. 3 (January 1981).

Wasserman, Mark. "Oligarquía é intereses extranjeros en Chihuahua durante el Porfiriato." *Historia Mexicana* 22, no. 3 (Enero-Marzo 1973).

———. "Chihuahua: Family Power, Foreign Enterprise, and National Control." In *Other Mexicos: Essays on Regional Mexican History, 1876–1911,* eds. Thomas Benjamin and William McNellie. Albuquerque: University of New Mexico Press, 1984.

Young, Ernest P. "Nationalism, Reform and Republican Revolution: China in the Early Twentieth Century." In *Modern East Asia: Essays in Interpretation,* ed. James B. Crowley. New York: Harcourt, Brace and World, 1970.

Unpublished Works

Bryan, Anthony. "The Career of General Bernardo Reyes: Continuity and Change in Mexican Politics, 1905–1913." Master's thesis, University of Nebraska, 1967.

Campbell, Richey Barron. "Taft, Díaz and Oil: You Can't Always Get What You Want." University of Houston, 1981.

Córdoba Pérez, Fernando. "El movimiento anarquista en México (1911–1921)." Licenciado thesis, Facultad de Ciencias Políticas y Sociales, Universidad Nacional Autonoma de Mexico, Mexico City, 1971.

Cott, Kenneth. "Porfirian Investment Policies 1876–1910." Ph.D. diss., University of New Mexico, 1979.

Cruz Valdés, Reina. "Levantamientos populares en Tlapa en los años 1842–1849."

Ford, John Salmon. "Memoirs." BTHC.

Friesell, Susan. "John W. Gates: A Study of Railroad and Industrial Consolidation 1900–1911." University of Houston, 1984.

Gómez Quiñones, Juan. "Social Change and Intellectual Discontent: The Growth of Mexican Nationalism, 1890–1911." Ph.D. diss., University of California, Los Angeles, 1972.

Graf, L. E. "The Economic History of the Rio Grande Valley 1820–1875." Ph.D. diss., Harvard University, 1942.

Gunder Frank, André. "Growth and Productivity in Ukrainian Agriculture and Industry from 1928–1955." Ph.D. diss., University of Chicago, 1958.

Hart, John Mason. "A Social History of the Mexican Peasant Wars, 1810–1910."

———. "Empire and Revolution: The United States and Mexico 1876–1910."

Hu-DeHart, Evelyn. "Indians and Immigrants: Rebellion and Assimilation in Sonora." American Historical Association, Washington, D.C., 29 December 1982.

Katz, Friedrich. "Francisco Villa and the Mexican Revolution." The Woodrow Wilson Center, Smithsonian Institution, Washington, D.C., April 1984.

Kromov, Pavel Alexeyevich. "The Economic Development of Russia in the Nineteenth and Twentieth Centuries." Trans. Fabian Vaksman.

La France, David. "A People Betrayed: Francisco I. Madero and the Mexican Revolution in Puebla." Ph.D. diss., Indiana University, 1982.

Lockman, Zachary. "Class and Nation: The Emergence of the Egyptian Workers' Movement." Ph.D. diss., Harvard University, 1983.

Maclachlan, Colin M. "Spain's Empire in America: The Effect of Ideas on Social and Political Change."

Meyers, William K. "Interest Conflicts and Popular Discontent: The Origins of the Revolution in the Laguna, 1880–1910." Ph.D. diss., University of Chicago, 1979.

O'Brien, Thomas F., Jr. "Anti-Commercialism in China: The Changsha Riot of 1910." University of Connecticut, 1970.

Schmidt, Arthur P., Jr. "The Railroad and the Economy of Puebla and Veracruz, 1877–1911: A Look at Agriculture." Southwestern Social Science Association, Dallas, 1973.

Stowe, Noel. "The Tumulto of 1629: Turmoil at Mexico City." Ph.D. diss., University of Southern California, 1970.

Tutino, John. "Agrarian Insurrection: The Hidalgo Revolt and the Origins of Agrarian Violence in Modern Mexico."

Valles, Gilberto. "Crop Failures in Mexico 1900–1910." University of Houston, 1977.

Villaseñor Cornejo, Jorge. "Origines del Movimiento Obrero Mexicano, 1870–1880." Thesis, UNAM, 1980.
Walker, David. "The Martínez del Río Family: An Elite Mexican Family: 1839–1963." University of Chicago.
Wells, Allen. "Henequén and Yucatán: An Analysis in Regional Economic Development, 1876–1915." Ph.D. diss., State University of New York at Stony Brook, 1979.

Interviews

Antonio Salazar Pérez, Cronista de la Ciudad, Veracruz, 28 July 1983.
Billy Marshall III, Owner, Hacienda de Corralitos, Corralitos, Chihuahua, 23 February 1984.
Eric M. A. Jasso Herrera, Consejero Agrario, Secretaría de Reforma Agraria, Oaxaca, Oaxaca, 2 August 1980.
Franz Schryer, Houston, Texas, 16 April 1984.
Ignacio Mendoza, Comisario y presidente de varios trabajos en el pueblo, Ayahualulco, Municipio de Chilapa, Guerrero, 7–8 August 1980.
James B. Hughes, Jr., Owner Deep River Armory, Houston, 3 August 1982.
Lois Archer, Pacific Palisades, California, 8 January 1984.
Leticia Reina, Austin, Texas, 17 July 1984.
Manuel García Rodríguez, Supervisor de Servicios Portuarios, Veracruz, 17 August 1983.
Oliver Scott Bluth, local historian, Casas Grandes Viejo, Chihuahua, 23 February 1984.
Rosendo Salazar, Tlalnepantla, 10 August 1969.
Paul Vanderwood, Las Cruces, New Mexico, 27 July 1985.

Documents

Daily Consular and Trade Reports, Bureau of Manufactures, Department of Commerce and Labor, Washington, D.C.
Diario de los Debates del Congreso Constituyente, Tomo 1. Mexico City, 1922.
Diplomatic and Consular Reports, Numbered File 1906–1910.
Fall Committee Reports, Investigation of Mexican Affairs: Preliminary Reports and Surveys, 66th Congress, 2d sess. Washington, D.C.: Government Printing Office, 1921.
Hanrahan, Gene. *Documents on the Mexican Revolution,* vol. I, pt. II. Salisbury, N.C.: Documentary Publications, 1976.
"Manifiesto de la Convención Nacional Liberal." In Manuel González Ramírez, *Fuentes para la historia de la Revolución Mexicana,* Tomo IV, *Manifiestos políticos (1892–1912).*
Report of the Commissioner of Corporations on the Petroleum Industry, Part III: Foreign Trade. Washington, D.C.: U.S. Department of Commerce and Labor, 1912. New York: Arno Press, 1976.

INDEX

Designer: U.C. Press Staff
Compositor: AutoGraphics, Inc.
Text: 10/13 Galliard
Display: Galliard
Printer: Maple-Vail Book Mfg. Group
Binder: Maple-Vail Book Mfg. Group